The Elementary School Journal

THE UNIVERSITY OF CHICAGO PRESS
CHICAGO, ILLINOIS

Agents

THE CAMBRIDGE UNIVERSITY PRESS
LONDON AND EDINBURGH

THE MARUZEN-KABUSHIKI-KAISHA
TOKYO, OSAKA, KYOTO

KARL W. HIERSEMANN
LEIPZIG

THE BAKER & TAYLOR COMPANY
NEW YORK

THE ELEMENTARY SCHOOL JOURNAL

VOLUME XV

SEPTEMBER, 1914—JUNE, 1915

THE UNIVERSITY OF CHICAGO PRESS
CHICAGO, ILLINOIS

Published
September, October, November, December, 1914
January, February, March, April, May, June, 1915

Composed and Printed By
The University of Chicago Press
Chicago, Illinois, U.S.A.

INDEX TO VOLUME XV

INDEX TO ARTICLES

[The asterisk indicates authors or editors of books reviewed]

INDEX TO AUTHORS

[The asterisk indicates authors or editors of books reviewed]

VOLUME XV NUMBER I

THE ELEMENTARY SCHOOL JOURNAL

CONTINUING "THE ELEMENTARY SCHOOL TEACHER"

SEPTEMBER 1914

EDUCATIONAL NEWS AND EDITORIAL COMMENT

Change in Name and Arrangement of this Journal

The *Elementary School Teacher* contained in its early days a large amount of material which was intended to influence directly the practice of the classroom teacher in the conduct of her work with children, hence the reference in its name to the Teacher. This direct attack upon class problems was the natural beginning of a movement of reform which was intended to break up the traditions of the school of a generation ago.

As soon as the discussions of classroom methods were well under way, it became obvious that the general organization of the school was quite as significant a problem for scientific study as the conduct of each class. In fact, the elementary school of today needs to be organized rather than to be reformed. Readers of the *Elementary School Teacher* have observed for a period of years that this *Journal* has devoted itself largely to problems of general organization. Why children get behind in their grades is a problem of general organization which reaches beyond the limits of a single grade. How far industrial organization is to affect the life of the school is a problem that cannot be solved by the individual teacher, and this is one of the most urgent problems of the modern school. In view of the importance of problems of organization, it seemed wise to allow the individual classroom to sink into the background for the time being in the effort to develop a general science of elementary-school administration. The limited space which the editors of this *Journal* had at their disposal further contributed to the emphasis on one particular kind of material. Fortunately, the editors have now reached the point where they can begin an enlargement of the *Journal*. Eight pages will be added to each issue and it is expected that this enlargement will later be carried farther. From this time on the *Journal* will aim to co-ordinate so far as possible the interests of the individual classroom with the interests of the school as a whole.

The organization of the *Journal* will be somewhat modified in order to include material of various types. The news notes and editorial comments will continue as for the last two years. A new section will be added covering the leading books and educational articles. No attempt to review these individually will be made, but instead all of the material will be thrown together in a single discussion. A third section will be devoted to reports of experiments in classroom methods. The remainder of the *Journal* will be devoted to articles of the type which has become familiar to readers of the *Journal*.

In view of these enlargements and changes it has seemed wise to give the *Journal* a broader title so as to include all interests and express somewhat more clearly the relation of the *Journal* to the different aspects of elementary-school work.

It is appropriate also to emphasize in this connection the general fact that this *Journal* is not the organ of any single institution. The *Journal* invites the co-operation of all who are interested in the scientific organization of elementary education. Short reports covering different aspects of school work will be very welcome from every possible source. A good deal of material will be presented which issues directly from the laboratory schools of the University of Chicago and naturally the school people who have been in contact in one way or another with the department of education of the University of Chicago will contribute to both the news notes and the other departments. But it is hoped that the *Journal* may serve to stimulate in a general way a broad, scientific interest in elementary-school problems.

Federal Subsidy of Agricultural Instruction

The federal government has taken a long step in the direction of subsidizing educational activity throughout the states. The so-called Smith-Lever bill has been passed and has been approved by the President. This bill makes available in the next nine fiscal years an aggregate sum of $23,120,000 of federal funds to be expended in instruction and practical demonstrations in agriculture and home economics. The states which are to enjoy the advantage of this appropriation are called upon to make state appropriations to supplement the funds furnished by the federal government. The work is to be carried on through the Department of Agriculture and is to be done through the co-operation of the agricultural colleges in the several states. It is the expectation that the instruction thus provided will influence in a large way the elementary schools as well as the higher schools. Indeed, this fund is explicitly restricted to use for the benefit of those who are not registered in the agricultural colleges.

The entrance of the federal government on this field of general education is a mark of progress which will be observed with great interest in all parts of the country. There are those who have been opposed to the participation by the central government in any large plans of local education. The next question that is to arise is the question of a central subsidy for vocational training in the various states. A bill now pending covering this matter may be made the subject of further comment.

The Federal Government and Vocational Education

In the June number of the *Elementary School Teacher* a report was given of the work of the Commission on Vocational Education. The work of that commission resulted in the preparation of a bill which was presented to Congress by Senator Smith and is known as the Smith bill. This bill provides for a gradually increasing subsidy for vocational and agricultural education in elementary schools. The bill leaves each state free to organize this work in its own fashion, requiring only that the state shall contribute a certain amount of money to supplement the funds given by the federal government. The sum of money which the federal government is called upon by this bill to expend is very large in the aggregate. For the year ending June 30, 1924, the total amount to be expended by the government for the conduct of the schools will be $6,000,000. An immediate appropriation of $500,000 is made available for the training of teachers. This amount is to be increased to $1,000,000 for the year ending June 30, 1919, and annually thereafter.

The bill also provides for a board to administer this fund. This board is made up of the Postmaster-General, the Secretary of the Interior, the Secretary of Agriculture, the Secretary of Commerce, and the Secretary of Labor, with the Commissioner of Education acting as the executive officer of the board.

The novel features of the bill are the large amount of federal money given to the purpose and the freedom with which the commission has dealt with the problem of internal organization of the schools. No effort has been made to force upon the different states any preconceived theories of the administration of this kind of education. This seems to the present writer to be a very wholesome and satisfactory method of dealing with the situation. If anyone is willing to have federal funds given to education at all, this seems to be the wise way of giving these funds. There will be some who will question the propriety of the entrance by the federal government upon this field of education. On the other hand, it is to be said that the government has already entered upon this field in its treatment of agricultural education and there seems to be no reason why the country at large should not interest itself in the solution of the difficult problem of industrial education.

Opposition to the Smith Bill

Violent opposition to the Smith bill has appeared from that valiant defender of his own views, Mr. H. E. Miles. Mr. Miles issues, under the clear designation of his offices as president of the Wisconsin State Board of Industrial Education and as chairman of the Committee on Industrial Education of the National Association of Manufacturers, a protest against the bill. In the first place, he thinks one of the prime faults of the bill is to be found in the fact that the bill tries to require vocational schools to employ teachers who have had experience. Mr. Miles is so thoroughly committed to taking teachers directly from the industries by some process of careful selection which he evidently knows about that he thinks it altogether unsatisfactory that this bill should require experience in teaching. Mr. Miles of course recognizes the difficulty of getting artisans who know enough about children really to take care of the needs of children, but he provides for this difficulty in the simple words "careful selection." One needs only to go out into the industries and with some high power of selection he can get what he wants. Training is all right in the industries themselves and a foreman undoubtedly ought to be prepared for his work, but the teacher can be secured by a "careful selection."

In the second place, Mr. Miles indulges in his usual offhand statements about educational matters in a criticism of the *ex-officio* board. He says:

> The form of board proposed reduces itself to a mere *ex-officio* board having a single head of a bureau as the power. It is not fair to ask any single man to distribute money under the shadow of great names and to assume the responsibilities involved. Thirty-five states now have boards of education and all but six are of this character, consisting of the state superintendents and other state officials. These boards have been almost utterly without consequence or influence.

It is doubtful whether the country at large will be prepared to submit to Mr. Miles as chairman of the Committee on Industrial Education of the National Association of Manufacturers the final verdict with regard to the efficiency of state boards. We should all be prepared to admit that these boards have not always been of the highest degree of efficiency, but that the difficulty lies in the fact that they do not conform to the type of organization that would be acceptable to Mr. Miles, president of the Wisconsin State Board of Industrial Education, is hardly to be believed. In fact, the probabilities are that one of the difficulties in these boards has been that the people who have talked about educational matters have not been prepared to give themselves a careful training in the real characteristics of an educational situation; and it is to be suspected that even the president of the Wisconsin State Board of Industrial Education and chairman of the Committee on Industrial Education of the National Association of Manufacturers might gain something by conferring with others who have in charge the educational organization of the country. He would then doubtless find that any appropriations supervised by the Commissioner of Education of the United States would probably be made with the advice of experts and after careful consultation with those who are trained in educational matters. It is even to be assumed that the chairman of the Committee on Industrial Education of the National Association of Manufacturers might have a voice in suggesting plans, provided these plans could be seen by the people of the country in advance and could be recognized as formulated with reference to the interests of children rather than with reference to manufacturing interests, which, on the whole, seem very often rather remote from the intellectual and moral life of these children.

The reorganization of the elementary schools has been emphatically suggested in many different quarters during the past summer.

Criticism of the Upper Grades

The superintendent of schools of the city of Chicago makes in her report a vigorous attack on the present method of conducting the upper grades of the grammar school. The following quotation indicates the type of argument which she presents against the present organization:

> Boys and girls cannot acquire by the close of the sixth grade sufficient power to meet satisfactorily the requirements of the positions into which they will strive to enter upon leaving school. It is not repeating and reviewing which makes one proficient; it is the attack made in accord with the period of growth and development that brings power and efficiency. The need of a junior high school is not urgent.
>
> There is, however, pressing necessity for a readjustment, a reorganization of the work in the grammar grades and the first and possibly the second years of the high school.
>
> The greatest drawback to the successful solution of this problem is the failure of principals and upper-grade teachers to see it, to feel the pressure of present conditions intellectually.

A committee of the Minnesota Educational Association appointed some years ago has recommended a reorganization of the

Elimination from the Elementary Course

elementary course through an elimination of a very large body of material. The report of this committee is published in *Bulletin No. 51* of the State Department of Minnesota and contains the following introductory statement:

The committee presents herewith certain recommendations for the elimination of various topics or parts of topics from the elementary curriculum. Owing to the difficulty of always stating definitely just what should be omitted, the recommendations are made affirmatively or negatively, according to the topic under consideration.

The committee began its work by sending out a letter to the 3,700 members of the Minnesota Educational Association. This letter called for suggestions along certain definite lines with reference to elimination of subject-matter in arithmetic, grammar, geography, reading and composition, and United States history. The number of replies received were as follows: 110 pertaining to arithmetic, 30 to grammar, 80 to geography, 114 to reading and composition, and 60 to United States history. The suggestions varied considerably in clearness and definiteness, but in so far as the committee has been able to determine their value, they have in the main been incorporated in this report.

The committee report then gives in detail a number of items which should be eliminated from the elementary course.

Possible Misuse of Economy in Elementary Schools

There is grave possibility that the suggestions of the superintendent of the Chicago schools and of the Minnesota committee will be misinterpreted. It may be assumed by those who read these reports that the educational world is bent merely on reducing the elementary course, whereas, in fact, it is directing its attention to the elimination of the unnecessary materials in order that it may include higher forms of training. The possibilities of a complete misunderstanding of the situation are clearly represented in the following editorial, which is clipped from the *Tribune*, of Duluth, Minnesota:

One section of the National Education Association, in session at St. Paul last week, was concerned with reducing the elementary public-school course two years. From the newspaper reports we judge this was to enable those who need to become earners to do so, and still complete a definite school course.

The public schools accept children for entrance at six years. The grades cover eight years; the high school four more. This would make the average boy or girl eighteen years old at graduation. If this could be reached at sixteen very many would complete the work who now stop at the high school because of the financial inability of their families.

A boy or girl at sixteen years should have considerable earning value. They could have, if properly trained and equipped by ten years of application, with no wasted time or effort. To reduce this elementary-school life two years is therefore important, if it can be done without material educational loss.

That this can be done is a growing conviction. One very simple way is by all-year sessions, which, if continued from the third grade, would of itself give two full years without the sacrifice of a single subject in the course of study.

Another way to gain a year is to accept children at five years instead of six. If we must have the present kindergartens, they could better take children at four years than at five, and instead of dissipating their powers of concentration and natural inclination to do something developing, by useless and largely senseless plays, they should begin the teaching of reading and numbers.

Still another way is to give vocational courses to be covered in the present ten-year period. That such courses can be framed, who can doubt? It is not complimentary to our children to hold that thinking hurts them; that mental effort is debilitating; that concentrated attention to what they can understand, intelligently grasp, and so like, is physically weakening.

The emphasis in this editorial is on mere reduction. The true emphasis is on extension. If we reduce the elementary course two years it is for the purpose of allowing children to get higher work of a type which the elementary school does not now offer.

Treatment of Abnormal Children in St. Louis

Dr. Wallin, who has for a number of years past been giving courses in the University of Pittsburgh on clinical psychology, has accepted a call to the St. Louis public schools, where he will organize a clinic for special children. For some years St. Louis has been very active in the training of defectives, and the removal of Dr. Wallin to that city means an extension and enlargement of the type of work which has been going on. Dr. Wallin will give courses of lectures on abnormal children at the Harris Teachers College and will thus spread among the teachers of the city an intelligent view of the methods of detecting abnormality and also of treating these cases. The clinic itself will be a clearing-house for the public schools and will be the instrument which will be used by the officers of that system in segregating abnormal children from the normal classes.

Politics and Education

The city of Cleveland has for some time past been confused in its school administration by political issues. The teachers decided to organize a union and the Board of Education forbade the joining of the union. The Board of Education has attempted to abolish German from the elementary school and has aroused the German population and the German teachers to a vigorous protest and to court proceedings to prevent the taking of this step. In general, the city of Cleveland is reaping the reward of a long period of the mixture of education and politics. One might express the pious hope that the people will ultimately see the disadvantage of this mixture and clear up the situation so that they may have a system of education free from political interference. If not, the only hope that one can properly entertain is that the situation will get so utterly bad that they will have to divorce the two whether they will or not.

Summer Sessions

The superintendent of schools of Hutchinson, Kansas, has hit upon a very fortunate plan of appealing to the community in favor of a summer session with the following statement, which is quoted from the *Gazette* of that city:

The time for the making of the annual school levy is but two weeks away, and the efforts of the board and the superintendent are all directed toward gaining a new building, needed even now, and a necessity in another year, without a bond issue. It comes as good news to the taxpayers to know that the summer school, as conducted last year and during this summer, for the backward pupils or those who had been forced to lose their grades through illness or some other cause, is an actual saving of money. The five weeks' school cost less to make its pupils ready for their advanced work than carrying them through regular sessions again would cost, and the superintendent's figures show the actual amount, $11.61 for each of the 161 promoted, besides their school gain. Superintendent Hall concludes his résumé of the results and costs with the remark: "I feel that in view of these results, the summer session may now be considered an established and regular part of the Hutchinson school system." The total saving was $1,868.

Spelling

The committee of Chicago teachers and principals which undertook as its special mission the survey of the spelling in the city system has made the following interesting report, which is quoted from the *Chicago Daily Tribune:*

The committee on spelling believes that the complaint of business men that public-school graduates can't spell is unjust. It found that the vocabulary of every business is different. In asking business firms to send lists of words which it was thought the pupils of seventh and eighth grades ought to be able to spell it was found that only seven words out of 125 sent in were repeated.

"This experience should discount very considerably," reads the report, "the complaint said to emanate from the business houses concerning the inability of pupils, fresh from the schools, to spell in terms of their employer's business."

The committee prepared lists of words and submitted them to pupils of the fifth, sixth, seventh, and eighth grades. Fifth-grade pupils made an average of 74 on their list. Sixth-grade pupils averaged 82 on the same list. The average of 1,800 pupils of the seventh grade was 75 for its list, and of the same number in the eighth grade was 76.

In a group of 78 eighth-grade pupils the following words were misspelled as indicated: alleys (45), competent (40), definite (37), garage (26), engineer (8), privilege (44), changeable (11), curable (26).

In another group of 196 eighth-grade pupils the following words were misspelled by the number of pupils indicated: constitution (22), representative (67), submarine (39), necessary (35), cupful (129), chocolate (73), Mexican (27) senators (34), luxury (65).

In a group of 90 fifth-grade pupils the following words were misspelled as indicated: arithmetic (37), answered (43), erase (51), relative (58), Illinois (66), vegetable (59), truant (62).

It was shown that the children are good spellers when they are spelling in their own vocabulary. In their own compositions their spelling averaged as follows: fifth grade, 91 per cent; sixth grade, 94 per cent; seventh grade, 95 per cent; eighth grade, 97 per cent.

"In a language spelled with such absurd and contradictory forms as we find in English," reads the report, "nothing but constant drill and close attention to a reasonably limited number of words can guarantee correct spelling of one's useful vocabulary."

School Savings Banks

Several cities report at the end of the year the success of the school savings bank. Dubuque, Iowa, for example, reports that 298 students availed themselves of the opportunity of learning thrift last year by becoming depositors in the school savings bank. In West DesMoines, Iowa, over $10,000 was deposited in the state savings bank through the organization of the pupils of the schools. In Kankakee, Illinois, a formal statement of the banking activities of the schools goes to show that during the year just past more than $5,000 was deposited in the bank. Since the move began in 1907, more than $32,000 has been deposited by school children. Sterling, Illinois, reports itself as very well satisfied with the school plans for teaching the children how to save. The following statement from the *Standard*, of Sterling, Illinois, shows the attitude of the people of that city toward this enterprise:

The report of the Penny Savings Association showing such excellent work in saving by school children caused much favorable comment since last evening, and the parents were amazed at the thrift shown by the pupils during the year.

The superintendents and teachers in the schools have done much in keeping up the interest in the work and their efforts have been of great assistance to the officers of the association.

Educational Scholarships

The city of Pittsburgh is fortunate in having an educational fund which sends the teachers of its schools to various institutions where they can study during the summer. This educational commission, which has John A. Brashear as its president, awarded the following list of scholarships for the present summer. It is worthy of note that the students enjoying these scholarships have been sent in all directions and will bring back to the city of Pittsburgh the benefits of a very wide series of courses given in different parts of the country:

Commonwealth Art Colony, Boothbay Harbor	4
University of Michigan	2
North American Gymnastic Union, Indianapolis, Ind.	1
Chautauqua Institution, Chautauqua, N.Y.	10
University of Chicago	11
Columbia University	21
Cornell University	16
Dartmouth	4
Harvard University	14
Zanerian College of Penmanship, Columbus, Ohio	3
Ocean City Summer School	3
University of Pennsylvania	4
Pennsylvania State College	7
University of Vermont	4
University of Pittsburgh	4
American Institute, Northwestern University	1
University of Wisconsin	11
University of Berlin, Germany	1
University of New York	1
New York School of Fine and Applied Arts	1
Munich Trade School, Germany	1
Total number of teachers sent in 1914	124

An educational fund of this sort can be of great value to a school system. There is certainly no larger opportunity for those who are seeking ways and means of endowing American education than the creation in all of our great cities of funds that shall keep alive the teaching profession after the period of preliminary training for admission to the profession is past.

EDUCATIONAL WRITINGS

With this issue of the *Journal* a division on "Educational Writings" is inaugurated. This division will be devoted to review and comment on various types of educational literature relating to elementary schools. It happens that during the summer just past an unusually large number of new books have appeared which may be classified as general educational literature. A brief review of these books is here presented as the first instalment of this department. The *Journal* receives from educational publishers their significant books. It will welcome, however, the reactions of readers as well as publishers, and if its readers will express their views on any books which they have found to be of special use, the *Journal* will welcome the opportunity of transmitting these views to others who are looking for helpful educational discussions.

This book[1] may be divided into three sections. The first deals with the physical characteristics of the child. It reports the investigations which have been made on growth and it contains also a full account of the nervous system. Following this is a section dealing with general psychology. This section contains the usual topics that are discussed in psychology, such as instinct, habit, association, memory, attention, etc. Finally, the last division of the book, which is relatively short, gives an account of school activities, beginning with a discussion of the different periods of school life and concluding with a discussion of the psychology of all of the fundamental school processes.

The book is intended to be used as a general textbook and to this end summarizes a large part of the recent technical literature on these various subjects. It is as comprehensive a book as has lately appeared on these subjects. There are no important contributions made by the author himself except the formulation

[1] *The Mental and Physical Life of School Children.* By Peter Sandiford. Pp. 346. New York; Longmans, Green & Co.

of the results of other workers. The large emphasis which is laid upon the physical nature of the child is in a measure a departure from the conventional treatment of educational psychology and will undoubtedly be useful in calling attention to an important phase of child-study. The psychology of the second part of the book is of the familiar, conventional type. Although the treatment begins with the discussion of instinct and habit, it passes very soon into the type of association psychology which has long been familiar to English readers. The results of the child-study investigations are included as far as possible in the text, but the relation of the psychological treatment to the later discussion of school subjects is not intimate. The section on school subjects is the best brief summary of this material that has yet been prepared. This section will be found to be very useful to teachers, more useful probably than the middle section of the book, which attempts to summarize psychology.

On the whole, the book may be described as the best elementary review of this material now at hand. The book ought to take the place that was filled for a time by Kirkpatrick's *Fundamentals of Child Study*. It is more up to date than any summary of the child-study movement and contains the new material on the psychology of reading, spelling, arithmetic, and other school subjects.

Professor O'Shea of the University of Wisconsin has undertaken the editorship of a series of educational volumes which are intended to appeal to lay readers as well as to teachers. These volumes are all to be about 250 pages in length and will deal with different aspects of the school and social situation. Four volumes of this series have already appeared. One of them can be passed with a mere mention as it relates primarily to the high-school period and is likely to be of interest to elementary teachers only in so far as they are concerned with the transitions from the elementary school to the high school.[1] It ought to be remarked, however, in this connection that elementary teachers would profit by cultivating more interest in the upper schools than they usually exhibit. Mr.

[1] *The High-School Age*. By Irving King. (Childhood and Youth Series, edited by M. V. O'Shea.) Indianapolis: Bobbs-Merrill Co. Pp. 233.

King gives a brief summary of the mental and physical characteristics of adolescent youth. He discusses a number of the high-school problems, such as the difficulties which arise from outside engagements. He has some original investigations on this topic. On the whole, the volume is a very useful summary of the more elaborate discussions on the high-school period.

The second volume of the series[1] is a popular exposition of the experiments which have been performed on the learning process. Mr. Swift summarizes his own investigations and those of others, giving a number of typical learning-curves, together with a description of the experiments which were made in securing these learning-curves. He discusses also a number of the important problems of school hygiene, such as economy in learning and the best methods of memorizing and arranging materials which are to be mastered through school work.

His final chapter on "New Demands on Schools" attempts to state in a brief, popular form the significance of the general doctrine of development and variation for school work. There is a plea for recognition of individual differences and for an accommodation of the school work to the changes that have been going on in social organization.

This book exhibits the virtues and at the same time the difficulties of a series of brief, popular treatises on education. Many of the author's opinions appear to be mere assertions of individual belief because in a volume of this compass it is necessary to leave out the evidence which lies back of these views. At the same time the statement of these views undoubtedly has some value in that it will call the attention of many readers to the changes that are going forward in modern education.

The third volume of the series[2] comes from the pen of a mother who has devoted very large attention to the training of her daughter. The editor compares the book to Rousseau's *Émile*. Mrs. Stoner began preparing her child for the career which she had planned for

[1] *Learning and Doing*. By Edgar James Swift. (Childhood and Youth Series, edited by M. V. O'Shea.) Indianapolis: Bobbs-Merrill Co. Pp. 249.

[2] *Natural Education*. By Winifred Sackville Stoner. (Childhood and Youth Series, edited by M. V. O'Shea.) Indianapolis: Bobbs-Merrill Co. Pp. 295.

her by quieting her restlessness in the cradle with lines from Vergil's *Aeneid.* The child very soon accumulated so much Latin and other foreign languages that she seems to be a leader in the Esperanto movement. In fact, we are told that the eight-year-old girl gives lessons in this subject and apparently is one of the most proficient disciples of this cult. She has acquired a large mastery of numbers through various games which the mother evidently plays with her as one of the common forms of amusement. The child writes jingles and indeed has written them since she was four years old. She copies on the typewriter and writes compositions on natural objects which she observes. She is described as being unusually husky and athletic, evidently more than a match for all of the small boys in the neighborhood.

The fundamental theory on which she has been brought up is at times a little vague. In one part of the book we find Mrs. Stoner objecting to the learning of the names of all of the different capes and bays around the coast of Africa, while on another page we are assured that the child knows the names of all of the capitals of the states in the United States.

There is a good deal of quotation from various authors who have evidently been of encouragement to the mother in the work she has undertaken. On the whole, the book, like a number of others which have recently appeared, will persuade those who read it that children can accomplish a great deal more than is ordinarily expected of them in school work. Like most of the ambitious tutors of children supposed to be extremely precocious, the mother evidently regards foreign language as a matter of very large importance. One thinks of the historical examples of children who mastered long lists of foreign languages. There is relatively little in the book to show any clear appreciation of the necessity of training the child in methods of reasoning. Where the book deals briefly from time to time with such problems, there is evidence that there is no very definite notion of what reasoning consists in or how it can best be trained.

There can be no doubt that home training of this intensive type would do much to improve schools, and Mrs. Stoner's contention that the school is seriously handicapped because parents fail to do their duty by their children will be heartily seconded by the technical reader of the book.

The fourth volume[1] reports, as does the monograph described below, a series of investigations of the methods of teaching spelling. It also presents a number of word lists which will be useful to teachers in determining the vocabulary which the child ought to acquire during his school work. The various simple rules which can be utilized in remembering the arrangement of letters in confusing words are briefly reviewed. The types of error which children commonly make are pointed out. The relative value of word lists and composition work in teaching spelling was investigated by one of the authors.

The improvement of spelling ought certainly to follow upon investigations of the type of those here recorded. One wonders how long the investigations which deal with the present form of English spelling will be necessary before it becomes apparent to everyone that a change in these matters ought to be introduced into the language as well as into school practice.

Spelling is one of the subjects in which the material is perfectly definite and capable of exact description. One hardly knows how to describe the topics in geography because they may include a great deal or they may include very little. But the list of words to be taught in spelling is capable of definite determination. Mr. Jones[2] has with great industry prepared a list for the different grades of the elementary school on the basis of compositions written by many children through a long period of years. This list he has arranged according to the various grades so that it is possible to determine from the actual practices of children in the school something of the expectation which the school should entertain regarding the vocabulary of children. Incidentally the pamphlet throws a good deal of light on the number of words used in different grades and by different individuals. The vocabulary of children in the

[1] *The Child and His Spelling.* By W. A. Cook and M. V. O'Shea. (Childhood and Youth Series, edited by M. V. O'Shea.) Indianapolis: Bobbs-Merrill Co. Pp. 282.

[2] *Concrete Investigation of the Material of English Spelling.* By W. Franklin Jones. Published by the University of South Dakota. Pp. 27.

eight grades consists of 4,532 words. When it is remembered that these are words which the children actually use and not a full list of the words which they are able to understand, we realize that the task before the elementary school is a large one. The details of the distribution of these different words are of great interest to those who have to deal with children. Perhaps the list of the 100 words most commonly misspelled in these compositions is the most interesting part of the pamphlet. The first four words in this list of 100 are "which," "their," "there," and "separate."

Mr. Jones has prepared a speller on the basis of his investigation which is published by the Capital Supply Co., Pierre, South Dakota. This book has a somewhat ambitious title, *The Spelling Problem Solved*.

One recognizes the limitation in this kind of a list since it does not include words which the children ought to have but which are not now given in the ordinary course of school life. Business words and general words may enlarge the list beyond those which Mr. Jones now has at hand. Other investigations such as this and the earlier work of Mr. Ayres, as well as the later work of Cook and O'Shea, ought shortly to realize Mr. Jones's ambition of solving some of the school's spelling problems. Whatever the addition to the list from these other sources, it is evident that Mr. Jones has attacked in a definite, empirical way one of the problems of the school curriculum. There is no reason why a number of other subjects should not be attacked with the same spirit of definiteness and finality. The topics in geography can be enumerated even if they cannot be worked out with the same degree of exactness as that exhibited here in the spelling-book.

For some time past the movement in the direction of using the schoolhouse for the general purposes of community life has been under way. Meetings of all sorts are now very common in school buildings, and the grounds of schoolhouses are often utilized for general recreation purposes. The relation thus established between the school and the community has, however, operated in the reciprocal direction of bringing to the school co-operation of various types which in the past were not common.[1] The physicians of the city, for example, have interested themselves in the sanitary conditions in and around the school, and in the personal health of the children; the playgrounds have been enlarged; pictures and other works of art have been brought into the school because the community has come to realize the barrenness of an undecorated building.

These various forms of co-operation with the school are enumerated and described by Mrs. Cabot in a way to make it clear that the school profits very greatly by cultivating relations with the community. She points out that every school officer is besieged by people who interfere with the school unless they are given something to do, and she suggests that such people be utilized to make contributions of all sorts. "Such people," she writes, "cling like a burr; we cannot do away with them. It is a temptation to pull them off one's sleeves once." Better, however, is the plan of appealing through reports and studies to such people and thus inducing them to contribute to playgrounds, social training of children, decoration of the buildings, and improvement of the physical conditions of schools.

The first excitement which followed the description of the Montessori system has somewhat subsided. Partisan feelings with regard to the merits and demerits of this system are somewhat less pronounced than they were a year ago, and the commercial interests which control the apparatus are more reasonable. Kindergartners are seeing the advantage of adopting any suggestions which the discussion brings, while the special schools that grew out of this movement are approaching more and more in character the well-organized American schools which deal with little children. It is very interesting at this stage of the movement to have a painstaking diagnosis of the movement such as Professor Kilpatrick has worked out in this monograph.[2]

Professor Kilpatrick went to Rome for the purpose of becoming personally acquainted with the Montessori schools. He speaks,

[1] *Volunteer Help to the Schools*. By Ella Lyman Cabot. (Riverside Educational Monographs.) Boston: Houghton Mifflin Co. Pp. xi+136.

[2] *The Montessori System Examined*. By William Heard Kilpatrick. (Riverside Educational Monographs.) Boston: Houghton Mifflin Co. Pp. viii+71.

therefore, with the insight of observation as well as on the basis of a careful reading of the Montessori books.

The monograph is divided into a number of chapters which deal with the general principles advocated in the Montessori system. Professor Kilpatrick finds as a result of his analysis that the interpretation given the general doctrine of development is inadequate. He regards the doctrine of liberty as a reiteration of the principle familiar to all students of the kindergarten. Self-expression and auto-education are recognized as valid principles but the means furnished by the Montessori system for working out these principles are regarded as too limited. The exercises of practical life which the system employs are regarded as altogether beneficial. In discussing sense-training as advocated by the Montessori system, Professor Kilpatrick enters into a labored discussion of formal discipline which seems hardly in place. One theoretical position can hardly be refuted by another theoretical position. The ordinary reader will not feel that Professor Kilpatrick has contributed very much to the exposition or criticism of sensory training. There is enough independent evidence in the hands of educators to make it possible to discuss this problem of sensory training without any reference to formal discipline. Finally, Professor Kilpatrick discusses the school arts of reading, writing, and arithmetic and regards it as one of the probable contributions of the method that these arts have been undertaken at so early an age. He finds, however, that the simplicity of the Italian language makes it somewhat easier to carry on this type of training in Italy than in America and he questions the wisdom of any attempt to imitate here this phase of the work.

It is difficult to understand why any author should attempt to deal with the problem of industrial education in the elementary school unless he has some very definite and clear-cut ideas on the matter. No one has any right to discuss this problem who is not able, first of all, to determine with a good deal of definiteness the point in the elementary school at which such training should be undertaken. At the present time the secondary school is the institution commonly held responsible for industrial education. In the second place, no one has any right to talk on this topic unless he is prepared to say with a good deal of clearness what method shall be adopted in carrying on the work.

Mr. Cole[1] has written on the problem in what must be described as a vague, general way. In the latter part of the monograph he has given one example of what might be done in the way of studying industry in the elementary school. Briefly stated, this example includes some theoretical instruction about a local industry, some observation of the plant itself, and, finally, a little constructive work which consists in making models of the devices which have been observed in the factory. All of this is to be part of a course in industry. This course is to absorb the regular manual-training work of the elementary school and is also to have some of the time now devoted to geography, reading, and the other subjects. We are confidently informed that the introduction of such a course as this will be a renovating influence to modify the spirit and character of the whole elementary work.

There are throughout the book paragraphs which criticize the present school as a school bent upon culture and not practical in its character. The manual-training movement seems to this author to be very formal and unproductive. In short, there is a wholesale criticism in all directions of everything done at the present time by the elementary school, and the remedy offered is this course in industry. Whether this work should be done in the third grade or in the seventh grade is not stated by the author. In fact, one goes through the book with a good deal of doubt as to the author's acquaintance with the difference between the third grade and the seventh grade.

Page after page of general discussion seems to indicate that the author is extraordinarily foggy in his thinking about the different processes on which he delivers final opinions. For example, on p. 46 the author is dealing in a summary way with culture. Here are a few sentences which indicate the scope and depth of the discussion.

> According to the traditional opinion, a study that is useful cannot also be cultural. Culture consists of philosophy, literature, and the fine arts.

[1] *Industrial Education in the Elementary School.* By Percival R. Cole. Boston: Houghton Mifflin Co. Pp. xviii+63.

. . . . We need a new theory of culture. The old definition may be retained—culture is the study of things worth while in themselves. It is the content, not the form, of the definition that must be changed. Things worth while in themselves include all great matters, whether useful for external ends or not. The industrial life is a great matter. It lies at the root of all civilization. It calls for the highest mental powers. It enriches the moral life with opportunities for the exercise of the economic virtues.

This eulogy of industry and its easy introduction into the group of cultural subjects is interesting; but one wonders whether executing a single process in a factory does involve the highest powers. One wonders whether the author would not have done well, before trying to persuade us in a wholesale way that industry is identical with culture, to have spent a little time in private thought distinguishing between various different kinds of industry. There are certain types of industry which are elevating; there are others which are not. If the educational world is to be persuaded to give adequate attention to industry, these distinctions must be recognized. It is not enough to dash into print with a wholesale eulogy of everything industrial. The book serves as a striking evidence of the complexity of this whole problem of dealing with industrial education. It certainly does not clear up the situation.

CLASSROOM METHODS AND DEVICES

Articles reporting concrete classroom exercises are very difficult to collect. From time to time the editors of the *Journal* have sought material of this type. They usually find themselves checked in their effort by the desire which seems to possess most people to discuss school problems in a broad, theoretical way. If a teacher has a good method of teaching nature-study or long division, he commonly feels the impulse to explain the theory of his practice and leave the reader to guess at most of the details of actual classroom work. The *Journal* hopes that it will be possible to overcome in some measure this impulse toward theory. The editors will make an earnest endeavor to get statements both of practice and of the fundamental principles which underlie practice. Materials that are available for classroom work and are to be classified under the general head of methods and devices will, therefore, be very welcome. But in each case these methods and devices should be accompanied by some statement which will make clear what is the aim of instruction.

How to Study

The difficulty which children experience in learning their lessons is very often due not so much to the subject-matter on which they are at work as to their inability to get at the meaning of what they read. My attention was drawn to this fact in connection with the geography work of the fifth grade. The weekly schedule provided six thirty-minute periods—four recitation periods and two study periods. During the recitation periods the class co-operated well, but the results from the study periods were very unsatisfactory. An analysis of the situation showed some of the difficulties to be: (1) a decided slowness in the rate of silent reading; (2) inability to select the essential and to disregard the unessential data in an assignment; (3) lack of facility in making proper use of table of contents, index, appendix, maps, etc., and (4) inability to organize data upon a single topic.

In short, the group had to be taught how to study. The whole organization of the class was accordingly turned to meet this need. The study periods for a few weeks were used for purposes calling for little initiative, but a high degree of precision, such as making maps, drawings, and written summaries of phases of the problems worked out by the class as a whole. The regular recitation periods were turned into "study" recitations with a view to training the children under supervision to study properly. The text was read silently, a paragraph at a time. At first the reading was made definite by requiring the children to find the answer to specific questions.

It was noted at once that the rate of reading varied considerably. Furthermore, it was noted that the fastest readers grasped the thought of the paragraph more frequently than the slower ones. The latter constantly pleaded for oral reading, saying, "We can understand it better." The slow readers were stimulated to read more rapidly. By gradually decreasing the time allowed, the slow readers were helped to increase their speed and with it their ability to get the thought.

Ability to organize material was cultivated as follows: At the beginning of the lesson the main topic of the problem being considered was placed on the board. As each paragraph was studied and discussed the results were summarized and placed as subtopics under the main topic. For further training in arrangement of materials the tables of contents and the indexes of various supplementary readers were critically studied.

Training was also given in the collection of new material. Newspaper clippings and magazine articles served to elaborate or explain or illustrate topics inadequately treated in the text. In using this latter type of material it was not always possible to have duplicate copies, but by giving out different articles upon the same general topic the pupils reading silently were forced to study independently each paragraph and then asked to state to the class what the clipping contributed to the problem under discussion. This information was discussed and sometimes questioned by the other members of the class. If after re-reading the passage the pupil still made the same interpretation, the passage was read aloud.

Not infrequently at such times it was found that the dictionary was needed as the court of last resort. Occasionally inaccuracies were found and many facts in supplementary readers were found to be out of date.

As the class gained in ability to study independently, the study periods were used for gathering information and the recitation periods became more and more a time for bringing together ideas for comparison, correction, and organization into a final solution of the problems relating to the study.

KATHARINE McLAUGHLIN
UNIVERSITY ELEMENTARY SCHOOL

ON PREPARING TO WRITE A LETTER

Maria intended a letter to write,
  But could not begin (as she thought) to indite,
So went to her mother with pencil and slate
  Containing "Dear Sister," and also a date.

"With nothing to say, my dear girl, do not think
  Of wasting your time over paper and ink;
But certainly this is an excellent way,
  To try with your slate to find something to say.

"I will give you a rule," said her mother, "my dear,
  Just think for a moment your sister is here,
And what would you tell her? Consider, and then,
  Though silent your tongue, you can speak with your pen."

ELIZABETH TURNER
(*English Book for Children*)

FORMAL LANGUAGE TRAINING IN THE PRIMARY GRADES

It is not difficult to get teachers to admit that forms of language are important; that they should be fixed in the pupil's mind and habits as early as is possible; but the questions with most teachers are: What forms shall be fixed? How can the end desired be attained?

The answer to the first question can be found in local conditions. An investigation held in a western city a few years ago revealed the following facts: Practically one-half of the errors of speech were those of verb-forms; one-half of the verb-form errors arose from confusing past tense and perfect participle; about one-fifth of the errors were due to misuse of pronouns; double negatives, adverbial errors, and even colloquialisms were relatively inconspicuous in the sum total of errors. Why one class of errors should be so pronouncedly greater in number than the other class is evident when we reflect upon the constant use we make of the one class of words. Could not a teacher, however, in order to satisfy herself respecting the right use of the pupils' time, make just such a classified list of errors among her pupils; could she not quickly discover whether it is the verb-form or the colloquialism that is most stubborn, and could she not decide which verb-form or which colloquialism she should most vigorously attack? No teacher can take a list of general errors made out for another locality and do the most effective work. A special study of her own field not only informs her at what she should aim, but it also assists her to do the aiming. Success here, as elsewhere, demands its price.

When the errors have been discovered the question arises, What method can be adopted to overcome these errors? Doubtless there are many devices which could be employed. One device which has proved very successful is the language game. In it the child is wholly unconscious of the ultimate aim of the teacher, though fully aware of the fact that a certain form must be used in order that the game be won. The teacher, however, is more successful with results than if she were to explain her intentions. She secures the functioning of language at the time when it is needed. The drill is not isolated; it is interesting on account of the activity; repetition is called forth by a natural situation, and the desired expression is in the focus of attention.

GAMES AND EXERCISES FOR USING VERB-FORMS CORRECTLY

WHAT I SAW

Leader stands in front of room and calls child's name. Class says, "Go to the window and you will see while we are counting, 'one, two, three.'" Child goes to the window, looks out, then turns and names things, e.g., "I saw a house, some pretty trees, and a man."

Should the incorrect form be used, the leader says, "Wrong," and calls another child to the window. The game is varied by, "Tell what you see," or "Tell what you have seen."

WHAT HE DID

Leader calls child's name and says, "Do three things." The child obeys. Leader says, "What did John do, Mary?" Mary answers, "John jumped, hopped, and ran."

WHO DID IT?

Leader says, "Follow me, John." John does as leader says. The leader says to third child, "Who did it?" [Who is doing it, or has done it?] Third child answers, "You and John did it." [Are doing it, or have done it.] Third child follows John, the new leader, who performs another act. Leader asks fourth child, "Who did it?" [Varied.] Fourth child answers, "You, John, and — did it." [Varied.]

The game continues by each child who answers correctly joining the procession and following the leaders. The "you" must be put in the right place, the children must be named in the order of their standing in line, the proper verb-form must be used, and the "and" must be used correctly before the child is entitled to join the procession. Naturally this answer must be given very quickly, else the march will seem to be more of a funeral than a game.

The foregoing devices may suggest others for the forms of "to go, "to be," "to have," "to come," "to give," "to take," "to throw," "to ride," "to ring," "to sing," "to choose," "to freeze," which seem to be the most troublesome verbs.

MAY

Children are told to think of any animal which they may wish to represent.
First child: "May I be a bird?"
Leader: "You may." [Child flies around the room.]
Second child: "May I be a frog?"
Leader: "You may." [Child hops.]
All of the children are finally engaged in some action.
Leader: "You may all be children." [Seats.]

CAN

This game is played as the previous ones, only child asks, "Can I be a frog," "bird," etc., and leader answers, "We shall see if you can," etc.; "We shall see if we can all be children." [Seats.]

GAMES AND EXERCISES FOR USING PRONOUNS CORRECTLY

YOU AND I SHALL DANCE TOGETHER

Children in a circle. Leader in the center goes up to child and bows. They both say, "You and I shall dance together." They dance around circle with piano accompaniment, after which each one goes up to another child and says, "Dance with him [her] and me." All four then say, "You and I shall dance together." Choices are made until all of the children are dancing.

WORDS IN SERIES

Leader: "Tell three things that you can do, and do them."

Child: "I can mark on the blackboard, run around the room, and sing." [Child does the three things.]

Leader: "Name three things in the front of this room." [Chair, picture, *and* chalk tray.]

Leader: "I am thinking of something in this room that is long and light brown. You may guess three things." [Is it the piano, the window shade, *or* the window stick ?]

Leader: "Name as many things as you can think of. Use 'and' before the last one." This may be turned into a contest.

DESCRIPTION. ADJECTIVES IN SERIES

Teacher holds up picture of fruit or vegetable (though the real thing is preferable). One child uses an adjective to describe it, e.g., "That apple is red." Another child takes it up and adds another word to describe it, e.g., "That apple is red and round." The game stops when some child fails to find a descriptive word. The sentence which has "and" incorrectly used is not counted in the game.

The games should, of course, be quick and full of life. Those who are slow in responding or who respond incorrectly should be penalized by being made to wait for another turn. These illustrations will serve only as suggestions, not as cut-and-dried devices.

Before leaving the subject of formal language work, however, it is impossible to forego making other suggestions, more specific in their application.

1. Make a list of errors of speech common among the pupils. Add to it as incorrect forms appear.
2. Concentrate upon certain types of errors until they are fairly well corrected.
3. When working with difficult forms, allow several sentences containing the correct form to remain upon the board, e.g., "The little boy doesn't need a sweater" [*doesn't*].
4. Do not display the incorrect forms to the children.
5. In fixing correct forms, have some studied and some unstudied dictations.
6. Have children repeat the dictated sentences, sometimes singly and sometimes in concert.
7. Remember that writing the correct form does not fix the speaking habit.

8. Be systematic in planning oral exercises to overcome faults on the list.
9. Make the exercises short and lively—about five minutes in length.

MATTIE LOUISE HATCHER

KENTUCKY STATE NORMAL SCHOOL
BOWLING GREEN

RATIONAL PRACTICE IN WRITING

It is a matter of common observation in the teaching of writing that the greatest retarding factors are (1) irrational practice, (2) the absence of a critical standard on the part of both teacher and pupils, and (3) the monotony that inevitably arises in connection with routine work. The following analysis of the common defects of writing and their respective causes is an attempt to apply some of the principles of the psychology of practice to the problems of writing. By being taught to recognize the defects of writing and to discover the causes, the pupil develops a critical standard for judging his own work and that of other members of his class, and he becomes interested in his progress, for he can understand why he is or is not succeeding. As a result monotony is minimized, because practice becomes a rational process.

DEFECT	CAUSE
Too much slant	1. Writing arm too near the body. 2. Thumb too stiff. 3. Point of nib too far from fingers. 4. Paper in wrong position. 5. Stroke in wrong direction.
Writing too straight	1. Arm too far from body. 2. Fingers too near nib. 3. Index finger alone guiding pen. 4. Incorrect position of paper.
Writing too heavy	1. Index finger pressing too heavily. 2. Using worn pen. 3. Penholder of small diameter.
Writing too light	1. Pen held too obliquely or too straight. 2. Eyelet of pen turned to side. 3. Penholder of too large diameter.
Writing too angular	1. Thumb too stiff. 2. Penholder too lightly held. 3. Movement too slow.

DEFECT	CAUSE
Writing too irregular........	1. Lack of freedom of movement. 2. Movement of hand too slow. 3. Pen-gripping. 4. Incorrect or uncomfortable position.
Spacing too wide...........	1. Pen progresses too fast to right. 2. Too much lateral motion.

W. C. Reavis

Pierre Laclede School
St. Louis, Mo.

A Map of the United States

In 1904, when visiting the World's Exposition at St. Louis, I was very much interested in a miniature exhibit of the irrigated gardens of the West. People generally are attracted to large things worked out on a small scale. At any rate, the beautifully laid-out fields and gardens growing in actual soil, showing the irrigation ditches, made such an impression on my mind that some years afterward, in searching for a way to present a study of the United States to a sixth grade in the public schools, the thought came to me, why not plan the United States as I had seen the irrigated western lands depicted? I did so, and the method worked out very successfully. I had in mind a general purpose, but having then had very little experience in teaching, I was not able to develop it in the organized way that I have done this year, working with a smaller group of children and having more conveniences in equipment. The class of this year, however, was composed of low-fifth-grade children instead of sixth.

When we began our study of the United States this year I told the class just what we were going to do after we had finished the subject. I described to them fully the plan of procedure, and told them that as a result of our study we should make a real map of the United States in soil, one large enough to show everything of importance that grows in our country and to indicate all the leading industries in some way.

From the first they had no trouble in picturing the map and were delighted with the plan. All the year they had wanted to give a play in connection with their Roman history and as I knew it would be impossible to work up the play and the map both, I was somewhat worried over the course I should take in persuading them to give up the play; but as soon as they understood the map project they voted unanimously to work that up instead of the play. This of course meant the centering of the geography work around this unit for the entire second semester of the year. Five thirty-minute periods a week were given to geography and during the last three weeks of the semester I allowed the children to take the study period each day, which was also thirty minutes, to work on the map.

From the beginning everything was done with reference to the map. We worked on the general shape, outline, and physical characteristics with the idea of modeling them in soil. The climate, highlands and lowlands, the location of the important rivers, and the Great Lakes were studied with interest because everyone in the room had to have a sufficient knowledge of these points to be able actually to help in the formation of a model of our country. After they had worked at their seats with relief and physical maps before them, and had taken part in general discussions of the physical characteristics, they went to the blackboard and drew the map of United States, showing the mountains and lowlands in relief. Drill in this was continued until the map was drawn from memory.

Next came a study of the different industries, special studies being made of the different regions of the United States where each industry is most fully developed. This work included a review of place geography.

We first took up agriculture and grazing. This included a study of cotton, tobacco, peanuts, sugar-cane, rice, corn, and wheat as the important crops. The study involved a detailed account of the conditions necessary for growth and all the stages from the planting to the manufactured product. Then specimens of grains and the finished product were examined; pictures were used showing the different processes of harvesting and manufacturing, and the children were encouraged to look up different topics at home or in the library at school and make reports on them. One little girl who used her father's new set of *Britannica* was one of the leaders in giving outside information. One of the boys, rather enviously, said, "Well, no wonder she knows so much about sugar-cane, she looks up everything at home." I asked, "Can't you look up things too?" The next day he came to school and proudly announced that he had been reading a lot about sugar-cane that Ellen hadn't told and wanted to give his report to the class. So the spirit of investigation grew through social emulation and natural interest in the products under discussion, and I am sure that eighth-grade children could not have gone at things with any better attitude of research than did these fifth-grade children when they wanted to find out about geographical facts with a definite purpose in mind. One child, who was on the Grazing Committee and had to place the tiny animals in the states where they belonged to show the great grazing-areas, brought to me one morning several pages of statistics which she had copied from the agricultural bulletin at home, showing the number of horses, cows, sheep, and mules in each state of the Union.

Why should not children of this age know facts definitely? They should get a correct knowledge of the resources of our country and I think the fifth grade is not too soon to give them this exact information. This does not mean that they must learn these statistics, but they should be able to understand them, and so be capable of judging the relative wealth of our country. The members of this class had a much clearer knowledge of the distribution of live stock in the different sections after hearing this report and helping to place the models where they belonged than if they had read monotonously in their geographies about grazing. It was knowledge put to a definite use immediately upon acquisition.

After the topics were read and discussed sufficiently, the children were given small maps of the United States and asked to color certain areas to show the greatest wheat-growing regions, corn regions, sugar-cane regions, etc. This was done to test their knowledge of the previous discussions, and, of course, with no assistance from maps or books. During this period of study I told them that when we were ready to make the real map certain committees would be appointed to show the different industries on the map, and that these committees must not only be able to work out the representations of their industries, but they must also be able to tell everything about each industry.

Various topics were used for the basis of composition work, and since the children were studying them with a definite purpose in mind, they wrote with the real interest that comes when there is something to say. At this time, when we were discussing the

PEANUTS

COTTON

different agricultural products, the class planted several window-boxes with sugar-cane, cotton, peanuts, grapefruit, and lemons. These were studied and watched during their growth, drawings were made of them, and compositions were written about them. The following are types of compositions which were written by the class a few weeks after the window-boxes were planted. This was almost a month before the map was begun. The purpose of these compositions was to get from the children expressions concerning their observations of the growth of the plants, rather than stories of the industries involved.

DOROTHY May 1, 1914

PEANUTS

Ronnoc and Norris planted peanuts on April 10, 1914. We will transplant them for our map around Virginia and the Carolina's. Today they are about $2\frac{1}{2}$ inches high. An acre sometimes produces from twenty to one hundred bushels. Oil is sometimes made from the peanut. When they come up they open up in the middle. They were planted about one inch deep. Norfolk is the biggest port for shipping them.

ELIZABETH April 29, 1914

COTTON

Dorothy and Ellen planted the cotton for our soil map April 10, 1914. In about three weeks it has grown $2\frac{1}{2}$ inches to $3\frac{3}{4}$ inches. It is grown mostly in Texas and around the Gulf States. Cotton is so important that if all the gold which is mined in one year from all over the world was stacked up in a pile and all the cotton that we ship to Europe in one year was stacked up beside it the cotton would be worth more than the gold.

SORGHUM

We thought at first that we might have to transplant these window-box plants to the soil map, but as a matter of fact we were able to begin with all the crops from the seeds. Indeed, most of the plants grew so fast that we had to harvest and replant them three times in the three and a half weeks of the existence of the map. We had to use sorghum seed instead of the real sugar-cane, which was a great trial to the children, necessitating constant explanations and apologies when they were pointing out the sugar-cane region to visitors. The corn also was a source of regret to them because it insisted on growing so fast that most of the time it was higher than the mountains.

It was not possible to include everything on the map. We had ordered it made as large a size as could be accommodated in the schoolroom, but still many facts had to be indicated in relation to those industries which were really worked out. For instance, most of the big cities had to be located and discussed with reference to whatever industry was going on about them, as Minneapolis in the wheat region, and New Orleans in the cotton region.

Mining and manufacturing considered in relation to the map were taken up next. Different specimens of ores were brought by the children and exhibited; iron in the various stages of manufacture was brought from the museum, and pictures of mining

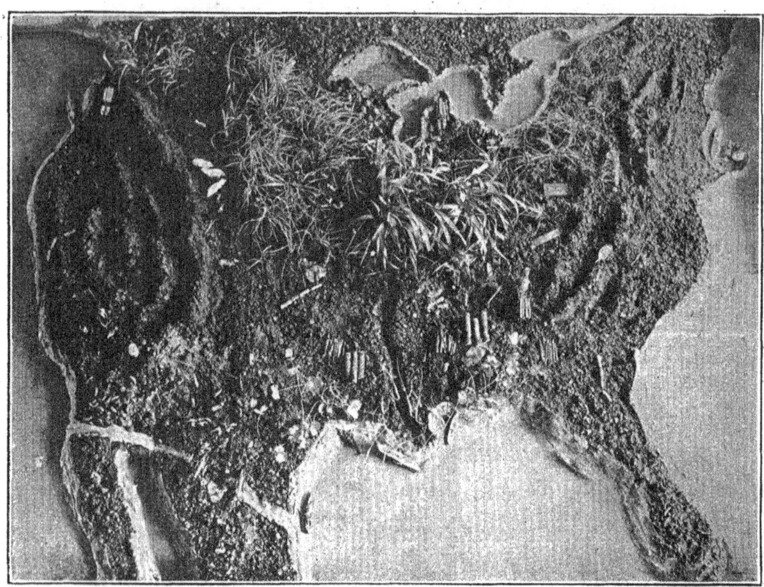

camps and mining processes were studied. Carpenter's *Geographical Reader of North America* was used as a text for the whole study, and, as before, the children were asked to look up different topics and give to the class a report of what they had read. In indicating the industry on the soil map, iron ore was placed in Tennessee, Alabama, Georgia, Pennsylvania, and around Lake Superior; coal in the Appalachian Mountains, Indiana, and Illinois; gold in California and Colorado, and silver in Colorado and Utah.

The lumbering industry was one of the most absorbing topics studied. Two of the pupils whose fathers were engaged in that business each brought about fifteen specimens of wood. Of course they were able to supplement the study with many interesting facts told them by their fathers. These two pupils were placed on a committee to work out the lumber industry on the map. They placed groves of tiny pine trees to show the pine forests and had minute chips cut from their samples of wood which were labelled and set in the places where they were supposed to grow. Then they showed the lumber camps by placing in the North small sleds filled with little sticks cut just like lumber, and in the South little wagons of lumber drawn by horses. Although I made no conscious effort to have the pupils study very many of the different trees, it was surprising to see how quickly they learned to recognize these from the specimens brought. We had a map made indicating in different colors the various vegetation belts of the United States and where the important trees were found. This was hung on the wall where it could conveniently be seen by the children. They would examine the samples of wood which were marked with the names of the trees they represented, and they would go to the map to see where each tree grew; and as a result, when the woods were placed on the map every child in the room knew in what state each grew, and was eager to display this knowledge. It was not at all surprising that the lumbering industry was one of the favorite topics for composition work chosen by the class.

The study of commerce had to be taken up with the study of the industries. Small boats were brought and placed at points on the water to show the big shipping ports. Of course, in telling about these ports each one had to know why it was important. Several railroad lines were represented by toy trains—the Illinois Central, the New York Central, the Florida East Coast, and the Southern Pacific.

The fisheries along the New England and eastern coasts were studied, also the salmon industry on the northwestern coast. The different methods of fishing were discussed—the trawl, the seine, and the hand line. This industry was not as well indicated on the map as some of the others. A small basket of fish was set at Cape Cod to show the fishing along that coast.

I have gone ahead of my point and in discussing the preparation of the map I have at times mentioned what we actually did after the study was finished. This has seemed necessary to get the connection between the study of the subject-matter and its application. When we had finished the investigating period of our study we were ready for the final result, which was the testing of the knowledge and ability of the pupils to put into practice what they had learned.

We decided to use for the map a zinc pan seven by five feet by six inches deep which we had made to order. It occupied the middle of the schoolroom, the children's desks being grouped around it. Needless to say, it was the center of attraction. In fact, from the time the map was first mentioned, life for the children seemed to be one series of exciting and eventful happenings. When the pan was brought into the room it was hard to act as if school were an ordinary affair; when the soil was carried in by the janitors and dumped into the pan every child in the room begged to be one of the first to begin work.

The first thing was to clear the dirt of all foreign particles and then to shape the country. This took three or four days. Everyone in the room was allowed to help. Some parts of the coast were extremely difficult to outline correctly. I allowed the children to work without help and then to compare what they had done with a map and to correct the errors. The Great Lakes caused them more trouble than any other thing, unless it was the New England coast; the former took at least ten trials. I looked for signs of discouragement and loss of interest, but none came; some child was always ready and eager to try where others had failed. They came to school at eight o'clock in the morning, were most unwilling to leave at recess or noon, and would not go home in the afternoon until I compelled them to do so by locking up the room.

When the shape was at last completed, clay was used to bank in the coasts and to form the basins for the Great Lakes. Of course water had to be put in the Pacific and Atlantic Oceans and the Great Lakes; this was one of the most important things to be done. In making the mountains the results of the careful map work were shown in getting the relative heights and directions. The Great Basin took some time. What was most pleasing was to see the attitude which the children took in regard to different questions which were discussed. It was no uncommon thing for one child to criticize some detail of another's work and then to secure a proof of his statement from some atlas or book.

Then I divided the class into sections or committees to work out the different industries. It was understood, however, that

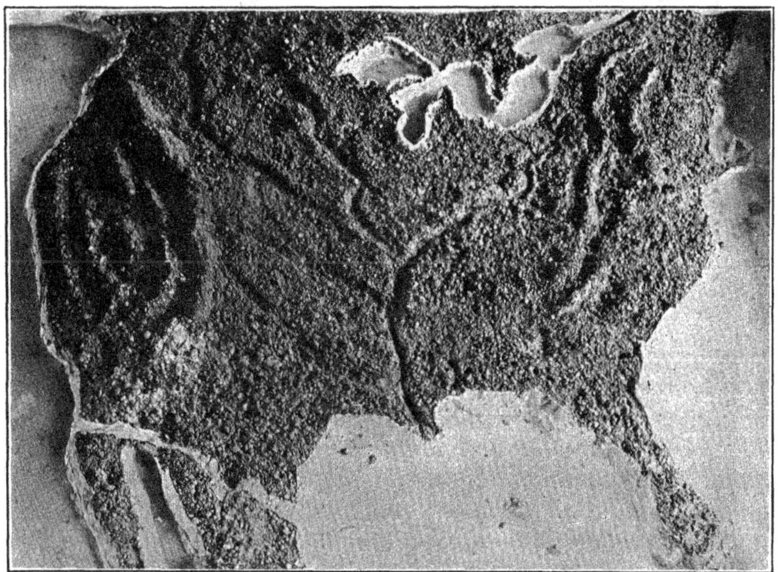

everyone in the room should contribute in any way he could to everything that was needed. The Agricultural Committee planted the crops: corn, wheat, cotton, tobacco, rice, grapefruit, oranges, lemons, and grass for the cattle to graze upon. The morning after the seeds were planted, almost every child in the room asked me the same question on entering: "Well, are they up yet?" They came up all too soon; in a week's time the corn was higher than the mountains, and had to be pulled up and replanted.

The tiny animals were brought and put in their appropriate places by the Grazing Committee. The stockyards were constructed to represent Chicago; there was an automobile for Detroit, and a basket of apples in New York to show the fruit district there; the lumber camps were set up; the arid regions of the West and Southwest were shown by the sandy stretches of country covered with cacti; the lofty mountains with their snow-covered summits (salt-covered) stood tall and imposing; the minerals were deposited; derricks were constructed showing oil deposits, and gas wells were shown by tall escapes of clay; bananas, grapefruit, and lemons were growing in Florida and California; boats were sailing on the Great Lakes and ocean steamers were leaving the big ports; even the tiny cannon were on the border pointing toward Mexico—the United States was a real country to the children and geography was the easiest of all subjects to teach.

It is unnecessary to say anything more about the interest aroused by the method of presentation. I had live children with whom to work, and I know the results obtained are permanent.

Another important outcome of this work was the spirit of investigation and research which it fostered: the children saw the necessity of careful study and of testing the results of that study. They had a reason for finding out facts and a real use to make of them.

It was a tragic moment when the time came for the janitor to remove the map so that the room could be used for summer school. The children insisted on keeping it in the room until the last minute. Finally everything was taken from the surface and the soil and water were being removed: there was a dead silence in the room save for the creaking of the pan and the shoveling of the dirt—it was a sad and serious moment. Suddenly the stillness was broken by a small voice whose owner had been very much interested in the Norse stories we had just finished: "Miss Storm, this is the twilight of the gods!"

Here are some compositions written about the various industries and the making of the map. All the written work presented is shown just as it was when handed in by the children. There has been no attempt to correct mistakes in spelling or punctuation. The children were allowed to look up the spelling of difficult words in their geographies, and in instances where words could not be found they were written on the blackboard.

5 B GEOGRAPHY

ELLEN June 3, 1914

GRAZING COMMITTEE

Our grade the 5 B class had studied the United States this year and we made a map of the United States in soil.

I was on the grazing committee and I looked up the states where the different animals were raised in a book of the Agricultural Bauea and found that Texas raised one million four hundred and thirteen swine. Illinois one million five hundred and ninty five horses. And Wyoming five million eight hundred and eighty five sheep.

I placed the little animals which were only one inch high in the states just named and learned them so I could explane it to visitors.

Some of the otheres childern helped me. Martha and Norris gave me some tiny animals which I also placed in the map.

5 B GEOGRAPHY

KENNETH U.E.S.

MINING

We made a soil map of the United States. I was on the mining committee and I put some iron in the Lake Superior reigon, in Sout Carolina and Pennsylvaina. I also put some gold in colorado and California. I put some coal in Pennysvania, Indiana, North and South Carolina, New York and Nebraska. I put some copper in the Kewahnee peninsula. I put some zink in Missouri also.

5 B GEOGRAPHY

WARREN University Elementary School

OUR SOIL MAP

We have been studying the United States in Geography and our teacher sugested that we make a soil map of the United States.

We had the janitors put the soil in a pan which we had made seven by five feet, and we started to model the map. We all helped to model it. When we got the shape the best we could we put clay in little strips around the shape so that the water when put in the oceans would not swamp the soil. We had a lot of trouble with Maine and the Great Lakes. Miss Storm did not help us but told us whether the shape was good or not. She told us the Great Lakes were not good. We tried again and again until we got the shape to suit us. Then we made the Apalachian mountains and the Rocky Mountains. Then we put salt on them to repersent snow. And then we put the water in the ocean and Great Lakes. We put the little trains to show the important railroad centers and boats to show the transportation all over the United States coast. New York is a great apple region so we put apples there. And fish on Cape Cod to repersent the fishing the fishing Industry. We also put cactus in Texas and Florida and Wherever it grows. We thought it would be best to have water in the Mississippi River so we put in clay. But we found it better not to have it so we put in silver paper.

NORRIS U.E.S.

LUMBERING IN OUR SOIL MAP

Our roum in Geography had been studying the United States. Our teacher promised us we could make a map of it in soil so we did. We had two or three pans but none were of good size. Finally we had a good zinc pan made. Then we modeled it and put in the different industries.

Elizabeth and I were on the lumber comittee She got some little pieces of lumber and so did I, I got some yellow pine and put it where it should be which is in Georga, Mississippi and Arkanses. I got some basswood, maple, aspen, chestnut, spruce, beech, Ash, Tamarock, birch, Oak and White and Northern pine. In the central states there are white, black and Red Oaks cherry, elms and hickory trees. In the south yellow pine, cypress, cedars, gums and Oak. In the west fir, balsom, spruce and western hemlock. I got a tiny wagon and put lumber in it and put it in washington to show the lumber there. I put a small sleigh in Michigan filled with lumber and a wagon in the south filled with yellow pine for the pine region and some yellow pine logs in the south.

ELIZABETH June 3, 1914

OUR SOIL MAP

Our grade the 5 B class has worked very hard in geography and at the end of school we made a soil map of the United States showing the different industries in these states. All most every one has brought and done something for it. We planted corn where most corn is raised in Illinois, Indiana, Iowa Nebraska and Kansas. We put the Wheat where most of it is raised in North and South Dakota and Minnesota. Then we planted cotton, sugar cane, tobacco and rice. We also planted some trees: orange, lemon and grapefruit trees. Beatrice made little bananas out of yellow clay and laid them in Florida and California We put cacti where they are found Norris brought a basket of apples and fish. We put but the apples in New York and the fish in Cape Cod to show the fishing industry. First the jainitor put a lot of soil in a little pan which was very much to little. We then had a lot of trouble in getting a large enough pan. At last we had one made which was 7 feet by 5 feet and 6 inches deep. We then modeled our map. We had a lot of trouble with Maine and the Great Lakes. We put salt on the mountains so as to make them look as if snow was on the top of them. We have the stockyards in Chicago and we put little ships to show where the most commerce is. We have little trains scattered over the United States they are the Florida East Coast, Illinois central and the northern Pacific railroads. There are little lumbering wagons and of course we have water in the two ocean and the Gulf of Mexico. We have little canons on the border to procted us from Mexico.

GRACE STORM

UNIVERSITY OF CHICAGO ELEMENTARY SCHOOL

THE SCHOOL SURVEY: FINDING STANDARDS OF CURRENT PRACTICE WITH WHICH TO MEASURE ONE'S OWN SCHOOLS

JOHN FRANKLIN BOBBITT[1]
University of Chicago

The superintendent of schools in a certain city found that his schools were unable to attract the quality of teachers that he wished to employ. He found also that the city was unable to hold many of its best teachers. They were continually resigning and going to cities that placed a higher valuation upon their services. He was continually being compelled to accept inferior teachers, to expend an undue proportion of time in getting them into shape for efficient work, only to find that a large portion of those that became efficient moved on to other cities, leaving the poorer quality of teachers for his service. The harder he worked to bring his teachers up to high standards of teaching ability, the sooner were they ready to leave him, and the sooner had he to begin the work over again with another batch of inferior material. The city could not hope to have effective teaching so long as this was the situation.

He asked the board to raise the general schedule of salaries. They replied that they raised many teachers' salaries every year; that they seemed to be always raising teachers' salaries. If they were unable to hold the teachers, this was simply due to the migratory nature of the teaching profession. In the nature of the case, teachers move about from city to city, and it is looked upon as being best for all concerned. In their opinions teachers' salaries were as high in their city as in other cities of their class. Moreover here was teacher A in their city receiving a full two hundred dollars more than teacher B over in their neighbor city

[1] The writer is indebted to Mr. E. G. Walker and Mr. E. C. Stopher for most of the computations, and to Mr. Harry Fultz for the graphical representation.

with whom one of them was acquainted; so if anything they were paying higher salaries than their neighbors.

Now most school board members are honest, well-meaning men; but, like the rest of us, they find it impossible to think clearly and to judge rightly on any question without a proper supply of the facts that bear upon the situation in hand. Like everybody else, they cannot think until they have the raw materials of thought. Now it is the business of the superintendent to supply the board in generous measure with these raw materials of thought. He must supply something more than his mere opinions, however; it must be an array of incontestible objective evidence. Moreover, it must not be presented in crude undigested form. It must be so assembled and organized that the meaning lies clearly upon the surface. So variable are the educational conditions concerned in the discussion of any problem that it is usually necessary to have a rather large quantity of facts; yet the whole must be so presented that the full significance of all of it, and of every part of it, can be taken in at a glance, and used as the basis of thought, discussion, and ultimate judgment.

The purpose of this article is to show the kind of facts that a superintendent situated as the one mentioned above should gather, and ways in which he might organize them in order to show the board the relative position of their city.

For this purpose the superintendent needs facts from many cities of the class to which his city belongs. Since conditions in different states vary, and teachers easily travel across state lines, the examples should be drawn from many states. The group of states must not be too dissimilar, however, in educational conditions. A superintendent in a northern city in the Middle West, for example, would best not include the states of the South. He possibly should not include cities west of the Rockies, owing to the greatly different economic conditions in those regions. For his purposes cities in the northern states east of the Rockies would constitute a reasonably homogeneous group.

In doing the work, one must at every stage keep in mind all the *purposes*. One of the purposes is always the finding of norms of current practice, applicable to his city for the immediate purposes of administration. Since educational standards in the South are of a different type from those of the North, salary conditions there also are of a different type, and salary practice in that region cannot be employed for finding the standards of practice for the northern states. In setting up norms of salary practice, the superintendent must consider only cities in that part of the country where the general educational standards are of relatively the same level with those of his own city.

Salary facts ready for the superintendent's use are presented in the recent National Education Association bulletin published by the United States Commissioner of Education entitled *The Tangible Rewards of Teaching*. This presents the salaries of all teachers in most cities of the country of 5,000 population and over. The facts are classified by cities, in each case giving the number of teachers receiving each grade of salary It is an array of crude data classified only for the convenience of publication. It is not digested and organized for the superintendent's use. One cannot get from the bulletin norms of practice on the basis of which to judge one's city. The averages as given include cities in all parts of the country, and are not, therefore, applicable to any part of the country. The bulletin does, however, provide the city superintendent with an invaluable mass of hitherto inaccessible data. He must, however, organize the portion of it that can be of service for his particular school system into the finished product that can be used as an instrument of thought and judgment. Our purpose here is to show how to organize such data. We shall assume that each superintendent has a copy of the bulletin, and shall not therefore reproduce here any of the crude data.

Let us suppose that it is the superintendent of the city of Reading, Pennsylvania, who is making the study, and that his purpose is to convince his school board that the salaries paid in his city are below standards of ordinary current practice; that they are below what responsible men in most cities consider a proper level. School board members do not like to see their city lagging behind the usual practice of cities of their class. What such board members usually need is information. The finished statistical product giving this information, which the superintendent might well prepare from the National Education Association report, is shown in the following tables and charts.

TABLE I

MEAN SALARIES OF ELEMENTARY SCHOOL TEACHERS IN 34 CITIES HAVING A POPULATION OF 50,000 TO 100,000

	City	Median Salary	Upper Quartile	Lower Quartile	Quartile Range	Relative Range
1	Hoboken, N.J.	$1,104	$1,200	$792	$408	37 per cent
2	Bayonne, N.J.	910	950	720	230	25
3	Youngstown, Ohio	800	900	700	200	25
4	DesMoines, Iowa	800	850	700	150	19
5	Springfield, Ill.	800	800	650	150	19
6	Fort Wayne, Ind.	776	800	720	80	10
7	Duluth, Minn.	750	800	650	150	20
8	Springfield, Mass.	750	800	725	75	10
9	Somerville, Mass.	750	750	750	0	0
10	New Bedford, Mass.	750	750	700	50	7
11	Lawrence, Mass.	750	750	750	0	0
12	Evansville, Ind.	750	750	600	150	20
13	Passaic, N.J.	750	850	700	150	20
14	Lynn, Mass.	700	700	700	0	0
15	Holyoke, Mass.	700	700	700	0	0
16	Canton, Ohio	700	750	425	325	46
17	Utica, N.Y.	700	700	675	25	4
18	Waterbury, Conn.	700	800	600	200	29
19	Kansas City, Kan.	684	793	540	253	37
20	Pawtucket, R.I.	684	722	532	200	29
21	Terre Haute, Ind.	680	680	660	20	3
22	Trenton, N.J.	680	840	520	320	47
23	Wichita, Kan.	675	675	585	90	13
24	Elizabeth, N.J.	675	750	505	245	36
25	East St. Louis, Ill.	650	700	550	150	23
26	St. Joseph, Mo.	607	720	513	207	34
27	Schenectady, N.Y.	600	675	500	175	29
28	Saginaw, Mich.	600	600	450	150	25
29	Wilkes-Barre, Pa.	600	700	550	150	25
30	Harrisburg, Pa.	570	641	499	142	25
31	Manchester, N.H.	550	650	450	200	36
32	South Bend, Ind.	540	702	414	288	53
33	Altoona, Pa.	540	585	495	90	17
34	Reading, Pa.	510	550	510	40	8

By reference to Table I and Chart I it is particularly easy for the school board in Reading to see at a glance the relative levels of salaries paid in each of the several cities, and to see the exceptionally low position of their city.

The quarter of cities doing the best by their teachers are paying mean annual salaries of more than $750. The quarter of cities doing second best by their teachers are paying median salaries ranging from $700 to $750. The quarter of cities that stands

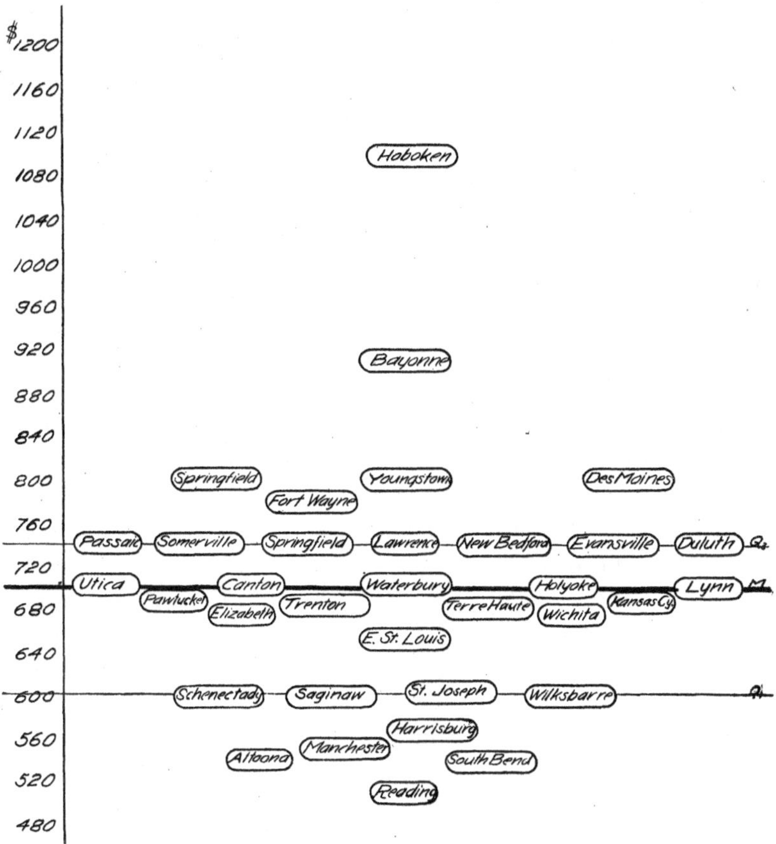

CHART I.—Showing the relative position of 34 cities of 50,000 to 100,000 population in the matter of mean annual salary paid elementary teachers. Data from U.S. Bureau of Education bulletin, *The Tangible Rewards of Teaching*, 1914.

third from the top are each paying a mean annual salary somewhere between $600 and $700. The quarter of cities paying the lowest salaries are paying less than $600. Of these the city of Reading stands at the very bottom. The school board does not exist that is not convinced by such an array of facts. They can be made to see clearly the exceptional nature of their judgment as to what constitutes a proper salary schedule. They may plead excuse; but they cannot deny.

What should be taken as the standard of practice for cities of this class? The general standard of practice may very well be represented by the median, the measure of the city which stands in the middle of the list—the city which has an equal number of cities above it and an equal number below it. There being an even number of cities in our list, there is no single middle city, but rather two middle cities, Waterbury and Utica, each with an average salary schedule of $700. Seven hundred dollars may be taken as a measure of the general average practice of this entire group of cities. With this measure one can see at a glance whether his city stands in the more progressive half of cities or in the less progressive; whether near the general average of practice, or whether far removed from it above or below.

If one should like to use the progressive half of the cities as the basis for finding a standard of current practice, then he might take the median of the upper half of the cities. This is called the quartile, since it is the measure of that city which stands one quarter of the distance from the top. Taking only the highest half of the cities, the quartile is the measure of that city that stands at the middle of that half, with an equal number above and below it in that particular half. In this case the ninth city from the top, Somerville, Massachusetts, is at the middle of the upper half. The average salary paid in Somerville is $750. This we may regard as a standard of current practice in the most progressive half of the cities. It is represented in the chart by the upper horizontal line, and marked Q_3. It is called the third quartile.

If, however, a city finds itself very low in the scale, as for example Manchester, and wishes to employ for its immediate purposes a standard of current practice derived from that half of the cities that are most backward in their salary schedules, then one should take the lower quartile, which is the measure of the city that stands just at the middle of the lowest half. In this case it is St. Joseph, Missouri, with an average salary schedule of $607. This lower quartile is shown by the lower horizontal line, and is marked Q_1. It is called the first quartile.

If the superintendents of Reading, Altoona, South Bend, Manchester, Harrisburg, Wilkes-Barre, Saginaw, etc., should have such a chart as this, put up in neat, attractive form, hung on the wall in the school board rooms, so that, meeting after meeting, their incontestible relative situation is permitted to sink deeper and deeper into the board's consciousness, then—the human mind is so made—they might in time be impelled toward an effort at least to lift their city into the class a quarter next higher. It may well be an aid in developing a proper feeling of discontent with the inferior relative position of their city.

Likewise if the superintendents of East St. Louis, Elizabeth, Wichita, Trenton, Terre Haute, Kansas City, Kansas, etc., will prepare such a chart in attractive, effective form and hang it on the walls of their board rooms, their boards may also be impelled in time to exert themselves and get their city over the dead line of mediocrity represented by the median. They may well be impelled to get out of an inferior class into a class that is above the average, since they are so very near the line of crossing anyway.

As cities of the lowest quarter climb into the second quarter, and the cities of the second quarter climb above the line of mediocrity into the third quarter, the standards themselves will be carried upward, since they are determined by current practice. Some that are now in the third quarter may thus be passed and dropped down into the second. Thus the process may in time begin to stimulate some of them.

The superintendents in the cities of Hoboken, Bayonne, Youngstown, DesMoines, and Springfield, Illinois, will not need to use the data upon their school boards. It may be that the less their school boards know about their position on the scale of current practice the better it will be for the schools. These superintendents, however, need to draw up the same array of facts; but they will use them in another manner. They will, if their teachers are suffering from a proper measure of divine discontent, find them, as usual, dissatisfied with the salary situation in their cities, and clamoring for increases of pay. While the teachers' claims may be justified on the basis of certain kinds of facts, it will be a developer of patience and moderation in their demands to show them how high above current practice their city already stands. The teachers can be convinced that if injustice is being done their profession on the side of remuneration, to them at least less injustice than usual is being done.

In a previous paragraph we referred to Table I and Chart I as being finished statistical products ready for the consumption of those for whom prepared. They are not quite complete, however. While showing the average position of each city upon the scale, they do not show the range of salaries over which the entire schedule is distributed. This range may be too narrow or too wide. If too narrow, injustice is being done the teachers, in that the poorer teachers are receiving altogether too nearly the same remuneration as the better teachers. Not enough reward for effort is given the better class of teachers; not enough stimulation to effort is given the poorer class of teachers. On the other hand the range of distribution may be entirely too wide. The city may be altogether too generous to a portion of the teachers who are particularly favored, and it may be altogether too parsimonious with another portion of the teaching body at the bottom of the schedule. Injustice may thus be done in just the reverse manner.

Now how can we compare the ranges of the salary schedules in different cities? The most convenient way and perhaps the best way is to take the quartile range for each city, and to compare these quartile ranges. By quartile range we mean the difference between the lower quartile and the upper quartile. We can illustrate the mode of calculation by taking the data of St. Joseph, Missouri. Salaries received in St. Joseph as shown by the bulletin are as follows:

12 teachers at $810
45 teachers at 765
18 teachers at 720
10 teachers at 693
19 teachers at 675
16 teachers at 657
15 teachers at 630
9 teachers at 603
7 teachers at 585
9 teachers at 567
11 teachers at 540
15 teachers at 513
29 teachers at 495
19 teachers at 450

The number of teachers in St. Joseph is 234. The teacher who stands one-quarter of the distance from the lower end of the scale is the 59th in the series. The salary of this teacher is $513. This is the lower quartile for St. Joseph. The teacher who stands one-quarter of the distance from the highest salary paid is the 59th in the series from the top. The salary of this teacher is $720. This is the upper quartile for St. Joseph. The quartile range therefore for the city is from $513 to $720—or $293. This is the difference between the mean salary of the upper half of the teachers and mean salary of the lower half of the teachers.

The upper and lower quartiles and the median for each of the cities above considered are shown in columns 2 and 3 in Table I. The facts of columns 1, 2, 3, and 4 of Table I are all shown in graphic form in Chart II. This chart shows exactly the same facts as Chart I, but in addition it shows graphically the quartile range of salaries in each of the several cities. The cities are designated by numbers because of the exigencies of space. The numbers used are those which correspond to the names of the cities in Table I. (In general it is necessary to use numbers or an abbreviation to represent the name of the city in this form of chart in order to bring the whole within a reasonable space.)

Table I and Chart II show that the quartile range of teaching salaries in Holyoke is zero, and that in Hoboken it reaches the large sum of $408. In Duluth the range seems to be about midway between the two extremes. It is clear that in Holyoke and in Hoboken the standards of current practice are not being followed. If the moderate range of the majority of cities represents the range that is most just and most stimulating to the teachers, then either the two cities referred to have an exceptional range in the qualifications and merits of the teaching body, or some injustice is being done one or another of the classes of their teachers. It is clear that Holyoke and Hoboken, as well as others similarly situated at the ends of the scale, should make an examination into the workings of their salary schedules to see whether adjustment may not be desirable.

Now it is a bit difficult to read directly from Table I or Chart II the standing as regards current practice of the majority of these cities. Really, however, each city should be able to see its standing as to quartile range, as clearly as it can see its standing in the matter of average position as shown in Chart I. This can best

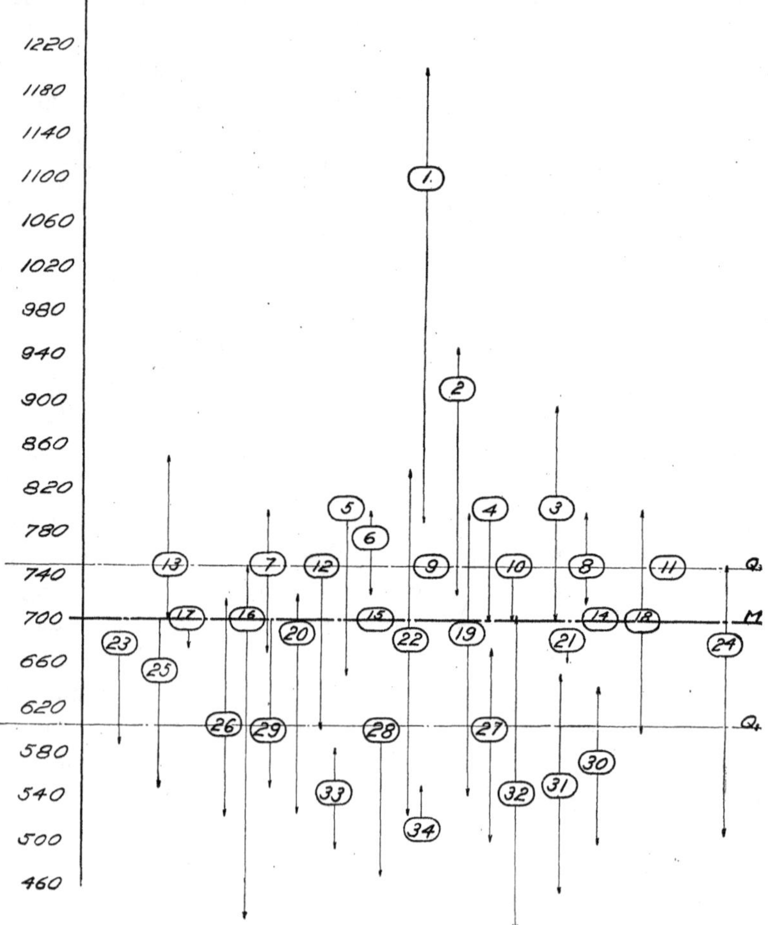

CHART II.—Showing the quartile range of elementary teachers' salaries for the 34 cities. Inclosed numbers refer to names of cities, Table I. The tips of the downward lines indicate the lower quartiles for the cities; the tips of the upward lines, the upper quartiles.

be shown by a chart built on exactly the same pattern as Chart I, using the data in the fourth column of figures in Table I, which shows the quartile range. The quartile ranges in order of rank are shown in Table II, from which each chart might be made.

TABLE II

SHOWING ABSOLUTE QUARTILE RANGE FOR EACH OF THE 34 CITIES

City	Range	City	Range
Hoboken	$408	Canton	$325
Trenton	320	South Bend	288
Kansas City, Kan	253	Elizabeth	245
Bayonne	230	St. Joseph	207
Manchester	$200		
Pawtucket	$200	Waterbury	$200
Youngstown	200	Schenectady	175
Wilkes-Barre	150	Saginaw	150
East St. Louis	150		
Passaic	$150	Evansville	$150
Duluth	$150	Springfield, Ill	$150
DesMoines	150	Harrisburg	142
Altoona	90	Wichita	90
Fort Wayne	80		
Springfield, Mass	$75		
New Bedford	$50	Reading	$40
Utica	25	Terre Haute	20
Lynn	0	Somerville	0
Lawrence	0	Holyoke	0

Table II shows a median salary range to be $150. The lower quartile of the salary ranges is $75, and the upper quartile is $200.

The "zone of safety" for range in salary schedules is perhaps represented by the zone between the two quartiles; that is to say, probably the salary range of a city should not be over $200, nor under $75. This means that such cities as Evansville, Duluth, Saginaw, Schenectady, Fort Wayne, etc., are playing safe when judged by the norms of current practice. It means that in the cities of Hoboken, South Bend, Canton, Trenton, etc., the quartile salary range is entirely too wide, if the general current practice is correct. It means further that in the cities of Holyoke, Somerville, Lynn, Utica, etc., the quartile range of the salary schedule is entirely too narrow. It needs to be widened, so as to do proper justice to meritorious teachers and properly to penalize those who are not sufficiently exerting themselves.

It is possible that the figures of Table II are sufficiently accurate for practical purposes. There is, however, an element of error that in doing very careful work should be taken into account and corrected.

It is altogether probable that in a city like Hoboken, where the general salary schedule is relatively high, the absolute quartile range should rightly be considerably wider than the corresponding quartile range of a city like Reading, where the general salary schedule is less than half as high. The figures therefore in Table II ought to be in some way related to the median level of practice in each city so as to take this difference into account. The simplest mode of procedure is to represent the quartile range of a city as a percentage of the median of that city. These percentages are shown in the last column of Table I. Their relative order is shown in Table III, and graphically in Chart III.

TABLE III

SHOWING THE RELATIVE QUARTILE RANGE OF ELEMENTARY TEACHERS' SALARIES IN THE 34 CITIES

City	Range	City	Range
South Bend	$53	Trenton	$47
Canton	46	Kansas City, Kan	37
Hoboken	37	Elizabeth	36
Manchester	36	St. Joseph	34
Schenectady	$29		
Pawtucket	$29	Waterbury	$29
Harrisburg	25	Bayonne	25
Youngstown	25	Wilkes-Barre	25
Saginaw	25		
East St. Louis	$23	Passaic	$20
Evansville	$20	Duluth	$20
Springfield, Ill	19	DesMoines	19
Altoona	17	Wichita	13
Fort Wayne	10		
Springfield, Mass	$10		
Reading	$8	New Bedford	$7
Utica	4	Terre Haute	3
Lynn	0	Lawrence	0
Somerville	0	Holyoke	0

When the absolute quartile range is thus transformed into relative quartile range, the order of the cities is very considerably

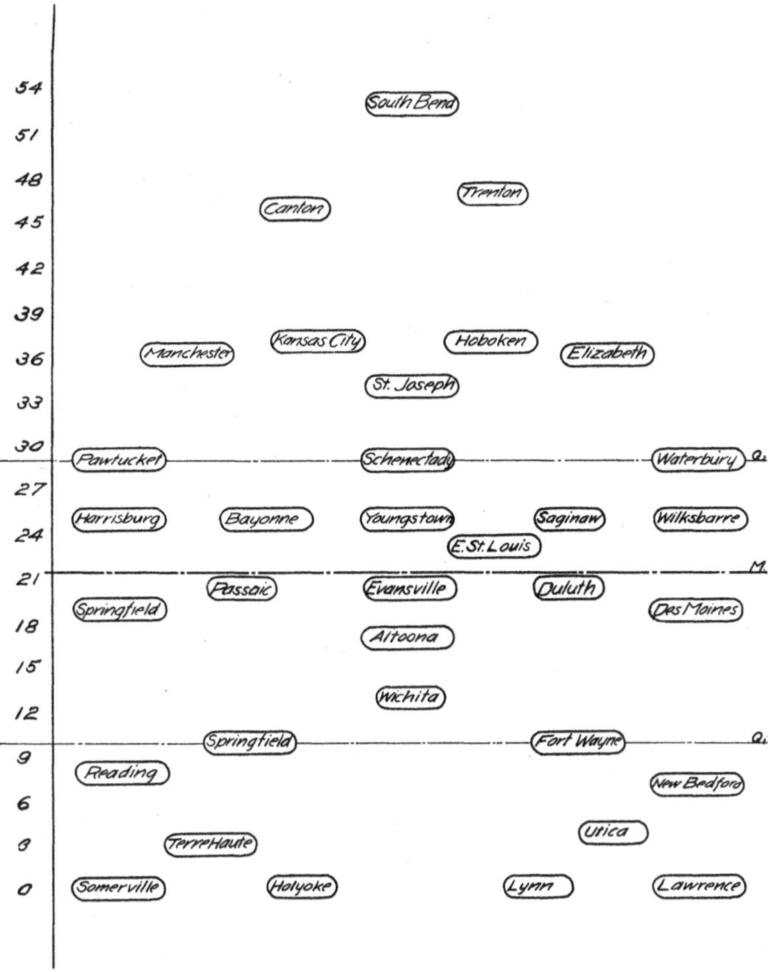

CHART III.—Shows graphically the relative quartile range of elementary teachers' salaries in the 34 cities.

changed. The cities within the "zone of safety" as judged by current practice are those in which the quartile ranges of salaries lie somewhere between 10 and 29 per cent of the medians. The names of these cities are shown on Chart III lying between the lines that designate the lower and upper quartiles. The cities lying outside of these lines, whether above or below, clearly have something to explain to themselves. Exceptional conditions may justify them in their exceptional position. They should be fully informed of such exceptional conditions, however, before being satisfied with their positions.

CURRENT EDUCATIONAL LITERATURE IN THE PERIODICALS[1]

IRENE WARREN
Librarian, School of Education, University of Chicago

Barnes, Horace Richards. The further history of some troublesome boys. Psychol. Clinic 8:107–13. (Je. '14.)

Bateman, W. G. A child's progress in speech, with detailed vocabularies. J. of Educa. Psychol. 5:307–20. (Je. '14.)

Bean, Robert Bennett. Reform in education. Pedagog. Sem. 21:284–86. (Je. '14.)

Boring, Edwin G. The marking system in theory. Pedagog. Sem. 21:269–77. (Je. '14.)

Boyer, Philip A. Class size and school progress. Psychol. Clinic 8:82–90. (My. '14.)

Buckingham, B. R. The Courtis tests in the schools of New York City. J. of Educa. Psychol. 5:199–214. (Ap. '14.)

Burnham, William H. A health examination at school entrance. Pedagog. Sem. 21:219–41. (Je. '14.)

(The) Carnegie Foundation for the Advancement of Teaching. Science 39:780–81. (29 My. '14.)

Clark, Lotta A. Pageantry in America. English J. 3:146–53. (Mr. '14.)

Cody, Sherwin. The ideal course in English for vocational students. English J. 3:263–81. (My. '14.)

Cosulich, Gilbert. The anatomy of scholarship. Pedagog. Sem. 21:290. (Je. '14.)

Dallenbach, Karl M. The effect of practice upon visual apprehension in school children. Part I. J. of Educa. Psychol. 5:321–34. (Je. '14.)

Davis, Anne. Occupations and industries open to children between fourteen and sixteen years of age. Educa. Bi-mo. 8:377–92. (Je. '14.)

Dew, Louise E. Making cripples into workingmen. Tech. World M. 21:842–43, 936. (Ag. '14.)

Dyer, Walter A. School gardens: in helping the children the nation profits. Craftsman 26:286–91. (Je. '14.)

[1] *Abbreviations.*—Atlan., Atlantic Monthly; Educa. Bi-mo., Educational Bimonthly; Educa. R., Educational Review; English J., English Journal; Indust. Arts M., Industrial Arts Magazine; J. of Educa. Psychol., Journal of Educational Psychology; Outl., Outlook; Pedagog. Sem., Pedagogical Seminary; Pop. Sci. Mo., Popular Science Monthly; Psychol. Clinic, Psychological Clinic; Tech. World M., Technical World Magazine.

Dyer, Walter A. Teaching country teachers to teach country life. World's Work 28:175–79. (Je. '14.)

Farrell, Elizabeth E. A study of the school inquiry report on ungraded classes. Psychol. Clinic 8:57–74; 99–106. (My. and Je. '14.)

Felter, William L. On reconstructing the curriculum in secondary schools. Educa. R. 48:37–48. (Je. '14.)

Fish, Susan Anderson. What should pupils know in English when they enter the high school? English J. 3:166–75. (Mr. '14.)

Fitzpatrick, Edward A. The second balcony of education. Educa. R. 48:49–63. (Je. '14.)

Flagg, Maurice I. Making farm life popular: what Minnesota is doing for her own youth. Craftsman 26:311–16. (Je. '14.)

Fulton, Martha J. An experiment in teaching spelling. Pedagog. Sem. 21:287–89. (Je. '14.)

Gale, Zona. What of coeducation? Atlan. 114:95–106. (Jl. '14.)

Graves, Frank Pierrepont. Is the Montessori method a fad? Pop. Sci. Mo. 84:609–14. (Je. '14.)

Gray, Roland P. The correlation of English with other subjects. English J. 3:299–302. (My. '14.)

Hall, G. Stanley. Contemporary university problems. Pedagog. Sem. 21:242–55. (Je. '14.)

Hall, G. Stanley. Some psychological aspects of teaching modern languages. Pedagog. Sem. 21:256–63. (Je. '14.)

Hubbard, James Mascarene. Education in Vermont. Atlan. 114:119–22. (Jl. '14.)

Johnson, Franklin W. Waste in elementary and secondary education. Pop. Sci. Mo. 85:40–55. (Jl. '14.)

Keyes, Helen Johnson. A one-room school. Outl. 107:205–8. (23 My. '14.)

Kline, Linus W. Some experimental evidence in regard to formal discipline. J. of Educa. Psychol. 5:259–66. (My. '14.)

Kohs, Samuel C. The Binet-Simon measuring scale for intelligence: an annotated bibliography. J. of Educa. Psychol. 5:279–90; 335–46. (My. and Je. '14.)

Kuno, Yoshi S. A classification of universities and colleges in Japan as compared with the universities of the United States. Pedagog. Sem. 21:264–68. (Je. '14.)

Lamon, Harry M. Uncle Sam and the country children. Craftsman 26:302–5. (Je. '14.)

Leavitt, Frank M. Manual training teaching as a vocation. Indust. Arts M. 1:211–12. (Je. '14.)

Lippert, Em. Some reports from Bohemia. Pedagog. Sem. 21:291–92. (Je. '14.)

Lyon, E. P. Principles of curriculum making. Science 39:661–72. (8 My. '14.)

VOLUME XV NUMBER 2

THE ELEMENTARY SCHOOL JOURNAL

CONTINUING "THE ELEMENTARY SCHOOL TEACHER"

OCTOBER 1914

EDUCATIONAL NEWS AND EDITORIAL COMMENT

A New Bureau of Efficiency

Oakland, California, has worked out in a systematic way a plan of co-operation between its public-school system and the two universities which are situated near at hand. The plan is fully described in a circular issued by the Board of Education. This circular is accompanied by a detailed statement of the various research problems which are to be taken up. The statement of problems is too lengthy to quote here, but may be secured by writing to the Bureau of Information.

There are many other centers where higher institutions of learning could be utilized in the same way. Where a university or college with a department of education is not at hand, normal schools are very frequently near enough to enter into the same type of co-operation. Furthermore, school superintendents will find that institutions not in their own cities but in the neighboring part of the state are very frequently glad to make the kind of arrangement that is here suggested. The following is the full statement from the Oakland Board of Education.

On July 1 of the present year, the Oakland Board of Education created a new bureau to be known as the Bureau of Information, Statistics, and Educational Research. As intimated in the title, it is the duty of the director of this bureau to look after the research work done in the school department.

This general duty falls naturally into about three divisions as follows:

1. The conducting of research studies suggested by experience or ordered by the Board of Education or the superintendents.

2. The encouraging of the research or scientific spirit in teachers and principals, and the direction of the studies undertaken by them when such direction is needed. (This work is described in detail in *Information Circular No. 3* of this bureau, which will be sent on application.)

3. The protection of the schools against unnecessary interruption by research students whose problems are unimportant or whose training is inadequate, and the assistance of properly qualified students who wish to investigate important problems in the schools.

In accordance with the last-named duty, arrangements have been made whereby advanced students of the University of California and of Leland Stanford Junior University may undertake research studies in the Oakland schools under the supervision of their own instructors and with the assistance of the director of the new bureau. Other properly qualified persons will also be allowed to conduct studies which are worth while upon obtaining the written permission of the director.

Interested students of the University of California should consult the appropriate instructors as follows:

1. Students of education, any of the staff.
2. Students of psychology, Professors Stratton or Brown.
3. Students of social economics, Professor Peixotto.
4. Students of hygiene, Dr. Force.
5. Students of pathology and bacteriology, Dr. Meyer.

At Leland Stanford Junior University, students should consult:

1. Students of education, any of the staff.
2. Students of psychology, Professors Angell or Martin.
3. Students of social economics, Professor Wildman.
4. Students of bacteriology and immunity, Professor Manwaring.

School Surveys

The surveys which are being organized at the present time differ from the earlier examples of such inquiries in that they are being undertaken before any emergency arises which compels the survey to be carried on under the adverse conditions of haste and partisan feeling. When a school system is under violent criticism, a survey must, of necessity, reflect the fact. When, on the other hand, a survey is undertaken for the purpose of finding out in a large and deliberate fashion what the needs of the schools are, there is very great promise that the outcome will be scientific and productive.

The following quotation illustrates the different types of activity of this sort which have been announced during the month of August. The first is from the *Times* of Seattle, Washington:

A Vocational Education Survey

Under the direction of Dr. Herbert G. Lull, professor of education in the University of Washington, the state commission on vocational education, of which Dr. Lull is chairman, is preparing to undertake an extensive survey of Washington for the purpose of assembling every essential fact bearing upon this phase of educational work. Such facts as are derived from the survey are intended for the guidance of the state legislature in the drafting of laws establishing vocational schools in Washington.

For the purposes of the survey, typical counties of the state will be selected. King, Pierce, Snohomish, and Whatcom counties will be fields of investigation in western Washington, while several representative counties in eastern Washington will also be included in the area to be surveyed.

Broadly speaking, the survey will seek data along social, industrial, and educational lines. One of the first aims of the commission is to ascertain the opinions of leading men, commercial organizations, labor unions, granges, and women's clubs concerning vocational education. The number of pupils in each locality likely to attend these vocational schools will also be ascertained as accurately as possible.

The advantages of each community with reference to its adaptability to the purposes of a vocational school will be investigated. For this purpose its industrial and agricultural status, its transportation facilities, its natural resources, and its position as a central point for a given district will be considered.

From a social standpoint the character of the population will be made a subject of study. Whether or not the people of the community are for the most part native or foreign born will be a factor for consideration. The intellectual standards of the community, its standard of living, and its various other sociological attributes will be closely studied.

In agricultural communities attention will be given to the extent and the character of the land surrounding a given center. The number of farms under cultivation, the estimated productivity of the district, and the principal products of the soil of the section will be listed and filed for reference.

School equipment possessed by each city or district will also be made a subject of study during the survey to be undertaken by the commission.

From the data which the survey will give to the commission, plans for a system of vocational schools in Washington will then be drafted. It is expected that this survey will have been completed and plans prepared in time to lay the matter comprehensively before the legislature when that body convenes early in 1915.

The second is from the *Times* of Dubuque, Iowa:

The University of Iowa's extension division will help the public schools of Iowa. E. J. Ashbaugh, former principal of the high school at Bartlesville, Oklahoma, has been selected to take charge of an educational survey in Iowa. He will study specific problems presented to him by school authorities, and will make recommendations after complete investigation. He will be in a sense an educational "efficiency engineer." Mr. Ashbaugh received his M.A. and B.A. degrees from the University of Indiana, and he has had twelve years' experience in public-school work.

A State Survey

"Educational survey work by the extension division is our first step in an effort to serve more effectively the public-school system of the state," said O. E. Klingaman, acting director of the extension division, yesterday. "This survey will take up all phases of public-school instruction, and later will endeavor to present in printed form the best ideas for educational improvement derived from the actual experience of the most representative schools."

The third is from Madison, Wisconsin:

To ascertain the exact needs demanded by industrial education and to suggest plans for best meeting these needs, a board of five persons has been named to make a survey of the city. Superintendent A. W. Siemers of the industrial schools will direct the work. Trips will be made to the manufacturing districts and to the foreign settlements. "Our intention is to find out just what the needs of the school are," said Superintendent Siemers. "We want to be of assistance to the employee and to the employer. We feel we cannot be of much help as a school until we find out the actual conditions in the city." Included in the report of the survey board will be information bearing on sanitation, moral surroundings of workers, and opportunities for advancement.

A Local Survey

Wherever a school survey has been carried out, interesting educational news has issued from that center during the year following. Very frequently the survey has excited adverse criticism. Even in this case the effects of the survey have been traceable during the succeeding year.

Effects of a Survey

The survey made at Springfield, Illinois, appeared only a short time ago. A review of this survey will be found on another page of this issue. In the meantime, the following items clipped from the *Evening News* of that city indicate that an immediate response is being made along lines that suggested themselves during the survey.

For the first time in the history of the public schools of Springfield each teacher will have to undergo a physical examination and be able to present a teacher's health certificate before he or she will be allowed to take her position when the schools open. The signed health certificates are now arriving in the office of the Board of Education. They show that the teachers have no contagious or infectious diseases. The examination is especially concerned about symptoms of tuberculosis. The certificate, which must be signed by an examining physician, is as follows:

> This is to certify that I have examined . . . . (name) . . . . and find no evidence of tuberculosis and that the physical condition is such as not to be prejudicial to the health of pupils or associates.
>
> Signed by
>
> *Examining Physician*

The opening of school this year in Springfield marks an epoch in the educational life of the city. The new junior high-school plan will be inaugurated, two buildings being turned over for the purpose of carrying out this plan. Also the schools, as nearly as possible, will be modeled after ideas advanced in the social survey, and, where criticisms have been directed with force and understanding, corrections will be made. Then, too, the physical condition of both teachers and pupils will enter more largely than ever into account. A physical director and supervisor of hygiene will have charge of the physical direction in the schools and during the summer months will supervise the playgrounds.

Practically all the districts of the schools have been changed this year and because of new buildings, the junior high schools and the new portable schoolhouse, there will not be an overcrowded building in the city.

The high-school building will be well filled, for, while the junior high-school plan has relieved it of about one hundred pupils, the number of out-of-town students and the growth of the city will keep it comfortably filled.

The following official announcement is clipped from the *San Francisco Examiner:*

American Montessori Courses

Madame Montessori, the greatest figure in the field of child education since Froebel, will be in San Francisco during the Panama-Pacific Exposition. For four months she will supervise the operation of the model Montessori school, which will be a part of the educational demonstration work of the exposition. Much of the credit for bringing her here is due to the officials of the National Education Association and to one of Madame Montessori's favorite pupils, Miss Katherine Moore of Los Angeles. Miss Moore has been chosen by Madame Montessori to take active charge of the class work at her model school on the exposition grounds.

Writing from Rome, Madame Montessori's secretary, Miss Harriet Barton, says: "You will be glad to hear that out of all the many parts of the world to which Madame Montessori has been invited for the purpose of giving a training course, her choice has fallen upon the great exposition in San Francisco. This course will continue during the four months of the exposition, in 1915, following her course of lectures in London and her return to Rome to initiate the pupils into the higher stage of the work. The children to be instructed should be quite tiny, without any previous teaching. It would be well to have a small number of already well-prepared children in another school engaged in all stages of the work. This last could be a school for observation by the general public and should also have a roomy gallery all around it. Many of the directoressa's friends and disciples will co-operate in organizing and preparing the work at San Francisco.

"It is wonderful to see how rapidly the great movement is making headway. It is said that no work on education has in a short time found so many readers as the lately published translation of Madame Montessori's work. The Japanese translation is about to appear, and Dutch and Spanish translations are in hand. With all the forces calling for the educational salvation of the children, it cannot be long before governments and educational authorities will be forced to see that only in this way can they be saved. Toward this consummation the work in San Francisco, she believes, will help."

It is expected that the pupils, not only for the Montessori classes, but for the many other model schools at the exposition, for which a special building will be erected, will be furnished by California, Oregon, and Utah.

Of similar importance to the educational world is the announcement made by Director Barr of the division of congresses that plans are maturing whereby it is hoped that an international congress on Montessori methods will be held at the exposition under the management of the National Montessori Association of Washington D.C., in connection with the already assured International Congress of Education, representing the whole civilized world.

An Educational Press Agent

The following clipping taken from the *Pioneer* of St. Paul suggests the very great desirability, not only in Minnesota but throughout the United States, of acquainting the people of every community with school activities. Frequently occasion has arisen, in the past few years, to draw attention to the fact that many controversies about school policies rest upon a general ignorance of the character and purpose of these policies. If school officers could forestall these difficulties by systematically putting before their patrons an account of what they are doing and attempting to do, there would frequently be sympathy for policies that are now opposed by an uninformed public.

Minnesota soon may have the work of its state educational department heralded and explained throughout the state by a press agent. Superintendent

C. G. Schulz probably will ask the legislature in 1915 to increase educational appropriations sufficiently for the establishment of a publicity bureau in the department of education. The educational department publicity man will be very unlike the circus press agent. It will not be his duty to sing the praises of the department and extol its work in adjectives long and picturesque. The press agent of the Minnesota schools will place before the people of the state plain, unvarnished facts about the educational work the state is doing. Parents will be informed of what is being accomplished.

That the school systems of the country are in dire need of the offices of a press agent was suggested by Philander P. Claxton, United States commissioner of education. While in attendance at the National Education Association convention here in July, Mr. Claxton spoke of the need of some medium of acquainting the public with what the schools are doing.

The work of the press agent for Minnesota schools, as outlined by Mr. Schulz, would be largely of an editorial nature. He would prepare bulletins and pamphlets telling of the work of the educational department. Editorial matter for newspapers and short news articles would be prepared by the publicity man. "There are no authentic figures showing the cost of teaching at hand now," Mr. Schulz said. "We have approximate figures showing what it costs to put a pupil through the grades or through the high schools." Mr. Schulz is anxious to establish a statistical bureau in connection with his department.

Compulsory Education for Continuation Students

The community is so vitally interested in the complete education of its boys and girls that we cannot rest satisfied with the present legislation regarding compulsory attendance. The following account of the changes which are to be inaugurated in the city of Boston ought to encourage people in other parts of the country to consider an extension of the present compulsory education law.

As a result of a bill passed by the Massachusetts legislature in 1913 and confirmed by the Boston school board last December, continuation schooling in Boston will be made compulsory in September, when all pupils between the ages of fourteen and sixteen who obtained their employment certificates since last January will be forced to attend a designated continuation school. It is expected that between 5,000 and 6,000 workers will be affected by this order. These pupils must attend the school during a period of four hours a week, the hours to be arranged to meet the convenience of the employees as far as possible.

The investigations which were carried on preliminary to the passage of the bill to determine the attitude of the employers toward compulsory education of this nature brought to light the fact that, instead of being unfavorable to the bill, the employers were almost unanimously in favor of it. They stated that they would not deprive the pupils of any wages because of the fact that they would be absent from work for four hours during the week. Most of the employers agreed that they expected to get as much work from the pupils in forty-four hours as they would get in forty-eight. Their reasons for this statement were that the gratitude of the workers who know that their employers are giving them four hours without any decrease in pay would force them to do more and better work while they were in the shops, department stores, or wherever they happen to be employed.

It is also planned to use the schools as a sort of clearing-house, so that one boy who is employed in a department store and desires to be a machinist may change his position with a boy who is employed in a machine shop but wants to work in a department store. It was learned that the attitude of the boys was very favorable toward the school, as they could take up any line of vocational work that they desired.

The instruction in the trade departments will be under men who have earned their living by working at the trade which they will teach. The teachers will spend but a part of the time in instruction, and the remainder will be devoted to visiting the homes and places of employment of the individual pupils. There will be no more than twenty in a class, men teachers being provided for the boys and women for the girls.

It is expected that from 2,000 to 2,200 pupils will start September 9 in the five-story building at 25 La Grange Street. The school will open at the same time as the regular schools, but will have a longer Christmas vacation to allow the pupils to devote their entire time to their employers' interests at a period when the business is rushed.

Open-Air School

Movements in education very frequently progress in a steady but unnoticed degree in different cities. One community tries an experiment and feels sufficiently satisfied with its success to make the experiment a permanent part of its school organization. Another community is slowly affected by the example of the success, and so on. After several years of gradual development of a given educational movement, in different communities, somebody discovers the fact that the movement has been going on and prepares a monograph showing how widespread it is. The following clipping will be of use to some later historians of education who wish to record one of the important forms of school organization now gradually spreading over the United States. It is from the *Times* of Racine, Wisconsin.

The Board of Education has voted in favor of continuing the open-air school, which was started as an experiment about four months ago. The committee reported that it had found, through the reports of those interested, that the school is doing a great amount of good, and that the need of such a school in this city is clearly demonstrated. They recommend therefore that the open-air school be made a regular part of the public-school system and that it be recognized with other special schools.

Vacation Courses in New York City

Reports from vacation schools in all parts of the country show that this movement is steadily increasing in scope. The following extracts from a long article in the *Globe* of New York City may be regarded as typical of reports that come from all parts of the country.

The vacation schools conducted by the Board of Education closed the summer season for 1914 on Friday, August 14. This has been the most successful season the vacation schools have ever known. The industrial classes have been more largely attended than in other years, and there has been a gratifying improvement in the number of children who wished to take advantage of the industrial subjects provided for them.

For the boys there were provided Venetian iron, elementary bench work, whittling, advanced bench work, basketry, chair-caning, and hammock-making. For the girls the following useful vocational subjects were taught: Cooking, housekeeping, knitting and crocheting, elementary sewing, advanced sewing, dressmaking, millinery, embroidery, hammock-making, and basketry. In the cooking classes much valuable work was done by the children, bringing their own materials and, under the supervision of efficient teachers, using the materials to make preserves. Hundreds of pints of canned fruits and vegetables were thus prepared for winter use. Every day homemade bread was made in each school and the children were encouraged to use their cooking ability at home as well as at school. In the sewing and dressmaking classes they made dresses for themselves. In many cases children made three or four dresses during the season. The material for these dresses was, of course, furnished by the children themselves. Many a proud mother will wear a dress this fall which was made through the efforts of her daughter. In the millinery classes the children were taught to make bonnets not only for themselves, but for their mothers also, and caps for their little baby brothers and sisters. The following shows the list of completed articles: Elementary sewing, 11,462; advanced bench work, 7,589; dressmaking, 2,289; millinery, 7,324; embroidery 4,772; knitting and crocheting, 5,024.

District Superintendent Stitt was specially pleased with the results accomplished in the summer trade school, conducted by the Board of Education in the educational alliance. These classes were opened for girls over fourteen years of age who had completed the educational requirements for working-certificates. These girls would naturally go to work in the fall in factories in which they obtain only about three dollars a week. However, when they have been taught how to use machinery and the elementary principles of trade workmanship, their earning capacity is more than doubled. Miss Sara Elkus, the supervisor in the educational alliance, has arranged places in factories for many of the girls who have completed the course, so that they will start on salaries of seven, eight, or nine dollars a week. The innovation of this trade school has been entirely successful.

The opportunity classes have been wonderfully successful. These classes were intended primarily for the following children: (1) "Holdovers" or "left backs" who had failed of promotion in June. (2) Children who needed to complete the 130 days' necessary attendance as required by the state law before they could go to work. (3) Foreign children similar to the "C" classes in day school. (4) Exceptionally bright and over-age children who had been specially recommended by their principals as being able to take up advanced work. The class of children thus named had B plus or A on their report cards for the term. Thousands of children who simply had a B record in day school were anxious to take up the advance work. However, it was not thought possible that these children, naturally slow, could in such a short space of time do the full amount of the grade work. In addition to this there were not funds sufficient to provide teachers for this class of pupils. Many of these children, however, entered the industrial classes. In the opportunity classes the children were examined in English, arithmetic, history, and geography. Those who received a satisfactory rating and who had attended 90 per cent of the number of sessions were granted promotion certificates. In many cases the children were present every day. Dr. Stitt, in his visits to all of those classes, found many of them with perfect registers.

An Advertisement

We are not sure that the following clipping does not serve as an advertisement for somebody, but we venture it even at the risk of falling into the familiar newspaper trap of giving advertisements circulation as though they were news items. If the houses here described are not too expensive, they may be of use to kindergartners and others who are looking for simple and interesting material for school children. The item is from the *Ledger*, of Tacoma, Washington.

Many Tacoma children are taking advantage of a national advertising campaign being conducted by a company selling an article of building material, and as a result there are probably more doll playhouses in the city today than there ever have been before. They are sure-enough houses, too, exact replicas of the real article and attractive enough to make a grown-up stand back with admiration. A small advertisement in a recent national publication started the thing and then it was discovered that a local building-material concern was the agent for the advertiser and could supply the demand. A rush was made and the dignified-looking building-material sample office has been having every appearance of a new department store for several days.

It seems that the same craze has hit many other cities of the country. The public schools of Winona, Minnesota, have ordered fifty of the miniature houses for use in the kindergarten and primary classes. St. Paul and Minneapolis schools have also placed orders. But the rush of the schools is nothing compared to the rush of the kiddies themselves through their parents.

The child houses come knocked down, and almost any youngster with a knack for tools can put them together.

EDUCATIONAL WRITINGS

Any adequate review of educational writings must take account of the fact that there are published in the United States more than a hundred education periodicals. The directory of the Commission of Education gives a list of a hundred and twelve such periodicals ranging from quarterly to weekly publications. The possibilities which are presented in this long list of periodicals are so distracting that it frequently is difficult or quite impossible for the individual teacher to secure the kind of reading-matter which is most helpful in organizing his work, because this matter is distributed through so many different publications.

One might begin a survey of these journals by commenting on the state journals. Almost every state has an educational journal and in some of the states two or three local journals try to occupy the field. These journals are commonly characterized by the news notes which they contain and by the reviews which they give of the questions used by the local school authorities in teachers' examinations and examinations of students. It is customary for such local journals to give in every issue a series of answers to the questions employed at the last examination. The rest of the reading-matter is made up of editorials which may in some cases deal with local educational issues but in general deal in a large and platitudinous way with broad educational matters. Then follow extracts from educational books and addresses. Indeed, one may say that the chief sources of material for such journals are educational meetings where inspirational addresses are presented by speakers who have prepared very little for the occasion and have very little to say that is either new or significant. Finally, such journals usually contain several pages of devices for teachers to employ in classroom work. These devices frequently relate themselves to the seasonal celebrations that are imminent at the time of the publication of the particular issue.

It may be that these local journals serve a valuable purpose, but one has difficulty, as he tries from month to month to discover in them something really significant for the teaching profession, in understanding why teachers spend their money for many of them. If one goes to local institutes and sees the methods by which subscriptions for these journals are secured, he realizes that a great deal of pressure is brought to bear upon teachers to show loyalty for local publications. It is very frequently promised that these journals will give a survey of all of the important interests that are being developed in education throughout the country. Contrasting these journals with the publications of other professions, it must be admitted that the teaching profession is badly represented by the trivial and personal character of most of what appears. There ought to be some combination of these journals. The National Education Association is the natural center from which some serious, general school journal should issue. So long as the matter is left to private enterprises or is carried on in a purely local way, educational journalism will continue to give the most striking evidence of the lack of organization of the American teaching profession. One does not get in these journals any serious reviews of educational literature. One does not get a discussion of the larger issues of education.

Furthermore, the example which is set by the type of articles which commonly appear in these journals is so bad that the teaching profession may be said to lack, more than any other profession in the country, the ability to record its experiences and discoveries. One finds that a serious superintendent or principal who has a good method which he has worked out in his school is afraid to describe it for some educational journal for fear that he will be regarded as self-seeking and as an advertiser. The scientific spirit which prevails in medical publications and in publications which are used by lawyers has not yet manifested itself in the teaching profession. The editors of this *Journal* have frequently had occasion to comment on the difficulty of getting teachers to write in an impersonal way about school experiences. This difficulty is very largely to be charged to the character of present-day educational periodicals.

In sharp contrast to these local journals are serious scientific journals which try to get together studies, particularly those of a type which are worked out in scientific laboratories. This material is commonly looked upon by practical school people as "heavy" and "unpractical." It is indeed impossible to make use of many of these studies in classroom work and in school organization. They represent the remoter, scientific principles which will have to be indirectly brought over into school processes. The taste for this sort of material has to be cultivated through a study of the sciences related to education. The criticism which is legitimately to be made of many such studies is that their authors have not attempted to point out the possible applications of their studies. The articles are unnecessarily remote from the sphere of interest of the ordinary teacher and superintendent. There is no reason at all why a practical science like applied psychology or applied sociology should not consciously aim to make its results accessible to all who are working in the practical field. Up to this time there has been very little of this conscious effort to make scientific studies appear to the ordinary reader available for his immediate task.

The earliest of the rigidly scientific publications is the *Pedagogical Seminary*, published at Clark University. This periodical has printed a very large body of material in its twenty-one volumes. It represents today a somewhat modified but ever vigorous form of the Child-Study Movement which has long been characteristic of Clark University.

A second publication containing much serious material is the *Teachers' College Record*. This publication has passed through fourteen volumes and has contained a great variety of articles, both for the elementary teacher and for the secondary teacher. It is not so much a journal as a series of monographs. Each issue is a unit in itself, and in many cases a unit supplies material which special teachers can use without reference to other issues of the *Record*.

The *Journal of Educational Psychology* is a younger member of this group of periodicals. It is published by psychologists who are interested in working out applications of their science to practical school problems. It is published in Baltimore by Warwick & York. Many of its articles relate to elementary-school work.

Three other journals may be mentioned in this connection, although they differ somewhat in type from the three that have already been commented upon. The *Educational Review*, which is now in its forty-seventh volume, has long been known as a general educational periodical, discussing in a broad way problems of the higher schools. From time to time it includes matter which is relevant to the elementary school.

The *School Review*, which is in its twenty-second volume, devotes its attention entirely to matters related to the high school, including from time to time articles referring to admission requirements and other such relations between the high school and the college.

In recent years the *School and Home Education* has, especially in its editorial columns, taken on a more scientific character under the editorship of Professor Bagley. This journal was founded by Dr. George Brown and is published in Bloomington, Illinois; it has a long, historical record of influence in the Middle West.

The most striking development in recent educational journalism is the appearance of departmental journals. One can pick out, for example, the two journals which are published from the same center and promote the interests of handwork and vocational work in schools. These are the *Manual Training Magazine* and *Vocational Education*. The first is in its fifteenth volume and the second is in its third. They are published by Mr. Bennett and his associates in Peoria, Illinois.

Home economics has several journals. The journal published by the Home Economics Association is entitled *The Journal of Home Economics* and is in its sixth volume. The Boston Cooking School now publishes its magazine under the title, *American Cookery*. *Good Housekeeping* is a somewhat more popular journal which gives much attention to educational problems as well as to general phases of home-making.

Defective children are receiving, not only in educational publications but in state legislation and in practical school organization, much attention. Three journals may be mentioned as discussing topics relating to the training of defectives. The first is the *Training School Bulletin*, published in Vineland, New Jersey. The second is the *Psychological Clinic*, published by Professor Witmer of the University of Pennsylvania. The third is the

Journal of Psycho-Asthenics, published quarterly by the American Association for the Study of the Feeble-Minded. The first is the organ of one of the most progressive institutions in the United States for the study and treatment of defectives. The second has served as the medium for general discussions of psychological and educational problems; the third as the organ of an association is somewhat less distinctive in character.

Physical education is represented by *Mind and Body*, published in Milwaukee, and the *American Physical Education Review*, published by the American Physical Education Association, as well as by *The Playground*, published in New York by the Playground and Recreation Association of America.

There is a *Kindergarten Review* published by Milton Bradley Company, Springfield, Massachusetts. The *School Arts Magazine* is published in Boston by Mr. Bailey and his associates. The *Nature Study Review* is edited by Professor Downing and published in Chicago. The *English Journal*, published by Professor Hosic and others, is issued from Chicago. *Religious Education*, published under the auspices of the Religious Educational Association of America, is issued in Chicago. The *History Teachers' Magazine* is published in Philadelphia. A new venture is the *Rural Educator*, published in Columbus, Ohio. *School Science and Mathematics* in its fourteenth volume is published in Chicago and makes an appeal chiefly to those who are interested in problems of secondary education. Geography has a whole list of journals devoted to its interests. Of these perhaps the one most used by teachers is a journal which is not edited chiefly for school purposes, namely the *National Geographic Magazine*, which is published in Washington under the auspices of the National Geographic Society.

One might go on mentioning other special journals which aim to promote the interests of various departments, but those listed serve to emphasize the scope of this kind of publication. There are some advantages and some disadvantages in specializing educational publications. The advantages are obvious. Material is created which is of special use to specialists, and the departments concerned are more rapidly advanced than they would be if left to find a place in the miscellaneous publications which include all sorts of material. Special teachers feel through these journals a closer contact with their departmental allies. On the other hand, the teacher or supervisor who is interested in developing his work on all sides is hindered by the necessity of getting hold of a series of departmental publications. Departmental journals tend to set up in the school distinctions and lines of separation which are harmful to the unity of the educational process. So far as the individual child is concerned, there ought not to be favored, or especially aggressive, departments. Even in the upper grades and in the high school where the work is departmentalized, every student of education realizes that the special teacher must cultivate broad, general interests if his department is to succeed. The separate publications make it increasingly difficult to satisfy this rational demand for unity in the course of study.

There are several journals which are to be classed as national rather than local in their circulation. One of the most interesting of these is the *Journal of Education*, published in Boston under the editorship of Dr. Winship. Dr. Winship is not only an editor; he is also a very active participant in all sorts of educational meetings. He lectures in different parts of the country and spends a large part of his time visiting educational experiments and coming in contact with people engaged in different phases of school work. Dr. Winship finds in the excursions which he makes about the country many interesting school experiments. Some of these he describes with the most unqualified enthusiasm. The result is that those experiments which he indorses are likely to have a large and in some cases an undue recognition. One does not like to be criticized by an educational speaker and writer whose audiences are as extensive as are those of Dr. Winship. Dr. Winship's type of judgment becomes therefore a matter of interest. He has not been converted to a belief in educational surveys and other forms of scientific study of education. His skepticism regarding these activities is in keeping with the general conservative attitude of practical educators in all parts of the country. Dr. Winship is disposed to regard the "expert" as less competent to determine school policies than is the Board of Education. The student of scientific education is disposed to be critical of a publication which reinforces a skeptical attitude toward scientific methods and brings to such prominent attention experiments that are by no means complete and have not been tested except by personal inspection. On the other hand, such a student of education sees the enormous importance of educational publicity in the influence exercised by a single aggressive editor.

A second journal which has a large national circulation is the *American School Board Journal*, published in Milwaukee. This journal has for some years specialized on problems that are related to supervision. Supervision is a very inviting field for the publisher because if there is any class of school people who have reached the professional stage it is school superintendents and supervisors. The teacher in our public schools is so transient in his tenure of office and so shifting in his actual work and place of residence that he does not gain any large influence over the schools. Furthermore, he is not likely to be in a position to control in any great degree his own practices. Superintendents and supervisors, on the other hand, do exercise a very large influence in the management of schools, and their salaries are high enough so that they can afford to subscribe for journals and can take some part in an influential way in educational meetings. The American School Board has made its appeal to this administrative class and has served a very useful purpose in disseminating information about the educational situation in different parts of the country. Its methods are somewhat different from those of Dr. Winship in that it does not undertake to pass personal judgment upon many of the doings of the schools.

Finally, reference may be made to the *Normal Instructor and Primary Plans*, a journal which has recently united under one cover two publications which were formerly issued separately. It makes an appeal to teachers who need devices for classroom work. Every imaginable kind of aid to classroom work is to be found in this journal. It makes no pretense to a critical or scientific study of educational problems. It is a handbook and a guide for the teacher who needs devices. Such a journal as this has both its value and its danger for the educational profession. The young teacher who finds that she can secure ready-made a large number of devices each month is very likely to give up preparing material in terms of her own immediate environment and in terms of the needs of the children whom she has in charge. She loses, accordingly, the initiative which she ought to cultivate if she is to be an independent, strong teacher. On the other hand, many a teacher who is not adequately supervised and whose training has not given her the degree of independence which would make possible the preparation of material is greatly aided by the coming once a month of this series of devices.

The general child-welfare movement which is of interest to teachers but includes institutions outside of the school is represented by several publications that deal with various aspects of public care of children. The most pretentious of these publications is a journal entitled *The Child.* This is an English publication, but includes references to the child-welfare movement in America as well as in England. The *Child Labor Bulletin* is published quarterly by the National Child Labor Committee which has its headquarters in New York City. A local publication which shows the enterprise of a single community is the *Child Welfare Bulletin*, published by the Child Welfare League of Peoria, Illinois. This publication contains discussions of many municipal activities which have to do with the children of Peoria and the neighboring country.

One series of publications which should not be omitted in any general catalogue of this type is the series of *Bulletins* published by the Bureau of Education of the United States. The statistical and descriptive information which the Commissioners of Education have collected for many years is unique among civilized nations. The countries of Europe are beginning to imitate the example of the United States in making accessible information about the schools. The Commissioner's *Reports* have gradually increased so that they were becoming unwieldy. Accordingly, a part of the material has in recent years appeared as a series of special studies. These studies deal with all sorts of topics. One may select from the list of 1913 *Bulletins* such important numbers as the following: No. 2, *Training Courses for Rural Teachers.* There are *Monthly Records of Current Publications.* Nos. 6 and 14 deal with *Agriculture Instruction in Secondary Schools.* No. 17 describes *A Trade School for*

Girls. No. 19 gives an account of *German Industrial Education*. Other titles are as follows: No. 20, *Illiteracy in the United States;* No. 23, *The Georgia Club;* No. 31, *Special Features in City School Systems;* No. 32, *Educational Survey of Montgomery County*. One can find topics of interest to all classes of teachers.

These publications are accessible only in small editions because the Bureau is not at the present time supplied with adequate funds for publication. Furthermore, the committees of Congress are not persuaded that publications of this type are demanded by American teachers. Teachers and supervisors will render a distinct service by calling upon the Bureau for those numbers of the *Bulletin* which they can advantageously use. The Bureau will thus get definite reactions from the different parts of the country upon its publications which it can use in securing the necessary funds to carry on this work. At the present time the Bureau is the only agency that is able to print elaborate monographs on various educational topics. The importance of its work in this respect cannot be overestimated. The other publications which have been referred to are dependent upon private enterprise or upon subsidies from institutions. They are so limited in scope that it is almost impossible for serious educational studies to come to light with any degree of promptness. If the Bureau could be supported in its effort to develop a serious body of educational material, it would undoubtedly succeed by this method in raising the tone of all American publications.

If the foregoing review of publications has served its purpose at all, it has called attention to the great importance of the consolidation and organization of these publications. Most teachers do not know how to find out about the journals which they ought to read. Many of them are undoubtedly misled by the energy of aggressive agents who come in contact with them but are not inspired by the desire to serve the teacher's interests in selecting the best possible journal for the teacher to read. The competition that exists between these journals is wasteful in the extreme. The repetitiousness of the publications is very great, and the trivial character of much of the output is obvious to even the casual reader. The struggle for improvement of these journals will undoubtedly go on in its present form until consolidation through associations or through some central agency such as the Bureau of Education can be effected. In the meantime, teachers can do much to bring about a better state of affairs by making a careful study of the situation before they subscribe for journals. If instead of allowing an agent to sell them journals which do not serve their purposes teachers would canvass the matter with the aid of some such general list as that which we have aimed to present above, or by writing to all of the publications mentioned in the *Educational Directory* of the Commissioner of Education for samples, there would be very shortly a selection of stronger journals and an elimination of the weak, which would be very helpful in reducing the competition and in raising the standards and character of those journals which survive on this comprehensive and comparative basis.

A report[1] of the survey made of the city schools of Springfield is published by the Russell Sage Foundation. Dr. Ayres undertook this survey at the request of the board of education of that city. The survey differs from others which have been made up to this time in the amount of time and energy which was devoted to coming into actual contact with the school. We find the statement, unique in school surveys, that some member of the survey staff visited every class of the city. The report is a complete, general statement of the organization and present conditions of the schools and contains a number of recommendations for changes to be made. The report is also illustrated very fully by diagrams, charts, and pictures, evidently intended to give the people of the city a complete notion of their school system and of its comparative standing among the school systems of the country.

The recommendations which stand out as most conspicuous are those which call for a change in the course of study, bringing it into more intimate relation to the present-day life of the people, and introducing more vocational work. The industrial training should not be theoretical in character but practical, establishing an intimate relation between the children and the school system by allowing them to make the supplies which are needed for the school system. It is also recommended that the upper grades

[1] *The Public Schools of Springfield, Illinois.* Russell Sage Foundation. Pp. 152.

of the elementary school be included in a junior high school, thus reorganizing the high schools as well as the elementary schools of the city. The reasons for all of these recommendations are elaborately set forth in terms of the findings of the survey committee.

Special interest will attach to two features of the report. There is a very full account of the children who are thirteen years of age in the school system. Their home antecedents and their probable vocations are studied so as to show in detail how the opportunities of the school may be adjusted to the needs of these pupils. As a vocational survey of the schools this chapter will be very useful in setting the example to other school systems.

As a second feature, Dr. Ayres has repeated a type of investigation which he has made before. He took some of the material that is being employed for instruction in spelling, geography, and arithmetic directly out of the school program and asked some of the leading citizens of the city to pass an examination on these subjects. The result was that these respectable leaders in the community failed deplorably to exhibit any of the knowledge which the children in the schools were supposed to be accumulating. This is a very vivid way of showing the inadequacy of some of the work done in the schools. It is rather dangerous, however, to commit one's self to the implied theory which lies back of these tests. An ordinary citizen is likely to infer that the surveyor holds that the school ought to deal only with those subjects that can be shown to have direct relation to later life in the person of leading citizens. One could defend some useless words on the ground that they train the pupil in the fundamentals of phonetic analysis. It may be that the school program will sometimes depart from the activities of later life in order systematically to cover all the facts in a certain branch of knowledge, most of which will be forgotten so far as the details are concerned. To be sure, it would be better to find, if possible, examples drawn from the actual life of society. But as a method of determining exactly what kind of material shall be used, this testing of the ordinary citizen is not adequate.

The school survey is a problem which is of interest to all school officers. Many school systems are being surveyed either by their own corps of teachers or by outside agencies. It is very desirable that the movement should be guided by a general discussion of principles and by a clear insight into the lessons which are to be derived from the many surveys which have up to this time been carried on.

The *Yearbook*[1] will be very serviceable in bringing to the attention of all who are interested the various surveys which have been made. Mr. Smith's paper concludes with an excellent bibliography on educational and community surveys. His own discussion makes it clear that there should be a careful outline of each survey before it is undertaken. The list of topics which he gathers from the different surveys as important for consideration will serve as a guide to those who are engaged in organizing such movements.

A brief account of the surveys that have been undertaken up to this time is appended to Mr. Smith's article. This summary was originally prepared for the Committee of the National Council on Tests and Standards of Efficiency.

Two thoroughly typical English books come to hand, one dealing with a system of education,[2] and the other a textbook on psychology.[3]

Mr. Whitehouse's book is a familiar type of political document. When Parliament is about to enact new school legislation the various parties get out programs of legislation which are intended to sound the public wishes. We have in this book virtually such a preliminary statement of a party program. If this book excites favorable attention throughout the country, it is likely to be

[1] *The Thirteenth Yearbook of the National Society for the Study of Education.* Part II. "Plans for Organizing School Surveys with a Summary of Typical School Surveys." By H. L. Smith and Charles H. Judd. Chicago: The University of Chicago Press. Pp. 85.

[2] *A National System of Education.* By John Howard Whitehouse. Cambridge University Press. Pp. 92.

[3] *Know Your Own Mind.* By William Glover. Cambridge University Press. Pp. 204.

influential. If not, it has served its purpose of drawing the opinion of people, and the legislation which is ultimately formulated will have the advantage of the preliminary discussions.

Such a book succeeds in presenting in vivid form the current problems of English education. The first and most significant of these problems is the reorganization of the school system in such a way that the elementary school shall lead to higher schools. The parallel system of education in which the children of the poorer classes go to elementary schools and the children of the rich have the advantage of secondary education is breaking down rapidly in a democratic country like England. How to overcome the traditions of the older system is a grave problem. Such matters as the support of the secondary schools must be considered, for at the present time these schools are tuition schools. It is obvious that the selection of students for higher education through the present examination system is by no means satisfactory. The universities evidently do not conform to popular demands, and the discussion of a commission to look into the activities of Oxford and Cambridge is renewed in this preliminary statement of a legislative program. Industrial education and the place of local and central authorities are also pointed out as important problems. As in all of the present-day official discussions of the religious question, the attempt is here made to avoid the bitter partisanship which commonly attaches to these religious discussions.

While Whitehouse's book gives us a view of the problems of legislation, Glover's book presents a most typical example of abstract, theoretical British thinking. Everywhere in England one sees clear evidences that the practical training of teachers is a matter of apprenticeship. The training colleges and university departments are not homes for the cultivation of educational science any more than is the traditional American normal school. When, however, an English writer discusses education in a book he seems to betake himself into another world. He forgets all about the apprenticeship system of training teachers, he forgets children and other people, and writes with such extreme devotion to theory that an American reader has difficulty in understanding how he came to regard his work as having any connection with practical life.

Mr. Glover has written in this book a very sketchy outline of the kind of psychology which is taught by Sully and Bain and Herbert Spencer. The book contains a few general illustrations, but practically nothing that would be of direct use to teachers. The discussion of the nervous system is reduced to the barest outline, and the nature of apperception is evidently taken up merely because of the traditional interests that education has always had in this concept. The book will be of very little use to the American teacher who is interested in psychology, but it is so typical of the whole English situation that one cannot take the book in hand without realizing that this is nothing more nor less than a perpetuation of the tradition which has grown up in English theoretical writing on psychology and educational topics.

CLASSROOM METHODS AND DEVICES

A Sixth-Grade English Unit

Search for a topic which would be of genuine interest to eleven- and twelve-year-old boys and girls, and which would, moreover, open to them a broader view of some of today's work in the world, led to the selection of the subject "Ships and Ship-building." The purpose of this article is to sketch the development of the topic as worked out with a group of sixth-grade children.

The children's own experiences with boats or ships of any kind were utilized to introduce the topic. These stories were told orally to the class. The variety of experiences was surprising, and interest increased steadily as the stories multiplied. Use of the suspense element in interesting others and clever selection of titles were two of the several good points discovered by the children in the following accounts.

A Vessel in Distress

One evening at dusk, on our way home from Europe, the look-out reported that he had seen sky rockets in the distance signifying distress. According to the rules of the sea, the captain was compelled to find out the trouble and, if necessary, send help. He changed the course of his vessel toward the sky-rockets. After two hours we sighted the vessel. The captain of our ship tried to speak to the vessel through a megaphone, but they failed to hear us on account of the severe storm which had been raging for two days. Six men then volunteered to go over to them in a life-boat. The sea was so rough that it took them over half an hour to lower the boat. It was now dark and very soon the little boat was out of sight. For two hours we waited. Their return was greeted by cheers from the passengers. After being taken aboard, they reported that the vessel was a tramp steamer bound for Holland with a cargo of oil from South America. She had lost her propeller and wished to be towed. As we were going in the opposite direction, they had to wait for another vessel.

A New Kind of Sail-Boat

When my father was a little boy, he always spent the winter in New Orleans and the summer in Kentucky. One autumn when the family were going up the Mississippi River, a very funny thing happened. Father was on the top deck looking up the river when, all of a sudden, he heard a scream from the nurse who was standing near him. A few minutes before, she had been holding a chubby baby in her arms. Now she was empty-handed. She stood there screaming and pointing to the water. There was the baby floating along the river. The baby's dress had a very long, full skirt, and a strong gust of wind had carried the baby from the nurse's arms to the water. There the skirt, being full of air, helped the child to float gently along until it was rescued. The baby had enjoyed the ride, and was none the worse for its wetting.

SAND FROM THE BOTTOM OF THE SEA

One day while crossing the Atlantic Ocean, I was up early enough to see them take the soundings. They do this to find out how deep the water is. To take the soundings, they used a long rope with a tape measure running the whole length of it, and a heavy weight on the end, surrounded by a thick layer of fat. This sank quickly to the bottom of the ocean as they let out the rope. Then the captain gave an order to haul it up, and many sailors tugged on the rope until the weight came into sight. The fat was now covered with a grayish layer of tiny grains of sand. The captain, when I asked him for it, gave me some of the sand, so that I could bring home with me a bottle of sand from the bottom of the sea.

In these reports, mention had been made of boats and ships as widely different as tugs, colliers, yachts, schooners, ocean liners, war ships, and canoes. Distinctions were discussed orally, and many of the children started scrap books containing pictures of as many as possible of the kinds discussed. Though the subject of shipbuilding had at no time been mentioned to the children, pictures of ships in construction soon began to appear in these scrap books—particularly in those of the boys. "Building a Three Decker"; "The 'Rivadavia,' Nearing Completion at Quincy, Mass."; "The Latest Work in Shipbuilding—The White Star Line's New 'Brittanic'"; and "Turbines Being Hoisted on Board the 'Aquitania,' now building at Clydebank" were titles of some of the illustrations secured.

To all the class, excepting two boys particularly interested in hydroplanes and hydro-aeroplanes, the great ocean liners seemed more attractive than any other vessels. This preference directed the course of procedure and led the class to write letters to the best known ocean steamship lines for further information. Each child chose the company to which he or she wished to write. Many asked permission to write to several. The substance of all the letters was much alike. The two below give some idea of the individuality of expression exhibited. Answers were awaited with much interest.

CHICAGO, ILLINOIS,
Jan. 19, 1914

Hamburg American S. S. Co.,
New York, N.Y.

DEAR SIRS: I am finding out all I can about ocean liners, and am collecting pictures of them. Would you be kind enough to send me some pictures of your largest steamships and information concerning them and the routes they sail?

Yours truly,
——— ———

——— K. AVE.
CHICAGO, ILL.

CHICAGO, ILL.,
Jan. 21, 1914

Cunard S. S. Co.,
New York, N.Y.

DEAR SIRS: Will you please answer for me the following questions concerning your steamships? What are the names of your largest boats? How large are they? Where and how are they built? What are your principal sailing routes? I shall be grateful for any pamphlets about them or pictures of them which you can send me.

Yours truly,
——— — ———

——— W. AVE.
CHICAGO, ILL.

While awaiting the replies to these letters, the class read the stories of the two famous prehistoric boats, the Ark and the "Argo." The biblical version of the Ark story was read, talked over, and re-read. Additional motivation for expressive reading of the passage lay in the knowledge that one child was to be chosen by the others to read the story in the morning exercise on ships that the class had been asked to give before other classes.

After the reading of the story, opportunity was given for two modes of self-expression. First, the written story of the Ark was reproduced in the children's own language. Then a crayon drawing of the Ark, as the child conceived it, was made. Owing to individual differences, the amount of biblical diction which was carried over into the children's accounts varied widely. The two copied below were chosen to illustrate this particular point.

NOAH'S ARK

The Lord requested Noah to build an Ark, so that when the flood came, he could preserve himself, his family, and the various animals. It was built of gopher wood, which we now call conifer cypress. The Ark was five hundred twenty-five feet long, eighty-four feet wide, and fifty-two feet high. It was not built for travel, and merely floated about until the flood subsided.

NOAH'S ARK

Many, many years ago, not long after the time of Adam and Eve, the Lord saw that there was nothing but evil in the mind of man whom he had created. So God determined to send a flood and wash the face of the earth bare from man. In this dreadful time, there was but one patriarch who won favor in the sight of the Lord. This was Noah. He only had not forsaken the Lord, and therefore God came unto him saying that a great flood would drown everyone on earth. But God bade Noah build an Ark, which was to be three hundred cubits long, fifty cubits wide, and thirty cubits high. The Ark was to have a window, a door, and three stories. Noah was to go into the Ark when the waters began to rise and with him he was to take his wife, his sons, and his sons' wives. God said he was also to take a male and female of every animal, bird, and creeping thing on earth. And just what the Lord commanded him to do, Noah did.

In the working out of the crayon drawings in the art period, questions such as those of proportion, of coloring, of placing of door and window, of showing three stories, and of the general shape of the boat presented individual problems to be met. The decision was unanimous and no less amusing that no steering gear was necessary because Noah desired only to float. The finished drawings were most interesting.

The "Argo" story was similarly treated. The sources used for this tale were Lowell's *Jason's Quest* and Baldwin's *The Golden Fleece*. Since only one copy of each was available, each child read in turn to the rest of the class. English periods did not come often enough to satisfy their desire for the completion of this story, and the class voluntarily held after-school sessions to hear it finished. The little accounts reproduced after just the one hearing were unusually good. Some chose to write of the building, some of the launching, and some of the return of the famous craft.

THE BUILDING OF THE "ARGO"

Jason walked through the land crying, "Who will build me a ship large enough for fifty men?" Men laughed at the idea of so huge a boat, but at last a man called Argus volunteered to try. One day as he was at work among the timbers on the beach, a beautiful woman came toward him. As she approached him she asked, "What kind of a thing is this?"

"I am trying to build a ship," he answered humbly.

She told him that so poor a craft could never sail the seas and the next moment disappeared. But in her place there stood Athena, the goddess of wisdom. She showed him how to use strong cedars for his hull and for the prow she bade him secure a bough from the talking oaks of Dodona. Before long, with such help, he completed a sea-worthy vessel, wonderful to behold, and after its builder it was named the "Argo."

The Launching of the "Argo"

When the "Argo" was well finished with its head figure of sacred oak, the time came to launch it. With all their might men pushed, but the boat would not stir. Then Hercules was called. With all his mighty strength he pushed, but the ship was not to be moved. Pretending that he had not even tried, he bade his comrades push hard with him. In this way they slightly shoved the stubborn ship, but the men now said their strength was giving out. As they paused for breath, they were astonished by exquisitely soft strains of music. Its sounds stopped the warriors in wonder and suddenly the boat began to move gently and swiftly to the sea. Then they saw that a young bard stood at the prow of the boat playing sweetly on his lyre. They clambered quickly up her sides and were off. Orpheus had charmed the "Argo" with his heavenly music.

The Return of the "Argo"

When the "Argo" sailed into the harbor with Jason and the other heroes it was not the shining craft which had started out, but an old storm-battered, weather-beaten vessel. The face on the prow was bent. The sails were torn. The hull was gray. Nobody knew it was the "Argo."

By the time the "Argo" stories were finished a mass of material (truly alarming in quantity from the teacher's standpoint) had been accumulated from the steamship companies. Several very large pictures had been sent, and pamphlets and small pictures of every description. More delightful to the children than anything else, however, were the personal letters which they received answering some of their many questions. Much clamoring to be first to tell about and show their treasures ensued. The coveted permission was given to the one who showed the best simple outline of facts to be presented. A class hour was spent discussing organization and selection of material. When two or three children wanted to talk about ships of the same company, they decided among themselves upon the division of the subject to be made. For example, of the three who wrote to the Hamburg American Line, one talked upon the "Imperator," another upon the trip of the "Cleveland" around the world in 1915, and a third upon the "Vaterland"—at that time still in process of construction at the great shipyard of Blohm & Voss, Germany. Several of the children laboriously made extra diagrams and maps of routes to help them picture effectively the exceedingly great size and merit of their respective ships. A mere skeleton of one of these oral reports, taken down by a student assistant as the child talked, is included below.

CUNARDERS

This large picture is of the "Lusitania." This ship is 790 ft. long and has a tonnage of 32,000 tons. If you look down to the water from this deck, you are looking down a distance of 80 feet to the water. Here is a diagram I have made of the Auditorium Hotel. If the "Lusitania" were put down Michigan Avenue in front of the Auditorium, it would reach this far. If you put one of these funnels down on the street, two street cars could run through it at once on double tracks the usual distance apart.

The "Lusitania" has a sister ship, the "Mauretania." They are both fast ships and sail weekly between New York and Liverpool. The "Lusitania" was built on the Clyde, Scotland, and the "Mauretania" on the Tyne, England.

The Cunard Company are now building the "Aquitania" and "Transylvania." The "Aquitania" is already launched. The hull of the "Transylvania" is just being built. This picture shows the fourth funnel as it is being put into place on the "Aquitania." These new boats will be the finest and largest on the line. The names of all the large Cunarders end with "ania."

Needless to say, all this information was divulged to the rest of the class with no small degree of pride on the part of the possessor. As reports multiplied, the children made it a point to learn the names and sailing routes of the great liners, not only of their own, but of all the companies discussed. Then they began, also quite of their own accord, to bring in reports from the daily papers as to the whereabouts of the various ships that day. Atlases were consulted more eagerly than in the geography class. That the "Cleveland" had arrived in Bombay late the preceding night was a subject of before-school conversation.

Perhaps the most interesting report made was upon the French line. This told how all these liners could be converted into war vessels by the French government, and how they were built at the St. Nazaire yards, although they could be built much more cheaply in England, and why these things were true.

As soon as a child had given the report on his material a subject for later report was chosen. This was to be based upon reading done in the library. Unless special request for a different kind of a topic was made, the assigned reading was upon some of the great ships of history. All read and illustrated a chapter upon the evolution of a boat. Individual instruction was given in the use of the card catalogue in finding the books referred to. *The American Sailor*, *The Boy's Wonder Book of Ships*, and E. Keble Chatterton's two volumes were found particularly adapted to children's use. Some of the topics assigned were: "The Norse Boat of Gokstad"; "The Golden Hind"; "The Bucentaur"; "The Great Harry"; "The Blessing of the Bay"; "The Clermont"; "The Great Western"; "The Constitution," etc.

"The Merrimac and the Monitor" was written up by one lad upon his own request.

The children, already not a little familiar from their various reports with the chief shipbuilding regions of the world, and with the parts of a great ship, were now quite ready to study the "Shipbuilding" chapter in Allen's *Industrial Europe*. The personal touch—the picture of the ship-builder as well as of ship-building—was supplied by the teacher's stories of Peter the Great, Phineas Pett, Robert Fulton, and other great ship-builders. Many shipbuilding articles from magazines were brought in by the class, the best of which was from the *Scientific American* of January 31, 1914. It was entitled "The Most Modern Ship-building Plant in the World." Early in the discussion of building ships of iron and of steel, the children were puzzled as to how an iron ship could float. The following is one boy's volunteered effort to explain.

Why an Iron or Steel Ship Can Float

If you put a piece of wood on the water in a basin, like this, you see it floats. We found out in our study of primitive boats that logs floating down stream gave early suggestions of boats. Therefore people were not surprised when a boat built of wood floated. But if you put a lump of iron in the water in the basin, like this, you see it instantly sinks. So when people first heard of steel ships, they were sure they would sink. I am going to try to show you why they do not. When I put this little iron cup in the water, you see it floats. The secret is in its shape. You see this is not a solid piece of iron but a shell of iron filled with air. The air and the iron together are light enough to be held up on top of the water just as the wood was. The cup sinks to within half an inch of the brim. Then we know that it is lighter than an amount of water just the size of the cup would be. Steel ships are hollow like the cup.

The class next read together Longfellow's "The Building of the Ship" and liked it. Modern ship-building methods were often compared to those of the "master." The parts of a ship named presented nothing strange. The thought-content was easily mastered.

During the study of the poem, five or ten minutes each day were taken up with the reports based on the library work. Some of these were oral and some written. The following one was written.

THE "BUCENTAUR"

Venice is built on islands, with the sea upon all sides. For this reason, and because she had obtained most of her wealth by commerce, she grew to love the sea. Venice felt that the sea loved her, too, and would protect her. From this idea there came to be held a beautiful ceremony called "The Marriage of Venice and the Sea."

Once every year the Doge, or chief ruler of Venice, accompanied by the priests and many attendants, sailed out into the harbor to perform the marriage service. It was the most important of all the holidays of the Venetians and the harbor was gay with throngs of people and bright decorations.

The "Bucentaur," the boat in which the Doge sat, was a beautiful boat. It had two floors or decks. Upon the lower deck sat the men who rowed the boat. The upper deck was covered with velvet and adorned with much gold braid and many tassels. At the stern was a small window from which the Doge cast a ring into the sea, while the priest solemnly read the words of the service.

For almost four centuries this beautiful ceremony was performed every year and many different boats were made to be used for it. Always, however, the boats were named the "Bucentaur."

As a final step, the class wrote original poems about any phase of ships or ship-building that they chose. The results exceeded expectations, especially in the distinctly ethical content embodied in such an attempt as the following. Such a "moral" had never in any way been pointed out or mentioned in class.

For us the steel is glowing,
For us the ribs are bent,
For us are hammers plying,
For us are labors spent.

The builder in his office
With master mind does plan
But every little labor counts
Down to the lowest man.

Many rather long rhymed stories of ships and wrecks and building were composed, but more pleasing than any of them was this little four-line production.

If you were but a fairy,
And could grant me wishes three,
I'd choose to be an architect
Of ships that sail the sea.

Last of all came Kipling's story of "The Ship That Found Herself." The children, already familiar with his "007," were rejoiced to know that he had written a ship story too. It was read to them by the teacher during the last two days of the twelve-weeks' period over which this unit of English work had extended. They seemed to enjoy every word of it.

When the unit of work was over, the children realized only that they had found out some very interesting things about ships and ship-building, and that they wanted and intended to know more. The adult onlooker knew, however, that training in oral composition, in writing stories, both reproduced and original, in oral reading, in proper use of a library, in letter-writing, in spelling and dictionary work, and in outlining and organizing of material had been given them as well as a knowledge of some of the world's mightiest carriers, and a glimpse of one of her greatest industries.

EDITH PUTNAM PARKER
UNIVERSITY OF CHICAGO ELEMENTARY SCHOOL

DRILL IN MULTIPLICATION

I have found it advantageous to substitute for drill in the multiplication tables a series of problems. These problems can be prepared rapidly and in great numbers in the following way. The method also has the advantage of giving complete drill in all the combinations.

The selection of the multiplier is dictated by the steps previously developed. Two's and three's having been developed, the multiplier may be 2, or 3, or, if two-place multiplying be known, 23. Four's having been developed, and multiplication by three places known, the multiplier can be 234, or 432, or 423, or 324. A multiplicand is then selected as follows: 369—. Successively around the school I give out to replace the dash the figures 1, 2, 3, 4, etc., up to 9. The first child's multiplicand, then will read 3691; the second child's, 3692; the third child's, 3693, etc., a condition that alters the result of each child's example and so puts each child on his own resources. His neighbor cannot help him and he finds the necessity of doing his own work.

Quickly working the first example, I add the multiplier to the product and get the answer to the second example. Adding the multiplier to that answer gives the answer to the third example, and so on.

This is the device partially worked out:

```
   3691
    432
-------
   7382
  11073
 14764
-------
1594512    First child's answer.
    432
-------
1594944    Second child's answer.
    432
-------
1595376    Third child's answer, and so on.
```

The facility with which each child can be given a separate example and be immediately examined is the feature that recommends the device for at least examination.

JAMES O. LUCAS

WASHINGTON, D.C.

A Course in Agriculture

Many schools are introducing, at the present time, instruction in agriculture. The course of study in this subject is sufficiently experimental to justify the distribution of information regarding possible lines of work which can be taken up in this course. The following statement issued in Springfield, Missouri, gives so complete an account of a possible course in agriculture that it is here reproduced in full.

E. A. Cockefair, Greene County farm adviser in co-operation with County Superintendent J. R. Reberts, has written a course of study which includes each month of the year. It will be printed in pamphlet form and distributed to students.

Sowing crimson clover, sweet clover, winter oats, alfalfa, and vetch should be done the first two weeks of September. Plots of ground on the school grounds, four feet square, should be dug for these experimental beds. Winter wheat, rye, Durum wheat, speltz, timothy, and orchard grass can be sown the third and fourth weeks in September. These are a few of the facts the children will learn. For advanced pupils, uses of fertilizers, including nitrates, acid phosphates, ground rock, potash, ashes, and lime, will be studied. Demonstrations of treatment of wheat for smut are suggested. A bushel of wheat can be taken to school, placed in a loose burlap bag, and immersed for ten or fifteen minutes in a solution in a barrel or tub, then spread to dry.

Study of acreage and yield of hay, grain, and pasture crops for the school district, with location of fields and reports of yields, set out on maps of the district, is part of the September course. These maps afterward can be displayed at the annual county show in December contests.

October is the month of seed-corn selection. Visits of the students to fields, with lessons in marking the stalks carrying the best ears will be made on Friday of the last quarter. Some of the older students may be interested in obtaining fair exhibits.

Corn-judging from samples furnished by pupils will be part of the studies in November. Planting of tulip bulbs will be taught. The older pupils and high-school students will be instructed in a tree nursery. A strip of ground twenty feet long will be prepared, and seeds from the wild cherry, walnut, butternut, hickory, pecan, chestnut, white oak, black oak, and ash of the forest trees, and apple, plum, apricot, and peach of the fruit trees will be planted. Girls of the school can interest themselves in planting roses, lilacs, barberry, and other shrubs.

Stock-judging is scheduled for December. A horse and a cow will be taken to the grounds for expert judging as to points. The children will go to a neighboring pen to judge swine. Purchase of a filt and care of it and its increase until January, 1916, is suggested for the boys. Girls will be taught to interest themselves in cows and poultry. Stock-feeding will be a theme for January lessons and visits will be made to pens. Reports on feeding balanced rations will be made to the schools. Statistics as to number of head of stock produced the last year, value and average price per head, must be recorded. Milk records for cow-testing will be taken from home by pupils.

The first pruning lesson will be given in February. Pupils will be asked to practice on grapevines and apple and peach trees at home and to submit reports. Examination of seeds for impurities will be a part of the study for that month.

Seed-testing of oats and treatment of potatoes for scab will be done in March. A contest in growing potatoes on vacant lots will probably be started and prizes given for the best crop.

Planting flowers and improvement of school yards will be done in April. Stimulation of the growing of prize acres of corn for the annual county contest will be featured this month. Growing tomatoes, with lessons on canning, for the girls, also will be featured. Popcorn- and peanut- growing will be taught. Adviser Cockefair believes the parents and pupils should join in Arbor Day exercises, planting trees and shrubbery.

Summer cultivation and care of live stock on summer pasture will be included in the May studies. Instruction on siloes and cost of their construction, and methods of combating drouth and maintaining feed and water for live stock, will close the year's studies.

Penmanship Recommendations

New York City is about to improve the penmanship of its school children. It would be interesting to record the number of new systems of writing that have been introduced in American schools in recent years. The explanation of these frequent experiments in penmanship is undoubtedly to be found in the fact that penmanship furnishes one of the most concrete examples of the success or failure of teaching. Since the problem is one which commands the attention of many teachers in different parts of the country, it is interesting to note the recommendations which have been officially sent out as the basis for the new system. The *Globe* of New York City summarizes on August 24 the official pamphlet which is to go to teachers as follows:

MATERIALS AND POSITION

a) Pupils should be trained to be discriminating in their choice of writing materials. The best results can be secured only by the use of proper equipment.

b) Penholders with metal tips should be avoided. Pupils using such holders are likely to grip them too firmly, making it impossible to relax the muscles sufficiently to develop freedom of movement.

c) Pens should be of the style commonly called "business pens," with a medium point and slight flexibility.

d) Ink should be of a quality that flows freely and makes a strong, clear line when first used.

e) Paper should be of a quality that will present a smooth writing surface and of a texture that will not permit ink to pass through it.

f) Charts, showing the approved letter-forms, should be placed in each room, in order that a distinct image of each letter shall be indelibly impressed upon the mind.

g) Each pupil should be provided with an appropriate copy showing the exact size of the writing required.

Proper position at the desk should be insisted upon at all times by the teachers to obtain the best possible results. The rules for position are as follows:

a) What is known as the "front position" at the desk should be taken. If this is impossible, the pupil may sit with the right side toward the desk, but it should be avoided, if possible.

b) The feet should rest upon the floor, the body inclining slightly forward at the hips, holding the back straight.

c) The hands should rest in a comfortable position, with the wrists turned slightly to the right.

d) The penholder should be held against the second finger, with the first finger on top and the thumb well curved pressing the penholder against the two fingers.

e) The point of the pen should be at least one inch from the end of the first finger. The top of the penholder should be held near the large knuckle of the first finger.

f) The paper should lie so that the right arm crosses the ruled lines at right angles.

The paper should be so placed that it will be convenient to swing the pen along the writing line, using the muscular rest as a pivotal point.

MOVEMENT

a) Movement drills are logically divided into general and specific; the general movement drills being of a nature to develop effective power in action, while the specific drills lead directly to letter-forms. Proper preparation for the presentation of any letter-form implies the use of both classes of drills. The rate of speed used in movement drills should be the same as that used in actual writing. Pupils should not be given the impression that movement drills should be executed rapidly, and that writing should be done slowly.

b) Each lesson should be introduced by a brief drill upon the oval- and straight-line exercises, which should be followed by practice upon a specific movement drill preparatory to the lesson proper.

c) Movement drills may be considered to be of four forms:

1. The general movement drill, such as the oval- and straight-line exercises.
2. A letter used as a drill, such as a group of small *o*'s joined.

3. A word movement drill, such as the word "mine" being repeated several times.

4. A sentence movement drill, such as "Nine men are now mining in a new mine."

d) While the use of muscular movement is paramount, drill on movement exercises alone must not be carried to an extreme.

e) The requirements of motivation demand that the usefulness of each movement exercise be shown, whether it be general or specific.

f) As the writing muscles are located in the arm, shoulder, and back, the exercises at first should be very large. As control is developed, the size may be diminished until it reaches the letter size. No attempt should be made to apply muscular movement to a letter-form until the movement drill from which the letter is generated has been mastered.

g) Little time need be devoted to the larger movement drills after the learner has acquired sufficient skill to make the smaller ones, as skill in executing the one-spaced or half-spaced movement exercises implies skill in executing the larger ones.

h) Until pupils have acquired a fair degree of control and a light, elastic touch, oval- and straight-line exercises should not be made very compact. The rule should be to let each down-stroke pass just to the right of a preceding down-stroke. The rate of speed on the simple drills should be about three down-strokes per second.

i) The amount of time devoted to movement drills exclusively in each lesson will depend upon the progress made by the class. Until a satisfactory degree of freedom and ease has been developed a large portion of the time should be used for movement drills exclusively.

LETTER-FORMS

a) While legibility is generally of first importance, yet greater success will come from the writing drills if the teacher develops: first, ease in writing; second, rapidity; and third, legibility.

b) Whenever legibility is represented as the chief essential, failure is sure to result.

c) Letter-forms acquired slowly lose their identity under speed pressure, scribbling being the invariable result.

THE RELATION BETWEEN THE PHYSICAL AND THE HEALTH CONDITIONS OF CHILDREN AND THEIR SCHOOL PROGRESS

W. C. REAVIS
St. Louis, Missouri

The question of the correlation between the physical and health conditions of school children and their mental progress is one that has received a great deal of attention from educators and the medical profession during the past twenty years. It has been the subject of numerous investigations and much speculation, but no altogether satisfactory answer has yet been given. Some have maintained that there is a positive correlation between mental precocity and good physical development and condition, and between dulness and poor physical condition; while others have declared that the relation in the one case is inverse, and in the other slight, if there is any at all. However, the data so far gathered do not warrant the acceptance of a causal relationship between bodily and mental defectiveness, although they do clearly justify the belief that bodily condition is an important means to mental welfare, and that attention given to the investigation and treatment of physical conditions of children often results in the elimination of wasted effort in education and in the improvement of school work.

The following study makes no attempt to prove or disprove a theory, or to establish a mathematical correlation between physical defects and school progress. It merely presents a statement of the relationship that was found to exist in a certain city school, (1) between the physical condition of the children and their mental progress (*a*) as measured by standing in class, (*b*) as measured by completed work; (2) between the nutritional and developmental conditions of the children and their standing in class; (3) between physical defects, attendance, and class standing; (4) between the social status of the child and each of the above topics.

In the first place, a careful medical examination of all the children of the school was made by a well-qualified school physician. The following facts were recorded: number and condition of carious teeth; condition of eyes and vision; throat obstructions, such as enlarged tonsils, adenoids, and nasal abnormalities which obstructed respiration; ear defects; and general bodily condition.

Secondly, each teacher was asked to submit a list of her pupils by grades, arranged in the order of their ability to do the regular work of the class. These lists were then divided into equal tertiles, and all of the first tertiles of the different lists were grouped, as were the second and third. These are designated throughout the study as Rank I, II, and III. Thus, the group marked I was supposed to contain the best third of each class, and likewise the groups marked II and III the middle and poorest thirds respectively. This method of classification is certainly more reliable than either general averages based on the results of examinations, or the arbitrary judgments of teachers on such criteria as bright, average, and dull. Furthermore, as the lists were made out near the end of the school year, the chances of a reliable judgment of the ability of each pupil were increased, as pupils who were members of the school at that time should have been doing either their best or poorest work.

PHYSICAL DEFECTS AND CLASS STANDING

Chart I that follows was compiled from data gathered from 122 children having dental caries (Fig. 1); from 181 children who had other defects in addition to decayed teeth (Fig. 2); from 35 children who had throat obstructions only (Fig. 3); from 64 children who had other defects plus those of the throat (Fig. 4); from 56 children who had defective vision only (Fig. 5); from 105 children who had other defects in addition to those of vision (Fig. 6); from a total of 256 children having the different kinds of defects (Fig. 7); and from 172 who appeared to be physically normal, i.e., they had no evident physical defects (Fig. 8).

It was my intention to construct figures showing the distribution of pupils having carious teeth and defective vision, carious teeth and throat obstructions, and defective vision and throat obstructions; but the cases of such combinations were too few in number. Such a series would have shown clearly and completely the cumulative effect of the different physical defects on class standing and would have made possible a more minute analysis and a more thorough comparison than can be made from Chart I.

An examination of the first seven figures of Chart I shows a consistent relationship between the different physical defects and

CHART I

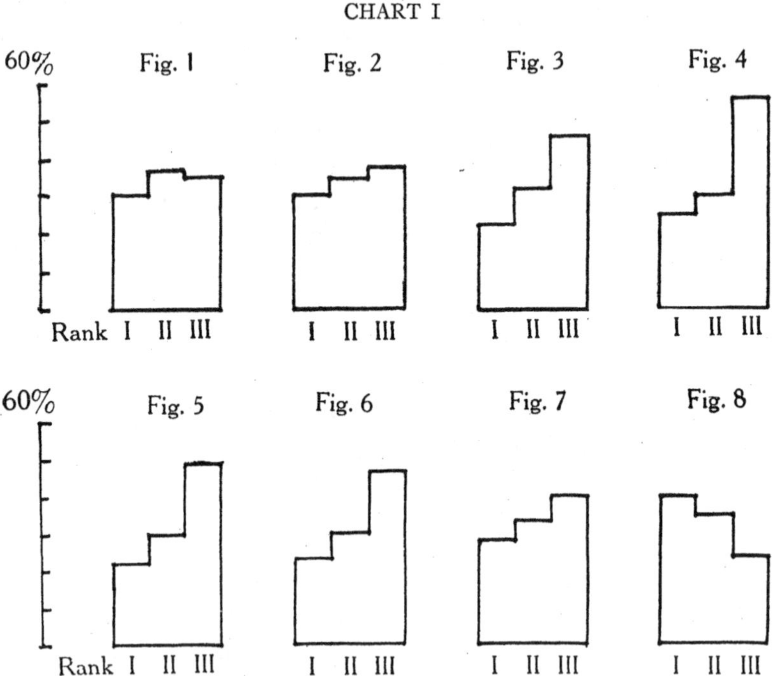

The abscissa shows the first, second, and third tertiles of the classes; and the ordinate the percentages of children. Fig. 1 shows that 30 per cent of 122 children having defective teeth belonged in the first third of the classes of the different grades, 36 per cent in the second third, and 34 per cent in the lowest third.

class standing. The uniformity of the skew in the curves toward the foot of the class rather than the exact percentages makes the relation significant. It becomes even more significant when compared with Fig. 8, which shows the distribution of the children who were considered normal physically. In Fig. 8, the skew is toward the head of the class and is almost identical in degree with that of Fig. 7, which shows the distribution according to class standing of all the children who had physical defects.

PHYSICAL DEFECTS AND COMPLETED WORK

The bearing of physical defects on school progress as measured by completed work is a problem with which it is more difficult to deal, especially with any degree of accuracy. This is self-evident to those who know the extent to which promotion in our schools is influenced and controlled by administrative problems. As a result the general statistics of promotion are unreliable when dealt with in mass, regardless of the facts which determine their validity. As a matter of fact the only statistics worth considering in this connection are those in which the personal record of each child considered is known by the statistician.

The school in which these data were gathered is a fourteen-room, eight-grade elementary school located in a fairly populous district of people of moderate means. It is well adapted for a study of this kind, as a well-established precedent for individual promotion prevails among the teachers. The unit of work is so small (four quarters of ten weeks each) that retardation is minimized, and the classes as a rule are not overcrowded. However, the difficulty lies in the fact that it was impossible to secure either a large number of records, or those covering more than a single year's work.

In Chart II that follows, the abscissa shows the number of quarters of work completed during the year by 172 pupils who were considered normal physically (Fig. 1), and by 278 pupils who had physical defects (Fig. 2). The ordinate shows the distribution of pupils in percentages.

The curves of Chart II show, as do those of Chart I, that the normal children excel those having physical defects, although the advantage in completed work is not so marked as in class standing. The height of the apex of the curve is not so significant, as it is determined largely by the regular class promotions; but the distribution on either side showing gain or loss in finished work, by individuals, in comparison with the class, is important; for it is the measure of individual progress. Here, on the lower side we find

18.5 per cent of the normal children (Fig. 1) against 27.5 per cent of the children with physical defects (Fig. 2), while on the higher side we see 19.5 per cent of the normals (Fig. 1) against 16.5 per cent of the children who had defects (Fig. 2).

NUTRITION, DEVELOPMENT, AND CLASS STANDING

A second examination of all the children was made by the school physician, in which special attention was given to nutrition and development. In grading nutrition, the color of the visible mucous

CHART II

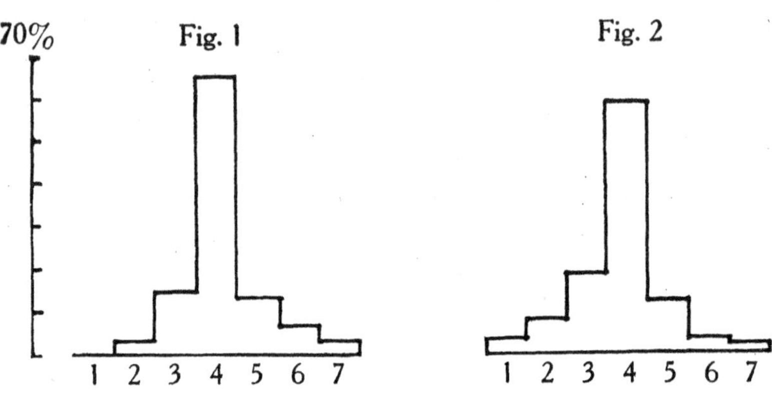

membranes, conditions of the skin, muscular tone, and carriage of the body were carefully observed; and in grading development, approximate height and weight for age, muscular and adipose proportion, formation of mouth, and general contour of the body received attention. As we had no scale by which to be guided in this undertaking, it was agreed to rank all pupils who appeared to grade above 85 per cent on the above points as first class, all between 85 per cent and 70 per cent as second class, and those below 70 per cent as third class. In order to have a check on the physician's grading, we compared his judgments with the results of a blood test that had been made with the Haemoglobin Scale, in the case of 15 pupils. The judgments conformed in each case; 8 who had been classed I by the physician tested above 85 per cent on the Haemoglobin Scale; 6 who had been classed II graded between 85 per cent and 70 per cent, and 1 who had been rated III graded below 70 per cent.

In compiling the following Chart III, it was found that the cases marked below 70 per cent in either nutrition or development were so few in number that it was thought best to drop them and consider only those graded I and II.

A comparison of Figs. 1 and 2 of Chart III shows that the children marked I in nutrition stand somewhat higher in the class than those marked II; and a comparison of Figs. 3 and 4 show

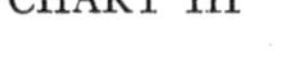
CHART III

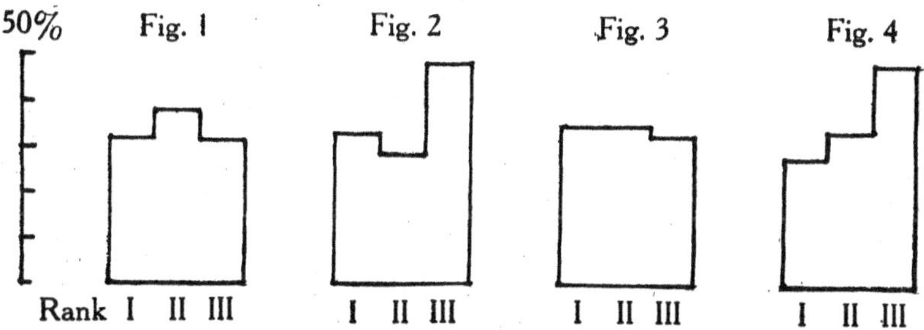

Fig. 1 shows class standing of 297 pupils graded 1 in nutrition
Fig. 2 shows class standing of 168 pupils graded 2 in nutrition
Fig. 3 shows class standing of 310 pupils graded 1 in development
Fig. 4 shows class standing of 155 pupils graded 2 in development

similar but more marked results in regard to development. The flattening of the curves in Figs. 1 and 3 seems to have been caused by the fact that the line of demarkation between the two classes in both nutrition and development was not properly drawn. Group I in nutrition contained 65 pupils that should have been in Group II, while Group I in development contained 77 that should have been classed with Group II. The probability is that this rearrangement would have increased the skew of the curves in Figs. 1 and 3 toward the head of the class, and would have decreased the skew in Figs. 2 and 4 toward the foot of the class.

In Table I (p. 102) which shows the distribution of the various groups of children distributed according to their percentage of attendance, two facts of considerable importance stand out:

(1) the correlation between good physical condition and a high percentage of attendance; (2) the bearing of attendance on class standing.

PHYSICAL DEFECTS, ATTENDANCE, AND CLASS STANDING

TABLE I

	Percentage										
	100–95	94–90	89–85	84–80	79–75	74–70	69–65	64–60	59–55	54 and Less	No. Cases
Normal children.......	31.2	24.0	15.0	9.1	4.5	5.2	4.5	2.6	1.3	2.6	154
Physically defective....	24.5	26.8	13.8	10.4	8.9	5.7	4.6	1.1	0.0	4.2	261
Nutrition I............	28.7	24.4	13.9	9.7	7.0	6.2	4.6	1.6	0.4	3.5	258
Nutrition II...........	24.2	28.0	14.6	10.2	7.6	6.6	6.6	1.9	0.6	3.8	157
Development I........	27.8	22.2	14.8	10.4	8.5	6.3	4.8	1.5	0.4	3.3	270
Development II.......	25.7	32.6	13.2	8.3	4.8	4.2	4.2	2.1	0.7	4.2	144
Rank I in class	39.4	27.7	13.1	3.6	5.8	5.1	3.6	0.7	0.0	1.0	137
Rank II in class.......	25.5	28.5	15.3	12.4	8.0	2.9	2.2	1.5	1.5	2.2	137
Rank III in class......	16.3	21.2	14.2	13.5	7.8	8.6	7.8	2.8	0.0	7.8	141

NOTE.—The percentage of attendance is based on the actual days attended out of a possible 200 days, the length of the school term.

The fact that 31.2 per cent of the normal children attained a percentage of 95 or above, against 25.4 per cent of the children who had physical defects is no statistical accident, as is likewise true of the children graded higher in nutrition and development. Physical defects and poor nutrition and development are conducive to intermittent absence which in the course of a school year is destructive to a high percentage of attendance.

The results of intermittent attendance may not be seen in the progress of a pupil from grade to grade, yet they are quite evident in the standing of the individual in class. This is clearly demonstrated by the percentages given above, in which 34.9 per cent of the pupils of Rank I in class have a percentage of attendance of 95 or more against 25.5 per cent of Rank II, and 16.3 per cent of Rank III. It is further demonstrated in the case of pupils attending 54 per cent or less of the time, where we find 7.8 per cent ranking III in class against 2.2 per cent ranking II, and 1 per cent ranking I.

These facts indicate a causal relationship between physical condition and attendance, and a close correlation between high standing in class and a high percentage of attendance. They offer ample justification for the existence in every modern school system of a competent attendance department and an active efficient department of hygiene.

SOCIAL STATUS AND EACH OF THE ABOVE TOPICS

The question now arises, Are physical condition and attendance independent factors in influencing school progress, or are they the result of some other influence, such as environment? The only data at hand in which an answer to this question might be found were the occupations of the parents. It was therefore decided to arrange this material in a similar way to that employed by Dr. Porter[1] in working out his conclusions regarding the correlation between the physical and mental attainments and the social status of the pupil, as determined by the occupation of the parent.

The parents were divided into two groups designated as (1) professional men and the mercantile class, and (2) manual tradesmen. It was found that there were 135 parents in the first group, and 280 in the second (including duplications where the parent had more than one child in the lists). The children of these parents were then distributed according to the parental occupation, class standing, and physical condition.

TABLE II

Parentage	Percentage		
	Rank I	Rank II	Rank III
Professional men and mercantile class....	44.7	27.7	27.6
Manual tradesmen....................	27.1	37.3	35.7

Table II, giving the distribution according to class standing of the children of the two groups, shows that parentage (in the sense of the home maintained by the men of different occupations) bears a relation to the character of the work done by the pupil in

[1] Porter, "Growth of Saint Louis School Children," *Transactions of the Academy of Science of Saint Louis*, Vol. VI.

school. This may be due to the attitude of the men of different vocations toward the content of our course of instruction in the public schools, or to reasons more closely related to the topics previously considered. The latter point calls for further analysis, on account of the close similarity in distribution between the above groups, and those of the normal and physically defective children respectively. See Figs. 7 and 8 of Chart I.

By separating the normal children and the physically defective according to parentage, and then distributing according to class standing, we see that physical conditions still appear to influence class standing regardless of the supplementary or counter influences that may result from different home conditions. However, the influences of the homes do appear to accentuate in their respective direction the correlation between physical condition and standing in class. See Tables III and IV.

TABLE III

NORMAL CHILDREN

PARENTAGE	PERCENTAGE		
	Rank I	Rank II	Rank III
Professional and mercantile class........	58.7	19.6	21.7
Manual tradesmen.....................	37.7	45.9	16.4

NOTE.—In the group of normal children, 48 came from homes of the professional and mercantile class, and 98 from the homes of manual tradesmen.

TABLE IV

CHILDREN WITH PHYSICAL DEFECTS

PARENTAGE	PERCENTAGE		
	Rank I	Rank II	Rank III
Professional and mercantile class........	37.5	32.9	29.6
Manual tradesmen.....................	21.4	32.4	46.4

NOTE.—Of the children who had physical defects, 88 came from the homes of the professional and mercantile class, and 182 from the homes of manual tradesmen.

The children of the two classes of parentage were next distributed according to their percentage of attendance, and arranged in Table V. By comparing this distribution with that of the normal and physically defective groups in Table I, we see that the different homes assert their influence on attendance, although in no more marked degree than on standing in class.

TABLE V

PERCENTAGE OF ATTENDANCE

PARENTAGE	PERCENTAGE									
	100–95	94–90	89–85	84–80	79–75	74–70	69–65	64–60	59–55	54 and Less
Professional and mercantile class	37.0	26.0	12.6	6.7	6.6	6.0	1.5	7.0	0.0	2.1
Manual tradesmen	22.2	25.8	14.6	11.4	7.5	5.3	6.1	2.1	0.7	4.3

These data clearly show that physical condition, attendance, and home environment are as a rule related factors, and that they seldom act as units on the work of the children in school. Because of this, a correlation that would even approach mathematical accuracy would be very difficult to establish, as in most cases it would be impossible to isolate the different influences in their bearing on school progress. However, the study does point out that the correlation between any of the factors and the character of work done in school is positive, and as such merits the careful consideration of administrators, supervisors, and teachers.

A PLAN FOR TRAINING TEACHERS WHILE IN SERVICE

W. S. DAKIN
Inspector of Connecticut State Supervision System

The training of teachers for rural schools has become a vexing problem. Many states are attempting to solve it by the establishment of county training classes and special courses in high schools. Teachers prepared in these ways, however, must lack the inspiration which comes from attendance at a good normal school, and they can have but few opportunities to secure practice.

A unique system for training teachers while in service has been developed in the country schools of Connecticut. All new teachers are considered as apprentices. Their apprenticeship has been organized and made to count toward sound training much as is the practice in many large industrial concerns of today. Only in this way can adequate practice be secured. The adjustment between theory and practice can also be kept reasonably constant.

By a law passed some years ago, towns having fewer than twenty teachers may secure on application to the state board of education the services of a supervisor to direct their schools. The supervisors assigned to this duty are engaged and paid by the state. According to the terms of their contract they must give two hours of instruction each month to all teachers in their district and must visit all schools at least twice during the same period. Although a supervisor may be assigned to the management of schools in several small towns, the total number of teachers in his territory is seldom allowed to exceed thirty-five, in order that he may have ample time to make the necessary visits to schools and meet with the teachers of each town monthly.

A certain amount of training is gained by teachers under any system of careful supervision, but in order that their development may be made surer there must be opportunities for the observation of good teaching as well as for practice. To supply this need a law was passed by the last legislature providing for the establishment of model schools in the small towns to be used as adjuncts to the system of training through supervision outlined above. A copy of this law follows.

TRAINING OF TEACHERS

CHAPTER 277

SECTION 1. One school in each town having twenty teachers or less may be organized as a model school for observation and instruction of the training class conducted by the supervisor.

SEC. 2. The state board of education may make application to the comptroller for an order on the treasurer for a sum not exceeding three dollars a week for each teacher in such model schools. No application shall be made to the comptroller under the provisions of this act unless the town in which said model school is located shall pay to the teacher of the model school a wage of not less than ten dollars a week or not less than the wage which was paid for teaching in said school during the previous year.

The assistance thus offered makes possible the placing of a strong teacher in every small town. The use of model schools for observation purposes enables young teachers in the most remote rural districts to see excellent teaching and through imitation acquire correct methods in their own work.

The approval of a school as a model is made only after a careful inspection by an agent of the state board of education. Even after approval the school is visited at intervals by an inspector to note its use for training purposes as well as to see that the desired standards of teaching are being maintained. The requirements for approval of a school as a model are here given:

The rural model school should be a one-room school in a situation accessible to all teachers of the town.

The building must be in good repair with sufficient blackboard space.

There must be ample equipment of aids to teaching, including a hektograph and a complete set of wall maps.

There must be a suitable selection of supplementary reading—at least fifteen sets.

There should be not less than fifteen pupils registered and five grades represented to include one first grade and at least one grade above the fifth.

The teacher must be able to secure results with well-defined and approved methods.

She must have a good program and keep a book of lesson plans.

She must prepare in some detail one model lesson outline each week for the instruction of visiting teachers.

She is to consider herself as an assistant to the supervisor and be prepared at all times to consult with him relative to the needs of teachers sent to observe her work.

During the present year forty-two towns have applied for the establishment of model schools. Twenty-five schools have been approved thus far. The schools already approved serve a territory employing 227 teachers, all of whom have enjoyed the benefits of observation in them and conferences with their teachers.

Some suggestions issued for the guidance of supervisors in the use of model schools are given below. New plans are being worked out continually, and it is hoped that still wider possibilities for the use of these schools will be developed the coming year when the system has become more widely established.

The supervisor shall interpret the course of study and determine the methods to be used in the school.

He shall confer frequently with the model-school teacher and send other teachers to her school for observation and instruction. He shall conduct teachers' meetings in the model school and have frequent demonstration lessons with classes of children at such meetings. Teachers sent to observe shall be given definite points to consider on which they are required to report.

Work by pupils of the model school shall be frequently sent to other schools of the town.

When new charts, seat-work devices, etc., are introduced, the model teacher will prepare samples for distribution to other schools.

The close correlation between the semi-monthly visits of the supervisor, the monthly meetings with all teachers, the observations at the local model school, and the daily practice in her own school rapidly develop the young teacher so that she soon acquires confidence and some real skill. Scores of Connecticut young women are now being prepared in this way for successful service as teachers. This is being done, too, while they are actually earning a livelihood during the apprenticeship. Through the correspondence courses with the Willimantic and Danbury normal schools and the Danbury summer normal classes other opportunities for improvement are offered.

This plan for the preparation of teachers for rural schools is working so successfully that it is believed its essential principles can be applied in any school system where there is intelligent supervision. An organization of the daily activities of a beginner so that the work becomes educative and leads to real improvement of the worker is coming to be recognized as furnishing a very economical and satisfactory means for vocational training. It is now being demonstrated that this principle can be used to advantage in training beginners in the vocation of teaching and even in improving those long in the service.

BOOKS RECEIVED

THE MACMILLAN CO.

City, State, and Nation. By William L. Nida. Cloth. Illustrated. Pp. 331. $0.75.

The Continents and Their People: Africa. By James Franklin Chamberlain. Cloth. Illustrated. Pp. 210. $0.55.

Elementary Exercises in Agriculture. By S. H. Dadisman. Cloth. Illustrated. Pp. 105. $0.50.

How Man Conquered Nature. By Minnie J. Reynolds. Cloth. Illustrated. Pp. 249. $0.40.

Literature for Children. By Orton Lowe. Cloth. Pp. 298. $0.90.

New American Music Reader: Number One. By Frederick Zuchtmann. Cloth. Pp. 151. $0.25.

New American Music Reader: Number Two, Part One. Cloth. Pp. 104. $0.25.

New American Music Reader: Number Two, Part Two. Cloth. Pp. 148. $0.30.

New American Music Reader: Number Three, Part One. Cloth. Pp. 150. $0.35.

New American Music Reader: Number Three, Part Two. Cloth. Pp. 147. $0.35.

Primary Handwork. By Ella Victoria Dobbs. Cloth. Illustrated. Pp. 124.

School Arithmetic: Primary Book. By Florian Cajori. Cloth. Pp. 285.

PUTNAM

The Corner-Stone of Education. By Edward Lyttelton. Cloth. Pp. 242. $1.50.

Die Familie Buchholz. Edited by G. H. Clarke. Cloth. Pp. 75. $0.75.

The Heroes. By Charles Kingsley. Cloth. Pp. 157. Illustrated. $0.30.

Journal of a Voyage to Lisbon. Edited by J. H. Lobban. Cloth. Pp. 116. $0.45.

L'Invasion ou le Fou Yegof. Edited by A. Wilson-Green. Cloth. Pp. 344. $0.90.

Livy: The Revolt and Fall of Capua. Edited by T. C. Weatherhead. Cloth. Pp. 166. $0.50.

Livy: Book xxvii. Edited by S. G. Campbell. Cloth. Pp. 218. $1.00.

Prima Legenda: First Year Latin Lessons. By J. Whyte. Cloth. Pp. 64. $0.40.

The Preface to Dryden's Fables. By W. H. Williams. Cloth. Pp. 36. $0.25.

J. B. LIPPINCOTT CO.

At the Back of the North Wind. By George Macdonald. Simplified by Elizabeth Lewis. Cloth. Illustrated. Pp. 126.

Daily English Lessons. By Willis H. Wilcox. Cloth. Pp. 252. Illustrated.

GINN & CO.

Outlines of European History. Part II. By James Harvey Robinson and Charles A. Beard. Cloth. Illustrated. Pp. 555.

CHARLES E. MERRILL CO.

Jan and Betje. By MARY EMERY HALL. Cloth. Illustrated. Pp. 122. $0.30.

RAND McNALLY & CO.

Chats in the Zoo. By TERESA WEIMER and R. G. JONES. Cloth. Illustrated. Pp. 139.

HINDS, NOBLE & ELDREDGE

How to Appreciate the Drama. By THOMAS LITTLEFIELD MARBLE. Cloth. Illustrated. Pp. 180. $1.25.

G. E. STECHERT & CO.

Stammering and Cognate Defects of Speech. (Vols. I and II.) By C. S. BLUEMEL. Cloth. Pp. 365 and 391.

SCHOOL ARTS PUBLISHING CO.

Something to Do. Vol. I, No. 1, September, 1914. Paper. Illustrated. Pp. 64 $0.10.

THE UNIVERSITY OF CHICAGO PRESS

Religious Education in the Public Schools of the State and City of New York. By ARTHUR JACKSON HALL. Paper. Pp. 111. $0.50 net.

CURRENT EDUCATIONAL LITERATURE IN THE PERIODICALS[1]

IRENE WARREN
Librarian, School of Education, University of Chicago

Anderson, William L. The stimulative and correlative value of a well-balanced course in commerce and industry. School R. 22:455–64. (S. '14.)

Bennett, Charles A. How may manual training retain its earlier educational values? Man. Train. M. 16:9–15. (S. '14.)

Bobbitt, John Franklin. The school survey: finding standards of current practice with which to measure one's own schools. El. School J. 15:41–54. (S. '14.)

Butler, Nathaniel. Report of the Twenty-sixth Educational Conference of the Secondary Schools in Relation with the University of Chicago. School R. 22:465–77. (S. '14.)

(The) classics and a "bad education." Outl. 107:957–62. (22 Ag. '14.)

Education: the tools and the purpose. Outl. 107:949–51. (22 Ag. '14.)

Gathany, J. Madison. Using magazines in history classes. Outl. 107:1053–56. (29 Ag. '14.)

Giles, F. M. Investigation of study habits of high-school students. School R. 22:478–84. (S. '14.)

Hervey, William Addison. How to test a practical command of French and German. Educa. R. 48:141–50. (S. '14.)

Jones, Adam Leroy. Entrance examinations and college records. Educa. R. 48:109–22. (S. '14.)

Judd, Charles H. Standards in American education. School R. 22:433–43. (S. '14.)

Macdonald, Alice B. Some reflections of a Philistine. Educa. R. 48:123–40. (S. '14.)

Mason, Gregory. Teaching by the movies. The uses of motion pictures in education and an interview with their perfector, Thomas A. Edison. Outl. 107:963–70. (22 Ag. '14.)

Osgood, Edith W. The development of historical study in the secondary schools of the United States. School R. 22:444–54. (S. '14.)

Payne, E. George. The German meisterkurse. Man. Train. M. 16:1–9. (S. '14.)

Raymond, Anan. The new university. Educa. R. 48:151–65. (S. '14.)

Yocum, A. Duncan. The determinants of the course of study. Educa. R. 48:166–83. (S. '14.)

[1] *Abbreviations.*—Educa. R., Educational Review; El. School J., Elementary School Journal; Man. Train. M., Manual Training Magazine; Outl., Outlook; School R., School Review.

VOLUME XV NUMBER 3

THE ELEMENTARY SCHOOL JOURNAL

CONTINUING "THE ELEMENTARY SCHOOL TEACHER"

NOVEMBER 1914

EDUCATIONAL NEWS AND EDITORIAL COMMENT

National Society for the Promotion of Industrial Education

The annual meeting of the National Society for the Promotion of Industrial Education is to be held this year in the city of Richmond, Virginia, December 9–12, 1914. The city has been carefully surveyed during the past months with reference to its industrial and educational activities, and reports will be presented at the coming meeting covering the whole situation. Opportunity will also be given to those in attendance at the meeting to make direct observations of interesting matters related to industrial education in the city.

It is very important that school people take an interest in this organization. There has been a tendency in many of the papers which have been presented in recent years to point out that school people are not competent to deal with the problems of industrial education. There has been a strong party within the organization that has been working for a dual system which should separate the control of industrial education altogether from the control of ordinary education. It is therefore highly desirable that those who are interested in dealing with this problem of industrial education within the school system should be on hand to present their case and see that it is properly recognized.

In connection with this meeting the United States Commissioner of Education has called a conference of specialists in charge of departments in state universities, normal schools, and other institutions for the training of teachers for vocational schools. This conference will be held in the rooms of the Richmond Business Men's Club on Friday evening, December 11. The conference will be preceded by an informal dinner at six o'clock. Tickets are one dollar. Application for copies of the program of the conference and charge of admission should be addressed before December 1 to W. T. Bawden, specialist in industrial education, of the United States Bureau of Education in Washington, D.C.

This conference on the training of teachers is also one of great importance. A recent bulletin issued by the National Society makes it very clear that the officers of that Association feel that one of the most important elements in the training of the teacher who is to have charge of industrial classes is acquaintance with the trades. There can be no doubt at all that training in the trade itself is of value to an industrial teacher, but there can be no doubt, on the other hand, that the experience of other nations and the experience of this country have made it clear that it is quite impossible to rely upon trade people to do adequate work in industrial schools unless at the same time they have some training which will acquaint them with the problems of presenting material to immature minds. The need of a full discussion of this problem is therefore very great and there should be on hand for this conference called by the Commissioner all who can make any contribution to the discussion.

The Junior High School

Indications come from all parts of the country that the junior high-school movement is rapidly gaining in momentum. We have commented in earlier notes to the effect that in many cases the change is very slight from the present organization of the seventh and eighth grades. On the other hand, there are many indications that the movement even in those centers where it begins with slight change is rapidly carried forward, so that the character of the work done in the seventh and eighth grades is very different from that which has been common in these upper grades. A number of quotations will serve to make clear the character of this movement in different centers. The

Boston Transcript gives the following statement of the change which is this year being inaugurated in Somerville, Massachusetts:

One of the greatest changes in the course of study is at the Forster School. Here has been established what is termed a junior high school. The program of studies is so arranged for the pupils of the sixth, seventh, and eighth grades as to give them the opportunity to take studies that will enable them to decide what higher courses they wish to take up later on. In this way it gives the pupils instruction in foreign languages at an age when study can be more easily carried on. The school is to be in charge of Joseph A. Ewart, the present master. The course taken by the pupils in this school does not prevent them from taking a different course after they enter the high school. The courses will comprise preparatory, commercial, manual arts, and grammar courses, all of which courses will devote approximately two-thirds of the time to the regular studies of the curriculum and one-third to the differential courses.

In the preparatory course this year Latin will be taught, but no modern language will be taken up. In the commercial course typewriting will be offered in connection with elementary bookkeeping and business arithmetic. In the manual arts course the handwork will be of a practical nature, while in the household arts course for girls the course in cooking will aim to give the girls practice in making articles of food that would be serviceable for family use. Each of the courses will be so planned and so taught as to connect with corresponding courses in the high school.

Press dispatches from Rochester, New York, widely quoted, indicate that a similar change is being made in the schools of that city:

Rochester, N.Y., is about to establish a reorganized school system under which it will operate junior and senior high schools.

The new system is classified in this way:

a) Elementary schools, each containing a kindergarten and six grades.

b) Junior high or intermediate schools, each consisting of three grades, the seventh, eighth, and ninth.

c) Senior high, or high schools, each consisting of three grades, the tenth, eleventh, and twelfth.

The number of grades is not changed, but there is a new stopping-point.

It is claimed that in arranging the two courses—one leading to completion of the senior high-school course and the other the junior—there will be no interference with the continuance through the former of the graduates of the latter, if they elect to remain in school. But it is also insisted that a better course can be outlined for those who expect to quit school with the ninth grade—and a majority do it—if plans are made with that result in view.

The *Jacksonville Courier*, after commenting at length upon the accommodations that have been provided in connection with the high school for the seventh and eighth grades, makes the significant statement which is repeated in the following paragraph:

When the schools are opened and have had time to adjust themselves to new conditions and surroundings, it would be well for parents of the pupils in the new establishment to visit the school, not only in order to become acquainted with the physical equipment, but to encourage both the pupil and the teacher in their work. The seventh grade is possibly the most vital spot in the entire school system—the point which may decide the educational fate of the child. Let the boy once gain headway and make progress sufficient to give him further advancement and he probably will go on and through the high school.

The clear recognition which this paragraph gives to the principle that one must prepare for the adolescent period and for vocational needs before these become pressing is the significant part of the whole discussion.

In a long article in the *Journal*, of Topeka, Kansas, there is a discussion of the economy which can be effected by this type of organization. A junior high school established in one of the elementary schools serves a larger community than the seventh and eighth grades when conducted separately. This economy will also, it is hoped, serve to make it possible to furnish better courses for those children who continue with the work.

In Clinton, Iowa, the discussion is carried on in great detail in a recent issue of the *Herald*. Here again it is pointed out that the relief which the high school will experience by the organization of the junior high school is of importance for both the Seniors and those who are taking the Junior work. It will be possible, for example, to organize supervision in the study-room as it was not possible before the organization of the junior high school. This organization of supervised study is due to the fact that there will be space and there will be teachers who can be turned to this problem.

The following statement from Clinton describes another advantage:

Another favorable condition is that the boys and girls of the junior high school will be associated with others of their own age and not in contact with those four years older and possibly more fixed in habit, all of which may prove to be detrimental to the younger and more susceptible students. It is a matter to which educators at present are giving a good deal of attention. Segregation of boys and girls will also be started. There are to be four rooms with boy students and four rooms with girl students—each year by itself. So far as possible lessons will be conducted for the boys and girls separately, with the idea that especially in literature work there may be a very definite selection of subject-matter and discussion.

Whether one agrees with the principle that is laid down in this quotation or not, it is evident that the real reorganization of the school is taking place with much greater freedom and with much greater willingness to modify the lines of work done by different classes of students than ever before in the history of public schools.

Finally, reference may be made to the fact that Superintendent Spaulding, of Minneapolis, has made the organization of a junior high school one of the subjects of extended discussion with his new constituency. While the plan is not yet carried out in Minneapolis, it is safe to assume that the vigorous beginning which Superintendent Spaulding has made in his initial address to the Parents' Association will result in a change in the organization of the schools in that city. We may therefore quote the plans which he has together with the grounds for his position:

"The plan is entirely tentative," said Dr. Spaulding, "and that is why I am glad to place it before the people for suggestions. In public-school work we must not only do what is best for the children—we must educate the parents to understand it is the best. There can be no question but that pupils, teachers, and parents are agreed the cut-and-dried methods of holding each child to so many subjects in the first eight years, making each take the same dose, has not given satisfaction. Too many children drop out at the end of the grade work. They have not been given a stimulus to enter high school.

"To be sure, we have the compulsory education law to force children to attend school until they reach the age of 16 years. We may be doing more harm than good by compelling attendance of children at work they do not like or are not fitted for. Under our present plan if a boy has no talent for grammar we cram it down his throat. If he fails to pass in that subject we force him to take the distasteful subject over again and with it all the rest of the subjects in which he already has shown himself capable.

"We should retain the first six grades very much as they now are as each child beginning school needs to learn certain fundamentals. The next three grades should form an intermediate school. In the intermediate school there should be three courses: literary, including some modern language as French, German, or Scandinavian; commercial, offering business training for office work;

vocational, offering an outlet for study by the boy or girl who has aptitude with hand in excess of alertness of head. Every child should be advanced in accordance with the subjects covered. This would allow pupils to specialize in the three years in the intermediate school and be prepared to carry out the specialty in the high school.

"The economy of the plan is that we could use ten or a dozen schools located in different sections of the city to care for the intermediate pupils, thus relieving congestion in some of the grade buildings, and also relieving the high schools the first year. These intermediate schools could be within walking distance of pupils attending them. They could be equipped to meet the needs of such pupils. By making a gradual change toward the plan as outlined there would temporarily be an economy as buildings would be equipped for definite needs. As it is now each grade building is demanding that it be made a center for cooking and manual training. These departments could be better provided in the intermediate schools and grade buildings would be devoted exclusively to the classroom work of the lower grades."

Dr. Spaulding said he already has made a start toward a plan by consolidating seventh and eighth grades. Dr. C. M. Jordan, superintendent emeritus, is to visit a number of cities to ascertain how best to care for the intermediate classes. The board of education has authorized the tour of inspection and it will be started early next week.

Health in Rural Schools

For some years past a joint committee on health problems of the National Council and of the American Medical Association has been examining the physical condition of school children. The latest material collected by this committee refers to the physical condition of children in rural districts. A comparison was made, for example, of the children in about two thousand of the rural districts in the state of Pennsylvania with children in the cities of Harrisburg, Pittsburgh, and Altoona. This investigation showed that a larger percentage of the rural children are in need of medical attention than of children in the city districts. This general statement holds also in detail. It was found in contrasting the children of Orange County, Virginia, with the children of New York City that a very much higher percentage of children in the rural district are defective in their lungs. The exact figures are for New York City a fraction of 1 per cent, while 3.7 per cent of the country children had affection of the lungs. Malnutrition also appears to be more common among the rural children than among children in city districts. This goes to show that the food which is supplied to the children in the rural districts is coarse and less nutritious than the food which is commonly provided even among the poorer classes in the great cities.

This material collected by the American committee is not different in its results from the material which appeared as a result of English investigations. The English and American reports both throw light on the rural problem, not only as it confronts the educator, but as it confronts the student of general social conditions.

The American committee has furthermore undertaken to inform rural districts of the standards which they ought to aim to attain. A pamphlet entitled *Minimum Sanitary Requirements for Rural Schools* has been prepared and a large edition will be distributed as widely as possible. Copies of this may be had by addressing the chairman of the committee, Dr. Thomas B. Wood, at Teachers College, Columbia University. The pamphlet gives in exact form a statement with regard to the location and surroundings of buildings, with regard to the construction of the school building itself, lighting, cleanliness, water, furnishing, toilets, and other improvements that are necessary for model, sanitary, rural-school buildings.

The Economic Side of Buying

Buying and selling have for the most part been taught as a part of arithmetic in the public schools. There is, however, another and a very important side to the operation of buying and selling which has nothing to do with numbers or their combination and recombination. One ought to have some knowledge of the sources of material to be purchased and some knowledge of the qualities of material. In other words, the purchasing of commodities in the market is an economic problem more than it is a problem in calculation of change. The following step taken in New York City is therefore of large interest and ought to be of encouragement to teachers of home economics in all parts of the country and ought at the same time to suggest to all school officers the importance of getting a real view of the articles with which people have to deal in ordinary life:

Beginning next week an educational plan will be inaugurated in the public schools of New York City, with the view of teaching the pupils how to buy food supplies. This announcement was made today by the chairman of the mayor's food supply committee.

More than 800,000 circulars, the first of a series on the subject, will be distributed among the public schools Monday. The first will deal with practical suggestions on "How to buy." Others will deal with "What to buy," "When to buy," "How to save waste," and the like.

School Survey

A hopeful example of the co-operation between a higher institution of education and a public-school system is furnished in the following clipping, which is taken from the *Star*, of Kansas City, Missouri:

The University of Missouri is conducting a survey of the grammar courses in the Kansas City public schools. This has been in process for a year and thousands of papers prepared by pupils have been submitted. A report is being printed now. It is expected that it will result this fall in a standardized course in all grades with much of the unessential and mechanical theory left out and with more of the essential, practical methods of teaching language put in.

The Detroit Department of Research

The new Department of Educational Research of the Detroit Public Schools has issued a pamphlet defining very clearly its purposes and problems. It may be well, in view of the importance of this kind of organization in connection with public schools, to repeat briefly the introductory statement of the aims which this department of research is to serve in the Detroit schools.

1. To measure the efficiency of the teaching in the Detroit schools.
2. To increase the number of children benefiting by school work.
3. To eliminate waste in subject-matter and methods.
4. To aid in the adjustment of school training to the world's needs.
5. To help teachers give greater assistance to individual children in accordance with their peculiar weaknesses.
6. To set up objective standards, reasonable because based upon the measured ability of children, so that each child may have the pleasure of success.
7. To aid the superintendent and others in the preparation of reports.
8. To aid in the continued professional training of teachers.
9. To supply any information about the Detroit System that may be wanted.
10. To maintain year after year a critical study of the Detroit public schools in order that each year the same may be made more efficient.

Politics in the School Board

We had occasion in an earlier news note in the *Journal* to comment on the situation in regard to the appointment of teachers in Detroit. While the local situation in Detroit is undoubtedly difficult for an outsider to interpret, the following quotation, which is part of a long article published by the *Detroit News*, is of more than local significance. It portrays a situation which has from time to time arisen in all American cities. There ought to be some educational organization which could take a hand in such a situation as this and exercise some general influence to alleviate the condition which is here described. There can be little doubt that even if the description here given is exaggerated, the fundamental facts are essentially as stated. We quote the article, then, as a description of an important educational problem:

In killing a resolution at its last meeting to put the power of initiating appointments to the army of 2,000 teachers in the public schools in the hands of the superintendent, the Detroit Board of Education put itself in absolute opposition to the best educational thought of the age, the removal of educational affairs from the contaminating influence of ward politics by centralizing control in the hands of an expert. Members of the school board machine frankly acknowledge that the passage of the resolution last Thursday would have been a probably fatal blow at the source of their power.

"If that resolution had passed we might just as well throw up our hands and have a small-man school board," said Inspector Kunz, the spokesman of the machine on the floor of the board.

Kunz admitted that if the resolution had passed there would be nothing left to do but to put out of existence one of the four great money-spending committees—one of the five-man political cliques that meet behind committee doors to spend $5,000,000 of the tax-payers' money each year. If this entering wedge of reform had stuck, Kunz shudders to think what might have followed. Leaving the Committee on Teachers and Schools without any further excuse for existence might possibly be followed by the destruction of the other three great money-spending committees, the Committee on Real Estate and School Buildings, the Committee on Textbooks and Course of Study, and the Committee on Janitors and Supplies.

In a government by five-men cliques such as the Detroit Board of Education has come to be, the places of greatest power are the chairmanships of these four money-spending committees. These chairmanships are eagerly sought for by the ward politicians of the board. To get one of these positions is to be on the glittering heights of far-reaching influence for a ward politician, one of the controlling forces at the purse strings of a five-million-dollar wad, an autocrat in command of an army of teachers, janitors, and scrub women.

What payments of old political debts this means, what new footholds on the ladder of municipal politics! A man who has been chairman of one of the great money-spending committees of the Board of Education can look forward to being an alderman at the very least.

The bargaining for committee appointments begins immediately after the annual meeting on the first of July, when the president of the board, who appoints all standing committees, is elected. The machine leaders gather around a table in a nearby saloon as soon as the meeting is over and parcel out the committee places. Unhesitating loyalty to the machine at all times is the one great test of fitness for a big committee chairmanship. The inspector of independent mind who is courageous enough to speak a word of criticism now and then can expect no favors. Once in a while a reformer may be given a place on an important committee, but there is never more than one. If a reformer gets a chairmanship, it is the chairmanship of the Committee on Sanitation or the Committee on Rules. These committees spend no money.

Attention to the Teeth

Students of school hygiene have for some time past been calling attention to the importance of the teeth as affecting the general physical condition of school children. The following report shows how these theoretical discussions of the students of hygiene may be utilized in effective organization within the schools themselves:

A movement has been started in the grades of the schools of Geneseo, Illinois, the object of which is to promote greater care of the teeth among the children. On Monday morning each child was handed a slip of paper on which was printed the following: "Good Teeth Pay. I have a toothbrush of my own and I cleaned my teeth this morning." After this came a blank which the pupil was asked to sign if he had cleaned his teeth.

The slips were handed the children without any previous warning, so that an accurate estimate of the number who habitually cared for their teeth could be obtained.

The investigation brought the following results:

The third grade of the North Side school had the highest percentage, 63 per cent of the children being able to sign the slips. The poorest grade was the first grade on the North Side which had not a single member who had cleaned his teeth. Most of the grades averaged around 30 per cent.

In order to encourage the practice of cleaning the teeth, Tuesday, September 22, has been set apart as clean teeth day, and at that time the slips will again be distributed. Suitable banners have been provided for the grades that show the highest percentage on that day.

The movement is commendable, and the teachers should have the united support of the parents and children in their campaign for clean teeth. It is anticipated that there will be a large increase in the sales of toothbrushes this week.

EDUCATIONAL WRITINGS

REPORTS OF CITY BOARDS OF EDUCATION

More and more we are coming to perceive that social control in a democracy grows out of enlightened public opinion. The more complicated the social organization, and the more important its labors, the greater is the necessity for this public enlightenment. Of all community functions, education ranks first on both counts. It probably is the most complicated social enterprise requiring the control of public opinion, and it probably also is the most important of the various social enterprises.

School officials in a city have various modes of keeping the general public informed as to the work of the schools. The public press offers an opportunity that is much utilized. Talks before parents' associations, business men's associations, women's clubs, civic organizations, etc., present other opportunities. Information given the public through these media tends to be fragmentary, disconnected, and even superficial. The addresses at their best in a city can reach but a limited audience. The medium of publicity *par excellence* employed by school officials is the annual or biennial report of the board of education. This report offers the superintendent, the clerk of the board, the architect, the auditor, and the other officials an opportunity to lay before the public the things which the public needs to know in order rightly to judge of the effectiveness of the service.

An important practical question arises: What kinds of facts, in what form, and in what quantity should each of the school officials lay before the general public for its enlightenment concerning the activities of his department? It is important that the essential things be presented, and that they be presented in a way that can be effectively grasped by the general public. The facts must lie pretty well upon the surface, so that they can be taken in without effort; and the things that belong together in judging the effectiveness of the school work should be placed together.

Professional men even are sufficiently uninformed as to statistical presentation of facts; laymen are still less informed. They cannot be expected to pore over meaningless statistical tables. They need figures reduced, digested, and organized, so that their significance lies clearly upon the surface and can be taken in at a glance.

It is always interesting to inquire into what superintendents think the community needs to know about the affairs of its schools. An examination of the reports of superintendents and other officials reveals their judgment in the matter. They seem not to be very well agreed as to what should be presented, nor as to the mode of presentation. A valuable and practical piece of research would be an examination of the city reports of all of our cities and a determination of the consensus of opinion as to what ought to be given to a community for its enlightenment on school questions, and as to the mode of organizing and presenting these materials. In the present article we are examining a few reports taken at random to see what they deem advisable.

The last report of the schools of Newton, Massachusetts,[1] drawn up by Superintendent Spaulding just previous to his departure, is addressed definitely "To the Citizens of Newton and especially to His Honor, the Mayor, and to the Honorable, the Board of Aldermen." Former reports had been addressed to the School Board. This one, however, is somewhat more clearly designed than previous ones to furnish information needed by the citizens in passing judgment upon the work of the schools. In Mr. Spaulding's opinion the public needs to know just one thing. He says: "This report will confine itself to one single issue. Indeed there seems to be but one issue today concerning the Newton schools. That issue, while difficult to solve, is simple to comprehend. It concerns the cost, not the details of expenditure but the total cost, of maintaining the school system." His report attempts to answer the two questions: Why are the schools so expensive? How can expenses be reduced? On the basis of the information presented in the report he then presents a question

[1] *The Newton Public Schools.* Annual Report of School Committee, Newton, Massachusetts, No. 74, 1913.

on which he desires community judgment: Shall school expenditures be reduced; or shall the present educational policy be maintained?

The question at issue seems to have been raised by a minority of the Board of Aldermen as to the annual appropriation for public schools. It is this board that makes the actual appropriations. It is, however, only the agent of the general community, and in the long run, at least, must obey the dictates of the citizens of the community. Public enlightenment clearly is necessary in order that the efficiency of the schools be not impaired by a group of men intent upon diverting money into other and perhaps for them more profitable channels. Under the circumstances it is natural that the superintendent should attempt to focus attention entirely upon this one large problem and to confine his message solely to its discussion. This he does with his usual effectiveness. He presents in clear, connected, readable statements the policy that has guided educational thought and labors in Newton for many years. He shows how the attempt has been made to provide educational opportunities adapted to the individual needs of every boy and girl from four to eighteen years of age. He shows the need, in order to do this, of a special school for abnormal children, special individual help for the 10 per cent of weaker pupils, high schools opened to all pupils of high-school age who are preparing themselves for any vocational destiny whatsoever, evening schools, summer vacation schools, kindergartens, playgrounds, and the vocational school, which is designed for pupils who do not take the high-school work. The report also shows that although living costs have been increasing during the past five years the expenditure for schools per pupil in every department of the Newton system is now less than it was five years ago. The Board has increased the size of classes and increased the number of periods taught by teachers without greatly increasing teachers' salaries. In some cases teachers' salaries have been actually reduced. Comparisons with other cities are introduced showing that the classes in the high schools, for example, are larger in Newton than in almost any other city in the entire state of Massachusetts. Comparisons with other cities as to the length of the teachers' day or as to the salaries of teachers in Newton are not presented. They would certainly be of service.

The reports of the Newton schools for some years past have in fact dealt chiefly with this very same problem, and in a manner not greatly different from that of this latest report. It would appear that the question has been before the community for some time. Very little place is given in any of the recent reports to the curriculum, to the student population, to the teaching population, to parents' associations, to social activities of the schools. It seems that current discussion of these and other similar things should also be presented to the community. Developments are rapid in these days, and competing interests are so numerous that even an informed public soon has its information pushed out into the margin of consciousness or even into complete oblivion. Current reports should deal with the various aspects of the work of the schools. The various labors must be understood and appreciated by the general community before the community will be in a position to sanction their continuance and to pay for their support. The topic of finance cannot in fact be handled separate and apart from the other educational activities. The need of continued support cannot be made clear by discussing finance directly. It is made clear only by showing the social needs of those particular things for which the finances pay.

The form of the report presents a valuable suggestion. It handles only one topic. It looks at this matter from many angles. Understanding is not confused by the introduction of a multitude of different kinds of materials looked at from different points of view. It is not so much like an encyclopedic reference book of facts as it is like a readable news article. It possesses unity and sequence and is therefore a document that the citizens can read. Most reports, built on the plan of the *World Almanac*, are valuable chiefly as reference documents. The suggestion referred to is the putting out by a superintendent, not of a formal and often formidable volume of relatively disconnected material without news interest, but in its stead a series of smaller pamphlets, each dealing with a single aspect of the school's work and distributed over the entire school year. A compact document of from 300 to

600 pages, such as some of our city reports with their array of figures and statistical charts, looks altogether too formidable even for the wide-awake, public-spirited citizen. If there could be a series of reports on the different phases of the work presented at different times in the year, each one of them simple, unified, and possessing news interest, there is far greater probability that these publicity documents would serve the purpose for which they are printed.

The Louisville publicity document[1] contains messages to the community from the city superintendent, the business director, the medical department, the secretary-treasurer, and the parent-teachers' associations. The superintendent first calls the community's attention to twenty-four kinds of improvements that have been effected during the past few years. To this only four pages are given. If these twenty-four new movements have been adequately presented to the community in previous documents, such a summary presents an excellent retrospective survey of past accomplishment. If, however, this constitutes the original statement of work to the community, each topic is handled so briefly that it can scarcely make any impression upon the community consciousness. It certainly does not give the facts necessary for community judgment. To this summary is appended nine further educational improvements yet to be accomplished.

Following this introductory statement the attention of the community is called to the million-dollar bond issue recently voted and it is announced that this additional revenue is to be employed in carrying forward the nine projected improvements. One expects at this point to find the report taking up a discussion of these various improvements in order that the community may be prepared to understand and to co-operate with the work as it proceeds. This, however, is not done. In the portion of the volume that follows there are brief discussions of a great number and variety of unrelated topics. Each one deals with a matter of interest to the community. When the various aspects of

[1] *Second Report of the Board of Education of Louisville, Ky.*, covering the period from July 1, 1912, to June 30, 1913.

education are treated so briefly, abstractly, and disconnectedly, the report, while it may be intelligible for the professional educator, in many cases at least does not seem to present the facts in such a manner and in such quantity that laymen can read and form intelligent judgments as to the work of the schools. And publicity documents are intended for laymen. Some of the topics here treated relate intimately to certain of the nine proposed improvements. Sometimes the relation to the improvements is shown and sometimes it is not.

Many of the facts are presented very effectively. In treating the need of playgrounds, for example, a full-page photograph is presented showing the school yard at one of the schools to be but a narrow, brick-paved passageway between two brick walls about six feet apart. Relative expenditures per pupil in elementary and high schools is made clear by very effective pictograms, and by tabular historical comparisons showing the trend of expenditures in both types of schools for the past six years. In showing the need of increased salaries among elementary teachers there is presented a table showing the average salary of elementary teachers for each year from 1896 to 1914; the percentage of increase of salary each year over that received in 1896; Bradstreet's price-index number for each of those years; the percentage of increase of this price-index year by year over that of 1896; and the resultant actual decline of teachers' salaries since 1896. During this time, the figures show, teachers' salaries have increased 42 per cent while the cost of living has increased 56 per cent. This relative decline of teachers' salaries is shown effectively in graphic form as well.

Rightly to judge of this publicity document for Louisville one must put himself in the place of the business man, the mechanic, the grocer, the banker, the housewife, etc., to whom such a document is, or at least ought to be, addressed. When one considers the public as the audience addressed, it is a serious question whether a publicity document should attempt so comprehensive a task as the treatment of so many aspects of the school work in a single issue. Fewer topics treated at a time, more continuity of treatment, more news interest, more of the effectiveness produced by presenting facts in charts, diagrams, pictograms, and tables of figures so arranged that the meaning can be seen, and shorter intervals between publications would appear to be desirable for more effective community enlightenment.

A very comprehensive report comes from Rochester, N.Y.[1] The report of the president of the Board, which introduces the volume, is addressed "To the Board of Education." The reports of the secretary and the architect are not addressed to any one but presumably they are directed also to the Board of Education. The major portion of the volume is by the Superintendent of Schools, and is addressed to the Board of Education. Attention is called to this fact because the practice is so common in these publicity documents. It makes a large difference whether the audience is the general community, which is relatively uninformed, and in no great degree interested in the facts concerning the public schools, or whether it is the members of the Board of Education, who are already pretty well informed as to the work of the schools and whose interests are fully awakened. If the report is published for the Board, it seems to be an altogether superfluous waste of money. It contains nothing but what can be obtained by the members of the Board at their meetings and from the records of the offices of the Board and Superintendent. The only justification, it would appear, for so ponderous a volume is the enlightenment of those who are being served by this field of public service, and who are maintaining the service. An examination of the content of the volume does not reveal to whom it is addressed. Much of it certainly cannot be intended for the consumption of the general public. Most of the facts presented—and it bristles with facts—are organized in such a way as to indicate that the volume may be intended for the school officials and other members of the school organization, rather than the general public. On the other hand, from its general spirit and form of organization it may be intended

[1] *The Fifty-sixth Report of the Board of Education of the City of Rochester*, for the years 1911, 1912, 1913, comprising the reports of the President of the Board of Education, the Secretary of the Board, the Architect, the Superintendent of Schools, and the Directors of Departments. 364 pages.

simply as a reference book, and is not addressed to anybody in particular. It would be interesting to know who would obtain copies of a school-publicity document that is a near-reference volume, and what use is made of them by those who receive them. It is not probable that the public who pays the bills and receives the service receives very much enlightenment from a mere reference book. There may be sufficient justification for the expense in the uses made of it by teachers and school officials. It may be desirable to have a volume designed simply for the members of the profession, but it seems desirable also to have the facts presented in such way that they can be understood and appreciated by laymen as well. If this is for the profession, there should be another volume, or better, a series of bulletins, dealing with special aspects of the work, written in form and spirit designed for community consumption. Rochester not long since had occasion to complain that progressive educational school movements were being stifled by the opposition of powerful sections of the community. It is altogether probable that neither Rochester nor any other city will wilfully oppose any movement which really makes for the general welfare. When the movement is really a valuable or necessary one, opposition is probably the fruit of ignorance, and this in turn is the result of the failure of the leaders of the educational movements adequately to take the lay community entirely into their confidence. No valuable educational movement can succeed permanently unless it represents the will of the large majority of a community. Will in such case is the expression of judgment, and judgment requires facts. A publicity document that gives the facts in ways that can be grasped and that will be grasped by the laymen seems to be an absolute necessity.

The Rochester report, when compared with the average publicity document, is a superior piece of work. The facts are presented in quantitative terms so far as possible, and these are often represented in effective graphical form. The figures are in very many cases reduced to unit-terms, thus permitting comparisons of schools with schools within the city and of the schools of the year of the report with those of preceding years. The units chosen are often of a type more accurate than those in current practice. In comparing the cost of the various types of schools—elementary, high, professional, normal-training, open-air, etc.—the unit used is the *per capita cost per hour* based on actual attendance. This is far more accurate than the usual cost per pupil based upon enrolment or register, and which does not take into account the length of time the pupil is in school per day. In considering the cost of operation, the cost of fuel, and the cost of janitor service, the unit employed is the hundred square feet of floor space. Cost of repairs is given in terms of percentages on the original cost of the building. The volume is also abundantly supplied with excellent graphical representations, which facilitate the making of comparisons. The most serious statistical defect of this report is one that is common to all publications of this class. Facts are presented as to the situation within the given city. They do not, however, show in any degree whether the work of the city is efficient or inefficient. Efficiency is wholly a relative matter. Only by comparing the situation within this city with the standards of current practice can either professional men or laymen judge of the effectiveness of the work. Such standards of current practice can be had by superintendents for use in these reports the moment they decide that they want them. This report, for example, presents the pupil-hour cost of each type of school in Rochester. No one in the community, however, can tell from the facts presented whether the costs there recorded are high, medium, or low. It cannot be expected that each of the various types of school should have the same cost per hour. A standard for the regular high schools must be determined from a study of a large number of city high schools in many cities. Only upon the basis of such a standard of current practice can the work in Rochester be actually judged. The figures presented have relatively little meaning simply because of their isolation. This is one of the two or three most serious defects to be found in practically all city-school reports.

J. F. B.

The theory and organization of the Fielden Demonstration School of the University of Manchester, England, is interestingly described in the *Demonstration School Record*,[1] edited by J. J. Findlay, professor of education in that university. This volume is very similar in general character to the *Elementary School Record*, edited by Professor John Dewey in 1900. The latter consisted of a series of monographs which contained descriptions of the curriculum and activities of Professor Dewey's laboratory school at the University of Chicago. In the theoretical discussions in the present volume the influence of Dewey is very prominent. In fact, the Fielden School might well be regarded as an exponent of Dewey's theories. The book contains relatively little Herbartian theory. This is quite striking in view of the fact that Professor Findlay might have been considered in earlier years to be as strong a Herbartian as was Frank McMurry in this country. Other sources of influence are mentioned, such as the writings of G. Stanley Hall. The acceptance of the latter's view of the characteristics of the child's life during the period from eight to twelve years of age seems rather incongruous, in view of Hall's contention that this is the period for "arbitrary memorization, drill, and habituation with little appeal to interest, reason, or understanding."

The chapters dealing with the special subjects of the curriculum contain much concrete and interesting material which should prove very helpful and stimulating, especially to teachers of children from nine to fifteen years of age. It is to be hoped that the so-called experimental schools of the type described in this volume will soon be in a position to become really experimental in the scientific sense by instituting exact measurements of the results of their endeavor. In the past, educationists thought they were conducting scientific experiments when they simply modified the conditions of instruction, entirely disregarding the necessity of precisely measuring the influence of these modifications. They might be compared to an amateur chemist who would start out to produce a certain substance, but would entirely lose sight of the final result in his interest in the intermediate processes of boiling. "Isn't it fine!" he might say; "see how it bubbles!" Similarly, the pseudo-educational experimentalists are prone to say, "Isn't it a fine experiment! See how interested and active the children are!"

S. C. P.

[1] *The Demonstration School Record, No. 2.* Edited by J. J. Findlay. London: Longmans, Green & Co., 1913. Pp. 283. $1.60 net.

CLASSROOM METHODS AND DEVICES

Motivation of Reading

A common procedure in teaching reading in grade schools is to have one pupil read aloud and the others read silently the same subject-matter at the same time. This practice is open to criticism because, in the first place, it is not the normal life situation for oral reading. We read orally when we have something to read to somebody. In the procedure that is common in schools there is no real audience depending upon the reader for the thought. Hence the reader is not reading something to somebody, but merely reading because he has to read, or to please the teacher, or to show how well he can read. It is evident that the real motive for oral reading, that of reading something to somebody, is not present. So in the second place, since the situation under which the child reads in such procedure is artificial and since the motives are artificial, the result is that the reading is oftentimes artificial, sometimes with the voice pitched high, sometimes with incorrect emphasis, sometimes with considerable stumbling and repeating. Under such a situation the child is oftentimes unconscious that oral reading is for the purpose of conveying thought.

After some experience in teaching reading and in the observation of the teaching of reading, I became convinced that the oral reading should be placed upon its true basis, that of a reader and an audience that must depend wholly upon the reader for the thought. During the last two years, in conjunction with my teachers, I have worked out certain devices for doing this from the third to the eighth grade.

In each room the teacher uses one thirty-minute period a week for miscellaneous reading with the whole room. The pupils bring in reading matter of various kinds—jokes, riddles, poems, clippings from papers, short selections from Christmas books and library books—and read to the room. Oftentimes the pupil is asked to state a reason for his choice of selection. This is most successful when it is managed so that a large number of pupils contribute.

Generally fifteen to twenty-five pupils will read during the thirty minutes. The skilful teacher will see that all pupils are interested in making a contribution and will have some reserve material on hand to encourage the pupil who has not been resourceful.

Another plan used for having a reader and an audience that has not read the subject-matter is as follows: In a third-grade room, one class was given the *Fifty Famous Stories* and the other class *Great Americans for Little Americans*. The first class read a story to the second class, which had no books and so constituted the audience. Then the pupils of the second class were allowed to take their books and read to the first class. Under the plan the reading is necessarily at sight, as the time ordinarily used in study is consumed in listening to the other class read. The poorer readers are encouraged to prepare at home. Under this plan the pupils of the class having the books have the advantage of seeing the words in the book and at the same time the reader has the advantage of an audience (the other class). This plan works best with two sets of books with comparatively short selections. This same plan is also used with one class at a time by giving half the class one book and half another book. With this arrangement the pupils have their study time for preparation.

The main difficulty in applying the scheme of always having a real audience comes in the regular textbook work where all the pupils are using the same selection and have of course read the subject-matter previous to the recitation. But we have not found the difficulty so great as it first appears. An eighth-grade class had studied and discussed "Rip Van Winkle" (*Baldwin's Eighth Reader*). For the next study each pupil was allowed to select a paragraph and make a drawing illustrative of it. At the next recitation the drawings were exhibited and it was evident that some had put the real feeling and spirit of Rip into the drawing, while others had not. So each pupil was allowed to read the subject-matter which he had illustrated and at the same time the drawing of the pupil was exhibited so the pupils could see it. The other pupils had been asked to close their books. Then they were asked to judge whether or not the picture was a true illustration of the word picture read by the pupil. One pupil had a picture of Rip fixing his fence. It didn't take the other pupils long to convince him that his picture needed revision. In the light of the suggestions and criticisms made by pupils and teacher, the pictures were revised with great improvement in representation of the character of Rip. Each pupil had read to an attentive audience with a view to giving the listeners a picture. The audience had a specific purpose for listening. It should be borne in mind that this situation of a reader and an interested audience was produced in connection with reading-matter that the pupils had studied.

Plenty of other illustrations might easily be given of lessons observed to show that, although all the pupils of a class have studied the same selection, there is plenty of thought undiscovered by the pupils for a basis of interest on the part of those who close their books and listen to the reader, provided the teacher is skilful in utilizing a specific purpose in the form of an attractive problem.

Oftentimes it is not wise to have continuous oral reading of the selection, but, as the discussion of the selection proceeds, to have certain parts read orally to settle arguments or disputed points. In reading-lessons as ordinarily taught, there is probably too much time given to the oral calling of words and too little time devoted to purposive thinking.

Practically all of the oral reading done in our grades above the lower third is done under a situation of a reader and a really interested audience, and we believe that this plan is bringing about a gradual improvement in the pupils' ability to get thought out of subject-matter and also in their ability to convey it to others by means of thoughtful oral reading.

C. R. STONE, *Principal*

HORACE MANN SCHOOL
ST. LOUIS, MO.

OUR SCHOOL PRINTSHOP

Every subject in a school curriculum should justify itself, either as a humanistic study or as one that meets the ends of manual or vocational training. While these ends are distinct one from the other, they are not in themselves antagonistic; so that some subjects, properly directed, may lead to any one or to all of them.

Printing is such a subject. It occupies a unique position. In the training it gives and in the finished products it turns out, it meets the demands of those who advocate vocational studies; in subject-matter it draws upon history, civics, science, mathematics, and English, thus establishing a natural kinship with the other subjects of the school curriculum; while from the standpoint of art, on the one hand, it is dependent upon art, and on the other it is art expression itself.

Its purely educational value secured its introduction into the University Elementary School, and is based upon the same general principles which underlie all the manual arts in school, the fundamental principles, namely, of a public-school curriculum. It offers a general training which fits the child not only for printing as a vocation, should he in later life elect it, but also for any other vocation demanding power to think in terms of objects, a cultivated artistic sense, and the training of the hand in the expression of ideas susceptible of such treatment.

The initial equipment of the School of Education printshop cost about $600.00. It consisted of an 8×12 Gordon press, one stone, a small paper-cutter, two case stands with a sufficient supply of 12-pt. Caslon to enable four pupils to work at one time, and a cabinet containing 25 job cases of type of various styles and sizes, ranging from 8-pt. to 48-pt. For three years no money was available for current expenses except what could be earned through the printshop. A school calendar, Christmas cards, reading-lessons, poems, words to songs, college outlines, and other work for which there was a demand in the school were printed and sold. The calendar alone netted $385.00. The proceeds were invested in a motor to run the press and in additional case stands and type. Although this commercial work was more or less an expedient, it served a purpose, and when later it became possible to secure the necessary supplies through the regular school channels, the lesson of buying only what was needed, and when it was needed, had been so thoroughly learned that the shop today contains only such things as are in constant use. The present equipment consists of six single- and five double-case stands, one furniture case, three lead and slug cases, sixty-seven cases of type, two stones, two galley racks, forty galleys, fifty composing sticks, six chases, and the usual smaller articles that are necessary for the work.

Printing is taught two hours a week for a half-year in each grade beginning with the sixth. The preliminary work consists in learning the case and in learning to pick up and put the type into the stick. From the first lesson the pupil is trained to take a correct position at the case and move economically, although at no time in the course is stress laid upon speed. The classes number from eighteen to twenty pupils who work together on their first piece of work, so that they may quickly see the result, a matter of importance to young children who do not project their aims far into the future. This first copy is some poem needed for use in the English or music classes; for only those things are printed which are of social value. Each pupil sets up the first line which he immediately submits to the teacher for criticism. The first perfect line is taken from the stick and put into a galley to be printed. The rest of the poem, line by line, is set up in the same way. When the poem has been all set up, a new poem is chosen, and the good workers are assigned "takes," but the weak pupils continue working together until they are able to do accurate work. If at this point emphasis is placed upon "clean work," "outs" and "doublets" and misspelled words will cause much less trouble later on; for this is the nascent period for establishing good habits and proper standards.

Through this drill the teacher may justly expect the pupils to gain some facility in handling materials, to space evenly (apparent even spacing comes later), to use quadrates and spaces properly in filling out a line, to know when to indent lines, to use leads, and to read type in the stick. Poetry rather than prose is chosen for this work because it presents fewer technical problems than does prose.

When the pupil begins to work alone, he is assigned a galley marked with his name in which to keep his work. He determines the length of his stick by setting up the longest line in the poem, and records on his copy this length and the size and style of type he is using. He is taught to tie up and put away his work at the close of the lesson and to return to its proper place his individual stick and all other material he has used. When his poem is in type he takes a proof, which he reads and corrects.

At first the pupils observe while the teacher "makes ready" their work for the press. No effort is made to teach this process earlier than in the seventh grade, although whenever any pupil wishes to attempt it he is permitted to do so. The presswork is taught as a class exercise, each working in turn, while the others look on and note the criticisms and suggestions given to the one at the press. This process is divided into three cumulative steps, first, putting the paper in with the right hand; secondly, adding to this step its removal with the left hand while continuing to place with the right; and, thirdly, adding to these the control of the lever. The press, run by motor, is operated at a very low speed. The first consideration is the safety of the child (no accident has ever occurred), and the second, the securing of correct movements so that there shall be nothing to unlearn hereafter.

In prose composition the problem of spacing becomes important. In beginning it the teacher examines each line set requiring even spacing between the words, the ending of the line on a completed word or syllable, and the justification of the line. With this also begins the work in distribution, though the pupil's skill and sense of responsibility largely determine when he is able to distribute. Distribution is always irksome, and if demanded too early in the training or in too great quantity results in a temptation to dishonesty. The act of "mixing the case," however, brings its own punishment clearly to the mind of the child and teaches its own lesson.

Throughout the learning of these processes, the child's work is "laid out" for him; that is, he is told what size and style of type to use, how long to set the lines, how to arrange his title, etc. He is thus left free to attend wholly to the process. But as soon as he becomes familiar with the process, can handle his material in a printer-like manner, knows in some degree the possibilities and limitations of his material, he makes his own plan for his work and submits it to the teacher (see Figs. 1, 2, 3). This plan may be printed by hand or it may be a pencil sketch or paper may be cut out and pasted on a card. Every type case in the shop is marked by a label printed in the kind and size of type it contains, so the pupil can intelligently choose the type he wishes to use and mark the name and size on his plan. This process, this making a plan, means that the child has in his mind a realized thought before

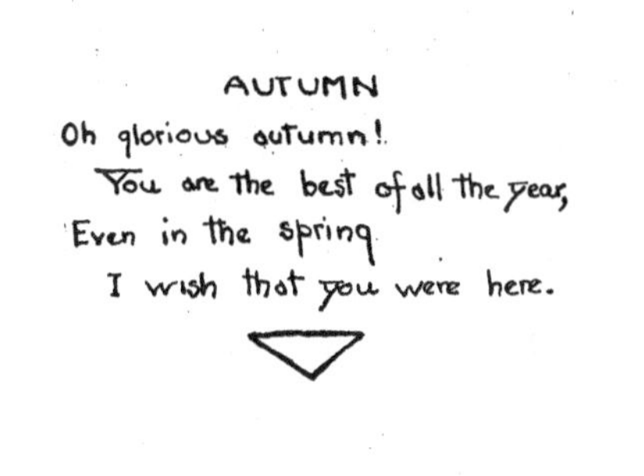

FIG. 1

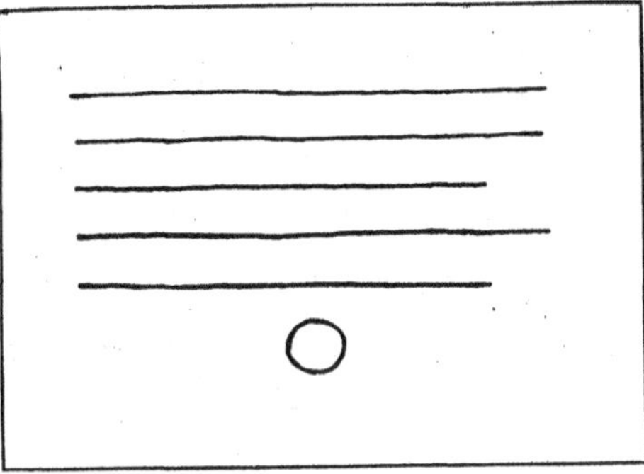

FIG. 2

FIG. 3

he touches type. He comes to his work with a clear image of type of definite size and style carefully arranged on paper of given dimensions. In other words, he has stated the problem which he has set himself to work out with printshop materials. When he can do this there is no "fumbling" in his mind, and every move he makes will be direct, filled with purpose and meaning.

In the carrying out of this plan, the teacher's function is that of adviser and critic. To illustrate: If, for instance, the child in planning a Christmas or an Easter card chooses a type adapted only to commercial display, the teacher explains to him the correct use of such type. If he has selected Cloister Black type for an

Fig. 4.—Plan

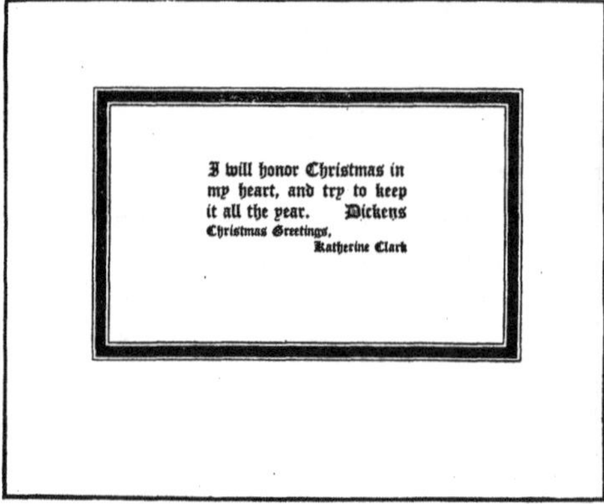

Fig. 5.—Proof

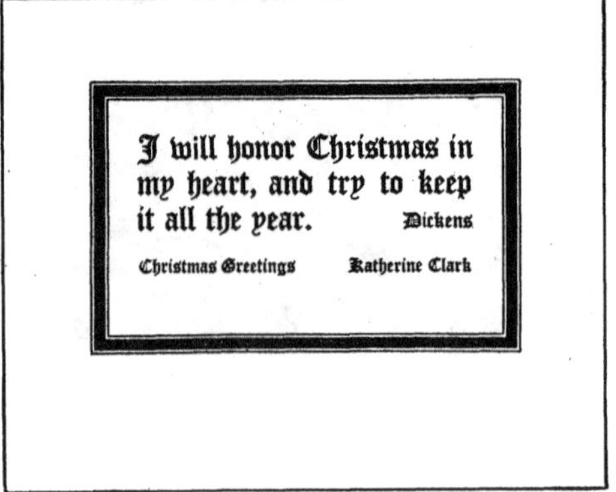

Fig. 6.—Result

advertisement, he is told that Cloister Black is a text type and reserved for such uses. But if his mistake is not due to ignorance of the use and origin of types, but is owing to imperfect judgment, he is allowed to set his type and discover his mistake (see Figs. 4, 5, 6). When the child has discovered his mistake, either of two courses is open to him: first, to choose another size of type which will fill the desired space, or, second, to use the type chosen and from the proof make a new dummy, adjusting paper and margins to this. In every case a second dummy should be made from the proof, thus allowing the child to revise his first arrangement.

From this point, the work becomes more refined. This is shown, not only in the results, but also in the selections printed. Design, illumination of letters and ornaments, illustrations, harmonious combinations of colors, harmony of type faces, proportion and balance, one or all, enter into the child's future problems. To acquire good taste, to know and to recognize good typography, is one aim of the work.

The nature of the work varies with the social demands. It may take the form of a program, an invitation, an announcement, reading-lessons for grades, labels, letters to parents, post cards, cooking-receipts, library cards, plays, booklets, a collection of original verses, anything for use by the whole school or some part of the school; or it may be something needed in the home or outside life, a business card, a social-settlement announcement, a Sunday-school program; or possibly something for personal use, a Christmas, valentine, Easter, or birthday card, a bookplate or a booklet of original work. Anything of distinct social value which the child recognizes, if it be within the capacity of our press and not beyond the ability of the pupil, may be found in the list.

In 1905 the University Elementary School began the publication of a school magazine called *The Reporter*. This has been financially supported entirely by the pupils of the Elementary School, at first by subscriptions and advertisements, later by subscriptions only. The pupils write all the articles and draw all the pictures that appear in it. A professional engraver makes the plates and a linotype machine sets up the "straight matter," but the children do all the rest of the work. It is possible for them to do everything in connection with its publication if it were advisable to use their time in that way. But the solution of a variety of problems seems more vital than much repetition, and the demands of other forms of handwork and of the academic studies make professional assistance necessary.

THE SCHOOL REPORTER

OF THE

UNIVERSITY ELEMENTARY SCHOOL

FIG. 7.—Cover

The School Reporter

of the

University Elementary School

SPRING

VOLUME X, 1914 NUMBER 3

RETURNED WITH INTEREST

"Clarn'ce," said that individual's mother, "Clarn'ce, what you did wid dat dime Mr. Frank done gib you?"

Clarence shuffled his bare toes uneasily and replied evasively as he felt that precious treasure deep down in his breeches pocket: "Safe an' soun', ma."

"Han' it ober den," commanded the head of the house, "ef yo-all wants any red beans an' rice fo' yo' suppah."

Unwillingly he pulled it out. He knew the dire consequences of refusing. And then red beans and rice could not be resisted.

Stately Corinne, his mother, worked for Mr. Frank, as he was called by the negroes. They had known him from a child, and such familiarity could readily be excused.

That very day Clarence had helped Mr. Frank mend the roof of the chicken house, and been rewarded with a shiny new dime. Now he sat on the wash-house steps and reflected on the cruelty of mankind until his mother, passing by on her way to the house

FIG. 8.—First page

62 *THE SCHOOL REPORTER*

The School Reporter

Editorial Staff

EDITOR-IN-CHIEF—Beatrice Marks
ASSISTANT EDITOR—Fritz Carpenter

Reporters

FOURTH GRADE		FIFTH GRADE	
Elizabeth Crandall	Eugene Lyden	Ella Marks	Carol Magenheimer
Beatrice Michelson	Herbert Skinner	Donald Dodge	Rosalind Wright

SIXTH GRADE
John Jones — Vories Fisher

SEVENTH GRADE
Richard Flint — Thorndyke Hilton — Mary Edith Stahl — Everett Walker

H. S. PREPARATORY
Barbara Bent

Business Staff

BUSINESS MANAGER—Ernest Loeb — TREASURER—Miss Stilwell

THE REPORTER, issued quarterly at 50 cents a year, is sold by subscription only, and is supported by the children of the Elementary School. They write all the articles and draw all the illustrations. The professional engraver and the line-o'-type machine lend their help, but the arranging of the articles in the magazine, the paging, the composition of the running heads, the titles, the signatures and the cover, and all press work are done by the children at the school.

REPORT OF A LECTURE

Dr. Headland lectured on the children of China in Mandel Hall. Many elementary school children attended. The following is a report of his most interesting lecture:

Are the Chinese children like those of America? Some call them "little heathens," but they really are nothing more or less

FIG. 9.—Editorial page

58 *THE SCHOOL REPORTER*

LIFE SAVING

It was a dark, stormy night. The waves rushed high upon the lonely beach as if driven by a great impulse. The sky overhead was dark and sinister; the moon, afraid of the dark and stormy night, did not so much as peep to the angry waves. Here and there along the beach could be seen a tiny, twinkling light, suggestive of a warm fireside and young and old telling stories.

It was a nice picture indeed that Jake Brown, beach patrol, visioned, as he tramped up and down his lonely beat of two miles. The wind playing with the waves made a ghastly noise as it swished and screeched to the lonely man. Now and then a huge breaker would roll and tumble up to his rubbered feet.

All was black out toward the sea, but as Jake looked he imagined a tiny light shoot up far out, toward the Douglas rocks.

"I wonder what that could mean," he soliloquized. "It's funny, yet it couldn't mean anything except a boat in distress. Gad! There goes another! I wonder if I should report to the station."

"Hello, there!" came a voice from the dark that was scarce audible in the roar of the wind, "Is that you? Pretty bad night out. I pity the poor sailors at sea, and those—," and the rest was drowned in the roar of the wind.

"Say, Jim," as the bulky form made a hole in the dark, "I saw a rocket go off out there. Do you think it could mean anything?"

"It might mean a ship in distress, but I think that all ships are safe and snug in harbor by this time. They wouldn't be out in this storm for love or money."

"Now, I'm not so sure, Jim! It goes to say that a rocket would mean a ship in distress. Quick, Jim, there goes another."

"You're right, Jake. It's a ship in distress, and mighty much in distress, if I'm any judge."

"What shall we do, with both of our stations two miles off?

FIG. 10.—Page of prose

In the past we have taught the history of printing. Today we are giving the children an opportunity by actually doing some printing to assimilate this knowledge and to make it a power in their own lives. For along with the work of printing, history must be studied to give meaning and value to the shopwork. The

ELEMENTARY SCHOOL REPORTER

AWAY, SPEED AWAY!

(A song written on a boat crossing to America in the fifteenth century.)

II

Away to the land where thoughts are free;
Away to the strange land over the sea;
Where red men are and kings are not,
Where flee the pilgrim and Huguenot.
Oh, away, speed away!

III

There roams the red man, nature's child,
And his ways are cruel and harsh and wild.
We battle the wilderness for our life,
And the forest wild resounds with strife,
But, away, speed away!

IV

The country is new and rich and free,
And there is plenty for thee and me,
So fly, speed our bonny boat,
And sail her faster than all afloat.
Oh, away, speed away!

DORIS BENTLEY, *7th Grade*

73

FIG. 11.—Music composed in the seventh grade in 1910

pupil should learn of the various ways in which this has been carried on from the days of the clay tablet to the making of a modern newspaper. Much of this historical material is not available in suitable form for elementary pupils, and our printshop is proving its commercial as well as its social value in helping to provide for this need. The pupils themselves are printing stories, translations, articles, and selections containing the necessary information. Another source of information is found in visits to modern printshops, engraving establishments, paper mills, type foundries, and other allied industries. The relation of the school printshop to outside life is so vital that the child is instinctively conscious of it. But visits to modern plants do much to enlarge his vision and give him a broad idea of printing and its position in the world today.

The most obvious result of the printshop is its effect upon the English work. The conscious attention to form in typesetting leads to close observation of all form. Through printing the

FIG. 12.—Cartoon: "When a Feller Needs a Friend," after Briggs

child comes to a knowledge of paragraphing, to the meaning of punctuation marks, to correct spelling, and the right use of capital letters. He notices the forms of verse and the style of expression. He becomes careful and accurate because his work demands care and accuracy, and children naturally respond to the inherent demands of their own work. They resent only the imposition of standards from outside.

The study of mathematics is directly strengthened by its practical application in the printshop. Besides the constant measuring, it furnishes practical problems, such as computing the number of ems to a given page, finding the amount of type necessary to set a required piece of copy, calculating the number of pages

The Trolls' Christmas

FIG. 13.—Cover page of booklet

ORIGINAL VERSES

BY THE THIRD AND
FOURTH GRADES
OF THE UNIVERSITY
ELEMENTARY SCHOOL

THE PRINT SHOP
THE SCHOOL OF EDUCATION
1913

FIG. 14.—Title-page

the manuscript copy will cover, finding the percentage of spoilage in the presswork, determining the cost of a zinc plate, and the amount and cost of paper for a desired piece of work. All these enter intimately into the regular shopwork.

But no less important is the connection between art and the printshop. The first real art problem which the child there faces is that of spacing between words, and he soon learns that well-spaced lines are more legible and therefore more pleasing than unevenly spaced ones; that neither choice type nor initial letter, colored ink nor attractive paper can hide the holes made on a page by irregular spacing. Since print is used as a means of communication between one person and many persons, legibility is the chief consideration of the printer, although it should not be the only consideration unless the word be made to include all that

FIG. 15.—Illustration for "The Drawing of the Sword"

adds to it. The child should be led to see that the page of type is most legible when it is most beautiful; that legibility depends upon choice of type, length of line, spacing, arrangement, page proportions, margins, quality and color of paper, good ink, and good craftsmanship; that good craftsmanship means clear and even impression of the type on the paper; and that the form of the expression should harmonize with the thought. Any page which fills these requirements is readable and beautiful. Decoration may make it more beautiful only if it emphasizes these points, if it is subordinate to the design, and does not attract attention from the print to itself.

Art problems which present themselves legitimately and which grow out of regular social work include cover designs (see Figs. 7 and 13), title-pages (see Fig. 14), margins, arrangement of text (see

Fig. 10), illustrations (see Figs. 15 and 16), and head and tail-pieces (see Fig. 17). Decorations and borders should be used sparingly, even when designed by the pupils themselves. They should learn first to see the beauty in the well-printed page, in the harmony of ink and type and paper.

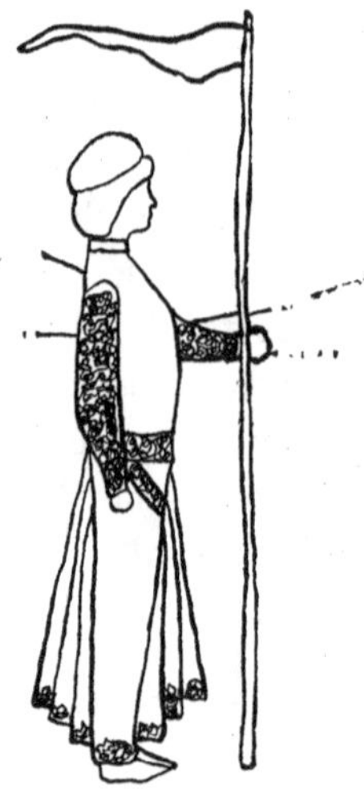

FIG. 16.—Illustration for "The Drawing of the Sword."

The value of this art training lies just in the fact that it is related to the printing. The principles of design which the pupil may have studied in his art lessons are emphasized and vitalized because they are needed. The child wishes to use them and feels the necessity for knowing them. So he comes to the art class a questioner with real problems that have grown out of his own experience in the printshop.

The question most frequently asked in regard to the printshop is "Does it pay?" The answer is unqualifiedly in the affirmative. It even pays financially. A record kept of the expenses compared with the value of the product estimated at current rates shows a balance on the side of credit.

It pays educationally. It gives to the pupils some technical training in the subject of printing. It offers a mental training equal to any other subject in the curriculum. It affords a knowledge of one of the world's industries, which is an acknowledged factor in civilization. It demands on the part of the child a practical application of his knowledge of grammar, rhetoric, history, mathematics, and art, and thus enhances that knowledge.

FIG. 17.—Tail-piece for "Our Greek Gods and Heroes."

But the highest value of the printshop can be estimated neither in terms of money nor of knowledge; there is a result above and beyond that of intellectual attainment—the strengthening and upbuilding of the moral character. The printshop does its part in producing the *esprit de corps* which prevails in the school. It makes for unity in the school because its problems are school problems, of interest to the entire school. Its effect is evident in a general desire to participate in some sort of social service, in appreciation of honest and efficient work, in power to co-operate with others for a common end, in a regard for property rights, and, most important of all, in that self-respect which comes from the consciousness of being identified with the world's workers in the doing of useful, creative work.

KATHARINE M. STILWELL

SCHOOL OF EDUCATION
UNIVERSITY OF CHICAGO

SCHOOL SUBJECTS AS MATERIAL FOR TESTS OF MENTAL ABILITY. I

CLARA SCHMITT
Assistant, Department of Child-Study, Board of Education, Chicago

In several large cities the school child, because of his unfavorable reactions to the school situation, comes in for clinical diagnosis of mental and physical condition. Since it is the child's reaction to the school situation which is at fault, it is well to test him along the line of the special abilities which he is expected to develop under the conditions of the school situation. The school subjects may be made to form a series of tests which can be used from year to year to measure or check up the development of special abilities. The curriculum of the school forms a serial arrangement of accomplishments proceeding from the simplest subject-matter of the first grade to the complexities of the eighth grade. Such an arrangement of tests derived from the school subjects as forms a psychological serial arrangement from that which is simplest to that which is complex may be derived from the curriculum as it exists. The following series of tests and suggestions for the evaluation of the child's development with reference to the school curriculum has resulted from an examination of several hundred children considered by the school to be unfavorable in their reaction to the school situation, and comparison of them has been made with children considered normal with regard to their reaction to the school situation. The subjects chosen for this series of tests are those of reading, writing, and arithmetic. The tests pertaining to reading are discussed in this article.

READING

The most important accomplishment in the school life is that of reading. The child's progress throughout the school is dependent entirely upon his attaining it. Upon it depends his progress, to a large extent, in arithmetic and almost entirely in history and geography and other such subjects which consist of classified or organized groups of facts.

The accomplishment of the child in this subject may be arranged with reference to *quantity* and *quality*. A defective child may be deficient in one or both of these two characteristics of the reading accomplishment. He may be incapable of learning to recognize the words of the printed page; he may show himself capable of learning words only very slowly or of forgetting them quickly and easily. He may show himself capable of learning words with some facility in memorizing them, and so of becoming a good reader, but incapable of gaining ideas from the words which he reads. It is this latter characteristic which one is to understand as included in its various aspects under the term "quality."

The child may show an ability to recognize words from the printed page to a greater or less extent, but this recognition with the defective child consists, largely, merely of a mechanical type of visual memory which serves as a stimulus for its associated vocal prototype. The child who learns words in this way only is always dependent upon his teacher, since he can acquire for himself no new or unfamiliar word from the printed page. He can become somewhat independent of his teacher only if he learns phonetic values. Defective children are sometimes capable of acquiring very large visual vocabularies, but show themselves quite deficient in perceiving phonetic relationships. Children of the first grade may be expected to acquire the simplest phonetic elements of the English language.[1] The child who can obtain a visual vocabulary with facility, who gains a perception of the simple phonetic values, and who learns to combine them correctly for the independent learning of new words is considered a favorable reactor so far as the subject of reading in the first grade of the public schools is concerned. The various steps from the early period of the reading accomplishment to its complex fulfilment are indicated as follows:

I. *Quantity*.—1. Knows no words: This is the condition of the average child when he enters school at six or seven years of age, and is one persisted in by the low type of defective child for several years. This low type of defective child shows himself incapable of

[1] Cf. Chicago Public Schools, Course of Study for the Elementary Schools, 1912.

perceiving the fine differences which serve to distinguish one word from another on the printed page, though he is able to use spoken language. Some knowledge of the degree of his defectiveness may be gained when one knows the length of time in which he has persisted in this disability.

2. Can recognize a few unrelated words: This is the accomplishment of the average normal child after a few days spent in the school. It is a *condition* persisted in by many defective children sometimes for years. In such case, the defective child has learned a word here and a word there which has stuck in his memory, and he recognizes them wherever he sees them. He shows himself, however, incapable of gaining sufficient words to make his reading a consecutive process with regard to meaning. The words which he does learn bear, perhaps, no relation to the amount or type of teaching that has been given. The learning of them is largely a matter of chance, and just why certain words have been learned, and many others imparted at the same time in his instruction have been forgotten, cannot be determined.

3. Can read entire sentence in the first or some other reader: This step in its simplest form is attained by the child after a few weeks in school. The reader which he has in school—if because of being a defective he is placed in an ungraded room—compared with the number of years that the child has been in school is some measure of his defectiveness in learning to read.

4. Can read at sight any material such as newspaper, etc.: This is the highest grade which may be attained in the ability to read, with reference to quantity. It is attained by the normal child with the fifth grade. The phonetics which underlie the reading process is the great stumbling-block of the defective child. Seldom is one found who has this accomplishment. He may be able to learn a very few of the simplest combinations, such as consist of one or two consonants and a vowel. The normal child progresses in his knowledge of phonetic values to such an extent that he becomes independent of the teacher in so far as the illogical complexities of our English spelling permit. At the fourth grade the normal child is able to work out new and unfamiliar words with approximate phonetic correctness.

II. *Quality*.—1. The defective child may be able to accomplish with reference to quantity in reading anything between the limits set above from the lowest to the highest stage of accomplishment. However great his accomplishment in the quantity of his reading, he is unable to read a new passage other than mechanically, that is, all he can do is to use a familiar popular phrase, parrot-like. This type of reading may be described as a straight line association between the visual and vocal centers. The child makes no, or few, other associations with the ideas gained from the printed page before him. The words or ideas which he reads do not relate themselves in his mind with anything else he has read, or with other experiences he has had, to the extent that a complex of related ideas is formed in his mind which he can reproduce orally or otherwise. He can reproduce few, if any, of the ideas which the page contains. Upon being asked what he has read about, he remains dumb or answers with merely a word or phrase contained in what he has read. This type of reading may be suspected from the monotonous tone with which it is delivered. An extreme example of this type was that of a girl of eleven, found in the second grade. She had attained the fourth step in quantity, and was very proficient in her rendering of phonetic values. She read a long paragraph, of which the following is the beginning sentence: "It was in the spring of the year 1826 about 10 o'clock, when Mr. Amos Bliss, manager and one of the proprietors of the *Northern Spectator*, was in the garden behind his house planting potatoes," etc. This selection was taken from a Fifth Reader which she had never seen. She pondered over the unfamiliar words "spectator," "proprietors," and "manager," and pronounced them correctly, with very little loss of time. The other words in the selection were read with little or no hesitation. Upon being asked what she had read about, she made no reply; and when the question was repeated she finally said, "It was about a horse." The selection contained no reference to a horse, but the opposite page contained a picture of a horse. The normal child, when reading material which is not familiar to him must give much attention to spelling and deciphering unfamiliar words. He will often, because of this distraction, be unable to give the sense of the selection read. A judgment of the quality of the child's reading should, therefore, in every case, be deduced only from material which he reads with reasonable facility and which contains few if any unfamiliar words.

2. Appreciative: This type of reading is the opposite of the mechanical type just discussed. With this type there is usually expression of tone in reading which shows the child's understanding or appreciation of the selection read. Upon being questioned, he can tell in a sentence or more the essential elements of a selection. It is usually a sure sign that the reading has been appreciative if pleasure is shown. However, expression is not an infallible test. Defective children may be trained to read selections with expression, and if the circumstances of the training have been pleasant the child may incorporate these pleasant associations into the reading process itself, so that he seems to be enjoying the ideas derived from the selection. In such a case, however, he fails to read with expression or to reproduce the sense of the meaning when the same material is arranged in unfamiliar form.

3. Apperceptive: This is a grade of performance above the *appreciative*, in that there is a relating of what is read to a larger complex of knowledge or experience in addition to the reproducing of content. In this type of reading the child can reproduce orally without further prompting the essential details and can give an interpretation of a selection. Fables lend themselves readily to such an interpretive test. Defective children often can answer correctly any question asked about a selection read, but are unable to organize it for themselves and are unable to give an interpretation of its meaning when the material is of a literary type other than that of didactic narrative.

4. Initiative; reads voluntarily: Many children who attain the highest stage as relates to quantity in reading may at the same time really be able to gain so little from such abstractly represented ideas that they never voluntarily read for their own pleasure. Many children who have not yet gained the highest stage as relates to quantity still read voluntarily because of a desire to gain knowledge or to meet certain social demands. It is seldom that a defective child reads from any other motive than to please his teacher.

RESULTS OF READING TESTS FOR NORMAL AND DEFECTIVE CHILDREN

Two selections to test ability in reading were given to seventeen children of each grade from the first to the sixth chosen from five public schools of Chicago. Three from each grade were chosen from four schools and five from another. These schools were situated in foreign-speaking districts. Of the eighty-five children tested, thirty-eight came from homes which were counted as English-speaking, since the mother was able to speak English. In the remaining forty-seven homes, according to the testimony of the children and the teachers who knew them, the mothers could not speak English.

The teachers were given the following directions for choosing the children for the test:

Select children who are average good readers for the grade; do not select the very best readers you have. Select them from that age of which you have most; that is, if you have more nine-year-old children than any other age select nine-year-old ones.

The first-grade teachers were asked to select only those who had begun school in September. The teachers consulted the record of ages upon entrance in September. The tests were given during the six weeks of May and June. The children of the first grade were, then, near the seventh birthday; the second grade were near the eighth; the third grade were near the ninth; the fourth grade were near the tenth, and the fifth grade were near the eleventh.

The defective children who were given the tests at the same time and in the same way were between the ages of ten and sixteen who had been in the special rooms for defective children for at least one year. Many of them had been in these rooms for several years. With one exception the rooms were situated in the schools in which the normal children were tested. There were five such rooms. Forty-six children of the eighty who constituted the membership of these rooms fell within the conditions chosen. None of them had uncorrected defects of sight or hearing.

The first of the selections chosen was the story of "The Fox and the Grapes."

THE FOX AND THE GRAPES

One day a fox went down the road.
"How hungry I am!" he said. "I wish I could find something to eat."
Just then he saw a grapevine. It had ripe grapes on it.
"Oh, how good those grapes look! I will have some," said the fox.
But he could not reach the grapes. They were too high on the vine.
He jumped high up in the air, but he could not get them.
At last he went away hungry.
The birds heard him say, "Those old grapes are sour.
They are not good for a fine fox like me."
But the birds knew better.

This selection was made in order to give each child something to read that he had been taught in school. The story is one of the lessons of the First Reader taught at the end of the first year. All but the first group of the first-grade children tested had read it. The general practice of the school with such stories as this is to read, recount, and discuss and in some instances dramatize the story. If the children had not all had an opportunity to recount the story individually they had heard some of their classmates do so and had joined in the discussion of it. All the defective children had had opportunity to hear it and read it and doubtless to recount it several times, since much attention is given to such work with the defective children. Each child had spent at least two years in the first grade before entering the special room.

The defective children were all mentally at least seven years of age according to the Binet scale. With the exception of the stamp-counting test with which three failed, all could pass all the tests of seven years of age. All could do the Thorndike *a* test with no more than three errors. All could do the Healy-Fernald Test I, as well as the average of the first grade. With tests of greater complexity there was much variation.

The data recorded include time for reading the selection, errors of pronunciation, verbatim reproduction of the story, and the correctness or falseness of the interpretation of the motive of the fox in saying the grapes are sour. This last item was obtained by asking after the child had given his reproduction of the story, "Were the grapes sour?" If the answer was "No," then "Why did he say so?" The interpretation was considered correct when the child indicated that the fox was disgruntled at not being able to get the grapes. The idea was not always expressed in words, but sometimes in an inflection of the voice in the answer, "Just because he couldn't get them." If the answer to the first question was "Yes," then the question was asked, "How did he know?" To this question there was sometimes an attempt to make an explanation such as that of one child, "He looked at them," but generally there was silence.

The reproduction was classed under the following heads, *scant*, *adequate*, and *full*. That reproduction was classed as *scant* which did not contain a sufficient number of the essential details to tell the story, or which had them so mixed or otherwise wrong that the story was not correctly rendered. An *adequate* reproduction contained enough detail to indicate the story, but with little or none of the embellishing details of dramatic setting. The *full* reproduction contained all or nearly all the items of the original story.

The two following reproductions were classed as *scant*.

"The fox couldn't reach the grapes; he went away hungry, the birds knew better."

"The fox was hungry, he wanted something to eat, so the birds said them grapes are not good, they are sour."

It should be remarked here that no reproduction was classed *scant* if the child could answer a series of questions which would bring out his understanding of the story, such as, "What did he try to get?" "What did he say?" etc.

The following is one of the poorest in the matter of detail of the reproduction classed as *adequate:*

"About the fox, he was hungry, and he wanted some grapes to eat, they were too high and he could not get them and he said those grapes are sour."

The following is a *full* reproduction:

"One day the fox went down the road, he was very hungry, he said I wish I had something to eat, then he saw a grapevine, it had ripe grapes on it, how nice it looked, I will get some, but he could not get any, then he went away hungry, the birds heard him say, those grapes are sour, those grapes are not good for a fox, but the birds knew better."

In recording mispronunciations those words which the child could not decipher in ten seconds were classed with the mispronounced. Words mispronounced in reading such as "then" for "they" were called to the child's attention with the question, "Is it 'then'?" If he pronounced it correctly the word was not classed with the mispronunciations. The time record for normal children includes time taken up in this way. For the defective children a time record was seldom of any significance because of the many corrections and helps necessary to get the child through the selection.

The first-grade children of the first school tested varied so widely from the other first-grade groups that their record could not be included in the averages. Their performance supported the assertion of the principal that this particular group of foreigners was very slow in learning to read. It is possible that their record would have been nearer the average if they had been tested last. The same backwardness in reading was evinced somewhat by the second grade of that school, but not sufficiently to make necessary their elimination from the averages. The third grade showed no variation.

Table XXXIV shows the data gained from selection I.

TABLE XXXIV

DATA OF READING TEST I

Grade	Number of Children	Average Time	Average Number Errors	Reproduction			Interpretation	
				Scant	Adequate	Full	+	−
I.....	12	82″	5	3	9	0	6	6
II.....	17	62″	0	0	9	8	6	11
III....	17	48″	0	0	4	13	13	4
IV.....	17	48″	0	0	5	12	15	2

The time average for the first grade of Table XXXIV had a range as follows: 2 took between two and three minutes to read the selection; 6 between one and two minutes; 3 less than one minute. The error average was made up of one child's 5 errors and 2 other errors made by two children.

The time average for the second grade ranged: 1 between two and three minutes; 4 between one and two minutes; 7 less than one minute. There was little variation in the time of the third and fourth grades.

It is rather significant of the small child's ability to understand the point of the fable type of story that though all these children had been taught this story and had discussed it more or less, it is at the third grade that it is understood. The children of the first and second grades who gave correct interpretation probably only reproduced their teaching.

The errors in pronunciation made by the normal children in this and the second reading test were always in favor of a word which had considerable visual or phonetic resemblance to the correct word. The errors made by the defective children with the first selection which was perfectly familiar to them in content, at least, were absurd so far as visual or phonetic values were concerned, but were calculated to fill in the context. The defective child reads, for instance, that the fox saw a vine with *berries* on it. Because of the great prevalence of this type of variation the performance of the defective group cannot be compared with that of the normal. Another type of comparison will be made below.

The second selection was chosen because of its unfamiliarity, its wide range of verbal difficulty, and simplicity of content, which at the same time possessed a definite unity. It was taken from p. 177 of Jones's Fifth Reader. This reader is not used in the schools, and probably had never been seen by any of the children who read the selection. Since the verbal expression is rather complex and the words used are not those of the ordinary child's everyday vocabulary, it was desirable to keep the content-matter simple, that not too many difficulties would confront the child at the same time. The paragraph selected was:

It was a fine spring morning in the year 1826 about ten o'clock when Mr. Amos Bliss, the manager and one of the proprietors of the *Northern Spectator*, might have been seen in the garden behind his house planting potatoes. He heard the gate open behind him, and, without turning or looking around, became dimly conscious of the presence of a boy. But the boys of country villages go into whosesoever garden their wandering fancy impels them, and supposing this boy to be one of his own neighbors, Mr. Bliss continued his work and quickly forgot that he was not alone.

The same data as for the first test were recorded, except that there is no interpretation for this one.

Following is an example of a reproduction classed as *adequate:*

"A man was planting potatoes in his back yard and a boy came in and he thought it was one of his neighbor boys and he didn't pay any attention to him and forgot he wasn't alone."

The following reproduction was classed as *full:*

"Mr. Bliss was planting potatoes behind his house, he looked up suddenly and there was a boy coming in his yard, but in that country the boys go whereever their fancy impels them and he thought it was one of his neighbors and kept on with his work and after awhile he forgot that he was not alone."

No child grasped the significance of the title, "manager and one of the proprietors of the *Northern Spectator*."

Table XXXV shows the data of the second selection.

TABLE XXXV

DATA FOR READING, TEST II

Grade	Number	Average Time	Average Number Errors	Reproduction		
				Scant	Adequate	Full
II	17	194″	7.8	14	3	0
III	17	91″	2.8	13	4	0
IV	17	74″	1.0	6	7	4
V	17	54″	.5	0	9	8

The words most frequently mispronounced were, "manager," "proprietors," "Northern," "Spectator," "conscious," "whosesoever," "impels," "continued." The mistakes of the normal children consist, for the most part, of misplaced accent, the omission of an obscure syllable in long words, or giving a different phonetic value than is the right one for the word in which the letter is found. Thus "manager" becomes "manāger"; "proprietors" becomes "prop′rietors," or "propetors," etc.

RESULTS OF READING TESTS FOR DEFECTIVE CHILDREN

The reading of the defective children presents such irregular characteristics that averages which would present any meaning are difficult to obtain. The children tested had been much drilled in the story of the Fox and the Grapes. Nevertheless 24 of the 46 could read it with less facility than the first-grade children. They made many errors of the absurd type discussed above. Their reading consisted of some unerring recognition of words and more or less filling-in to supply a remembered context. Nine of the defectives could give only a scant account of the story and an incorrect interpretation.

Twelve defective children were graded as equal to the first-grade child in reading ability. Ten were graded equal to the second-grade child in ability as regards the mechanical and qualitative aspects of the second reading test. Two of the defectives of the second grade could give an adequate account of the matter read. One of these children was ten years of age and by reason of this test and others was reclassified on his record sheet as only backward and returned to the regular grades of the school. The other, twelve years of age, was so deficient in other tests that he was retained in the special room.

Table XXXV shows that it is only with the fourth grade that sufficient mechanical skill in reading has been attained to admit of sufficient attention to content to give an adequate reproduction of an unfamiliar selection. With the fifth grade, such skill has become general.

GRADE FOR INTRODUCTION OF A TEXT IN ARITHMETIC

WALTER A. JESSUP
College of Education, State University of Iowa

The supervisor who has been interested in finding out the practice of his neighbor in connection with the introduction of a textbook in arithmetic has no doubt been impressed with the fact that wide variations exist in this particular. Any investigation, covering a small number of cities only, presents such wide variations as to make it impossible to form an intelligent opinion as to the practice in this connection. However, with data from hundreds of superintendents distributed throughout the country, it is possible to make certain generalizations in regard to the prevailing practice. Professor Lotus D. Coffman of the University of Illinois, and the writer, in connection with the report of the Committee on Economy of Time in Arithmetic, received replies from 754 cities in regard to this item. The data are presented in the following tables.

TABLE I

Showing Grade in Which an Arithmetic Text Is Introduced
(by geographical divisions)

	I	II	III	IV	V	VI	Total
North Central	1	18	160	64	22	2	267
North Atlantic	2	9	122	78	15	0	227
Western	0	6	25	17	2	0	50
South Central	0	13	44	17	1	0	75
South Atlantic	0	4	19	5	2	0	30
Counties	2	16	53	28	4	3	106
	5	66	423	209	46	5	754

The meaning of Table I becomes clear when read as follows: Of the 267 cities reporting from the North Central territory, 1 introduced a text in the first grade, 18 in the second grade, 160 in the third grade, 64 in the fourth grade, 22 in the fifth grade, and 2 in the sixth grade. Again, of the 5 cities introducing a textbook in the first grade, 1 is in the North Central territory, 2 in the North Atlantic territory, and 2 in the country schools reported by the county superintendents. Of the 66 schools introducing a textbook in the second grade, 18 were in the North Central territory, 9 in the North Atlantic territory, 6 in the Western territory, 13 in the South Central territory, 4 in the South Atlantic territory, and 16 in the counties reported by the county superintendents. Attention is directed to the wide variation as represented by isolated cases. The 5 superintendents who introduced a textbook in the first grade are at wide variance with the 5 superintendents who introduced a textbook in the sixth grade. Again the 66 superintendents who introduced a textbook in the second grade are clearly at variance with the 46 superintendents who introduced a textbook in the fifth grade. However, despite this variation, it is of distinct significance to note the fact that there is a prevailing tendency to introduce a textbook in the third grade or in the fourth grade; thus experience seems to point to these as the standard grades for the introduction of a textbook. (It should be noted that the distribution resembles the distribution to be expected by chance.)

Table II shows the same facts reduced to percentages. The third and fourth grades are even more clearly shown to be the dominant grades for the introduction of a textbook. Almost 85 per cent of the cities introduce a textbook in one or the other of these grades. In this particular there seem to be no striking differences due to geographical location, the third grade being the modal grade in each section of the country, and the fourth grade standing second in each section of the country.

TABLE II

PRECEDING TABLE REDUCED TO PERCENTAGES

	I	II	III	IV	V	VI	Total
North Central	.3	6.8	60.0	24	8.2	.7	100
North Atlantic	.9	4.2	53.8	34.4	6.7	0	100
Western	0	12.0	50.0	34.	4.0	0	100
South Central	0	17.3	58.7	22.7	1.3	0	100
South Atlantic	0	13.3	63.3	16.7	6.7	0	100
Counties	1.9	15.2	50.0	26.4	3.7	2.8	100
	.7	8.7	56.1	27.7	6.1	.7	100

The meaning of Table II becomes clear when read as follows: In the North Central territory .3 per cent of the schools introduce a textbook in the first grade, 6.8 per cent in the second grade, 60 per cent in the third grade, 24 per cent in the fourth grade, 8.2 per cent in the fifth grade, and .7 per cent in the sixth grade.

In the absence of striking sectional differences, the question arises as to whether or not differences in the year in which a textbook is introduced may be due to the size of the city. Table III represents replies from the schools above (excluding the country schools). The meaning of this table becomes clear when read as follows: In the one city of 1,000,000 and over reporting, the textbooks are introduced in the third grade. Of the fifteen cities of 200,000 to 999,999 reporting, one introduced a text in arithmetic in the second grade, nine in the third grade, five in the fourth grade, etc.

TABLE III

Showing Grades in Which Arithmetic Text Is Introduced (by size of city)

Population	I	II	III	IV	V	VI	Total
I. 1,000,000..............	0	0	1	0	0	0	1
II. 200,000 to 999,999......	0	1	9	5	0	0	15
III. 100,000 " 199,999......	0	0	8	4	1	0	13
IV. 50,000 " 99,999......	0	2	20	8	1	0	31
V. 30,000 " 49,999......	0	2	22	12	3	0	39
VI. 20,000 " 29,999......	1	1	26	11	3	0	42
VII. 15,000 " 19,999......	0	1	30	9	1	0	41
VIII. 10,000 " 14,999......	0	10	45	26	7	0	88
IX. 8,000 " 9,999......	0	4	41	25	7	2	79
X. 4,000 " 7,999......	2	29	168	81	19	0	299
	3	50	370	181	42	2	648

It is interesting to note that the variations are in the smaller cities. All the cities introducing arithmetic in the first grade are in towns with a population of 30,000 or less. Four-fifths of the cities introducing a textbook in arithmetic in the second grade are in cities of 15,000 or less. Three-fourths of the cities introducing a textbook in arithmetic in the fifth grade are in towns of 15,000 or less. The variation is revealed even more clearly in the table of percentages (Table IV).

The meaning of this table becomes clear when read as follows: In cities of 1,000,000 population or over, 100 per cent introduce a textbook in the third grade; in cities of 200,000 to 999,999 population, 6.7 per cent introduce a textbook in the second grade, 60 per cent in the third grade, 33.3 per cent in the fourth grade, etc.

Here again it is noteworthy that experience has been so standardized that in cities of every size, the third grade is the modal grade for the introduction of a textbook, with the fourth grade standing second.

TABLE IV

TABLE III REDUCED TO PERCENTAGES

Population	I	II	III	IV	V	VI	Total
I. 1,000,000	0	0	100.	0	0	0	100
II. 200,000 to 999,999	0	6.7	60.	33.3	0	0	100
III. 100,000 " 199,999	0	0	61.5	30.7	7.8	0	100
IV. 50,000 " 99,999	0	6.5	64.5	25.8	3.2	0	100
V. 30,000 " 49,999	0	5.2	56.4	30.7	7.7	0	100
VI. 20,000 " 29,999	2.4	2.4	61.8	26.2	7.2	0	100
VII. 15,000 " 19,999	0	2.5	73.2	21.8	2.5	0	100
VIII. 10,000 " 14,999	0	11.3	51.1	30.	7.6	0	100
IX. 8,000 " 9,999	0	5.2	51.9	31.7	8.7	2.5	100
X. 4,000 " 7,999	.8	9.6	56.2	27.1	6.3	0	100
	.6	7.7	57.1	28.	6.2	.4	100

From the foregoing presentation of replies from the superintendents distributed throughout the various parts of the United States, and throughout the cities of different size, we can arrive at the following conclusions: a superintendent who introduces a textbook as early as the first or second grade, or who postpones the introduction of such text as late as the fifth or sixth grade will do so in the face of generalized practice at the present time. While we do not know absolutely the best time to introduce a textbook in arithmetic from the standpoint of scientific investigation, because very little investigation has been made thus far in this connection, we do know that in the experience of the thousands of teachers and of the hundreds of superintendents represented in this study, the third grade is the best grade for the introduction of this subject, with the fourth grade standing second. It would be of great administrative importance for us to know about the results obtained in arithmetic work that is done in a school which postpones the introduction of a textbook until the fifth or sixth grade. From an investigation of isolated instances, where the textbooks have been introduced very late, we have reason to believe that much of the arithmetic work which is commonly associated with the textbook is done at about the same time that it would have been done had the textbook been introduced. In other words, the extreme postponement indicated in Table IV in all probability represents an attempt to get away from the use of the textbook, rather than an attempt to get away from the actual teaching of arithmetic. Again the students of this problem are concerned with the question as to which is the better grade for the introduction of a text, the third or the fourth grade. This can only be determined by careful tests, but the amount of time to be saved is of sufficient importance to justify the attempt to determine the better practice. This experimentation is going on, as is shown in the foregoing tables. What is needed now is a thoroughgoing co-operative investigation of results attained under the different systems.

The advocates of the policy of concentration of the energy of the school toward the mastery of reading in the first three grades have much to encourage them in this report. If a third of the schools are already postponing the introduction of a textbook in arithmetic until the fourth grade, there need be little difficulty in getting more time for reading during the first three grades.

The fact that the introduction of a textbook in arithmetic is as late as it is no doubt represents a more or less conscious acceptance of the theory proposed by the psychologists a few years ago that formal instruction in arithmetic be postponed until a later period in the life of the child.

On the other hand, the student of educational administration who takes cognizance of the wide variation in age and maturity of the children in a particular grade may be led to question the advisability of postponing formal instruction in arithmetic until the upper grades. Again, the student who is conscious of the enormous amount of elimination which goes on in the early grades may question the policy of allowing children to postpone the introduction of a textbook in arithmetic until so near the close of their scholastic career.

The school superintendent needs the help of the experimental educationist in finding out whether or not the variation in time of introducing the textbook in arithmetic is paralleled by the variation in arithmetical efficiency. Is not this a problem of sufficient practical importance to challenge the student of educational administration?

CURRENT EDUCATIONAL LITERATURE IN THE PERIODICALS[1]

IRENE WARREN
Librarian, School of Education, University of Chicago

Boshart, E. W. The day vocational school. Man. Train. M. 16:65–73. (O. '14.)

Broome, Edwin C. Vitalizing the high-school course of study. Educa. 35:12–15. (S. '14.)

Brown, H. A. The function of the secondary school. Educa. R. 48:227–40. (O. '14.)

Dakin, W. S. A plan for training teachers while in service. El. School J. 15:106–9. (O. '14.)

Dallenbach, Karl M. The effect of practice upon visual apprehension in school children. II. J. of Educa. Psychol. 5:387–404. (S. '14.)

Dyer, Walter A. Our public schools. Craftsman 26:599–605. (S. '14.)

Earle, Samuel C. English courses in the small college. English J. 16:422–26. (S. '14.)

Estee, James B. Interesting children in civic betterment through instruction by mayor and city officials: teaching them to work for public good. Craftsman 26:584–87. (S. '14.)

Fitzpatrick, Edward A. The universities and training for public service. Survey 32:614–15. (19 S. '14.)

Fitzpatrick, Frank A. James M. Greenwood: an appreciation. Educa. R. 48:288–93. (O. '14.)

Fontaine, Mary B. Articulation of English teaching in the elementary and high schools. English J. 3:416–21. (S. '14.)

Griffin, Caroline. One hundred plus in the reading book. Educa. 35:21–25. (S. '14.)

Hartshorn, Helena E. The college entrance examination in English. Educa. 35:43–55. (S. '14.)

Hay, Ian. The lighter side of school life. Liv. Age 283:28–38. (3 O.'14.)

Hetherington, Clark W. The training of the physical educator and play director. Educa. R. 48:241–53. (O. '14.)

[1] *Abbreviations.*—Atlan., Atlantic Monthly; Educa., Education; Educa. R., Educational Review; El. School J., Elementary School Journal; English J., English Journal; J. of Educa. Psychol., Journal of Educational Psychology; Lit. D., Literary Digest; Liv. Age, Living Age; Man. Train. M., Manual Training Magazine; Pop. Sci. Mo., Popular Science Monthly.

Heuser, Frederick J. W. College entrance examinations in German. Educa. R. 48:217–26. (O. '14.)

Hill, David Spence. Minor studies in learning and relearning. J. of Educa. Psychol. 5:375–86. (S. '14.)

Hippensteel, H. S. The problem of the training school. Educa. 35:1–11. (S. '14.)

Kiernan, Frank. The great adventure of democracy: preparing for it by self-government in the public schools. Craftsman 26:626–30. (S. '14.)

Kirkpatrick, E. A. An experiment in memorizing versus incidental learning. J. of Educa. Psychol. 5:405–12. (S. '14.)

Lewis, Howard T. The social survey in rural education. Educa. R. 48:266–87. (O. '14.)

Lind, Samuel C. Medical inspection in the schools. The children's point of view. Educa. 35:39–42. (S. '14.)

McCleery, Wm. J. The attendance officer, his qualifications and work. Educa. 35:16–20. (S. '14.)

MacDougall, Robert. The picture and the text. Pop. Sci. Mo. 85:270–83. (S. '14.)

O'Shea, M. V. Determining educational values. Pop. Sci. Mo. 85:284–91. (S. '14.)

Patterson, Herbert P. Ideals in present day education. Educa. R. 48:254–65. (O. '14.)

Paul, Harry G. On handling supplementary reading. II. English J. 16:427–36. (S. '14.)

Reavis, W. C. The relation between the physical and the health conditions of children and their school progress. El. School J. 15:96–105. (O. '14.)

Roorbach, Eloise. A picturesque Japanese finishing school where girls are taught to be charming women and good housekeepers. Craftsman 26:620–25. (S. '14.)

Sanders, Frederic W. The organization of education. Educa. 35:26–36. (S. '14.)

Schoolmasters and schoolmistresses. Liv. Age 282:700–702. (12 S. '14.)

Strunsky, Simeon. School. Atlan. 114:546–55. (O. '14.)

(The) war as an educational topic. Lit. D. 49:633. (3 O. '14.)

Williams, Jessamine Chapman. Subject-matter in home economic courses for high schools. Man. Train. M. 16:71–81. (O. '14.)

VOLUME XV NUMBER 4

THE ELEMENTARY SCHOOL JOURNAL

CONTINUING "THE ELEMENTARY SCHOOL TEACHER"

DECEMBER 1914

EDUCATIONAL NEWS AND EDITORIAL COMMENT

Night Schools

If we may judge from the number of newspaper items that have come to hand during the past month, the most important single item of school activity during the latter part of October and the beginning of November is the organization of night schools. Everywhere in the country this problem is vigorously discussed by school officers and by organizations of citizens.

One is impressed as he reads these statements with regard to night schools with the variety of work which is offered. Many of these schools devote themselves to the training of foreigners and give, for the most part, the ordinary academic subjects, with a good deal of emphasis on instruction in English. Others devote themselves to the industrial arts and have the greatest variety of courses for all sorts of people. They are virtually continuation schools, with a strong bias in the direction of industrial subjects.

The sources of support are quite as varied as the courses offered. In some cases the state department makes a contribution to the local community's effort to maintain such schools. In many cases private philanthropy of one sort or another is drawn upon to enlarge the scope of the work which can be supported by the public board of education. In some cases one reads of discussions held by the board as to the feasibility of finding the funds for such enterprises. The board finds that it must retrench in some quarter and determines that the night school is the most easily dispensed with portion of its work, whereupon a group of citizens immediately passes resolutions to the effect that this is the most important part of the work.

One hardly knows how to deal with the mass of information which is at hand. Possibly quotations from the headlines of a number of these clippings will serve the purpose of giving a general impression of the scope of the movement.

The *Times*, of Erie, Pennsylvania, has an article entitled, "State Will Be Asked to Aid Night Schools." The *Chicago American* has an article entitled, "Teach Spanish in Evening Schools and Aid Business Men." The *Globe Democrat*, of St. Louis, has an article entitled, "Night-School Circulars Sent to Employers."

At Lansing, Michigan, as reported by the *Press* of that city, a discussion has arisen as to the desirability of allowing day students to enter the night school. It has been decided that it is undesirable to duplicate effort by allowing these day pupils this additional privilege. At Rockford, Illinois, the night school is described as a foreigners' school. At Dayton, Ohio, the *News* reports that twelve hundred pupils have been enrolled in the night school. The Y.M.C.A. is frequently mentioned as contributing to the general educational opportunities. Minneapolis, as reported by the *Tribune*, is one of the cities that has found it difficult to organize night schools. The disappointment of citizens is expressed in a number of articles following the first announcement. At Grand Rapids, Michigan, the *Press* reports that band music will be taught in the night school. Drawing is a very common subject mentioned. It is explicitly mentioned in a report from Spokane, Washington. In Santa Barbara, California, the superintendent reports that he has secured enough volunteer teachers to carry on the work so that there will be no additional expense in opening night schools. At Dubuque, Iowa, emphasis is laid upon the practical courses. The *Herald* of that city reports shop mathematics, shop drawing, carpenters' and builders' arithmetic, and other subjects of the same type. From points as distant from each other as Everett, Washington, and Terre Haute, Indiana, the papers report large increases in attendance. At Toledo, Ohio, night schools have to be curtailed, owing to the shortage of funds for salaries.

The geographical distribution of these clippings makes it clear that activities of this type are more common in the northern schools than in southern cities. This is undoubtedly an expression of the better economic support of schools in the northern states, although Kentucky has been conspicuously brought to the attention of the whole country by its night schools, which are making an effort to overcome illiteracy, and the *Oklahoman*, of Oklahoma City, describes in a long article the reopening of the night schools with large attendance.

State School Funds in Minnesota

The state of Minnesota has a larger school fund than any other state in the country. It is interesting to note that the effect of such a large school fund upon the organization of schools is dependent entirely upon the mode of distributing the money. Superintendent Barnard pointed out years ago, during his superintendency of the state of Connecticut, that a large state fund may become a menace to good school organization in the community. If local communities come to depend upon the central state subsidy and do not do their duty both in contributing to the support of the local schools and in seeing that the state money is well expended, the large state fund may become an embarrassment to the community rather than a help. The following extract from an item published in the *Pioneer*, of St. Paul, gives an account of the situation which now exists in the state of Minnesota:

A report to be made to the next legislature by the commission was made public yesterday by C. G. Schulz, state superintendent of education. The commission was created by the legislature of 1913 to recommend a plan for the reorganization of the educational system of the state.

The commission in its report takes occasion to decry the present policy of distributing state aid to rural schools in no uncertain terms.

"State taxes for the support of local schools," the report says, "are levied either to equalize the burden or to provide a stimulus. The state gives to some districts more than it collects and takes from others more than it returns, on the ground that the guaranty of a common-school education is the state's concern.

"The state levy is designed to spread more equally the burden of common education or to diffuse more equally, through every district, facilities for education—in either case that the efficiency of the schools may be promoted for the sake of all.

"From the most comprehensive study that the commission has been able to make, based on fourteen counties comprising 1,011 school districts, it does not appear that this distribution of the state school fund has anything to do with the efficiency of the schools, especially the rural schools.

"The apportionment has no discoverable relation to the amount of local school taxes, no relation to the scale of salaries, no relation to attendance. It cannot be shown that it stimulates better support of the schools, as shown by taxation; better maintenance of the schools, as shown by teachers' salaries; or better work by the schools, as shown by average attendance.

"It does not act as a stimulus nor does it operate to equalize the burdens. There are poor districts that tax themselves heavily and richer districts that tax themselves lightly. Where the burden is heaviest, the school fund gives no more than where it is light. Where it most ought to be a spur, it becomes rather a subsidy to civic indolence."

The commission recommends that half of the school apportionment basis be on an attendance of 100 days a year instead of forty days a year by each pupil as at present. The other half should be distributed in proportion to teachers' salaries, which can not be less than $400 a year for the school to receive state aid under the new plan.

"It is the rural school that needs skilled supervision most and gets it least," the report continues. "The rural school is dependent solely on the county superintendents for the sort of oversight that strengthens the weak teacher and tones up the school. It is of highest importance that the county superintendent should have knowledge, capacity, and experience.

"The engaging of county superintendents by popular vote does not reasonably insure good choice. The commission, therefore, recommends that all the territory of each county outside the independent school districts shall constitute a common school district; that its government shall be in a common school board, to be elected by the district, which will choose the superintendent.

"The common school board will develop a trained body of school directors. Economy will also be possible to a degree seldom attainable by the limited experience of the local school board in the small districts."

It is the opinion of the commission that St. Paul, Minneapolis, and Duluth school districts should retain their charters and that all other special districts should become independent districts under the general law.

Early in October the state of Indiana celebrated a "Disease Prevention Day." In response to a proclamation of the governor, setting aside the day for public celebrations, many cities organized parades and other forms of activity aimed to promote among school children and among the population at large a greater interest in hygiene. Parades were held in all cities and towns of size, safety-first motion pictures were exhibited free of charge, and lectures on disease prevention were delivered by physicians. In one city 8,000 persons are said to have participated in the parade. There were floats gaily decorated, bearing messages of health and hygiene, teaching lessons in the care of babies and in housing problems. Some of the banners carried by the children were "One Window Open" and "Too Much Fresh Air Is Just Enough." One wagon bearing a load of children was marked "We Are Fed On Pure Food." There were other floats and banners indicating that the house should be freed from the deadly fly, the rat, the cockroach, and the insanitary drinking-cup. There were mottoes urging personal cleanliness and the proper sanitary regulation of all public places.

Hygiene and Publicity

It is the belief of those who are interested in promoting a movement of this sort that a public celebration of this type once a year will be of great service in bringing to the attention of the whole community the importance of the problem of health.

The Board of Estimate of New York City has as usual pronounced on various educational matters in making its provisions for expenditures for the coming year. One of the pronouncements of the Board of Estimate which has attracted most attention on the part of the teachers in Greater New York is the cutting out of an item of $65,000 from the budget for the payment of teachers' salaries in vacation schools. The Board takes the opportunity to recommend to the Board of Education that teachers be required to teach during the summer without additional compensation.

Discussion in New York of the All-Year School

The implication of this recommendation is that the present vacation of teachers is too long. The idea which the Board of Estimate has in this matter was undoubtedly borrowed from the visit made by the mayor of the city of New York and some of the other members of his official staff to Gary, Indiana. Superintendent Wirt, of Gary, has been employed by the Board of Estimate to come to New York City and contribute during the year by his advice and counsel to the reorganization of the city school system. It is evident why, with the example of Gary before them, the Board should consider seriously the desirability of an all-year-round school. On the other hand, the teachers have been very vigorous in their protest against the mode of administration suggested by the Board of Estimate. Practically all of the organizations of teachers have expressed themselves volubly as opposed to the procedure recommended.

Some discussions have been held with regard to the desirability of keeping children in the school much longer than at the present time. Physicians have expressed themselves on both sides of the discussion. But, on the whole, the balance of opinion seems to be in favor of a much longer school year. Certainly any consideration of the example of the older civilizations of Europe would lead us to believe that children can without harm attend the school much longer than is common in American cities. The difficulty which is presented by the ruling of the Board of Estimate is, however, somewhat apart from the general academic question whether we should have longer schools. Whether teachers should be required to contribute these schools to the public or the public should recognize the importance of longer schools and be willing to pay the larger price necessary for a continued program of school work is in part an economic and not altogether an educational question.

One finds himself, therefore, sympathizing with both parties to the New York discussion. If the Board of Estimate could find some way of carrying out the laudable plan of a school all the year round, great advantage would come to the school children of New York. But the teachers certainly have a right to feel that the present rate of compensation was established for the shorter year and that they ought not to bear the burdens of the community in developing the very desirable result of a longer school period for the children of the city.

Two quotations clipped from the *Globe and Commercial Advertiser*, of New York, show how difficult it is to discuss a question of this sort without bringing in issues that are not altogether relevant. For example, one teacher, writing to the *Globe*, says:

> If I taught during these two months [July and August] I should need a vacation for the remainder of the school year for the restoration of my health. I wouldn't teach in those two months for $1,000 a week. I need that time for rest and recuperation. I entered the teaching profession with the understanding that such a rest was available. If I were engaged in some other line of work I should be quite content without even a week's vacation. But being a teacher I have found that this relaxation from work is an absolute necessity.

A little later in the same letter the writer goes on to say:

> When a few ignoramuses began to whine about the teachers' "long" vacations, the Board, instead of combating the evil, encouraged it by drawing up plans for running all-year-round schools. As a matter of fact, we only get about twenty days more than the other city employees, and even the worst foes of the profession concede that we are entitled to this time.

Contrast with a statement of that sort the remarks made by Professor Hetherington in arguing in favor of attendance by children through 365 days in the year. He says, basing his experience upon the school conducted at the University of California, that it is altogether possible to organize summer work and work throughout the year so that it shall be advantageous to children to have this kind of experience every day in the year.

> In a six weeks' session in Berkeley, California, held under the auspices of the University of California last summer, three hundred children between the ages of three and twelve, gathered from every social class and ranging from precocious infants to children bordering on feeble-mindedness, went to school in a beautiful eucalyptus grove. All the work was out of doors. And the children were so absorbed in the delightful play work that they never paid any attention to the two hundred visitors a day who observed them so closely.
>
> These tots mastered twice as much reading and writing as is usually mastered in twice the time. They made headway in foreign-language acquisition, all as a part of their daily "play."

Finally, the New York teachers must recognize the fact that the Board of Estimate has set itself in harmony with tendencies that are exhibited on every side to extend in a very proper way the school opportunity of the children of New York City. The method may be open to criticism, but the end should not be described as in the letter above quoted, for the simple reason that the method of objecting to a longer school program adopted in that letter will in the long run give way before the more rational demand that children and teachers alike shall organize the program so that it will not be necessary for the teaching profession or the children to relax during a period of two months from an unnatural type of schooling.

There are two large commercial interests that attach themselves to school organization. One is the publishing interest and the other is the teachers' agency. It is the judgment of a number of states that the textbook business should be taken over by the school system itself. On the other hand, it is argued that private competition makes, in the long run, better textbooks for the schools than would public supervision. The discussions of textbook matters have been carried on with such vigor that it is hardly necessary to repeat the arguments pro and con. The public has been interested in the publishing business and politicians have frequently been very much involved in the business transactions that attach to the supplying of books.

Teachers' Agencies under Public Control

Teachers' agencies, on the other hand, have been somewhat narrower in their scope of operation and have attracted less attention on the part of the public in general because their fees are commonly extracted from the teachers whom they serve.

Teachers' agencies represent, however, an unsolved problem in educational organization. If teachers' associations or if state departments were able to cope with the problem of supplying teachers and giving information with regard to available candidates, there would hardly be a place for these outside commercial agencies. It cannot be denied that in many cases these commercial agencies are at the present time serving an important function. A superintendent who needs a teacher can commonly get more information and better information by going to a teachers' agency than he can by applying to any public institution. On the other hand, teachers are certainly paying an enormous price in the aggregate for the kind of service which is rendered by these agencies.

It is interesting, therefore, to reproduce the report recently compiled by the Bureau of Education with regard to the tendencies that are operating in the direction of taking the whole matter of the appointment of teachers out of the hands of commercial agencies:

NOVEMBER 2, 1914

CITY SCHOOL CIRCULAR NO. III, 3

STATE TEACHERS' EMPLOYMENT BUREAUS

A. Three states have special laws establishing state teachers' employment bureaus:

Massachusetts.—By an act of the legislature of 1911 (Chapter 731, Sec. 1–2–3) a teachers' registration bureau was established under the control of the state board of education. A fee of $2 is charged each applicant. The applicant must be a graduate of any high school or normal school in the commonwealth or of any other school considered by the board of education of equal grade, or a graduate of a reputable college. Printed lists of applicants with a brief statement of their qualifications are sent to the school committees in the different cities and towns. The law as originally passed was for teachers who were residents of the state, but this restriction was removed in 1913.

The work was started upon its present basis in October, 1912. From that time until November 30, 1913, 101 positions were filled. To November 30, 1914, probably 200 positions will be filled. On December 31 there were 142 high-school teachers, 149 elementary-school teachers, and 73 special teachers registered with the bureau.

Minnesota.—The Minnesota State Teachers' Employment Bureau, authorized by the act of April 25, 1913, began operation June 1, 1913. The registration to August 1, 1914, was 830, divided as follows: rural, 71; grades, 315; supervisory, 94; high school, 235; special, 115.

The salaries of the teachers already placed and reported amount to $260,-310. A registration fee of $3, payable at time of registration, entitles the person enrolled to the services of the bureau for 12 months from date of registration. Receipts from these fees for the first year amounted to $2,490, with expenses amounting to $2,000. The items of expense do not include the salary of the director of the bureau, who is listed as state school inspector and draws his salary from a separate fund. The fiscal year closes August 1, but since that time during the present year (1914) 112 teachers have enrolled and 165 teachers have been located whose salaries amount to $68,000.

Michigan.—A law has been upon the statutes making the department of public instruction an employment bureau for teachers, but it is a dead letter.

B. Three state departments of education maintain employment bureaus without special state laws authorizing them:

Connecticut.—A teachers' employment bureau has been conducted by the state board of education for a number of years. A complete set of cards is kept in the state office with records and credentials of each applicant. Records of normal-school graduates are kept on white cards so that they may easily be distinguished from the records of those not having normal training. A special form (No. 8) is filed by superintendents and committees desiring teachers. A list of the best available candidates is sent and a notice of the vacancy is sent each teacher on the list by a special circular (No. 2). Superintendents and committees are requested to notify the state office as soon as a teacher has been secured. During the year 1913–14, 544 applications for positions were filed and 159 for teachers to fill vacancies were received from superintendents and school committees.

New Jersey.—The state board of education maintains a "bureau of information for teachers and school officers, which was established January 15, 1898, to act as a medium between competent teachers and boards of education in the state of New Jersey without charge for the services rendered." Special forms are used for filing the teacher's application for a position and the board's notice of a vacancy. "Teachers keep the bureau well informed of their movements, and by so doing the management is in a position to supply teachers at 24 hours' notice, from September 1 to June 1, each year."

Indiana.—An employment bureau for Indiana teachers is a part of the state department of public instruction. No charge is made for services and only a few vacancies are filled.

C. In the following states special files or informal lists of teachers who apply for positions are kept in the office of the state department, and these lists are sent to boards of county superintendents desiring teachers:

Louisiana.—Hundreds of applications are received yearly from teachers who apply for positions to teach in the state. About twice each month a list containing the names of these applicants is sent out to the parish superintendents, giving educational qualifications, teaching experience, etc., of each applicant.

Maryland.—No bureau is maintained by the state department, but all applicants for a position who address the state office are given lists of county superintendents or other school officials to whom they may apply, and from time to time mimeographed lists of applicants are sent to school officials.

D. The other states that aid teachers in a more or less direct manner are Alabama, California, Florida, Mississippi, Nebraska, New Mexico, North Carolina, Oklahoma, Oregon, Rhode Island, Vermont, Virginia, and West Virginia. These states maintain no separate bureau or department in the state office, but aid boards in securing the services of competent teachers, without vouching for the teachers except in special cases where the qualifications are well known to the state office. The work done by this state office is free from any fee whatever and only serves to accommodate both teachers and boards.

EDUCATIONAL WRITINGS

Of making books there is no end. This year the collection we have arranged on the shelves from which to choose the children's Christmas gifts proves that childhood has appropriated much from the greatest of the world's literature. Modern writers, with imagination, facility in writing, and a marvelous insight into the child mind, have added to this all sorts of stories, verse, and more serious narratives and description which give joy and profit to the young.

Many of the best illustrators have found this field of literature an excellent medium for their flights of fancy and their wonderful skill in drawing and the use of color. The commercial houses have vied with each other in the excellency with which they have made the reproductions. Even the binders are trying to make good-looking exteriors that will wear.

Hundreds of the world's greatest men and women in all lines of endeavor have paid tribute to the influence of the printed page, so I need make no plea for the reading of books. Perhaps it will not be amiss, however, to call your attention to the great beauty of many children's books which are now appearing and to urge that you choose editions of old favorites with care. Sometimes at this season of the year, when all sorts of beautiful and dainty things are displayed to tempt us, we forget for the moment the *lasting* joy of a good book. This little list may be a reminder and I trust a convenience to you in selecting.

BOOKS ABOUT CHRISTMAS

Dickens, Charles. A Christmas carol; illustrated by A. C. Michael. Doran. $1.50.

———. A Christmas tree; pictured by C. E. Brock. Doran. $0.50.

Dickinson, A. D., and Skinner, A. M., editors. Children's book of Christmas stories. Doubleday. $1.25.

Field, Eugene. Christmas tales and Christmas verse. Scribner. $1.50.

Howells, W. D. Christmas every day. Harper. $1.25.

Irving, Washington. The old English Christmas; illustrated by H. M. Brock. Jacobs. $1.25.

Lagerlöf, Selma. Christ legends. Holt. $1.25.

Moore, C. C. "'Twas the night before Christmas"; illustrated by Jessie Willcox Smith. Houghton. $1.00.

Olcott, F. J. Good stories for great holidays. Houghton. $2.00.

Pyle, Katharine. The Christmas angel. Little. $1.25.

Wiggin, K. D. The birds' Christmas carol. New holiday edition. Houghton. $1.00.

BIBLE STORIES

The Bible for young people. Century. $1.50.

Chisholm, Edwin, editor. Old Testament stories. Dutton. $0.50.

Hodges, George. The castle of Zion; stories from the Old Testament. Houghton. $1.50.

———. The Garden of Eden; stories from the first nine books of the Old Testament. Houghton. $1.50.

———. When the King came. Houghton. $1.25.

Kelman, J. H., editor. Stories from the life of Christ. Dutton. $0.50.

Moulton, Richard G., editor. Bible stories. (Modern reader's Bible, children's series.) Macmillan. 2 vols. $0.50 each.

Tappan, E. M. The Christ story. Houghton. $1.50.

———. An old, old story-book, compiled from the Old Testament. Houghton. $1.50.

PICTURE BOOKS

Aldin, Cecil. Merry party series. Doran. 6 vols. $0.40 each.

"Forager's hunt breakfast," "Rag's garden party," "Master Quack gives a water picnic," "Tabitha's tea party," "Peter's dinner party," "Humpty and Dumpty give a fancy dress ball."

Also published complete in one volume, $3.50.

Brooke, L. L. The golden goose book. Warne. $2.00.

Each of the stories in this book is also printed separately as a paper picture book. $0.50 each.

———. The golden goose and the three bears. Warne. $1.00.

———. Johnny Crow's garden. Warne. $1.00.

———. Johnny Crow's party. Warne. $1.00.

———. The three little pigs and Tom Thumb. Warne. $1.00.

Burgess, Gelett. The goop directory. Stokes. $0.50.

———. The other "Goop books" are also published by Stokes. $1.50 each.

Caldecott, Randolph. Picture books. Warne. 4 vols. $1.25 each.

Miniature edition, 4 vols. $0.50 each.

Each of these rhymes, 16 in all, may be had separately in paper covers for $0.25 or in board covers for $0.50.

Cox, Palmer. The Brownies, many more nights. Century. $1.50.

There are eight other Brownie books.

Crane, Walter. The baby's own Aesop. Warne. $1.50.

———. Picture books. Lane. 9 vols. $1.25 each; paper edition, $0.25 each.

Dean rag books. A. B. C. Quaint Zoo. Cupples & Leon. $0.15.

———. Noah's A.B.C. Cupples & Leon. $0.25.

Teaches the alphabet.

———. Jungle. Cupples & Leon. $0.75.

A good animal book.

Greenaway, Kate. Birthday book for children. Warne. $0.60.

———. Little Ann and other poems, by Jane and Ann Taylor. Warne. $1.00.

———. Marigold garden. Warne. $1.50.

———. Mother Goose. Warne. $0.60.

———. The pied piper of Hamelin, by Robert Browning. Warne. $1.50.

———. Under the window. Warne. $1.50.

Monvel, Boutet de. La civilité. Brentano. $2.35.

———. Girls and boys. Duffield. $2.25.

A translation of "Filles et Garçons." The price of the French edition is $1.25.

———. Joan of Arc. Century. $3.00.

———. Nos enfants. Brentano. $1.25.

———. La Fontaine; fables choisies pour les enfants. Brentano, $2.35.

The Society for promoting Christian knowledge, London, publishes a translation for $2.50.

Perkins, Lucy Fitch. The Eskimo twins. Houghton. $1.00.

Mrs. Perkins' Dutch twins, Irish twins, and Japanese twins are well known by the children.

Smith, E. B. The early life of Mr. Man. Houghton. $2.00.

Mr. Smith has most successfully illustrated many children's books, including:

The chicken world. Putnam. $2.00.
The circus and all about it. Stokes. $1.50.
The farm book. Houghton. $1.50.
Santa Claus and all about him. Stokes. $1.75.
Story of Noah's ark. Houghton. $1.25.
The railroad book. Houghton. $1.50.
The seashore book. Houghton. $1.50.

FOR THE OLDER BOYS AND GIRLS

Aesop. Fables, selected by Joseph Jacobs. Macmillan. $1.50.

———. Fables; illustrated by Arthur Rackham. Doubleday. $1.50.

There is also an edition with 40 illustrations by E. Boyd Smith, published by the Century Company. $2.00.

Alcott, L. M. Little men; illustrated by Reginald B. Birch. Little. $2.00.

———. Little women; illustrated by Alice Barber Stephens. Little. $2.00.

———. An old-fashioned girl; illustrated by Jessie Willcox Smith. Little. $2.00.

———. Under the lilacs; illustrated by Alice Barber Stephens. Little. $2.00.

Andersen, H. C. Fairy tales; illustrated by Helen Stratton. Caldwell. $1.00.

———. Fairy tales; illustrated by W. H. Robinson. Holt. $3.50.

———. The snow queen and other stories, with illustrations by Edmund Dulac. Doran. $2.00.

Arabian Nights. Arabian nights entertainments; edited by Andrew Lang. Longmans. $2.00.

———. The Arabian nights; edited by Kate Douglas Wiggin and Nora Archibald Smith; illustrated by Maxfield Parrish. Scribner. $2.50.

———. Stories from the Arabian nights, retold by Laurence Housman; with drawings by Edmund Dulac. Doran. $1.50.

———. Arabian nights; edited by Frances J. Olcott. Holt. $1.50.

Barrie, J. M. Peter Pan; illustrated by Arthur Rackham. Scribner. $1.50.

———. Peter and Wendy; illustrated by F. D. Bedford. Scribner. $1.50.

Bunyan, John. Pilgrim's progress; illustrated by the Brothers Rhead. Century. $1.50.

Carroll, Lewis. Alice's adventures in Wonderland; illustrated by John Tenniel. Macmillan. $1.00.

This is the edition of "Alice" with the original pictures.

There are a number of others, the best being the one illustrated by Arthur Rackham. Doubleday. $1.40.

Peter Newell has illustrated an edition published by Harper's at $3.00.

———. Through the looking-glass; illustrated by John Tenniel. Macmillan. $1.00.

Cervantes, Miguel de. Don Quixote, retold by Judge Parry; illustrated by Walter Crane. Lane. $1.50.

Collodi, C. The adventures of Pinocchio. Ginn. $0.40. Holiday edition. $1.00.

Cooper, J. F. The last of the Mohicans; illustrated by E. Boyd Smith. Holt. $1.35.

Dana, R. H., Jr. Two years before the mast; illustrated by E. Boyd Smith. Houghton. $1.50.

Defoe, Daniel. Robinson Crusoe, with drawings by the Brothers Rhead. Harper. $1.50.

France, Anatole. Honey-Bee; translated by Mrs. John Lane. Lane. $1.50.

Another translation called "Bee: princess of the dwarfs" is published by Dutton. $2.50.

Grimm Brothers. Fairy tales, translated by Mrs. E. Lucas; illustrated by Arthur Rackham. Doubleday. $1.50.

———. Household stories, translated by Lucy Crane; illustrated by Walter Crane. Macmillan. $1.50.

Harris, J. C. Uncle Remus, his songs and his sayings. Appleton. $2.00.

Hawthorne, Nathaniel. Wonder book; illustrated by Walter Crane. Houghton. $3.00.

The stories are published separately in The orange tree series. Houghton. $0.50 each.

Hawthorne, Nathaniel. Wonder book and Tanglewood tales; illustrated by Maxfield Parrish. Duffield. $2.50.

Hughes, Thomas. Tom Brown's school days. Cranford edition. Macmillan. $2.00.

Jacobs, Joseph. Celtic fairy tales. Putnam. $1.25.

———. English fairy tales. Putnam. $1.25.

———. Indian fairy tales. Putnam. $1.75.

Kipling, Rudyard. Captains courageous. Century. $1.50.

———. The jungle book. Century. $1.50.

———. The second jungle book. Century. $1.50.

Lagerlöf, Selma. The wonderful adventures of Nils; illustrated by M. H. Frye. Doubleday. $2.50.

LaMotte Fouqué, baron de. Undine; illustrated by Arthur Rackham. Doubleday. $2.50.

Lang, Andrew. The book of romance. Longmans. $1.60.

———. The red romance book. Longmans. $1.60.

———. The Lang fairy books. Longmans. $1.60–$2.00 each.

MacDonald, George. At the back of the north wind. Caldwell. $1.50. Maria L. Kirk has illustrated At the back of the north wind and also Princess and Curdie. Both volumes have been simplified by Elizabeth Lewis and are published by Lippincott.

Maeterlinck, Madame Maurice. The children's Blue Bird; illustrated by Herbert Paus. Dodd. $2.50.

Masefield, John. Jim Davis. Stokes. $1.25.

Mulock, D. M. The little lame prince; illustrated by Hope Dunlap. Rand. $1.25.

Parish, J. C. The man with the iron hand. Houghton. $1.25.

Pyle, Howard. The merry adventures of Robin Hood. Scribner. $3.00.

———. Pepper and salt. Harper. $1.50.

———. Story of King Arthur and his knights. Scribner. $2.00.

———. Story of Sir Launcelot and his companions. Scribner. $2.00.

———. Story of the champions of the Round Table. Scribner. $2.00.

———. Story of the grail and the passing of Arthur. Scribner. $2.00.

———. The wonder clock. Harper. $2.00.

Quiller, A. T. Couch-, editor. The sleeping beauty and other fairy tales; illustrated by Edmund Dulac. Doran. $2.00.

Remington, Frederic. Pony tracks. Harper. $1.75.

Rhead, Louis. Robin Hood. Harper. $1.50.

Rostand, Edmond. The story of Chanticleer; retold by E. M. Hann. Stokes. $1.50.

Sabin, E. L. On the plains with Custer. Lippincott. $1.25.

Scott, Sir Walter. Ivanhoe; illustrated by E. Boyd Smith. Houghton. $2.50.

———. Kenilworth; illustrated by H. J. Ford. Holiday edition. Lippincott. $1.75.

Sewell, Anna. Black Beauty; illustrated by Cecil Aldin. Stokes. $2.00.

Spyri, Johanna. Heidi. Ginn. $0.40.

Stevenson, R. L. Kidnapped; illustrated by N. C. Wyeth. Scribner. $2.25.

———. Treasure Island; illustrated by N. C. Wyeth. Scribner. $2.25.

Swift, Jonathan. Gulliver's travels; illustrated by Louis Rhead. Harper. $1.50.

There is also an edition published by Dent of London and Dutton of New York which contains a dozen or more colored illustrations by Arthur Rackham.

Twain, Mark. Adventures of Tom Sawyer. Harper. $1.75. Holiday edition, $2.00.

———. The prince and the pauper. Harper. $1.75.

Wilde, Oscar. Happy prince and other tales; illustrated by Charles Robinson. Putnam. $3.75.

Wyss, J. R. von, and Montolieu, baronne de. The Swiss family Robinson; illustrated by Louis Rhead. Harper. $1.50.

POETRY

Dodge, Mrs. M. M. Rhymes and jingles; illustrated by Sarah S. Stillwell. Scribner. $1.50.

Field, Eugene. Poems of childhood; illustrated by Maxfield Parrish. Scribner. $2.50.

Lear, Edward. Nonsense books. Little. $2.00.

Mother Goose. The big book of nursery rhymes; illustrated by Charles Robinson. Dutton. $3.00.

———. A nursery rhyme picture book; illustrated by L. Leslie Brooke. Warne. $1.00.

———. The old nursery rhymes; illustrated by Arthur Rackham. Century. $2.50.

Palgrave, Francis Turner. Golden treasury of songs and poems; illustrated by Maxfield Parrish. Duffield. $2.25.

Shakespeare, Willliam. The Ben Greet Shakespeare for young readers. Doubleday. Cloth, $0.60; leather, $0.90.

———. Tales from Shakespeare, by Charles and Mary Lamb; illustrated by Arthur Rackham. Dutton. $2.50.

Stevenson, R. L. A child's garden of verses; illustrated by Charles Robinson. Scribner. $1.50.

IRENE WARREN, *Librarian*

SCHOOL OF EDUCATION
UNIVERSITY OF CHICAGO

CLASSROOM METHODS AND DEVICES

Adaptation of Regular School Subjects to the Needs of Prevocational Boys[1]

A series of brief articles will be prepared for the readers of the *Elementary School Journal* which will be descriptive of the material and methods employed in presenting ordinary school subjects to boys of about fourteen years of age in the upper elementary grades who have but meager prospects of entering high school at a *reasonable* age, or possibly of even completing the work of the grades.

Several cities have developed "prevocational" work as a part of the school system, and, while such work varies in organization and content, a common *purpose* and similar *methods* are found in all these examples. As the term "prevocational" has come to have a commonly accepted meaning in these cities, and as it is rapidly coming into use elsewhere, it has been employed in the title of this series and will be defined or discussed later.

It is believed that the material presented in these articles will be valuable not only to teachers of prevocational classes, but as well to teachers in the elementary grades of those schools where no special provisions are made for the pupils who are failing in the usual school work, or who are apparently hopelessly behind grade, or are certainly out of harmony with the aims and methods of so-called "general" education. Since prevocational work is almost invariably given for the benefit of such children, doubtless many teachers in the elementary schools will be glad to learn of some of the concrete material which the special schools are utilizing in teaching the so-called "regular" school subjects, as, for example, reading, history, civics, hygiene, elementary science, arithmetic, and manual work.

[1] This paper introduces a series of reports of material employed with an industrial class of boys. It seems necessary to precede the statement of concrete material by some general definitions.

In order to help in organizing such material, the University of Chicago has conducted, for more than two years, an experimental "industrial class." It is not the purpose of these articles to describe this experiment in detail, but the material presented has been worked out either in this class or by the teachers who have given the instruction in it, most of whom have had valuable experience in other schools.

Subsequent articles will appear monthly and each will take up in detail some one school subject, setting forth the methods which have been found to be measurably successful, the object which has been paramount in presenting the subject, some of the concrete material which has been used and reference to sources of other similar material, and some estimate of the efficacy of the work in inciting the boys to genuine intellectual effort. The present article merely seeks to furnish a setting for the more concrete studies to follow by discussing in a general way the meaning of the term "prevocational," the purpose of establishing such work in the elementary grades, and the more prominent characteristics of the pupils to whom the work is usually given.

That the term "prevocational" needs some explanation is evident to anyone who sees in how many different ways it has been used. It is not possible to give an exact definition which will accurately describe the characteristics of the school work which is now being done under that name, but these characteristics themselves may be noted as this series of articles progresses. It is desirable however, at this time, to trace the evolution of the word during the five or six years of its existence.

Perhaps some clearer understanding of the term can be gained by reflecting on the nature of a prelegal or premedical course as offered in a university. Such courses are intended to be as markedly cultural as any other college work, but are expected to give the *kind* of cultural training which will furnish the best foundation for the subsequent legal or medical course. There is recognition of the fact that of two subjects which are equally cultural one may have more practical value than the other for certain individuals.

In much the same way prevocational work is intended to be as cultural and as inspirational as any of the regular school work for the children to whom it is given, but it is believed to be more valuable as a preparation for the occupational experiences of these children, most of whom enter "vocations" at an early age.

While it must be admitted that professional education is "vocational" education, the term "vocational," as commonly used, refers to the education which prepares somewhat specifically for the humbler occupations, those which do not require an education of college grade. The occupations for which this humbler or non-professional vocational training was first given were generally industrial in their nature. For this reason "industrial education" was the term first used to designate all kinds of practical education for those who could not have or did not need a professional training, but who, nevertheless, needed an educational preparation for the work which they would soon be called upon to do. The term "vocational education" came into prominence only after the term "industrial education" was seen to be too narrow to cover all the school activities carried on under that name.

Thus "vocational education" refers to educational programs which contemplate school training of less than college grade and relate to the humbler vocations or occupations. Such training is, furthermore, intended for pupils fourteen years of age or over.

With this conception of the meaning of the term "vocational," it becomes clear that "prevocational" simply means the type of general education which will lay a better foundation for the vocational courses than is commonly provided by the regular school work. While the term has sometimes been loosely used and has been made to apply to widely different courses of study, there can be no doubt that in recent years it has come to have a commonly accepted place in educational nomenclature. The work which is done under this name in a number of the large cities enables one to say without fear of contradiction that a prevocational course is a modification of the work commonly found in grades seven and eight, or possibly in grades six, seven, and eight, in order to make that work more vital and purposeful for three types of children. While these three types vary in their marked characteristics, they are alike in this, that they are predisposed to leave school at an early age. Again, while they desire to leave school for a variety of reasons, one reason is practically common to all, namely, a distaste for school work *as they know it.*

These three types comprise, first, concrete-minded children who are more easily stimulated by doing than by reading; second, pupils who have been seriously retarded because they have never been awakened; and third, those who are hopelessly behind grade for one or the other of the above reasons or because of incapacity.

While it can be said truly that children selected for prevocational classes are "concrete minded," "seriously retarded," "anti-book," etc., the most pronounced thing about such children is that they are strongly individualistic and can never be grouped successfully under any narrowly limiting classifications.

It has been customary to consider most of these children as somewhat subnormal. May it not be that our general school methods appeal to one rather commonplace type of mind, albeit a type which is wholly praiseworthy and of great value to society, in that it can be counted upon to react in a definite and predetermined way to any given set of conditions or experiences, and that the boys for whom prevocational work is being urged, while different from the others, are nevertheless quite as normal, frequently more interesting, and possibly of even greater potential value to society at large if their energies are directed into the proper channels? A study of these children may reveal such charming, lovable, human characteristics as to show that no reasonable effort on the part of society to save them for subsequent training and education is too great in the light of their potential worth. It is only as this human, personal element dominates prevocational work that such work fulfils its true mission.

These children are individualistic and do not easily adjust themselves to the "system"; therefore the system must be adapted to the several individuals. These individuals need the fundamental "book subjects" as much as the others, and if the "bookish" way of teaching does not make it appeal strongly to these children the problem is to *vitalize* such work by devising other methods and by accepting new standards of attainment, not necessarily lower than, but at least different from, those by which school work is generally measured.

It is not so important that these children learn certain prescribed facts as it is that they gain a desire to learn *something*. What that something is does not matter so much in the beginning, and so more attention is given to developing individual differences than to securing uniformity.

It is not necessary that all become interested in the same studies, but it is fundamentally important that each becomes intellectually active—vitally and dynamically interested—in some of the school work; so much interested that the whole scheme of education takes on a new meaning and becomes a genuine pleasure.

In the experimental industrial class referred to above, the boys attended school during the whole summer seven and one-half hours daily. Some of the parents expressed a doubt as to whether the work could be really valuable because the boys liked it so well. It must be confessed that teachers sometimes have the belief that school work should be filled with hard, unpleasant drudgery if it is to be truly educational, a belief which is evidently shared by children of the prevocational type and one which has led most of them to decide that school is to be avoided and attendance to be discontinued as early as possible.

The purpose of giving prevocational training to such children, therefore, is always dual. It prolongs their school life and it also fits them somewhat better to meet the conditions of occupational life provided they enter it, as they commonly do, before seventeen or eighteen years of age.

From the foregoing it will be seen that the establishment of prevocational work is merely one of the features of the great social movement toward universal education. Perhaps the final outcome of this movement may be the opening of our palatial high schools throughout the country, not only to the small minority who are now receiving the benefits of the opportunities there afforded, but to the vast *majority* of boys and girls of high-school age, many of whom are hopelessly stranded in the grades. It may be that we shall come to see that what we have considered our high standards of admission to the people's high schools are really evidences of the relentlessness with which we have excluded from the beneficent influence of these institutions the very children who need it most.

When our high schools shall become democratized it may well be that prevocational work will pass off the stage, and that the term will no longer have its present significance. At this time, however, "prevocational" must stand for a symbol of liberality in providing, either in our upper elementary grades or in our high schools, appropriate types of educational activity for all children and for a promise that such work will be administered in a spirit of impartial sympathy. Such a procedure will be of untold benefit to the future industrial workers of the country, and, when we shall have ceased to prate of the dignity of work and shall have made provision for dignifying the workers by giving them an honored place in a truly democratic school system, we shall have done much more than advance the industrial interests of the United States; we shall have helped to make our schools mighty forces for social improvement, which they can never be to the same extent under the educational conditions which obtain very largely throughout the country today.

FRANK M. LEAVITT

A WISCONSIN EXPERIMENT IN VOCATIONAL EDUCATION AND SOME OF ITS LESSONS[1]

HOWELL CHENEY
State Board of Education, Connecticut

Mr. John R. Commons, a member of the Wisconsin Industrial Commission, speaking before the Social Service Institute in Milwaukee on April 10, 1913, on the subject of industrial education, concluded with the following words: "It is the business of those who do the planning [referring to industrial education] to know in advance what the results will be, otherwise reactions occur and the program goes farther back than it was at the beginning. This is especially true of such a profound and far-reaching reform as industrial education through the continuation school."

In view of this utterance at the close of an address which evidently saw quite clearly some of the unfortunate as well as the fortunate reactions of a great social experiment, it would be as unnecessary as it would be valueless to examine the results of Wisconsin's experiment in vocational education with a view to pointing out individual cases of failure. The correction of these failures as instances of a proper lack of methods must be for that state to work out which has assumed the responsibility for them. The traditions between our various states differ so greatly as to the forms in which legislation shall express itself that mistakes are often made in criticisms because they go no deeper than a comparison of the forms and leave the vital principles unaffected. While, therefore, the forms which are peculiar to Wisconsin are its own responsibility, the vital principles are a matter for every state's concern—no less for Connecticut than for Wisconsin.

The industrial education problem had, previous to 1911, been largely a work of promoting an idea. Massachusetts had, in a

[1] It is to be noted that this article was written in January, 1914, before the receipt of the last report of the Wisconsin Commission, which makes mention of some material changes in conditions.

limited way, worked for the establishment of all-day trade schools under state aid. Connecticut had authorized an experiment in trade schools entirely under state control. These were all-day schools as well and were realized to be tentative experiments. New York had made valuable demonstrations under institutional management without state aid. In all of these cases, and in other states where similar experiments had been under way, the aim was confessedly to attempt to give those who had not yet entered industry the elements of a trade training. The report of the Massachusetts Commission on Industrial Education had made a shibboleth of "the two wasted years," and the evil effects of this discovery were rung from one end of the land to the other. No very clear ideas had been expressed in the legislation as to how to get at the problem, though numerous studies of the European and especially German experience had been made and able reports had been written which had vitally affected public opinion.

While it was realized that the all-day trade schools could not reach a very large number of pupils, the hope was thrown out that an adaptation of the German idea of continuation schools could reach a far greater number of individuals. Trade schools had become either weak imitations of an actual trade training or frankly manual-training experiments under the control of schoolmasters who had a vague and hazy notion that by pursuing handwork for a cultural purpose the practice and theory of a trade could be taught.

The able report of the Wisconsin Commission, on which its later law was predicated, reflected the above conditions and further emphasized the industrial situation which, to a greater extent than in our eastern states perhaps, lacked opportunities for skilled training. With a large vision, Wisconsin in one law determined to write the following principles into her legislation: first, that she would assume the responsibility for some form of an education of her children up to the time they were sixteen years of age; second, that the trade experience of all children in industry should be supplemented by a school training in the years between fourteen and sixteen; third, that the state would regulate an apprenticeship system in a way that would guarantee a real training in all of the processes of a trade to all workers in the skilled industries until they were sixteen years of age.

A comparison of the ideas governing the control and conduct of industrial education and apprenticeship in Wisconsin and Connecticut would show the following:

Wisconsin meant to create a dual control of her educational system and has so widely published it. Statewise, she has not, as we understand it in eastern states, much direct supervision of her common schools. She has a state superintendent who is charged with the general inspirational as well as the statistical duty, but in effect he lacks power, except through his general influence, to alter or direct the standards of the common schools. In creating a new state board Wisconsin legislators made it practically an advisory board, but gave the state superintendent, as regards industrial education, a considerable degree of supervision when money shall have been appropriated to support it. They left to him the appointment of all assistants, except that the salary of the first assistant must be approved by the board.

Connecticut, Massachusetts, and New York have state boards of education which are administrative and not advisory bodies. The secretary of each of these boards is its executive officer, but without a vote, and so is in theory a servant of the board.

Wisconsin has paralleled her theoretical idea of dual control statewise as regards the local boards. The local industrial board is appointed by the school board, and the superintendent of the common school board is ex officio a member, without a vote, of the industrial school board. In practice he has been the expert and necessarily the executive officer in the direction of work in which the other members of the board were inexperienced. In consequence he has been given a degree of independence and responsibility to which he was foreign as superintendent of the common schools, and to a greater degree than probably exists in any other state system. As regards the state control, it may, therefore, be said that as far as it exercises the supervisory power which it has in theory, but which it has not been able to exercise for lack of funds, such supervision is in the hands of the state superintendent, who looks to his industrial board, if at all, as an advisory board and not as an administrative one.

Connecticut and Massachusetts have clung to the single control, both locally and statewise. Their boards are, however, administrative bodies, backed by the power of appointment of their executive officers and assistants, and backed by the even greater power of making many grants conditional upon the compliance with standards which they enforce, subject of course to statute.

In the control of trade training Connecticut created no dual boards. At the start she conceived of her trade training as being limited to all-day trade schools, but in its development she has made these trade schools centers of influence for the training of teachers and for evening schools, continuation schools, and part-time schools. To this factor more extended reference will be made later. In this connection it is only necessary to point out that, while Connecticut has the single control, her efforts have gone toward creating centers of trade educational influence; that is, toward creating men who had practical experience in the trades to be taught, and providing them with the tools necessary to duplicate practical trade conditions in instruction. It was not an accident that, in seeking to avoid the pitfalls caused by intrusting an industrial training to school teachers, she retained the form of a single control, but set herself sincerely to work to create an experience and spirit, as far as her trade education was concerned, of men trained in the industries.

In the creation of the apprenticeship system Wisconsin may have hoped to create, through fiat of law, an effective system of trade training under state-controlled indentures. This purpose is expressed in many of the writings on the subject.

It is noticeable that even in Wisconsin's analysis of the elements of apprenticeship there is little emphasis laid upon the ability to produce work under commercial conditions, on manual dexterity and skill, or on applied mathematics, physics, and drawing.

The insertion of this legislation in regard to apprenticeship would have indicated that Wisconsin had a serious purpose in mind and really meant to depend upon this form of apprenticeship for the actual trade training. It could hardly, however, have been supposed that a system which had already vanished would have been automatically created by advising employers of their ability to do certain things which they were not already doing if they would only undertake greatly increased burdens. It would have seemed necessary, if she meant to re-create a system of apprenticeship by the fiat of law, to create some new advantages in it for the employer, or to penalize him by some new disadvantages if he did not establish such systems of apprenticeship. An incentive which would have been in harmony with the rest of the legislation might have been the idea that no one could employ any children under eighteen years of age except in establishments which freely offered systems of indenture and apprenticeship under state supervision, but that in such establishments the state would provide the supervision and reimburse the employer for the $50 bonus.

In the absence of any reasonable hope for its success, I have not considered the system of apprenticeship as a serious part of the Wisconsin plan, and have not believed that it was intended that it should be.

The principles involved in the above legislation would seem to be the following:

Wisconsin sought to offer a form of vocational training to all pupils between fourteen and sixteen years of age who were engaged in industry. She conceived that the function of such training was primarily the teaching of the theoretical, artistic, and scientific aspect of a trade—of the cultural side of a trade in its best sense; the practice of a trade she left to industry to give. She aimed at centering the control of the vocational training in school boards separate from those intrusted with the conduct of the common schools, to the end that it might be inspired by men who were experienced in the trades and industries taught. She made the obtaining and the continuance of employment between the ages of fourteen and sixteen dependent on the attendance upon some form of vocational school for a minimum of five hours a week for six months in a year. She believed that actual experience and skill in employment, whether manual dexterity or knowledge of processes, products, and tools, or the ability to co-operate effectively with fellow-employees, would be developed in industry.

She endeavored to enforce the attendance and certificating laws through several and distinct legal officers, which excluded the schoolteacher, in theory, but left it in large part to his discretion, in fact.

She expressed a purpose to terminate compulsory school attendance on the basis of a certain standard of mental attainment, but of permitting employment practically on the basis of age only.

Such were the theoretical forces that were to abolish the deadened employments and the two wasted years. The ultimate exclusion of children from real industry until they were sixteen was the logical aim, and the initial substitutes offered were instruction in reading, writing, arithmetic, hygiene, civics, English, citizenship, mechanical drawing, and manual training.

Connecticut's purpose is not so strongly contrasted in aim as it was in the principles and methods employed. In developing a training applicable to the many, she started on an experimental basis with a few, and she devoted herself to teaching the practice as well as the theory of a trade. She did not attempt to separate the control of the vocational schools from that of the existing common schools. Starting with an all-day trade school, she used the building, equipment, and teachers for continuation schools, evening schools, and part-time schools. The secondary aims have become as important and valuable as the original aims. Instead of taking cultural-school teachers for trade-school teachers, she made her trade schools also training schools for teaching men who had had experience. She definitely insisted that mental and physical ability to undertake employment were the essential tests above an age of fourteen, rather than an increased age. She declared against the exclusion of children from real industry until they were sixteen, and attempted to supply opportunities for trade training as a substitute for necessary restrictions. She attempted to duplicate ideal trade conditions as a possible basis for developing a system of the state's actually supervising children in industry. She enforced her attendance and certification laws through one central state authority and took away from the schoolmasters the power of passing on their own work. She held the common schools up to a definite standard of performance and tried not to create new agencies to make good ancient and shirked responsibilities.

In brief, Connecticut started to develop her system with a few rather than with the many, but for the benefit of all; to create vocational teachers rather than separate vocational boards; to test pupils both in school and at work by ability rather than by age; to hold the common schools up to a definite performance of their old ideals, and to put up to the vocational schools the developing of a new training for the practice and science of a trade.

Wisconsin's legislation looked toward the exclusion of children from real industry until they were sixteen; Connecticut's looked toward developing the physical and mental ability necessary to the entering of industry without injury as soon after fourteen as was practicable. Wisconsin laid small emphasis on the teaching of a trade, more on the teaching about a trade, and considerable on making good the deficiencies of the common schools. Connecticut tried to hold the common schools responsible for their failures, and in its vocational schools frankly laid the emphasis on the trade training.

If the above analysis of the purpose for which the two states were legislating is true, it has shown that they were both sincerely working for a common purpose—the connecting of a child's school training with his life training. With this clearly in mind, let us examine the reactions from the methods that were employed, always remembering that these are not as vital as the common principles. The results in Wisconsin have been widely published in both the spoken and the written utterances of the chairman of the State Board of Industrial Education, Mr. H. E. Miles. Coming from her responsible leaders, it represented the state's attitude toward the problems that had arisen under the enforcement of the law. Let me enumerate somewhat in detail the claims which the most ardent believer in the system, Mr. Miles, has made for it, as illustrated in his article in the *World's Work* of October, 1913.

Mr. Miles claims:

1. That it is possible to organize education "so that good vocational teaching costs only $10 per year per pupil."

2. That for the last year 17,000 pupils in the state of Wisconsin were given free vocational education for five hours a week; that this year 25,000 pupils will be given the same, and next year, 40,000.

3. That the "continuation schools have solved, in a simple yet highly efficient and practical manner, the biggest educational problem confronting the United States."

4. That the "dual form of control was working out admirably from an educational point of view," as well as from a social side.

5. That with a continuation school opened in every industrial community there will be no idle children learning the vices of the street.

6. That the extent of the failure of the common-school education was a surprising revelation.

7. That in the continuation schools every child was given instruction in the theory and practice of the industry in which he was engaged.

8. That it takes "only from four to twelve weeks to start a substantially perfect industrial school, which will operate at one-half of the cost of the common schools, or, on an average for the entire state, of $10 per year per pupil."

9. That an abundance "of competent, enthusiastic, and up-to-date teachers can be found in the shops."

10. That the Wisconsin schools "aim to give to every person of every age in the state the training that he or she needs."

11. That the Trade School in Milwaukee is only half full and costs $300 per year per pupil, as contrasted with $10 per year in the continuation schools; that Connecticut is running its trade schools for 250 pupils at a cost of $250 per year per pupil.

12. That "85 per cent of the children have gone into blind-alley jobs on leaving school," but that compulsory attendance at the continuation school will save the boy or girl from the blind-alley job.

13. Finally, that Wisconsin was trying, through its conception of vocational education, "to stop the 50 per cent waste in our present educational system" and was trying "to remove from America the stigma that there is thirty-eight times as much illiteracy among our native white people as in Northern Europe and eleven times more among the children of our native whites than among the children of our immigrants."

On the basis of these and similar statements coming from the authoritative head of the Wisconsin Board of Industrial Education, an issue has been frankly joined with the eastern states, on the following claims:

1. That a good vocational education could be given to industrial workers for $10 a year.

2. That the content of this training should not be the practice but the theory and art of a trade.

3. That good teachers could be found in abundance, of this content, in the shops.

4. That the leaven of this new education would react upon and revolutionize our common-school systems.

5. That, finally, Wisconsin had a vision which would abolish the blind-alley jobs, lead idle children away from the vices of the street, remove the sting of illiteracy, and give to every person in Wisconsin, from children to gray-haired men and women, "the special training that he or she needs."

Stated as boldly as above, these claims would doubtless now seem as exaggerated to their authors as they here appear. That of getting a good vocational education for $10 has already been retracted by its author. Nevertheless, the gist of these claims has been vigorously defended, and because of their source they were taken up by practical business men all over the land, as well as by progressive school men. The eastern men were pointed to as reactionaries who had missed the vision of real education and were spending enormously unnecessary amounts for a type of vocational education that was as mistaken in purpose as it was unsuccessful in reaching working people.

WISCONSIN CONTINUATION-SCHOOL PUPILS RECEIVED LESS THAN FORTY HOURS' VOCATIONAL TRAINING PER YEAR

The annual report for the school year 1912–13 does not show an enrolment of 17,000 pupils, as Mr. Miles claims, but 12,219. The weekly attendance for the thirty-two weeks the continuation schools were in session, and for the twenty-four weeks the evening schools were open, was 6,335 pupils. About half of this whole attendance was in the evening schools, and of pupils over sixteen years of age, consequently not coming under the study of the conditions governing pupils from fourteen to sixteen. In evening schools, further, about one-half of the pupils were in classes called vocational, that is, in classes which were learning about a trade more accurately than practicing it.

In the continuation schools proper there were in weekly attendance 192 pupils in the classes for indentured apprentices; 221 in those of the temporarily unemployed pupils; and 3,263 of permit children, that is, children between fourteen and sixteen years of age legally employed, but not indentured. About three-quarters of the time, on an average, of the continuation-school pupils was spent upon what we would consider non-vocational studies—more than that if we except mechanical drawing and typical school manual training. The average attendance in hours on the various classes has been estimated by the writer. He has assumed that every child in weekly attendance averaged 4 hours for thirty-two weeks, or 5 hours for twenty-six weeks, which is hardly supposable, as it is a practical maximum. In the evening schools the average hours of attendance for pupils was 40. In the continuation schools the average for permit pupils was 62 hours, and for the very small number of apprentices and unemployed pupils, 90 hours and 86 hours respectively. Figured to a numerical average, the general average would have been about 52 hours per year for each pupil in average attendance, of which, very roughly, three-eighths, or say 20 hours per pupil for the year, was given to vocational work. To guarantee an overstatement, rather than a possible understatement, let us assume that twice this amount, or 40 hours a year per pupil, was spent upon work which had some relation to a vocation. On this basis the children of Wisconsin received as much vocational training, measured in time, in one year, as the pupils in an all-day trade school would receive in one week.

THE COST OF TRAINING IS HIGH

The cost of the Wisconsin system is shown in the 1912–13 report to have been $120,831.73, of which the state contributed $49,924.83, or 41+ per cent. On the basis of an enumeration of 12,219 pupils the cost per pupil was a few cents under $10 per year, which is the figure taken as the basis for the statement that a good vocational education could be given for $10 a year. On the basis of weekly attendance, however, it was nearly double this, or $19.07 per year for approximately fifty-two hours of instruction. There was an estimated total of approximately 707,072 student hours costing $120,831.73, or an average cost per student hour of 17¼ cents. The cost per student hour net average attendance in our common schools is now about 4 cents, and in our high schools from 6 to 7 cents. In Wisconsin, the cost of what is called vocational training is more than four times as great as a similar class of instruction in our public schools and 2½ times greater than the cost in our trade schools, and nearly three times as great as in our high schools, estimated on a unit basis of student hours. The cost in our trade schools per pupil in net average attendance for a year of 2,450 hours would be $171.50. The cost in Wisconsin, to duplicate an equal amount of student hours, would be $322.65. The cost, even for the full number of hours which the Wisconsin law prescribed (130), would be $23.15, but slightly less presumably than it costs Wisconsin to maintain her common schools for a year of over six times as many hours.

MAKING GOOD THE FAULTS OF THE COMMON-SCHOOL SYSTEM

Much that has been written on the Wisconsin situation has emphasized the imperative necessity which the continuation schools found themselves confronted with—of first making good the deficiencies of the common-school system. It was further found that they devoted from five-eighths to three-quarters of their time to purely common-school subjects. Assuming, however, that it is only one-half of the time, was it good economy or good educational efficiency to create an entirely new system of schools in order to get twenty-five hours of instruction in common-school subjects at four times the cost of providing for these same subjects in her existing system, and then to hand these schools over to the authors of her previous failures? Further, how much has she permanently weakened her common schools by accepting a condition of failure as necessary, and without making a determined effort to bring them up to a higher level of accomplishment?

It has not been my thought to imply that the East has not the same problem of school efficiency to contend with, or has had a better common-school system, because I have not sufficient basis of comparison upon which to express an opinion; but when Connecticut awoke to a realizing sense of the possibilities of failure in her common schools and was faced with the same problem, instead of accepting failure she said to her schools, her parents, and her employers that thereafter no child should leave school to go into employment unless he had a grasp of the three R's as expressed by an ability to read intelligently, write legibly, and to perform the simple operations in numbers, including decimal fractions. This law has had a stimulating effect upon the worst conditions and has aroused many parents to seek for the causes of failure which prevented their children from becoming wage-earners at fourteen. The further causes will be found in the quality of the teaching itself. During the last year, however, it is more than significant that nearly 12,000 children passed this test without the imposition of a new school burden on this commonwealth, while Wisconsin spent $120,000, of which somewhere near $75,000 went toward trying to overcome the failures of the older and existing system.

INVESTIGATIONS AGREE

Three expert examinations have been made of the Wisconsin system and seem to be in agreement on the following points:

1. That the day continuation schools of Wisconsin are doing a fine work, which vitally needs to be done, in trying to make good some of the deficiencies of the common-school system. They question only the success of the methods chosen to attack this purpose.

2. That the character of the instruction is mainly along traditional and cultural-school lines and is not vocational in the sense of specialized training for useful occupations, but is to a limited extent manual training.

3. That, notwithstanding the dual form of control, the continuation and evening schools are generally organized, directed, and supervised by school superintendents who have been given more responsibility and freedom in their direction than they have ever

had in the supervision of the common schools. In other words, dual control exists more in theory than in practice.

4. That the system of indentured apprentices, which had 192 pupils in weekly attendance for the whole state, has been ineffective, as was expected, in offering a real vocational training on any considerable scale, and no new all-day trade schools have started since the enactment of the law. Wisconsin has practically made little new progress in training boys or girls in the practice of a trade since the law went into effect, and is apparently not now interested in that phase of the problem. There are exceptions to this statement in Racine and Milwaukee.

5. Little attempt has been made even to group children according to the occupations they were engaged in. They are usually classified according to the grade from which they left school, and the instruction is similar for children working at radically different employments.

6. Wisconsin has failed, as has every other state, in providing a valuable course of training for children over fourteen who were temporarily out of employment. No system on a large scale has yet been perfected for really helping the drifting children.

7. Most of the teachers are not qualified for vocational or trade work. The teaching problem is just as difficult a one in Wisconsin as elsewhere.

Can we now point to any conclusions from the experience we have been studying? Has any light been thrown upon the vexed problems of public education, from either these laws or their reactions, which can be stated in terms of general principles?

There has in recent years grown up in the minds of many earnest and sincere people what has amounted almost to a hysteria in regard to child labor. In the face of a very real evil, existing under certain conditions, a campaign has been conducted for the enforcement of the universal principle of the exclusion of all children from all gainful employments practically until they are sixteen years of age, and this exclusion is to be based on the age limit alone. With the enforcement of an age limit of fourteen years, the writer is heartily in accord. The sixteen-year age limit has already been enforced in whole or in part in Illinois, Ohio, Wisconsin, New York, and possibly in other states, and is being vigorously pushed in all of the northern states. The success of this movement can be attributed to three forces: the real humanitarian consideration for the protection of children; the earnest desire of labor to exclude competition from immature workers; and the evident desire of traditional educators for the state to assume the entire responsibility for the child's development until he is sixteen years of age.

This whole question of our attitude toward child labor has such an important bearing upon the subject that it is not possible to avoid its consideration. As regards age, we all recognize that it is a relative matter; that maturity of mind and body—the factors necessary to protect the child in industry—are positive standards. It has been insisted that age, largely because of tradition and existing records, was the only possible basis of enforcement; the only factor that could be readily known; the measure most easily applied. The evils of this attitude pushed beyond the fourteen-year age limit have been threefold. It has put up neither to the schools nor to the state the necessity of furnishing the really valuable factors of mental and physical maturity as possible measures of restriction. The increasing age limit has thrown back upon the schools the product they had already failed with, while it brought no practical compulsion upon the schools to do more effective work with the oncoming generations and ever more heterogeneous races, creeds, traditions, and conditions. With an almost blind and sentimental confidence in the efficacy of age, it did not point the way to building up where it had torn down nor acknowledge the responsibility for the substituting of opportunity for restriction.

The foregoing evils cannot always be clearly recognized or kept separate in their effects. The result we see most often is that restriction has condemned a class of pupils to a school which has nothing to feed them with. A concrete example, which approached to the tragic, was the driving of the pupils out of the excellent Cincinnati continuation schools by the enforcement of the more drastic Ohio age law. The medicine has always been more school—ever more school of the same kind—and failure has fed upon failure with small attempt at fixing responsibility or insisting upon achievement. The wail of the two wasted years ending in blind alleys was laid at the doors of industry entirely, perhaps properly so, and a school blind alley or idleness was substituted in its place. The opportunity to do the thing the boy or girl might do, and through the doing of which only can he realize the incentives of achievement and reward, is being shut out. The defense has been that when the problem was put up to the school it would find a solution. The raw material of the product was put up to the school in abundance, but not the means for handling it. On the other hand, an accumulating number of failures in the school, for which the school has been held to no definite responsibility and from which it saw no relief except in the passing of them on for others to struggle with, has been the result.

The first lesson of the experiments we have been witnessing is that society should not exercise a restrictive or prohibitive power alone. It should not forbid an exercise which is not necessarily wrong for great numbers of individuals without offering some substitute in its place which will reach an equally great number. The second lesson is that the place to stop failure is at its source. If a school is allowed to cover up its failures by passing them on to someone else to bury, it will surely do it. On the other hand, if you hold the school up to an accounting to parents for a definite achievement, it will set its strength to meet the bill. The way to improve your common schools, to speak in plain language, is not to create more schools of the same kind to do their work over; it is to begin in the old schools and insist that every department shall do its task and not hand it on to other schools as a legacy of failure. Not until our common schools have been held to a more definite performance can we lay the foundation of a good vocational education. There Wisconsin was correct in her conception, but from that point she went on to lay a faulty superstructure. Her vision has been in part blinded by the age-restriction idea. In part she lost her clearness of vision in her anxiety to create practical boards of control rather than practical teachers. Finally, she has lost her bearings in the fog of pedagogy which she tried to escape. In the end practical boards may find practical teachers. For the time being, one of the greatest problems confronting the providing of a real vocational education is the providing of practical men and women experienced in the trades and industries taught, who have the ability to teach, and this is true of every state in the Union. They cannot be found among the ranks of the school teachers because these are too old to be trained in the practice of industry. They will be found slowly in the shops, as Wisconsin believes, but Connecticut was right in making her trade schools centers for the training of teachers for the creating of trade ideals of instruction as well as centers for the trade training of its pupils.

Next, can we seriously question that it is better to work out social experiments on a small scale before attempting them as of universal application? The reply that you never will prove a principle which is meant for all until it is applied to all has a basis in theory, but you never can produce a product for all until you have created the tools to work with. There must come a time in the near future for Connecticut to face the test of applying to all what she has done for a few, and that test will be watched with great anxiety. It will succeed in proportion as her working drawings are correct, her tools are available, and her men are capable of applying both.

The question as to whether our solution shall lie in continuation schools, part-time schools, or trade schools, neither Wisconsin's nor Connecticut's experience can answer conclusively. It is more likely to be a combination of them all. A continuation school for general improvement in culture can do certain definite things for adult workers who have begun to find themselves. Its real province is of much the same character for pupils between fourteen and sixteen that evening schools are for more adult workers. To be effective it must exercise upon pupils who have become conscious of a lack in themselves and can appreciate the application of theory to the practice of the occupation they are following. To those who are already in line for promotion it can be a direct inspiration and help to self-betterment. We shall look to it in vain, however, if we expect it to raise boys and girls out of blind alleys and idleness, because, in the first instance, such boys and girls cannot get their feet on the ladder unless they can learn some of the things the trade demands of them. Hygiene, citizenship, trade ethics, and political economy will be all the more robust if they have bread to feed upon. You cannot secure bread without performing some service that society needs. You cannot be valuable to society without learning some trade or profession that is essential to its support. We cannot all follow the professions. We can all come into a realizing sense of some of our needs for the application of the principles of science and art through learning to do first one or more useful things. Can we ever learn to do that useful thing effectively except under conditions similar to those we find confronting us when we are thrown upon society's tender mercies? When we have felt her spurs we may then appreciate both the technical theories related to our work and the broader and more general culture to be found correlated with work as well as with study.

It is coming, therefore, to be realized that that vocational education can most probably raise a boy out of a blind-alley employment, i.e., unskilled occupations offering no road to promotion, which first provides its pupils with some skill. A general improvement continuation school alone cannot do this, and general courses in hygiene, civics, manual training, physics, drawing, mathematics, etc., "are usually ineffective and uneconomical in contributing to trade efficiency." Anything is unproductive of any real training which is limited to fifty hours spread over a year. Trade continuation courses of five hours a week, twelve months in the year, will be effective in developing trade ability in those starting at industry, if they offer practical trade processes and methods under as nearly commercial conditions as is possible. General continuation schools will be valuable, particularly in the machine trades, in showing the application of mathematics, physics, and the allied sciences to actual products to those who have a start and have had some little experience in a trade. Evening continuation schools will be valuable both as trade continuation courses and as general improvement courses. They will be most valuable in making good known deficiencies through short-unit courses. To the man who has the ability to make good at the next stage of promotion they are invaluable. But when all of the above has been said and done, there remains much to be accomplished in all-day trade schools in adapting children to living and working conditions.

Many of the mistakes which have followed attempts to initiate vocational education have come from losing sight of the fact that the purpose of vocational education is to prepare children to enter useful occupations and vocations at as high a stage of development as their abilities will allow them and with the least waste of time to themselves. Its intent should be clearly differentiated from that of cultural education, in that while one prepares the child in a general way for his future and the happy maintenance of his position in society, the service of the other is the much more definite one to make it possible for a child to enter that place in the industrial organization to which he is best adapted through a specific trade or occupation.

It is true that the whole content of neither the cultural nor the vocational education is exclusive one of the other. The intent, however, of both should be limited to their peculiar fields as clearly as possible, to the end that each should be kept to a distinct purpose and performance, and that particularly vocational education should be saved from that vague and shadowy realm of theory and fads and indefinite performance which is the worst enemy today to our cultural educational system.

There is great danger of grants for vocational education being used for common schools without commensurate benefits if the two systems are not sharply differentiated. We certainly do not want more of the same kind of public education as at present. We must insist upon a distinctly higher quality of performance on the part of the present establishment, and in addition to that we must create a definite, distinct training for useful occupations.

I do not doubt that we shall come to enforce vocational training by compulsion, as Wisconsin has attempted, with as little opposition finally as now follows compulsory attendance at grammar school. Every child has as inherent a right to be taught the elements of a useful occupation or vocation as he has to be taught the elements of reading, writing, and arithmetic. The method and degree of compulsion to be exercised is a matter for every state to determine for itself, but compulsion without enforcement is infinitely worse than a voluntary system, because it endangers all of the laborious advantages gained in the enforcement of our compulsory attendance and child-labor laws. It weakens respect for all laws, though it may be partially successful. Also, compulsion without the material and financial support which offers a reasonable prospect of meeting the demands is a confusing rather than a clarifying method. It is of course as ridiculous to delay compulsion until every contingency is covered as it is to force it without the knowledge, experience, support, and equipment or facilities to meet it. State compulsion must be a progressive and intelligent development enforced just as fast as it can be practically achieved.

Finally, whether vocational education shall be conducted in continuation schools, part-time schools, trade schools, apprenticeship schools, or evening schools, singly or together, is not yet a question to be decided as a matter of principle so much as a matter of wise adaptation to the particular occupations to be taught and the working conditions of the pupils to be provided for. That system is best which will give the pupils the best training primarily, and secondarily, which causes the least disturbance to their employment, with the least duplication of facilities and the least expense to the public.

VARIATIONS IN STUDY STANDARDS

FRANK P. BACHMAN, PH.D.
Committee on School Inquiry, New York City

ACADEMIC STANDARDS IN THEORY AND IN FACT

Workers in the several fields of education speak of academic standards as if these were something fixed and well defined. The primary teacher affirms with confidence that A is below grade in beginning reading. With equal assurance the grammar-grade teacher declares that B is a failure in sixth-grade arithmetic. So accustomed are teachers to pronounce on the fitness or lack of fitness of pupils for advancement that we have come to assume that there exists among teachers a body of clear ideas of what the achievements of pupils should be before they are to be passed in a given study. If, however, the results of a survey of the failures by studies in a city school system of size can be taken as symptomatic, it can be affirmed with some assurance that we have no academic standards in the sense that our ideas of academic achievements are well defined and that the same standards of achievement are accepted and held by any considerable number of teachers. Whatever academic standards we have seemingly vary, even within the same system, with the school, the study, the study-grade, and the teacher. In a word, talk about academic standards as if these were well defined and generally accepted is educational cant. Such standards in all probability do not exist. What we have and what we use to measure the achievements of children and to judge of their fitness or lack of fitness to pass are more than likely the opinions and bias of particular teachers.

These assumptions are based on a study of the failures by studies and grades in the elementary schools of Cleveland for the fall term of 1910. A partial report of this study is here submitted.

VARIATIONS IN PERCENTAGE OF FAILURES BY STUDIES AND GRADES

Table I gives by subjects and grades for the fall term of 1910 for all elementary schools of Cleveland the percentage of failures and the minutes per week allotted.

TABLE I

Subject	First Grade		Second Grade		Third Grade		Fourth Grade	
	Percentage of Failures	Minutes per Week	Percentage of Failures	Minutes per Week	Percentage of Failures	Minutes per Week	Percentage of Failures	Minutes per Week
Reading	17.80	500	12.89	500	11.26	440	7.81	310
Spelling	3.74	75	15.06	100	9.97	125	6.21	100
Language and grammar	11.16	125	13.51	150	17.50	125	15.85	165
Arithmetic	9.69	60	16.54	315	21.47	225	19.70	240
History	......	......	......	......	3.63	30	24.24	40
Geography	......	......	......	......	3.54	45	25.11	160

Subject	Fifth Grade		Sixth Grade		Seventh Grade		Eighth Grade	
	Percentage of Failures	Minutes per Week	Percentage of Failures	Minutes per Week	Percentage of Failures	Minutes per Week	Percentage of Failures	Minutes per Week
Reading	5.86	255	5.16	215	3.54	240	2.51	240
Spelling	5.21	80	3.67	75	2.19	75	1.24	75
Language and grammar	16.32	190	21.49	190	24.90	200	25.82	200
Arithmetic	28.18	225	37.03	245	32.07	225	23.44	250
History	9.02	40	12.76	80	25.03	135	17.30	135
Geography	22.78	200	17.68	200	21.03	90	13.92	90

It will be observed that the percentage of failures in the above subjects varies with the grade. The percentage of failures ranges in:

Reading, from 17.80 per cent in the first grade to 2.51 per cent in the eighth grade.

Spelling, from 15.06 per cent in the second grade to 1.24 per cent in the eighth grade.

Language and grammar, from 25.82 per cent in the eighth grade to 11.16 per cent in the first grade.

Arithmetic, from 37.03 per cent in the sixth grade to 9.69 per cent in the first grade.

History, from 25.03 per cent in the seventh grade to 3.63 per cent in the third grade.

Geography, from 25.11 per cent in the 4th grade to 3.54 per cent in the third grade.

A part at least of the variation from grade to grade in the percentage of failures in a given subject may readily be accounted for. For example, the high percentage of failures (17.80) in first-grade reading is doubtless due somewhat to the difficulties of the subject for beginners and to the importance placed on beginning reading. Again, the difference between the percentage of failures in third- and fourth-grade geography (3.54 and 25.11 per cent respectively) results at least partially from the difference between the emphasis placed on this subject in these two grades and the difference in the subject-matter taught, whereas the difference between the percentage of failures in sixth- and eighth-grade geography (17.68 and 13.92 respectively) may be due to differences in the ability of the children instructed. Similarly, the high percentage of failures in sixth-grade arithmetic (37.03 per cent) might be due to overloading the curriculum in this study in this grade. Finally, the difference between the percentage of failures in any two grades might be due to differences in methods, hence in the efficiency of the teachers in the respective grades. In a word, such variations in the percentage of failures in different grades of the same subject might exist even though standards of achievement were well defined and uniform, and these variations might be due to the inherent difficulties encountered by children in taking up a subject for the first time, to the differences between the emphasis placed on the same subject in different grades, to the differences between the requirements of the course of study in different grades, and to the differences in the abilities of the children instructed and the efficiency of teachers.

VARIATIONS IN STUDY STANDARDS BY SCHOOLS

These explanations of the variations in the percentage of failures in the several grades of the same subject lose their weight to a considerable extent if the percentage of failures in the same grade and subject in different schools are considered.

READING

Table II gives the several percentages of failures in sixth-grade reading and the number of schools failing a given percentage of pupils.

TABLE II

Percentage of Failures	Number of Schools	Percentage of Failures	Number of Schools	Percentage of Failures	Number of Schools	Percentage of Failures	Number of Schools
0	26	5	4	10	2	16	1
1	10	6	5	11	3	18	1
2*	7	7	1	12	3	21	1
3	7	8	2	13	1	26	1
4	5	9	3	15	2	29	1

* Median percentage.

The percentage of failures in sixth-grade reading ranges, it will be noted, from 0 to 29 per cent. Twenty-six elementary schools were, however, able to pass all of their pupils, while one school was constrained to fail 29 out of each hundred. All of these schools were following the same course of study and had the same textbooks; hence there were but two variable elements: pupils and teachers. It is scarcely probable that the differences in the percentage of failures can be accounted for by the differences in the abilities of the children enrolled in these several schools and in the efficiency of the teachers in question. The more reasonable explanation of at least a good part of this variation is that standards of achievement in sixth-grade reading vary almost with the school, and that, since in most of these schools there are but one or two teachers, standards of achievement vary with the teacher. Similar variations in the percentage of failures in the same grade in other subjects point to the same conclusion.

HISTORY

Table III gives the several percentages of failures in sixth-grade history and the number of schools failing a given percentage of pupils.

TABLE III

Percentage of Failures	Number of Schools	Percentage of Failures	Number of Schools	Percentage of Failures	Number of Schools	Percentage of Failures	Number of Schools
0	11	9	4	17	1	32	1
1	3	10*	5	18	1	33	1
2	7	11	3	19	3	35	2
3	2	12	2	20	3	38	2
5	4	13	5	22	1	45	1
6	3	14	3	24	1	50	1
7	3	15	4	25	1	61	1
8	1	16	4	27	2	....	....

* Median percentage.

ARITHMETIC

Table IV gives the several percentages of failures in sixth-grade arithmetic and the number of schools failing a given percentage of pupils.

TABLE IV

Percentage of Failures	Number of Schools	Percentage of Failures	Number of Schools	Percentage of Failures	Number of Schools	Percentage of Failures	Number of Schools
0	5	23	2	38	2	57	2
5	2	24	1	40	2	58	1
9	2	26	2	41	3	59	1
11	1	25	1	44	3	61	1
12	2	29	2	45	1	62	2
13	1	30	2	47	1	63	2
15	2	32	4	48	1	65	2
17	1	33	3	49	1	69	1
19	2	34*	1	50	4	73	1
20	1	35	3	54	1	75	1
21	2	36	2	55	1	78	2
22	2	37	2	56	1	80	1

* Median percentage.

That the percentage of failures in the several schools of any modern system should range in the sixth grade in a subject like arithmetic from 0 to 80 per cent is almost unbelievable. Equally astounding is the relatively uniform distribution of the several schools at the different points in the scale of failures. These data on failures in sixth-grade arithmetic indicate, therefore, even with greater clearness than the foregoing data on reading and history, that standards of achievement vary with the school and teacher.

VARIATION IN STUDY STANDARDS BY SUBJECTS

Not only do study standards vary with the school, but they seem also to vary with the particular branch. For example, of the 86 elementary schools in question, only 20 had in each of the following sixth-grade subjects, reading, spelling, language and grammar, history, and geography, a percentage of failures lower than the sixth-grade average in all schools for the respective studies, and only 8 had a percentage of failures higher than the average for the respective branches. In a word, only 28 out of 86 schools had anything like a uniform and constant standard of achievement for the above-mentioned studies.

If the sixth-grade averages for all schools of the per cent of failures in the respective studies in question are made the basis of grouping, the variation in study standards by studies becomes even clearer. For example, of the 55 schools failing below the city average in sixth-grade reading, only 40 also failed below the sixth-grade average in spelling. Of the 40 schools failing below the sixth-grade average in reading and spelling respectively, only 33 also failed below that average in language. Of the 33 schools failing below the sixth-grade average in reading, spelling, and language respectively, only 27 also failed below this average in arithmetic. Of the 27 schools failing below the sixth-grade average in reading, spelling, language, and arithmetic respectively, only 21 also failed below this average in history; and of the 21 schools failing below the sixth-grade average in reading, spelling, language, arithmetic, and history respectively, only 20 also failed below this average in geography.

Conversely, of the 31 schools failing above the average in sixth-grade reading, only 20 also failed above the sixth-grade average in spelling. Of the 20 schools failing above the sixth-grade average in reading and spelling respectively, only 14 also failed above this average in language. Of the 14 schools failing above the sixth-grade average in reading, spelling, and language respectively, only 9 also failed above this average in arithmetic. Of the 9 schools failing above the sixth-grade average in reading, spelling, language, and arithmetic, only 8 also failed above this average in history and geography.

Similarly, of the 46 schools failing below the average in all schools in sixth-grade arithmetic, only 37 also failed below the sixth-grade average in reading. Of 37 schools failing below this average in arithmetic and reading respectively, only 28 also failed below the average in spelling. Of the 28 schools failing below the sixth-grade average in arithmetic, spelling, and language respectively, only 26 also failed below this average in language. Of the 26 schools failing below the sixth-grade average in arithmetic, reading, spelling, and language respectively, only 21 also failed below this average in history; and of the 21 schools failing below the sixth-grade average in arithmetic, reading, spelling, language, and history respectively, only 20 also failed below this average in geography.

Conversely, of the 40 schools failing above the average in all schools in sixth-grade arithmetic, only 22 also failed above the average in sixth-grade reading. Of the 22 failing above the sixth-grade average in arithmetic and reading respectively, only 12 also failed above the average in spelling. Of the 12 schools failing above the average in arithmetic, reading, and spelling respectively, only 11 also failed above the average in language, and of the 11 schools failing above the average in arithmetic, reading, spelling, and language respectively, only 8 also failed above the average in history and geography.

Similar variations in study standards by subjects appear when the average percentage of failures in the other sixth-grade studies is made the basis of grouping and when the variations in the percentage of failures for the same studies in the other grades are considered.

In view of these variations in study standards by subjects, and since in the elementary schools of Cleveland there is as a rule but one teacher to the grade, there are strong indications that, in Cleveland at least, study standards not only vary with the branch, but vary with the teacher; that is, a given teacher may hold a high standard of achievement with respect to certain branches and a lower standard of achievement with respect to other studies of the same grade.

VARIATION OF STUDY STANDARDS BY STUDY-GRADES

While it might be admitted that study standards vary with the branch, it might not be admitted that standards of achievement vary in the same study with the study-grade; that is, a different standard of achievement held for fifth- and sixth-grade language or arithmetic, or for seventh- and eighth-grade reading, etc.

In comparing standards of achievement in the same study in different grades, there are at least four factors which may vitiate any conclusions made on the basis of such comparison: differences in pupils, in teachers, in the methods of instruction, and in emphasis. Yet the facts at hand are symptomatic of such variations. For example, 190 minutes per week were assigned in the elementary schools of Cleveland in the fall term of 1910 to fifth- and sixth-grade language, but the average percentage of failures was 16.32 and 21.49 per cent respectively. Similarly, the percentage of failures in fifth- and sixth-grade arithmetic, with a time allotment of 225 and 245 minutes, were 28.18 and 37.03 per cent respectively. Under similar time conditions, 200 minutes per week, the failures in fifth -and sixth-grade geography were 22.78 and 17.68 per cent, and in seventh- and eighth-grade, with 90 minutes per week, 21.03 and 13.92 per cent respectively.

Not only do the differences in the percentage of failures in different grades of the same subject, under similar time allotments, suggest a variation in study standards by study-grades, but there are also indications of this in the lack of uniformity in different grades in the number of schools failing a given percentage of pupils in the same subject. Take, for example, arithmetic in the fifth

TABLE V

Percentage of Failures	Number of Schools Failing		Percentage of Failures	Number of Schools Failing		Percentage of Failures	Number of Schools Failing	
	Fifth Grade	Sixth Grade		Fifth Grade	Sixth Grade		Fifth Grade	Sixth Grade
0	2	5	23	1	2	46	1	0
1	2	0	24	0	1	47	0	1
2	1	0	25	1	0	48	1	1
3	1	0	26*	2	2	49	0	1
4	1	0	27	3	0	50	2	4
5	0	2	28	4	1	51	2	0
7	3	0	29	2	2	55	2	1
8	1	0	30	0	2	56	0	1
9	1	2	31	1	0	57	0	2
10	2	0	32	4	4	58	1	1
11	2	1	33	3	3	59	0	1
12	0	2	34†	0	1	61	0	1
13	3	1	35	1	3	62	1	2
14	1	0	36	1	2	63	1	2
15	2	2	37	2	2	64	1	0
16	2	0	38	3	2	65	0	2
17	2	1	39	1	0	69	0	1
18	3	0	40	3	2	73	0	1
19	2	2	41	0	3	75	0	1
20	1	1	42	3	0	78	0	2
21	4	2	44	0	3	80	0	1
22	2	2	45	1	1			

* Median percentage for fifth grade.

† Median percentage for sixth grade.

and sixth grades when the time allotment is 225 and 245 minutes per week respectively.

Table V gives the percentage of failures in fifth- and sixth-grade arithmetic and the number of schools failing a given percentage of pupils in each grade.

The range in the percentage of failures in the fifth grade, it will be noted, is from 0 to 64 per cent, but in the sixth grade from 0 to 80 per cent. Again, the median percentage of failures in the fifth grade is 26, whereas in the sixth it is 34 per cent. Moreover, there is no one percentage of failures distinctively common to the two grades. In only 7 cases out of a possible 65 is there a common number of schools failing a given percentage of pupils. While these differences are not conclusive, they at least point toward the fact that the standards of achievement are higher in the sixth- than in fifth-grade arithmetic—in a word, that study-standards vary with the study-grade.

CONCLUSIONS

The foregoing facts warrant, we believe, the tentative conclusion that within a given school system study-standards vary with the school, the subject, the study-grade, and the teacher. These facts also show the need of collecting such data if school officials are to know what is going on in the schools. They show, besides, the need of making such data the starting-point at least of determining to what particular factor or factors such variations are due, whether due, either singly or collectively, to differences in emphasis, difficulties in materials, overloading, differences in methods and teachers, differences in the abilities of children, or to lack of clear and well-defined standards of achievement. They make clear what a go-as-you-please business teaching is, and how much the advancement of a pupil depends on the teacher he happens to have and the school he happens to attend. Finally, they reveal the need of developing objective standards of achievements in each of the several subjects and grades of the elementary schools.

AN INTERESTING EXPERIMENT

E. H. DRAKE
Superintendent of Schools, Elkhart, Indiana

The grade teachers of the Elkhart public schools tried out an experiment during the past year with what may be called a system of minimum-maximum assignments of lessons. The purpose of the system was to provide a course to meet the different abilities of different children and thus to increase the promotion rate among them; also to test out the scheme as a forerunner to the planning of a course of study along the same lines.

The minimum assignment was that expected of all pupils in a given class, while the maximum was the assignment given to the more capable. The former was planned to be as rich in content in proportion to the quantity of subject-matter assigned as the latter. The two were supposed to differ merely in the quantity of subject-matter. For example, in a geography lesson on Germany, the minimum assignment was a certain portion of the text, with an addition, for the maximum, of reports on such information as the German government, its military system, the growth of certain centers of industry, effect of certain physical features, points of historical or artistic interest, etc. A certain minimum arithmetic assignment consisted of ten problems in local banking, while the maximum provided several additional problems, one or two of which were more difficult; also an assignment of a future report on a special study of banking. A seventh-grade history assignment had as the minimum the causes of the Revolutionary War, while the maximum provided for a more intensive study of certain causes, for instance the British idea of taxation and representation; also a search in reference books for causes not commonly stated. Maximum assignments in the above or other subjects might provide merely more extensive subject-matter in a lesson or more intensive preparation of certain phases of it. The minimum assignment in every case was the quantity of work it was reasonable to expect of the majority of the slower ones in the class. The sum total of such assignments for the term had to be sufficient to give at least the minimum preparation for the next term's work, otherwise there was no promotion.

The results of the experiment were tabulated at the close of the school year and show the following outcome. In some few schools there was no noticeable difference in the promotion rate, due in most instances to the fact that the teacher was inexperienced or was new to the city and accordingly had no previous experience on which to base her judgments as to whether children deserved promotion. In a few cases the absence of change was due to the fact that the teacher for good reasons had always had a high promotion rate; and finally in a few cases the absence of change may have been due to the inability of the teacher to take up readily with the newer ideas. At least nine-tenths of the corps found that the scheme has greatly increased the promotion rates. The average gain for the entire city was 18 per cent. That for three large schools taken together was $19\frac{3}{8}$ per cent. One second-grade teacher, who had a school of 2B's only, worked out the plan very skilfully during the year and had a gain of 50 per cent. Many teachers reported a gain of 25 per cent. By grades the average gains for the city were: first grade, 21 per cent; second, 23 per cent; third, 15 per cent; fourth, 18 per cent; fifth, 15 per cent; sixth, 20 per cent; seventh, 20 per cent; and eighth, 20 per cent. The plan operated easily and brought best results where the teacher had all pupils of one half-grade and in grades organized on the departmental system where there were several sections in each half-grade.

That there are some objections to the scheme and some difficulties in the way of its execution goes without saying, but none of these difficulties proved insurmountable. The objections which seemed most serious are as follows: There was a tendency to overstimulate the too-nervous child who is bright in mind but weak in body. Difficulty was experienced in planning all subjects to meet all needs. Extra labor for teachers was entailed in working out the scheme. Lack of co-operation of parents existed in some instances. The difficulty of manipulating the plan was greater where there were two grades in a room. There was a loss of the stimulus from competition with brighter minds in the slower classes.

The degree in which these difficulties will hamper depends largely upon the teacher. If she is lacking in the sympathetic understanding of the needs and abilities of both classes of children the success of the plan will be hindered. Many teachers are drawn to the more capable in the class, which is natural with them as it is more interesting and easier for them to teach these children. It is necessary for them to be equally interested in the less capable who call for exhaustless perseverance, persistence, and thoroughly planned instruction on the part of the teacher.

In working out the details of the system various plans and devices were brought into use. At times classes were organized by dividing into working groups. In some cases part of the class engaged in written work while the other section was given oral work. As occasion demanded, a study period was provided, when the teacher gave individual help to those needing it. Occasionally the recitation period was devoted to leading the children in the method of study. The recitation became less a recital of the lesson than formerly and more an occasion for thinking. Sometimes the more capable children helped the less capable in preparation of the work. A larger amount of freedom than had been customary was granted the children in working together. The spirit of helpful co-operation was encouraged and used to advantage in achieving the results sought. The successful execution of the system would be facilitated by smaller classes, by frequent meeting of teacher and supervisor to discuss schedules and methods, and by close supervision.

While the system is open to some of the objections mentioned above, these are far outweighed by the advantages in its favor. In the first place, it adjusts the course to the different abilities of the children. Each child is kept working at the level of his best. Brighter pupils are not held back in their progress; the slower ones are not crowded forward, and they do the work more thoroughly. Self-confidence and self-respect are inspired in the slower ones, who are encouraged to do their best. They are enabled to grasp to greater extent the fundamentals. Oftentimes a backward pupil can become so well grounded in his work that he is enabled to work up to the maximum grade. Time is economized to advantage, greater interest is shown, the number of promotions is increased, and the amount of elimination is reduced.

Enthusiasm of the teachers for the system has been marked. One teacher's written report said: "We have all disliked to sentence to failure a child who has studied hard and honestly, who has been regular and punctual in attendance, but whose rate of speed is less than that of others in the class. We have been equally loath to make the bright child mark time while we struggled with some who needed only a little longer to fully understand the lesson. It is a long step up in behalf of the many who are not in the capable class at the beginning of their school life but who may rise to that later, and also in behalf of those who probably will leave school before finishing the grades. The work we do will be more efficient and satisfactory." Another teacher's report said: "Grades and systems tend to crowd out many individual children who could keep up if there was a chance for them. It helps the children who need the greatest help from the public schools." A third report reads: "The brightness that shines in a child's face when he finds the encouragement that he can do more than he thought he could is evidence that the system brings a result worth striving to attain." A principal said: "The teachers speak with enthusiasm for the plan, nearly always with a high degree of enthusiasm. My own opinion is that it is not yet an unqualified success, but almost so."

CURRENT EDUCATIONAL LITERATURE IN THE PERIODICALS[1]

IRENE WARREN
Librarian, School of Education, University of Chicago

Andress, J. Mace. Solving country life problems in Massachusetts. Educa. 35:91–95. (O. '14.)

Bellamy, Raymond. A professor in a small college. Atlan. 114:608–19. (N. '14.)

Bland, Henry Meade. David Starr Jordan and his message of peace. Educa. 35:77–81. (O. '14.)

Boggs, A. M. Visualized opportunity. Ped. Sem. 21:445–53. (S. '14.)

Brett, George P. The reading of books nowadays. Atlan. 114:620–26. (N. '14.)

Brigham, Carl C. An experimental critique of the Binet-Simon scale. J. of Educa. Psychol. 5:439–48. (O. '14.)

(A) children's market. Outl. 108:407–8. (21 O. '14.)

(The) conduct of the universities. Liv. Age 283:378–80. (7 N. '14.)

Coulter, Vincil C. The redistribution of the content of some high-school courses. English J. 3:490–99. (O. '14.)

Curtis, Henry S. Physical training in the normal school. Educa. 35:82–90. (O. '14.)

Day, Lorey C. Alphabet friendships. Ped. Sem. 21:321–28. (S. '14.)

Day, Lorey C. The child god. Ped. Sem. 21:309–20. (S. '14.)

Did Nietzsche cause the war? Educa. R. 48:353–57. (N. '14.)

Dilworth, G. L. The electric high school. Sci. Am. 111:320, 325. (17 O. '14.)

Feingold, Gustave A. Suggestions toward a study of mediocrity. Ped. Sem. 21:336–42. (S. '14.)

Fitzgerald, Clara P. Notes on the scalp and hair. Ped. Sem. 21:329–35. (S. '14.)

German university teaching and the war. Educa. R. 48:341–46. (N. '14.)

Hailman, W. N. Adjustment of the common school curriculum to the present vocational needs of today. Man. Train. M. 16:129–38. (N. '14.)

Hasty, Philip S. The present status of vocational work in the elementary school. Man. Train. M. 16:139–45. (N. '14.)

[1] *Abbreviations.*—Atlan., Atlantic Monthly; Educa., Education; Educa. R., Educational Review; English J., English Journal; J. of Educa. Psychol., Journal of Educational Psychology; Lit. D., Literary Digest; Liv. Age, Living Age; Man. Train. M., Manual Training Magazine; Outl., Outlook; Ped. Sem., Pedagogical Seminary; Pop. Sci. Mo., Popular Science Monthly; Psychol. Clinic, Psychological Clinic; School W., School World; Sci. Am., Scientific American; Teach. Coll. Rec., Teachers College Record; Tech. World M., Technical World Magazine.

Hay, Ian. The lighter side of school life. II–VI. Liv. Age 283. (10 O.–7 N. '14.)

II. The house-master. pp. 85–92.
III. Some form-masters. pp. 152–62.
IV. Boys. pp. 225–34.
V. The pursuit of knowledge. pp. 284–92.
VI. "My people." pp. 338–47.

Horowitz, B. The ultra-scientific school. Pop. Sci. Mo. 85:463–66. (N. '14.)

Keech, Mabel L. Our girls and their training. Educa. 35:95–98. (O. '14.)

Kuno, Mrs. Emma E. How a knowledge of the characteristics of the adolescent boy may aid one in directing his conduct. Ped. Sem. 21:425–39. (S. '14.)

Lyans, C. K. The doctrine of formal discipline. Ped. Sem. 21:343–93. (S. '14.)

Mead, Cyrus D. Height and weight of children in relation to general intelligence. Ped. Sem. 21:394–405. (S. '14.)

Mensel, Ernest H. The one-unit preparation in a modern language for admission to college. Educa. 35:65–76. (O. '14.)

Morgan, J. H. The academic garrison of Germany. Educa. R. 48:347–52. (N. '14.)

Morrison, Carolyn E. Speech defects in young children. Psychol. Clinic 8:138–42. (O. '14.)

Patrick, G. T. W. The psychology of play. Ped. Sem. 21:469–84. (S. '14.)

Pease, Joseph A. Education and the war. School W. 16:361–63. (O. '14.)

Perry, John. The science of education. Pop. Sci. Mo. 85:504–15. (N. '14.)

Price, W. Cecil. The practical utility of the boy scouts during the war. Liv. Age 283:72–80. (10 O. '14.)

Pyle, W. H. A study of delinquent girls. Psychol. Clinic 8:143–48. (O. '14.)

Quisenberry, George R. Where the school pays the board. Tech. World M. 22:420–22. (N. '14.)

Reaney, M. Jane. The psychology of the boy scout movement. Ped. Sem. 21:407–11. (S. '14.)

(The) response of our universities. Lit. D. 49:741. (17 O. '14.)

Rowe, E. C. Five hundred forty-seven white and two hundred sixty-eight Indian children tested by the Binet-Simon tests. Ped. Sem. 21:454–68. (S. '14.)

Sanders, Frederic W. The organization of education. Educa. 35:98–106. (O. '14.)

Snyder, Alice D. Notes on the talk of a two-and-a-half year old boy. Ped. Sem. 21:412–24. (S. '14.)

Spaulding, Thomas Marshall. Federal aid to military education in colleges. Educa. 35:107–14. (O. '14.)

Taylor, E. H. A comparison of the arithmetical abilities of rural and city school children. J. of Educa. Psychol. 5:461–66. (O. '14.)

VOLUME XV NUMBER 5

THE ELEMENTARY SCHOOL JOURNAL

CONTINUING "THE ELEMENTARY SCHOOL TEACHER"

JANUARY 1915

EDUCATIONAL NEWS AND EDITORIAL COMMENT

Chicago Dinner

The Department of Superintendence holds its annual meeting in Cincinnati during the week of February 22. A number of affiliated societies will meet with the general organization. This *Journal* takes the opportunity of announcing to all former students and graduates of the University of Chicago that there will be a Chicago dinner early in the week of the meeting. A special announcement of the place and time of this dinner will be posted in the hotels and places of meeting. Information can also be secured by writing directly to the University before the date of the meeting itself.

Boston Department of Educational Measurement

The first output of the Department of Educational Investigation and Measurement of Boston has appeared as School Document No. 8, under the title, *Provisional Minimum and Supplementary Lists of Spelling Words for Pupils in Grades I to VIII*. This document emphasizes the significance of the general movement which is going forward in a number of the large cities of this country where bureaus of research are being organized as part of the office of superintendent of schools. The document further shows how scientific investigations can be made of immediate use to the school system. The first part of the pamphlet contains a summary of investigations on spelling made in the Boston schools. The second part contains lists of words which are to be used in the different grades as spelling lessons. This fortunate combination of scientific work and practical suggestion is encouraging both to students of science who are interested in seeing the plan of investigation through the office of superintendents succeed, and also to teachers who are looking for practical results from the work of these bureaus.

How Superintendents Are Made

We shall depart from our common practice of giving explicit information as to the source of a news item and print with names omitted a quotation from a city daily. The reason for printing this news note in this fashion is that it calls attention to a situation so common that the omission of names renders the news note interesting as a statement of a very general condition in the public schools of this country. Why superintendents should be willing to accept positions under conditions like those described in this clipping when a little co-operative organization would tend to clear up the situation is a continual source of surprise to anyone who is in contact with school people.

WILL THE HANDS OF THE NEW SUPERINTENDENT BE FREE?

For the first time in many months the Board of Education seemed to reach a point Saturday night when its members were agreed. By a unanimous vote they selected a superintendent who will begin his duties shortly. The loud praises the members of the board have for the new man would indicate that they believe they have found a superintendent who, like Mr. ——, understands his business.

Mr. —— comes with fine recommendations. His experience has been extended for a man of forty. He should be able to do much for bettering the standing of —— schools, the rejuvenation of which was started by Mr. ——. Owing to the fact that the latter was determined to manage the schools, to pass upon the ability of the teachers in the schools, and that, despite the chance of losing the support of some of the members, he continued to follow a course which was contrary to their wishes, he lost his position. Under this trying situation Mr. —— steps in. If he has the make-up of a genuine superintendent he will not permit himself to be dictated to by members of the board, not one of whom is an expert in educational matters.

The old board members made the error, considered hurtful to the welfare of the schools, of thinking that after they hired a superintendent they could dictate to him as to how the schools should be managed. The position the board took was contrary to custom in other cities. A superintendent of schools is supposed to be a manager, and not a piece of dough in the hands of a school board. If the present board is made up of the same class of material as the old board, with ideas of the same sort, Mr. ——— can figure at the outset that he is going to have a hard row to hoe just as soon as he clashes with the ideas of the members of the board. If Mr. ——— finds the new board of the same caliber as the old, it is hoped he will not play policy in order to make a good fellow of himself and retain his job. He will not be serving the people of ——— as he should if he pursues that course.

All of the members should give Mr. ——— a free hand to raise the standard of the schools of ———. If he is the man for that purpose, as the members say he is, they will not follow the policy of dictating to him or hampering him when he has an idea of his own to develop to the advantage of the school system.

Indiana State Teachers' Association

The reorganization of state teachers' associations is going forward very rapidly. A number of these associations have organized themselves as corporations. Some have permanent secretaries to take care of the interests of teachers in the state. The following resolutions adopted by the Indiana State Teachers' Association, together with the notes of the committee reporting on the plan, present one case of a reorganization under the district plan:

WHEREAS, The scientific study and investigation of educational problems has become a necessity, and

WHEREAS, The multiplicity of larger meetings which we now have does not furnish adequate opportunity for such study, therefore be it

Resolved, That we adopt the following

PLAN OF ORGANIZATION OF THE STATE TEACHERS' ASSOCIATION

A. STATE MEETING

That a two-day meeting of the Association be held annually in the city of Indianapolis in the month of October.

1. The first day and the first evening to be given to section meetings. The main purpose of these meetings to be the presentation and discussion of reports of work done under the district organization, as indicated below (B 1).

These sessions to give wider opportunity for discussion and criticism of the field work being done in the different districts; to secure state organization of the field work on a given problem; and to prevent unnecessary duplication.

2. The sessions of the second day and of the second evening to be general sessions and the speakers to be selected on account of extraordinary ability in

their respective lines of educational investigation, study, or accomplishments. The purpose to be the broader consideration of educational topics of general interest.

B. DISTRICT MEETINGS

1. The state to be divided into districts, using the present congressional districts as nearly as may be practicable; the teachers of each district, in so far as their interests incline them, to organize for the study of specific problems in education. Such study to be carried on during the school year by individuals or groups in co-operative investigation or experiment.

2. A district meeting to be held annually, preferably in late spring, for the purpose of hearing and discussing reports; for the discussion of new specific topics and the setting and assignment of new problems for study. This annual meeting to furnish a "clearing-house" opportunity.

3. Reports of studies, research, etc., when approved by a committee to be appointed by the State Association, to be recommended for publication and distribution by the State Association.

Also be it further

Resolved, That as a part of this plan the General Association appoint each year a Committee on Resolutions, whose duty shall be to report at the next annual meeting on any needed change in, or additions to, the Association's policy or principles; to present larger problems that concern the Association; to study the larger work and welfare of the Association. This committee to consist of five members of the Association.

COMMITTEE'S NOTES ON THE PLAN

1. The plan here proposed is made for the one purpose of giving opportunity for co-operative, systematic, and scientific study of education.

2. Several returns objected to the "district" plan because not all teachers are interested in scientific investigation and experiment. This is also the view of the committee. The idea of the district meeting is to break the body of teachers of a district into small working groups, each member of each group to be present at the meeting because of his genuine interest in the specific problem of his group. By this system of grouping, the teachers grade themselves by interest and ability. It is even desirable that the groups in very many instances should be small, so that the group may form a more effective working body.

3. The "district" lines are not meant to be rigid. The congressional districts are used because such division gives groupings of fair size for working bodies, and because it is the most satisfactory division the committee could devise.

Reorganizing Institutes

The Superintendents' Association of Indiana, working on the problem of the county institutes, plans to render these institutes more systematic by having a textbook which shall be assigned early in the year and shall be made the subject of study on the part of the teachers before they come to the institute. The plan, as adopted by the superinten ents, is too long to print in full. Certain of its essential elements, however, can be briefly outlined by quoting the following paragraphs:

PLAN OF PROCEDURE

1. The textbooks should be purchased and at least carefully read before the week of county institute.

2. The instructor should furnish to each teacher, on the first morning of the institute, outlines of the week's work, the outlines to be based on the books chosen.

3. In following the outline of the text dealing with general principles, discussions should be given before the institute as a body, for economy of time, if nothing more.

4. If possible, these general lectures should be followed by section meetings, in which specific and practical application of general principles to the problem in hand is made. This is perhaps best accomplished, generally, by lectures and conferences.

5. If possible, there should be an examination and correction of notebooks at the end of the week, not for the purpose of grading, but to help the teachers.

6. During the year following this work in institute the teachers should make systematic study of the problems from the texts and notes, and in connection with their actual school work.

Efficiency in City Schools and Rural Schools

The State Department of Education of New Jersey has been conducting tests on the relative efficiency of school children in the cities and rural districts of that state. The following quotation from *Educational Bulletin*, Vol. I, No. 3, together with the comments of explanation from the Commissioner's office, throw a good deal of light on the condition of rural schools. The table which is referred to in the text is not quoted in full because of its length. The facts, however, come out in the brief summaries which are given in the quotation:

The table shows that in every subject in which eighth-grade pupils were tested pupils in cities made uniformly higher averages than pupils outside of cities.

For example, in arithmetic more than 42 per cent of city pupils received 90 points or more, and in the territory outside of cities only a little more than 34 per cent received 90 points or more. On the other hand, of those who received 69 points or less in arithmetic 22 per cent were in the territory outside of cities and only 17 per cent in cities.

Even in spelling the city pupils outranked pupils in country schools. In the cities more than 65 per cent received 90 points or more, whereas only

51 per cent in the territory outside of cities received 90 points or more. Of the pupils who received 69 per cent or less in spelling less than one-half of 1 per cent were in cities and about 1 per cent in the territory outside of cities.

How may we account for these differences in the results obtained by pupils in city schools and those in the territory outside of cities? There are, of course, many good teachers in the rural schools. The differences in results noted cannot be explained by difference in the natural ability of the children. How, then, can this difference be accounted for?

It is believed that the answer is found in the differences in school opportunity that children have. The plain fact is that some of the rural schools suffer from the following causes:

1. Poorly equipped and poorly trained teachers.

2. Too frequent changes in teachers. More than half the teachers in one-room schools in some counties are changed every year.

3. Poor attendance. In too many schools attendance is not only irregular, but there is much unnecessary and prolonged absence. No teacher can teach the children if the children are not in school.

4. In ungraded schools the teacher has too many classes to teach.

5. In many schools there is a sad lack of equipment and apparatus for teaching.

6. There is often a lack of enthusiasm and interest in the smaller schools which is found in larger schools.

7. Lack of adequate, helpful, constructive supervision of instruction for those teachers who need it most. The county superintendent cannot give an adequate amount of supervision.

The Oakland Bureau of Research

The following extract from a letter written by the director of the Bureau of Information, Statistics, and Educational Research of Oakland, California, describes the progress of research under the direction of this Bureau:

I believe that the most important thing the Bureau has accomplished since its organization is the interesting of the principals of the city in the scientific study of school problems.

The elementary-school principals of the city have organized themselves into a Principals' Study Club and have adopted as their program for the year the study of the subjects of the school curriculum. It is their opinion that the prime function of the school principal is supervision, and so they are going to try to find out what a principal ought to know concerning each school subject.

The first subject to be studied was spelling. They have reviewed all of the best literature on the subject, have had reports on leading experimental studies, and have conducted some studies of their own. The final culmination of the plan was the undertaking of a wholesale study of the teaching of the subject throughout the city, the various factors involved, and a number of other matters which will be used as a basis for investigating the other school subjects in the various schools. For their direction in this work, they secured the services of Professor J. B. Sears of Stanford University.

Professor Sears donates his time to the city, and uses the city as a sort of laboratory for his students who are studying various phases of education. The data gathered together in the Oakland spelling test have been divided up into several minor studies, each of which has been assigned to a student who is interested in that particular phase of the problem. Twenty-five students came up from Stanford, a distance of nearly 50 miles, on the day of the test to see that the conditions were kept as uniform as possible. The School of Education of the University of California also co-operated, nearly forty students from this institution donating their services on the day of the test.

We hope soon to have some results for publication.

Universities and Rural Schools

The State University of Missouri has a fund of $10,000 which it is spending in attempting to give the boys and girls in the rural common schools of that state as much advantage from the agricultural work at the state university as it is possible to supply with this fund of money. An officer has been appointed by the state university, whose business it is to organize throughout the state various clubs and associations and to supply the children of the rural schools with as much reading-matter and concrete material as can be sent out from the university.

This is another example of the way in which the great universities of this country are accomplishing the purpose which was explicitly adopted by the University of Michigan at the time of its organization, when this institution declared its purpose of becoming a part of the common-school system of the state. If more institutions would realize that the interests of the university are rooted in the common schools as well as in the high schools, great advantage would come to the whole school system and the university itself.

Junior High-School Courses

A circular issued by the Bureau of Education gives in full the recently adopted program of studies for the public schools of Oakland, California. This program is worth reproducing because it shows very definitely the tendency which has been commented on before in the *Journal* toward the introduction into the elementary schools of a program which shall modify radically the work of the upper grades. The large amount of elective work which is provided in the seventh and eighth grades of the Oakland schools by this new program is distinctly in keeping with the movement going on all over the country to develop junior high schools.

The following time schedule in hours per week has been adopted recently in the schools of Oakland, California:

Subjects	Grade							
	1	2	3	4	5	6	7	8
English and penmanship	15	15	15	10	9	9	5	8
Arithmetic	2	3	5	5	5	5	3	3
History and geography	......	......	......	5	5	5	5	5* 2½†
Nature-study, physical training, and hygiene	1	1	1	1	1	1	....	2½‡
Music: Vocal, or band, or orchestra	2	2	2	2	2	2	2	2
Drawing	1	1	1	1	1	1	2§ or 5	2§ or 5
Manual training	1	1	1	1	2	2	2§ to 10	2§ to 10
Science	......	......	......	......	......	......	5§	5§
Literature, or Latin, or French, or German, or Spanish, or Italian	......	......	......	......	5‖	5‖	5§	5§
Typing	......	......	......	......	......	......	....	5§
Unassigned	3	2	......	......	......	......	....	....
Total	25	25	25	25	25 or 30	25 or 30	25 or 30	25 or 30

* First term, history and geography. † Second term, civics. ‡ Second term.

§ Electives 10 or 15 hours, to be chosen from subjects marked §.

‖ Modern languages, elective, at present offered only in the university school.

We are very glad to give currency to the following communication, which comes from the National Child Labor Committee with the plea that it be published in the *Journal:*

Child Labor

The first social Sunday in the New Year is Child Labor Sunday, which has been observed for the past eight years, and which falls in 1915 on January 24. In issuing its appeal for the observance of the day the National Child Labor Committee refers to the fact that nearly half of all the children ten to thirteen years of age in three southern states are at work instead of in school. In spite of the rapid progress in legislation between 1900 and 1910, the Thirteenth Census reports that nearly 100,000 children ten to thirteen years of age were at work in non-agricultural occupations throughout the country in 1910, or considerably more than half of the number of such working children in 1900.

One of the Committee's investigators this fall found in a North Carolina mill two little spinners whose grandmother said that they were six and seven years old, and scores of older children at work below the legal age limit, which is thirteen years in that state. Canneries in New York state have persisted in violating the child-labor law, because the state Department of Labor has found it impossible to get judgment in local courts against canners who employ small children. Moreover, there are still six states in the Union with no fourteen-year limit whatever for children at work in factories, six states with no compulsory school attendance law, and fifteen states whose fourteen-year limit for factories is practically nullified by exemptions.

For these reasons, and others, the National Child Labor Committee is asking that special attention be given on Child Labor Day to the Palmer-Owen bill now pending in Congress. It has been favorably reported by the House Committee on Labor, so that it is on the House Calendar for the present session, and there is reason to hope that it will also come to a vote in the Senate. This bill, which has received the indorsement of prominent men of all political parties, proposes a fourteen-year age limit in all factories, mills, canneries, and workshops manufacturing goods for interstate commerce; an eight-hour day and no night work for children fourteen to sixteen years old in the same occupations; and a sixteen-year limit for mines and quarries.

But besides working for the Palmer-Owen bill, the Committee is continuing its campaign for improved state laws, since the federal bill contains only the basic standards and, moreover, cannot regulate those forms of child labor in which interstate commerce is not involved. The Illinois law, for instance, already contains the four provisions of the federal bill, but allows boys of sixteen to work as night messengers, and has no age limit whatever for boys and girls in other street trades; while immigrant children of fourteen may go to work without a knowledge of English, provided they can read and write in their native tongue. Iowa does not require work permits at all, but throws the burden of proving the child's age upon the employer. Maine and West Virginia have a 14-year limit for factories but not for stores, and no higher age limit for the commonly specified dangerous occupations.

Other state laws have similar defects, which can be regulated only by the states themselves. The National Child Labor Committee will try to secure improved child-labor laws in fifteen states this year, and believes that the 12,000 clergymen, school superintendents, and teachers from every state in the Union who co-operate in the observance of Child Labor Day are among its most powerful allies in securing legislation, whether state or federal. Those who wish to observe Child Labor Day in their churches or schools can obtain literature on the subject, free of charge, from the National Child Labor Committee, 105 East 22d Street, New York City.

EDUCATIONAL WRITINGS

Educational reform is of two types. There is one type of reform which grows out of a violent discontent with existing institutions. Authors of such reforms usually believe that anything is better than that which is now at hand, and they make radical changes with easy consciences, contending that they can improve matters whatever they do. Such reformers usually learn a great deal by their experiments.

The second type of reformer is one who makes a careful, sympathetic study of existing institutions and, building together all that he can find of excellent practices, devises a coherent plan of organization. Such a reformer usually accomplishes more in the long run than his more radical brother.

Professor Cubberley[1] is a reformer of the second type. He has allowed himself the freedom which comes from describing an imaginary state, the state of Osceola. Here he has been of enough influence to secure the adoption of a new and ideal school code. The code or constitution describes the organization of the school system from the state board to the classroom teacher. The schoolhouses are described, and all of the supplementary agencies for vocational education and training of all the people in matters of health and labor are provided. As one reads these laws of Osceola one sees the influence of existing institutions. The system has a state university, for example, which serves the rest of the system in the way that our better state universities are now doing. One finds reading circles for the carefully certificated teachers. One finds provision for increasing state funds and for their distribution on an equitable basis. One finds statutes bringing into the state system those private educational agencies which have always played a large part in the education of American children.

It is well for the individual teachers as well as for the administrative officer to look into such a book as this, for after all the

[1] *State and County Educational Reorganization.* By E. P. Cubberley. New York: Macmillan, 1914. Pp. xx+257.

work of a single classroom is very intimately dependent on the system to which the class belongs. Some teachers think of the state system as remote and unfriendly, administering examinations and now and then conferring some distant benefit. It is encouraging and illuminating to see in an ideal organization how the central authority can come into helpful contact with all who are involved in the educational system.

The original form of the New York City Survey is not available for common use in the schools. It is well, therefore, that an independent publishing company has undertaken to give to teachers and superintendents the results of the New York Survey. The World Book Company is publishing under the title *School Efficiency Series*, under the editorship of Professor Hanus, a series of books which are virtually reprints of the New York report with some elaborations by the authors of the different sections. We have several such volumes now in hand; some have been incidentally mentioned in earlier connections. *The School Training of Defective Children*,[1] by Professor Goddard, is an interesting statement of the work done in New York City and recommended for other school systems in ungraded classes and classes for children who are below the normal in mental development. The kind of work that ought to be undertaken in these classes and the way in which they should be organized to advantage are set forth on the basis of the concrete examples of New York experience.

Another number of this series, namely, *Elementary School Standards*,[2] by Professor McMurry, is sympathetically reviewed by Professor Paul J Kruse, of the University of Washington. We are very glad to present his review as follows:

The title is not misleading. The author has set up some standards for the testing of the efficiency of instruction, course of study, and supervision in the elementary school. He applies these standards to the New York City schools, showing wherein those schools fail to measure up to the standards,

[1] *The School Training of Defective Children.* By Henry H. Goddard. (School Efficiency series, edited by Paul H. Hanus.) Yonkers-on-Hudson: World Book Company, 1914. Pp. x+97.

[2] *Elementary School Standards.* By Frank M. McMurry. (School Efficiency series, edited by Paul H. Hanus.) Yonkers-on-Hudson: World Book Company, 1914.

and offers recommendations for improvement. However, the usefulness of the standards is not limited to the New York schools; but, as Professor Hanus says in the editor's Preface, "His formulation of the standards on which his judgments are based and his detailed descriptions of the application of those standards to the actual work of the schools will be useful, we believe, to earnest teachers everywhere. Professor McMurry did not attempt to make the standards all-embracing, but they are so fundamental to satisfactory plans and procedure in elementary school work that, whatever limitations as to scope and variety they may possess, all good elementary schools must conform to them. Further, they point the way to progressive improvement where improvement is desirable." That the New York City schools did not show up well when measured by these standards does not necessarily carry with it the conclusion that they are less efficient than the schools of other large cities, but rather that they are less efficient than they should be and might be, a condition not peculiar to New York City.

In a brief discussion of standards in general the author proposes the principle that: "Purposes in any field of activity should be the standards of value in that field." He assumes therefore, "that the leading purposes of instruction must form the basis for judging its quality." As to what the aims of instruction are, the conclusion reached is that as "the more immediate purpose of instruction must be to impart the knowledge and power and to form the habits that determine a well-ordered daily life, we must look directly to the life about us to find what subject-matter the school should offer and how this should be treated."

The following four factors are selected as aims of school instruction: (1) motive; (2) consideration of values; (3) attention to organization; (4) initiative. It is granted by the author that these are not all-inclusive, the only claim being that they are universal and "sufficient to test the general effectiveness of teaching." The value of these standards is urged especially as tests of habits formed, of thoroughness of knowledge, of instruction in the three R's, as sources of suggestion for improvement, and as tests of the curriculum. Two planes of instruction are recognized: the higher, on which facts are comprehended as means—efficiency on the part of the pupils being the goal; and the lower, on which comprehension and retention of facts and mechanical skill are the ends to be attained.

The book is divided into three parts dealing, respectively, with Standards and Instruction, Course of Study, and Supervision. In the first section, after four chapters devoted to a statement of the standards, an exposition of their value, and an explanation of the method of applying them, follows a chapter on the standards to particular recitations. This is one of the most interesting and valuable chapters in the book. It is a real study of actual recitations.

In the section on Course of Study the author applies the same standards, testing the curriculum and syllabi for the various subjects as to provision for motive, organization of subject-matter, consideration of relative values, and provision for individuality. He definitely recognizes that "probably no curriculum in existence ideally meets any one of the four tests we have employed," but maintains that "it is, therefore, their partial successes and the endeavor they show to achieve such successes that make the distinction between acceptable curricula and those that should be condemned."

The author's treatment of Supervision is based upon the proposition that the principal's "main relationship as an educational leader is to his teachers, and the influence that he exerts upon them in kind and degree is the chief measure of his worth to the school." He points out that the principal should be "working for the same ends as the classroom teacher," but that his pupils are the teachers themselves. Therefore he is to be judged by the same standards as the teachers. The author assumes that the principal's time will not be devoted to clerical work, but that he is really a supervisor of teaching.

The book will undoubtedly be of great value to teachers, principals, superintendents, and all students of education who are concerned with the actual work in the schoolroom. It helps the teacher to test his work in a very definite way, and it certainly, if wisely used, will aid the supervisor in his efforts to detect and correct the bad and to recognize and give due credit for the good in classroom work. It is such a book as many have been looking for, and for those who do not expect more of it than the author claims for it the book will be a real help. It should be read and studied by every teacher who wants to improve his work.

It should be said that Professor Kruse's sympathy for the McMurry report is hardly shared by the New York people themselves. A very interesting document entitled *Reply of the Superintendents*[1] gives an account of the attitude of the New York superintendents toward various parts of the New York report. The reply is directed in the main to the two reports issued by Professors Elliott and McMurry.

Professor McMurry comes in for a large part of the discussion. The discussion becomes very personal at points, it being the belief of the superintendents that they must in some way explain why their critic has the confidence of school people in general while they cannot accept his standards. On p. 35 they say, "It is not his four standards or characteristics of good teaching, which he only recently invented for the purpose of testing our schools. Professor McMurry *is* his method, just as Socrates was his method, as every artist teacher is his method." This quotation from the

[1] *Reply of the Superintendents.* Prepared by a Committee. Edited by Joseph S. Taylor, Ph.D. New York, 1914. Pp. 116.

Reply of the Superintendents seems to us to exhibit concretely the difficulty in the whole matter. Professor McMurry did not succeed in making his standards sufficiently objective and impersonal to convince the school population of New York City, and those teachers demand, not that there shall be the judgment of a single individual on the efficiency of their work, but that there shall somehow be the kind of objective definition of what is wanted that will make it unnecessary for a teacher to appeal to any authority for confirmation of his procedure.

In this respect Mr. Courtis' book which is to be a part of this series, setting forth his tests on arithmetic, is more convincing by far than any of the other sections of the report. It is interesting to note that no one seems to deny what Mr. Courtis says in his report. That may be due in part to the greater intellectual effort necessary to prepare one's self to discuss that report, or it may be due—and we think it is—to the objective character of his results.

Three books have appeared which may be grouped together because they deal in a general way with the training of children in reading and in general oral exercises. The first[1] is a summary of the various methods of teaching reading and a brief discussion of the theoretical problems related to their methods. Mr. Klapper has brought together a statement of the various methods employed in teaching primary reading and has added a few chapters on reading in intermediate grades and the methods of teaching a literary masterpiece. The review of primary methods is preceded by a brief study of the hygiene and physiology of reading and the psychology of reading. The introductory chapters, as the author says in his Preface, are intended not as profound studies of the subject, but rather as introductory discussions suitable for the teacher who is interested in an elementary way in matters of method. The review of different methods will be gladly received by students of education as well as by teachers, because there is such diversity in the methods of dealing with primary reading that a summary of these different methods is always acceptable.

[1] *Teaching Children to Read.* By Paul Klapper. New York: D. Appleton & Co., 1914. Pp. 213.

We shall devote our own attention, so far as a critical discussion of the book is concerned, to those chapters which aim to deal with the methods of teaching reading in the intermediate grades. Here Professor Klapper seems to be very conscious of the fact that there is a distinction between oral reading and silent reading and that this distinction ought to be recognized by the intelligent teacher. It is interesting to note, however, that all of the positive suggestions which he has to make with regard to methods refer primarily to the oral method, although he recognizes the fact that the oral method is by no means the only method that ought to be cultivated. When it comes to cultivating silent reading, Professor Klapper is almost helpless. He recommends that children be encouraged to read at home, but there is no detailed statement of the methods that ought to be employed in making these children efficient readers. They ought, as he recognizes, to read more rapidly than they do. He quotes Huey and other earlier writers and recognizes in his argument that there is much to be said regarding the limitation of oral reading exercises, although in the main his argument is in favor of the continuation of that sort of work.

Furthermore, during this critical intermediate period of school life Professor Klapper would have a continuation of the sort of literary reading which is now common, and there is very little evidence that he has made a study of intermediate children which would suggest to him the desirability of bringing in a large body of material that is not like that which is to be found at the present time in ordinary reading books.

It is to be regretted that books of this type simply review practices and do not subject them to careful, constructive criticism. Anyone who is acquainted with the work of schools will agree very heartily with the comment that is made by Professor Klapper in various places that the reading of the upper grades is a blank failure, but why it is a blank failure he does not seem to be able to tell us, and he certainly does not give us the formula by which we could improve the reading, for his suggestions are of the conventional type.

The second book, dealing in an entirely different way with the problem, is a book entitled *Literature for Children.*[1] This book, after giving a brief introduction discussing the desirability of learning lyric poetry as an important branch of literature in the school, devotes something like one hundred pages to the repetition of familiar extracts of poems which are to be committed to memory. The only value in such a collection as this is that it makes the material easily accessible to teachers who are unwilling to look up the references that are always at hand in any school. Furthermore, the emphasis upon poetry is from many points of view open to criticism. Why should children, if they are going to learn English by heart, be confined to poetry? It is so much more important that they should get standard prose forms, and yet in the main their work of memorizing is always turned in the direction of poems just because these are a little easier to remember.

There follow a few discussions on the owning of books and the desirability of reading books and finally we find from p. 239 on about fifty pages of bibliography which is the best part of the book. This bibliography turns the attention of teachers to a number of good references that might be used. The criticism which suggests itself here again is that the author has confined himself almost exclusively to pure literature. Anyone who knows the elementary school realizes that there is a very large demand for another type of reading-matter, and teachers need suggestions with regard to this other type of reading-matter so sorely that it seems a waste of time and energy to pile up again and again the references of pure literature.

Finally, in this connection attention may be called to *Morning Exercises for All the Year.*[2] This book is a miscellaneous collection of various kinds of material. Possibly the best part of this book is the bibliography at the end which makes it possible for teachers to look up reference material that will serve their purposes. There

[1] *Literature for Children.* By Orton Lowe, Assistant Superintendent of the Allegheny County, Pennsylvania, Public Schools, New York: Macmillan, 1914. Pp. 298.

[2] *Morning Exercises for All the Year.* A Day Book for Teachers. By Joseph C. Sindelar. Chicago: Beckley-Cardy Co., 1914. Pp. 251.

is in this present volume such material as brief accounts of Benjamin Franklin and James Watt, some stories about care of animals and about manners, exhortations to industry and cheerfulness. Extracts of poems are distributed throughout the book suitable to reinforce the teachings of the stories.

The morning exercise is an important part of school work and undoubtedly a volume of this sort will suggest sources of material to teachers. It would be a great pity if most of the exercises should dominate the morning exercise. The danger of having in hand easily accessible material of this kind which has been collected by somebody remote from the actual situation in which the leader of the morning exercise finds himself is the common danger which always threatens human beings of doing the easy rather than the productive thing. There is grave danger that such exercises will become purely formal. On the other hand, the variety which the book supplies may in some measure compensate for the dangers of formalism. The material is at least suggestive. Again we call attention to the fact that most of the work is of a strictly conventional type. There is no suggestion here that it would be a good thing to give children vocational guidance in the morning exercise. There is no suggestion here that the problems of local social organization or civic life might serve as the best possible type of morning exercise. Indeed the morning exercise can be made so fruitful by the ingenious teacher that the type of suggestion which comes from the inspection of a book of this kind is to be criticized rather than praised.

It has sometimes been assumed that motives of work are natural, that all one has to do is to expose children to things and they will be impelled to productive activity. It is interesting, therefore, to note a title[1] which emphatically calls attention to the fact that motives must be trained. The yearbook which appears under this title serves also to emphasize another fact: Expression includes reading and composition. There is grave danger in these days of trade training and manual work that some will think of academic courses as passive or receptive.

[1] *Expression as a Means of Training Motive.* Third Yearbook of the Francis W. Parker School of Chicago. Published by the Faculty of the School. Pp. 188.

The description supplied by the authors gives the following summary of the book:

The present volume contains a general introductory article on expression in school work and its intimate relation to motive; an article on children's play as fundamental in education; one on oral reading; one on imaginative writing in school; one on the utilization of the dramatic instincts on the part of children in school work; one on clay-modeling; one on metal-working; and one on art. In addition to these, a page of references to articles in former volumes of the Yearbook, dealing with expression, is given.

One may add the comment that the introductory article is a very interesting interpretation of Colonel Parker's teachings regarding activities in the school and regarding the nature of movements. The rest of the volume contains a great deal of illustrative material which will interest teachers who are looking for practical suggestions to aid them in their work.

Social gatherings in schoolhouses must be organized if they are to be successful. The pamphlet prepared by L. J. Hanifan,[1] of West Virginia, will be of large service to anyone in charge of such gatherings in rural schools. It contains a number of detailed programs.

[1] *A Hand Book Containing Suggestions and Programs for Community Social Gatherings at Rural School Houses.* Prepared by L. J. Hanifan. Published under the direction of M. P. Shawkey, state superintendent, Charleston, W.Va.

CLASSROOM METHODS AND DEVICES

SCIENCE FOR PREVOCATIONAL BOYS

The major purpose of the work in science for prevocational boys is not to turn out scientists capable of doing elaborate scientific work, but to create a rudimentary interest in scientific facts and principles; to call attention to and explain the more obvious and simple phenomena which the boys meet in their daily surroundings; to lead the pupils to see that science means the substitution of real knowledge for mere guesswork—the development of rational procedure in the place of the antiquated rule of thumb; to give an idea of the important part which the development of scientific knowledge has played in our modern industrial progress; and to give practice in reasoning and in applying some of the principles of science.

A secondary but important purpose of giving the so-called science work to these children is to utilize their interest in scientific phenomena as a basis for English composition, spelling, drawing, and mathematics. It is believed that the work in science can be organized in such a way as to furnish this correlating principle.

Since only a limited amount of time can be devoted to science, and since the purpose of giving it is slightly different from that which is usually urged for high-school science, for example, it is desirable to note the way in which the subject is presented, especially as the laboratory method is not employed. In defense of the method which is described in the following paragraphs, it may be said that as only four hours a week are devoted to the subject, this brief period would be rather unproductive if divided between laboratory work and classroom instruction. If the time were devoted entirely to laboratory work it is doubtful whether any more would be accomplished. Even if we grant that a few more scientific facts and principles could be learned through laboratory work, the loss incurred by the employment of the proposed method is more than compensated for by the gain in the pupils' ability to interpret the printed page and to express themselves in writing and in drawing, and, moreover, the work in the shops provides considerable concrete information of a scientific nature. This makes the demand for laboratory work in science less imperative.

A method which has been found successful is to have the pupils study a general science textbook and other supplementary material, and make notebooks which, when completed, constitute illustrated textbooks covering almost the entire work given in the subject. Demonstrations are given by the teacher to arouse interest and to make the work concrete. They are such as can be performed with relatively little apparatus, or at least with such equipment as can be used in an ordinary classroom.

The textbooks are used as reference books and for the purpose of supplementing information given by the teacher during the demonstrations. Multiple copies of direct questions based on the text and on the demonstrations are prepared and each pupil is supplied with a copy. The nature of these questions will be seen from typical illustrations which appear below.

The usual classroom procedure is to begin with the demonstration and to follow this by the reading of the texts and by notebook work guided by the question sheets. When there is no demonstration, the teacher makes an assignment in which he tries to arouse a desire on the part of the pupils to study the text. This is followed by recitation work in which the pupils answer orally the questions on the question sheet. During these oral recitations the slower pupils have an opportunity to profit from the recitations of the brighter ones, and the difficult parts of the text are cleared up for all. Then the lesson is concluded by notebook work.

At this point the character of the question sheets, upon which the notebook work is based, must be described. At first the questions follow the text rather closely and are designed to aid the pupil in mastering the text by focusing his attention on the main thoughts. These questions are so worded as to encourage the pupil to use his own vocabulary rather than the words found in the text. Often they break up the thought of a long and rather involved sentence into several shorter sentences, thus enabling the pupil to get the meaning of the paragraph which was obscured by the long sentence. Often a question is so worded that its answer involves giving the thought of a whole paragraph. In the early part of the work subordinate questions are placed under these major questions, to assist the pupil in formulating a logical and intelligent answer.

A typical question of the latter kind is the following, which is based upon a paragraph describing how a Fahrenheit thermometer is graduated. The main question and its subordinates follow:

Q. (*a*) How is a Fahrenheit thermometer graduated?

A. Begin: A thermometer is graduated in the following way: Then answer the following:

(*b*) How is the 212° mark found?

(*c*) How is the 32° mark found?

(*d*) How many degrees are there then between the 32 mark and the 212° mark?

(*e*) Now if we want each space between the melting point of ice and the boiling point of water to represent two degrees, how many spaces will there be between the 32° mark and the 212° mark?

(*f*) How long, then, will each space be?

(*g*) How is this length of space made use of?

As the pupils improve in their ability to write in better form, and reach the point where they can dispense with the subordinate questions, the questions follow the text less closely, become less specific and particular in character, and involve the composition of several related sentences, comprising a paragraph. Toward the end of the year's work, outlines are prepared from which the pupils write shorter or longer compositions on scientific subjects.

Correlation between science and drawing is secured by so wording a question that it calls for graphic expression in connection with the answer. Mathematics is correlated with the science by inserting among the questions problems concerning levers, the inclined plane, pulleys, the differential pulley, the wheel and axle, the screw, the lifting jack, gears, the bicycle, the geared windlass, etc. These problems involve the use of the processes of addition, multiplication, division, and subtraction of whole numbers and especially of common fractions and decimals.

Practice in reasoning is afforded by inserting questions and exercises which call for the application of principles found in the text. As a rule the answers to questions of this type are not found in the book. The following are samples of the exercises of this kind: If you were a track foreman on a railroad, what directions would you give your gang for laying rails in the winter? Why? If you were a lineman for a telephone company, how would you string the wires in summer? Why? How does the boiler-maker take advantage of contraction due to cooling when he rivets boiler plates together?

In some cases, instead of following the above method, the inductive development lesson precedes the study of the text.

While the pupils are studying the texts and answering the questions, the instructor has an opportunity to give individual instruction on points which are not made entirely clear in the demonstration, or which the pupils find obscure in the text. He has also the opportunity of calling attention to mistakes in spelling, sentence structure, punctuation, and erroneous answers; and to make suggestions in regard to figures which the pupils draw.

One feature of the instruction which it is believed accounts largely for its success, and which should be characteristic of all prevocational work, is that the boys are continually encouraged when they show the least interest, accomplishment, or improvement in their work, and are almost never told that they are doing poor or worthless work. Instead they are shown by example how they can improve, and are given the commendation they deserve.

A word must be said in regard to the motivation of the notebook work. In order that ownership of the texts by the boys may not remove the motive for making the notebooks, all the reference books are furnished by the University. The sources of information are numerous enough to prevent the boys from coming to the conclusion that the notebook work could be made unnecessary through the purchase of a textbook. Furthermore, the fact is pointed out that each boy will in reality be compiling a book for himself which will contain information drawn from many sources, the purchase of which would involve considerable expense. Some emphasis is laid on the fact that an attempt will be made to put into the notebooks only the most valuable information, the less valuable and too technical being disregarded. Special emphasis is laid on the fact that the boys have an opportunity to create something which will be of value to them; which they may exhibit with pride to their parents, if they choose to make it creditable; which will be representative of the work of the class and which, in case of a school exhibit, may be shown with considerable credit to themselves and the class.

Several encouraging results have been obtained. First, there is an added interest in reading about scientific facts, and an added ability to learn facts from the printed page. Second, there is an acquisition of a few fundamental and useful facts. Third, the work develops an interest in, and to some extent an understanding of, the scientific features of industrial processes many of which can be illustrated in the shop work. Fourth, there is acquired by the pupil added ability to express himself in writing and drawing. Fifth, the observation of the simple rules of punctuation and capitalization tends to become habitual, and the pupils become more efficient in the fundamental operations of arithmetic. Sixth, the boys frequently acquire a keen zest in writing and rewriting their notebooks, some of which finally reach a point of genuine excellence.

The following illustrative material is planned to show in a concrete way how a given topic is treated; for example, heat. Under this general heading are given, among others, the following:

Introduction.
General Effects of Heat.
Expansion and Contraction.
Uses of Expansion and Contraction.
Methods of Heating Buildings.
Ventilation.
Methods of Transmitting Heat.
Measuring Heat.
Sources of Heat.

The following questions are selected from a total of 98 questions covering this general topic and are illustrative of the principles which have been described above.

Heat

A. Introduction

1. Show how heat and fire do damage every day.
2. Tell how heat is used for good purposes.

B. GENERAL EFFECTS OF HEAT

1. Expansion and Contraction.
   a) Tell how you could prove that heat makes water expand.
      (1) First tell what things you would use.
      (2) Then tell how you would use them.
   b) How could you show that heat makes air expand?
   c) Make up an experiment to show that heat causes expansion.
      (1) Tell first what materials you would use.
      (2) Then tell how you would use them.
   d) How do you think things act when they are cooled?
   e) What in general may we say is the general effect of heat and cold?
2. Exceptions. Heat does not always cause expansion.
   a) Does ice for example expand or contract when heated?
   b) How does water act when cooled from 39 Fahrenheit to 32?
   c) Are there any metals that contract when heated?

C. USES OF EXPANSION AND CONTRACTION

1. How does the blacksmith make use of heat to make iron expand?
2. How does he make use of the contraction due to cooling?
3. How do boiler-makers make use of contraction due to cooling?
4. If you were track foreman on a railroad, what directions would you give for laying the rails in winter? Why?
5. How would you order them to be laid in summer? Why?
6. If you were lineman for a telephone company, how would you string wires in summer? Why?
7. What causes cement walks to hump and crack in summer?
8. How could this be prevented?

. . . .

E. METHODS OF HEATING BUILDINGS

1. In early times before stoves were invented, how were buildings heated?
2. Explain why smoke goes up the chimney.
3. Why is the open fireplace a healthful way of heating?
4. In what respect was the stove an advance over the fireplace as a means of heating?
5. What part is played by the draft or inlet of a stove?
6. What harm is done by having the damper of the stove wide open all the time?
7. Which is the better way of heating a building: by stoves or by a hot-air furnace? Give two reasons why you think as you do.
8. Explain by means of a diagram how a hot-air furnace works.
9. Explain by means of a diagram how the hot-water heating system works?
   a) What would you say led to the invention of hot-water heating systems?

b) Draw a diagram of a two-room house with a hot-water boiler in the basement and explain how the water circulates.
c) How does the hot water in the radiators heat the rooms?
d) What does a hot-air furnace do that a hot-water heating system does not do?
e) How is ventilation provided for in connection with some hot-water heating systems?
f) Why is ventilation necessary?
g) In what respects are hot-water systems better than hot-air furnaces?

10. The steam-heating system.
a) Draw the cross-section of a two-room house which is heated by steam and explain how system works.
b) What device is used to prevent boilers from blowing up? Show how it works.
c) In what respects is heating by steam better than heating by hot water?
d) On the other hand what advantages has hot water over steam heating?

11. Make a short summary on the three ways of heating.

Begin: We may summarize on the three ways of heating by saying (*a*) First, give the advantages of the hot-air furnace. (*b*) Then give the disadvantages of the same. (*c*) Third, give the good points of heating by hot water. (*d*) Then tell its weak points. (*e*) Close with a statement of which system you prefer.

. . . .

G. METHODS OF TRANSMITTING HEAT

1. Convection.
a) Define convection.
b) How does the Gulf Stream illustrate the transference of heat by convection?
c) Give two more examples of heat transferred by convection.

. . . .

2. Conduction.
a) Define conduction.
b) Give two examples of heating by conduction.
c) Define good and poor conduction of heat.
d) Show how poor conductors of heat are made use of.
e) Show how good conductors are made use of.

3. The fireless cooker.
a) Explain the construction of the fireless cooker. (Draw diagram.)
b) Upon what principle did its invention depend?

4. Radiation.
a) Explain radiation of heat.

5. Describe the processes which take place when rooms are heated by steam.

H. MEASURING HEAT

1. Show that while the temperature of a body tells how hot the body is, it does not tell the amount of heat in the body.
2. Tell how heat is measured.
   a) The calorie.
   b) Calculation of number of calories.
   c) The British thermal unit.
   d) Calculation of number of B.T.U.'s.
3. Specific heat.
   a) Introduction.
   b) Definition.
   c) What does the specific heat of a substance tell you?
   d) Give several examples to make this clear.

F. M. Leavitt
L. A. P. Harms

University of Chicago

TESTS IN READING IN SYCAMORE SCHOOLS

KARL DOUGLAS WALDO
Principal, East Aurora High School, Aurora, Illinois

INTRODUCTION

A short time before I became superintendent of the Sycamore Public Schools (in 1909) the Ward Rational System of Reading had been adopted in the first and second grades. Most of the teachers were enthusiastic over the innovation and declared this system to be superior to the old plan of having each teacher work out her own plan of instruction. Soon, however, one teacher became dissatisfied with the character of the subject-matter in the Ward readers, her objection being the lack of interest shown by the children for the reading material offered. She heard W. W. Howe give an exposition of the phonic method developed by him and used at Whitehall, New York; this discussion was before the regular bimonthly teachers' meeting. Soon afterward she asked to be allowed to try that system of reading. This she was permitted to do.

As supervisor, I naturally watched the reading as it was developed through the phonic method and compared it with the work done under the Ward plan and also with the reading of the higher grades which had started their reading with no regular system. With notebook in hand I endeavored to keep a record of the individual work of the three systems for the purpose of comparison. These records were not very satisfactory and were based upon oral reading only, with no attempt to determine the comprehension by the children of the passages read other than that which could be shown by the oral expression.

When I saw how inadequate the comparison, made in this way, proved to be, I looked for some better method of making a record of the work. The attempts of Ayers, Courtis, Thorndike, and others to formulate standard tests suggested the formation of a plan for more scientific testing of the reading work. I also wished to test the silent rather than the oral reading, for the former is of much greater importance, not only later in school, but in future life.

I have not endeavored in this investigation to formulate a series of standard tests. If this study should prove to be of any help toward that end, however, I shall feel amply compensated for the effort expended. These statistics may be of some help in the study of children's reading habits and may aid in determining future plans for the teaching of reading.

Working from day to day upon the same problems and in the routine of the school it is often difficult to see that the young people have made any distinct increase in efficiency. The results of this test in showing the large progress made in reading during a period less than six months are of great value. Every teacher was delighted with the improvement made and felt rewarded for her efforts. Even the children were pleased at their own increased efficiency and set to work with a will, vowing to do even better in the future.

An example showing how these tests created an interest in the reading work may more clearly show their value as a means of motivation. Miss Finnegan's third grade, one of the places in which the check tests were given, was found to have the poorest average reading ability of all the third grades in the September test (see Table III). It was not planned originally to give her room any test in the spring. She set to work to bring her grade up to standard and asked that her room might be given a test later with the others. A special test with somewhat similar material was arranged for her. She emphasized the reading work and at least once a week asked the children to reproduce in writing an account of what their reading lesson had contained for that day. No set day was used for this exercise, so that the young people never knew when they might be expected to remember and understand all the reading lesson. This written exercise was done in the language period and correlated these two branches of the curriculum. The children were incited to do their best so that the superintendent never again would find them to be the poorest readers. With these third-graders this plan was a success, for the children fell in with the spirit of competition and soon greatly improved their work. By spring they had made the greatest percentage of increase in reproduction and were up to standard in every way when the tests were given. Miss Finnegan's room is not quite typical of the rest of the rooms, yet it shows how a skilful teacher can use such tests to improve the work in her room.

The majority of the teachers welcomed such tests, which gave them an opportunity to measure the results of their own work and to compare these results with the work of other teachers and children. An example of the teacher's attitude is shown by the teacher just mentioned, Miss Finnegan, who offered to count, record, and average the words read and reproduced by the children of her room in order that her grade might in the spring be compared with the other third grades.

The weakness of any phonic system of reading usually is found in the tendency to neglect the thought element because of the desire to perfect the mechanics. Such a test measures both elements of the reading much better than could be done by listening to the oral reading of the children, as is usually done in supervision.

These statements show that as a means of supervision and administration tests like this one are of much utility. Some teachers may doubt the value of the superintendent's criticism or may feel that his opinion of the work in their rooms is unwarranted. After such a test there is no need for the superintendent to criticize. The facts found in this test were shown in the bimonthly teachers' meeting and, after discussion, were accepted by the teachers as indicative of the true situation in the reading work. Knowing the situation is the first step in the direction of effective work, and after that is taken both teachers and superintendent can, in cordial co-operation, set about improving the reading work.

DESCRIPTION OF METHOD

The method used in these tests was simple and closely resembled the regular work of the school. Each test took about an hour of school time. No attempt was made to emphasize this work, yet the children seemed delighted with the test and many asked for their record afterward.

The first issue for the year 1913–14 of *Current Events*, a school weekly paper, was used for the tests. This paper is taken regularly by all the children above the fourth grade. However, this issue was not distributed, so that the children never read it except during the two tests. Owing to a mistake the papers were distributed in the eighth grades and were in the possession of the pupils a few hours previous to the test. Not even the teachers knew of the coming test, and as the time was well occupied by the school work only a few of the children in the eighth grade had read any in these papers. Several in each eighth-grade room, when asked whether they had read the paper, replied that they had "looked it over."

A careful description of the method of conducting the tests should be given. The same person gave all the tests and made the directions uniform in all the rooms. After stating to the young people that a reading exercise in the nature of a test was to be given to their room for the purpose of comparison with the other rooms, the papers were distributed face down upon each desk. Then the directions were given that on a signal all were to read silently, beginning with the first column on p. 3, for a period of five minutes, after which they would be examined upon what they had read. A signal to stop would be given, after which each one was to mark the place where he or she finished reading. They were cautioned not to try to memorize figures or reread any of the difficult parts, and were ordered to proceed as they would do in reading any newspaper article in which they might be interested. When all were at attention the signal was given to begin, and for five minutes there was no interruption of any kind while all were reading.

When the signal to stop was given each pupil checked the last word read and wrote his or her name on the paper. Then these were collected. The children were next supplied with paper and were asked to write a complete account of what they had just read. In future references this exercise will be called the word test. They were allowed all the time desired, except in a very few cases where individuals wrote an unusual amount. After these papers were collected a set of ten questions, covering the subject-matter just read, was placed upon the blackboard and the children were asked to answer them briefly. These papers will be referred to as the percentage test. About two of the columns of the reading were covered by the questions, which might consequently extend over more ground than some had read. If so, each one was directed to answer only as far as he or she had gone in the reading. For instance, if a child read 506 words he would answer or attempt to answer only seven questions. These last papers were graded upon a percentage basis, like regular test work in school. If a pupil read only far enough to answer five questions, each answer counted 20 per cent; while if he read as much or more than was covered by the questions, he could answer all ten questions, each answer being valued at 10 per cent.

The attempts to reproduce an account of what was read, or the word tests, were recorded by counting the total number of words written. So there were two tests of reproduction, one for words reproduced in a narrative form and one graded by percentage on the answers to questions. Thus it will be seen that an attempt was made to measure both the quantity and the quality of the reproduction or comprehension. The percentage basis of judging comprehension was somewhat more satisfactory, in that it is a more common form of rating. In many cases the record of the number of words reproduced means practically nothing regarding the ability of the child in comprehension, for some wrote many meaningless phrases and jumbles of words. Often the phrases written related to other subjects called to mind in some way by the reading material. Others wrote briefly, telling excellently in a few words what was read. In general, however, the number of words reproduced is a fair test of the ability in comprehension. Yet most of the comparison is made on the basis of percentage method of judging the comprehension of the subject-matter read.

The same plan of procedure was used in all the grades except that the third and fourth grades had different material and read in the first test a story of Daniel Boone in Eggleston's *Stories of Great Americans for Little Americans* (American Book Company, 1895), beginning with p. 76.

Late in March, after nearly six months of school work, the second set of tests was given in the same manner. The material was taken from a different page of the same periodical; the matter was, therefore, different from that used in the fall. The four upper grades read p. 1 instead of p. 3 in the same issue of *Current Events;* while the third and fourth grades read the story of Audubon, beginning with p. 111, instead of the one about Boone. So in all cases the subject-matter was new to all concerned and of about the same relative difficulty. The greater part of the fall test in *Current Events* was an account of some special elections for Congress, while in the spring it consisted chiefly of an article upon the tariff.

Check tests were given to prevent any errors, to show the relative character of the subject-matter, and to enable the experimenter to secure previous experience in their conduction. The check tests were given in a third- and fourth-grade room in the same school system, which room was not included in the later tests, and in the first-year English class in the high school. The same reading material given to the four upper grades in the fall and spring tests was given to this high-school class on consecutive days; and the lower-grade reading based upon the stories of Boone and Audubon were given but a day apart in the third- and fourth-grade room. These tests show the material for the lower grades to be relatively equal in difficulty for reading and comprehending; and the same fact to be true for the upper-grade tests.

TABLE I

SHOWING COMPARISON OF THE TWO CHECK TESTS: PERCENTAGE OF GAIN OR LOSS

	Change in Rate	Change in Reproduction	Change in Percentage of Correct Answers to Questions
Freshmen	+3.6	+ 3.8	+ 42
Fourth grade	+3	+ 0.7	− 4.4
Third grade	−2.4	+186	− 6

Table I shows the percentage of gain or loss as found in the two check tests given on consecutive days. The small percentage of difference in most cases shows the material to have been fairly well selected. As an example, the Freshmen read 3.6 per cent lower, wrote 3.8 per cent more words, and averaged 42 per cent better in the percentage grades on the second test than in the first.

Over half of the children in the third grade made no attempt at reproduction in the first test, which explains the gain there in word reproduction. This result may have been due to the fact that the children had never been requested to attempt such a thing; for they told the teacher afterward that they did not understand what was wanted.

There was a large increase in the first-year high-school percentage grades in the check test. In this class were ten tuition pupils who said afterward that they were not used to having anyone other than their regular teacher give tests and were consequently confused on the first occasion but "knew better what to do" in the next one. This may account in part for the big gain, which the second test shows over the first one. These two records practically are the only places where the check test did not show results which were nearly the same. Better directions and a somewhat different method of approach were gained by the experimenter from this experience with the check tests.

The words each child read were counted and tabulated, together with the number of words reproduced and the percentage grade upon the questions answered. In addition to making the averages for each room and each grade, the mean variation was figured for each child and the records include also the variation from the average, as suggested by Thorndike in his *Manual of Mental and Social Measurements* under the head of "Reliability of Measures." That is, the average mean variation is divided by the square root of the number of cases involved. The medians for each room are also included; and then to make the figures for the reading rate correspond with other experimenters, the result has been expressed in the number of words read per minute.

In order to get a single unit of measurement for comparison of all the grades, the percentage grade was multiplied by the number of words read per minute; for the reading ability depends both upon the rate of reading and the ability to comprehend. The one who can read rapidly and comprehend equally well certainly is a better reader than one whose comprehension is the same, but who reads more slowly.

Table II gives an illustration of the results from the pupils of one teacher, and Table III gives a summary of the results from all the grades which were tested.

TABLE II

THIRD GRADE (MIDDLETON)

	September						March						Gain Amount Read	Gain Amount Reproduced	Gain Percentage
	Amount Read	Variation	Amount Reproduced	Variation	Percentage	Variation	Amount Read	Variation	Amount Reproduced	Variation	Percentage	Variation			
1	484	34.7	35	8	16	27.5	1,138	409	85	29	45	9.3	654	....	29
2	80	369.3	90	3	75	32.5	850	121	125	11	35	0.7	770	35	*40*
3	344	105.3	75	18	74	31.5	575	154	190	76	40	4.3	231	115	*34*
4	284	165.3	158	65	35	8.5	714	15	150	36	35	0.7	430	*8*	....
5	484	34.7	120	27	33	10.5	841	112	105	9	44	8.3	357	*15*	11
6	484	34.7	150	57	33	10.5	732	3	105	9	38	2.3	248	*45*	5
7	1,112	662.7	75	18	40	35.0	850	121	150	36	40	4.3	*262*	75	....
8	484	34.7	45	48	0	43.5	432	297	70	44	25	10.7	*52*	25	25
9	360	89.3	55	38	48	5.5	742	13	85	29	38	2.3	382	30	*10*
10	484	34.7	80	13	55	11.5	605	124	115	1	33	2.7	121	35	*22*
11	274	175.3	66	27	80	36.5	540	189	75	39	20	15.7	266	9	*60*
Totals	4,874	1,740.7	999	322	489	221.5	8,019	1,558	1,255	319	393	61.3	3,459 *314*	324 *68*	70 *166*
Averages	443	158.2	90.8	29.3	44.4	20.1	729	141.6	114	29	35.7	5.6	286	23.2	*8.7*
Median or variation of average	484	47.9	80	8.9	40	6	732	42.9	105	8.8	40	1.7	....	....	....
Words per minute	886	31.6	....	....	....	....	145.8	28.3	....	....	....	....	57.2	....	....

FOURTH GRADE (MIDDLETON)

	September						March						Gain Amount Read	Gain Amount Reproduced	Gain Percentage
	Amount Read	Variation	Amount Reproduced	Variation	Percentage	Variation	Amount Read	Variation	Amount Reproduced	Variation	Percentage	Variation			
1	360	91.2	63	50.6	56	6	400	288	140	12.8	40	21.4	40	77	16
2	561	109.8	110	3.6	50	0	770	82	90	62.8	40	21.4	209	*20*	*10*
3	782	330.8	115	1.4	90	40	1,040	352	275	122.2	75	13.6	258	160	*15*
4	683	228.8	100	13.6	50	0	850	162	225	72.2	77	15.6	167	125	*27*
5	643	182.8	132	18.4	25	25	658	30	75	77.8	60	1.4	*15*	*57*	35
6	882	430.8	215	101.4	85	35	962	274	160	7.2	60	1.4	80	*55*	*25*
7	714	257.8	65	48.6	50	0	1,165	477	150	2.8	100	38.6	451	85	50
8	450	301.2	40	73.6	0	50	132	456	90	62.8	60	1.4	*18*	50	60
9	484	32.8	115	1.4	50	0	746	58	150	2.8	62	0.6	262	35	12
10	561	109.8	96	17.6	30	20	850	162	265	112.2	50	11.4	289	169	20
11	484	32.8	110	3.6	45	5	744	56	130	22.2	70	8.6	260	*20*	25
12	360	91.2	175	61.4	58	8	473	215	120	32.8	33	6.4	113	*55*	*3*
13	425	26.2	115	1.4	15	35	643	45	123	27.8	70	8.6	218	10	55
14	220	231.2	103	10.6	40	10	300	388	75	77.8	38	23.4	80	*28*	*2*
15	311	140.2	235	121.4	80	30	1,129	441	280	127.2	80	18.6	818	45	....
16	233	218.2	175	61.4	64	14	870	142	160	7.2	70	8.6	637	*15*	6
17	160	291.2	75	38.6	85	35	240	248	65	87.8	55	6.4	80	*10*	*30*
18	360	91.2	130	16.4	47	3	692	4	170	17.2	55	6.4	332	40	8
Totals	8,573	3,193.0	2,169	645.0	910	316	12,383	3,880	2,705	935.2	1,106	213.8	3,843 *33*	796 *260*	298 *102*
Averages	476.2	177.4	120.5	36	50.6	16.4	688	215.5	152.8	52	61.4	11.8	212	32.3	9.8
Median or variation of average	450	42.2	110	8.5	50	4	692	51.3	140	12.4	60	2.8	....	....	....
Words per minute	95.2	35.5	....	....	....	....	137.6	43.1	....	....	....	....	42.4	....	....

Figures in italic show loss.

TABLE III

SUMMARY OF THE RESULTS OF THE SEPTEMBER AND MARCH TESTS

	September						March						Gain Rate per Minute	Gain Repro-duced	Gain Per-centage
	Rate per Minute	M.V.	Words Repro-duced	M.V.	Percent-age	M.V.	Rate per Minute	M.V.	Words Repro-duced	M.V.	Percent-age	M.V.			
Middleton	88.6	31.6	90.6	29.3	44.4	20.1	145.8	28.3	114	29	35.7	5.6	57.2	23.2	*8.7*
Overocker	70.4	25.2	57	27.7	42	25.1	140.9	35.1	173	38	45.4	8.6	70.5	116	3.4
Haygreen	76.2	25.9	65.5	38.7	47.5	25.3	147.4	45.4	118	43	57	18.1	90.4	52.5	3.5
Third	76.4	27.6	71.1	31.9	44.6	23.5	149.1	36.3	135	36.7	44	10.8	72.7	63.9	*0.6*
Middleton	95.2	35.5	120.5	36	50.6	16.4	137.6	43.1	152.8	52	61.4	11.8	42.4	32.3	9.8
Overocker	82.7	24.5	152.2	47.2	58.1	21.8	157.8	47.3	284.7	87	64.1	15.7	88.8	132.5	5.9
Haygreen	101.3	46.5	128.7	56	61.5	25.3	180.7	51.9	201.3	54.2	57.3	19.8	79.4	72.6	4.2
Fourth	92.7	35.6	133.8	46.4	56.7	21.2	163.3	47.4	212.9	64.4	60.9	15.8	70.2	79.1	6.6
Hopkins	107.2	40.2	37.8	24.5	13.3	14.2	116.8	53.3	76	28.5	25.1	14.3	9.6	38.2	11.8
Van Galder	118.8	58.2	66.6	23.8	19.4	15.2	141.6	46.2	65	25.6	26.1	14.2	22.8	*1.6*	6.7
Fifth	113	49.2	52.2	24.2	16.3	14.7	129.2	49.8	70.5	27.1	25.6	14.3	16.2	18.3	9.8
Clinch	134.1	41.5	52.6	22.6	24.4	15.9	130.9	39.3	89.2	30.5	32.3	11.8	*3.2*	26.6	7.9
Gross	127.5	39.9	51.6	18.7	29.4	14.2	129.2	47.6	82.9	26.5	37.4	12.7	6.4	31.3	8
Sixth	128	40.6	52.1	20.6	27.1	15	130.1	43.8	85.3	28.4	35	123	2.1	33.7	8
Nilson	131.8	34	81.3	40	46.4	19	144.8	41.8	128	44.4	48.2	15.7	35.5	46.7	1.8
Harrington	125.9	35.9	69.9	36.7	39	20.2	131	44.9	123.1	49.3	48.4	18.4	5.1	53.2	9.4
Seventh	122.7	34.9	75.6	38.8	42.7	19.6	142.8	42.8	125.5	46.8	48.3	17.1	21.8	49.9	5.6
Hall	151.8+	33.9+	112.4	31.8	51.3	18.5	140 +	37.9+	182.2	61.8	62.6	13.5	*1.5*+	69.8	11.3
Chamberlain	149.1+	28 +	120.6	56.6	59.4	22.3	174.1+	42.4+	177	59.4	62.4	14.3	24.9	56.4	3
Eighth	147.2	31	116.5	44.2	55.3	20.4	158.9	40.1	179.6	60.6	62.5	13.9	11.7	63.1	7.1

Figures in italic show loss.

Hall and Chamberlain reversed for figures marked with +.

DESCRIPTION OF RESULTS

Variations in same grade.—One of the most noticeable results is the wide variation within single grades, both in rate of reading and in reproduction. Courtis found this in his test as far as he had gone, but these variations are even greater than those found by him. Table IV, taken from the spring test (Freshmen were excepted, although the work was the same as was taken in the fall), shows this remarkable variation without further comment.

TABLE IV

VARIATIONS WITHIN SAME GRADES

Grades	Rate of Reading		Words Reproduced		Percentage Grades	
	High	Low	High	Low	High	Low
Freshmen.........	1,014	399	260	85	100	27
Eighth grade......	1,720	233	425	60	98	29
Seventh grade.....	1,365	233	275	17	100	0
Sixth grade........	1,105	185	180	35	90	0
Fifth grade........	1,545	233	160	0	68	0
Fourth grade......	1,736	110	450	65	100	30
Third grade.......	1,183	356	280	70	85	10

TABLE V

VARIATIONS IN DIFFERENT GRADES

Percentage of Children in Lower Grades Doing Better Work than Those in Upper Grades

	Third Grade Exceeding Fourth								
	Rate			Words Reproduced			Percentage		
	35.1			10.8			13.5		
	Upper Grades								
	Rate			Words Reproduced			Percentage		
	6	7	8	6	7	8	6	7	8
Fifth grade......	42.6	36.1	29.5	24.6	8.2	0	26.2	13.1	0
Sixth grade......	......	35.5	29.4	......	15.7	2	......	15.7	4
Seventh grade....	......	......	27.7	......	......	14.8	......	......	24.1

Table V, taken from the pupils' spring test, shows another phase of the variation, namely, that of individuals in different grades. It will be seen from this table that many children in lower grades excel their schoolmates in higher grades. Thus 29.5 per cent of the fifth-graders excel the average rate in reading of the eighth grade; 36.1 per cent of them excel the seventh-grade average, and 42.6 per cent excel the average for the sixth grade.

In reproduction there are smaller numbers of children who are superior to those of higher grades; but sixteen children, or 26.2 per cent, excel the average of the sixth grade; and but eight, or 15.7 per cent, exceed the seventh-grade average, and none are superior to the eighth. Other interesting comparisons may be found by a study of the table.

Need for standardized material.—This test clearly shows one fact: that it is not possible, in a test of this kind, where two different passages are used, to compare all grades with each other; for with two different kinds of reading material it is impossible to get a relative comparison for the grades which read different matter. Comparisons can be made, therefore, in this case only within the two groups. This is shown by the table giving the summary for all grades (Table III), where it will be seen that the fourth grades exceeded the fifth, sixth, and seventh grades, not only in the rate of reading, but in the number of words reproduced and in the percentage grades for comprehension. Of course, this is caused by the difference in reading material.

Improvement from lower to upper grades.—One would expect to find an increase both in speed and reproduction from the lower grades to the higher. This increase is not shown fully in this test because of the difference in the material, as has already been pointed out. However, increase of ability in general is shown in most cases, though there are a few exceptions. The rate of speed, ability in reproduction as measured by words, and the comprehension measured by percentage marks, for both the fall and spring tests, are easily deducible from the tables. One notices the regularity of the improvement from grade to grade in quality of comprehension. It is very striking, on the other hand, that in the reading rate there is little increase after the fifth grade. Courtis found the same fact for careful reading in the one school which he has reported in the April, 1914, number of the *Elementary School Teacher.*

These figures show that the lower grades are very important in the development of reading, for there were made the greatest gains in the mechanics of reading. The third and fourth grades nearly doubled their reading rates from September to March. In ability to write the story about what was read the third grade nearly doubled in efficiency, while the fourth grade increased about 50 per cent. The tables show a great increase in composition and comprehension everywhere except in one fifth-grade room, where there was a slight loss.

TABLE VI

SHOWING PERCENTAGE INCREASE OF THE SPRING TEST IN THE READING RATE

Grade	Fall Rate	Spring Rate	Percentage of Increase
3	76.4	149.1	95.2
4	92.7	163.3	76.1
5	113	129.2	14.3
6	128	130.1	1.2
7	122.7	142.8	16.4
8	147.2	158.9	8

As shown in Table III, the third grades declined in the percentage grades in the second test, owing to a heavy loss in one room, which was not overcome by the slight improvement made in the other two rooms. The loss, however, was but six-tenths of 1 per cent. This was the only grade in which the average efficiency in comprehension decreased between the fall and spring tests. One fourth-grade room had a poorer average, but it was offset by the other two fourths, which showed marked improvement. One sixth grade and one of the eighth grades read in the spring at a slower rate than they did in the fall, showing an average loss of 3.2 words per minute and 1.5 words per minute, respectively. These were the only rooms in which there was any loss in rate or comprehension.

Table VII, based upon the product of the rate of reading in words per minute times the percentage grade, shows this great improvement clearly. All the grades increased materially. One room, an eighth, showed a lower efficiency in the spring than in the fall, but the other eighth increased more than enough to make the average, for the whole grade showed an increase.

Comparison of the different systems of teaching reading.—All the children below the sixth grade started with the Ward system of reading, except about one-half of Miss Middleton's third-grade room, which had the Howe system. One reason for putting the

TABLE VII

Showing Reading Ability Based upon a Single Index, the Product of the Rate Times the Percentage Grade

	Fall	Spring	Gain
Third grade—			
Middleton	39.4	52.1	12.7
Overocker	29.6	64	34.4
Haygreen	36.2	75.2	39
Average	34.1	65.6	28.5
Fourth grade—			
Middleton	48.2	84.5	36.3
Overocker	48.1	101.2	53.2
Haygreen	76	103.5	27.6
Average	54.6	99.5	44.9
Fifth grade—			
Hopkins	14.3	29.3	15.1
Van Galder	23	37	13.9
Average	18.4	33.1	14.7
Sixth grade—			
Clinch	32.7	42.3	9.6
Gross	37.2	48.3	11.1
Average	34.7	45.5	10.8
Seventh grade—			
Nilson	50.6	69.8	19.2
Harrington	49.1	63.4	14.3
Average	52.4	68.9	16.5
Eighth grade—			
Hall	76.5	111	34.5
Chamberlain	90.2	87.4	*2.8*
Average	81.4	99.3	17.9

Figures in italic show loss.

rather difficult reading material offered in the *Current Events* down so low in the grades was for the purpose of comparing the fifth and sixth grades upon the same reading material; the former learned to read by a severe phonic system (the Ward), while the latter was taught to read by whatever plan the teacher chose to develop. The figures for these two grades show a relation quite similar to the relations of the other similar grades; so that it is impossible to draw any conclusion regarding the relative merits of the two different plans for starting the reading work. In other words, there seems to be no more difference between a fifth grade which has had the Ward method and a sixth that has not than there is between the sixth grade and the seventh, neither of which has had the phonic system.

It will be seen that the third-grade children who learned to read by the Howe method did the best reading work in the fall test, 39.338 being its single-index measurement, compared with 29.40 and 34.07 for the other third-grade rooms; while in the spring test it had lost its leading position, scoring 52.05, which put it into third place, for the other figures totaled 75.174 and 63.969. This cannot be attributed to the Howe method entirely, for the teacher in that third grade, although she tried to work both systems, did not carry on the drills as thoroughly as she might, being more interested in the Ward method. Here was clearly shown the loss occurring in a single system when different plans of work are carried out in the same grade. Miss Middleton, the teacher, explained this weakness of her grade by the fact that she had a fourth grade in the room at the same time which was twice as large as her third and somewhat backward. In trying to bring this fourth grade up to standard, she thinks that she might have neglected the third grade somewhat.

Effect of tests.—The children in the spring about reach the plane of development which the grade above them had at the beginning of school in the fall. There should perhaps be some correspondence between spring tests of the grade below and the fall tests of the grade above. Attention should be drawn to two facts which complicate the comparison: that the spring test was given about three months before the close of school, and that the upper-grade children in the fall test were on an average about six months older. With these facts in mind, one would expect the children of the greater maturity, who had had three months more of school work, to do much better work than their younger rivals. In the fall, however, these older children had just returned from their vacations and doubtless lost somewhat in efficiency from the lack of regular school reading exercises.

In the majority of cases the lower-grade record exceeds that of the grade above in spite of the lack of maturity. This probably is due to the stimulus caused by the test and bears out Woodworth's conclusion in his report, found in the *Proceedings of the Mental Hygiene Conference and Exhibit for 1912*, on p. 217, where he urges the value of such tests to prevent dawdling over the school tasks. The apparent superiority of the fourth over the fifth grade is due to the difference in the character of the subject-matter read and is not real. This superiority of the lower grade does not show in the percentage tables nor in the single-index measurement. The latter, however, is largely determined by the former. In speed and word reproduction there is but one place where the younger children did not do better, and that is in the eighth grades, where, as has been before mentioned, some of the children in the fall had seen the paper in advance.

These results furnish a good argument for the value of regularly conducted tests in reading, although the evidence shows that ability in comprehension is less easily stimulated in this way than is the reading rate. Yet by increasing the reading rate, which can be done without any loss in comprehension, the pupils in general would be much stronger readers.

TABLE VIII

SHOWING SINGLE-INDEX RATING

Gain by Grades for September and March	Words Read per Minute	Words Reproduced	Percentage Reproduced	Single-Index Rating
Third, spring test	149.1	135	44	65.6
Fourth, fall test	92.7	133.8	56.7	54.6
Fourth, spring test	163.3	212.9	60.9	99.5
Fifth, fall test	113	52.2	16.3	18.4
Fifth, spring test	129.2	70.5	25.6	33.1
Sixth, fall test	128	52.1	27.1	34.7
Sixth, spring test	130.1	85.3	35	45.5
Seventh, fall test	122.7	75.6	42.7	52.4
Seventh, spring test	142.8	125.5	48.3	68.9
Eighth, fall test	147.2	116.5	55.3	81.4

Table VIII and Chart I present a summary of the gains in efficiency from the fall to the spring tests for each grade taken as a whole.

The conclusion to be drawn from Table VIII is that speed and ability to reproduce words are more easily stimulated by tests than the real mental development, if such be measured by the percentage marks. However, it seems to the writer to be a good argument for holding such tests, for it gives a goal toward which to work, for

CHART I

GRAPHIC REPRESENTATION OF THE FACTS PRESENTED IN TABLE VIII

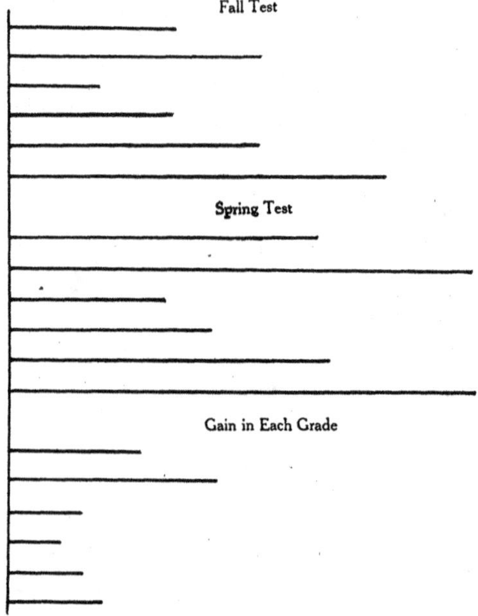

both the children and teachers, and tends to do away with the dawdling over the reading tasks. Altogether it is a safe conclusion from all these statistics to state that the real comprehension depends more largely upon regular mental development and is less easily stimulated than the rate.

Relation of speed to comprehension.—The work previously quoted of Quantz, Abell, and others interested the writer in an attempt to find the correlation between the reading rate and the comprehension. No definite result can be stated, but it would seem that the rapid readers usually are strong in comprehension, although there are many exceptions. The high-school Freshmen show the most correlation, but that is far from perfect. Of course it must be borne in mind here, as has been pointed out before, that high speed with an equal percentage of reproduction represents much higher general efficiency than a lower speed with the same reproductive ability. That is, the boy who reads a thousand words in five minutes and reproduces 50 per cent of it has a much higher reading efficiency than the one who reads but five hundred words with the same power of comprehension. So a rapid rate is greatly to be desired, and being more open to stimulus it can be secured by special emphasis, such as tests of this kind.

SUMMARY

The conclusions drawn from this study are not stated dogmatically and may have to be altered, should further investigation be made. However, the author believes the following conclusions are justified by the evidence developed:

Great variation exists in reading ability between different individuals in the same grade, and many children in lower grades are much better readers than the average of the upper grades.

In developing a standard reading scale to show the relative efficiency of different grades it will be necessary to use the same subject-matter for all grades, or else the materials should be so standardized that their relative difficulty is known and can be used in judging the results, or else there should be some overlapping tests.

In careful reading the rate increases but slowly in school work after the fifth grade. The increase in comprehension, however, increases regularly from the lower to the upper grades.

The third and fourth grades are places with the possibilities for wonderful development, especially in the mechanics of reading. The effects of starting the reading with a phonic system like the Ward are not evident in the reading of the upper grades. Tests tend to stimulate the work in reading, but have more effect upon the reading rate than upon the ability to comprehend what is read.

No definite conclusions were obtained upon the correlation between speed and comprehension; yet it is safe to say that an increase in the rate of reading does not decrease ability in comprehension.

BIBLIOGRAPHY

Abell, Adelaide, "Rapid Reading, Advantages and Methods," *Ed. Rev.*, VIII (1894), 283.

Bowden, Josephine H., *Learning to Read.* Doctor's Dissertation, University of Chicago, 1911.

Brown, H. A., "Measurement of the Efficiency of Instruction in Reading," *Elem. Sch. Teacher*, XIV (1914), 477–90.

Courtis, S. A., "Standard Tests in English," *Ibid.*, 374–92.

Dearborn, W. F., "Psychology of Reading," *Columbia Contributions to Philosophy and Psychology*, XIV, No. 1 (1906).

Huey, E. B., *Psychology and Pedagogy of Reading.* New York, 1909.

Judd, Charles H., "Reading Tests," *Ibid.*, 365–73.

Quantz, J. O., "Problems in Psychology of Reading," *Psych. Rev.* (Mon. Supp.), 1897.

Reudiger, "Field of Distinct Vision," *Columbia Contributions to Philosophy and Psychology*, XVII, No. 1 (1907).

THE USE OF AN OBJECTIVE SCALE FOR GRADING HANDWRITING

HERSCHEL T. MANUEL
Greencastle, Indiana

For the last few years a great deal of attention has been given to the problem of educational measurement. Attention has been called repeatedly to the need for objective bases for the evaluation of school products. As a result of this movement a number of objective scales designed to furnish such bases have been published. These published scales have in turn furnished an opportunity for experimentation and test from which a better understanding of the general problem is emerging. The writer has been engaged in a study of the Ayres Measuring Scale for Handwriting (Russell Sage Foundation, New York City, 1912) from the viewpoint of the variability in the grades assigned to the same writing when the scale is used. It is the purpose of this article to report very briefly some of the main results of this study and their apparent implications for the problem above mentioned.[1]

The Ayres scale, it will be remembered, consists of reproductions of samples of school handwriting arranged in order of quality on the basis of legibility and assigned certain numerical values. In all, twenty-four different specimens of handwriting are used. These are arranged in eight groups of three specimens each and printed on a rectangular sheet of heavy paper. Above the groups appear the numbers 20, 30, 40, ... 90, respectively. These numbers indicate the comparative value of the writing displayed below them. The legibility of the samples was determined by actual timed readings of a number of paid investigators reading a

[1] The writer acknowledges with thanks his indebtedness to a large number of different persons, whom space forbids to mention by name, in the study underlying this article. Special thanks are due to Dr. Frank N. Freeman. For a fuller discussion of the investigation see the Master's essay by the writer in the library of the University of Chicago.

large number of samples of elementary-school writing. The grading of handwriting by the use of the scale is simply a matter of comparison of the sample being graded with the samples on the scale, and the giving of an appropriate numerical value in terms of the values appearing above the specimens on the scale. The directions on the scale are very simple: "To measure the quality of a sample of handwriting slide it along the scale until a writing of corresponding value is found. The number in black at the top of the scale above this represents the value of the writing being measured." For purposes of this discussion the expression "to measure the quality of" may be considered synonymous with the phrase "to grade."

The investigation has consisted of the collection of a fairly large number of handwriting grades assigned by different persons working under various conditions and of a study of the variability among them. It has been the intention to use the grades of such persons as might be expected to use the scale in practical work and yet who have had no training in its use other than independent practice. Neither the number of papers graded nor the number of graders contributing to these results in the different parts of the investigation can be detailed here. It will be sufficient to state that the grades of a total of more than a thousand papers are used and that more than two hundred persons contributed to the grading, grading sets varying from eight papers to one hundred and seventy-six, some with the scale and some without and some by both methods.

Briefly stated, the direct conclusion from the investigation is that miscellaneous graders vary rather widely in their use of the Ayres scale when their only training in its use is independent practice. Table I shows how extreme this variability may be among persons presumably expert in their judgment of handwriting. The table shows the grades of eight samples of writing (numbered 1–8) given by three supervisors of writing using the Ayres scale. The figures at the bottom represent scale values. The figures above are the identification numbers of the samples graded and are placed above the values given. Each row represents the grading of one of the three supervisors. The table should be read as follows: One judge rated paper No. 2 at 20 on the Ayres scale, a second judge at 40, and the third at 75. The same judges rated paper No. 4 at 20, 30, and 50, respectively.

TABLE I

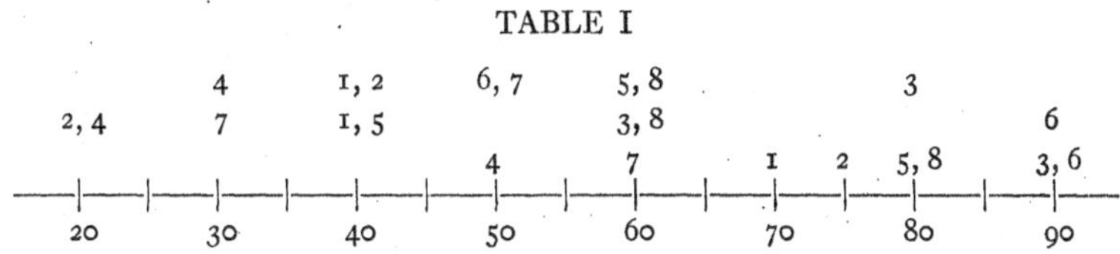

Fig. 1 shows graphically the distribution of values given to paper No. 6 of this series by nineteen members of a class in experimental education after considerable practice with the scale. The heights of the columns represent the percentage of the number in the group (19) assigning the Ayres-scale values indicated below. The second part of the figure gives for comparison the average values of handwriting in the various school grades as proposed by Dr. Frank N. Freeman for tentative standards (*Elementary School Teacher*, XIV, 170).

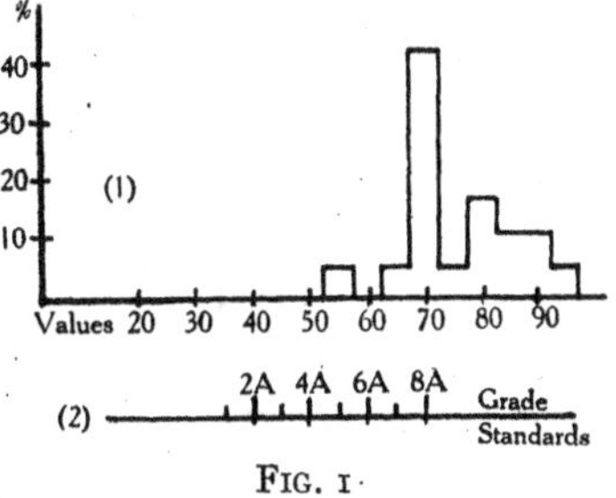

FIG. 1

The characteristic distribution of the grades assigned to separate papers graded in a series is illustrated in Fig. 2. The same eight papers as appeared in Table I are the basis of the grades here represented. The first part of the figure shows the characteristic distribution of values by one hundred eighteen persons, most of whom were relatively unfamiliar with the scale; the second part by a group of nineteen after practice with the scale and after a suggestion of the possibility of using 5's as well as 10's in the grading had been given; the third part by a group of sixty-five grading the papers by the ordinary school method of grading, i.e., on the basis of the advancement of the pupils producing the writing and the passing-grade of the school. The heights of the columns represent, as in Fig. 1, the percentage of the number in the group assigning the values indicated below. The values are indicated in terms of deviations from a middle value. In the first two parts of the figure the middle value taken is a multiple of ten lying near the median of the distribution of the grades given by the various graders in the group, and in the third part the middle values are multiples of five lying near the median. Suppose, for example, in a group of six graders three give the value 70, two 80, and one 60. The middle value in this distribution would be taken as 70. The table would show then that 50 per cent of the graders assigned a value deviating from the middle value by 0, $33\frac{1}{3}$ per cent by 10, and $16\frac{2}{3}$ per cent by -10. It will be observed that the same absolute differences in grades are represented by longer differences on the base line in the third part of the figure than in the other two parts. This change of scale is made to enable one to make a direct comparison of the real significance of the distributions and is made necessary by the fact that the same absolute differences in the two methods of grading form different proportionate parts of the ranges of values used in each.

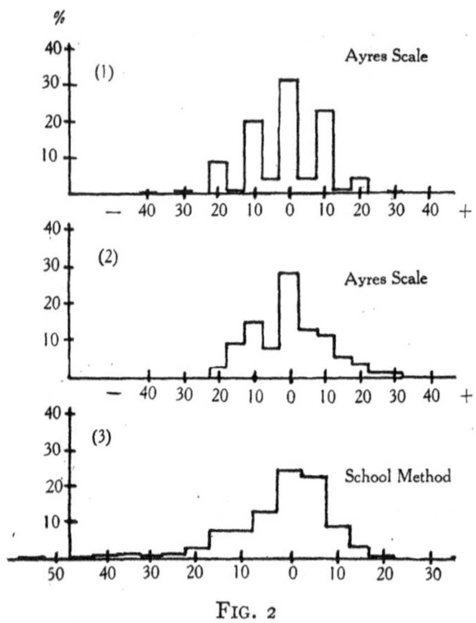

FIG. 2

The curves in Fig. 3 represent the Ayres-scale grades of the writing of two schools of the same city as assigned by two different persons, the same two persons grading each school. The figures at the left indicate the values given to the papers of the school grades indicated below. The grades are based upon from twenty-three to twenty-six papers from each grade. The dotted line represents the grades of one grader and the unbroken line those of the other.

So much by way of illustration; a summary of some of the leading facts brought out by the study follows.

With reference to the variability of the grades of the separate papers of a series it has appeared that:

On the average the chances are more than one in two that two graders after practice in the use of the scale will assign values to the same paper differing by 10 or more, and more than one in six that the values will differ by 20 or more.

The average deviation of the grades of individuals from the group average in grading a single paper with the scale may be as low as 3 or as high as 11.

In general the grades of the same individual at different times may be expected to vary about one-half as much as do the grades of different individuals.

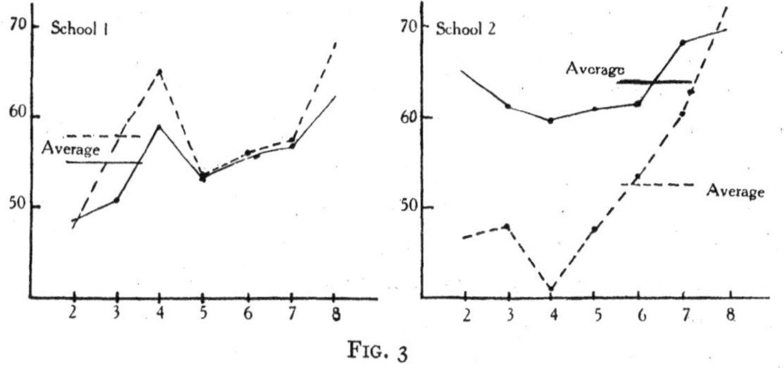

FIG. 3

In general there is a greater variability in the absolute values assigned to writing by the ordinary school method of grading than in those assigned on the basis of the scale. This variability is more marked on the papers that are judged to be below passing.

From the viewpoint of variability the scale appears to have little or no superiority over the other method of grading as a means for finding the relative rank of papers.

With reference to the average grades of series of papers such as are used in comparisons of the writing of groups it has appeared that:

A difference of as much as 10 (a full step on the Ayres scale and twice the difference between the averages of the writing of two successive school grades as shown in Fig. 1) in the averages assigned to a series of twenty-five papers by different persons after practice is common.

In terms of deviations from group averages the variability in the use of the school method is about three halves as great as that in the use of the scale, and the variability in the use of a subjective scale in which only the zero and one-hundred points are defined almost twice as large as the Ayres-scale variability.

Independent practice in the use of the scale without instruction or exchange of experience may not be expected to reduce the variability if 5's as well as 10's are used in the grading from the first.

The deviation of an individual from a group may be radically modified by experience, but two gradings of the same papers by the same person close to each other in point of time and unmodified by special experience with reference to the grading of handwriting tend to be, from the viewpoint of averages, approximately the same.

The deviation of the average given by a single individual from the group average may be quite different for different sets of papers.

The obtaining of and use of a "personal equation" for correcting the grades of various individual graders that the results of their work may be directly compared require elaborate tests and carefully controlled conditions as to the character and number of the samples graded and the time and experience in grading that intervene between the various gradings used. The evidence at hand does not indicate that such "personal equations" will be generally useful in work with the scale.

In comparisons of the averages of the grades of sets of twenty-five papers graded by different persons any real difference in quality should not be assumed unless the difference in the averages is as much as 7½, three-fourths of a step on the Ayres scale.

In comparisons of the writing of various schools based on the averages of sets containing not to exceed twenty-five papers from each grade from grades two to seven, if the grading is done by different persons using the Ayres scale, any real difference in quality should not be assumed unless the difference in the averages is as much as 5, one-half step on the Ayres scale.

In averages of twenty-five papers given by different groups of four graders each differences less than 5 should not be considered as representing real differences in quality without information as to the characteristic grading of members of the groups.

Such are the facts; what do they mean? The opponent of attempts at exact measurement in education will be inclined to say, "I told you so! Scales may be all right for the *theorist*, but they have no value for the *practical* man." Another who would be unwilling to go quite so far may say, "No, the fundamental idea of scales is sound, but I never did believe that this particular scale is a good one." Still another who views with grave doubts the ability of the ordinary school man to do anything well may say, "It is merely an evidence of the gross inability of those who did the grading." It would, however, be a long jump indeed to the conclusions just quoted from the real net result of the investigation, viz., that miscellaneous graders vary rather widely in the use of the Ayres scale when their only training in its use is independent practice. The real significance of the results, it appears, is twofold: first, they furnish experimental data for the interpretation of the results when the scale is used under the conditions described in this experiment, and in the second place they furnish a basis for a clearer understanding of the general problem of the scale in educational measurement. The first of these is sufficiently clear from the results themselves; the second will justify some further discussion.

It will hardly be necessary to say anything in support of evaluation as a factor in the work of the schools. Very few, I suppose, would deny that some estimate of the results of educational practice is desirable. Indeed, the absence of all evaluation in school work would set that field off in opposition to all of the rest of human life, which is characterized everywhere by implicit or explicit judgments of value.

Grading is a form of evaluation. In judging the output of any productive system two considerations arise, expressed by the terms quantity and quality. Grading has to do with the determination of and expression of the latter. Quantity is *one* attribute or aspect of a thing. The quality of a thing is the same as the being of the thing itself—it is a complex of *all* the attributes. The accurate expression of quality in quantitative units necessarily involves the quantitative description of each and all of the separate unit factors which constitute the object the quality of which is being determined. The measurement of quality is a measurement of the unit factors which make the object just what it is. The determination of the quality, therefore, will vary in difficulty with the number of separate factors to be considered and the difficulty of evaluating them.

Measurement consists in a comparison of the thing to be measured with a standard unit of the same thing. To measure, for example, a linear distance we make a comparison of the distance with a unit of distance, and to measure an angle we use a unit angle. Any such distance or angle may, of course, be employed as a unit, but the advantage of having certain well-established standard units is universally recognized in this field, and such units are employed.

Consider now the measurement of the quality of handwriting. It is clear from the analogy that the measurement must be in terms of a unit of quality, and, of course, any quality may be used as a unit for measurement. To carry the analogy a bit farther, just as the meter is described as the distance between certain transverse lines on a certain bar, so a unit of handwriting may be merely some specimen published so that it will be generally available and named so that it may be referred to conveniently. Suppose in the absence of another name we call the unit for the measurement of the quality of handwriting a "scrib." Then in the expression of the quality of a sample of handwriting we are measuring we should say that the quality is, for example, two scribs, meaning that the quality of the sample measured is twice that of the unit sample.

The difficulty with this form of measurement for the quality of handwriting is that the quality of handwriting is not *immediately* quantitative. The quality of handwriting involves a number of factors, including the slant, the alignment, the legibility, the beauty, etc. The use of a unit of handwriting, therefore, necessitates the isolation and comparison of all the separate factors (except as these may be arbitrarily limited by definition). This complexity makes impractical any attempts to evaluate handwriting in terms of the quality of a single specimen such as described. Instead, scales consisting of a number of samples have been devised. The real unit of measurement is the difference in quality between the successive specimens on the scale, but the quality is expressed in terms of the samples themselves by means of certain identification symbols (such as the 20, 30, etc., of the Ayres scale), rather than directly in terms of the unit.

Now it is evident that an enumeration of all the separate factors of handwriting would be rather difficult. Moreover, as the number of these to be considered in the evaluation of the writing increase, the difficulty of accurate use of a scale increases. There is still a further difficulty in the impossibility of comparison of the various factors by actual physical superposition or even juxtaposition. It is not strange, therefore, that persons without special training vary in the use of the scale. Consider, for example, how complex the use of a red maple rule with a brass edge would be if all of these factors had to be considered in measuring a table! A truer analogy than measurement of dimensions would be that of the grading of agricultural products.

Several conclusions may now be stated:

1. It is clear that generally accepted standards in terms of which the quality of writing may be determined and expressed are desirable.

2. For practical purposes the publication of samples of handwriting is a serviceable part of the description of such standards.

3. The publication of samples must be accompanied by accurate quantitative descriptions as far as possible in terms of the factors to be considered in the grading. A description of the basis for the selection of the samples will not be sufficient unless it is the same as that to be used in the comparisons involved in the process of grading.

4. Those who use the scale with the purpose of accurate comparisons of results must be technically trained for such work, just as poultry judges, for example, find training necessary. On the other hand, such scales, though used with somewhat different results, will be valuable in ordinary schoolroom practice.

5. The scale itself should be based upon the factors to be considered in the grading.

6. Elaborate efforts to establish a zero of quality in order to have a "perfect scale" analogous to simple physical measures are quite unnecessary. Ideally, any two samples may be taken as fixed points and other samples may be defined in terms of their difference.

7. The definition of samples should be based upon the best available schoolroom practice, rather than upon an attempt to represent a progressive increase in the perfection of various factors which may or may not represent writing in its various stages of growth. The samples on the scale should represent the various degrees of excellence as they actually mature. I am inclined to believe that the factors of production need to be given more weight in the determination of scales, as some have urged. The excellence of a product is not to be determined by a consideration merely of the ratio certain factors bear to the same factors in the finished product, but by a consideration of its general scheme of growth toward that end. Moreover, it is worth while to measure the process as well as the product. In the grading of the product, then, the characteristics of the process should have consideration in the degree that desirable or undesirable features of the process are shown by peculiarities of the product.

8. The next step, therefore, is to determine and to describe in objective terms the characteristics of handwriting as found in the best practice of different systems. This would better be the work of specialists in handwriting who are willing to devote themselves faithfully to this end. On the basis of these studies the essential factors of handwriting could be selected and defined by a representative body of school men. After the objective definition of the grades of writing to be recognized, the number of actual publications known as scales may be as numerous as the different systems of writing, and yet all would have the same foundation, just as many styles of thermometers may read in Fahrenheit units. Such scales will furnish common terms for the discussion of handwriting and at the same time a fairly true picture of the thing it is really worth while to measure—namely, the progressive accomplishment of a pupil toward the acquirement of a certain ability in a particular line of activity. Meanwhile, however, let us realize that we have made progress, and let us make the best use of the tools so far available.

BOOKS RECEIVED

BECKLEY-CARDY COMPANY, CHICAGO

Bow-Wow and Mew-Mew. By GEORGIANA M. CRAIK. Illustrated. Cloth. Pp. 95. $0.30.

Progressive School Classics ($0.05 each):

Longfellow's "Courtship of Miles Standish"
Tennyson's "Enoch Arden"
Longfellow's "Evangeline"
Hawthorne's "Great Stone Face"
Ruskin's "King of the Golden River"
Irving's "Legend of Sleepy Hollow"
Hale's "Man without a Country"
Irving's "Rip Van Winkle"

MACMILLAN, NEW YORK

American Literature for Secondary Schools. By WILLIAM B. CAIRNS, PH.D. Illustrated. Cloth. Pp. 341. $1.00.

Dramatic Readings for Schools. By MARION FLORENCE LANSING. Illustrated. Cloth. Pp. 242. $0.50.

A Handbook of Vocational Education. By JOSEPH S. TAYLOR, PH.D. Illustrated. Cloth. Pp. 225. $1.00.

Stories from Northern Myths. By EMILIE KIP BAKER. Illustrated. Cloth. Pp. 276. $1.25.

AMERICAN BOOK CO., NEW YORK

Business Arithmetic. By C. M. BOOKMAN. Illustrated. Cloth. Pp. 250. $0.65.

Principles of Cooking. By EMMA CONLEY. Illustrated. Cloth. Pp. 206. $0.52.

HENRY HOLT & CO., NEW YORK

A Book of English Essays. Selected and edited by C. T. WINCHESTER. Cloth. Pp. 405.

An English Grammar. By ALMA BLOUNT, PH.D., and CLARK SUTHERLAND NORTHRUP, PH.D. Cloth. Pp. 375. $0.80.

J. B. LIPPINCOTT CO., PHILADELPHIA

Daily English Lessons. Book Two. By WILLIS H. WILCOX, PH.M. Cloth. Pp. 293.

ORANGE JUDD CO., NEW YORK

Farm Animals. By THOMAS FORSYTH HUNT and CHARLES WILLIAM BURKETT. Illustrated. Cloth. Pp. 534.

D. C. HEATH & CO., NEW YORK

First Notions of Geography. By JOHN H. HAAREN, LL.D. Illustrated. Cloth. Pp. 154.

CURRENT EDUCATIONAL LITERATURE IN THE PERIODICALS

IRENE WARREN
Librarian, School of Education, University of Chicago

Baldwin, Bird T. The normal child, its physical growth and mental development. Pop. Sci. Mo. 85:559–67. (D. '14.)

Beard, Frederica. Ethical standards in the high school. Educa. R. 48:444–51. (D. '14.)

Cooley, Edwin G. Bishop Grundtvig and the people's high school. Educa. R. 48:452–66. (D. '14.)

Cooper, Clayton Sedgwick. Domination of athletics. Educa. 35:129–39. (N. '14.)

Cummings, Robert A. A study of defective pupils in the public schools of Tacoma, Washington. Psychol. Clinic 8:153–69. (N. '14.)

Hawes, James Anderson. The collegiate side shows. Educa. R. 48:433–43. (D. '14.)

Hayes, Edward C. Education for personality. Educa. R. 48:475–86 (D. '14.)

Hill, David Spence. Educational research in New Orleans. J. of Educa. Psychol. 5:499–510. (N. '14.)

Keech, Mabel L. House-keeping as a public school study. Educa. 35:164–66. (N. '14.)

Klapper, Paul. Efficiency in class instruction. Educa. R. 48:498–513. (D. '14.)

Phelps, Alice Starkey. What shall we eliminate from the high school course? Educa. 35:140–42. (N. '14.)

Pintner, Rudolf. A comparison of the Ayres and Thorndike handwriting scales. J. of Educa. Psychol. 5:525–36. (N. '14.)

Rapeer, Louis W. Industrial hygiene and vocational education. Educa. R. 48:467–74. (D. '14.)

Sanders, Frederic W. The organization of education. Educa. 35:178–83. (N. '14.)

Shreves, Rolland M. The psychologist in the class room. Educa. 35:152–56. (N. '14.)

Thorndike, Edward L. The foundations of educational achievement. Educa. R. 48:487–97. (D. '14.)

Wallin, Wallace J. E. The hygiene of eugenic generation. Psychol. Clinic 8:170–79. (N. '14.)

Warren, Irene. Teaching the use of books and libraries. Educa. 35:157–63. (N. '14.)

Weiss, A. P. A modified slide rule and the index method in individual measurements. J. of Educa. Psychol. 5:511–24. (N. '14.)

Wyer, James I. Text-books and some others. J. of Educa. (Bost.) 80:427–28. (5 N. '14.)

VOLUME XV NUMBER 6

THE ELEMENTARY SCHOOL JOURNAL

CONTINUING "THE ELEMENTARY SCHOOL TEACHER"

FEBRUARY 1915

EDUCATIONAL NEWS AND EDITORIAL COMMENT

The Richmond Conferences

Between the 7th and 12th of December, Richmond, Virginia, entertained the delegates to two national conventions. The first was that of the National Vocational Guidance Association and the second the annual convention of the National Society for the Promotion of Industrial Education. Of the first conference little need be said except to record that it bore evidence of an ever-increasing interest in the movement to make vocational guidance, in all of its different phases, an integral part of the public-school system. The employment of vocational counselors, the gathering and distribution of vocational information, the establishment of placement bureaus, and the exercising of employment supervision were all discussed and approved. There can be no doubt that the movement is gaining in definiteness and consequently in general support.

The eighth annual convention of the National Society for the Promotion of Industrial Education was unique in the meetings of this society. In the first place, it was more nearly "national" than ever before both in the delegates attending and in the speakers on the program, eleven states and the District of Columbia being represented by the latter.

In the second place, the entire program was based upon an extensive survey which had been in progress in Richmond during the eight months preceding the conference.

In the third place, the deliberations brought to the surface nothing but the most harmonious opinions, regarding industrial education, from representatives of corporations, organized labor, and educational authorities, and from legislators and social workers.

And finally, the conference revealed the growing influence of the National Society and also indicated the general lines along which this influence is to be exerted.

The Richmond "Survey" was made, at the request of the city of Richmond, under the direction of the National Society. The Society had the assistance, however, of many important organizations, among them being the United States Bureau of Education, the United States Bureau of Labor Statistics, and the Russell Sage Foundation, besides the following local bodies: the Board of Education, Board of Trustees of the Virginia Mechanics Institute, Business Men's Club, Chamber of Commerce, Rotary Club, Central Trades and Labor Council, Metal Trades Council, and a number of employers' associations.

The total cost of the survey is estimated at from $15,000 to $20,000. Of this the amount of $10,000 was subscribed locally for the expenses of the survey and of the convention, and the remainder was borne by the Russell Sage Foundation, which made the school survey, and the Bureau of Labor Statistics, which bureau gave the services of its expert, Mr. Winslow, and will print the final report.

The amount and nature of the co-operation indicated by these statements are highly suggestive and need no further comment.

The school survey was made under the direction of Dr. Leonard P. Ayres. The work contemplated the examination of such facts only as related specifically to education and to industrial employment. It consisted in the examination, tabulation, and interpretation of statistics already available, and the collection of certain information about the employment of the older brothers and sisters of the thirteen- and fourteen-year-old school children. This information was secured by means of questionnaires, submitted to the children in question, and relating to the kinds and conditions of labor in which these brothers and sisters were engaged and to the progressiveness or non-progressiveness of wages.

The school survey revealed the fact that Richmond, a wealthy city, was doing far less than most cities of her class for education in general, and little or nothing for the children who would profit most by industrial education. It showed that, while a well-enforced child-labor law kept children out of the factories and many other places of employment until sixteen, a very small fraction of these children remained in school after reaching twelve years of age. It showed clearly that the kind of education most urgently needed was of a prevocational nature.

The industrial survey was a more elaborate affair, though it is to be doubted whether it will be more productive of good than the school survey. Its purpose was to make careful analyses of several industries to ascertain all pertinent facts relating to the conditions of labor under which the industrial wage-workers of Richmond were employed. Among other facts sought were age distribution of apprentices, amount and cause of loss of time, extent of part-time employment, age of entry upon wage-earning occupations, relation of years of experience to wages, extent to which workers receive proper training in the shop while learning the trade, misfits in present positions, conditions causing strain or impairing health, and lack of *general school training* of present workers. This part of the survey also attempted the minute analysis of the processes of manufacture in several important industries.

A preliminary report says:

> Eight months' time was given to the survey, which was directed by Mr. Charles H. Winslow and a corps of twenty workers, of whom seventeen were men and three were women. In addition there was an office force of five clerks and stenographers. The field work required six months, during which time at least six people were continuously employed. All the agents were regularly employed, no volunteer help being utilized in this portion of the survey.

It would be well within the facts to say that this industrial survey was made with the full co-operation of organized labor, a most important consideration. Mr. Winslow is a recognized champion of organized labor as well as an expert on industrial education. In one of the most notable addresses of the convention, Mr. Samuel Gompers, president of the American Federation of Labor, said that, for the first time, a sufficient basis in industrial facts had been established to support a practical plan of industrial training. There can be no doubt that he intended his address to be construed as an authoritative indorsement of the whole Richmond program. This fact alone may be worth to the cause of industrial education all that the survey cost, and it will make it much easier to secure the indorsement of local unions to any plan which follows the Richmond scheme.

This scheme, which, it must be remembered, is supported by all the parties to the survey, includes a much more effective general education, the establishment of prevocational schools, vocational courses in the high schools, and a complete system of day and evening part-time and continuation schools.

In organizing this survey and in bringing together in practical unanimity the employing interests, organized labor, and the school authorities, the National Society has rightfully secured for itself a greatly increased influence, but this increased influence is coincident with a broadening in its own point of view and with the attainment of catholicity in its propaganda. In its pronouncements regarding the introduction of industrial education it has advanced from the position, held five years ago, that such education was a thing apart which needed protection from the narrow-mindedness of the professional educator, and now maintains that all vocational education is a local and not a general question, and, furthermore, is a co-operative matter which should unite all who are genuinely interested in child welfare.

And so the survey must be acknowledged to be a great success. It is not that hitherto unknown or unsuspected facts and conditions have been brought to light by the studies of the several experts. It would have been possible for half a dozen students of the industrial education movement to have foretold all the essential findings after a week's study and conference on the grounds, but the findings now have the moral force of well-nigh unassailable authority and, what is of even greater importance, the testimony of all these experts points inevitably to the logic of the solution recommended by the survey committee and shows that, to be successful, any plan must adequately represent the worker, the employer, and the teacher, and must be adjusted to local conditions of industry and of the present public-school system.

Frank M. Leavitt

University of Chicago

The Meeting of Section L of the American Association for the Advancement of Science

The meeting of the Education Section during the Christmas holidays at Philadelphia showed a remarkable growth in the scientific study of education since the time this section was founded a few years ago. There was a very large attendance at most of the sessions and the papers which were offered were numerous and in the main of high character. In the three days of the meeting there were 48 papers and two general addresses. Besides the separate meetings of this section there were two joint meetings, one with the American Psychological Association and one with the American Federation of Teachers of the Mathematical and Natural Sciences.

Not only the attendance and the number of papers, but also the character of the papers was of great significance. The majority of the discussions consisted in either reports of scientific investigations or critical discussions of experimentation. Two groups of papers were especially prominent. The one was concerned with the development of tests either of mental ability or of efficiency in some phase of school work. The interest in tests as a means of measuring the product of education as reflected in these meetings is very widespread and intense. This was reflected not merely in the account of new tests, or in the application of tests, but also in certain critical discussions. It becomes apparent that the principles which govern the reliability of such scientific means of measurement become of great importance, as these tests are used by a wider group of people. If tests are used without an appreciation of the errors which are possible, there is danger that an exaggerated opinion of the value of the results will be held. It is therefore appropriate that certain of the papers of the meeting had as their aim the effort to determine the exact reliability of the results obtained by tests.

Another large section of the meeting was concerned with the study and education of exceptional children. Investigations in this field are still concerned mainly with the backward child in spite of the fact which is theoretically recognized that the superior child is of greater importance than the deficient child. The deficient child, however, awakens the greater attention because his failure to adapt himself to the work of the school is the more evident. The superior child finds no difficulty in keeping up with his grade in the school and the fact that he is wasting opportunity because his capacities are not fully made use of does not particularly strike the attention of the teacher or the administrator.

In addition to these general types of papers there were some upon the subject of methods of teaching or concerned with methods of learning in general or in particular subjects of the school.

There would not be space to give even a summary account of the individual papers, but a few may be taken as illustrations of the general classes of papers which have been mentioned. A number of papers dealt with the description of new tests or with the investigation of the reliability of certain tests. Professor Yerkes of Harvard University described a method of the diagnosis of the degree of mental development or of intelligence which he calls the *point scale method*. This is intended as a substitute for the well-known Binet-Simon series of tests. It differs from that series in two main ways. In the first place, an answer to a question is not graded merely as right or wrong, but is given a weight according to the character of the answer. Thus a person may gain one, two, or three points according as his answer is of one kind or another to a particular question. Another point of difference is that the tests are not grouped according to different ages, but a child is put through as many tests as there is any chance of his passing and his total score is found by adding the points which he makes on each individual question. This takes account of the difference in the type of mental life of different children. A child may be able to progress to a high point in one type of tests and be low in his ability in another type. Such difference would not lower his score in the point scale, although it might by the Binet method.

Two other interesting mental tests were described, one of them a picture-arrangement test in which pictures of the type of the "Foxy Grandpa" series are placed out of their order and the child is required to place them in the order which makes a connected story. No words, of course, appear to guide the child in this arrangement. This test was described by Professor Fraser of Cornell. Mr. Trabue of Columbia described the standardization of a sentence completion test. This consists in a series of sentences from each of which one or more words are omitted and are to be supplied by the child. Fifty-six sentences have been put in order according to their difficulty based upon the response of school children to the test.

Considerable interest was manifested in handwriting scales. A paper by Mr. H. T. Manuel indicated the extent to which we may expect reliable results from the use of the Ayres scale when papers are graded by a single judge and the results are to be compared with those obtained by other judges. The same general principles would hold for the Thorndike scale. It appeared from extensive tests that if two persons measured a group of papers by such a scale there would be one chance out of two that they would differ by as much as a step on the Ayres scale. This amount of difference is equal to more than twice the difference between successive school grades. This paper was followed by one by the present writer in which an analytical method for grading handwriting was described; that is, a method according to which five characteristics were judged one at a time with a chart for guidance in grading each characteristic. Professor Thorndike in commenting upon the discussion said that undoubtedly it would be necessary to develop such analytical scales when one desired to do more than make a rough determination of pupils' standing.

A number of papers described the application of tests, as, for example, in the working-out of norms for college Freshmen or in the development of means of measuring the efficiency of children in reading. One paper by Professor B. T. Baldwin reported the application of the Courtis arithmetic tests to college students. Two papers which appeared in the same meeting were of interest because of the contrasting point of view they represented toward school tests in general. The one by Superintendent Bliss of Montclair, New Jersey, expressed a very optimistic attitude toward scientific measurement of educational products. The other, by Professor E. A. Kirkpatrick of Fitchburg, Massachusetts, Normal School, while approving of the tests in general, called attention to the necessity of taking account of their limitation or at least of observing certain principles in their application. He mentioned, for example, the danger of overemphasis by the teacher of the phase of school work which is the subject of test, of the danger of losing sight of the individual child in the attempt to bring up a class average, and of the fact that the measurement of results and the determination of average attainment of pupils in the school do not automatically give us standards which should be set up as ideals of attainment. In order that we may determine what the standard should be, it is necessary to know the social demand for the product of the school. With reference to the need of paying regard to the individual pupil he mentioned the well-known psychological principle that after a certain point in the practice curve has been reached further effort will be wasted. Therefore, if the teacher has in view merely the standard and not the individual progress made by the pupils, a pupil may be kept practicing long after the limits of profit have been exceeded. The chief aim as Professor Kirkpatrick sees it in educational tests is to enlighten both the pupil and the teacher as to the progress which is being made, and this is a very strong point. By the old method neither teacher nor pupil knew definitely what he was striving to attain, nor the extent to which he was succeeding. By means of an objective test both teacher and pupil may become aware of the change which takes place from month to month and of the degree to which the standard's aim is being reached.

An interesting paper by Dr. L. P. Ayres raised the question of the cost of educating the backward child. After presenting figures to show the number of children who repeat grades and the consequent duplication of work and therefore waste of money in carrying the same child through a grade more than once, Dr. Ayres made the point that the significance of these facts is not so much in the money cost of such repeating, as in the fact that the condition shows the need of an entire reorganization of the graded system. Dr. Ayres then showed the amount of overlapping in the abilities of pupils of different grades as exhibited by tests in number, writing, spelling, etc., indicating that many children of the lower grades have ability which is superior to many of those in the higher grades. This condition, he said, cannot be met merely by attempting to prevent repeating, but must be met by some sort of flexible organization which permits the different children to progress through the school at about the same rate of speed, but allows the better endowed to do a much larger amount and higher grade of work than the more poorly endowed children. He expressed the matter by a figure of speech. "We may assume," he said, "that the elementary curriculum is represented by a field of grain to be mowed. All the children, then, should complete a swath from one end of the field to the other, but some children will take a very wide swath and others a very narrow one." How this might be worked out in detail he did not say.

A number of technical papers dealt with the diagnosis of treatment of deficient children. One particularly interesting paper was given by Dr. M. P. E. Groszmann of the National Association for the Study and Education of Exceptional Children. This paper was of interest because it dealt not with the backward child, but with the various kinds of children who were superior or had superior capacities. These children, as Dr. Groszmann showed, require in many cases special treatment in order that their peculiarities or eccentricities may not produce some abnormality in mental development which will impair their usefulness. The children to whom he had reference are not merely those of rapid development, but those in whom there is some exceptional ability in particular directions which is likely to disturb their mental balance. Such children if given proper treatment will exhibit high ability, but if left to themselves may become cranks or even insane.

This report serves merely to suggest some of the more striking subjects which were discussed in the meetings. Many other papers of much interest were given. The high character of the meeting as a whole must be ascribed in large measure to the industry and intelligence in formulating the program and in getting papers which were displayed by the secretary, Mr. A. S. Courtis. The movement for scientific education is clearly growing rapidly and the time is at hand when such gatherings as this will assume the greatest importance to the educational world.

F. N. Freeman

University of Chicago

EDUCATIONAL WRITINGS

There is in England an active nature-study society known as the School Nature-Study Union. This association was founded in 1903; it devotes itself to furthering the interests of nature-study in the schools and to popularizing scientific studies. The official organ of the Union is *School Nature-Study*, the editor of which is Miss C. von Wyss, of the London Day Training School, and the headquarters of the Union are at 1 Grosvenor Park, Camberwell, S.E., London. *School Nature-Study* is published five times a year and its price is 6*d.* per number.

The School Nature-Study Union is publishing also a series of leaflets that are designed primarily for the use of the teacher. These cost only 1*d.* each if ordered in lots of twelve, otherwise 2½*d.* Here are a few of the titles:

No. 1. The Green Grocer's Shop and the Use That We Can Make of It.
No. 8. Tree Buds in Winter.
No. 9. The Nature-Study of Rocks.
No. 11. The School Aquarium.
No. 17. Some Common Moulds and How to Grow Them.
No. 18. School Pets, Their Wants and Ways.
No. 27. The True Inwardness of Nature-Study.
No. 30. The Esthetics of Nature-Study.

Many English publishing houses are turning out nature-study books now. Ernest Stenhouse's *First Book of Nature-Study*, by Macmillan; *The Aims and Methods of Nature-Study*, by John Rennie, University Tutorial Press; Scott's *Nature-Study and the Child*, by George B. Harrap & Co., are good samples.

Like our American publishers, the English houses are also putting out a good many books designed especially to help the nature-study teacher or the teacher of elementary science who does not want to attack the scientific books. Unwin's *Pond Problems*, published by University Press, Cambridge, is such a volume. The author endeavors to show how nature-study may use the pond materials and throw the work into problem form.

The author believes that it is only when the work is thrown into such problem form that it comes to have large value in education. As examples of the popularization of scientific work there may be mentioned several books in one particular field of nature-study, that dealing with the birds. H. B. McPherson's *Home Life of a Golden Eagle* is an exceedingly interesting study of the development of the golden eagle from the egg to the young bird ready to fly from the nest. The book is not voluminous—only 45 pages of printed matter—but this is accompanied by 32 plates—photographs of the animal's home life. A similar book by the same publishers is devoted to the home life of the osprey; C. G. Abbott is the author. F. W. Headley writes a book on the flight of birds which is the best presentation of the subject that has appeared, at least in anything like popular form. There are a number of plates illustrating the book that are quite wonderful. Then Bentley Beetham writes a very practical book on *Photography for Bird-Lovers*, in which he describes in detail the methods which he uses successfully in getting pictures of birds during all stages of their life-history. These four books, all from the press of Witherby & Co., are samples of what the English publishers are doing in the interest of nature-study.

It is very satisfactory to find that American schools are not alone in their efforts to use commonplace materials for educative subject-matter, and that the nature-study movement—progressing so satisfactorily in America—has its counterpart in equally successful movements in other countries as well.

Among the pamphlets referred to above the one on *The True Inwardness of Nature-Study* is by J. Arthur Thompson, one of the really great English biologists and a writer of eminence. It is impossible to give a summary of his discussion in so limited a space, for the pamphlet itself is an abstract, but an excerpt will make his meaning clear on one point at least.

> In our ways of prosecuting nature-study there is room for more of another quality which I cannot name—a certain humaneness and freedom. I stand by the heresy that a good deal of the nature-study and of the science generally of the school-days should be frankly recreative. Much of it is at present quite absurdly analytic; much of it is spoiled by an attempt to develop a premature grasp of principles, which is also psychologically wrong.

Now my point is that there should be more educational play and that nature-study is a good subject for this. The Germans have a fine word, *Abänderungsspielraum*—free play for variations—and we need this for the mind as well as for the body. And just as we must not inspect, criticize, peer into children's ordinary play too much, so we must not codify, rationalize, "examinify" nature-study too much. We must leave some room for unconventional exploration and intellectual adventure.

But let there be no misunderstanding. The last thing we wish to suggest is that we can countenance playing at nature-study, in the opprobrious sense of the word "playing." At times we must be as serve as the mathematician, as precise as the chemist. It is no easy thing to see clearly, to record accurately, to think scientifically—and unless we sincerely work toward these ends our nature-study is become as a tinkling brass or a sounding cymbal. My point, however, is that we are thinking this afternoon of the education of the citizen, and my recommendation is that we remember the need for a culture of feeling. Without losing hold on modern methods, may we not work back a little toward something simpler and less analytic—the old-fashioned but very real lore of the shepherd and the farmer, of the minister and the dominie in the country parish?

Another survey[1] which is notable because of the character of the surveyors and also because of the importance of the city in which the survey was made is that which was completed early in the summer of 1914 at Butte, Montana. This survey differs from the others which have been published in that it attacks the problem by first making a careful statistical analysis of the school population.

The first chapter, by Mr. Bachman, deals with the classification and progress of pupils. Contrasted with the Portland Survey, for example, the present report, instead of dealing with the general economic conditions of the population of the city, opens with a detailed account of the distribution of children in the schools. One is impressed by the fact that a report of the present type is less likely in its earlier chapters to command the interest of the people of the city. On the other hand, the material with which this report opens is perhaps better mastered by scientific students of education than any other single type of material that could be employed.

[1] *Report of a Survey of the School System of Butte, Montana.* Published by the Board of School Trustees of Butte. Pp. 197.

The second chapter, which is by Professor Strayer, the director of the survey, deals with the quality of instruction. In this chapter Professor Strayer has given with a good deal of detail the principles on which instruction should, in his judgment, be organized. The chapter impresses one as being somewhat theoretical, and the general question arises whether the surveys of various cities should be made the avenues for communicating to school people and to the local citizens broad, general principles of education. On the other hand, it may be answered that without the establishment of these general principles there is no possibility of judging the effectiveness of the work that is carried on in schools.

The third chapter, on the course of study, which was prepared by Professor Cubberley, deals in more detail with the various subjects of instruction. The tests, which were carried on by Mr. F. J. Kelly and are reported in the fourth chapter, seem to justify the contention of all of the contributors to the survey that the children in the schools are efficient in the formal phases of school work. They seem to be very rapid in addition and efficient in grammar and other formal subjects, but they are described as lacking in power of reasoning and in interest in broad, general considerations. This criticism of the children of Butte could probably be repeated for the children of most of the schools in the United States. How far one has a right to demand of children that they show ability to reason is a question that will remain open until investigation of many cities and schools can establish something like a standard for these more desirable and higher products of education.

It will be interesting to find out how far the present survey has proved to be a convincing document for the community to which it was addressed. The volume will serve as a handbook for students of education, and the many suggestions which it contains doubtless could be accepted with advantage by the school system of Butte. There is, however, much material in this report which is of doubtful propriety in a survey of a city. The scientific student of education will have to be on his guard lest he overload the reports which he has an opportunity to make with so much abstract material that the world at large will get the impression that he is making theoretical studies of education rather than practical surveys of particular situations.

The American Peace League has interested itself in a broad way in the problem of training children not only in the details of the campaign against war but in the general problems of community life. The members of this league have prepared a book[1] in which they have attempted to bring together the material which can be used in schools in giving a broad training in citizenship.

The early chapters of this book deal with such virtues as kindness to playmates and animals. The point of view is that of the home rather than the civic community. The second chapter takes a somewhat more comprehensive view of the school and the playground and deals with such matters as the childhood of great men, and the general virtues of obedience and helpfulness. In chap. iii, intended for the third grade, one begins to be acquainted with the neighborhood and to understand what is meant by neighbors and the possibilities of service to the whole community. In the fourth grade the town and city are introduced. Finally, the nation, general American ideals, the United States, and the world-family are presented for the different grades.

The book contains an abundance of references, so that material can be secured beyond the compass of the volume itself. The material is suitable for morning exercises or for class exercises, and many good stories are included in the text itself.

Superintendent Taylor has undertaken once more a general survey[2] of the activities in this country and abroad which are aimed at the development of vocational courses for children in the schools and in continuation classes.

Mr. Taylor remarks in his preface that there is no systematic treatise dealing with this problem. He attempts to supply what he regards as a deficiency in educational literature. He surveys

[1] *A Course in Citizenship.* By Ella Lyman Cabot, Fannie Fern Andrews, Fanny E. Coe, Mabel Hill, Mary McSkimmon. Houghton Mifflin Co., 1914. Pp. 386.

[2] *A Handbook of Vocational Education.* By Joseph S. Taylor. Macmillan Co., 1914.

the various types of industrial education in Germany, especially in Munich, and in Edinburgh, Scotland, and in some of the leading centers in the United States. It is, of course, a mistake to assume that these various school systems have not been adequately described. Indeed, in many reports all of the material which Mr. Taylor presents is available. The virtue of the present book is that it puts the matter in very simple and concise form within the compass of 179 coarsely printed pages. Mr. Taylor has touched upon most of the leading experiments along vocational lines.

Following the text are some forty pages including as appendixes documents of permanent value to the student of vocational education. Perhaps one of the most valuable contributions is the paper quoted from Professor Dewey, on p. 191 and subsequent pages, in which Professor Dewey, under the title, "An Undemocractic Proposal," opposes the bill which has been suggested by Mr. Cooley for the state of Illinois, according to which a separate school system is to be set up to give vocational training to the children of the state.

The problem of making scientific studies of school work available for practical teachers is one on which professors of education are at the present time busily engaged. During the last fifteen years a good deal of material has been accumulated in laboratories and in advanced courses on the different school processes. Some years ago Professor Huey attacked the most vital problem of the elementary school, namely, reading, and published a volume on the psychology and pedagogy of reading. That volume was criticized because it did not present the material in a sufficiently practical form. Professor Freeman has tried his hand at the presentation of scientific material on handwriting in a new volume[1] of the "Riverside Educational Monographs." The success with which he has accomplished the work must, of course, be judged by those who attempt to use his advice in organizing school work. The volume contains at all events a very large amount of practical

[1] *The Teaching of Handwriting.* By Frank N. Freeman. Houghton Mifflin Co., Pp. 156.

advice to teachers. The summary of scientific material is condensed and simplified so that no one can fail to see the importance and the character of the experiments which Professor Freeman reports.

The practical character of the book can perhaps be judged best by repeating Professor Freeman's statement of the way in which the movements involved in handwriting should be made.

> The form of movement, then, which best meets the requirements which may be laid down as the result of experiment and of practical experience is somewhat as follows: The hand and arm must be so adjusted that the hand progresses freely along the line during the formation of the letters and in the spaces between words. The hand must rest upon some freely sliding point or points of contact, such as the finger nails or the side of the little finger. When, on the contrary, the pen point is carried along from one letter to another by means of adjustments of the parts of the fingers and the hand, the hand continually gets into a cramped position.
>
> The movements of the arm and fingers should form a smooth and easy co-ordination in which there is a condition of flexibility in the whole member. The rotation of the arm upon the muscle pad of the forearm as a center carries the hand along, the upward and downward oscillatory movement forms the groundwork of the letter formation, and slight adjustments of the fingers complete the details of the letters. In addition to these chief elements of the movement the wrist may rotate to the side to supplement the sideward movement of the arm, and the forearm may revolve upon its axis in the movement of pronation as a corrective to the increase in slant at the end of the line. There is no good reason for seeking to eliminate any of these component movements. Each has some part to play. Moreover, room must be left for individual differences in their relative prominence and manner of combinations.

The last chapter of the book reviews the various efforts which have been made to furnish standards for the judgment of specimens of handwriting. Furthermore, Professor Freeman has worked out an elaborate series of charts which make it possible to analyze any specimen of handwriting into its elements. Thus the slant and spacing, the character of the alignment, and the form of the letters can all be distinguished from each other as distinct virtues or defects of handwriting. Instead of using a single scale to cover all of these different qualities, Professor Freeman suggests that teachers cultivate skill in the analysis of handwriting and the selection of particular defects to be corrected by special lines of attack upon each of the special aspects of the writing movement.

The first line of vocational education which was seriously attacked in the United States was the training of clerks and office assistants. The kind of training that was thus developed has commonly gone under the name of commercial education. It has for the most part been cultivated by private institutions. Only recently have the public schools taken over this work in any large measure. The elementary school has, in general, not included very much of this sort of work. A little bookkeeping has sometimes been introduced and the arithmetic of the upper grades has sometimes been described as commercial arithmetic and has been given a special character to meet the demands of those who are going into business.

With the development of the intermediate school and with the specialization that is now going on in the upper grades of the elementary school the problem of introducing commercial work into the upper grades is likely to be more and more vigorously discussed. Elementary teachers may, therefore, with profit look into some of the volumes which are now being prepared for those who are interested in commercial education chiefly from the point of view of high-school teachers.

In an earlier issue of the *Journal* Professor Farrington's volume on commercial education in Germany was reviewed. It is proper, therefore, to mention briefly a work[1] which has just appeared on the methods of commercial education in American schools, especially in the American high schools. This volume discusses with a good deal of detail the general principles of method as applied to business courses, and in Part II takes up business arithmetic, office practice and routine, bookkeeping, accounting, commercial geography, technique of commercial history, commercial law, economics, business English, stenography, and typewriting. Part III deals with the preparation of teachers for such work.

The careful reader misses in some of these discussions of method the maturity of judgment which has long been familiar in the discussion of methods in the conventional school subjects, such as

[1] *Principles and Methods in Commercial Education.* By Joseph Kahn and Joseph J. Klein. Macmillan Co., 1914. Pp. 493.

reading, arithmetic, and so on. At the same time, there can be no doubt that the methodology of commercial courses differs from the methodology of the other subjects, and it is well that this difference should be made a subject of explicit attention.

The time has passed when teachers are willing to devote any large amount of attention to the study of the history of education if that history is merely to be a résumé of books on theory. A history of education which repeats what Locke and Rousseau and other writers have said is relatively easy to prepare, because the author of such a book needs only to sit down with the volumes that he is reviewing and give an epitome of what each author has said.

Many students who have taken required courses in the history of education at normal schools and colleges have questioned the whole system of education of teachers because they have not been able to see the usefulness of any such historical studies. Gradually, however, the situation is being changed. Industrious students of history are finding material which is of genuine value to all teachers. It is important that we should know something about the development of the course of study as it has actually taken place in American schools. It is important that we know something about the mistakes and successes that have appeared in the administration of state school funds.

The collection of this kind of information entails, however, a great deal of research, and the ordinary student of the history of education finds himself handicapped because of the lack of material and because of the arduousness of the historical problem which is presented. There are so many local differences in different parts of the United States that any complete history of schools of the United States will involve the co-operation of many workers in different centers. It is very encouraging, therefore, to find that a new agency has arisen which is to co-operate in the collection of this type of historical material.

The state of Iowa has always been interested in its school system as one of the clearest expressions of the pioneer spirit which has dominated that state from the beginning. The Historical Association of that state has now put out two handsome volumes[1] dealing in detail with the history of schools in the state of Iowa. All of the agencies in the state that could contribute to the collection of material have been drawn upon, and we are promised subsequent volumes which will take up in detail other aspects of the school system.

It is not appropriate here to enter into any detailed account of these two volumes now at hand. Suffice it to say that they furnish an example which teachers in all parts of the country should set before their local historical associations with as much emphasis as possible. If agencies could arise in all of the different states for the collection and publication of an elaborate body of material of the type that is now at hand from Iowa, it would soon be possible to give a description of American education that would be of real use to teachers in training and of very great interest to those who are conducting present-day schools.

A very wide interest has been exhibited in the methods of individual instruction practiced in the schools of Batavia, New York. From time to time the so-called Batavia method has been discussed in this *Journal*. We now have a book from Superintendent Kennedy who inaugurated the system.[2]

This books consists of a series of chapters discussing various aspects of the system and giving an account of the reason for its continuance. The book is a description and something of an argument in favor of this sort of organization. Undoubtedly the argument would have been very much stronger if it had been supported by systematic objective evidences regarding the success of this system in the advancement of individual children. One misses in the book the type of material which has come to be familiar in recent school surveys where the efficiency of a system is tested out and recorded in objective terms. The time will doubtless

[1] *History of Education in Iowa.* By Clarence R. Aurner. State Historical Society of Iowa, 1914. Vol. I, pp. 436. Vol. II, pp. 469.

[2] *The Batavia System of Individual Instruction.* By John Kennedy. Batavia, N.Y.: C. W. Bardeen, 1914.

come when those who institute school reforms will find it necessary in persuading their colleagues to adopt their examples to give such objective evidence of their success.

The problem of keeping family accounts is not merely a problem in subtraction and division; it is in very large measure a problem of practical economics and a problem of mastering some of the devices that modern ingenuity has put at the disposal of the household. To rescue family accounts from the arithmetics and make a separate readable book on the subject was therefore a stroke of practical and pedagogical genius. Mr. Brookman's new book[1] has sections on house-furnishing, on reading the gas meter, on taxes, taking boarders, insurance, and other equally absorbing topics. Each topic is introduced by an explanatory text telling what is actually involved. There is a little mathematical work in each section.

[1] *Family Expense Account.* By Thirmuthis A. Brookman. Boston: D. C. Heath & Co., 1914. Pp. 98.

CLASSROOM METHODS AND DEVICES

Physiology and Hygiene for Prevocational Boys

In the introductory article of this series it was pointed out that the purpose of prevocational work was dual: first, to incite intellectual activity by means of a new and more vital interest in one or more of the regular school subjects, and second, to increase the pupil's potential occupational efficiency as an insurance against incompetency should he be forced into work at the earliest possible moment.

If properly conducted no subjects have greater possibilities in both respects than physiology and hygiene. Children of prevocational age may easily be interested in a study of the body and of the laws, both physical and social, which govern its development and secure the conservation of its powers.

At first thought it may seem unnecessary to present arguments in favor of introducing the study of physiology into the course of study when instruction in this subject is required by law in so many states. It should be appreciated, however, that physiology is seldom taught to the pupils with whom these articles are dealing, such instruction being reserved for the grades which they rarely reach, or, if given in the lower grades, being of such a nature as to make little appeal to the children of this type and to have practically no effect on their mode of living. Furthermore, where the subject is taught to industrial classes it is still in its experimental stage, which fact warrants a statement of our principles as well as of our practices. We would give briefly, therefore, the reasons why this instruction is peculiarly pertinent for prevocational pupils.

The study of physiology is, by its very nature, of genuine interest to pupils of this age, and this interest may be utilized in leading the children, not only to take better care of their bodies, but to appreciate the real value of other sciences which are more or less closely related.

The study of hygiene is perhaps even more effective as a means of developing occupational efficiency. Much thought, time, and money have been expended in developing courses of study which will contribute to the pupil's ability to take his place in the ranks of the world's workers. There are no means of evaluating this training in terms of increased efficiency, though careful observers have little doubt that such training actually enables the pupil to find his place in industry more quickly after leaving school and to fill it more acceptably. There must always be a question, however, as to just how great the advantage of this training may be over that afforded by the traditional school courses. But even a superficial examination of the facts will convince one that any improvement in the physical condition of the industrial worker will certainly increase his efficiency. Improper diet, unhygienic housing and working conditions, and any infringement of the laws of physical life result in a sapping of energy and a loss of time from sickness which often prove a serious handicap in the competitive struggle with those more liberally endowed by nature with strong bodies and by circumstances with more invigorating surroundings either at home or in the work-place.

While the efficiency and the period of usefulness of the workingman depends more largely upon his health than upon any other one thing, he rarely has any adequate knowledge of the effect which his mode of life and his surroundings have upon his physical health and strength. It would seem natural that the people's schools, especially those which exist primarily to secure greater efficiency in the future industrial worker, should devote a great deal of attention to a subject of such vital importance. An examination of the courses of study in the various industrial schools will convince one, however, that little consideration is usually given this subject. It will be seen, therefore, that any study or training which tends to improve the pupil's health or to make him more intelligent regarding the laws which society has enacted for the benefit of child or adult workers will possess real vocational value. As it will quite as certainly contribute to the pupil's culture, the study of physiology and hygiene is eminently suitable for all prevocational classes.

Authorities differ as to the best method of teaching the subject and especially as to whether a study of physiology should precede instruction in hygiene. Tolman, in his excellent book *Hygiene for the Worker*,[1] begins his preface with this sentence: "The teaching of hygiene fails when it is founded upon the assumption that a knowledge of anatomy is necessary."

Ritchie, in the preface to his *Human Physiology*, says: "Neither can the desired end be reached by teaching the rules of health without an anatomical and physiological basis; for without such a basis, hygiene is an intangible and an elusive subject."

There are many reasons why the course in hygiene should be preceded, wherever possible, by an elementary and eminently practical study of anatomy and the functions of the various organs of the body. Some of these reasons may be stated as follows:

1. Unless it is based on some knowledge of physiology, hygiene must be taught through mere memorizing and not through processes of reasoning.

2. To arouse the young worker's interest in hygiene without giving him some scientific knowledge of the different organs of his body may lead him to fall a prey to the first quack doctor with whom he comes in contact. If the technical and scientific terms are avoided altogether, the pupil is likely to be awed or unduly impressed by the first person whom he hears glibly using them on the street corners.

3. For children of the age with which we are dealing in these articles there is reason to believe that physiology will be more *interesting* than hygiene and therefore should precede and vitalize it. Dr. Peter Sandiford, in *The Mental and Physical Life of School Children*, says: "Curiosity about the mechanism of the human body does not awaken before adolescence, hence it is worse than useless to try to teach physiology to ten-year-old children. But physiology to fifteen-year-olds is one of the most fascinating subjects in the curriculum."

4. There are many devices for teaching physiology which make a strong appeal to motor-minded children. For example, the mechanics of the respiratory system may be shown by means of a

[1] William H. Tolman, *Hygiene for the Worker*. American Book Co.

glass tube, the air pump, and a small rubber bag.[1] *The Human Mechanism*, by Hough and Sedgwick, will be found helpful in dealing with the various systems of the body from a mechanical standpoint.

A study of such physiology as time will permit, together with the personal hygiene which quite naturally grows out of the discussions, leads logically to some consideration of "industrial hygiene" which ought to be of interest to all future industrial workers. It can be made especially valuable to them through the assistance which it may give in choosing an occupation, or, perhaps, in refraining from doing so. Such a study should seek to inform the children about their own physical powers, or lack of such, and it should also show that the peculiar advantages or dangers of a given position ought to be considered as carefully as circumstances will permit before any occupation is entered. Gradually the schools are coming to assume some responsibility in this matter. Miss Florence M. Marshall, principal of the Manhattan Trade School for Girls, says: "It would be little short of criminal neglect to permit a girl to train for a standing trade who has a flat foot." Letting this serve as a simple illustration of the two factors involved—the physical condition of the worker and the physical demands of the occupation—it is clear that a variety of data can be secured which the teacher may classify and present as best suits the educational and economic conditions of his own pupils. Further illustrations are given in one of the class talks outlined later in this article.

It is to be regretted that industrial hygiene today deals more with disease than with health. Since its line of attack is to abolish unhygienic conditions, it must necessarily call especial attention to the dangers and diseases which inhere in so many occupations. It may appear, therefore, that the details presented herewith serve as warnings to avoid certain positions rather than as guides to suitable occupations. It is sometimes affirmed that, since children *must* enter more or less dangerous and debilitating occupations, there is little value in taking this merely negative attitude and in warning them against doing so—that the more important thing is

[1] Hough and Sedgwick, *The Human Mechanism* (Ginn & Co.), "Mechanics of Breathing Movements," p. 169; "Mechanics of the Heart Beats," p. 138; "Apparatus to Illustrate Circulation," p. 152.

to instruct young people how to minimize the dangers and the harmful effects of their occupations. It must be remembered, however, that society is regulating more carefully year by year or even prohibiting the entry of children into dangerous trades, and is also seeking to reduce the dangers. The surest way to induce industry to ameliorate these unfortunate conditions is to put an embargo on the supply of necessary labor or, by other means, to render the practices expensive. The truth of this statement is amply sustained by the attitude of employers toward the "safety first" movement after the passage of a workingman's compensation law.

There is no economic necessity for this species of human sacrifice and the schools should ally themselves uncompromisingly with all other child-saving agencies in its curtailment or its entire abolition. Of course, for some time to come children will enter such occupations, and so the teacher should present also the positive side of the question and show the potential workers how to protect themselves in every possible way.

While, as above stated, a general interest in the subject may be assumed, it is desirable to vitalize or popularize this interest by some initial lessons intended to show the children the economic or money value of the proper care of the body. The following are suggested as sources of material for such lessons:

Bulletins of the National Safety Council, Continental and Commercial Bank Building, Chicago. There are hundreds of employers who are members of this council. They receive weekly bulletins relating to the prevention of industrial accidents and diseases as well as those common to all walks of life. The bulletins are posted in the factories or other places of employment for the information and guidance of the workmen. Membership may be secured by the payment of an annual fee of $5.00. A copy of one of these bulletins is shown on p. 306.

The Metropolitan Life Insurance Company, New York, distributes, free of cost, pamphlets on "The Health of the Worker," "First Aid in the Home," "Milk," "Teeth, Tonsils, and Adenoids." This fact clearly indicates the money value of preserving the health, and the pupils will find in the pamphlets much excellent advice.

The Sanitol Educational Company, St. Louis, Missouri, publishes a set of drawings by H. Reichard which show the growth of the teeth and indicate how necessary it is to care for them.

With judicious use, an advertisement published by Colgate & Company, Jersey City, New Jersey, entitled "Dental Hygiene," will be found valuable.

(Distributed by NATIONAL SAFETY COUNCIL, Chicago, Ill.)

To All Our Employes:

CONCERNING PNEUMONIA

The Pneumonia season has arrived.

Not because the weather is colder—Arctic explorers do not get Pneumonia until they return to 'Civilization.'

Not because of raw winds, though these chill the body and thereby reduce resistance to the disease.

Pneumonia comes at this season because people close doors and windows to keep out cold air, and thereby condemn themselves to breathe foul air in which the Pneumonia germ rejoices and multiplies.

Keep your houses as warm as you like. People in this country are accustomed to warm rooms, and it would be foolish to make a sudden change.

But see that the place where you live and work has as much fresh air as possible.

A closed window shuts sickness IN, not OUT.

As mentioned above, the presentation of such material as this impresses the pupils with the fact that it "pays" to keep well.

Another method of giving a practical introduction to the subject of physiology is to discuss industrial fatigue. In this connection the teacher would do well to consult Miss Goldmark's authoritative work, *Fatigue and Efficiency*.[1] Answers to questions like the following may be brought out in the course of informal discussions supplemented by assigned readings from a few reference books, in which case particular pages and paragraphs should be selected to simplify the work:

QUESTIONS

1. What is fatigue? (Goldmark, p. 22; Hough and Sedgwick, p. 55.)
2. Of what importance is its study to the industrial worker?

[1] Josephine Goldmark, *Fatigue and Efficiency*. Published by Charities Publication Committee, 105 East 22d Street, New York.

3. To what is muscular contraction due?

4. Can it be shown that this contraction of the muscles is a form of combustion?

5. What is necessary for combustion?

6. How is oxygen brought to muscles?

7. How is this oxygen carried in the blood?

8. What part in this process is played by the food we eat?

9. What are the elements in the carbohydrates?

10. What are the results of the union of oxygen and glycogen? (Goldmark, p. 22.)

11. What is energy?

12. What becomes of the heat?

13. What becomes of the carbon dioxide and other wastes?

14. What is meant by the fatigue poison? (Hough and Sedgwick, p. 60.)

15. What is the remedy for fatigue? (Goldmark, p. 25.)

Although there are no text or reference books just suited to the needs of the prevocational work in this subject, the following are recommended for use in the above and in similar lessons: *Good Health*, *Emergencies*, *The Body at Work*, *Town and City*, *Control of Body and Mind*, by Luther Halsey Gulick, and published by Ginn & Co.; *Primer of Hygiene*, *Primer of Sanitation*, *Human Physiology*, and *Primer of Physiology*, by John W. Ritchie, published by the World Book Co.

The practical phases of the question of fatigue may be made very real to the pupils by telling them of the studies of accidents in factories and their relation to fatigue. The results of one such study are given herewith.

It might be claimed with justice that eternal vigilance is the price of safety in some industries. It is necessary that the operative come to his work with mind alert and muscles under good control. That he fails to present himself in this condition accounts for many industrial accidents, as the following will show:

Statistics covering accidents in the factories of Illinois for a period of one year show that between the hours of eight and nine o'clock in the morning there were 120 accidents, and that this number steadily and progressively increased until, during the hour between eleven o'clock and noon, 257 accidents were recorded. In the hour following the noon rest, or between one and two o'clock, there were 111, the number again increasing hour by hour until, between four and five o'clock, the maximum of 260 accidents was reached. The most reasonable conclusion is that fatigue is responsible for the increase in the number of accidents in the late hours over the number in the early hours and raises the question why the first morning hour should not show a much lower record than it does. The difference between the early morning hour and the early afternoon hour is comparatively slight, but it is highly significant in that it points to possible personal negligence on the part of the operatives between five o'clock in the afternoon and the beginning of work the next morning. It brings to the front the subject of social conditions in general, opens the questions of personal hygiene in its relation to sleeping-quarters, habits of eating, drinking, smoking, and to the nature of such recreation as may have been taken.

In this connection it is perfectly feasible to teach the pupils something about the workingmen's compensation laws. While this may not be "hygiene," it grows directly out of "industrial hygiene," as it is a part of that movement which society is making to conserve the human element entering as such an important factor into the industrial problem. The whole "safety-first" movement is the result of this interest in conserving human life; and valuable material can generally be obtained from large manufacturing establishments where the movement has been placed in charge of one individual charged with the responsibility of reducing accidents.

This may seem a rather difficult subject for the children of prevocational age but, in reality, is it more so than much of the technical grammar and abstract mathematics which we have required children of this age to study? Does it not come nearer to life, as they know it, than much of the history and geography? And is it not the only possible foundation for such practical sociology and citizenship as the young industrial worker can possibly grasp? Concrete material for the discussion of this question can be had from many sources, but the bulletins of the American Association for Labor Legislation will be found sufficiently suggestive for the interested teacher.

In addition to the informaton which the pupils gain from text and reference books, from what may be called commercial material, and from personal observation, it will be necessary for the teacher to give class talks himself or to secure, from time to time, the voluntary assistance of men and women from the field. As an example of the kind of discussions which will be found interesting and valuable the two following are submitted.[1] They are adapted from Tolman's *Hygiene for the Worker.*

WHAT KIND OF POSITION SHOULD I SEEK?

Before taking any position the young worker should first submit to a thorough medical examination, such as is given in many schools today. This would furnish data regarding eyes, ears, chest, nose, throat, lungs, kidneys, back, hips, legs, and feet. If the individual is flat- or narrow-chested or afflicted with catarrhal or bronchial troubles, he should not work at file-cutting, painting, glass and metal grinding and polishing, stone-cutting, paper-hanging, gilding, some kinds of woodworking, grinding and cutting of mother-of-pearl and bone, nor in earthenware and china factories, because of the harmful dusts resulting from the processes employed in these industries. Neither should one seek employment as cigar-maker, tailor, shoemaker, engraver, or jeweler, because of the stooping position which must be taken in such work, thus cramping the lungs. Such persons should seek out-of-doors employment as far as possible.

Persons whose hearts are weak should not engage in occupations involving great strain upon this organ. They should not take work where there is much lifting or carrying of heavy loads, or where there is a constant strain on certain sets of muscles. Such persons are not physically fitted to become bakers, brewers, butchers, coopers, metal-grinders, millers, carpenters, weavers, stone masons, or machine-operators. They should engage in some light muscular work, but never neglect daily exercise.

Those having weak or inflamed eyes should avoid dusty trades, or those in which one comes in contact with heat, steam, vapors, and fumes. Persons who have vision in only one eye should not select an occupation where they are obliged to make accurate measurements on fine work requiring great care. Watchmakers, engravers, tailors, dressmakers, chemists, and draftsmen all require good eyesight, as the strain on their eyes is greater than in most other trades.

[1] Additional material of this nature may be found in such references as the following: Sir Thomas Oliver, *Dangerous Trades* (London: Murray); William H. Tolman, *Safety* (Harper & Brothers); George H. Ireland, *The Preventable Causes of Disease, Injury and Death in American Manufactories and Work-Houses* (American Public Health Association).

Persons who have broken-down arches or who suffer from varicose veins should not select occupations where they are obliged to stand for hours at a time. They should not become motormen, conductors, or bakers, nor seek work in stores or laundries.

Bricklayers, tanners, and butchers are subject to skin diseases through the handling of cement, hides, and much hot water. Persons afflicted with any inflammation of the skin should not engage in these occupations. Those who are liable to suffer from eczema should be careful not to come in contact with acids, dyestuffs, and other materials which might increase the trouble and make it necessary to give up the work entirely. Such persons are not fitted to become bakers, bricklayers, painters, lacquerers, polishers, cooks, or laundry-workers, or to do any work where the hands are kept long in water.

Persons whose hands perspire freely cannot do good work as engravers, watchmakers, fine-instrument makers, or as workers in any of the fine metals. They are particularly unfitted for the handling of delicate materials, such as laces and linens, and for such fine, clean handwork as millinery, embroidery, sewing, bookbinding, and fine leatherwork.

Industrial Poisoning

Industrial hygiene treats also of the various industrial "poisons" and of how to protect the worker from their harmful effects. One illustration only will be given here, namely, lead poisoning.

Of all the metals employed in the arts and industries, none is so widely and generally applicable as lead. Potters, cutlers, file-cutters, glaziers, lead-workers, painters, operators in electric works, typographers, plumbers, glass-workers, earthenware- and tile-makers, lead-foil-makers, shoe-finishers, employees in mirror and silvering works, some chemical workers, and those who wash lead-workers' clothing are all subject to lead poisoning.

Lead is a subtle poison. Most of its salts have no unpleasant taste or odor, are easily soluble, and produce their baneful effects so gradually and insidiously that the worker often becomes seriously ill without any preliminary warning. The symptoms need not be discussed here, but the way or ways in which the poison enters the human system and the means which may be taken to safeguard the worker will be noted briefly.

The metal gains an entrance to the body through the respiratory organs, the digestive canal, or, occasionally, the skin. Inhaled as dust, it is drawn into the respiratory passages, where it is dissolved and passed into the blood, or it may be suspended in the saliva and swallowed. On reaching the stomach it is acted upon by the hydrochloric acid of the gastric juice, converted into a soluble salt, and absorbed.

To prevent lead poisoning the worker should keep himself in as good general condition as possible, exercise care in the selection of food, avoiding acid fruits and using plenty of milk, come to his work with his stomach well filled, and especially practice rigid cleanliness on leaving the works and before eating. A few months ago the Pullman Company, by the simple expedient of compelling the employees to bathe their hands and faces in hot water for ten minutes, both before luncheon and before going home, reduced its cases of incipient lead poisoning among its painters from seventy-five to none. One white-lead manufacturer advocates giving a free breakfast to the operatives before the beginning of the day's work, while a certain British tile works furnishes hot milk free every morning. Cleanliness with regard to the clothing is also important. In Great Britain the employer of glaze-workers, for example, is required to furnish each of his men with a full suit of washable clothes and to wash and mend them at his own expense every week.

Conclusions

The most important and the ultimate purpose of all this work is, of course, to make good citizens. The employee often fails to see that he is a part of the great public which passes the labor laws and determines the efficiency of their enforcement by means of factory inspection and otherwise. The enforcement of state legislation for working-hours, proper water and milk supply, education of the children, sanitary tenement conditions, efficient health administration, is dependent upon the interest, activity, and intelligence of the public, of which the working class is a large and influential part.

The first and most important step in securing hygienic rights for workingmen is to make sure that they know the rights which the laws already give them. For example, the passage of the workingman's compensation law in 1913 marked a revolution in the treatment of industrial-accident cases in the state of Illinois.

Where previously the injured workman had been the prey of unscrupulous, ambulance-chasing attorneys, of unprincipled employers, and of heartless claim agents and casualty companies, today his legal status is definitely fixed and his compensation or his death benefit automatically provided for, and the field of activity of the lawyers, both reliable and dishonest, is reduced to the minimum. Mr. Samuel Harper, attorney for the Workingman's Compensation Committee, desires to give wide publicity to the fact that now no attorney need be retained by the injured workman, and also to the right which the workman has of appealing to the Industrial Board in case of dispute between the employer and the employee.

What the employee can do for himself as a citizen having equal health rights with employers he has never been taught to see. Perhaps the highest service which can be rendered to society by industrial hygiene is to educate the industrial classes to recognize unhygienic conditions, to co-operate with other citizens in eliminating them, and to secure the enforcement of health regulations. Where can this be done more effectively than in the schools?

FRANK M. LEAVITT
L. GRACE HUFF

UNIVERSITY OF CHICAGO

TESTING THE EFFICIENCY IN READING IN THE GRADES

E. E, OBERHOLTZER
Superintendent of City Schools, Tulsa, Oklahoma

The study discussed in this article was carried out in the Tulsa city schools after the teachers and principals had signified their willingness and anxiety to co-operate. The interest grew out of a series of grade meetings where the subject of reading in all its phases was discussed. As a result of this study the writer as well as all others concerned has received a new view of the subject and its possibilities. In the beginning the teachers were somewhat skeptical as to the purpose of the tests, some thinking that it was an attempt to check up the work of the individual teacher as a basis for determining his efficiency. However, as the work proceeded the purpose became evident, teachers and pupils alike entering upon it with a feeling that it was legitimate and profitable.

One must necessarily face many difficulties in such an undertaking. It was found necessary to change many minor details and to simplify directions. The value of the result of such a test depends largely on uniformity of selections and the similarity of conditions under which the tests were given. Such factors as the day of the week, whether Monday or Friday, the time of day, whether 9:00 A.M. or 3:30 P.M. were found to be significant. It was found desirable to have the study made as a part of the regular everyday work of the school and conducted by the regular classroom teacher in the presence of the principal. However, the principal must be a frequent observer in the classroom lest there be the feeling on the part of the pupils that something extraordinary is being undertaken. These factors, while they may seem minor in importance, are telling in the effect they have on the final results. Furthermore, the work should be carefully planned and discussed before the teaching body, so that the test may be given under "natural" conditions. Should there be evidence of coaching or an attempt of the individual teacher to "shine" in reporting results, the result will be unsatisfactory. By the person who has attempted such a study the difficulties spoken of above are fully appreciated. It may be said, however, that most of the errors are compensating rather than cumulative and diminish as the tests are carried forward.

It seems quite evident from this study that the child in learning to read is facing a multitude of difficulties without being guided by a definite notion of how to proceed. Methods of presenting the subjects, habits formed in visualizing the printed page, the span of attention, mental alertness, sense perception, vocal impediment, and many other individual differences are significant factors for the teacher's study and significant to the child's success in acquiring the ability to read.

The notion that the way to learn to read is to *read*, *read*, *read*, may be responsible for the establishment of many wasteful and careless habits. Reading should be constantly under the supervision of the teacher, both in the study period and the recitation. Lessons should be given in silent as well as oral reading, and the emphasis should be placed where the greatest advantage will accrue to the learner in adapting himself to his social needs. These and many other vital phases suggest themselves from the study herein presented.

The tests were given near the close of school. One building was under the direct charge of the principal. In the other cases individual teachers gave the tests as directed by the circular letter sent out. Some irregularities entered into the test which, in a way, affected the results slightly. On the whole the tests have demonstrated certain facts and revealed certain characteristics of the work in reading which are worth while emphasizing to teachers of reading. In all about 1,800 pupils were tested, distributed as follows: first grade, 350; second grade, 350; third grade, 240; fourth grade, 174; fifth grade, 157; sixth grade, 130; seventh grade, 165; eighth grade, 91.

DIRECTIONS TO TEACHERS

Get ready for the first test by having the children get out (1) the books containing the passage to be read and (2) paper and pencil.

Have them open the book to the page *before* the one on which they are to read. Tell them they are to read the passage in such a way that they shall be able to report to you. Do not tell them that you are going to time them. At a signal tell them to turn over the page and all begin together to read the passage. After two minutes (if you have chosen a passage which will surely last longer than that; if the passage is short, take a less time) have the reading stop, have the books closed, and have the children write at once the last words that they read. Now, ask them, for the space of twelve or fifteen minutes, to write what they can recall of the passage.

Second, try an oral test with another passage as though it were a regular reading lesson. Put your watch where you can readily refer to it, but where it will not attract attention, and note the time required for each pupil's reading. The passages in this case will, of course, be of different lengths.

The silent reading and the oral reading tests should now be tabulated for the whole class. Count the words in all cases and divide the number of words by the number of seconds required for the reading.

Try these tests with the following kinds of passages: (1) a familiar passage read sometime ago; (2) a familiar passage read recently; (3) a new easy passage; (4) a new difficult passage.

Repeat each type of test, reporting the first trial under x and the second under y. That is, let $1x$ designate the first trial with a familiar passage read long ago, $1y$ the second trial of such a passage; $2x$ the first trial with a familiar passage read recently and $2y$ the second trial, etc. Allow two days to elapse between x and y.

Find the averages of these several averages, reporting as follows:

Let $5x$ stand for average of oral.
$5y$ stand for average of oral and silent.
$6x$ stand for average on first trial of silent.
$6y$ stand for average on second trial of silent.

Make two averages for each child, averaging together those results which come from the silent reading and those which come from the oral reading. Thus, if in silent reading the child reads

250 words in 120 seconds, the rate is 250 divided by 120 equals 2.08. If he reads orally 90 words in 50 seconds, the rate is 1.8. The averages required are simple arithmetical averages. In making a table of results follow the scheme given below:

Name of school...................Teacher................Date.......

Name of Pupil........	Oral 1x	Oral 1y	Oral 2x	Oral 2y	Oral 3x	Oral 3y	Oral 4x	Oral 4y	Average ......

Average of Oral 5x Average of Oral and Silent 5y

Your principal will be given the selections chosen for each grade.

(Signed) E. E. Oberholtzer, *Superintendent*

The following is a sample of the results of the tests taken from average of grades:

TABLE I

Results of Tests

	Fifth Grade		Seventh Grade		Eighth Grade	
	Number of Pupils	Average Words per Second	Number of Pupils	Average Words per Second	Number of Pupils	Average Words per Second
1x..........	157	2.5	165	2.6	91	3.4
1y..........	214	2.3	159	2.9	64	3.9
2x..........	238	2.7	151	3.0	93	4.1
2y..........	231	2.7	153	3.1	87	4.6
3x..........	197	2.6	153	3.0	87	4.6
3y..........	172	2.6	153	3.3	72	4.4
4x..........	137	2.8	86	2.4	75	3.3
4y..........	139	2.8	105	3.0	74	4.8
5x..........	86	2.4	80	3.1	56	3.9
5y..........	63	3.1	209	3.6	25	3.8
6x..........	166	3.1	105	4.7	175	4.2
6y..........	139	3.0	81	4.8	140	4.8

In most cases the second trial with the same selection showed decided improvement. In a few cases there was a misunderstanding of the instructions, the teacher merely continuing the reading at the place where the first trial ended.

Table II shows the average of oral reading in a series of eight tests for each of the grades from third to eighth.

The following are the conclusions:

1. The difference in the rate of reading between the oral and silent method increases as the pupil advances in the grades.

In the first grade the oral reading is earliest developed and the child naturally depends on this means of expressing himself and of getting the thought. The rate of silent reading is much slower where he is required to grasp closely the content. This is perhaps due largely to the absence of vocal accompaniment and the auditory sensations, etc., to which he is accustomed.

TABLE II

SHOWING INCREASE IN RATE IN THE THIRD TO EIGHTH GRADES

	Pupils	Average
Third grade	250	2.1
Fourth grade	174	2.3
Fifth grade	157	2.4
Sixth grade	130	2.8
Seventh grade	165	3.1
Eighth grade	91	3.9

2. There seems to be a definite correlation of the rate of reading among the grades, the rate of silent reading increasing most rapidly as the grade is advanced. This is perhaps due largely to the child's being thrown more on his own responsibility; also to the fact that he realizes more fully the value of silent reading in giving him control over the printed page and in acquiring information. He has also ceased to practice the oral reading and begins larger utilization of silent reading.

TABLE III

	Oral	Silent
Third grade	2.1	2.3
Fourth grade	2.3	2.6
Fifth grade	2.4	3.1
Sixth grade	2.8	3.9
Seventh grade	3.1	4.7
Eighth grade	3.9	4.8

Table III shows a difference of 1.8 between the rate of the third grade and that of the eighth in oral reading, whereas the difference between the rate in the third grade and that of the eighth in silent reading is 2.5 (see III), or more than double the rate for the third grade. Two hundred and forty pupils were tested in the former and ninety-one in the latter. Thus it is seen that the rate in silent reading increases more rapidly than the rate in oral.

3. The rate of reading in all the grades is relatively lower than it should be if the habit of reading had from the beginning been acquired through conscious effort to improve the rate.

One room showed an increase of 50 per cent in the rate after two weeks' practice in rapid reading. These tests showed that oral expressions and the power to grasp the content were equally improved. Tests are now being carried on, both with the classes and individuals, in order to ascertain how far rate improvement may be carried and at the same time maintain a high standard in oral expression or grasp of content. Results of these tests we hope to report later.

4. Silent reading measured in terms of its usefulness to the individual has been sadly neglected.

Pupils must consciously strive to become efficient in silent reading, yet the teacher is the most potent factor in bringing about rate improvement. Much, of course, depends upon how well the child realizes the advantage an efficient reader has in the field of intellectual attainment or practical achievement.

5. The efficiency of reading, like writing, is very largely the result of the kinds of habits acquired in the early grades.

The child when he begins to read is prone to form many awkward and wasteful habits. Lip movement or any form of vocal accompaniment is a hindrance in rapid reading. Practice in enlarging the unit in the span of attention, as well as in forming accurate visual concepts, should be given early in the child's experience in learning to read. Word-study is not reading; in teaching reading the sentence is the unit. The sentence method seems to enable the child to read more rapidly. The kind of habits formed in reading will determine largely the efficiency of the reader.

6. Efficiency may be measured in silent reading in respect to the grasp of thought with as great a degree of accuracy as expression in oral reading

Experiments have shown that the rapid reader has more power and experience in grasping the content—in fact the rapid reader seems to have greater power in this respect. By choosing a simple selection where a few definite thoughts are expressed, it is possible to measure accurately the efficiency of the grasp of content. This is a more simple process than measuring expression in oral reading.

7. Few children are good silent readers. The rate decreases in proportion to the strictness with which the pupils are held for the content.

Upon examination we were surprised at the very small number of good silent readers. The power to grasp content was also notably lacking. Thus the tests seem to reveal the need of more attention in teaching silent reading.

8. Teaching silent reading is a subject yet to be developed in our system, and one which will receive closer attention.

One of the most interesting things about the series of tests was the revelation to both teachers and pupils. An attitude of zeal and determination among the teachers was generally shown. In summarizing I shall say that the few statements quoted in the following are sufficient to show the attitude of the teaching body giving the tests.

Reaction of Teachers

(*Quotations*)

1. We do not know how to teach silent reading.
2. We had not realized the importance of efficiency in silent reading as related to the rest of the subjects.
3. We are going to emphasize the silent reading and grasp of content.
4. We will not teach oral reading less, but silent reading more.
5. The problem is ours. We will assist in its solution.
6. We have new interest in teaching reading.

Selections for Reading Efficiency Tests To Be Held Tuesday Afternoon and Thursday Afternoon

1B

I. "The First Lesson," Wheeler Primer, p. 38.
"Gyp, Muffet and Flozzy," Wheeler Primer, p. 121.
"Dolly's Bed," Wheeler Primer, p. 73.

II. "My Dove," Ward Primer, p. 47.

III. "The Duck," Ward Primer, p. 22.
"Out for a Walk," Ward Primer, pp. 27, 38.

IV. "Little Will," Ward Primer, p. 76.
"Three Little Kittens," p. 35.

1A

I. Wheeler First Reader, pp. 61, 62.
II. Wheeler First Reader, pp. 103, 35.
III. Free and Treadwell Primer, pp. 89, 32, 38, 30.
IV. "Ugly Duckling," "Three Pigs," Household Stories.

2B

I. Wheeler First Reader, pp. 25, 32–33, 44–45.
II. Wheeler Second Reader, pp. 9–12, 31–33, 67–69.
III. Free and Treadwell Second Reader (or similar selection), pp. 11–12, 13–19.
IV. Free and Treadwell Second Reader (or similar selection) pp. 88–96, 105–22.

2A

I. Wheeler Second Reader: "Rainbow Fairies," pp. 49–53; "Miss Pussy Willow," pp. 70–72; "H. W. Longfellow," pp. 43–44; "Ceres and Persephone," pp. 19–23.
II. Wheeler Second Reader: "Shoemaker and Elves, pp. 138–41; "Lucky Loaf," pp. 142–45.
III. Free and Treadwell Second Reader: "Hans in Luck," pp. 58–66; "The Queen Bee," pp. 75–80; "Discontented Pine," pp. 35–37.
IV. Grade Literature Book, III, "Story of Columbus," pp. 22–29; "Hans the Shepherd Boy," pp. 30–34; "Benjy in Beastland," pp. 39–48.

3B

Silent Test

I. Wheeler Third Reader, p. 145.
II. Wheeler Third Reader, p. 184.
III. Heath Third Reader, p. 143.
IV. Heath Third Reader, p. 226.

Oral Test

I. Wheeler Third Reader, p. 83.
II. Wheeler Third Reader, p. 222.
III. Heath Third Reader, p. 12.
IV. Heath Third Reader, p. 210.

3A

Silent Test

I. Wheeler Third Reader, p. 104.
II. Rational Method in Reading, p. 98.
III. Heath Third Reader, p. 205.
IV. Stories of American Life and Adventure, p. 26.

Oral Test

I. Wheeler Third Reader, p. 164.
II. Rational Method in Reading, p. 127.
III. Heath Third Reader, p. 210.
IV. Stories of American Life and Adventure, p. 9.

4B

I. "To Be a Gentleman," Heath Reader, p. 318.
II. "The Village Blacksmith," p. 102.
III. "The Forest Fire," p. 126.
IV. "The Little Brown Baby," Seven Little Sisters, p. 5.
V. "The Georgia Volunteer," Johnson Fourth Reader, p. 243.

4A

I. Graded Classics, p. 62.
II. Graded Classics, p. 45.
III. How the World Is Fed, p. 46, beginning with "Our corn crop," etc.
IV. How the World Is Fed, p. 73.

5B

Silent Test

I. Heath Fifth Reader, p. 80.
II. Heath Fifth Reader, p. 324.
III. How the World Is Fed, p. 7.
IV. How the World Is Fed, p. 274.

Oral Test

I. Heath Fifth Reader, p. 170.
II. Heath Fifth Reader, p. 316.
III. How the World Is Fed, p. 56.
IV. How the World Is Fed, p. 308.

5A

Silent Test

I. Johnson Fifth Reader, p. 7.
II. Johnson Fifth Reader, p. 236.
III. Thomas Elementary History, p. 299.
IV. Johnson Fifth Reader, p. 315.

Oral Test

I. Johnson Fifth Reader, p. 10.
II. Johnson Fifth Reader, p. 239.
III. How the World Is Fed, p. 214.
IV. How the World Is Fed, p. 317.

6TH GRADE

I. Story of Europe: "Sparta and Athens," p. 15; "Successes of Columbus," p. 278; "Growth of Civilization," p. 349.
II. Story of the English: "King and Parliament, p. 260.

7B

I. Story of the English: "The Field of Cloth of Gold," p. 207.
II. "Courtship of Miles Standish," Curry's Reader, p. 63.
III. How the World Is Fed, p. 163.
IV. Curry's Reader, p. 49.

7A

I. Curry's Reader, p. 143, line 131.

II. "Vision of Sir Launfal," Curry's Reader, p. 217.

III. The Advanced History, p. 250.

IV. Curry Literary Reader, p. 374.

8TH GRADE

I. Familiar passage read some time ago: "Great Stone Face," Curry Reader.

II. Familiar passage read recently: "Enoch Arden," Curry Reader.

III. New easy passage: "How England Is Governed," Carpenter's Europe, p. 76.

IV. New Standard Encyclopedia, Vol. III (Chicago), for a new difficult passage.

AN INQUIRY INTO THE DEPARTMENTAL SYSTEM

JAMES H. HARRIS
Superintendent of Schools, Dubuque, Iowa

In connection with a study of the Six-and-Six plan and the reorganization of the upper grammar grades, it occurred to me that it might be of interest to ascertain the attitude of the pupils of the seventh and eighth grades toward the departmental system which has been in operation in these grades for about three years.

I accordingly prepared a brief questionnaire, which was distributed to all the pupils of the seventh and eighth grades in our public schools. The questionnaire was as follows:

AN INQUIRY AS TO THE DEPARTMENTAL SYSTEM

Name.................................School............Grade ......
Date.........................

Which do you like better, one teacher for all subjects, as you formerly had it, or different teachers for different subjects, as you have it now?

State, in a sentence or two, the reason for the answer you give.

The pupils were given the utmost freedom as to the nature and form of their reply, and no suggestion was offered that could in any way influence them in their expression of a preference. The replies may therefore be fairly interpreted to represent the untrammeled and candid sentiments of those who gave them, and, within the modest bounds set by the questionnaire, the results may be accepted as trustworthy.

The answers of the pupils disclose the fact that more than 80 per cent prefer the departmental to the one-teacher system. In other words, the majority for the departmental system is as four to one, with a little to spare. The exact figures are as follows:

Total number responding to inquiry	462
" " favoring different teachers for different subjects	382
Total number favoring one-teacher system	80
Percentage " departmental "	.82+

VOTE BY GIRLS AND BOYS

The girls show a larger percentage in favor of the departmental system than do the boys. In this respect the replies give the following results:

Total number of boys responding to inquiry	222
" " " " favoring departmental system	170
" " " " " one-teacher "	52
Percentage " " " departmental "	.76+

Total number of girls responding to inquiry	240
" " " " favoring departmental system	212
" " " " " one-teacher "	28
Percentage " " " departmental "	.88+

PREFERENCE BY GRADES

In studying the preferences by grades we find that the eighth grade is somewhat more strongly inclined toward the departmental system than the seventh grade. This is as it should be, assuming that the system is an improvement on the one-teacher-for-a-grade system. If the eighth grade showed a diminishing percentage favorable to the system, it would be an indication that it was not standing the test of time.

The statistics yield the following results:

Total number of eighth-grade pupils responding to inquiry	229
" " favoring departmental system	198
Percentage " " "	.86

Total number of seventh-grade pupils responding to inquiry	233
" " favoring departmental system	184
Percentage " " " (nearly)	.79

There is thus apparent an advance of 7 per cent in the showing favorable to the departmental system.

BY HALF-GRADES

Studying the figures by half-grades, we find that the A7, B8, and A8, are approximately the same, the percentages being respectively: 87, 86, and 87. There is a slightly lower percentage in the B8 than in the A7, but it is not enough to be significant. The percentage for the B7, however, is only 69; from which point it jumps to 87 in the B8. It is evident that many pupils have not become adjusted to the new methods in B7, where the departmental system is first put into operation, and as a result the number of those favoring it is considerably smaller. It is evident, too, that as soon as they become adjusted to it they show no diminution in fidelity. The figures bearing out the above percentages are as follows:

Total number of A8 pupils answering inquiry............ 108
" " favoring departmental system............. 94
Percentage A8 " " " .... .87

Total number B8 pupils answering inquiry............... 121
" " favoring departmental system............. 104
Percentage B8 " " " .... .86

Total number of A7 pupils answering inquiry............ 124
" " favoring departmental system............. 108
Percentage A7 " " " .... .87

Total number of B7 pupils answering inquiry............ 109
" " favoring departmental system............. 76
Percentage B7 " " " .... .69

THE GRADES BY BOYS AND GIRLS

When we study the grade replies by boys and girls, we find the results given in Table I.

TABLE I

	No. Replies	No. Favoring Departmental System	Percentage Favoring Departmental System
Eighth-grade boys............	106	86	.81
" " girls.............	123	112	.91
Seventh-grade boys...........	116	84	.72
" " girls...........	117	100	.85
By Half Grades			
A8 boys....................	52	43	.82
B8 "	54	43	.79
A7 "	63	53	.84
B7 "	53	31	.58
A8 girls....................	56	51	.91
B8 "	67	61	.91
A7 "	61	55	.90
B7 "	56	45	.81

Taken by solid grades, we see that the boys advance from 72 per cent who favor the departmental system in the seventh grade, to 81 per cent who favor it in the eighth. The girls advance from 85 per cent to 91 per cent.

When we study the progress by half-grades, we observe that the boys do not take to the new system, or do not adjust themselves to it, so readily as the girls. In the course of the four terms, however, they show a more rapid transformation of opinion than do the girls. They become "converted" very rapidly, after they have once made the adjustment. The girls adjust themselves more quickly and in larger numbers in the B7 grade and practically "strike their gait" in the A7.

REASONS FOR PREFERENCE

The second topic in the questionnaire: "State the reason for the answer you give," elicited many interesting replies.

Table II classifies the reasons as closely as it was possible to group them.

TABLE II

Reasons Favoring Departmental System

	Improved Teaching through Speciali-zation	Change and Variety	Prepares for High School	Easier for Teachers	Seems to Shorten Time	Custom	Gives Change to Teachers	Getting Along Better through Having *Several Teachers*	More Interesting	Miscellaneous	Total
Boys ...	131	31	7	10	2	2	0	2	0	4	189
Girls ...	138	69	7	10	0	7	5	3	3	7	249
Total.	269	100	14	20	2	9	5	5	3	11	438

Reasons Favoring One-Teacher System

	Dislikes Confusion of Chan-ging from Room to Room	Gains Time	Easier to Get Used to One Teacher	Knows Standing in Other Subjects	Better Teach-ing	Knows Pupils Better	Accus-tomed to Old Way	More In-teresting for Teacher	Miscel-laneous	Total
Boys	12	15	14	1	4	3	1	0	5	55
Girls	4	3	11	2	3	4	0	1	2	30
Total...	16	18	25	3	7	7	1	1	7	85

As will be seen, 269 of the 438 reasons assigned for preferring the departmental system had reference to improved teaching through specialization. "We learn more," said several, "because the teacher can teach two or three subjects better than eight or nine." "I like different teachers for different subjects," said one boy (and he was representative of many others), "because they know their subjects better and can teach them better." This view of the value of the departmental system bears out strongly, from the pupils' point of view, the a priori and theoretical argument advanced by those schoolmen who favored its introduction. The experience and testimony of the children themselves confirm the view that the departmental system means a measure of specialization with resultant better teaching.

The variety, change, and increased interest that come from having several teachers instead of one is the reason that appeals to 100 of those who favor the departmental system. This reason is expressed in various ways, but it usually falls back upon two forms: either they feel relief from the monotony of one teacher all the time, or they assert their liking and preference for several teachers as over against one, because it gives variety and affords change. It is not unlikely that the three who assert that it is "more interesting" to have several teachers than only one, and the two who say that it seems to "shorten the day," have the thought of variety in mind, but there was not enough certainty to justify classification under that head. The same thing is possibly true with regard to the five who prefer the departmental system because they can "get along better with several teachers than with one." On the other hand, this last-named reason may refer to "getting along" in studies and may properly be classified under "improved teaching." However, they have been listed as separate reasons in lieu of any positive means of identification.

That the departmental system means more effective teaching and gives greater variety and interest to school life is amply sustained by the responses of the pupils. Sixty-one per cent assign "improved teaching" as the reason for their preference and 22 per cent assign "variety and change." Grouping them, we find that these two reasons include 83 per cent of the replies.

It was noticeable that only 14 of the 438 assigned as the reason for their preference the better introduction to the high school afforded by the departmental system. In theoretical arguments for the departmental system this point is prominently stressed—and rightly so—but with the pupils themselves it involved an anticipation of experience which naturally did not occur to many of them.

Twenty are of a distinctly altruistic type and prefer the departmental system, not because it is of advantage to themselves, but because it is "easier for the teacher"! May their consideration for their teachers never falter! Five others have the teacher's comfort in mind when they give as their reason, "it gives change and variety to the teacher." These twenty-five have at least kindly hearts!

REASONS FOR PREFERRING ONE-TEACHER SYSTEM

Of the 85 reasons given for preferring the one-teacher system, 25 (29 per cent) named the fact that is was easier to get used to one teacher than to several. There is, of course, something to be said for this point—at least from the side of the pupil. Again, 18 were of the opinion that the one-teacher system was preferable because it saved time. Time is lost, according to them, in the movement of classes from one room to another. This parsimonious attitude toward time, in the light of the reckless way in which most young people of that age squander it, is a curious phenomenon. Allied closely with the time loss involved in moving from room to room, is the point made by 16 pupils that it also caused confusion and disturbance, and for that reason the one-teacher system was to be preferred.

Seven thought better teaching resulted from the one-teacher system—just the reverse of the argument offered by 61 per cent of those who favored the departmental system. Another group of 7 preferred the one-teacher system because it enabled the teacher to know her pupils better. There is doubtless an element of legitimacy in this reason.

The group of 85 who favored the one-teacher system were evidently not interested in the teacher's comfort or happiness, for only one considered the question from her point of view, and his only comment was that he thought the one-teacher system was "more interesting for the teacher."

The remaining ten reasons were of a heterogeneous nature and no classification of them was possible.

Many of the replies had an element of originality and humor in them, and a few of the choice ones are here reproduced. In expressing her preference for the departmental system, one girl said, "I would rather have three teachers than one because when you get into business you may have more than one 'boss' and you will be used to it because you had more than one teacher, and a person can learn more with different teachers because you get tired of seeing the same teacher every day and all day that you don't feel like studying."

A boy who felt that the departmental system involved a loss of time expressed himself as follows: "I prefer one teacher for all subjects, because in passing from one room to another we lose time and have to rush to make up this at the end of the term."

Another boy in giving his reasons for preferring different teachers for different subjects, said, "My reason is that it is nicer to hear different teachers' voices during school time."

"I like different teachers for different subjects," said still another boy, "because it makes the day shorter"—certainly a desirable result if it can be achieved!

Here is a young lady who got into deep water in her reply, but managed to drag herself out in the last sentence. "My reason is," she says, "for liking different teachers for different subjects, that I think I can learn better, and that they are more strict than the teacher I always have, and I like this better. Not saying the teacher I always have is not strict."

The girl next quoted expresses her reason in both a positive and a negative manner. "The reason I would like different teachers," she says, "is because we might learn more, or if we had one teacher why maybe we might not learn as much."

Here is a boy who has a curious notion of what one teacher is doing when a class is reciting to another. "I like different teachers for different subjects," he says, "because it gives our teacher time to mark papers while we are in the other rooms."

Next comes a boy who likes music, for he says, "I like different teachers for different subjects because in Miss M.'s room she has a piano, and for history it don't make much difference."

That the departmental system makes for variety and interest is expressed rather forcibly in several instances. One girl says, "It is kind of dreary having one teacher all day." Another one says, "It gets me tired to have one teacher all day." "We get tired," says another, "of being under the same control all day."

Here's a boy who evidently thinks the teacher who teaches all subjects is in a sadly distracted state. "I like different teachers," he says, "because one teacher doesn't know which study we need the most."

CONCLUSION

In conclusion it may be said that the advantages theoretically assumed by schoolmen for the departmental system have been abundantly confirmed by the evidence and experience of the pupils themselves. When 382 out of 462 young people, who are actually working and living under this system, indicate their preference for it, it may be accepted as at least collateral evidence that the system is successful; that it is meeting the situation it was designed to meet, and that it appeals to the intelligence and interest of the boy and girl of the upper grammar-school period.

The writer makes no claim that the data of this article are conclusive. The results of the inquiry are interesting and significant; they show how the children themselves feel about the system; they shed a little side light on the subject. That is all that is claimed for the inquiry.

CURRENT EDUCATIONAL LITERATURE IN THE PERIODICALS[1]

IRENE WARREN
Librarian, School of Education, University of Chicago

Barber, Fred D. The present status and meaning of general science. School R. 23:9–24. (Ja. '15.)

Bean, Robert Bennett. The eruption of the teeth as a physiological standard for testing development. Pedagog. Sem. 21:596–614. (D. '14.)

Bohn, William E. First steps in verbal expression. Pedagog. Sem. 21:578–95. (D. '14.)

Chapin, Henry Dwight. What animal experimentation has done for children. Pop. Sci. Mo. 86:55–62. (Ja. '15.)

Cooper, Lane. The teaching of English and the study of the classics. Educa. R. 49:37–47. (Ja. '15.)

Coulter, John M. The mission of science in education. School R. 23:1–8. (Ja. '15.)

Coursault, Jesse H. Standardizing the junior college. Educa. R. 49:56–62. (Ja. '15.)

Cutten George B. Moral influence of the curriculum. Relig. Educa. 9:520–27. (D. '14.)

Dodd, Alvin E., and Bawden, William T. Report on a plan for an elementary industrial school in the city of Richmond, Virginia. Man. Train. M. 16:271–77. (Ja. '15.)

Eckels, George H. The place of mathematics in the high school curriculum. Am. School Bd. J. 49:21, 58–59. (D. '14.)

Engleman, J. O. A survey of entrance requirements and recent tendencies in the courses of study of the normal schools of the United States. Pedagog. Sem. 21:532–58. (D. '14.)

Fitzpatrick, Frank A. The development of the course of study in American schools. Educa. R. 49:1–19. (Ja. '15.)

Hasty, Philip S. The present status of vocational work in the elementary school. II. Man. Train. M. 16:208–13. (D. '14.)

[1] *Abbreviations.*—Am. School Bd. J., American School Board Journal; Educa. R., Educational Review; J. of Educa. Psychol., Journal of Educational Psychology; Man. Train. M., Manual Training Magazine; Pedagog. Sem., Pedagogical Seminary; Pop. Sci. Mo., Popular Science Monthly; Psychol. Clinic, Psychological Clinic; Relig. Educa., Religious Education; R. of Rs., Review of Reviews; School R., School Review.

Jenks, Jeremiah W. University influence on civic life. Relig. Educa. 9:515–19. (D. '14.)

Judd, Charles Hubbard. The junior high school. School R. 23:25–33. (Ja. '15.)

Kayfetz, Isidore. A critical study of the Hillegas composition scale. Pedagog. Sem. 21:559–77. (D. '14.)

Kelley, Truman Lee. Comparable measures. J. of Educa. Psychol. 5:589–95 (D. '14.)

Kitson, H. D. Suggestions toward a tenable theory of vocational guidance. Man. Train. M. 16:265–70. (Ja. '15.)

Lanier, Henry Wysham. The educational future of the moving picture. R. of Rs. 50:725–29. (D. '14.)

Latham, Harris L. A study of falsehood. Pedagog. Sem. 21:504–22. (D. '14.)

Lewitin, Marie. The first Russian teachers' congress. Pedagog. Sem. 21:615–18. (D. '14.)

Lull, Herbert G. The relation of vocational to academic instruction. Man. Train. M. 16:201–7. (D. '14.)

Otis, Margaret. A study in the borderland of morality. Psychol. Clinic 8:201–7. (D. '14.)

Peterson, Harvey A. The generalizing ability of children. J. of Educa. Psychol. 5:561–70. (D. '14.)

Phillips, Byron A. The Binet tests applied to colored children. Psychol. Clinic 8:190–96. (D. '14.)

Pintner, Rudolph. One hundred juvenile delinquents tested by the Binet scale. Pedagog. Sem. 21:523–31. (D. '14.)

Pintner, Rudolf, and Patterson, Donald G. Experience and the Binet-Simon tests. Psychol. Clinic 8:197–200. (D. '14.)

Reuben, Milton Harold. An undergraduate's view of college education. Educa. R. 49:48–55. (Ja. '15.)

Rice, Melvin. The practical operation of school lunchrooms. Am. School Bd. J. 49:17–18. (D. '14.)

Russell, William F. Economy of time in secondary education. Educa. R. 49:20–36. (Ja.' 15.)

Scott, Fred Newton. Efficiency for efficiency's sake. School R. 23:34–42. (Ja. '15.)

Thorndike, Edward L. Measurement of ability to solve arithmetical problems. Pedagog. Sem. 21:495–503. (D. '14.)

Thorndike, Edward L. The significance of the Binet mental ages. Psychol. Clinic 8:185–89. (D. '14.)

Witham, Ernest C. School measurement. J. of Educa. Psychol. 5:571–88. (D. '14.)

VOLUME XV NUMBER 7

THE ELEMENTARY SCHOOL JOURNAL

CONTINUING "THE ELEMENTARY SCHOOL TEACHER"

MARCH 1915

EDUCATIONAL NEWS AND EDITORIAL COMMENT

A School Bulletin

The superintendent and the Board of Education of the schools of Kansas City, Missouri, issued early in January the first number of the *Kansas City School Bulletin.* The character and purpose of this publication are described in the leading editorial article, which we quote because it contains such a clear statement of a very legitimate social purpose that ought to be served by some kind of school publication. If other school systems would recognize with equal clearness the importance of keeping in close contact with the citizens of the community, many misunderstandings which come from school work could be avoided.

To the Citizens of Kansas City:

Annually the Board of Directors of the public schools publishes a report of several hundred pages giving in detail an account of all phases of public-school work. This report contains two classes of matter: (1) Statistical tables showing school expenditures and school attendance in detail. (2) Reports from the superintendent of schools and other officers of the Board of Directors setting forth the plans and policies of the Board and its officers.

The Board of Directors has long desired that the people should know more fully about the work of the schools. The voluminous character of the annual report and the cost of its publication render it unwise and extravagant to print these reports in sufficient quantity that one may be sent to every home in the city, and furthermore many of the statistical tables in such reports are necessarily dry, tedious, and uninteresting to the casual reader. Although each home is deeply interested in the policies and in the success of the public schools, many parents have not time for a thorough study of these complete reports, however valuable and necessary under the law they may be. In view of these facts, the Board of Directors in October of this year authorized the superintendent of schools to publish from time to time the *Kansas City School Bulletin.* It will be the purpose of this *School Bulletin* to give the parents and taxpayers of Kansas City brief summaries of the statistical tables of the *Annual Report* and of the articles of this report, and to publish from time to time such other plans and policies as may be adopted, and to keep the people more fully informed in regard to the work of the schools. The motto of this *Bulletin* is "For Increased Co-operation between Home and School." We believe that the home and school are striving for the same ends and that in fact the school is merely the agent of the home to perform certain work for the children that the home finds it impossible to do. Hence it is very fitting that your agents should report to you frequently. It will be the plan to publish enough copies of the *School Bulletin* to reach the home of every child in the schools. The Board of Directors, superintendent, and teachers desire the most hearty co-operation with the home. The superintendent especially in the opening number of the *Bulletin* desires to express personally his sincere appreciation of the hearty response that has come from the homes of Kansas City to all efforts at securing more efficient service and better school conditions. As will be told in the *Bulletin* from time to time, Kansas City has made wonderful progress in her schools in the past quarter of a century. There yet remains much to be done The noblest motive that actuates any parent or teacher is the desire to make life happier, better, and more helpful for the next generation than it has been for the present one. Such a motive eliminates self and lifts its possessor to a high plane of joyful service. You shall be told frankly of the achievements of our schools and of their possibilities. Their weaknesses and difficulties will be pointed out in order that you may help strengthen the weak places and remove the difficulties, thereby assisting in the betterment of the service rendered.

Educational Activity of the Department of Agriculture

The Department of Agriculture of the federal government has of late taken up a series of vigorous activities in connection with elementary schools. It will be remembered that Congress passed a law authorizing a much more general participation by this department and the related institutions in the general development of agricultural and technical education throughout the United States. It will not be possible to quote in full detail the bulletin which has just been issued, but the following extracts will serve to indicate the character and scope of the work which the Department of

Agriculture is now ready to undertake in connection with elementary-school work:

Mothers and teachers who wish to keep the young people cheerfully busy in useful tasks about the home or farm may be interested in a project of the United States Department of Agriculture for organizing farm and home handicraft clubs. Some of the arts and crafts in which the department's specialist in charge of club work for the northern and western states hopes to interest his boys and girls are as follows:

1. Rope-tying and -splicing.
2. Making seed testers (box, blotter, and rag-doll testers).
3. Making a hen coop and brooder.
4. Fruit-tree grafting and tree surgery.

. . . .

11. Sharpening saw, pair of scissors.
12. Making a medicine cabinet.
13. Making and laying a cement walk or floor.

. . . .

16. Drawing plan of 80-acre farmstead.
17. Forging—2 kinds, practical, related to farm work.
18. Welding—2 kinds, practical, related to farm work.
19. Horseshoe-making.
20. First aid to household furniture: (*a*) chair; (*b*) table; (*c*) picture frame; (*d*) door lock or hinge.
21. Pressing and cleaning a suit of clothes.
22. Papering a room.

. . . .

30. Show how to repair the cover or broken back of a book.
31. Art metal work for household.
32. Modeling in clay and plaster.
33. Leather work: repair of leather goods or art work.
34. Fabric-dyeing and -printing.
35. Pottery for use in the home.
36. Basketry for use in gathering and marketing vegetables and fruit.

. . . .

These are mere suggestions which have been sent out to different state and district leaders in the northern and western states. It is hoped this list will enable them to encourage lines of work that have an economic value in the farm and home management of any community.

The new clubs, it is expected, will be merely the agricultural clubs already organized among the young people and the new lines of industrial work will be taken up at times and seasons when corn, pigs, chickens, and vegetables do not need the special attention of the boys and girls. Under the new plan each club member will probably select about ten of the suggested tasks and do each of them during convenient moments. The results of the work of all the members of one club will be exhibited at the end of a year's time in a place where the rest of the community may see what has been attempted and may pass judgment on its value.

Any mother or teacher who would care to interest her children in any of the arts and crafts outlined above may write for further details to the Office in Charge of Club Work for the Northern and Western States, United States Department of Agriculture, Washington, D.C.

New Orleans Researches

A series of publications issued by the Division of Educational Research connected with the public schools of the city of New Orleans furnishes another example of the value of scientific work in connection with the office of a superintendent of a great city school system. Mr. D. S. Hill, who is the officer in charge of this division, issues in a pamphlet entitled *Measurements in Elementary Education* a study of the progress of children in the city of New Orleans. The relative age in the various grades, the rate of their progress, and other general information about the character of each one of the classes are presented in such form that each school can see its individual record and can make a comparison of this record with the general average of the city. The second division of the pamphlet deals with the educational laboratory, describing briefly its equipment and its purposes. The third part of the pamphlet deals with certain problems of industrial education.

Mr. Hill has also prepared at the request of the commissioner of public property a study of delinquent and destitute boys in New Orleans. This pamphlet gives in full detail the mental and moral characteristics of a number of boys who constitute a genuine sort of problem.

A third pamphlet issued by this division deals with the vocational survey for the Central Trades School and is entitled *Facts about Public Schools of New Orleans in Relation to Vocation.*

The Division of Educational Research in the city of New Orleans is one of six or seven such organizations in the leading cities of the United States. It is very gratifying to the student of education to see this movement spreading in all parts of the country. There can be very little doubt that the superintendent's office in every large city in the United States will shortly be equipped with facilities for the kind of investigation which is being pushed forward so successfully in New Orleans.

We are glad to give currency to the following notice sent out by the Barber Asphalt Paving Company, Land Title Building, Philadelphia:

An Exhibit on Asphalt

So many requests for literature, samples, and exhibits describing asphalt, its sources and uses, have reached us from primary schools, high schools, and colleges that it has been found desirable to prepare a school exhibit together with illustrated booklets especially for the use of schools. These appear to be used in teaching commercial geography. Apparently one teacher or school learns from another that this matter is available, and in this way the requests come to us, since we have never made an announcement previous to this that the exhibits and booklets were available.

Any requests for this material that may reach us from your readers will be gladly complied with. The exhibit and the literature are sent entirely without charge.

Sizes of Boards of Education in Different Cities

In the course of the discussion in New York City regarding the reduction of the large board of education to a small and more representative group, the Public Education Association of the city of New York has just issued a bulletin regarding the sizes of boards of education in cities of 100,000 population and over which reveals the following facts:

Twenty-three of these cities have boards of education of more than seven members, and only thirteen have boards of more than nine members. The common size is five. The tendency is distinctly toward the small board. In seven cases only has the board been enlarged, and in each of these cases the addition was small. In two cities, Chicago and Detroit, the addition occurred in the nineties, before the desirability of small boards was clearly recognized. In some cases, as in Boston, Baltimore, Cambridge, Cincinnati, Grand Rapids, Newark, New Orleans, Pittsburgh, Scranton, Syracuse, and Toledo, the decrease has been remarkable. The size of the board does not increase with the size of the city; the tendency seems to be for large cities to have smaller boards than the smaller cities of the group of 100,000 population and over.

The following table shows the sizes of school boards in cities of this class:

Size of Board	Number of Cities	Names of Cities
0..........	2	Buffalo,* St. Paul†
3..........	1	Albany
4..........	1	San Francisco
5..........	14	Spokane, Cambridge, Lowell, Memphis, Birmingham, Toledo, Portland, Denver, Rochester, Louisville, Indianapolis, Seattle, New Orleans, Boston
6..........	1	Kansas City
7..........	8	New Haven, Syracuse, Oakland, Columbus, Minneapolis, Los Angeles, Cincinnati, Cleveland
9..........	10	Nashville, Grand Rapids, Fall River, Paterson, Richmond, Scranton, Jersey City, Washington, Newark, Baltimore
12..........	4	Bridgeport, Omaha, Atlanta, St. Louis
14..........	1	Dayton
15..........	3	Milwaukee, Pittsburgh, Philadelphia
18..........	1	Detroit
21..........	1	Chicago
30..........	1	Worcester
33..........	1	Providence
46..........	1	New York

* In Buffalo, the commission charter recently adopted provides for a board of education consisting of five members.

† The schools of St. Paul are administered by one of the board of commissioners who appoints a superintendent of schools.

The following kindergarten letter issued by the Bureau of Education will be of interest to all who are concerned with the extension of the kindergarten movement:

Kindergarten News

The kindergarten is coming to its own in the state of California largely through the law recently passed by that state. The law provides that "upon petition of parents or guardians of 25 or more children between the ages of four and a half and six, residing within a mile of any elementary school," and with the approval of the school authorities, the board of education of the school concerned "shall establish and maintain a kindergarten." This law has already resulted in the presentation of 50 petitions with 36 kindergartens opened so far in 21 different cities, 19 of which never had a kindergarten. The legislation that accomplished this was the result of the efforts of the California State Congress of Mothers.

It is fitting that California should take high rank among the states in regard to kindergarten work. It was the Silver Street Kindergarten in San Francisco, conducted as far back as 1878 by Mrs. Kate Douglas Wiggin and her sister, that helped to give such popularity and celebrity to the kindergarten cause throughout the United States. The Silver Street School inspired the Golden Gate Kindergarten Association, identified in the public mind with its founder,

Mrs. Sarah B. Cooper. Mrs. Cooper's work, in turn, brought forth the first kindergarten legacy—that of Mrs. Leland Stanford. The first public lecturer to espouse the kindergarten cause was Felix Adler, who stirred Los Angeles and San Francisco in 1875–76, when visiting the Pacific Coast on a lecture tour. It is expected that California, now in the eleventh place among the states in kindergarten work, will, under the inspiration of the new law, move up to near the front, particularly because of the Panama-Pacific Exposition.

The exposition of Philadelphia in 1876 not only acquainted that city with kindergarten work, with the result that Miss Burritt, the "Centennial kindergartner," was retained there, but the exposition opened the eyes of the entire country to the principles and methods of the kindergarten. In like manner California at the Panama-Pacific Exposition will doubtless present a complete free educational system, including the kindergarten.

Illiteracy among Adults

Between 4,000,000 and 5,000,000 adults in the United States can neither read nor write, according to figures recently prepared from the census of 1910 by the United States Bureau of Education for the Panama-Pacific Exposition. There has been a notable decrease in illiteracy among children from ten to fourteen years of age, the numbers decreasing from 42 in each 1,000 in 1900 to 22 in each 1,000 in 1910. Most of the illiteracy among children is in the southern states.

The foregoing facts, together with the recent discussions in Congress in connection with the immigration bill, again raise the question of what the schools should do to decrease illiteracy in the country. For children between ten and fourteen years of age the problem is relatively simple. Adequate compulsory-attendance laws, rigorously enforced, will place such children in the regular schools. For illiterate persons above the compulsory-attendance age the problem is more difficult. Such persons are usually at work and find in the evening classes conducted in school buildings the only provisions generally made by the schools for instructing them in reading and writing. Such evening classes are in general voluntary and are attended only by the stronger and more ambitious among the illiterates.

In New York City an interesting experiment has been conducted the past two years in offering a part-time continuation course to non-English-speaking women at work in a clothing factory. The class meets in the factory. The employer furnishes the room and equipment and allows the employees to attend the class during working hours without loss of pay. The Board of Education furnishes the teacher and the supplies. In this case, both employer and employees are convinced that the factory efficiency of the employees is increased as a result of the class work, although the instruction is not vocational in the sense that it gives training in the factory processes. Instruction is given in English; simple hygiene related to the individual, the home, and the factory; accident prevention; and concrete civics comprising the relation of the employee to the employer, to the family, and to the community.

Similar continuation classes are conducted by the school authorities of New York City in hotels and settlements. The classes which meet in hotels are held in the evening and are attended by the hotel maids who cannot speak English. The classes which meet in settlements are day classes and are attended by night workers in the neighborhood who cannot speak English.

By thus securing the co-operation of employers the New York school authorities are carrying the instruction to the illiterate workers at their place of work. Such a plan seems necessary if any large reduction is to be made in the number of illiterates in the country who are beyond the compulsory-attendance age. At least one employer thinks it pays to give time for such instruction during working hours without loss of pay.

Religious Education

In spite of the war an international convention will be held in Buffalo in the first week of March. This is the convention of the Religious Education Association, discussing the topic, "The Rights of the Child," bringing one hundred speakers of national fame for its thirty different meetings on the days March 4–7. The association which holds this convention has members in all parts of the world and represents all the different faiths and churches.

Among the attractions of the convention will be an exhibit on child welfare in relation to education. Materials, pictures, charts, diagrams, gathered from all parts of the country, will be shown, illustrating present conditions and the best methods of providing for the proper development of children, especially as to their moral and religious lives.

Educational Progress in Virginia

The progress of education in the state of Virginia during the last decade is a source of considerable pride to the citizens of that state who are interested in education. In view of the fact that the population of Virginia has increased but comparatively little since 1905, the following facts indicate a substantial educational advance. They also probably give a rough measure of progress in the more progressive sections of the country.

Increase in enrolment	78,345
Increase in average daily attendance	82,345
Increase of state, county, and city appropriations	$4,025,386.77
Increase of high schools	427
Increase in salaries of teachers	$2,080,530.62
Number of new schoolhouses	2,412
Cost of new schoolhouses and grounds	$6,113,189.45
Number of schoolhouses consolidated	572
New normal training schools built	3

Of more significance than the quantitative progress represented by the facts just given is the qualitative progress indicated by the following list of new features introduced in the schools of Virginia during the past ten years: "School Fairs, School Leagues, Civic Leagues, Night Schools, Open-Air Schools, School Wagons, Industrial Supervisors, Manual Training, Domestic Science, Girls' Canning Clubs, Boys' Corn Clubs, Mothers' Clubs, Extension Work, Medical Inspection, Free Lunches, Industrial Surveys, Vocation Schools, School Inspectors, Schools for Adult Illiterates, Supervised School Athletics, Public Playgrounds, Literary Leagues, Debating Societies, Teachers' Reading Courses, School Gardens, Normal Training Schools, Agricultural Schools, and Classes for Backward Pupils."

The interesting fact clearly brought out by this list of innovations is that the conception of education has been rapidly changing during the twentieth century. A generation ago it would have been difficult to see the relation between public education and industrial surveys, girls' canning clubs, etc. The value of the school is coming to be measured by the extent to which it serves the community. The school is not an end in itself.

Comparison of Races

The *Honolulu Friend* reports a comparative study recently made on the grades of graduates of the three largest Honolulu high schools and grammar schools for five years to determine the relative standing by races. There were 804 graduates, of whom 251 were of American or North European parentage, 191 Chinese, 113 Japanese, 112 mixed white and Hawaiians, 77 Portuguese, 28 Hawaiians, 22 Chinese-Hawaiians, and 10 Koreans.

Of the 113 Japanese graduates, 30.1 per cent ranked A, or 90 on a scale of 100; of the 10 Koreans, 30 per cent; of the Chinese, 26.7; of the Chinese-Hawaiians, 18.2; of the white Hawaiians, 16; of the American and North European, 13.2; of the Portuguese, 11.7; and of the pure Hawaiians, 10.7 per cent.

The results of this test may cause the "superior" white race to ponder on the preparation their children are making to carry the white man's burden.

Industrial Monographs

A joint committee made of manufacturers is publishing a series of monographs which contain full information with regard to different phases of mechanics and physical science. *Monograph No. 5* is published by the Singer Sewing Machine Company and contains a full description of the mechanics of sewing machines. *Monograph No. 2* is published by the Weston Electrical Instrument Company of Newark, New Jersey, and gives an account of elementary electrical testing. *Monograph No. 3* is an account of the Edison storage battery. *Monograph No. 4* is an account of experimental electrical testing. These monographs dispense a great deal of useful information. Their purpose is described in a note in the preface as follows: "These monographs are intended to convey to teachers the point of view of men of affairs and the principles and facts worth teaching to students in each specialty."

The information will be very valuable to anyone who is interested in mechanics and in giving instruction to children in any grade of school. Some of the material is directly useful for seventh- or eighth-grade pupils. The rest of the information is of such a nature that it would be directly available for students in the early years of the high-school course.

Governor Brumbaugh's Report

Dr. Martin G. Brumbaugh, in the last report he made to the Philadelphia school board before assuming the duties of the governorship, recommends that the school system of the city be organized on the six-six basis with junior and senior high schools of three years each.

He also criticizes the schools of observation and practice used in the preparation of prospective teachers as made up of selected pupils and not affording real school conditions. While appreciating the pedagogic value of such schools, Dr. Brumbaugh thinks it would be much better practice for student-teachers to carry on their work under actual teaching conditions, and concludes by saying, "I hope the board will not increase or even continue the artificial and expensive machinery now used to train our young men and women to teach."

EDUCATIONAL WRITINGS

Two books[1] have recently appeared on school discipline. One is by Professor Bagley and the other by Miss Morehouse, supervisor of high-school teaching in the Illinois State Normal University.

The appearance of these two books shows that the problems of school administration are to be taken up in the future in more detail than has been possible in the general treatises on education which have been the accepted means of training teachers up to this time. A chapter on school discipline has been common in all of the books prepared for teachers and supervisors, but the appearance of whole volumes devoted to this subject suggests the possibility of subdividing the field of education so that there shall be special books on such topics as the promotion of children in the grades, the preparation of a lesson by the teacher, the organization of the study period in schools, and so on. The development of a body of material on each of these topics is sure to follow as soon as it becomes apparent that classifications of the type which appear in these volumes are helpful to the teacher in training and to the experienced teacher who wishes to formulate his experience in definite, scientific terms.

The two books in hand may be characterized by saying that Miss Morehouse's book is somewhat more general in its discussions than is Professor Bagley's. Miss Morehouse discusses the methods of school government in general. She then deals with the various types of disciplinary activity, with the different types of offenses, and with the punishments with which teachers attempt to check these offenses. Several chapters on disciplinary devices then follow which give help to the teacher in determining the methods of dealing with cases.

Professor Bagley's book, on the other hand, begins with a very concrete description of the unruly school. He aims to point out

[1] *School Discipline.* By William Chandler Bagley. Macmillan, 1914. Pp. 259.
The Discipline of the School. By Frances M. Morehouse. D. C. Heath & Co., 1914. Pp. 342.

the causes of unruliness in the school and then deals with the methods of treating this difficulty and describes in detail the various forms of punishment and reward. The final chapters deal with the characteristics of the orderly school and the types of pupils with which the teacher has to deal.

Both books make an effort to classify the cases. Professor Bagley gives in one chapter a very interesting account of the troublesome types of pupils. Here he classifies different pupils as stubborn, haughty, self-complacent, irresponsible, morose, hypersensitive, deceitful, and vicious. Each of these types is described in some detail and suggestions are given with regard to the methods of dealing with them. Any teacher who has had classroom experience realizes the importance of knowing human nature in its various manifestations far enough to realize that individual treatment of different pupils is necessary if their own advantage is to be gained and the discipline of the classroom maintained.

The service which these two authors have rendered in pointing out the detailed character of the problem of discipline is very great. The books are addressed to young and inexperienced teachers, it being assumed that they will find the problems of discipline most difficult to understand and deal with. Both books reiterate the general principle that there is no possibility of doing good intellectual work in a classroom until the conditions are favorable for attention to intellectual problems without serious distractions because of lack of order. Both books attempt to make the problems of the schoolroom subordinate to the general problem of instruction, and yet both books recognize the fact that it is quite impossible to deal with many of the cases that arise in school discipline merely through instructorial methods.

The first report of the General Education Board[1] is a descriptive summary of the work which has been done by this organization during the last twelve years. The report is a bound volume of 240 pages with many maps and illustrations showing the scope and character of the work that has been undertaken.

[1] *The General Education Board 1902–1914.* Published by the Board, 1915.

In the South the Board has been very active in developing first of all a large number of community activities which lie outside of the province of the ordinary school work. Experimental farming has been undertaken in a sufficient number of centers to furnish concrete examples to all of the communities in the southern states of the best methods of agriculture and of the disposition of products of agriculture. The boys and girls of the South have been encouraged to cultivate more intelligently the crops which are appropriate to their soil and they have been shown how the products can be canned and prepared for market.

As one reads the report of this work, he sees the grounds for the enthusiasm exhibited by the writers of the report. On the other hand, there is some danger of overemphasis of these types of work and their educational importance. The general educational theory which grows out of constant contact with these productive industrial experiments is likely to be an educational theory which depreciates the ordinary school subjects. Something of this temper is exhibited at various points in the report.

The second general type of activity in which the Board has been interested is the development of higher education, of secondary schools in the South and colleges and universities throughout the United States. Especially through the appointment of agents for the inspection and development of secondary schools in the southern states has the Board contributed to a rapid enlargement of the high-school opportunities that are offered to southern children. It has undoubtedly helped to raise the standards very much more rapidly than the communities could have done the work if left to their own unaided resources.

The giving to colleges has also been carried on with a view to raising standards, especially standards of financial administration. There is no group of institutions in the world with less feeling of public responsibility for funds than American colleges. The Board has taught many of these institutions how to keep their accounts and how to make reports that approximate the truth.

One sometimes wonders why the Board, which has been so insistent upon careful and complete accounting on the part of the institutions with which it deals, has never seen the importance of issuing a similar report of its own doings. The enormous body of funds handled by the General Education Board makes it a public institution in every sense of the word. It undoubtedly has a complete and accurate account of everything that it has done, but the public is admitted to its counsels only through a general summary of the funds which it has disbursed.

Finally, the General Education Board has done much to improve in recent years the status of medical education in this country. It has given liberally to a few centers with a definite understanding that at these centers medical education should be improved as rapidly as possible. The importance of this sort of benefaction cannot be overestimated.

The book concludes with chapters on negro education and some description of the experiments in rural education which are being projected outside of the southern states.

The preface contains a promise that other reports will from time to time follow upon this first statement of the Board's activities and plans. It is undoubtedly true, as the book states, that an earlier report would have been somewhat premature because the Board itself was feeling its way and attempting to find a proper sphere for its operations. A feeling of responsibility to the public manifested in a constant exhibition to the public of the activities and theories of the Board would be a very wholesome acknowledgment of the public interest in so large and influential an enterprise. It is to be hoped that later reports will deal in much greater detail with the work that is undertaken and will give also, in definite, quantitative form, some statement of the results which have been obtained.

The present report contains a large body of descriptive material. It differs from the conventional reports of institutions of this sort in the fact that it is a document which the ordinary laymen will read with great interest. But it lacks some of the precision and completeness which is to be expected in reports issued by great public agencies.

The body of periodical literature in education is so large that additions in the way of new journals are likely to escape attention.

Within the past few months two very notable additions have been made to the list of educational periodicals.

Professor Cattell, well known as the editor of a number of scientific journals, including the *Popular Science Monthly* and *Science*, has begun the publication of a weekly journal entitled *School and Society*. This new journal is uniform in its appearance with *Science*, and in its internal organization reminds one of that journal.

It has already reported in its first four numbers addresses by President Eliot, G. Stanley Hall, Commissioner Claxton, and others at various educational gatherings. It has given a large body of educational news from many different educational institutions. The discussions also indicate that there are many problems which are of importance to teachers of all grades. In general, it may be said that the appearance of this journal promises to give an avenue for immediate publication of important educational material from all parts of the country.

The suggestion has been made from time to time that the National Education Association devote its energies to a general publication which should appeal to all who are engaged in the schools and universities of this country. The National Education Association has for some reason or other not seen the importance of undertaking this work. It has remained for private enterprise and for institutions to organize all of the dignified educational journalism of the country.

One cannot help feeling some regret that *School and Society* is not the expression of organized interest in educational journalism. It would have been very much more appropriate for some great national institution such as the National Society to issue a weekly of this type. Since no public institution has undertaken the task, it is of the highest credit to Professor Cattell that he has seen the opportunity and acted on it.

Another new journal, entitled *Educational Administration and Supervision*, edited by Professors Coffman and Johnston, Commissioner Snedden, and Superintendent Van Sickle, is to appear monthly except in July and August. The first issue contains eighty pages and is to be devoted to the discussion of problems of importance to superintendents and supervisors. A statement of the purposes of this journal is given in an editorial comment as follows:

Educational Administration and Supervision will be a monthly journal covering fields which can roughly be distinguished as follows: (1) state and county systems of education, including rural education and also educational legislation; (2) city school systems, including chiefly problems of city administration, supervision, management, reporting, and educational statistics; (3) secondary education, including problems of organization, administration, inspection, curriculum-making, and internal supervision, management, and the pedagogy of the different subjects, and including also a consideration of those problems of higher education involving directly the interests of secondary education; and (4) elementary education, with the problems in this field analogous to those cited for secondary education.

In addition to these fairly distinct administrative fields there are those overlapping problems of vocational education and of school extension, the one including agricultural education, and all varieties of trade, of continuation, part-time, and evening schools; and the other including broadly the problems of school hygiene, of the school as a social center, and of the school's co-operative agencies.

The first issue shows the scope of the journal's interests by giving, first of all, a brief discussion by Professor Cubberley of the fundamental problems of school administration. The contrast between the interests of the community and of the larger unit of organization is pointed out by Professor Cubberley in the type of treatment which has become familiar to his readers.

The second article, by Professor Coffman, gives an account of the characteristics and the influence of the American school superintendent. This paper leaves a vivid impression in one's mind that the school superintendent is a factor of large importance in American education. He is a relatively permanent factor in school organization as contrasted with the teachers, who are much more transient in their connections with schools. He is at the center of the organization in a very influential degree.

The third article, on "The High School Issue," by Professor Johnston, is cast in the somewhat elaborate literary form of a dialogue between those who have interested themselves in the organization of secondary schools.

A short article by Professor Davis, of the University of Michigan, on "College Surveillance and Student Responsibility," exhibits the practices of a number of leading institutions with regard to reports and methods of dealing with college students.

Briefer discussions are to have a place in the new journal. Book reviews and editorial comments range in their topics from city charters of schools to discussions of the position of a superintendent as an educational expert and discussions of vocational tendencies in education.

The appearance of another journal which is to have high-grade, scientific discussions of school matters is an encouraging evidence of the development of a scientific attitude within the educational profession.

A little pamphlet[1] which gives definite suggestions regarding the measurement of various school activities will be useful to many teachers who are anxious to try out some of the methods of measurement.

The tests which have been performed by Mr. Courtis have come to be so widely known that it is unnecessary to comment on the possibility at the present time of securing test material from that source. The current articles in most of the educational journals make suggestions as to other methods of testing. The scales of handwriting prepared by Professor Thorndike, Mr. Ayres, and Professor Freeman, all make it clear that teachers are utilizing standardized tests much more frequently than they did a few years ago.

Professor Starch's contribution to this sort of work lies in the fact that he has brought together tests in reading, English, and spelling, these being perhaps the most difficult phases of school work to test, and undoubtedly the most important phases from the point of view of the elementary school. A great deal of work has been done in spelling and that is perhaps the line of work which can be most easily measured of any in the elementary school. Reading and English are very baffling because of the complexity of the problems which they present.

[1] *The Measurement of Efficiency in Reading, Writing, Spelling and English.* By Daniel Starch. The College Book Store, Madison, Wis., 1914. Pp. 33.

This *Journal* has made an effort during the last year to bring together as much material as possible on reading tests, and Professor Starch's work will be a welcome addition to the material which has thus been presented.

Mr. Davis[1] has been engaged for some years past in one of the most extended school experiments in vocational guidance that is to be found anywhere in the United States. He is an enthusiastic advocate of this type of work and believes that it will modify the whole of the school course and that the community can very properly devote a large amount of time and energy to informing its young people about industrial opportunity and placing them in lines of work which will be suited to their individual needs and training.

The book is written by himself and some of his colleagues. It contains an account of the work which has been going on at Grand Rapids. It is written very largely from the point of view of the secondary school, where most of this effective work has been carried out; but there are chapters in the book that will be very suggestive to elementary-school teachers. The general movement which is represented by the book is certainly of the greatest importance to all who are concerned with the education of boys and girls.

Mr. Davis believes that the best way to deal with the problems of school discipline is through an organization of responsible activities on the part of the students. He has therefore gone far beyond the ordinary range of school discipline in his organization of the boys and girls of the community in which he lives. He has also presented in this book some of the results which seem to him to justify all of the work which he has done.

The Russell Sage Foundation has issued two more useful volumes.[2] The first deals with working girls in evening schools and the second with the care and education of crippled children. Both

[1] *Vocational and Moral Guidance.* By Jesse Buttrick Davis. Ginn & Co., 1914. Pp. 303.

[2] *Working Girls in Evening Schools.* By Mary Van Kleeck. 1914. Pp. 252.

Care and Education of Crippled Children in the United States. By Edith Reeves. Survey Associates, 1914. Pp. 252.

of these books contain a large body of information about activities along the lines indicated by their titles. Through a careful review of existing institutions and their methods these books tend to stimulate more intelligent activity along similar lines.

The girls in night schools represent an ambitious class of workers who for the most part are struggling with a difficult problem of adjustment to the needs of society. These girls, many of them, are from foreign homes where they have had no adequate opportunity to prepare for American life. In most cases they are from poor homes where the domestic opportunities for self-improvement are very meager. How they do their work, what courses they take, how regularly they attend their classes, and what ought to be done for the improvement of their conditions are problems of the largest social importance.

The second volume is somewhat more detailed in its suggestions as to advantageous methods of treating those with whom it is concerned. Detailed descriptions are given of the organization of children's homes and hospitals. The principles which should govern their care and training are also given in detail. The book will be a source of valuable information to anyone who is interested in this type of philanthropy.

It is coming to be common for publishers and authors to address books to parents who wish to be intelligent about the training of their children. The recent enthusiasm which has been exhibited for the Montessori system is very largely due to the fact that many parents have wished to give their children during the early years of life prior to their entrance into schools all of the advantages that are to be expected from a systematic, educational training at home.

A new book[1] intended to satisfy this demand has just been put out by the Century Company. This book contains in very accessible form many of the familiar games and rhymes of the sort that parents have always employed, together with some discussion of the way in which these should be used.

There are chapters on habit drill and chapters on story-telling and physical education, chapters on rhythmical plays, and some statements concerning manual training and occupations. In short,

[1] *Child Training*. By V. M. Hillyer. The Century Co., 1915. Pp. 299.

the book contains a large amount of very definite, concrete material which can be used by any intelligent parent.

A useful new book[1] is accompanied by a set of cards which make it possible to carry out in a practical way the exercises which are described in the book itself. The author has been very skilful in taking a number of the tests which have been recently suggested as well as some of the formal grammatical exercises which have long been familiar in the school, and has turned them into drill exercises by putting into the hands of the teacher the material which will make it very easy to carry on the work.

There can be no doubt at all that one of the important additions to the classroom equipment much needed in American schools is printed material such as charts and cards which will make it unnecessary to do much writing on the blackboard. In getting together devices of this type, the author and the publisher of this book and set of cards have performed a distinct service for teachers.

The importance of play in the modern school has frequently been emphasized. The American Playground Association was very active some years ago in promoting the organization, both in schools and in municipalities, of systematic types of recreation. Educational theorists have also been very emphatic in their statements that the work of the school would be greatly improved if the natural example offered by play were more generally accepted as the model on which school work is to be patterned. A new discussion[2] of the matter, therefore, is by no means foreign to the spirit of the educational discussions. In a volume which touches all aspects of the matter of play Mr. Curtis renews the plea for an emphasis on this type of activity in the schools and in municipalities.

It is unfortunate that the attitude adopted by Mr. Curtis is one which tends to throw play in its different forms into opposition to the regular school work. On p. 48 Mr. Curtis writes as follows:

> Not only has it been true that the things taught in the schools have had no close relationship to either the business or the social life of the ordinary citizen, but it has never yet proven true that effectiveness has been in direct

[1] *Language Games for All Grades*. By Alhambra G. Deming. Beckley-Cardy Co., 1914. Pp. 80.

[2] *Education through Play*. By Henry S. Curtis. Macmillan, 1915. Pp. 359.

proportion to knowledge, as there are many other elements besides information that go to make the effective individual; and self-confidence, energy, and a fixed purpose, with a small amount of information, ofttimes accomplish vastly more than encyclopedic knowledge without these accompaniments. In fact, it may well be questioned if encyclopedic knowledge on general subjects adds greatly to the effectiveness of the individual anywhere.

Childhood is essentially the motor period of life, and every idea tends to immediate expression in some form of action. From all biological and psychological studies it would appear that the mind was not intended for a bin or granary in which to store a wealth of knowledge, but that it was intended for a workhouse where knowledge should be gathered for immediate use and wrought into action almost as soon as it is gathered. The typical "grind" in school and college often uses his energy so completely in the acquisition of knowledge that he has none left to make this knowledge effective.

The spirit of these remarks is one which will hardly promote the most productive relationship between play and the general intellectual life which it is the business of the school to cultivate. There can be no doubt at all that the world at large is satisfied that arithmetic and Latin and the other subjects dealt with in the regular school work have value in preparation for the serious activities of both the trades and the professions. It is not necessary for arithmetic to show that each one of its problems can be utilized in some later practical situation. It is enough for the experience of the race to make it clear that the whole science of mathematics is worth cultivating.

On the other hand, the descriptions which Mr. Curtis has given of the actual facts in regard to the introduction of play in American schools and in American public life tend to refute his own extreme attitude with regard to the place of play in the course of study. The various chapters in which he gives an account of the place of play in German and English schools and in American cities, his discussion of play activities in the rural school and in the Gary system, his account of athletics in secondary schools and in summer camps, all tend to show that there is the largest harmony between the regular work of the school and play.

The book will also be useful to teachers because it gives in the appendix rules of most of the common games, so that not merely the argument in favor of play but also the material which can be employed by those who wish to introduce play commends the book to the ordinary reader.

CLASSROOM METHODS AND DEVICES

PROBLEMS IN GEOGRAPHY—THE MAP

In a recent examination for a teacher's certificate given in a New England city, fifteen questions were asked; eleven and one-half of these, or nearly 75 per cent, were based on memory and belonged to the class of questions which have to do with location alone, two and one-half were economic in their intent and could be interpreted as geography questions only by the character of the answers, and one of the fifteen questions recognized geography as a relationship between the physical features and the organic inhabitants. If this may be taken as an index to the division of time devoted to geography in the grades and applied to a five-year course in geography from the fourth to the eighth grade inclusive, it would mean that nearly four years of the time should be devoted to the study of locations, about two-thirds of the remaining year to accessories or relevant items, and only one term to actual geographic presentation. Such a division of time cannot by any measure of efficiency be considered justifiable.

In the *Journal of Geography* for June, 1914, there is published a list of places recommended as suitable for thorough mastery by pupils in the schools of Springfield, Illinois, during their geography work of the fourth and fifth grades. In the list there are 371 places. The learning of these locations is not the geography work but a very necessary preparation for the work. It would be folly to use three-fourths of the time of the two years in learning and drilling on the list. The small number of names in the recommendation implies that there is something more to the subject, that there is a dynamic side as well as a static. This has been recognized in all our definitions of geography, whether relationship or response is the key-word, but teachers have not always acted accordingly. One difficulty which constantly arises lies in the inability to test with any degree of accuracy the stages of mental advancement. The examiner of teachers in the case stated at the beginning of this paper found it easier to test the memory than the reasoning power of the candidates. And in any examination in geography questions on locations call for a definite and unequivocal answer. On the other hand, it is possible to examine reasoning processes in geography as concisely as in geometry, providing proper emphasis is placed upon the work during the school year. There is the danger here lest the teachers believe that the thorough mastery of the list is the only requirement, while for true geography work it is the basal requirement only. The lists represent the requirements of static geography. The time is not ripe for making out requirements of dynamic geography, but teachers should at least face in that direction. To use the knowledge that is gained is an aim in education, much more, perhaps, than is the acquisition of knowledge. Thus, if some means can be devised of applying knowledge in geography it will naturally follow that the testing in this new field will not lag far behind. Problems on the three main requirements of the map, the scale, the direction, and the legend, are recorded here. No claim of perfection is entered for them but they represent a type of work which aims at the ability to use knowledge. With each a number of questions are introduced which show a different type from the purely memory question. The work on scale and direction is much narrower in its scope than that on legend. In the latter instance a large variety of problems involving relationships and responses is possible.

SCALE

Scale is taught at the beginning of map work and afterward it is relegated apparently to the background as far as any future map work is concerned. The pupil sees in turn maps of South America on many scales, but little confusion arises from this because he easily adopts a ratio scale; confusion arises, however, when he jumps from a map of South America to a map of some other continent, as Africa. The inference is that the scale is the same. Thus, as in one of our leading textbooks, North America at 760 miles to an inch, South America at 640, Europe at 470, Africa at 840, Asia at 890, and Australia at 1,000 are an unfortunate variety unless the pupils make use of the scale. There are a number of problems here of more or less value which can be used to emphasize the scale, and they are largely scale determinations.

1. *By comparison of lengths.*—An outline map which the pupils are to use appears on the blackboard or on paper without a scale attached. The problem is to find the scale. By finding the same map in the textbook, the length and the scale of the textbook map are noted. The length of the given map is measured. It is known that the larger the map, the smaller the scale, or, in other words, the proportion is an inverse one, and our equation reads: the length of the map in the textbook divided by the length of the given map equals the unknown scale of the given map (the x) divided by the scale of the textbook map.

2. *By latitudes.*—This is a variation of the above. From the map in the textbook the pupils find the latitude of the northern and southern tips of the continent along a meridian and this yields the length of the map in degrees. In round numbers, using seventy miles as the length of one degree of latitude, the length of the map in miles can be found. Now by measuring the length of the given map and dividing its length in miles by its length in inches a good estimate of its scale is made.

3. *By comparative areas.*—The result of this yields, not a definite scale, but a ratio, and it is most effective when two maps of different scales are in use at the same time. For instance, a map of South America and a map of Australia are before the pupils. Two of the latitude lines for each map may be inserted near the edge—for South America, the equator, and the southern tropic. By subdividing the distance between these points into twenty-four parts a near approximation to one degree is gained. The pupils will be able to sketch roughly their own state. Pennsylvania is about two degrees in latitude and five in longitude. Upon the subdivisions just made draw a sketch of that state. Do the same thing for Australia. The resulting comparison which appears before the eye will indicate the diversity in the two scales. We can recognize the fact that degrees of longitude vary in the number of miles in different latitudes by the use of latitude distances alone, as Pennsylvania is two degrees in latitude and twice as wide, linear measurement, in longitude.

Upon these as a background a great variety of problems can be based which will make the study, not a theoretical, but a practical one. For the upper grades, at least, it will call into use the knowledge which was gained in the earlier grade and will also emphasize the more important ideas concerning scale. And such questions as the following will show in their solution a process of reasoning rather than of memory.

1. Given a map of New England with political boundaries. If the northern boundary of Massachusetts is 42° 45′ N. Latitude and the northern boundary of Vermont is 45° N. Latitude, what is the scale of the map?

2. In the above map, knowing the scale, find the latitude of the northern boundary of Connecticut.

3. Draw an island 120 miles, north to south, by 40 miles, east to west, located at 43 S. Latitude and 75 W. Longitude, distances to be indicated by parallels and meridians.

DIRECTION

The most common mistakes in direction arise from the overlooking of the direction lines, parallels, and meridians on the map. This is the result of the bad habit of considering "up" as north, the "right" as east, and so on. The practical drill on direction must have for an objective the forming of a new habit strong enough to overcome the old; or better still the right habit in the first place. This means a recognition but not necessarily a training in the various nets for projection. For example, take the Mercator projection with horizontal parallels and vertical meridians, Flamsteed's with horizontal parallels and curved meridians, and the conic with curved parallels and straight but diverging meridians. The manner of making these nets need not be known, but it is well that the earmarks of each be learned so that the pupils may decide in most cases what the projection is. The drill in this case is to place two dots on the network and allow the pupils to state the direction one is from the other. Thus of two horizontal dots on the Mercator one will be east of the other, the same on Flamsteed's, but on the conic the direction will depend largely on the part of the map used, whether one point is northeast, east, or southeast of the other. The drill should be complete enough to show all the possibilities of the projections and the problem element based on the drill may reverse the operation.

1. Using two points marked *A* and *B*, draw a network which will make *B* east of *A*.

2. Using the same positions, make *A* southwest of B; northwest.

3. Using three points marked *A*, *B*, and *C*, draw a network making *B* south of *A* but west of *C*.

4. Using the same points, make *B* and *C* south of *A*.

LEGEND

While the interpretation of scale and direction is a part of map-reading and may properly be included under this heading, the term "legend" is usually confined to the conventional signs by which physical and political features are indicated. Many maps, especially the political, show little more than distribution. A few items like nearness to the sea and distance north and south of the equator are common to all maps. Political maps are the sources of most of the questions of static geography. Distribution is the result of physical conditions, and to the items already referred to as common to all maps there should be added as time goes on the general topography and the wind belts, the latter with the latitude yielding the climatic status. If, then, geography is really taught as a relationship or response, the general type of question which begins with "Where is" will give way to the type beginning "Why is." A great variety of drill exercises may be devised.

A. There is the class which is based on the resultant of the wind belts and the topography, including the migration of the planetary belts.

1. Draw the map of an area under the westerlies having a rainy and a dry region.

2. Draw a map of an area under the doldrums and the trades having a wet and a dry season.

3. Draw a map of an area with two rainy and two dry seasons per year.

4. Draw a map with an area with little rain throughout the year.

In drawing the maps, topography should be indicated by colors, the pupils using as nearly as possible the proper shades for mountains, highlands, uplands, and lowlands, and indicating the wind belts in the conventional way.

B. There is the class which has to do with the conditions of growth of vegetation and which differs from the above only in an added factor.

1. Rice demands warm temperatures during a long growing season and plenty of moisture. Draw a map of an area containing a rice area and a desert.

2. Grazing is carried on on mountain slopes not densely wooded and on semi-arid plains. Draw a map of a country having a rice area and a grazing-area.

C. To these may be added in turn a number of physical features.

1. Draw a map of a region including an area of interior drainage, a rice field, a coastal plain, and a heavily forested tract.

2. Draw a map of an area containing a manufacturing city dependent on the immediate neighborhood for its raw materials and shipping its wares to distant lands.

3. Draw a map of an area containing a large river and a seaport shipping hides.

4. Draw a map of a country growing coffee (on uplands in tropics under plenty of rain) and rice, with a large port and a city which may be used as a health resort.

As the experience of the pupils widens, most of the answers will represent actual places on the earth, although at the beginning the maps may be purely hypothetical.

In the preparation for this work, the teacher will find that her time limit will be a great restraint so that it will devolve upon her to select from a large array of examples. Each physiographic province of the earth may be treated in detail and many problems may be devised to test the pupils' grasp of the subject, but probably a typical case will be all that the teacher can afford to use because of other work, as, for example, the desert with its many variations: the desert under the trades; the desert on the leeward side of mountains; irrigation, the Nile case; irrigation, the Uncompaghre case; oases; and many others.

The result of such exercises as have been indicated will meet more nearly the requirements which geography workers should insist upon, and certainly the work of the schools both in place geography and in this study of relationships will receive thereby a better balance.

ROBERT M. BROWN

PROVIDENCE, RHODE ISLAND

THE WORK OF THE INTERMEDIATE SCHOOLS OF LOS ANGELES[1]

The principals of the Los Angeles City Intermediate Schools herein submit a brief report of the work undertaken in the intermediate schools during the school year 1913–14.

We take the liberty of quoting from the report of the Committee on Readjustment of the Course of Study and the Certification of Teachers, of which Committee Dr. Alexander F. Lange, dean of the College of Education, University of California, was chairman. The report as presented to the Council of Education and printed in the *Sierra Educational News*, September, 1912, refers among other matters of vital importance to the establishment of intermediate schools, in part, as follows:

In the judgment of the committee and in agreement with a growing national tendency, an adequate readjustment of the course of study calls for a revision of the traditional grouping of the grades constituting the "educational ladder." Both the first two years of the typical American college and the last two years of the typical American grammar school belong within the boundary lines of secondary education. In other words, the end of the sixth grade and the end of the fourteenth grade should be regarded as points of articulation, along with other points to be discussed later on. It is coming to be generally recognized that under our present arrangements secondary education begins too late and that for the majority of the high-school graduates it ends too early, while for those who take a full college course it again ends too late if the whole of such a course is devoted to purely cultural or man-centered aims.

The reason for selecting the end of the sixth grade and the end of the fourteenth grade as points of articulation may be summarized as follows:

1. On physiological and the psychological grounds, such regrouping is better adapted to the stages of development from childhood to manhood and womanhood.

[1] At the request of the editors of the *Elementary School Journal*, Superintendent Francis, of the schools of Los Angeles, California, has given his permission to publish a communication which was addressed to him in the form of a report by those who are responsible for the details of the organization of the intermediate schools of that city. The report is presented without any attempt to change the form in which it was originally submitted to the superintendent of schools of Los Angeles.

2. The economic conditions of modern American life are such that, by regrouping thus, more complete and more continuous educational opportunities can be devised for more individuals, both at or near the end of the elementary-school period and at or near the end of the secondary-school period.

3. The conception of a six- or eight-year secondary period renders it practically far easier to plan equitably and adequately for the complete needs, cultural and vocational, of all adolescents.

4. Such a regrouping is in agreement with the best European experience and practice, but voids the social cleavage of the old world. Moreover, American state universities already recognize more or less explicitly the end of the fourteenth grade as the turning-point from secondary education to university training.

The committee notes with satisfaction the progress of the plan whereby the pupils of the seventh, eighth, and ninth grades are grouped together. The plan tends to break up the traditional notions about the grouping of grades. It secures prolongation of formal education for many who would otherwise drop out of school. It furnishes an opportunity through optional courses for better occupational preparation as well as better preparation for the more advanced high-school grades. Above all, it facilitates the closing of the gap that now exists between the material and methods of the grammar school and those of the high school.

An examination of the percentage of attendance in the various grades of the Los Angeles City School, 1896 to 1911, shows that the average "dropping out" in the higher grades as based on relative enrolment of pupils was as follows: fifth grade, 18 per cent; sixth grade, 20 per cent; seventh grade, 30 per cent; eighth grade, 17 per cent; ninth grade, 54 per cent; tenth grade, 45 per cent; eleventh grade, 28 per cent.

It will be noted that most of the pupils completing the eighth grade entered the high school, but that more than three-fourths of them did not enter the eleventh year. The causes of this falling out are many, but lie chiefly in the fact that the average pupil has not been prepared through his experiences in the grammar school to meet the problems which enter his life as a high-school student.

In the ordinary grammar school we have pupils of all ages from six to sixteen, and if a kindergarten be connected with the school, as it usually is, from four to sixteen years. The extremes in such a case are very great, and it will be impossible to have a school which will return the most for either group, the adolescents or the preadolescents. A school to be successful must be a social unit; but if the extremes in the moral, physical, and intellectual development of its members be great the institution will usually develop at one end or the other. If the school be managed for the good of children who need motherly care and watchfulness (this is the case in elementary schools), then the older children are deprived of the freedom necessary for their development. The great majority of these pupils, lacking individuality and initiative, are not prepared for the freedom allowed them as members of a high school. This is evidenced by a neglect of lessons, irregular attendance, and a dropping out of school.

In the intermediate school, however, every precaution is used to avoid the break between the sixth and seventh years that formerly existed between the eighth and ninth. Here the transition from grade work to departmental work is more gradual.

The restless, changing period of adolescence covers about three years, including generally the period of the seventh, eighth, and ninth grades of school. In these grades the interests are similar and methods of discipline should be about the same for all but very different from those of the lower grades. Under careful guidance, children reaching out after the responsibilities of life are given an opportunity to assume them.

The teachers who would be the friends and advisers in this new plan must be chosen with great discrimination. The handling of children from eleven to sixteen years of age requires a broad sympathy that is founded only on wide experience, and preparation must be quite complete. Boys and girls of this age are prone to be critical of their elders, yet childlike and imitative. They are at the age when hero-worship is a great factor in their development. How important, therefore, that the personality of the teacher be an inspiration to them.

The work is specialized, and the general plan of organization is the same as that of a high school. The value of the mother-teacher of the elementary school is remembered, and the work is so planned as to avoid a break between the elementary and intermediate school.

COURSE OF STUDY

English.—The first and fundamental requirement in any process of education is the acquisition of the language. Its necessity is so imperative that English is made a solid in every course and year of the intermediate school. The subject is divided into five branches: technical grammar, composition, literature, oral expression, and spelling.

To create a love for literature is to provide the pupil with one of the most potent forces for future self-education as well as a means of ever-increasing enjoyment. By the use of literary masterpieces in the seventh and eighth grades as well as in the ninth, the scope of the reading-lesson is enlarged. The library, which is maintained in each school, supplies many magazines and books, and, since its management is largely in the hands of the pupils themselves, an intimate association with books is encouraged.

An increased interest in technical grammar is due largely to the fact that 70 per cent of the pupils in the intermediate school study a foreign language. As a language is usually begun in Grade VII B, the necessity for technical grammar as a basis of correct sentence structure is early emphasized. Special classes have been organized for backward pupils or those who have found difficulty in some phase of the English work.

Better opportunities are offered in composition through the school paper and programs given in the school auditorium. Oral expression is given special attention and is emphasized in book reviews, plays, and debates.

Spelling is made a distinct branch of daily work and every pupil is required to spell regularly.

Mathematics.—The work in mathematics consists of arithmetic in the seventh grade, algebra in the eighth and first half of the ninth, and geometry in the last half of the ninth grade. Commercial arithmetic is offered as a required subject for pupils in the commercial course in the ninth grade. Arithmetic is required of all pupils in the seventh grade. The VII B work includes the material usually offered in that grade plus a large amount of review work made possible by reason of the greater time devoted to the subject. In grade VII A the girls and boys are separated into different classes and the work is varied accordingly. With the boys the emphasis is put upon the practical side of arithmetic in connection with shop problems, etc., while the girls are taught household accounting, house furnishing, division of recipes, etc.

In algebra three terms are devoted to what is usually done in the first year in high school, the additional time being given to drill work, thus greatly reducing the percentage of failures.

The geometry offered in IX A is that commonly offered in the first half of the tenth year in high school.

Foreign languages.—The introduction of the foreign languages in the intermediate school has come as a result of the fact, long recognized by the best teachers of the languages, that students intending to take up such work should do so at an earlier period of life than is customary. Foreign schools have taken cognizance of this and placed the beginning of such study at least two years before the usual time of taking up language-study in this country.

Several reasons may be advanced for this contention, among which may be mentioned the greater imitative powers of the younger student resulting in better pronunciation, and an adaptability to the demands of a new language with little or no feeling of self-consciousness. The same methods are used as in the high school, but much more attention is given to the conversational side of instruction. Only those features of technical grammar are introduced at first which will serve to master the particular difficulty under consideration. The aim has been to base the work upon the interests of the child rather than upon conjugations and declensions, and the other intricacies of technical grammar. The course has been arranged so that the earlier part has much in it pertaining to the everyday life and environment of the student. By degrees the formal part of grammar is introduced until, at the end of the course, not only much practice in conversation has been given, but also the technical elements have received their proper amount of emphasis.

The languages offered are Latin, French, German, and Spanish, the entire course covering three years' work. The result of three years' experience has been on the whole gratifying, and pupils completing the intermediate work satisfactorily have been able to take up the work of the third year of high school, thus saving a year of the high-school course in foreign language.

History.—The reality of history is the life and progress of mankind; but this appreciation may be gained only through a broad knowledge of the world and a careful training in its records. Intermediate schools are privileged in having teachers trained for high schools, by travel and higher educational institutions, and in having well-equipped libraries.

Seventh- and eighth-grade history classes take a careful elementary survey of United States history and spend about five months on the study of civics, including topics of the day. Current events and the political situation are made real and alive by debates and class discussions, and an attempt is made to train boys and girls for the duties and obligations of citizenship by imposing questions of self-government and responsibility regarding the rights of others in the school itself as a democratic community.

Ancient history is introduced in the ninth year by a brief survey of the earlier civilizations, followed by the story of the Greeks to the Persian wars, when a more detailed study is made of the eastern nations. The rest of the term is devoted to the great and virile periods of the leading Greek cities; emphasizing art through pictures, literature through well-chosen selections, and Greek ideals through biography and story. The political and economic development of the Roman republic is followed by a study of the Roman empire in Italy and in the provinces.

Home economics.—The underlying purpose of the course in home economics is to create and develop individuality, efficiency, and self-dependence, giving the girl a better understanding of the duties of women as producers and consumers, and intensifying the interest in all matters pertaining to the home and the extension of its influence.

In sewing, our girls have been taught to make the garments they wear, to do fancywork, to design costumes, and are given lectures on textiles and on economy in the purchase and use of materials. Many of our girls wear simple dresses that they have made themselves.

In cooking, a systematic study is made of the production and manufacture of food materials, their wholesomeness and digestibility, nutritive value and cost. Constant training is given in order, neatness, methods of cleaning, care and use of utensils, and laundry work. The actual preparation and serving of simple meals—breakfasts as well as luncheons and dinners—each week, the careful consideration of their cost and proper balance in nutritive values, have shown splendid practical results. Throughout all the work an effort is made to keep a high ideal of the dignity of labor and to apply the principles learned to the problems of everyday life. Each school maintains a cafeteria in which pupils may secure a noon lunch at as near cost as possible. Much of the preparation of food, the serving, and the managing is done by the pupils. The cooking department provides such food as may furnish lessons for demonstrations in cooking classes. In most schools the general management of the cafeteria is assigned to the teacher of cookery, who supervises the various phases of the work.

Woodwork.—The intermediate school through its woodshop offers to the boy double the amount of manual training heretofore given in the seventh and eighth grades. In the ninth year he is permitted to elect the work if he so chooses. Well-selected type forms are first given, and to these the boy may add supplemental models as his peculiar ability and needs may direct. Independence, both in the form of design and in the peculiarity of construction, as well as in the work itself, is developed. Thus the boy gains through the woodshop the self-confidence necessary to the proper mastery of himself.

The addition of several of the elementary wood-working machines to the regular bench equipment has done much for the efficiency of this department.

Bookkeeping.—The subject of bookkeeping is an elective in the seventh grade and is continued throughout the three years' course. The strongest argument in favor of introducing it at this time is that the children like it and become more enthusiastic over it than do the pupils of regular high-school age. Many pupils of the seventh and eighth grades have not learned to get the exact meaning from a printed sentence or paragraph. They soon realize that only a partial understanding of even one sentence means failure. Here is their first opportunity for a practical application of their knowledge of arithmetic, and they soon learn that accuracy is essential to success.

Only the simplest elements of bookkeeping are presented during the first year, and the transactions are kept well within the experience and comprehension of the child. The aim is to educate the child rather than to make of him a professional bookkeeper. In the eighth grade the pupil writes checks, notes, drafts, etc. He learns the meaning and importance of leases, contracts, and deeds; how real estate is transferred; and how and why contracts and deeds are recorded. He keeps the accounts of business transactions involving the use of such papers, and by this time he has learned to make financial and business statements, and to close a set of books with a considerable degree of accuracy. In the ninth year, besides continuing the work of the previous grades, the pupil is expected to study something of the workings of a bank and to learn the purpose of corporations and how they are formed. The aim throughout the entire course is to give such training as will be of value to any boy or girl, whatever his or her position in life may be.

Stenography.—The subject of stenography seems peculiarly adapted to the intermediate schools. The shorthand satisfies the longing which comes to the heart of every child for a secret method. It satisfies his desire for "short cuts." He acquires with great satisfaction the ability to record whole sentences with but a few strokes of his pencil. The method used is simple, based upon syllabic sounds.

Typewriting requires neatness, accuracy, carefulness, and a knowledge of spelling and composition. The touch method only is used. Children at this age have the required ability and skill, and are delighted with this work which centers about the coordination of hand and mind.

While the power of children in the intermediate schools to grasp the subject of stenography is limited by their general development, the chief aim of the study consists in its educational power rather than in making expert office workers. As a factor in retaining the interest of the student, in developing the power of concentration and close application, in making familiar the terse, simple English and good business forms, it is unequaled.

Music.—Instruction in music is given in the seventh grade and half of the eighth grade and is made elective in the ninth grade. In addition to regular class work in music the schools organize choruses, glee clubs, orchestras, etc., and encourage individual effort. Instrumental as well as vocal selections by individuals and groups have a very beneficial effect upon performer and hearer. They inspire all to renewed effort and give a keener appreciation of the good in music.

Drawing and applied arts.—The object of drawing and applied arts is to stimulate the need for beauty in all the practical things of life. It strives to bring about perfection in line proportion and color while developing a perfect workmanship. It is the aim that pupils should observe, choose, and create things of usefulness and beauty, and having learned discrimination from the world of things to make finer choices in the mental and moral problems of life. They are expected to carry the subjects farther each year, and more opportunities are given to apply what they learn to articles of use to themselves and their friends or to the school. Designs are worked out in leather, metal, clay, embroidery, or stenciling, varying according to the conditions or equipment of the different schools.

Color harmony is studied in relation to dress, suitable combinations, for boys—suit, cap, tie, and shirt; for girls—dress, hair ribbons, coat, and hat. Designs for embroidery of underwear and simple dresses or collars are made in white and in colors and are carried out in the sewing department. Color is also studied in relation to the furnishing of a room and the arranging of a garden. The work is correlated with other school interests through book covers and posters.

Mechanical drawing.—The aim of the mechanical drawing course is threefold: to develop accuracy and neatness while forming a knowledge for making and reading plans and drawings; to stimulate the ability to sketch and to turn sketches into working plans; and to train boys who want to take up draughting as a business. The course includes freehand and block lettering, working drawings from woodshop and machine objects, sketching, a few geometric problems, projections, section, intersections, triangulation, architectural drawings, and lettering.

Penmanship.—Penmanship is required in the seventh year in all courses. It is an elective in the eighth and ninth years in the general course. In the commercial course it is required the first two years, and is an elective in the ninth year. The endeavor is to teach the pupil to write a good rapid style, combining ease, legibility, and endurance.

Geography.—In the first half of the seventh grade the pupil finishes the course in geography. The work consists of a brief summing up of the important facts concerning each of the grand divisions, but Europe is taught in detail. The United States, and especially California, are studied in their relation to other countries.

The interest in foreign countries is broadened by the abundant use of pictures, by short stories depicting the life of the people studied, and also by brief sketches of the lives of their noted characters. In some classes it has been possible to make use of the balopticon to great advantage in reflecting suitable pictures for class exercises. The school library has proved a great help in enlarging and making real the subject-matter.

Physiology.—Physiology is taught in grades VIII B and VIII A. Instruction is given in the science laboratory, where experiments before the class emphasize the subject-matter of the course. To help the developing boy and girl not only to know facts relating to the body but to make use of them at the most impressive period of his or her life is made the chief aim.

Physiography.—The work of the ninth year in physiography is identical with the first-year high-school science. The aim of the work is twofold, viz., to implant within the pupil a love for the study of science and to give him a better understanding of everyday phenomena. It introduces him to all the physical and biological sciences and thus gives him a foundation for an intelligent choice in further work in science.

Physical training.—The work in physical training is carried on under the direction of competent instructors employed on the same basis as teachers of other subjects. Two periods a week are required of all pupils unless excused on account of ill health. For the girls, the work consists of marching, running, calisthenics with or without apparatus, folk-games, gymnastic games, indoor and volley-ball. The boys are given work with dumbbells, Indian clubs, tactics, and free play in such games as soccer, basket-ball, volley-ball, indoor and outdoor baseball, and track work. In these games the boys are divided into three classes according to size so as to include everyone.

The attempt is made with both boys and girls to cultivate in them a desire for, and a love of, play, and to build up good, healthy bodies. Practically all the work is done in the open air. The endeavor has been to have all pupils enter into the games rather than to develop expert teams to represent the various schools in contests.

School activities.—The grouping together of the seventh, eighth, and ninth grades has placed in one school boys and girls of about the same age, tastes, and interests. This has made possible some form of student government in each school whereby students assume control of various student activities under their own officers and student administration. The policy here stated is in line with the present-day feeling that if our democracy is to prosper the beginnings must be laid in the public school, and students must early be taught the duties and responsibilities that fall upon the individual in a democracy. The adolescent child is at a most impressionable age and the ideals developed at this time are enduring in character. Because of this fact and the further fact that school life for many must terminate during these years, it is all the more important that the student become familiar as soon as possible with the life of the larger community of which he is later to become a member.

All of the intermediate schools have placed certain phases of school administration and school activity under student control differing in each locality according to the varying conditions that are encountered. It is the consensus of opinion that there has arisen in pupils a better attitude toward school and a greater desire to co-operate in those things that make for a more wholesome school atmosphere.

Debating teams, camera clubs, orchestras, and glee clubs have been organized. Athletics are largely inter-class rather than inter-school, the aim being to develop many instead of the few who make up a team. Physical directors have had charge of week-end hikes to the mountains or the seashore with groups of boys or girls. Student bookstores provide for exchange of textbooks, and lunch counters or cafeterias furnish generous hot lunches on the school grounds.

Adjustment of high schools to intermediate schools.—As might have been anticipated, the problem of adjustment was one of the first to confront those directing the two types of schools. The courses have been so arranged that pupils enter the intermediate school from the elementary school without question. The more serious problems lay in the proper adjustment between high and intermediate schools. The newness of the plan rendered it a difficult matter to judge accurately as to how much might be done in the new type of school. The question has been in the hands of a committee composed of both high and intermediate principals and teachers. A general desire on the part of the high schools to co-operate has helped materially to make the problem less difficult.

The more delicate phases of adjustment have arisen in the subjects which are found in the two schools, such as the commercial branches and the foreign languages. The beginner in the intermediate school, because of his greater immaturity of mind, will not be able to parallel the work of the beginner in the high school. In all cases, however, it has been found possible to recommend that students covering the full course of the intermediate school be allowed advanced standing in the high school; or, in other words, the work done herein carried the student farther than if he had delayed electing the subject until entering high school. The average number of high-school credits received by the pupils in Grade IX A in five schools, June, 1914, was 11.1, which was a saving of almost one half-year of high-school attendance.

Statistics relative to intermediate schools follow:

TABLE I

ENROLMENT OF PUPILS OF THE SEVENTH, EIGHTH, AND NINTH GRADES

Year 1913–14	Seventh	Eighth	Ninth	Total
In intermediate schools	2,774	2,339	948	6,061
In grammar schools	2,755	2,280	....	5,035
In night schools	628	1,515	....	2,143
In high schools	....	....	2,984	2,984
Total	6,157	6,134	3,932	16,223

TABLE II

NUMBER OF TEACHERS EMPLOYED AND THEIR CERTIFICATION

School	Teachers	High-School Certificate	Special Secondary Certificate	Elementary Certificate
Lincoln High School	49	33	15	1
Custer Ave. Intermediate	27	10	15	2
Virgil Ave. Intermediate	24	14	8	2
Berendo St. Intermediate	26	12	13	1
Sentous St. Intermediate	28	14	14	....
Thirtieth St. Intermediate	39	19	20	....
McKinley Ave. Intermediate	35	11	21	3
Fourteenth St. Intermediate	32	13	16	3
Boyle Heights Intermediate	43	17	18	8
Total	303	143	140	20

TABLE III

SALARIES RECEIVED BY TEACHERS (12 PAYMENTS)

Salary per month	$62	$74	$82	$86	$94	$98	$100	$105	$110	$115	$120	$125	$130
Teachers employed	1	1	2	1	1	1	22	7	21	22	16	21	187

TABLE IV

NUMBER OF PUPILS ENROLLED IN VARIOUS COURSES AND SUBJECTS, MAY, 1914

Grade	General Course	Commercial Course	Vocational Course	Total
VII B	1,386	89	10	1,485
VII A	1,360	140	1	1,501
VIII B	1,079	115	23	1,217
VIII A	974	131	49	1,154
IX B	658	123	52	833
IX A	501	87	31	619
Total	5,958	685	166	6,809
Boys	2,980	315	96	3,391
Girls	2,978	370	70	3,418

Subject	Number
Algebra	1,970
Arithmetic	2,986
Bookkeeping	1,643
Commercial arithmetic	482
Cooking	2,662
Drawing, freehand	3,347
Drawing, mechanical	500
English	6,809
Foreign languages:	
French	497
German	816
Latin	596
Spanish	2,819
Geography	1,485
History, United States	3,786
History, ancient	614
Music	4,407
Oral English	1,679
Penmanship	3,701
Physiography	615
Physiology	2,371
Sewing	2,993
Spelling	6,809
Stenography	1,737
Woodwork	2,773

TABLE V

AMOUNT OF HIGH-SCHOOL CREDIT ALLOWED TO PUPILS OF INTERMEDIATE SCHOOLS

Subjects	VII B	VII A	VIII B	VIII A	IX B	IX A
Algebra	......	......	½	½	1	......
Ancient history	......	......	......	......	1	1
Bookkeeping	½	½	½	½	½	½
Commercial arithmetic	......	......	......	......	1	1
Cookery	......	......	......	......	½	½
English	......	......	......	......	1	1
Freehand drawing	......	......	¼	¼	½	½
French	½	½	½	½	1	1
Geometry	......	......	......	......	......	1
German	½	½	½	½	1	1
Latin	½	½	½	½	1	1
Mechanical drawing	......	......	½	½	1	1
Music	......	......	......	......	⅕	⅕
Glee Club orchestra	......	......	......	......	⅖	⅖
Oral English	......	......	......	......	⅕	⅕
Penmanship	......	......	......	......	½	½
Physiography	......	......	......	......	1	1
Sewing	¼	¼	¼	¼	½	½
Spanish	½	½	½	½	1	1
Stenography	½	½	½	½	1	1
Woodwork	¼	¼	¼	¼	½	½

TABLE VI

AGE ON SEPTEMBER 1, 1914, OF PUPILS PRESENT OCTOBER 30, 1914, IN INTERMEDIATE SCHOOLS

AGES OF BOYS

Age	10	11	12	13	14	15	16	17	18	19	20	Total	Average Age
Grade VII...	7	104	350	429	313	137	39	6	0	0	1	1,386	13.11
Grade VIII..	2	28	118	279	383	222	59	6	2	1	0	1,100	13.78
Grade IX....	0	0	15	78	240	209	136	35	7	2	1	723	14.72
Total......	9	132	483	786	936	568	234	47	9	3	2	3,209	13.70

AGE OF GIRLS

Age	10	11	12	13	14	15	16	17	18	19	20	Total	Average Age
Grade VII...	8	108	387	403	250	82	30	2	0	0	0	1,270	12.9
Grade VIII..	0	6	96	368	186	57	9	1	0	0	0	723	13.3
Grade IX....	0	0	7	71	274	256	90	20	1	0	0	719	14.57
Total.......	8	114	490	842	710	395	129	23	1	0	0	2,712	13.4

TABLE VII

PUPILS GRADUATING FROM GRADES VIII A AND IX A OF INTERMEDIATE SCHOOLS

Grade VIII A	February, 1914		June, 1914		Total	
		Per Cent		Per Cent		Per Cent
Number of graduates.........	667		883		1,550	
Returned to the same school.	525	78.7	665	75.1	1,190	76.7
Transferred to intermediate schools..............	29	4.3	14	1.5	43	2.7
Transferred to city high schools..................	52	7.7	69	7.8	121	7.8
Entered private schools.....	10	1.4	14	1.5	24	1.5
Out on account of sickness, travel, etc..............	9	1.3	13	1.4	22	1.4
Left the city..............	15	2.2	57	6.4	72	4.6
Working..................	27	4.0	51	5.7	78	5.0

Grade IX A	February, 1914		June, 1914		Total	
		Per Cent		Per Cent		Per Cent
Number of graduates.........	355		479		834	
Transferred to city high schools..................	307	86.4	435	90.8	742	88.9
Entered private schools......	7	1.9	6	1.2	13	1.5
Out on account of sickness, travel, etc..............	9	2.5	8	1.6	17	2.0
Left the city..............	8	2.2	7	1.4	15	1.7
Working..................	24	6.7	23	4.8	47	5.6
Average high-school credits..	9.5		10.65		10.2	

Average high-school credits of the IX A pupils in the five intermediate schools maintained for three years was 11.1.

TABLE VIII

PERCENTAGE OF THE PUPILS IN VARIOUS GRADES AND YEARS

Year	In Kindergarten to Grade VI	In Grades VII–IX	In Grades X–XII
1896–97	84.4	13.3	2.6
1897–98	83.4	13.4	3.2
1898–99	83.0	13.8	3.4
1899–1900	81.7	14.2	3.4
1900–1901	83.2	13.7	3.2
1901– 2	83.5	13.4	3.1
1902– 3	82.8	14.3	3.0
1903– 4	82.4	14.9	2.8
1904– 5	82.3	15.2	2.7
1905– 6	79.6	16.6	3.0
1906– 7	79.8	16.6	3.4
1907– 8	78.0	17.8	3.8
1908– 9	....	....	....
1909–10	75.8	19.5	4.8
1910–11	74.9	19.9	5.1
1911–12	74.2	20.0	5.4
1912–13	73.8	19.7	6.3
1913–14	73.3	20.3	6.6
	Average of the first seven years:		
1897–1903	83.2	13.7	3.1
	Average of the second seven years:		
1904–11	79.0	17.2	3.6
	Average of the last three years:		
1911–14	75.8	20.1	6.1

ADVANTAGES OF THE INTERMEDIATE SCHOOL

1. It offers an opportunity to elect subjects suited to individual needs.

2. It gives departmental instruction under specialists and prepares students to meet the requirements of higher schooling.

3. It saves time by pursuing subjects rather than grades.

4. It provides better organization and equipment.

5. It encourages intelligent self-direction through student government and student activities.

6. It enables students to come in contact with more men teachers.

7. It furnishes an opportunity to correct mistaken judgments with regard to studies and courses with less serious results than in the high school.

8. It makes easier a second differentiation of work at the end of the three years.

9. It overcomes the temptation to drop out of school at the end of the compulsory period, or the eighth year. Pupils are doing high-school work and remain in school.

10. It provides more schools and hence makes them more convenient to all.

11. It takes the student at the beginning of the adolescent period, the most important period of life.

STANDARD TESTS AS AN AID TO SUPERVISION

HENRY A. LANE
Houghton, Michigan

During the latter part of October, 1913, the writer conducted the Courtis standard tests in arithmetic (Series B) consisting of four tests, one in each of the four operations, with a time allowance of six minutes for multiplication, four minutes for subtraction, and eight minutes for each of the other operations. The subjects were about five hundred pupils distributed in thirty-five classes in four schools in Houghton, Michigan. The results of the test for each class were tabulated and graphed; but as this gave groups that were too small, tabulations and graphs were made for the system as a whole, thus giving ten groups of approximately fifty individuals each. These results are shown in the accompanying graphs and table (Table I and Charts I and II). The abscissas represent the grades from 4B to 8A and the ordinates represent the number of examples. Full lines indicate the number of examples attempted and dotted lines the number of examples right.

Taking the curves for addition, it seemed a singular comment on the efficiency of our educational system that four years of arithmetic teaching should increase a child's score in attempts from 4.5 to 9.2, rights from 1.1 to 4.0, and in accuracy from 24 per cent to 43 per cent; that is, an 8A child can do only 5 more examples in 8 minutes than a 4B child, can get only 3 more right, and can work only 20 per cent more accurately. Furthermore, the shape of the curves indicated a very uneven development of ability through the school course.

These were the facts. What was to be done? Knowing what some of the best of the thirty-five classes tested had done, a curve was drawn for the number of addition examples attempted, allowing for a growth of from 5 examples in the the 4B grade to 12 examples in the 8A grade, and a curve for the number of examples right was constructed ranging from 2 examples in the 4B grade to 10 examples in the 8A grade; the growth in accuracy is thus from

TABLE I

Grade	Source of Score	No. of Pupils	Addition			Subtraction			Multiplication			Division		
			Attempts	Rights	Percentage of Accuracy	Attempts	Rights	Percentage of Accuracy	Attempts	Rights	Percentage of Accuracy	Attempts	Rights	Percentage of Accuracy
4B	October, 1913	44	4.5	1.1	24	4.5	0.8	18	3.0	0.9	30	......	......	......
	June, 1914	49	4.9	3.1	63	4.4	1.8	41	4.2	2.6	62	2.6	0.7	27
	Standard	....	5.0	2.0	40	5.0	2.0	40	4.0	1.6	40	4.0	1.6	40
4A	October, 1913	44	4.2	1.3	31	5.7	3.2	56	4.8	2.4	50	3.3	1.2	36
	June, 1914	52	5.7	2.4	42	5.5	3.4	62	4.4	2.9	66	3.3	1.6	48
	Standard	....	5.7	2.9	51	5.7	2.9	51	4.9	2.4	49	4.9	2.4	49
5B	October, 1913	60	7.0	1.9	27	6.6	3.5	53	4.9	2.3	47	3.9	1.2	31
	June, 1914	49	8.0	4.9	61	7.7	6.3	82	6.2	4.3	69	4.8	3.2	67
	Standard	....	6.5	3.8	58	6.5	3.8	58	5.8	3.4	59	5.8	3.4	59
5A	October, 1913	50	7.1	2.3	32	7.8	3.3	42	5.4	2.5	46	4.1	2.0	49
	June, 1914	53	7.9	4.0	51	8.7	6.7	77	6.5	3.9	60	5.9	4.7	80
	Standard	....	7.3	4.7	64	7.3	4.7	64	6.6	4.4	67	6.6	4.4	67
6B	October, 1913	48	7.0	2.3	33	7.5	4.6	61	6.1	2.6	43	4.0	1.5	38
	June, 1914	58	10.1	6.8	67	10.0	7.6	76	8.4	6.1	73	7.4	5.9	80
	Standard	....	8.0	5.6	70	8.0	5.6	70	7.5	5.3	71	7.5	5.3	71
6A	October, 1913	60	8.3	3.4	41	8.6	5.1	59	7.0	3.5	50	4.4	2.6	59
	June, 1914	48	9.7	6.0	62	10.3	8.0	78	8.6	5.3	62	8.0	5.7	71
	Standard	....	8.8	6.5	74	8.8	6.5	74	8.4	6.2	74	8.4	6.2	74
7B	October, 1913	68	8.6	3.4	40	9.5	6.0	63	7.9	4.1	52	6.6	4.6	70
	June, 1914	55	10.9	6.2	57	10.9	8.4	77	9.0	6.1	68	7.5	5.7	79
	Standard	....	9.6	7.4	77	9.6	7.4	77	9.3	7.2	77	9.3	7.2	77
7A	October, 1913	44	8.7	3.7	43	10.8	6.5	60	7.9	3.8	48	6.7	4.3	64
	June, 1914	72	11.3	7.5	66	12.8	9.9	77	10.8	8.1	75	12.3	10.1	82
	Standard	....	10.4	8.2	79	10.4	8.2	79	10.1	8.1	80	10.1	8.1	80
8B	October, 1913	46	8.0	3.1	39	11.5	7.2	63	9.4	4.4	47	8.5	5.7	67
	June, 1914	43	12.4	8.8	71	13.3	11.3	85	10.9	8.2	75	10.3	9.0	87
	Standard	....	11.2	9.1	81	11.2	9.1	81	11.0	9.0	82	11.0	9.0	82
8A	October, 1913	36	9.2	4.0	43	13.0	7.4	57	10.5	5.3	50	10.0	6.4	64
	June, 1914	44	12.3	7.6	62	13.5	11.3	84	11.5	8.3	72	12.7	10.0	79
	Standard	....	12.0	10.0	83	12.0	10.0	83	12.0	10.0	83	12.0	10.0	83

CHART I

HOUGHTON, MICH. 523 PUPILS

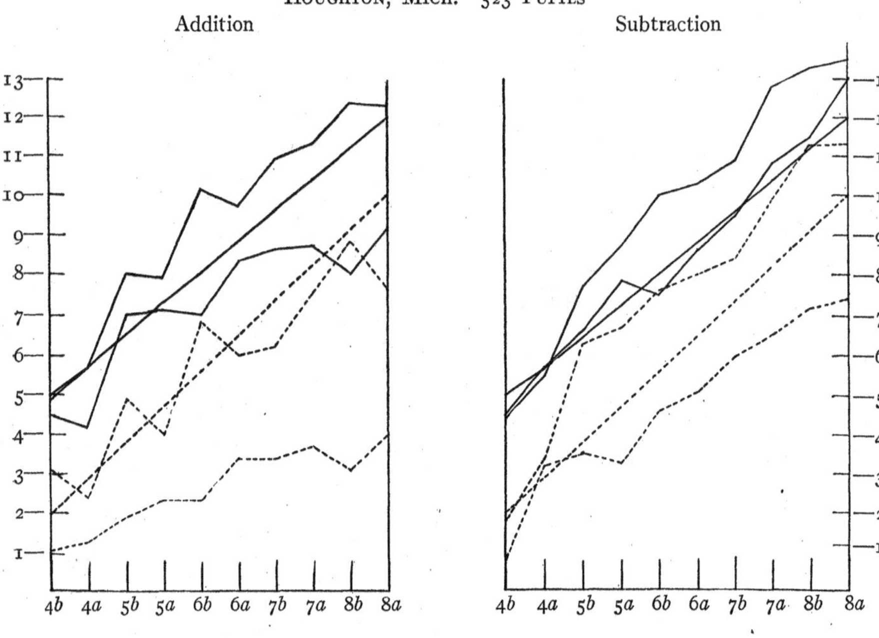

CHART II

HOUGHTON, MICH. 523 PUPILS

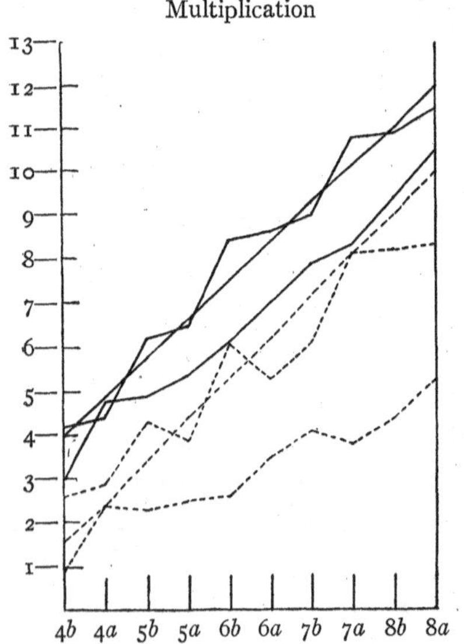

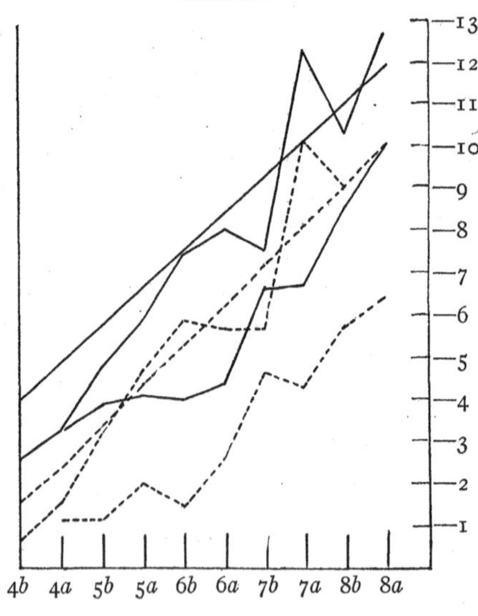

40 per cent to 83 per cent. To insure a uniform development throughout the grades, these curves were drawn as straight lines, and the scores for each grade were plotted from the curves. This gave goals to be attained by each grade at the expiration of the school year. Similar tentative standard curves were drawn for the other operations. The pupils as well as the teachers were informed what the standards are so that all could co-operate toward attaining them. Periodical tests similar in construction to the Courtis tests but with modifications in the time allotment were made a feature of the arithmetic course of study, the children keeping a record of their scores and watching their growth; and it was hoped that in June, 1914, the tentative standards would in the majority of the grades be attained. The writer was of the opinion that the inefficiency of arithmetic instruction was not due to faulty method so much as to the fact that teachers and pupils did not know definitely what was expected of them. He therefore placed in the hands of each teacher a copy of the following announcement:

In June there will be another Courtis test of the same type as the one given in October. At that time, the grades are expected to attain the following standards:

	Addition and Subtraction		Multiplication and Division	
	Attempts	Rights	Attempts	Rights
4B	5.0	2.0	4.0	1.6
4A	5.7	2.9	4.9	2.4
5B	6.5	3.8	5.8	3.4
5A	7.3	4.7	6.6	4.4
6B	8.0	5.6	7.5	5.3
6A	8.8	6.5	8.4	6.2
7B	9.6	7.4	9.3	7.2
7A	10.4	8.2	10.1	8.1
8B	11.2	9.1	11.0	9.0
8A	12.0	10.0	12.0	10.0

Work in the four operations must be stressed. These are tentative and minimum standards. They will very likely be raised next fall. The success with which classes achieve these standards will, in a sense, be a measure of teaching ability.

At the close of the school year in June, 1914, another measurement was made and the results were very gratifying, as can be seen by examining Table I and graphs (Charts I and II). The straight

CHART III

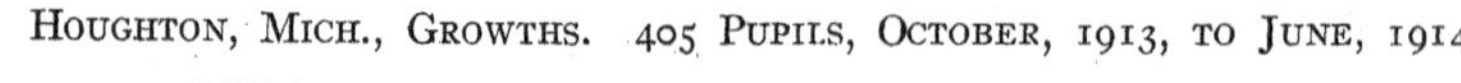
Houghton, Mich., Growths. 405 Pupils, October, 1913, to June, 1914

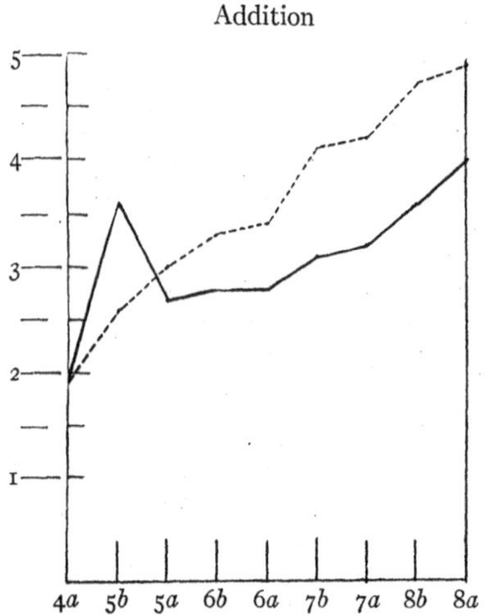

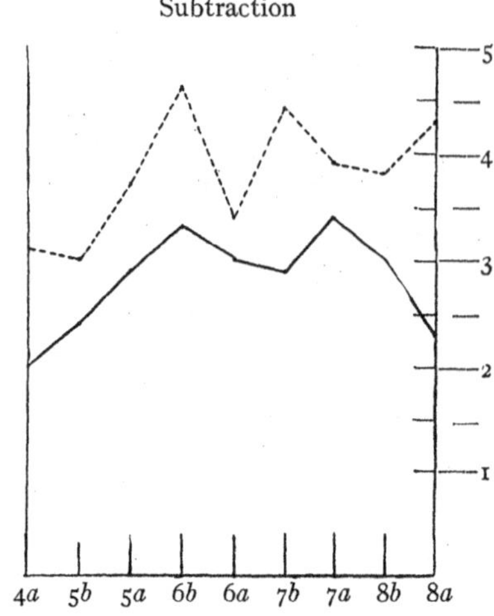

CHART IV

Houghton, Mich., Growths. 405 Pupils, October, 1913, to June, 1914

Multiplication Division

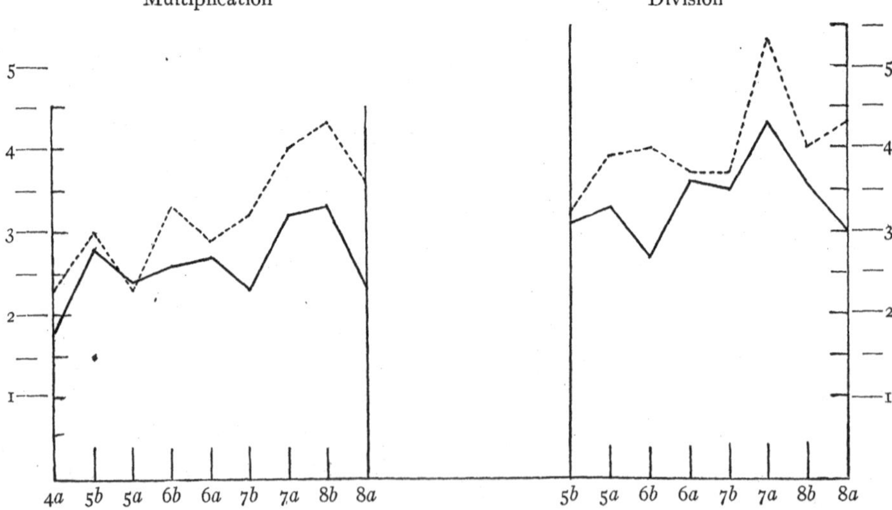

lines are the tentative standards, the lower curves are the October results, and the upper curves the June results. The graphs speak for themselves and they tell an instructive story. With very few exceptions, the standards set were attained and in some cases they were exceeded. It is interesting to note that the accuracy of subtraction and division is much greater than that of addition and multiplication. But the essential thing is that the June results were a remarkably close approximation to the tentative standards. One feels almost like stating as a proposition capable of demonstration that reasonable standards can in a very short time be attained.

A tabulation was now made of the growths from October to June, with the results shown in Table II and the accompanying

TABLE II

ADVANCE OF 405 PUPILS FROM OCTOBER, 1913, TO JUNE, 1914

Grade	Addition			Subtraction			Multiplication			Division		
	No.	Attempts	Rights	No.	Attempts	Rights	No.	Attempts	Rights	No.	Attempts	Rights
4A......	39	1.9	1.9	40	2.0	3.1	35	1.8	2.3	.....	.....	.....
5B......	37	3.6	2.6	37	2.4	3.0	37	2.8	3.0	30	3.1	3.2
5A......	46	2.7	3.0	46	2.9	3.7	46	2.4	2.3	46	3.3	3.9
6B......	49	2.8	3.3	51	3.3	4.6	51	2.6	3.3	50	2.7	4.0
6A......	41	2.8	3.4	41	3.0	3.4	41	2.7	2.9	41	3.6	3.7
7B......	44	3.1	4.1	44	2.9	4.4	43	2.3	3.2	44	3.5	3.7
7A......	65	3.2	4.2	65	3.4	3.9	66	3.2	4.0	66	4.3	5.3
8B......	40	3.6	4.7	40	3.0	3.8	40	3.3	4.3	39	3.6	4.0
8A......	39	4.0	4.9	40	2.3	4.3	39	2.3	3.6	40	3.0	4.3

graphs (Charts III and IV). Note that every grade showed growths in every operation and that the growth in rights exceeded the growth in attempts. Speaking roughly, the 405 pupils in a school year showed a growth of 3 examples in each of the four operations.

But there is also a dark side to the story. Table III and the corresponding graphs (Charts V and VI) show the individual growths by numbers and by percentages and display the wide variation. Thus in subtraction, 43 pupils, or 16 per cent of the group, suffered actual losses in speed and 26 pupils, or 6 per cent,

TABLE III

ADVANCE FROM OCTOBER, 1913, TO JUNE, 1914

Score	Addition				Subtraction				Multiplication				Division			
	Attempts		Rights		Attempts		Rights		Attempts		Rights		Attempts		Rights	
	No.	Per-centage	No.	Per-centage	No.	Per-centage	No.	Per-centage	No.	Per-centage	No.	Per-centage	No.	Per-centage	No.	Per-centage
13	1	......	1	......	1	......	......	......	......	......	......	......	......	......	1	......
12	1	......	......	......	1	......	1	......	......	......	......	......	......	......	3	1
11	......	......	4	1	1	......	3	1	......	......	......	......	1	......	4	1
10	......	......	6	2	1	......	5	1	......	......	......	......	7	2	5	2
9	3	1	3	1	3	1	4	1	1	......	2	......	4	1	10	3
8	1	......	13	3	6	2	16	4	......	......	8	2	6	2	20	6
7	12	3	17	4	14	4	25	6	4	1	18	5	22	6	20	6
6	30	8	34	9	10	3	27	7	13	3	33	8	25	7	22	6
5	32	8	44	11	25	6	36	9	19	5	36	9	28	8	42	11
4	50	13	56	14	59	15	63	16	45	11	47	12	44	12	44	12
3	65	16	49	12	55	14	67	17	81	20	61	15	61	17	52	14
2	76	19	62	15	85	21	62	15	90	23	77	19	51	15	42	11
1	65	16	45	11	63	16	44	11	74	19	60	15	59	17	49	13
0	35	9	37	9	35	9	23	6	42	11	40	10	23	7	30	8
−1	16	4	17	4	19	5	15	4	17	4	15	4	12	3	7	2
−2	5	1	12	3	8	2	5	1	8	2	3	1	5	1	5	2
−3	5	1	1	......	7	2	4	1	2	......	2	......	3	1	2	1
−4	......	......	1	......	5	2	2	......	2	......	......	......	2	1	......	......
−5	1	......	......	......	3	1	......	......	......	......	......	......	......	......	1	......
−6	......	......	......	......	1	......	......	......	......	......	......	......	......	......	......	......
Total	398		402		402		405		398		401		353		359	

CHART V

GROWTHS. 405 PUPILS, OCTOBER, 1913, TO JUNE, 1914

Full lines, attempts; dotted lines, rights

Addition

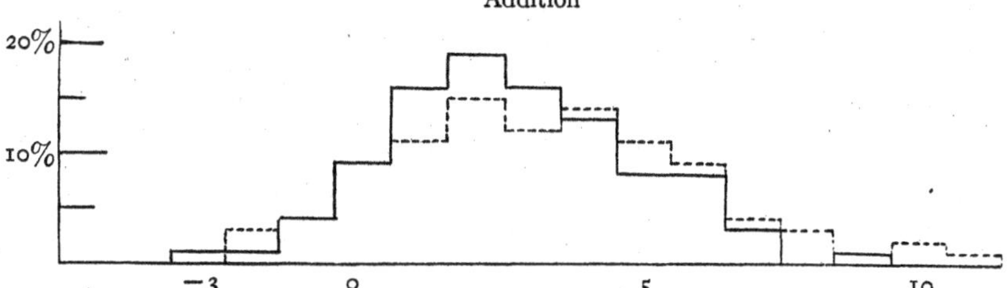

Subtraction

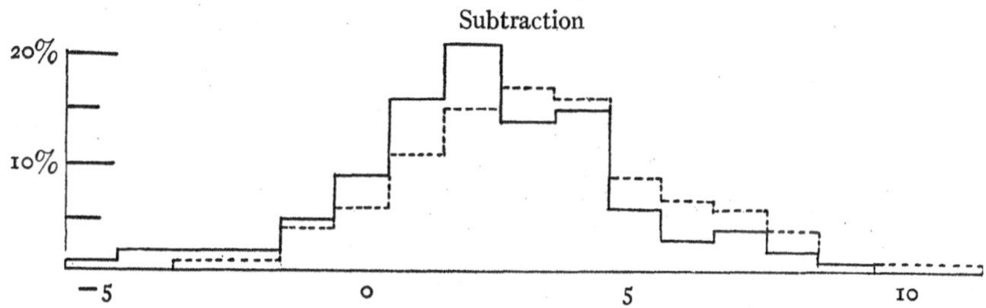

CHART VI

Multiplication

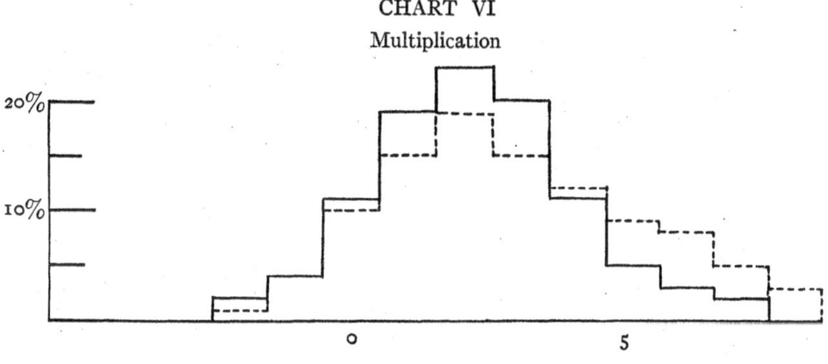

Division

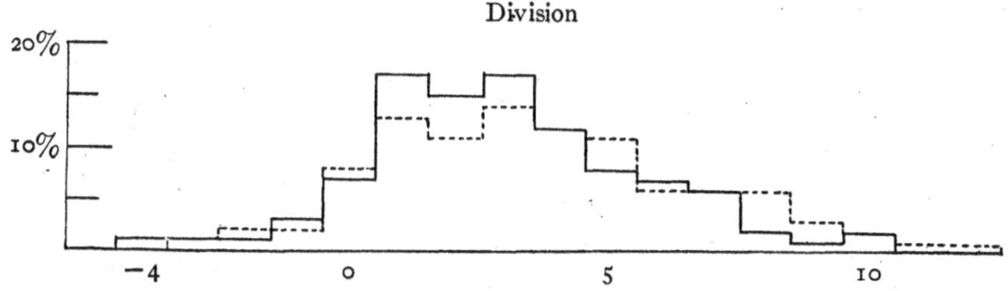

suffered losses in accuracy; 35 pupils, or 9 per cent, made no change in speed and 23 pupils, or 6 per cent, no change in accuracy. From 80 to 85 per cent of the group made growths varying from one to eleven examples. There is no reason why everyone who is not mentally deficient should not grow in speed and accuracy, and the problem to be attacked during the current school year is the attainment of standard scores by every individual.

CURRENT EDUCATIONAL LITERATURE IN THE PERIODICALS[1]

IRENE WARREN
Librarian, School of Education, University of Chicago

Arnold, Felix. Obstructed breathing and memory. Psychol. Clinic 8:234–46. (Ja. '15.)

Baker, Franklin T. High-school reading: compulsory and voluntary. English J. 4:1–8. (Ja. '15.)

Bowden, Witt. Education for the control and enjoyment of wealth. Educa. R. 49:147–67. (Fe. '15.)

Canby, Henry Seidel. The undergraduate background. Harper 130:466–71. (Fe. '15.)

Childe, Elizabeth. Teaching concentration. Outl. 109:155–59. (20 Ja. '15.)

Claxton, P. P. The American rural school. School and Society 1:37–50. (9 Ja. '15.)

Coulter, John M. The mission of science and education. School Sci. and Math. 15:93–100. (Fe. '15.)

Cubberley, Ellwood P., and Elliott, Edward C. Rural-school administration. School and Society 1:154–61. (30 Ja. '15.)

Cushman, Lillian S. A test of efficiency for the industrial arts. Indust. Arts M. 3:49–51. (Fe. '15.)

Dabney, Charles W. The movement for the modern city university in Germany. School and Society 1:150–54. (30 Ja. '15.)

Dewey, John. The American Association of University Professors: Introductory address. Science 41:147–51. (29 Ja. '15.)

Eliot, Charles W. Educational evolution. School and Society 1:1–8. (2 Ja. '15.)

Fitz-Gerald, John D. Languages and the college-preparatory course. Educa. R. 49:168–90. (Fe. '15.)

Foster, Wilfred L. Improvement of dental hygiene in the high school, with relation to efficiency. Psychol. Clinic 8:230–33. (Ja. '15.)

Foster, William T. The state-wide campus. School and Society 1:13–16. (2 Ja. '15.)

[1] *Abbreviations.*—Cur. Opinion, Current Opinion; Educa., Education; Educa. R., Educational Review; El. School J., Elementary School Journal; English J., English Journal; Hist. Teachers M., History Teachers Magazine; Indust. Arts M., Industrial Arts Magazine; Outl., Outlook; Pop. Sci. Mo., Popular Science Monthly; Psychol. Clinic, Psychological Clinic; School Sci. and Math., School Science and Mathematics.

Gerrish, Carolyn M. Secondary school composition. Educa. R. 49:126–35. (Fe. '15.)

Gruenberg, Benjamin C. Thought in science and in science teaching. Pop. Sci. Mo. 86:164–73. (Fe. '15.)

Hall, G. Stanley. Teaching the war. School and Society 1:8–13. (2 Ja. '15.)

Harris, James H. An inquiry into the departmental system. El. School J. 15:323–30. (Fe. '15.)

Hinckley, Alice C. Six weeks with a supposedly hopeless case. Psychol. Clinic 8:213–29. (Ja. '15.)

Johnston, W. Dawson. The library and history study. Hist. Teachers M. 6:31–33. (Fe. '15.)

Johnston, W. Dawson. The library and the teaching of English. English J. 4:21–27. (Ja. '15.)

Lovejoy, Owen R. Education and industry debating over children. Survey 33:399–400. (9 Ja. '15.)

Manuel, Herschel T. The use of an objective scale for grading handwriting. El. School J. 15:259–78. (Ja. '15.)

Oberholtzer, E. E. Testing the efficiency in reading in the grades. El. School J. 15:313–22. (Fe. '15.)

(A) physiological discovery that explains the formation of bad habits. Cur. Opinion 58:101–2. (Fe. '15.)

Prosser, C. A. The Richmond survey of the National Society for the Promotion of Industrial Education. School and Society 1:161–64. (30 Ja. '15.)

Royce, Josiah. The Carnegie Foundation for the Advancement of Teaching and the case of Middlebury College. School and Society 1:145–50. (30 Ja. '15.)

Sachs, Julius. The secondary school teacher and the college. School and Society 1:50–53. (9 Ja. '15.)

Sears, J. B. The problem of the rural school. Pop. Sci. Mo. 86:174–79. (Fe. '15.)

Thorndike, Edward L. The disciplinary value of studies: a census of opinions. Educa. 35:278–86. (Ja. '15.)

Waldo, Karl Douglas. Tests in reading in Sycamore schools. El. School J. 15:251–68. (Ja. '15.)

Wilgus, James A. The teaching of history in the elementary school. Educa. R. 49:136–46. (Fe. '15.)

Woodbridge, Frederick J. E. The university and the public. Educa. R. 49:109–25. (Fe. '15.)

VOLUME XV NUMBER 8

THE ELEMENTARY SCHOOL JOURNAL

CONTINUING "THE ELEMENTARY SCHOOL TEACHER"

APRIL 1915

EDUCATIONAL NEWS AND EDITORIAL COMMENT

Department of Superintendence

The meeting of the Department of Superintendence at Cincinnati during the last week of February was one of the most notable educational gatherings that has ever come together in this country. The attendance was larger by five hundred than ever before. It became apparent in the resolutions passed by the Department that a certain degree of independence will be sought for this meeting. It was resolved that hereafter only those should vote at the meetings of the Department who are directly concerned with the type of work that is represented by this meeting. This resolution has to be submitted to the general Association, but will undoubtedly act to give the Department a type of independence which it deserves.

Junior High School

The interests of school organization were also represented in certain of the other resolutions. It was voted that the differentiation of the school curriculum beginning with the seventh grade is desirable throughout our public schools. This is an indication of the growing tendency in all parts of the country to develop a junior high school.

Permanent Organization

A resolution was also adopted creating a committee to provide for some type of organization which shall carry the influence of the Association through the year between the meetings of the Department. If an organization can be effected which will promote the professional interests of superintendents and teachers, it undoubtedly will be a very large service. The general Association has never been compact enough to take in hand the serious problems of professional organization. The Department of Superintendence has reached the point in its history where it could become a very useful agency to this end.

Standards and Tests

Passing over the other resolutions which are important in themselves, but not characteristic of the particular meeting of this year, we may comment on several programs which were significant in determining the history of certain movements. The National Council evidently had planned during this meeting to give a full hearing to those who are skeptical about the desirability of standardization, tests, measurements, and other exact forms of evaluating school work. The first program of the National Council bore as its general title, "Standardization, Wise and Otherwise." Mr. Winship, President Pearse, Superintendent Nathan S. Schaeffer, and Professor Bird T. Baldwin appeared on the program. A telegram was read from Mr. John R. Kirk, president of the State Normal School at Kirksville, Missouri. The first three speakers on the program called attention to the fact that standardization has been going forward very rapidly through various agencies. A number of times outspoken criticism was expressed against the activities of some of the great educational foundations, but, beyond this criticism, the effort to show that there is harm or danger in standardization did not get very far.

Mr. Winship was very clear in his mind that different localities must be satisfied with different kinds of institutions. For some reason or other he seemed to believe that standardization was going to destroy the autonomy of different communities. Why standardization should be regarded as inimical to variation is difficult to see. If a community wants to have an institution like Valparaiso as distinguished from another institution like Yale or Harvard, these being the institutions to which Mr. Winship most frequently referred, then certainly the community ought to be allowed to do what it likes. Standardization simply means that the community will know what it is doing; if it wants to have these variations it will hardly be doubted that the choice ought to be made intelligently rather than by mere accident. There are some people who are likely to be misled by an institution that is not equally good with other institutions without knowing that the character of institutions differs as widely as it does. Consequently Mr. Winship's argument that various institutions ought to be different from each other is in nowise unacceptable to the most ardent advocate of standards.

Mr. Pearse followed the same general line, arguing that there is no possibility of standardizing families. This analogy represents perhaps the strongest point in his argument, but here again it ought to be pointed out that families will undoubtedly be interested, if they are at all scientifically minded, in comparing themselves with each other. A standard does not necessarily mean a final rule of action, nor does it demand that everyone shall conform absolutely to the principles set down by any single institution or family. Mr. Schaeffer called attention to the very encouraging fact that all of the professions are making use of educational institutions as a basis for their standardization. While the requirement of a high-school education as the basis of all professional courses may be called in question as a general policy, it is nevertheless an accomplished fact.

Mr. Baldwin pointed out some of the efforts which have recently been made in standardization. Mr. Kirk's telegram indicated that he has very little sympathy with the survey which is being made at the present time of the normal schools of the state of Missouri by the Carnegie Foundation.

No one attended the program under discussion without feeling that the attack upon standardization, if such was intended, was a complete failure. In the first place, those who attacked standardization apparently did not understand what is meant by standardiardization; and the evidences that appeared that standardization is going forward and is an important part of our American educational and social scheme were very strong.

Discussion of Surveys

Another general program which dealt with the same type of topic was the program of Friday morning of the Department of Superintendence. The title of this program was "The Investigation of the Efficiency of Schools and School Systems." It had been reported widely that the whole matter of surveys would here be handled without any reserve whatsoever, and so it was. Superintendent Van Sickle read a very impressive paper giving an account of the development of the movement for school surveys and reported with a good deal of detail the judgment of those who have been in contact with these surveys as to the profitable results for the school systems that have been surveyed. His verdict was unqualified that the result has been useful in American education.

Mr. Ayres of the Russell Sage Foundation followed with a very notable paper in which he gave an account of the development of the whole movement for social surveys. He indicated that the school surveys are part of the general scientific attitude which is being assumed by communities at the present time. Mr. Ayres also gave a number of characteristics of a good survey. The survey must be made by competent people; it must not be partisan in its character; it must be co-operative in its character, including the activities of the superintendents and principals; it must have public character; its results must be made available for the people in the school system. All of these maxims for the organization of a survey indicate that the movement has passed beyond the experimental stage and is coming to be recognized as a movement with definite public character.

Superintendent Young of Chicago followed with a plea for the internal organization of school surveys. She referred to the undertakings of the school officers of the city of Chicago and called attention to the value of a survey made by the officers themselves. She pointed out the difficulties that arise from the common attitude of over-criticism of what is found in the schools. Anyone who expected an attack upon the survey movement from this quarter was disappointed. To be sure, Superintendent Young did point out that there are many agencies now making surveys in the country that are unworthy. She included among those of whom she was skeptical the college officers who have been engaged in work of this type, but in the main her verdict was in favor of a rational, internal self-examination.

Commissioner Kendall followed with an elaborate discussion of the different kinds of surveys that ought to be developed. He also called attention to the dangers that arise from basing these surveys on mere opinion. There should be experienced, practical officers of school systems connected with every survey. Commissioner Kendall's discussion of the matter was very wholesome and encouraging to those who wish to see the survey movement promoted along rational lines. There was also in his statement a strong emphasis upon the desirability of continuity in the work.

The final number of this program was presented by Superintendent Maxwell. Superintendent Maxwell felt very sure that the surveys in the form in which they are now organized are open to many criticisms. He made the charge that the surveys were the result of the efforts on the part of college officers to secure employment, evidently assuming that college officers have very little else to do than to look for some perquisites in the way of opportunities to work outside their own field. Mr. Ayres's answer to this in the earlier paper was so complete that it is hardly worth discussing this particular point. The survey movement is a movement which grows out of the large social interest in public affairs. After Mr. Maxwell had disposed of those whom he criticizes for having organized surveys, he found the movement closely related to the historical fact that there has in recent years been a reaction against examinations. Mr. Maxwell regards scientific testing as merely a new form of examination. He thinks that this new form of examination will have its day and will ultimately be superseded by something better. He did not indicate what something better would be, but he did point out the very hopeful outlook of this present movement as the probable basis of that which is to come in later years.

The Survey Movement Established

Commenting on the whole problem from the point of view of the partisan of standards and measurements and surveys, it must be said that nothing but encouragement could be derived from the words which were spoken. If there are agencies which have been carrying on surveys in a fashion unworthy of the science of education, they ought to be suppressed and everyone will welcome criticism of such agencies and their modes of operation. On the other hand, there can be no doubt at all that the time has passed when surveys are open to general skepticism and the time has certainly passed when standards and measures will be looked upon as of doubtful value. The actual adjustment of the school situation will still involve complexities that we have not solved, but that the time has passed when one can scoff at standards and surveys was very apparent from the whole tone of the Cincinnati meeting.

Economy in School Work

It would hardly be fair to close the discussion without calling attention in a general way to the fact that in many of the meetings details were brought forward showing how economy can be effected, showing how reading and arithmetic and history and geography need to be reorganized, showing how in all of these fields there are vigorous activities going on in the schools through the agencies both of superintendents and of special students.

School Efficiency Bureaus

One very notable feature of the meeting was the organization of a National Society of Efficiency Men. Already there are nine school systems in the United States that have employed in connection with the office of superintendent men whose special business it is to measure the effects of school work and to give the superintendent the advantage of a scientific inquiry into the operation of the schools. That these men should organize and begin to promote the movement which they represent, each in his own city, is a historical event in the development of American education. There will be a meeting of these men next year at Detroit, where the Department of Superintendence is to come together, and we may soon look for a stream of publication from this source which will be of very great advantage to the educational world.

Reading Tests and Other Tests

One other comment may be added. The Committee for Determining Standards and Tests recommended that the work go forward, and this was voted by the National Council without a dissenting vote. The *Elementary School Journal* will attempt throughout the year to collect and publish material on reading, as it has during the past year. It solicits from its readers material of this type and will be very glad indeed to put anyone who is attempting to carry on tests in communication with others who are engaged in similar work, and it will so far as possible supply material to anyone who is undertaking tests of this kind.

The Value of Medical Inspection

The past few years have witnessed a widespread movement among the larger cities toward the introduction of medical inspection in some form into the public-school system. The experience of those cities in which medical inspection has been attempted in a systematic way indicates that the school in adding this to its list of functions is rendering a social service of the highest order. A few facts from Boston are of interest in this connection.

In 1907 the Division of Hygiene in the Boston School Department began the systematic testing of the eyesight of the children of the public schools. In that year it was discovered that 31.5 per cent of the 83,909 pupils examined were defective. "By continued testing, by following all cases into the homes, by prescribing glasses and remedial treatment, and by assisting indigent children to obtain glasses at a nominal cost, the Division has greatly reduced the number and the percentage of ocular trouble." An examination of 91,326 children, completed in January of this year, shows that 5,754 children are now wearing glasses, and 11,039, or 12.08 per cent of the total, have abnormal vision. Thus it is seen that careful inspection for eight years has resulted in the reduction of the percentage of defectives from 31.5 per cent to 12.08 per cent. These results most certainly point to a wise expenditure of public funds when we consider the relation of visual defect to retardation with its attendant social and economic evils.

The Need for Clerical Assistance

Those in control of public education in this country are frequently guilty of practicing a false economy; and probably in no instance is this tendency more pronounced than in the burdening of the superintendent with numerous clerical duties. Of course the members of school boards may be excused on the grounds that they are human and are merely exhibiting a perfectly natural human weakness. And possibly they are, so long as their attention is not directed toward the facts. Consequently, in order that this excuse may not long be a valid one, it might be profitable to give currency to a summary of the conclusions reached at a recent gathering of school-board members and superintendents from the parishes (counties) of Louisiana. A statement of these conclusions follows:

No business will succeed unless it is properly managed and supervised, and this is as true of the school business as of any other business. Even thoroughly competent teachers need the constant advice and co-operation of a wise superintendent; many of our teachers, however, are young and inexperienced, and they, especially, should receive constantly the help of the superintendent. In order that the superintendent may keep in close touch with the people of the various communities, and especially with all of his teachers, he should be able to visit each of the schools at least once or twice a month, and to spend sufficient time in each school to enable him to be of real service to the teachers in organizing and directing the work.

The school board cannot afford to pay the salary required to secure the services of a competent superintendent for clerical work in the office. The bookkeeping, compiling reports, typewriting, writing warrants, etc., should be done by a cheaper employee than the parish (county) superintendent, especially in parishes that employ a large number of teachers. It was the opinion of the conference that clerical help should be given the parish superintendent in order that the superintendent may spend his time in his schools directing the efforts of teachers and stimulating educational activity among the patrons.

An Experiment for the "Wasted Years," Fourteen to Sixteen

Boys and girls in New York City, between fourteen and sixteen years of age, who have secured working papers and have left school to go to work, but have failed to obtain employment or have lost their jobs after working for a time, are to receive special opportunities to continue their schooling. A small beginning has already been made by establishing in one public elementary school a "practical information class" designated as 7A–8B special, the teacher furnishing such instruction as seems to meet the special needs of the pupils. Since the class is intended for pupils temporarily out of employment, the number in attendance fluctuates greatly. Class sessions are five hours a day, but pupils may be excused for as many as three hours, when necessary, to seek employment.

The experiment is an attempt to reduce the deterioration which results during these years from the shifting about from one juvenile occupation to another with intermittent idleness for weeks at a time. Somewhat similar provisions are made for the work-permit children in Wisconsin in the all-day industrial school established as a part of the state system of industrial education.

Play Space for Children

The problem of securing for every child "a place to play" is a very serious one in large cities such as New York and Chicago. In Chicago, for instance, there are 334 regular school buildings, 43 branches, 19 schools occupying rented quarters, and 261 of the so-called portable buildings. In scores of cases playgrounds are either entirely lacking or inadequate. The deficiency is partly met by the establishment of small parks and special playgrounds, but it is found too expensive to provide a playground for every neighborhood.

The remedy which is being very successfully used in both Chicago and New York is a very simple one and costs but little money. In the crowded districts and near schools having no playground, a block or two of the street is roped off for certain hours of the day providing a safe convenient play space for the children. At other times the street can be used for regular traffic, and no one is seriously inconvenienced.

A Junior High School

A junior high school has recently been inaugurated in the little town of McMinnville, Oregon. The establishment of this institution has attracted much attention inasmuch as this is the first time that a junior high school has been organized in one of the smaller American towns.

The newly organized institution is described by Superintendent W. R. Rutherford in a recent bulletin entitled *Feasibility of the Junior High School in the Small City*.

The sum of thirty thousand dollars was appropriated for the erection of the building, which is located near enough to the regular high school to permit the regular high-school teachers to come to the building or to receive classes from it in their own classrooms at the high school.

The course of study differs but little, as yet, from the regular work of the seventh, eighth, and ninth grades except in the electives offered. These include music and art, German, typewriting, shorthand, printing, ancient history, and household accounting.

Compensation of Members of Boards of Education

In connection with the present discussion in New York City regarding legislation to reduce the size of the board of education from 46 to 9 numbers, the question has arisen whether the members should receive compensation in case the small board of 9 members is authorized. The following facts showing the present practice of cities of 100,000 population and over, with reference to the compensation of members of boards of education, have been gathered by the Public Education Association of New York City and published in a recent bulletin:

COMPENSATION OF MEMBERS OF BOARDS OF EDUCATION IN CITIES OF 100,000 POPULATION AND OVER*

Compensation	Number of Cities	Names of Cities
No compensation........	42	Albany, Atlanta, Baltimore, Birmingham, Boston, Bridgeport, Cambridge, Chicago, Cincinnati,** Cleveland, Columbus, Dayton, Denver, Detroit, Fall River, Grand Rapids, Indianapolis, Jersey City, Kansas City, Louisville, Lowell, Minneapolis, Nashville, Newark, New Haven, New Orleans, New York, Omaha, Paterson, Philadelphia, Pittsburgh, Portland, Providence, Richmond, St. Louis, Scranton, Seattle, Spokane, Syracuse, Toledo, Washington, Worcester.
Compensation..........	6	
$3000 per annum......		San Francisco
$1200 per annum......		Rochester
$ 40 per month......		Memphis
$ 10 per meeting, not to exceed $50 per month..........		Los Angeles
$ 10 per meeting, not to exceed $40 per month..........		Oakland
$ 3 per meeting, not to exceed $100 per annum..........		Milwaukee
Total..............	48	

*Only 48 of the 50 cities which had 100,000 population and over, according to the Federal Census of 1910, are included in this table, as 2 cities, Buffalo and St. Paul have no boards of education.

**Entitled to 5 cents per annum for each pupil enrolled, but none have collected the amount allowed them.

COMPENSATION OF BOARDS OF DIFFERENT SIZES IN CITIES OF 100,000 POPULATION AND OVER

Size of Board	Number of Cities	No Compensation		Compensation	
		Number	Cities	Number	Cities
3	1	1	Albany		
4	1			1	San Francisco
5	14	12	Birmingham, Boston, Cambridge, Denver, Indianapolis, Louisville, Lowell, New Orleans, Portland, Seattle, Spokane, Toledo	2	Memphis, Rochester
6	1	1	Kansas City		
7	8	6	Cincinnati, Cleveland, Columbus, Minneapolis, New Haven, Syracuse	2	Los Angeles, Oakland
9	10	10	Baltimore, Fall River, Grand Rapids, Jersey City, Nashville, Newark, Paterson, Richmond, Scranton, Washington		
12	4	4	Atlanta, Bridgeport, Omaha, St. Louis		
14	1	1	Dayton		
15	3	2	Philadelphia, Pittsburgh	1	Milwaukee
18	1	1	Detroit		
21	1	1	Chicago		
30	1	1	Worcester		
33	1	1	Providence		
46	1	1	New York		
Total	48	42		6	

EDUCATIONAL WRITINGS

Aids for Grammar-Grade History Teachers and Supervisors

During the past year or so there have come from the press many books and pamphlets of special interest to teachers of history in the upper elementary grades. While publishers make strenuous efforts to acquaint teachers with their publications, it often happens that much valuable information never gets beyond the office of the principal or superintendent; or should the class teacher chance to acquire some general information about a new book in history, this information is often too fragmentary to give her a basis for judging its value. Unless she is willing to buy somewhat recklessly, making no effort to distinguish between the good and the bad before purchasing, she needs some comparative statement which can be used as a basis for judging what will help her and what will not. She needs to have the special features of a half-dozen books on a topic pointed out in some detail. It is the purpose of this discussion to perform this service with reference to a body of material which has recently come from the press. Recency of appearance and the probable aid to grammar-grade history teachers and supervisors have been the two controlling principles of selection.

Two books on the teaching of history appeared during the closing months of 1914. One[1] (1) is a revision, the other (2) a first edition. While these books contain material of interest and value to history teachers other than grade teachers, yet they are primarily for history teachers in grades below the high school.

In his revised book Professor Mace has included some new material of great value, namely, the section on "The Picture-making Phase of History." The major part of this section deals with the materials for picture-making. It is not a discussion of illustrative material, as the heading might indicate, but a program for history in the grades based on the psychological doctrine that history should lead to the development of mental pictures. The

[1] The numbers refer to the list of books given at the end of the article.

program outlined is sufficiently concrete to be of great value to those who may be thinking of revising their course in history. It is the writer's opinion that this section alone is worth the price of the book. It is also his opinion that the remainder of the book is of little value to the upper elementary-grade history teacher.

"How to Teach American History" is a book much of which Professor Wayland has evolved from actual classroom experiments in a normal school in Virginia. The material thus evolved includes chapters on "The Visual Appeal in the Teaching of History," "Why Some Pupils Dislike History," "Making and Using History Question," "On Voyages of Discovery," "Devices for Review and Recreation," "The Teacher's Lesson Plan," and "The Teacher's Need to Know Himself." These chapters contain concrete material of value to history teachers, especially those who have had little or no experience. In all, the book contains thirty chapters of varying length and value. The style is simple—indeed too simple at times for mature students—descending not infrequently to the literary level of a high-school oration. The author's great enthusiasm for history, however, permeates the book throughout. If it succeeds in creating a similar enthusiasm in the teachers of history for the subject its existence will have been justified (3).

In a study (4) of history teaching in the elementary grades which the writer made two years ago, the problem of suitable texts in history for the sixth grade came to his attention again and again. While there was a great demand for history for this grade, there seemed to be a deplorable lack of suitable texts. Fortunately this condition of affairs has been materially remedied since the study was made. The epoch-making report of the Committee of Eight has had more influence in producing the present supply of texts in history for the sixth grade than any other single factor. As soon as publishers and competent textbook writers felt any degree of certainty about what was wanted in such texts, they were not long in preparing them. The report of the committee defined the demand with a definiteness altogether lacking in earlier discussions of the matter.

There have rather recently appeared six texts (5) suitable for the sixth grade, covering practically the material recommended by the Committee of Eight for this grade. Speaking in general, each of these seven texts follows, in the organization of the field and the individual topics selected for treatment, the course outlined by this committee. While this is true in general, yet the books differ somewhat in emphasis placed on certain phases of the material treated. For example, Miss Atkinson has told her story with England as a basis, more than half of her chapters containing material relating to English life and customs. Anyone desiring a book with such an emphasis will find it in this volume. Ex-Superintendent Gordy has followed strictly the outline proposed by the committee. He uses the general divisions suggested as the largest division of his book and the main subordinate divisions as chapters. His is a book in which the story suggested in the skeleton outline proposed by the committee has been clothed in language adapted to the sixth grade. Benton and Bourne have devoted eight of their twenty-one chapters to the discovery and exploration of America. It is their intention to treat this period in such a way that it will not be necessary to go over it again in the seventh grade. Their text for the last two elementary grades takes up the story where this introductory book leaves it. Since so much space is given to the period of discovery and exploration, the treatment of the topics connected with Greek, Roman, and mediaeval life is necessarily brief. The same is true of the Elson and MacMullen text, which gives 26 per cent of its treatment to the Western world. Professor Harding's book is what its title suggests, a story of Europe. Superintendent Nida's *Dawn of American History in Europe* belongs in the same category as Harding's *Story of Europe*. One finds here a strong emphasis on Continental European history.

There are a number of pamphlets which should be brought to the attention of history teachers. This type of material is usually privately printed, and for this reason never advertised to any extent. The following should be known more widely than they are: pamphlets by R. D. Chadwick (6), Gary, Indiana; Maurice C. Tex (7), Taylorville, Illinois; J. O. Hall (8), Hutchinson, Kansas; Lucy W. Glass (9), Jeannette, Pennsylvania; and W. J. Adams (10), Rensselaer, New York. A brief note concerning each of these will assist the teacher in estimating its value to her in her daily work.

Mr. Chadwick's little book contains material that was used during the school year 1912–13 in typewritten form in the evening continuation school of Gary, Indiana. The book contains a brief statement of the facts of United States history and a description of local and national government, adapted to foreigners who are expecting to become naturalized citizens. The historical part was planned for foreign men and women who came to the evening school. The description of government was planned for a like audience, but was also used with good results in two classes of eighth-grade history as an outline for the study of civil government. The value of the pamphlet is not in its historical accuracy, for it is not always accurate; but in the fact that it furnishes a splendid example of the possibility of adapting history and civil government to the needs of a large class of students in our evening continuation schools.

Miss Tex in her two pamphlets treats every topic in seventh- and eighth-grade history. Her topics harmonize in the main with those in the fifth general revision of the Illinois State Course of Study. The pamphlets contain material not commonly found in the regular texts for these grades.

Hall's outline is a revision of an older publication. It is strong on the period following the Civil War. Since many texts are weak on this period, the outline will be of service to the busy teacher who is yet feeling her way through this period.

Miss Glass has given us out of her own experience a comprehensive outline of United States and Pennsylvania history. The suggestions on state history are very helpful to those seeking suitable material on local history for the upper elementary grades.

The Regents' questions used in New York state are arranged according to periods by Adams. They are valuable from the standpoint of giving the teacher an idea of what phases of each period are considered essential by the authors of such questions. In doing this they may be considered as a form of standardization. It is the opinion of the writer that much information on the matter of standardizing history material can be gained from such questions.

On account of the increasing interest in the study of civics in the grammar grades, due in a large measure to the efforts of the

Committee on Social Studies, some mention should be made of recent material along this line. Four examples of this kind of material may be examined somewhat critically. These include a revision of a former book by A. W. Dunn (11), and original editions by A. G. Fradenburgh (12), Mabel Hill (13), and one edited by Ella Lyman Cabot (14).

Mr. Dunn has made but few changes in his original edition. A notable feature of the revised edition is an "Introduction for Teachers" dealing with aims and methods. In this discussion are included two type-lessons in which the author illustrates how the material in the text should be presented in order to achieve the best results. The entire discussion is full of excellent suggestions.

The book by Mr. Fradenburgh adheres closely to the old type of civics material, emphasizing chiefly local and general government.

Miss Hill's book is a real contribution to the cause of civics teaching. While it is more applicable to work of a high-school grade, yet the grammar-grade teacher will find in it an abundance of suggestions. Twenty-four lessons are worked out in detail. With the suggestions given in these lessons the teacher should be able to do some very effective work in civics. *A Course in Citizenship* is what its title suggests. The general topics for each grade in order, beginning with the first, are "Home," "School and Playground," "The Neighborhood," "Town and City," "The Nation," "American Ideals," "The United States and the World," and "The World Family." Work is outlined for each of these topics by school months. A very great deal of excellent material is given for each grade.

Fortunately for the subject of history in the elementary school the dry matter-of-fact textbook method is rapidly disappearing. Good teachers are attempting to make the subject as concrete as possible. One method by which this is being accomplished is through dramatization in its various forms. Some helpful books have recently appeared along this line. Space will permit the mention of but four of these. They are three books (15) on historical plays and one (16) on pageants and pageantry.

The three books on historical plays are very similar, all of them, as suggested by the titles, taking their material from the Colonial period of our history. The book by Bird and Starling is planned primarily for reading-lessons, with occasional formal presentation. Miss Shoemaker has aimed at simplicity. Her plays could be presented by the children with little formal memorizing of parts, since the speeches by the various characters are about what a sixth- or seventh-grade pupil would most likely say if he knew the history upon which the play was based. The plays by Tucker and Ryan are for fifth-grade pupils. They are suitable for either acting or reading. It is the writer's opinion that the chief value of all books of this type is that they furnish the busy teacher a model. With the ideas gained from the reading of such plays, she and the children can construct similar ones based on their actual history work. Plays in which the pupils have had no part in their construction are a very poor substitute for those that the children actually make. Pageants written and planned by the teacher without the assistance of the pupils are not worth the energy required for their presentation. To be of value to history teaching both plays and pageants must be largely planned and written by the pupils themselves. The three books mentioned above will be of great service to pupils in suggesting both form and content of historical plays.

The volume by Bates and Orr is useful in the hands of a teacher who is thinking of having her class construct a pageant. Besides a chapter on "The Making of a Pageant" it contains a Roman, a Mediaeval, and a Colonial pageant, all of which are very suggestive. The appendix contains a full bibliography which will assist the teacher in finding material on practically every phase of making and presenting pageants.

Such are some of the various aids for grammar-grade history teachers and supervisors. Every book or pamphlet mentioned is worthy of a place on the teacher's desk. If she gets but one idea from each of them, both her money and her time will have been well invested.

BIBLIOGRAPHY

1. Mace, W. H. *Method in History.* Rand McNally & Co., Chicago, 1914.
2. Wayland, J. W. *How to Teach American History.* Macmillan, Chicago, 1914.
3. If one is looking for the principles of history teaching in all the grades stated rather dogmatically, such may be found in:

McMurry, C. A. *Handbook of Practice for Teachers.* Macmillan, Chicago, 1914.

4. *Indiana University Studies, No. 17,* Indiana University, Bloomington, Indiana.
5. Elson and MacMullan. *The Story of the Old World.* E. P. Dutton & Co., New York, 1911.

   Benton and Bourne. *Introductory American History.* D. C. Heath & Co., Chicago, 1912.

   Gordy, W. F. *American Beginnings in Europe.* Scribner, New York, 1912.

   Harding, S. B. *The Story of Europe.* Scott, Foresman & Co., Chicago, 1912.

   Nida, W. L. *The Dawn of American History in Europe.* Macmillan, Chicago, 1913.

   Atkinson, Alice M. *An Introduction to American History.* Ginn & Co., Chicago, 1914.
6. *A Brief History of the United States.* Emerson School, Gary, Indiana, 1913.
7. *History for the Eighth Grade.* Published by the author, Taylorville, Illinois, 1914. *History for the Seventh Grade.* By the same author. A similar pamphlet.
8. *An Outline of United States History.* A. Flanagan Co., Chicago, 8th ed., 1913.
9. *A Comprehensive Typical Study of United States History and Pennsylvania History.* Published by the author, Jeanette, Pennsylvania, 1914.
10. *Up-to-date Regents' Questions in Elementary United States History and Civics.* Bardeen, Syracuse, New York, 1914.
11. *The Community and the Citizen.* D. C. Heath & Co., Chicago, 1914.
12. *American Civics for the Seventh and Eighth School Years.* Hinds, Noble & Eldredge, New York, 1913.
13. *The Teaching of Civics.* Houghton Mifflin Co., 1914.
14. *A Course in Citizenship.* Houghton Mifflin Co., 1914.
15. Bird and Starling. *Historical Plays for Children.* Macmillan, Chicago, 1912.

    Shoemaker, Blanche. *Colonial Plays for the School-Room.* Educational Publishing Co., Chicago, 1912.

    Tucker and Ryan. *Historical Plays of Colonial Days.* Longmans, Green & Co., Chicago, 1912.
16. Bates and Orr. *Pageants and Pageantry.* Ginn & Co., Chicago, 1912.

CLASSROOM METHODS AND DEVICES

Practical Lessons in Electricity for the Sixth and Seventh Grades

In the Elementary School of the School of Education many physical science topics are introduced in the natural history work, beginning definitely with a study of magnetism and electricity in the latter part of the sixth grade, and continuing these and other science topics in the seventh grade.

The work is presented in class as a series of problems which the children are led to solve, mainly by individual experimentation. Much of the apparatus used is made by the pupils, some is made by the teacher, and a small amount of it is purchased. Apparatus, therefore, is nearly all of the simple home-made type, intricate apparatus being avoided. From their own efforts and this home-made apparatus the children obtain results and get a clearer knowledge of the subject; also they acquire efficiency in constructive work, and at the same time develop the powers of observation and reasoning. No textbook is used, but notebooks are compiled in which diagrams are made and descriptions of the work the pupils have done are written.

Following are a few typical studies in electricity:

LESSONS ON THE ELECTRIC BELL AND THE BUZZER

Problem 1: What is the difference, in construction, between the bell and the buzzer?

Have pupils examine both carefully and they will learn soon that the only difference is that the bell has a gong and a long hammer while the buzzer has a short hammer and no gong.

Problem 2: What are the different parts of the bell or the buzzer?

The pupils, with bell or buzzer in hand, are asked in turn to point out one thing which they see, and if the correct name is not known to them, it is given by the teacher. A large diagram is put on the board by teacher or pupil, and the parts labeled and learned: Binding-posts *BP;* coils of wire *C;* connecting bar of iron holding the coils at one end *CB;* hammer placed across the other end of coils but not touching them *H;* small spring on hammers, one end of which rests against the connecting point of a small arm *A;* this arm, *A*, with connecting point, insulated (i.e., separated by rubber or other non-conducting material) from base *B;* rubber tube covering parts of the wire; insulation or non-conducting pad under one of the binding-posts; and gong *G*.

Pupils draw diagram of bell or buzzer in notebook and label parts. See Fig. 1.

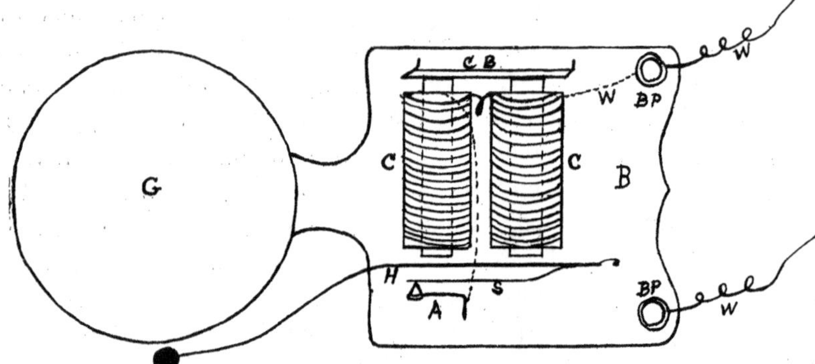

Fig. 1.—Electric Bell

Before learning how a bell or a buzzer works, or tracing the path of electric current through it, it is best to have the pupils make a cell and learn how to attach it to the bell so that the bell will ring.

Problem 3: How can a cell be made which will give sufficient electric current to ring a bell?

a) Pupils take an eight-ounce bottle, or pint fruit jar, and put into it 1 cup of water, 1 teaspoonful of potassium bichromate, and, always last, one-eighth of a cup, or 5 teaspoonfuls, of strong sulphuric acid. (The teacher had better measure and pour in the acid to avoid danger of burning hands or clothing.) A carbon rod and a zinc rod or strip, each from 4 to 6 inches long, are needed for the cell. The carbon is the kind used in arc lights and stereopticon lanterns, and may be purchased for a few cents, or taken from worn-out dry cells. Zinc rods or strips are inexpensive, and may be purchased from an electric or hardware store. For convenience the pupils fasten the two rods together with rubber bands in such a way that they do not touch each other. Next they attach one bare end of a copper wire, size No. 18 to No. 24, to the top of the carbon rod, and a second wire to the zinc rod, and connect the other ends of the wires to the binding-posts of the bell. Last of all the rods are put into the cell. See Fig. 2.

If the bell does not ring at once, vibrate or start the hammer with the finger.

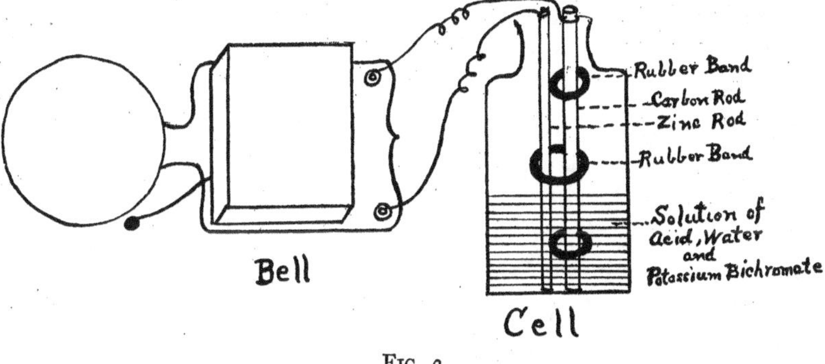

FIG. 2

b) Cautions in using this cell (called the Grenét or Bichromate cell):

1. Handle bottle carefully so as not to spill acid solution. Better fasten it into ring stand.

2. Make all connections before putting the rods into the cell. Have connections tightly made, with ends of wires bare and clean.

3. Remove rods from cell when it is not in use, to prevent the acid from eating away the zinc rod.

Problem 4: Trace the path of the electric current through the bell.

Pupils easily follow the wire from one binding-post of the cell to the bell, thence to the nearer coil, then to the second coil, and from that coil to the little arm whose contact point rests against the spring on the hammer. They may be able to see how the current now passes through the contact point to the spring on the hammer, thence through the hammer, from the hammer to the iron base, through the base to the second binding-post, thence through the second wire to the cell again.

Questions bring out the fact that the current cannot go through the bell base to the first binding-post because this binding-post is insulated from the base.

Problem 5: What makes the buzzer or the bell ring when an electric current goes through it?

A horseshoe magnet, such as is familiar to children, may be shown and its power to attract iron illustrated. Then a large round nail, or some other piece of iron, may be tested to see if it has magnetism and will draw iron (tacks, for example) to it. If not (and it will not unless previously magnetized), wind covered copper wire around it, connect the wire to a cell, and send a current around the nail. Test it while the current is on. Does it now pick up tacks or other iron?

Notice that the coils on the bell, with the bar of iron connecting them, resemble a horseshoe magnet with wires wound around each arm.

Will these coils attract tacks when a current runs through the wire around them? Try it.

What effect will this attracting force have on the hammer?

What prevents the hammer from being drawn to the ends of the coils and sticking there?

When the hammer is drawn away from the contact point of the little arm, is the electric current affected?

If the current is broken, do the coils remain magnetized?

When the hammer is pulled back by the spring at one end of it, to the contact point, does the electric current flow through the bell and coils again?

Now it is seen that the bell is made to ring by quickly breaking and making again the electric circuit at the contact point, thus magnetizing and demagnetizing the coils, alternately attracting and releasing the hammer.

Applications of the bell: Door bells, school bells, fire alarm bells, call bells, etc.

Applications of the cell: Ringing bells, running electric toys, telephones, furnishing spark for gasoline engines, etc.

LESSON ON THE PUSH BUTTON

As it injures most cells to run them continuously, a push button is needed so that the current may be turned off or on at will.

Problem 6: How may a simple push button be made?

Allow pupils to examine an ordinary push button, which may be purchased for ten cents, learning parts and connecting it in with bell and cell. Raise questions as to the principle involved, etc. It is seen that when the two pieces of metal in the push button are pressed together, the electric current passes through the wires which are attached to the two pieces of metal and thence to the bell and cell, thus completing the circuit. Next have the children draw a plan of a simple push button which they would like to make. Then give them a block of wood, two pieces of metal, a hammer, small nails, and tacks, and allow them to carry out their plan. See push button in Fig. 4.

Connect the home-made push button with bell and cell and work it. Keep for future use in school or at home.

LESSONS ON ELECTROPLATING

While the pupil's cell is still in good condition, it is well to give one or two lessons in simple electroplating. Copper plating can be done by the pupils with simple apparatus which they can put together.

Problem 7: How can a cell be used to copper plate something?

a) Pupils put a few crystals of copper sulphate (blue vitriol) in a metal dish with one-half a glass of water and heat to dissolve the crystals. Dilute to a faint-blue solution.

b) Let each fill a glass one-half full of this solution and put into it a narrow strip of copper and the object to be plated, after first attaching copper wires to each of them. Attach the other end of the wire which is on the copper strip to the carbon rod of the cell, and the second wire to the zinc of the cell. Within five or ten minutes the article being plated will show the reddish tinge of the copper. Preferably use first a piece of carbon rod to plate, then try other things, such as clean pieces of iron, steel, etc. See Fig. 3.

Problem 8: How can the plating be removed by electricity?

Try suggestions of the pupils, or lead them to reverse the connections so that the copper strip is attached to the zinc rod of the cell, thus reversing the direction of the current.

In discussions bring out the fact that all electroplating is done on this principle: nickel plating requires a certain nickel solution

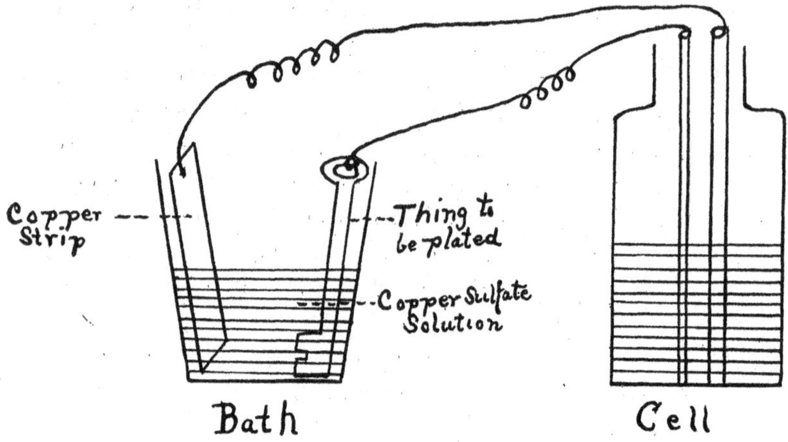

FIG. 3.—Electroplating

and a lump of nickel, or a nickel strip, instead of a copper solution and a copper strip; silver and gold plating require silver and gold solutions, and silver and gold strips respectively.

LESSONS ON THE GALVANOSCOPE

After the cell has been made and something has been learned about an electric current in its power to ring bells and do copper plating, another interesting problem is to make a simple apparatus to determine whether a cell has any electricity in it, and if so in what direction it flows through the wires. Also the apparatus will show whether the current is very weak or strong.

Problem 9: To make a piece of apparatus called a galvanoscope, that will detect a current given by a cell.

a) Pupils are given the general idea that a block of wood needs to be wound with a few coils of wire in such a way that a compass may be placed on the block directly under the wires. Sometimes a hole is bored in the block, in which the compass is placed. Again, small strips of wood are nailed to one surface of the block and the compass placed between them and under the wires. The children may devise other ways of getting the same results. See Fig. 4.

b) Pupils connect up the galvanoscope with the cell and the push button. Place the galvanoscope so that the wires run north and south, parallel to the compass needle, and press push button, watching the compass needle.

Does the north end of the compass needle move toward the east or the west? How far? Sharply to the east or west, or only part way?

Does it swing to the north again when the current is off?

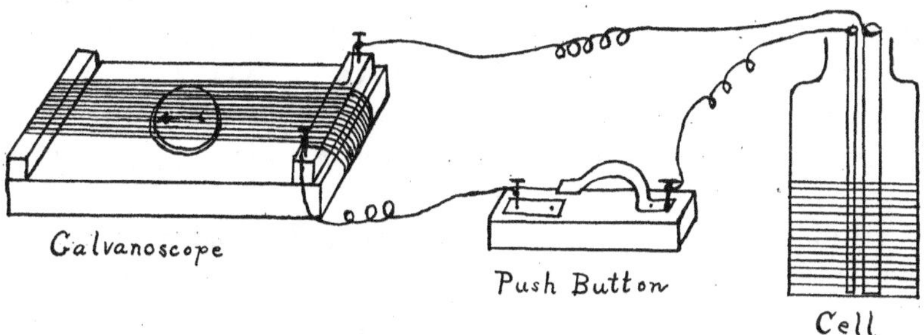

FIG. 4

This proves that the cell sends a current through the wire, and denotes somewhat its strength. If the current is weak the needle moves but slightly.

Problem 10: How can the direction of the current be determined by the galvanoscope?

Pupils put right hand over the compass, palm down, with thumb extended at right angles to the fingers, and so place the hand that the thumb points to the east if the north end of the needle points that way when the current is on, or toward the west if the compass points that way; then the extended fingers will point the direction the current is flowing in the wire.

Reverse the current in the wires by changing connections. For example, exchange ends of wires on copper and zinc rods of the cell. Does this alter the direction of the needle?

Problem 11: Does a stronger current through the wire affect the compass more strongly?

Pupils either connect two cells to the galvanoscope (connect the carbon rod of one cell with the zinc rod in the second cell), or have one strong cell. Turn on current and test compass. Result?

Problem 12: Do more turns of wire around the galvanoscope or a less number of turns affect the compass needle?

Pupils add more wire around the block and test the compass. Try only two or three turns of wire. Results?

LESSONS ON MAGNETIC FIELDS, OR MAGNETIC INFLUENCE

The question which naturally arises now is, How is it that the compass is affected when it is near wires which have a current running through them? Beginning with the magnetic field, or influence, of a bar magnet, the child can easily be taught that there is magnetic influence surrounding an electric current in wires.

Problem 13: How is it that a current in a wire is able to affect a compass placed near it?

If pupils have studied magnets, they understand what a magnetic field, or magnetic influence, about the magnet means. This influence is best shown by placing a magnet under a sheet of cardboard and sprinkling iron filings on the cardboard. If one gently taps the cardboard, the filings arrange themselves in curves about the magnet, thus outlining the magnetic field. If children have not studied magnets, have them perform this experiment.

The same magnetic influence may be shown to exist around a wire through which a current flows. Wind some covered wire in a rectangular loop, ten or fifteen turns, and place it in a slit in a sheet of cardboard so that one-half of the coil is above and the rest below the cardboard. Have two holes at proper distances along the slit so that the coils of wire will fit in, allowing the slit to close up.

Attach the ends of the wire to the home-made cell and the push button. Sprinkle some iron filings on the cardboard about the wires, then turn on the current and gently tap the cardboard. The filings will form concentric circles about the wires, showing the magnetic influence. See Fig. 5.

Place a small compass near the wire and turn on the current. Does the needle of the compass arrange itself parallel to the lines of magnetic influence or force? Move the compass along these lines around the wires. How does it behave?

Shut off the current; does the needle resume the north-and-south direction? Repeat.

Move the compass around the second coil of wire. Does the needle point in the same direction as when near the first wires, or in the opposite direction?

Does the magnetic field run around the two wires in the same direction?

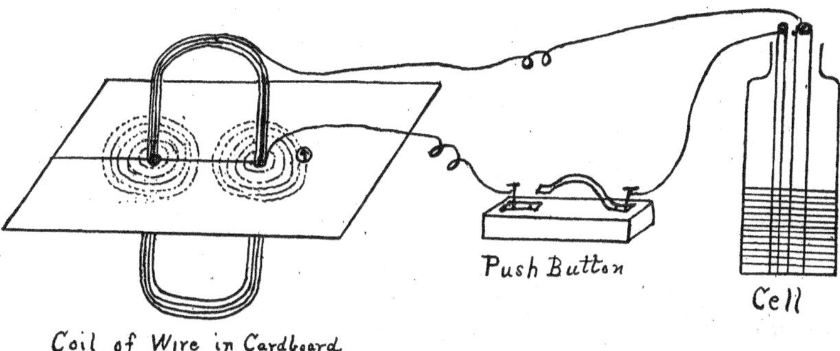

FIG. 5

Does the direction the current takes through the wires have any effect on the direction of the magnetic field?

Can you see now how the current in the galvanoscope wires affects the compass and makes it point at right angles to the direction of the wires?

LESSON ON THE SOLENOID

Having seen that a magnetic field exists around a wire whenever a current passes through it, we next make a magnet out of a coiled wire.

Problem 14: How may a magnet be made out of a coil of wire?

Pupils take a piece of covered wire about three feet long and wind it in a close coil around a pencil or large round nail, leaving

6 or 8 inches of each end of the wire unwound. See Fig. 6. Slip the coil off the pencil and attach it to push button and cell.

Put one end of the coil as near as possible to one end of the compass needle and turn on current. Is the needle affected?

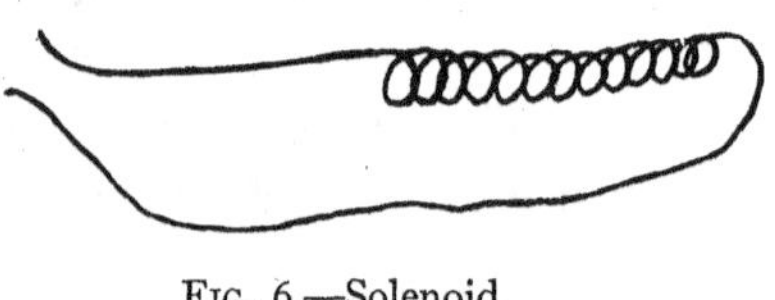

Fig. 6.—Solenoid

Try the other end of the coil near the compass. Is the effect different? Has the coil a north and a south pole?

Put one end of the coil on some iron filings. Do they adhere to the coil? Try the other end. Result?

The coil of wire with a current passing through it is called a solenoid, and it has a north and a south pole like a magnet, though it is very weak.

LESSONS ON THE ELECTROMAGNET

Problem 15: How can the solenoid be made into an electromagnet?

Allow pupils to put an iron nail, or other soft iron, through the solenoid which is attached to the cell and push button, first testing the nail in iron filings or with the compass to see that it has no magnetism in it, or but very little.

Now put one end of the nail, which is in the coil, into iron filings and turn on the current. Result?

Do many filings adhere to the nail when it is raised?

Does anything happen if the current is now shut off?

Try the other end of the nail. Try both ends on the compass needle.

Is this nail a magnet with north and south poles?

Does it remain magnetized when the current is off?

Unless the iron nail is very soft it will hold some of this magnetism.

Such a magnet, or solenoid surrounding a nail or other piece of iron, is called an electromagnet.

A piece of gas pipe, or a bundle made of pieces of soft iron wire of equal length and wrapped together by the wire, makes a good core in place of the nail.

Problem 16: Why has the nail strong magnetism when in the coil with current passing through, and none, or very little, when there is no current in the coil?

Pupils soon draw the inference that the magnetic field about the wire, when the current passes, enters the nail and magnetizes it.

Problem 17: Why use covered or insulated wire in making solenoids and electromagnets?

Pupils wind bare copper wire closely on a pencil so that the separate coils touch, and test with nail as before. Does it work as well?

Does the current go around each coil or cut across from one to the other?

If the latter is the case, is the circuit for the current shorter than or the same length as before?

If the current cuts across, it is called "short-circuiting."

Why is wire covered? Why use covered wire then for apparatus work?

Problem 18: Can an old bar magnet be made stronger by winding wire around it and sending a current through the wire?

Pupils try it, testing the magnet before and after the current is sent around it.

Can you make a new bar magnet by sending a current around a bar of hard steel?

Secure some hard steel from a blacksmith or a machine-shop and try it.

How then can bar magnets be made or magnetized?

Problem 19: How can a stronger electromagnet be made?

Pupils devise means, or the teacher leads them to wind more wire, another layer, on the electromagnet just made, and test it. Will it lift more tacks, nails, or heavier pieces of iron than before? Why?

Now add one or two more cells, so as to have a stronger current, and test again.

In what way, or ways, then, is the magnet made stronger?

Problem 20: How can the magnetic field of one pole of an electromagnet be shown?

Pupils stand the electromagnet on end, place sheet of cardboard on top, sprinkle filings on it, and tap gently while current is on.

Draw a picture of it in notebook.

Problem 21: Is the horseshoe-shaped electromagnet of the same strength as the straight one?

Pupils wind another nail, or bundle of six or eight wires, with same amount of wire as used in problem 15, putting nearly all the wire equally on the ends for about two inches, and very little wire in the middle.

Now carefully bend it all into a horseshoe shape without injuring the insulation. See Fig. 7, *A* and *B*. The bending may be done before winding the wire.

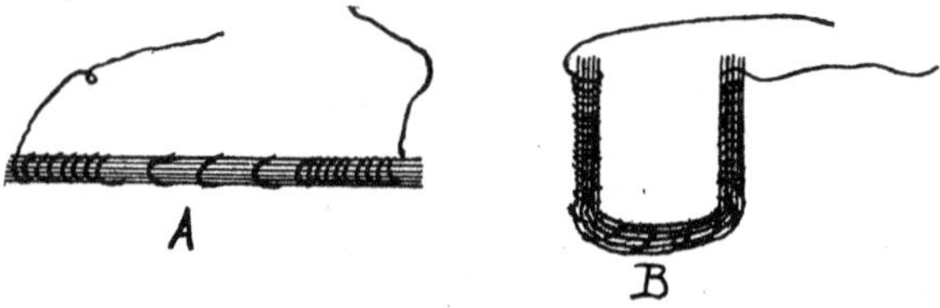

FIG. 7.—Electromagnets

See how much iron can be lifted by one end of the straight magnet and then lift as much as possible on the poles of the U-shaped magnet. Compare the strengths.

Test each pole of the U-shaped magnet by causing each in turn to approach the same end of a compass needle. Are the poles alike or different? What makes them so? (One pole should be north, the other south. If both poles are alike there has been some mistake in the winding.)

Do the windings on the poles of the horseshoe magnet seem to be in the same or in the opposite direction?

Recall the experiment showing the magnetic field around a wire (problem 13). Why then are the poles of the horseshoe magnet different?

Application of the U-shaped electromagnets: Bells and buzzers (review bell and note how it works), telegraph instruments, telephone receiver, arc lights, front-door latches in apartments, handling and shipping iron or iron products, mining iron ore, drawing steel from the eye in accidents, etc.

LESSONS ON THE TELEGRAPH INSTRUMENT

The use of the electromagnet in the telegraph instrument can be demonstrated easily by the pupils if they construct a simple instrument and use the magnets they made.

Problem 22: How has the electromagnet made possible the telegraph instrument?

Pupils fasten, with double-pointed tacks, the U-shaped magnet (*M*) to a block, 4×8 inches, two inches from one end. Support over the magnet a light stick 10 inches long (*A*) with a cross-piece of sheet iron (*I*), this iron to be just above the poles of the magnet. The stick is supported and pivoted on a piece of sheet metal at *P*. Make a push button on the block for a key (*K*), or use the push button already made. See Fig. 8.

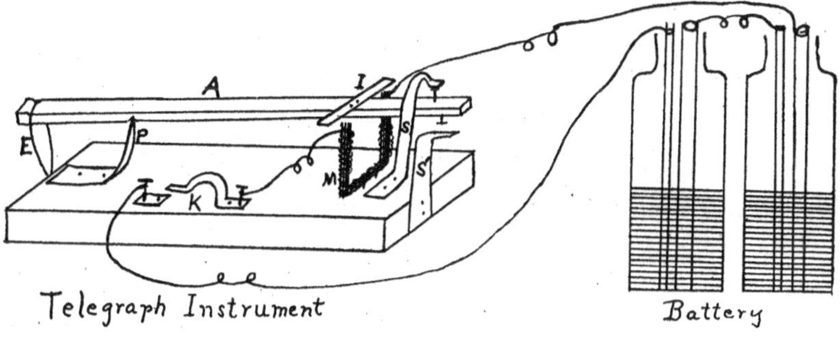

Fig. 8

The sounder consists of the stick (*A*) and two pieces of metal (*S* and *S′*) between which the stick vibrates. The narrow strip *S* curves up and over the stick, so that a small nail or tack in the stick strikes *S* and prevents the elastic band *E* from lifting the iron cross-bar on the stick too high above the magnet. Similarly the narrow strip *S′* prevents the stick from being drawn down far enough for the iron cross-bar to touch the magnet because of the tack in the stick just above *S′*. Allow the cross-bar to come as near the magnet as it can without actually touching it. One end of the wire from the magnet is connected to the push button, or key as it is called here, and the other end is attached to the cell. Another wire connects the cell to the other end of the push button.

The elastic band is so adjusted that it just barely lifts the stick and holds it against S. If the elastic is too tight or too strong, the magnet cannot pull the stick down. When the key is closed so that the current magnetizes the magnet, the iron cross-bar is attracted and pulled down until S' is struck by the tack on the under side of the stick. When the key is released, causing the magnet to lose its magnetism, the cross-bar is no longer attracted, and the elastic band raises the stick quickly until S is struck by the upper tack.

After the pupils can work such a telegraph instrument (our children always succeed after a little practice), two of them may connect their instruments with wire a few feet long, and send messages to each other. One pupil may take his instrument into the corridor, passing the wires under the door, and telegraph to his partner in the room. Either Morse's or the International code may be used. Our pupils often take these instruments home, and work them between houses if close together, or make a second instrument and telegraph from room to room.

Many other lessons in electricity are similarly given, as well as lessons in other phases of physical science.

A keen interest is aroused among both boys and girls by experimental work such as is outlined in this article, and one important result is that many of the children carry their interest in the science work to the home and continue it there.

C. F. Phipps

School of Education
University of Chicago

A STUDY IN RETARDATION AND ACCELERATION

CHARLES S. MEEK
Superintendent of Schools, Boise, Idaho

In most public schools, the curriculum for each grade of the elementary school contains a rather clearly defined body of facts and principles, the mastery of which is the necessary requisite of promotion. The marks that are given to each child are merely the teacher's estimate of the completeness of this mastery.

If a uniform test of ability is applied to all the children, they naturally fall into three groups: (1) those who fail and are compelled to repeat the work of one or more grades and thus require more than the regularly allotted time to complete the course; (2) those who make normal progress and complete the eight grades in eight years; (3) those who receive double promotions, skip grades, and complete the course in one or more terms less than the time assigned by the course of study. The second group, including all those who make normal progress, presents no very difficult administrative problems. It should contain the very great majority of all the pupils. In this class may be found the certain performers, those who respond readily to group instruction, who do not require special attention and individual methods of treatment. This group fixes the grade standards for the entire school. It is counted upon to complete the work of each grade in the allotted time and to advance regularly at each promotion period.

One of the most difficult administrative tasks is to adjust school machinery to fit the needs of all the pupils, to secure the most effective and successful work from the child of average ability and yet not neglect the interest of the unusually bright one or the exceptionally dull one. In the public schools as now organized, the three types of children are not adequately protected. According to a conservative estimate (*Pamphlet* 77, Russell Sage Foundation), there are in the average American city at least ten times as many children who are advancing more slowly than the normal rate than there are of those who are advancing more rapidly than the normal rate. This means that the course of study is not adapted to the slow child or to the one of average ability, but to the unusually bright pupil. Readjustment is, therefore, necessary until the number making slow progress is about equal to the number making rapid progress. The problem then remains to work out successful methods of caring for the needs of the exceptionally bright and the exceptionally dull pupils.

As a preliminary step toward the solution of this problem, a detailed investigation was made in 1909 of the amount of retardation in the Boise schools. The standard adopted was the one by which Dr. Maxwell rated as over age all children in the first grade who were eight years of age or older; all those in the second grade who were nine years old or more; and so on for each of the succeeding grades. (This standard is used by Dr. Leonard P. Ayres and is explained on p. 27, *Laggards in Our Schools.*) The investigation brought to the attention of the school authorities of Boise that 51 per cent of the children were retarded. Efforts were at once made to adjust the curriculum more nearly to the abilities of the average child and to give special attention to the exceptionally slow and unusually bright pupils. Two years of intensive work along these lines had, in June, 1911, reduced the amount of retardation from 51 per cent to 32.8 per cent. But there were yet too many over-age pupils in all the grades. These were far from being balanced by the number who were under age for their grade. Those making less than normal progress yet outnumbered those advancing more rapidly than the normal rate. Since the over-age pupils were in excess of the under-age for each grade, many children were making slower progress than they should make and were able to make. For a number of years, therefore, the double promotions would be in excess of the failures before a situation could be reached whereby the age and grade distribution would show the vast majority at the normal age for their respective grades and the remainder about equally divided into the over-age and the under-age groups. During the past three years, supervisors, principals, and teachers have been laboring to achieve this end, but before consistent teamwork could produce measurable results toward that achievement, all had to agree upon a standard of promotion. As stated above, the standard for the majority who were advancing at the normal rate is the mastery of the subject-matter of the curriculum for each grade.

But this standard could not be maintained for those pupils who were handicapped by limited educational opportunities or for those who were subnormal in intelligence. If these unfortunates must equal the achievements of the normal group before being permitted to advance, most of them would be condemned to the ranks of repeaters. A study of the performances of the failure in Boise has convinced the entire force that the repeater is generally a quitter and does about as poor work in his second attempt as in his first trial at the work of a given grade. The stamp of disapproval has been placed upon him. He starts on his second attempt with a grievance against the teacher and the entire institution. The parents as well as the child feel injured, so that the teacher must combat both the antagonism of the home and the hostility of the pupil, who has been trained for failure and not for success, and who becomes either morbidly sensitive or brazenly indifferent. What the laggard would probably do as a repeater is therefore quite definitely known. If he were permitted to advance, he could hardly do worse and he might do better. It is less expensive and more human to promote him than it is to degrade him. This view of the situation is generally accepted in Boise. The standard for promoting the dull pupil is entirely individual. He is not compelled to do all the work of his present grade before he is permitted to pass to the next. He is even allowed to pass on without manifesting enough ability to justify the hope that he may be able to do the work of the advanced grade. The question is reduced to the one consideration, Would he do better if advanced than he would as a repeater?

In every grade of twenty which is promoted in Boise, there is an average of two who have not satisfactorily completed the work of the lower grade. These are accepted by the teacher as special cases to which she is expected to give individual attention both in and out of school hours. She is not held responsible for the work of the special pupil, but is given credit for all progress that she can stimulate. She gets the enthusiastic co-operation of the home, for the parents know that their unfortunate offspring has been treated generously and leniently. They thus aid in every possible way to bring their child up to the standard. This policy of dealing with laggards has the indorsement of the great majority of teachers. The consensus of opinion is that those who are permitted thus to advance more nearly approach the standard of the advanced grade than they would of the lower grade had they been compelled to repeat. This is not surprising when one considers how little there is in the curriculum that is so connected and consecutive that one year's work depends upon the completion of the subjects of the previous year. The obvious objection to this plan is that it breaks down all grade standards, that it puts a premium on inferior work, that it takes away from the normal group the stimulus of being compelled to reach a degree of proficiency required of all for promotion. This false educational theory and the reluctance of teachers to promote weak pupils because they fear what the instructors in the advanced grade may say of their products have congested the primary grades with laggards and have eliminated from the schools 50 per cent of the children before they have completed the sixth grade and 75 per cent of them before they have completed the eighth grade.

In Boise, all grade standards are ignored in permitting weak pupils to advance, but the normal pupils treat these special cases with sympathetic toleration and do not relax in their own efforts because their handicapped companions are not held to the standard of work required of themselves. Standard tests of efficiency in which the work of these specially promoted pupils must be tabulated with the class demonstrate that the work of each grade is more thorough than it was three years ago before this policy of promoting the slow pupils had been generally adopted. Neither has this flexible standard of promotion increased the number doing unsatisfactory work. Early in December of the present school year all teachers were asked to send to the superintendent's office the names of all pupils who were unable to respond to such group and special instruction as could be given in the classes as now organized. From an enrolment of 2,700, but 48 pupils were so designated. A number test was later given, and three of those made 100 per cent where the standard for their grade was 85 per cent. A spelling test was also given which was submitted by Dr. Leonard Ayres. One of the 48 made 95 per cent, and the standard was 70 per cent. At a later conference with the teachers the list of 48 pupils was cut to 17. These will be placed in an ungraded room at the beginning of the second semester. Many other examples could be produced to show that the individual method of promoting slow pupils has not lowered the standard of the school. Ample proof could also be collected to demonstrate that never before have there been so few students who were not doing satisfactory work in their present grades.

TABLE I

PERCENTAGE OF CHILDREN IN EACH GRAGE ABOVE NORMAL AGE IN JUNE, 1911, AND THE PERCENTAGE ABOVE NORMAL AGE IN JUNE, 1914

Grade	1	2	3	4	5	6	7	8	Total
Percentage above normal age, June, 1911..........	12.6	19.5	32.2	43.1	44.1	45.3	40.4	34.6	32.8
Percentage above normal age, June, 1914..........	7.6	7.4	17.4	20.4	18.9	25.4	31.5	27.4	18.8

As appears in Table I, the amount of reduction in percentage of retardation produced during the three years is not so great for the seventh and eighth grades as for the lower grades. The reason for this is apparent when the high percentage of retardation in the fourth, fifth, and sixth grades, June, 1911, is observed. By double promotions, some of these retarded pupils had been brought up to normal in the three years. But many were so far behind that they could not be pushed into the normal group in the few remaining years of the elementary-school course. This reduction of percentage of retardation from 32 per cent to 18 per cent in three years is not, on the face of it, a distinctive achievement, but the difficulty of accomplishing decided results along this line is increased by the fact that a large percentage of the population of western cities shifts each year. More than 10 per cent of the pupils enrolled in the elementary schools of Boise this year have come from other schools. Of these new pupils, 35 per cent are over age as against 5 per cent under age. In 1911, the years lost by slow children were so in excess of the years gained by pupils making rapid progress that not only must the number making slow progress be reduced materially, but, also, the number of those making rapid progress must be decidedly increased before the number over age in each grade should be balanced by the number under age.

TABLE II

PERCENTAGE OF UNDER-AGE CHILDREN IN EACH GRADE, 1911, AND PERCENTAGE OF UNDER-AGE CHILDREN IN EACH GRADE, 1914

Grade	1	2	3	4	5	6	7	8	Total
Percentage under age, 1911..	0	8.4	9	9	9.3	7.7	7.6	8.1	7.8
Percentage under age, 1914..	3.7	16.4	16.2	21.4	22.5	18.7	17.7	14.1	15.2

Table II shows that the total percentage of under-age pupils has been doubled during the three years. The number of those in the under-age group is now almost equal to that in the over-age group. In June, 1914, there were 18.8 per cent over age as against 15.2 per cent under age. The present year will, without doubt, complete the balance.

Just as the number making slow progress was decreased by ignoring for the slow pupils the standards of promotion applied to those making normal progress, so the number making rapid progress has been increased by individual investigation and individual treatment. The report of 1911 showed a large percentage over age and a small percentage under age. It was, therefore, very obvious that fewer pupils should be in the slow group and more children should make rapid progress. To equalize this situation, the double promotions must exceed the failures. But to realize this desired end, pupils capable of making rapid progress must be found and pushed forward. Teachers were, therefore, asked to furnish a list of pupils who were maintaining their grades standing and yet expending less than the amount of energy required from the average child to accomplish the same purpose. When these pupils were reported to the supervisors of instruction, their ability to do the work of advanced grade was tested. The supervisors placed in the advanced grade all pupils who appeared to possess unusual ability. This policy has been in operation for three years. No definite time is fixed for double promotion. When a child of exceptional ability is found, he is promptly put forward. Those advanced are not always the younger pupils; often they are overgrown boys and girls, who in former years, have failed of promotion or who entered school late, or who have attended irregularly. No effort has been made to drill pupils thus advanced on the subject-matter of the curriculum they missed by the promotion. They were merely given an opportunity to try the work of the advanced grade. If they could do it, they remained there; if they were unequal to the task, they dropped back.

During the second semester of the school year, 1912–13, and the two semesters of 1913–14, 440 such double promotions were made. The pupils thus advanced constituted more than 10 per cent of all enrolled.

TABLE III

PERCENTAGE OF RANKS 1, 2, 3, AND 4, GIVEN TO THE 440 PUPILS THUS PUSHED INTO ADVANCED GRADES, COMPARED WITH THE PERCENTAGE OF RANKS 1, 2, 3, AND 4, GIVEN TO ALL THE PUPILS IN ALL THE GRADES IN THE JUNE REPORT, 1914

Grade	1	2	3	4
440 pupils receiving double promotions......	48	38	13	1
All the pupils in all the grades, June, 1914....	26	35	28	11

A comparison of the relative class-standing of the 440 pupils receiving double promotions with the average class-standing of the pupils in all the grades is enlightening. Each of the pupils who are eligible for promotion at any promotion period receives rank, 1, 2, 3, or 4. Rank 1 is the highest rank and rank 4 is the lowest passing mark. To determine the distribution of passing marks for all the pupils in all the grades as they are shown on the records in June, 1914, all the 1's, 2's, 3's, and 4's were counted and the percentage of each calculated. In the same way the distribution of the marks of the 440 pupils receiving the double promotions was calculated. The first marks they received in the class to which they were promoted in every case are taken as the standard. Reference to Table III will show that while the percentage of 1's given to all the pupils was 26, the 440 pupils advancing more rapidly than the normal rate received 48 per cent of the 1's. All the children received eleven times as many 4's, the lowest passing mark as, were recorded against the 440 pupils making rapid progress. Not a failing mark (rank 5) has been recorded against one of those pushed forward. This comparison demonstrates that the pupils thus advanced immediately assumed rank far above the average of the class to which they were promoted. They almost invariably maintained the same relative rank in the class to which they were promoted that they had held in the lower class from which they came. This is additional proof that the work of the elementary school is not so connected and consecutive that the curriculum of the advanced grade cannot be successfully mastered until all the work of the lower grade has been completed. This fact must constantly be impressed upon teachers if they are to be induced to adopt flexible standards of promotion.

The teachers in Boise realize that the ideal situation would indicate that the course of study and the system of promotion were so adjusted that most of the children would advance at the normal rate, the slow ones requiring more time to do the work, and an equal number of bright ones advancing more rapidly than the normal rate. But in years past, the number making slow progress has been so in excess of the number making rapid progress that the entire force is now working to reverse the situation until the number of over-age pupils in each grade is balanced by the number under age.

As indicated by Table IV, the percentage of double promotions is more than double that of failures for all grades but the first primary. Many children get into the first primary before they are six, and therefore cannot keep the pace set by the pupils of normal age. No official age record being available, the age given by the parents must be accepted. But the failures in the first primary do not materially increase retardation as most of the children who repeat are yet well within the normal age for their grade.

In estimating school expenditure the usual inquiry is the average expenditure for each child in the school system. The more significant standard is the average cost of advancing each child one grade. If the time lost by pupils advancing more slowly than the normal rate is equal to the time gained by children who make rapid progress, the average per-capita cost of keeping all children in school for one year and advancing all of them one grade is just the same. In school systems where time lost by children making slow progress is in excess of time gained by children making rapid progress, the cost of sending each child forward one grade is greater than the cost of keeping each child in school one year. The amount of excess cost of one year's advance over one year's schooling depends upon the ratio of years lost to years gained. In the average American city there are ten times as many children making slow progress as there are making rapid progress (*Pamphlet 77*, Russell Sage Foundation). The average cost of advancing the children one year is, therefore, considerably greater than the cost of keeping them in school one year.

TABLE IV

NUMBER ON THE PROMOTION LIST, NUMBER PROMOTED, NUMBER NOT PROMOTED, NUMBER RECEIVING DOUBLE PROMOTIONS; PERCENTAGE NOT PROMOTED, PERCENTAGE RECEIVING DOUBLE PROMOTIONS, FOR THE TWO SEMESTERS OF THE SCHOOL YEAR, 1913–14

Grade	On Promotion List	Promoted	Not Promoted	Percentage	Double Promotions	Percentage
I.	757	652	105	13.8	98	12.94
II.	609	598	11	1.81	41	6.73
III.	547	532	15	2.74	37	6.78
IV.	650	631	19	2.92	34	5.23
V.	631	624	7	1.11	23	3.65
VI.	611	597	14	2.29	42	6.87
VII.	603	586	17	2.82	4	.66
VIII.	542	532	10	1.85	1	.185
Total	4,950	4,752	198	4.00	280	5.65

(As there are two semesters in each term, each pupil is counted twice. The 198 and 280 represent, respectively, terms lost and terms gained.)

During the school year 1913–14, in Boise, there were 99 years lost as against 140 years gained. Hence, the cost of one year's advance was a trifle less than the cost of keeping the children in school for one year. The excess of years gained over years lost was 41. The average per-capita cost of one year's attendance was $38.00;

thus 41×$38.00=$1,558.00. The total cost of advancing all the children one grade was $1,558.00 less than the cost of keeping them all in school for one year (*Pamphlet 111*, Russell Sage Foundation).

Very few pupils can be kept in the elementary school after they are fifteen years of age. This is the age at which they almost invariably leave school, whether they have completed the course or not. If we wish to increase the number completing the elementary-school course and thereby swell the number entering the high school, we must get more children through the grades before they reach the age of fifteen.

TABLE V

GRADE DISTRIBUTION IN THE BOISE SCHOOLS, JUNE, 1911, AND JUNE, 1914, REDUCED TO A SCALE OF 1,000 FOR THE FIRST PRIMARY GRADE AND THE SAME RATIO MAINTAINED FOR EACH OF THE SUCCEEDING GRADES

Grade	I	II	III	IV	V	VI	VII	VIII
1910–11........	1,000	873	764	920	777	842	582	502
1913–14........	1,000	732	781	764	752	695	746	604

Table V shows that in 1914 the proportion in the first six grades was not so great as in 1911. This means that the reduction of the number making slow progress has decreased the congestion in the lower grades. The increased proportion of pupils in the seventh and eighth grades in 1914 shows that just as the number making slow progress is decreased and the number advancing rapidly is increased, the power of the school to retain the pupils until they have completed the entire elementary-school course is correspondingly increased. The proportion of pupils in the eighth grade, June, 1914, was 20 per cent greater than in June, 1911. For every five pupils who in 1911 completed the course, six children finished the eighth grade in 1914. The adjustment of school machinery to the needs and abilities of unusually dull children and exceptionally bright pupils has prevented one-fifth of the elimination or leakage.

The teachers of Boise feel, then, that their use of an individual standard for promoting pupils, rather than a uniform standard for an entire grade, has given the following results:

1. The average cost of advancing a pupil in school is somewhat reduced.

2. A larger proportion of the pupils is held in school during the entire elementary course.

3. Conditions of efficiency in the lower grades are improved by lessening the congestion there—congestion which means not merely too great numbers, but means also a group of laggards who are an undue drag on the work of the entire grade.

4. Exceptional pupils, both above and below the average, receive more nearly the kind of treatment which is suited to them.

AN ANALYTICAL SCALE FOR JUDGING HANDWRITING[1]

FRANK N. FREEMAN
University of Chicago

A number of experiences with the two handwriting scales which have been published led to the effort which is here described to construct a scale upon a somewhat different principle. The outstanding difficulty which was found with both the Thorndike and the Ayers scales is the lack of uniformity in the results which are obtained by their use. The question then arose whether some means might not be found by which this lack of uniformity might be overcome, and this led to the question as to the source of the variability in the results obtained in using the scales.

The critical statements which are made in this paper with reference to the Ayers and the Thorndike scales are not intended as a disparagement of their value for certain purposes; they are made rather for the purpose of pointing out the limitations in the use of these or similar scales. These scales are useful when it is desired to make merely a rough general survey of handwriting excellence. There is danger, however, that they may be used with an exaggerated confidence in the accuracy of results which are obtained by them. The considerations which are here given are for the purpose of preventing such uncritical confidence. It is the purpose of the paper, further, to indicate the directions in which a more reliable means of measurement is to be found.

The testimony of those who have used the handwriting scales leads to the conclusion that one important source of variability is the ambiguity as to the characteristics in writing which are to be used as the basis for judgment. Professor Thorndike, the author of one of the two widely used scales, makes the point that the use

[1] The scale itself is published in a volume entitled *The Teaching of Handwriting*, by the writer, published by Houghton Mifflin Co. This paper was read before the Section on Education of the American Association for the Advancement of Science at Philadelphia, December, 1914.

of a scale will give objectivity to the measurement of writing which cannot be had by judgment without the use of some such standard for reference. When a person attempts to judge a specimen of writing, however, by the use of the scale, the first question that arises is, What is to be taken as the basis of the judgment; what characteristic in the writing is to be looked for in order that it may be determined what part of the scale it corresponds with, and what rank is to be given to it? The answer which is given in the case of the Thorndike scale is that the judgment is to be based upon three characteristics; namely, legibility, beauty, and character.

The first difficulty with judgment upon the basis of these three characteristics is that of determining what relative weight should be given to each of the three. The judgment is a single one to be made upon the combined value of these three traits. If, now, one judge uses legibility as the chief trait in his rating, and another beauty, and another character, it will be seen that, even though each judgment may be perfectly reliable on the basis of the weight it gives to the different characteristics, yet the rating given to a particular specimen may differ widely.

Another difficulty is introduced, however, by the character of the three traits which are to be used as a basis of judgment. They themselves, even taken singly, are difficult to use in making a judgment, because each of them represents a complex characteristic which may be based on a variety of elementary characteristics in the writing itself. In brief, beauty and character and even legibility are not accurately definable characteristics so that we can be sure that different persons mean exactly the same thing by them.

A similar difficulty confronts the judge who attempts to use the Ayers scale. In this scale a distinction is not made between the different characteristics which are to be used as a basis for judgment. The term "general quality" is the only one which is given to guide the person who is to use it. Confusion arises, further, by the fact that the basis upon which the specimens for the scale were selected is not the same as that which is used by the person who attempts to grade specimens by means of it. The specimens for the scale itself were chosen on the basis of the rapidity with which ten individuals could read the specimens or other samples of writing by the same individuals who produced the specimens in the scale. The assumption then is that there is a correlation between the rank in specimen as determined by the rate-of-reading method and the rank based upon a judgment of quality.

Merely by the examination of the specimens on the scale one is led to a suspicion that this correlation is not complete, and it is a common complaint among those who use the scale that in some cases higher specimens do not appear to be of as good quality as some of those lower down on the scale. This naturally introduces confusion in the mind of the person who is attempting to use the scale. A further confirmation of this suspicion is obtained when we conduct an experiment to determine the degree to which the correlation exists. When a number of specimens of writing are graded by the Ayers scale and then by the speed-of-reading method by the same individual, it is found that little correlation exists between the series as arranged on the basis of the two types of measurement; in fact, the coefficient is so low as to be scarcely enough to be taken as evidence of a reliable correlation. It is evident, then, that legibility is not the basis for judgment with the Ayers scale and we are left at sea as to just what the basis is.

Both for the measurement of writing and for the guide of the teacher it is very desirable that we should obtain a more exact definition of the characteristics which make up excellence in writing. If this is not done, we cannot say that objectivity is reached. The analogy with linear measurement will not hold, because in the case of linear measurement, although there may be errors in the application of a scale, yet the notion of the characteristic which is to be measured is perfectly definite. There is no ambiguity as to what is meant by *length* or by *surface area* or by *cubic contents* in the same manner as there is an ambiguity as to what is meant by *quality* or *excellence* in writing. When this ambiguity exists we are confronted with a double difficulty in the measurement of such a product as writing. We have not only the difficulty in discerning the degree of the trait in question, but also in determining just what trait it is upon which the judgment is to be based. This latter difficulty, that is, the difficulty due to ambiguity, should be overcome so far as possible at the start. It is for the purpose of reducing, at least, this difficulty that the scale which is to be described was constructed.

When the attempt was made to determine the characteristics which should be used as the basis for judging the excellence of writing, the first one selected was uniformity. If writing is not uniform, it evidently suffers by such fact. That is, the slant of the writing, for example, should be the same throughout, and the height of those letters which are supposed to be of the same height should be equal. These illustrations suggest the two types of uniformity which can readily be determined; that is, uniformity of slant and uniformity in the alignment of the letters. These, accordingly, constitute the first two traits. The accompanying chart is a reduced copy of the first of the five charts which compose the scale. It may be referred to as an illustration of the general characteristics of the charts as a whole.

Uniformity of writing depends largely upon the fluency and the regularity of the movement by which it is produced. Another characteristic which depends also upon the ease and fluency of the movement is the quality of the line or the stroke. The line may be regular, smooth, and even, or it may be irregular, jerky, wavy in character. The one, then, constitutes excellence and the other a defect in writing. We may take quality of line, then, to be a third characteristic and one which depends largely, as in the case of uniformity, upon the character of the movement.

The movement may be smooth and regular, however, and yet the writing may be difficult to read because the letters are not well formed. We may ascribe this characteristic largely to the accuracy with which the form of the letters is perceived and the care which is taken to maintain the proper form. Letter formation has been commonly thought of as the chief form of excellence of writing. It certainly is an important one, particularly when we regard, not the deviations from an arbitrary standard of form, which are of no importance, but those deviations which make the writing difficult to read, as, for example, when one letter is made of similar form to another. The failure to round the top of the *m* or the *n* makes these letters resemble *u* or possibly *w*.

Finally, the appearance and the legibility of writing is determined very largely by the spacing between the letters or between the words or between the lines. Writing is sometimes met with which

Chart I. Uniformity of Slant

Group	Specimen	Sample
5	No. 90 M. V. 2.3	A quick brown fox jumps over the lazy dog. A quick brown fox jumps over the lazy dog. A quick brown fox
	No. 28 M. V. 2.7°	A quick brown fox jumps over the lazy dog A quick brown fox jumps over the lazy
3	No. 64 M. V. 4.3°	Some books are to be tasted, others to be swallowed and some few to be chewed and digested. That is, some books are to
	No. 91 M. V. 4.4°	Some books are to be tasted, others to be swallowed, and some few to be chewed and digested That is,
[illegible]	No. 6 M. V 8.0°	A quck brown fox jumps over the lazy dog A quick brown fox jump
	No. 83 M. V. 8.5°	A quite brown fox jump over the lazy dog

would be very legible if it were not so closely crowded together. The writer has confirmed this by tracing the letters of such writing, but spacing them farther apart. The writing also may present a scrawled appearance because the letters of the words are spaced too widely.

This, then, gives us five characteristics which are perfectly definable in their nature and in some cases at least, as we shall see, are measurable in their degree. One problem which arises is as to the relative weight which should be given to excellence in these five characteristics determining the total grade of the writing. For the present we shall not attempt to determine accurately what this relative weight should be. We can only give them an arbitrary weight, therefore, and wait for further investigations to determine which of these is the most important in determining the total quality of the writing. We may assume, however, as a starting-point that letter formation is somewhat more important than any one of the other characteristics. In order to express this increased importance this characteristic has been given double weight in the scale.

In the first attempt to construct a scale on the basis of these five characteristics it was assumed that when the characteristics were clearly defined, series of specimens could be chosen merely upon the basis of the judgment of a group of individuals. Accordingly a preliminary chart was first constructed for the purpose of illustrating different degrees in these traits, and this was used as a guide by a class in experimental education composed of advanced students, most of whom were experienced in supervision and teaching, upon which to rank a large number of specimens into ten degrees of excellence in each trait. After the specimens had been so rated, however, it appears to the writer that the order was not always the correct one. He therefore set about to find so far as possible objective measurements upon which to base the rating and with which to compare the rating made on the basis of the judgment of the graders.

In the case of uniformity of slant and of alignment objective measurement could be directly applied. It was only necessary to measure the angle of a series of letters and to find the mean variation among these angles, or to measure the vertical position of the tops and bottoms of the letters and to measure the variability among these positions. When this was done it was found that the order based on the variability as measured did not correspond to the order on the basis of the judgment made by the graders. The order based on objective measurement was therefore used as a basis for the selection of specimens for the scale.

In the case of quality of line no means was found upon which to base such objective measurement, but the characteristic in question was made more prominent by photographic enlargement. When this was done it was relatively easy to determine differences in the irregularity of the line of the writing. On this basis specimens for this chart were selected.

In the case of letter formation difficulty again was found, but some approach to objectivity was obtained through the assistance of Mr. R. R. Simpkins, of the State Normal School at Macomb, Illinois. Mr. Simpkins had developed a system of determining excellence in letter formation by the method of counting the errors in form. He was therefore requested to note the errors in the specimens of the scale which had been selected. In some cases the results of this measurement differed from the result of the judgment of the graders, and a compromise between the two methods of determination was used in selecting the specimens for the scale.

Some degree of objectivity in the determination of the best spacing between letters or between words was obtained in the following manner. Three widely differing styles of writing were chosen and the judgment of about fifteen people was obtained as to the most pleasing distance between the words in these three styles of writing. This was done by selecting pairs of words and placing one upon a transparent piece of paper so that it could be moved back and forth until the most agreeable distance between the words was found. This distance was then recorded by reference to a scale below the word.

It was found that this distance varied considerably with the different styles of writing, according as they differed in size or in slant. The slant, however, seemed to be the most important characteristic in determining the spacing which should be used. The length of the word seemed to have little effect in the matter. On the basis of this determination a standard spacing between words for these three styles of writing was selected. The spacing to be regarded as the standard between letters was determined in a slightly different way. In this case various specimens were constructed in which the spacing between letters was different, and the judges were asked to select that specimen in which the letters were the most agreeably spaced.

The chart was then constructed in the following manner. Specimens were selected which should conform to the standards of spacing between letters and between words. Then the lower grades were constructed by varying this spacing in a variety of ways. The middle grade was determined by varying one of the two characteristics, that is, spacing between letters or between words, and the lowest grade by varying two of the characteristics.

Each chart contains specimens of writing which represent three grades of excellence in the characteristics in question. This small number was chosen in order that the degrees of difference might be great enough to be perfectly evident, or at least to be as evident as possible. An experiment was first made with a larger number of differences and this was not found so satisfactory. The lowest grade is given a rank of one, the middle grade the rank of three, and the highest grade the rank of five. The exception to this is in the case of letter formation, in which double weight is given to each rank. The intermediate grades between these may be used, that is, the grades of two and four, or, in the case of letter formation, of four and six. The total rank of the paper is to be determined by adding the rank in each of the five characteristics.

As has already been said, the difficulty of grading such a product as handwriting is not completely met when we have defined and represented the traits to be measured. There is still the difficulty which a judge finds in selecting the trait to be used as the basis of judgment from the complex of those characteristics which make up the writing. In order to facilitate this selection, or abstraction, various devices were used to emphasize the trait which is represented in each of the charts. In the case of uniformity of slant a line is drawn parallel to the tall letters to catch the eye and to lead to an easy determination of variability. Furthermore, a transparent paper upon which are drawn lines of a certain slant is to be placed over the specimen which is to be judged in order that the variability may be seen by comparison with these lines, all of which have the same slant. The variability in alignment is brought out in the same way by a line above or below the letter. An effort was made to emphasize the variation in line or irregularities in line in the same way that they were emphasized for the purpose of selecting specimens for the scale, but it was found that in the reproduction of the specimens of the photographic enlargement the irregularities of the line were in a large measure smoothed out, so that this aid is of little avail. To facilitate the judgment in letter formation the errors in the first part of each specimen on the chart were indicated by small arrows. The judgment of spacing is facilitated by the artificial construction of specimens each of which illustrates a particular type of error in this respect.

It has already been remarked that all of the difficulties in using such a scale are not met when we have defined the characteristics. To place a scale before a person in which the characteristics are represented does not guarantee that he will see them. It is necessary, therefore, that some attention be paid to the training of a judge in order that he may learn to abstract from the complex written product the characteristic which is to be judged. I am convinced on the basis of my experience with a large number of persons in using scales that we cannot expect to find any device which can be used in a simple or mechanical manner or without care and some degree of preparation for the task. We do not expect people to be able to distinguish accurately between live stock or between ears of corn or any other complex object without having some training for the task. The assumption that anybody can judge handwriting or any of the other products of the school without the development of some degree of expertness will serve to amass a large number of facts which are in themselves highly unreliable and therefore to discredit the whole movement for scientific measurement of educational products.

The teacher also needs some degree of training or expertness in distinguishing the various characteristics of writing and in grading the writing of her pupils so as to determine their rank or to determine the direction in which their further efforts should be applied. In fact, the primary application of such a scale as this may be in the schoolroom where the teacher needs to distinguish, not only differences in quality of writing, but also the particular respect in which the differences exist and the particular feature of each pupil's writing which needs to be improved.

The scale as it stands appears to be cumbersome, but after a person has acquired some skill in the application of the judgment on the various traits one may grow independent of the need of actually consulting the specimens. That is, the specimens and their rating may be kept in mind and a judgment may be made on the five characteristics with considerable rapidity.

The purpose of presenting a description of this scale for judging handwriting is not merely to make known this particular example of measuring scales, but to use it as a type of the method which can be most profitably pursued in the construction of scales in general. This method involves, first, analyzing the product into fairly simple elementary characteristics; secondly, defining and measuring these so far as possible in objective terms; and, thirdly, constructing the scale in such a way that different degrees of the elementary characteristics may be made evident to the person who is to use it.

BOOKS RECEIVED

MACMILLAN, NEW YORK

Language Reader Series: Primer. By Franklin T. Baker, George R. Carpenter, and Fannie Wyche Dunn. Illustrated. Cloth. Pp. 118. $0.30.

Pinnocchio under the Sea. Translated from the Italian by Carolyn M. Della Chiesa. Edited by John W. Davis. Illustrated. Cloth. Pp. 201. $0.50.

Health and Cleanliness. By M. V. O'Shea and J. H. Kellogg. Illustrated. Cloth. Pp. 301.

The Body in Health. By M. V. O'Shea and J. H. Kellogg. Illustrated. Cloth. Pp. 324.

Indian Legends. By Margaret Bemister. Illustrated. Cloth. Pp. 187. $0.40.

Stories of the Golden Age. By Mary Gooch Anderson. Illustrated. Cloth. Pp. 231. $0.40.

RAND McNALLY & CO., CHICAGO

Robin Hood and His Merry Men. By Maude Radford Warren. Illustrated. Cloth. Pp. 290. $0.50.

Sunbonnets and Overalls. By Etta Craven Hogate and Eulalie Osgood Grover. Illustrated. Cloth. Pp. 84. $0.40.

Sunbonnet Babies in Holland. By Eulalie Osgood Grover. Illustrated. Cloth. Pp. 159. $0.50.

The Holton-Curry Readers. By Martha Adelaide Holton, Mina Holton Page, and Charles Madison Curry. Illustrated. Cloth.

First Reader, pp. 146, $0.30.
Second Reader, pp. 168, $0.35.
Third Reader, pp. 227, $0.40.
Fourth Reader, pp. 244, $0.45.
Fifth Reader, pp. 287, $0.50.
Sixth Reader, pp. 314, $0.55.
Seventh Reader, pp. 335, $0.60.
Eighth Reader, pp. 334, $0.60.

TEACHERS COLLEGE, COLUMBIA UNIVERSITY, NEW YORK CITY

Education Psychology: Briefer Course. By Edward L. Thorndike. Cloth. Pp. 442. $2.00.

Individual Differences in Ability and Improvement and Their Correlations. By J. Crosby Chapman. Cloth. Pp. 45. $0.75.

The Recapitulation Theory and Human Infancy. By Percy E. Davidson. Cloth. Pp. 105. $1.00.

Teachers' Marks: Their Variability and Standardization. By F. J. Kelley. Cloth. Pp. 139. $1.50.

A Comparative Study of the Intelligence of Delinquent Girls. By Augusta F. Bronner. Cloth. Pp. 95. $1.00.

Functional Periodicity. By Leta Stetter Hollingsworth. Cloth. Pp. 101. $1.00.

CURRENT EDUCATIONAL LITERATURE IN THE PERIODICALS

IRENE WARREN
Librarian, School of Education, University of Chicago

Ballou, Frank W. The function of a department of educational investigation and measurement in a city school system. School and Society 1:181–90. (6 Fe. '15.)

Brandon, Edgar Ewing. Recent educational tendencies in Argentina. Educa. 35:362–65. (Fe. '15.)

Brigham, Albert Perry. Problems of geographic influence. Science 41:261–80. (19 Fe. '15.)

Bronner, Augusta F. Effect of adolescent instability on conduct. Psychol. Clinic 8:249–65. (Fe. '15.)

Brown, Robert M. Classroom methods and devices. El. School J. 15:355–60. (Mr. '15.)

Butterworth, Julian E. An evaluation of methods for providing free high-school tuition. School R. 23:85–96. (Fe. '15.)

Carter, E. M. Pictures in the classroom. School W. 17:16–17. (Ja. '15.)

Claxton, P. P. The American rural school. School and Society 1:37–50. (9 Ja. '15.)

Coffman, Lotus D. The American school superintendent. Educa. Admin. and Supervision 1:13–28. (Ja. '15.)

Coulter, J. G. A four-year course in science in the high schools. School and Society 1:226–34. (13 Fe. '15.)

Crawshaw, F. D. Organization of teaching material. Indust. Arts M. 3:128–33. (Mr. '15.)

Cubberley, Ellwood P. Fundamental problems in educational administration. Educa. Admin. and Supervision 1:3–12. (Ja. '15.)

Davies, G. R. Spencer's philosophy of education. School and Society 1:269–72. (20 Fe. '15.)

Davis, Calvin O. College surveillance and student responsibility. Educa. Admin. and Supervision 1:50–54. (Ja. '15.)

Downing, Elliot R. The scientific trend in secondary education. Science 41:232–35. (12 Fe. '15.)

Foster, William T. Reed College. School R. 23:97–104. (Fe. '15.)

Fultz, N. F. The making of an alliance with a chamber of commerce. Indust. Arts M. 3:97–102. (Mr. '15.)

Gammans, Harold W. The pupil who fails in secondary high school English; how to teach him. Educa. 35:378–83. (Fe. '15.)

Graham, James. The training of an industrial and a commercial army. School W. 17:53–56. (Fe. '15.)

Groves, Ernest R. Clinical psychology and the rural schools. Psychol. Clinic 8:272–75. (Fe. '15.)

Hill, David Spence. Vocational guidance in the South. School and Society 1:257–63. (20 Fe. '15.)

Hinckley, Alice C. The Binet tests applied to individuals over twelve years of age. J. of Educa. Psychol. 6:43–58. (Ja. '15.)

Johnston, Charles Hughes. The high school issue. Educa. Admin. and Supervision 1:29–49. (Ja. '15.)

Kingsley, Maud E. Examination outline for language work. Educa. 35:366–70. (Fe. '15.)

Lane, Henry A. Standard tests as an aid to supervision. El. School J. 15:378–86. (Mr. '15.)

Lightley, Edmund. The place of the text-book in mathematical teaching. School W. 17:6–9. (Ja. '15.)

Luckey, G. W. A. The essentials in the training of a teacher. School and Society 1:263–69. (20 Fe. '15.)

Minnick, J. H. A comparative study of the mathematical abilities of boys and girls. School R. 23:73–84. (Fe. '15.)

(The) most notable school books of 1914. School W. 17:22–25. (Ja. '15.)

Perry, John. The need of a science of education. School and Society 1:114–26. (23 Ja. '15.)

Puncheon, Katharine E. The place of vocational and liberal studies in 1914. Educa. 35:341–49. (Fe. '15.)

Rapeer, Louis W. Standardization of the rural school plant. School and Society 1:217–26. (13 Fe. '15.)

Roman, Frederick W. Control of the German vocational schools. Indust. Arts M. 3:112–16. (Mr. '15.)

Rugg, Harold Ordway. A scale for measuring free-hand lettering. J. of Educa. Psychol. 6:25–42. (Ja. '15.)

Sachs, Julius. The secondary school teacher and the college. School and Society 1:50–53. (9 Ja. '15.)

Sanders, Frederic W. The organization of education. Educa. 35:371–76. (Fe. '15.)

Snedden, David. Problems of aim in elementary education. School and Society 1:253–57. (20 Fe. '15.)

Starch, Daniel. The measurement of efficiency in reading. J. of Educa. Psychol. 6:1–24. (Ja. '15.)

Strong, Frank. The opportunity of American universities. School and Society 1:109–14. (23 Ja. '15.)

Thompson, Frank V. Vocational guidance in Boston. School R. 23:105–12. (Fe. '15.)

Thorndike, Edw. L. The measurement of ability in reading. Teach. Col. Rec. 15:1–71. (S. '14.)

VOLUME XV NUMBER 9

THE ELEMENTARY SCHOOL JOURNAL

CONTINUING "THE ELEMENTARY SCHOOL TEACHER"

MAY 1915

EDUCATIONAL NEWS AND EDITORIAL COMMENT

University Conferences on Elementary Education

One of the most impressive manifestations of the growing unity of the American educational system appears in the fact that a number of the leading universities are organizing conferences with the superintendents and teachers of elementary schools. Conferences between officers of colleges and secondary schools have become familiar in all parts of the country. The motives for such conferences are not far to seek. The interest in the preparation of students for college classes is served best by direct contact between secondary-school and college teachers. The motives for these recent conferences between elementary schools and universities are altogether different from the motives that prompt the organization of secondary-school conferences. Conferences with elementary schools are due in part to the initiative of departments of education, but more fundamentally they arise out of the fact that the universities are beginning to recognize the general principle that the development of a science of education is a part of the business of every one of our higher institutions. For a long time the normal schools had a monopoly on the training and development of elementary education, but there is danger at the present time that the normal schools will drop behind unless they see the significance of this new movement which is appearing in the universities.

The University of Pennsylvania, for example, has organized a school men's week. Two days will be devoted to problems relating to the training of teachers, two days to rural-school problems, three days to the administration of city schools, and three days to matters in which the teachers of colleges and high schools are concerned. At Indiana University a conference on scientific measurements has been organized, continuing the work which was undertaken last year. At the University of Wisconsin the superintendents of the state are to come together for a week in what amounts to an educational short course. The same is true at the University of Minnesota, where the university has united with the State Department of Education to give the superintendents a week of discussion of problems of supervision. Earlier in the year the University of Iowa had a week for the superintendents and supervisors, separating them for the purposes of this discussion from all of the other school officers of the state and devoting the time exclusively to the problems of supervision. A number of other institutions, such as the University of Kansas, have organized in connection with their secondary-school conferences special conferences for school administrators.

In all of these cases the appeal to the influential body of school officers who were to be found among the state superintendents makes it clear that there is coming to be a recognition on every hand that the teaching profession has large problems of supervision which can be worked out only through the co-operation of practical school people and the theoretical students of education. That conferences of this sort are likely to become more common would seem to be indicated by the geographical distribution of the conferences now under way.

A National University

In this connection it is interesting to note that the House Committee on Education of the United States Senate has reported favorably an initial appropriation of $500,000.00 for the founding of a national university. The only justification for the establishment of such an institution as this would be the extension in research and the general improvement of educational organization in all of the states which would be promoted by a central institution equipped with all of the facilities for investigation which are to be found at the seat of government. The remarks of ex-President Taft at the meeting of the Department of Superintendence are significant in this connection, showing the conception which he has of the function of the Bureau of Education and of the national university which in some form is certain to be organized. Mr. Taft said:

What we need in the country is an opportunity for standardization and comparison of school systems in the different states and different cities. This, I think, we might have by establishing what Washington recommended, a national university in Washington. The Bureau of Education might well be enlarged into a university which should not be a teaching university, but one with a corps of experts who could offer to the people of all the states and the people of all local communities the opportunity of having their respective school systems examined and reported on as to proper scope, efficiency, thoroughness, and economy. The same university should hold periodical examinations in convenient parts of the country which any person might, upon payent of a small fee, take and if successful receive a certificate equivalent to a degree in certain established courses.

All this would be voluntary, but if the system were impartial, thorough, and wisely severe as it should be, the value of the reports and the value of the certificates would become great. They would assure the people of a community that they were getting their money's worth from a school system officially approved by such university, and by assuring them that the graduates of their school could obtain degrees from such examinations. Thus we should soon have a standardization of our school systems of the highest value.

The pressure of the taxpayers upon their particular school authorities to apply for an examination and report would be so great that it would soon become equivalent to a compulsory system. It would stimulate school authorities to earnest work. It would eliminate shoddy pretense and show, would minimize exploiting and publicity methods, and would give a proof of excellent and comparative high standing that would be incontestable.

School Surveys

Two notable school surveys have been launched. The first is a survey to be made of the state of Maryland under the auspices of the General Education Board. Dr. Frank P. Bachman is in immediate charge of the work, but the General Education Board will co-operate through its officers to make this survey a model of what should be done in canvassing the educational opportunities and difficulties of the whole state. We have had an exhibition in the state of Vermont of the way in which a state can be canvassed through the cooperation of a foundation. It is to be hoped that the General

Education Board with its great resources will be able to carry on even more completely the survey of the state of Maryland. The Carnegie Foundation investigation of the state of Vermont had some of the appearances of undue haste. The opportunity in Maryland is greater because there is no urgent demand in that state for a reorganization at the present moment of the school system. We may look to this school survey, therefore, for larger results than any that have been obtained heretofore from state surveys.

The second significant survey which is being planned is that of the city of Cleveland. A foundation has recently grown up in the city of Cleveland with funds that seem to promise the possibility of many types of investigation which will be to the advantage of that municipality. One of the first problems that the trustees of the Cleveland foundation recognized as important is the problem of the public-school system. From the point of view of the technical student of schools the survey of a city of the size of Cleveland has many advantages that cannot be supplied by a greater city on the one hand or a smaller city on the other. The survey of the city of New York encountered difficulties caused by the huge size of the school system to be surveyed. On the other hand, small school systems do not present many of the acute problems that appear in greater municipalities. Cleveland, standing as it does between the two extremes, with ample funds to secure the services of those who are competent to pass upon its school system, offers one of the best opportunities that has yet been afforded for a careful and complete study of the school system. We may here again look for results that are far-reaching in their significance, not only for that city itself, but also for the country as a whole.

The following bulletin is sent out by the National Child Labor Committee:

Bulletin on Child Labor

"North Carolina has the least effective Child Labor law of all the industrial states, and it was one of her senators who blocked the way to a federal law in the Senate that has just adjourned." This statement was made at the quarterly meeting of the Board of Trustees of the National Child Labor Committee by A. J. McKelway, southern secretary of the committee, whose headquarters have been in Washington ever since the Palmer-Owen Child Labor bill was introduced in Congress a year ago. Dr. McKelway said further:

"This winter the cotton manufacturers of North Carolina succeeded first in defeating all child labor legislation before the state legislature. They packed the Committee on Manufactures to which the Child Labor bill was referred. Their lobby, forty strong, appeared before their committee to urge the unfavorable report that followed. Then they became alarmed at the prospect of federal legislation and appealed to Senator Overman to defeat it. Under the antiquated rules of the Senate, when the bill was reached on the calendar, one objection was sufficient to prevent consideration, and Senator Overman objected. Thus with Senator Overman contending that child labor is a state problem, and his manufacturing constituents able to defeat state legislation, the young children of the North Carolina cotton mills make appeal to state and to nation in vain."

Owen R. Lovejoy, general secretary of the National Child Labor Committee, reported on the general work of the committee. He said: "We have helped to secure a fourteen-year limit in the cotton mills of Alabama, and a compulsory education law has just been passed in South Carolina. Important bills are still pending in several states, notably Pennsylvania, Michigan, Illinois, and Iowa. But our defeats in West Virginia and North Carolina, and our hot fights in Arkansas and Alabama, make us realize that what we have accomplished is easy and obvious by comparison with that which remains to be done. We need the power of the federal government to drive child labor from its worst strongholds and as soon as the new Congress meets we shall begin a fresh campaign for a federal law."

Felix Adler is chairman of the committee and the Board of Trustees includes Jane Addams, Howell Cheney, Homer Folks, Edward T. Devine, Mrs. Florence Kelley, Adolph Lewisohn, and Charles P. Neill.

Unit and Dual Control of Industrial Education

The foregoing note with regard to the difficulties that are encountered in securing legislation preventing the employment of children furnishes an introduction for the whole topic of the division of the school system into vocational schools and common schools. Some of the manufacturers of this country are very insistent that there be separate schools for the vocational training of children. The difficulties that would arise if such separate schools were established can be anticipated from the failure of the forces of education at the present time to control the matter of child labor. It is therefore altogether timely that the Bureau of Education should bring together in a single comprehensive statement the arguments which ought to determine judgment with regard to the unit and dual control of vocational education. Attention has been called repeatedly in this *Journal* to the fact that in the state of Illinois a crucial situation exists at the present moment with regard to school legislation. In other states, though the menace is not so obvious, there is nevertheless a strong tendency to put the control of vocational education into hands that are inexpert and into the power of those who are too often interested in exploiting children and young people for commercial purposes. The following statement issued by the Bureau of Education is, therefore, a matter of national importance and we are glad to give currency to this statement because of the intrinsic merit of the arguments themselves. The Bureau issues these statements in the form of a summary of the arguments that are presented in various papers.

1. Separate control would divide and duplicate the administrative educational machinery.

2. Separate control would tend to stop the movement now under way to vitalize general, academic education by the introduction of new activities. Separate vocational education would leave general education to stagnate in remoteness from the realities of contemporary life.

3. Separate control would tend to check the movement to keep pupils in school for a longer term of years, since many would leave a purely academic school at the earliest possible moment in order to get their "working papers," trusting to the part-time or evening schools for further training.

4. Separate vocational schools work to the disadvantage of the pupils because of the narrow type of work such schools would be forced to offer.

5. Industrial workers should not be subjected to a training for efficiency separate from education for citizenship, intelligence, and character.

6. Extreme subdivision of labor, rapid changes in industrial methods, and mobility of the laboring population are reasons against trade training which is not an integral part of a general plan of education for industrial workers.

7. Separate schools for industrial workers would not harmonize with a policy of discouraging undesirable class distinctions.

8. The experience of several states, but especially Massachusetts and Wisconsin, has not developed strong popular demand for separate vocational schools, independent of the regular public-school system. Massachusetts began by organizing a special commission on industrial education, for the purpose of administering the law and fostering the development of independent industrial schools. After experimenting with this plan for a time, the separate commission was abolished, and the responsibility for control and administration of all forms of educational effort was lodged with the state board of education, while local boards of education were given the power to organize vocational schools in connection with the regular public-school system.

The Wisconsin plan, which has been cited as a successful example of separate administration, does not, strictly speaking, afford separate, independent control of vocational schools. The state superintendent of public instruction is, ex officio, a member of the state Commission on Industrial Education. Wisconsin, it should be noted, has no state board of education. The city superintendent of public schools is, ex officio, a member of the local board of control for vocational schools, and it is provided by law that the other members of this board shall be designated by the local board of education. The state official in charge of the administration of the law governing vocational education is a deputy in the office of the state superintendent of public instruction.

9. The experience of agricultural college administration in the state seems to demonstrate the wisdom of developing such a college as a department of a university rather than as a separate institution. The presumption is that similar experience would be encountered in the secondary-school period.

10. The establishment of separate vocational schools would result in the subtraction from the regular public school of all the most energetic pupils, except those who are bent along literary lines, to the detriment of both types of schools.

11. If it could be shown that adequate vocational training can be given only in separate schools, it would still be financially impossible to establish as many schools as there are vocations, except in densely populated large cities.

12. Separate control of vocational schools would obstruct, if not prevent, that readiness of transfer from one type of school to another, so desirable for pupils during the early period of differentiation of courses, that would be facilitated by the organization of all forms of education under the control of a single board of education.

13. The experience of boards of education in handling drawing and manual training does not forecast with certainty what their experience will be with industrial education. Both boards of education and popular sentiment have changed materially since the early days of misunderstanding of the place of practical activities in an educational scheme.

14. The recommendations of the Commission on Federal Aid to Vocational Education and the provisions of the proposed act dealing with this subject, now pending before Congress, accept the centering of responsibility for all forms of educational effort in one office or board as the logical method of procedure.

The School Museum

The Bureau of Education has published a bulletin setting forth the work of the Educational Museum of the public schools of the city of St. Louis. A full description is given in this bulletin of the way in which the material is collected for this museum, the method of distributing the material to the schools, and the way in which this material is employed for classroom work. A very impressive account is also given in the bulletin of the increase in the use of this material which has appeared during the years of its organization. The accompanying table is worth quoting to show the importance of this new device of instruction which has been developed in St. Louis:

RECORD OF DELIVERY INCREASE

School Years	Museum Collections	Teachers' Library Books
1905	5,111	0
1906	11,830	300
1907	16,690	2,748
1908	19,153	3,368
1909	23,152	4,365
1910	29,039	4,790
1911	37,954	9,030
1912	42,994	12,471

Schools that have not realized the possibility of bringing concrete material into the classroom through the co-operation of a museum should certainly recognize from this empirical statement of the influence of the museum in the St. Louis schools how far they have failed to take advantage of one possible means of improving education.

The state of Indiana has a new law for the pensioning of teachers. The essentials of this law are presented in the following quotations:

Teachers' Pension Law in Indiana

Every teacher coming under the provisions of this act shall be assessed upon his or her salary for the school year in which such assessment is made as follows: For the first fifteen years of teaching service, $10.00 per year; for the next ten years of teaching service, $20.00 per year; for the next ten years of teaching service, $25.00 per year; for the remaining years of teaching service up to and including the fortieth year of such service, $20.00 per year. *Provided*, that should a teacher coming under the provisions of this act teach longer than forty years, no assessment shall be collected from such teacher for time taught beyond the period of forty years. . . . .

Any person coming under the provisions of this act who shall have rendered thirty-five years or more of teaching service in the public schools, twelve of which may have been in public schools outside of the state, who ceases to be in the employ of the public schools of the state from any cause, shall be entitled to an annuity in accordance with the following schedule:

For 35 years of service	$600.00
For 36 years of service	620.00
For 37 years of service	640.00
For 38 years of service	660.00
For 39 years of service	680.00
For 40 years of service	700.00

Provided, that any teacher in the service of the public schools of the state may be temporarily or permanently retired for disability on an annuity in accordance with the schedule in this act after he or she shall have served as such teacher as per the conditions of this act for a period of twenty-five years or more, and provided further, that when a teacher is retired for any disability before he or she has met with the conditions for permanent retirement under this act, such retirement shall continue only until such disability is relieved or removed, and no further annuity or benefit shall be paid to such teacher after medical examination made on demand of the Board of Trustees of the Indiana State Teachers' Retirement Fund and at the expense of said teacher shall establish that such disability is removed. No benefit for disability shall be paid for less than one-half of a school year.

The schedule according to which disability benefits shall be paid follows:

For 25 years of service	$350.00
For 26 years of service	375.00
For 27 years of service	400.00
For 28 years of service	425.00
For 29 years of service	450.00
For 30 years of service	475.00
For 31 years of service	500.00
For 32 years of service	525.00
For 33 years of service	550.00
For 34 years of service	575.00

Such annuities shall be paid upon the order of the Board of Trustees in four equal payments as follows: On January 1, April 1, July 1, and October 1 of each year.

In the event that any teacher coming under the provisions of this act for any reason leaves the services of the public schools of any unit of this state operating under this act, before said teacher is entitled to receive annuities under this act, such teacher shall be entitled to withdraw from the treasury of the Indiana State Teachers' Retirement Fund, such a sum as will equal all payments made by such teacher into the treasury of this fund without interest.

The following health note sent out by the New York State Department of Health is of general importance:

Health Hints

When an epidemic of diphtheria, or measles, or whooping-cough broke out in a school, the old-time health officer saw only one thing to do—to close the school; but today there are better and much more effective ways.

When a school is closed in the midst of an epidemic there is almost certain to be a number of the children who have become infected, but have not yet "come down" with the disease. When the school is closed these children are sent back to their homes where they are under no supervision. They play freely with their friends and with their brothers and sisters. In a few days the disease germs have grown in their nose or throat, so that they have a little sore throat or a slight running at the nose. This is the *most dangerous* stage of the disease when the germs are being discharged in the largest number and greatest activity. Yet the children feel fairly well. They are up and about playing with other children and freely *spreading the disease.* In particular they are likely to infect their little brothers and sisters who are specially in need of protection, since these diseases are much more serious for infants than for children of school age.

The modern way of dealing with school epidemics does not involve the closing of the school at all, but uses the school as a most valuable aid in *keeping the children under observation*, detecting the early cases of disease so that they may be isolated and kept from doing harm to anyone. Each school should have a school physician to carry out the necessary supervision. In the case of diphtheria, cultures can be taken from the throats of all the children, and all carriers of diphtheria germs at once discovered. In measles and whooping-cough outbreaks, the children can be examined by such a school physician, and the ones who are coming down picked out much sooner than they would be recognized at home. Then these dangerous individuals can be so isolated at home that they cannot spread infection to anyone else in the school or out. Last fall Sanitary Supervisor Sears of Onondaga County was called to a town where there was an epidemic of diphtheria. In one school of 240 pupils there were 32 children whose throats contained diphtheria bacilli. The Supervisor persuaded the School Board and the local Board of Health to keep the schools open and to obtain a good visiting nurse to inspect all the children daily and to see that those excluded from school were properly isolated. He had to overcome some opposition to the plan, but it was finally followed out and, in a very short time, the outbreak was checked.

The plan for closing schools in an epidemic was a blind shotgun sort of measure, which often did as much harm as good. The new way is precise, and scientific, and effective.

EDUCATIONAL WRITINGS

Professor Thorndike's work in educational psychology is so well known, both in character and in its general conclusions, that lengthy comment will be unnecessary to introduce his latest contribution.[1] The title, "Briefer Course," which he has adopted for this book, gives a clear impression of its relation to his earlier work. This single volume is a condensation of the three large volumes on educational psychology which appeared last year. The divisions of this book are the same as the titles of the three volumes of the larger work.

The first division of the book is devoted to a discussion of the natural capacities of man, dealing with his instincts and modes of behavior. Then follows a discussion of the different forms of learning. The last section deals with individual differences and their causes.

Throughout the book the technical methods of dealing with these problems are presented and critically discussed. One notes in this volume, as in the larger work, the negative character of many of the conclusions. This tendency of Professor Thorndike to express in a critical way the attitude of the scientific student toward many of the beliefs of the educational world has very wholesome influence on the too optimistic supervisor and teacher. One will feel, however, that the positive contributions of educational science ought to be emphasized so that the teaching force in schools shall have something to substitute for the uncertain practices of the past. To leave the student with critical views with regard to discipline and fatigue and to deny the validity of the ordinary doctrines that are accepted is indeed a service, but it is only a partial service.

Furthermore, one finds it difficult to accept Professor Thorndike's psychological scheme because of its utter neglect of those

[1] *Educational Psychology, Briefer Course.* By Edward L. Thorndike. New York: Teachers College, Columbia University, 1914, Pp. 442.

higher forms of activity which lie beyond the instincts and natural impulses. An educational psychology that does not recognize the fact that one of the chief subjects of instruction in the school is reading and that all of the activities of the school center about the development of language as a natural form of psychological behavior seems to the present writer to be a thoroughly deficient scheme of psychology.

The National Society for the Study of Education owes much to Professor Parker, who for a number of years has, as secretary of the Society, brought together in the yearbooks a body of very useful, scientific material. Professor Parker now retires from this position and gives place to Professor Whipple.

The last yearbook to be prepared by Professor Parker was worked out in collaboration with a committee of the National Education Association headed by Superintendent Wilson of Topeka, Kansas. This yearbook[1] is the outcome of investigations which the Committee on Economy has been conducting for some time past. Superintendent Wilson gives a summary of the different efforts which have been made to promote this general movement. Then follow some empirical discussions of the distribution of the subjects in the grades and typical experiments for economizing time in elementary schools. The particular subjects are then taken up: first, reading; second, hand-writing; third, spelling; fourth, composition and grammar; fifth, arithmetic; sixth, geography and history; and finally, literature. Each of these topics is discussed by an author who has devoted some special attention to the investigation.

There can be no doubt at all that educational science has now reached a stage where these detailed discussions of particular subjects promise the most productive contributions to the development of school work. The time was when general investigations were all that could be undertaken and the particular subjects were

[1] *Fourteenth Yearbook of the National Society for the Study of Education.* Part I, "Minimum Essentials in Elementary-School Subjects—Standards and Current Practices." Edited by S. Chester Parker. Chicago: The University of Chicago Press, 1915. Pp. 163.

allowed to work out their applications of the general principles resulting from these general investigations as best they could. At the present time the tendency is in the other direction. The particular subjects are being carefully analyzed with a view to determining in each case those processes which will be economical for the pupils and practical for the teacher who is training these pupils.

The papers published in this yearbook make it clear that further investigations are very much needed in each of the particular subjects. The present body of knowledge which is available is sufficiently encouraging so that the practical school man, as well as the scientific student, can find suggestions for his own work from the investigations that have been taken up by these various authors.

Among the various educational reformers whose influence is largely felt in the current practices of schools no one has been more significant than Pestalozzi. His influence in England and America is attested by the acknowledgments given to his influence in such writings as Spencer's *Essays on Education* and the emphasis which has been given in this country to object teaching and other concrete forms of instruction.

A general summary[1] of his theories and activities is, therefore, a very useful contribution to the body of historical material that can be put into the hands of students. Since Quick's *Educational Reformers* there has been a disposition to summarize the general historical movements rather than to lay emphasis upon particular workers in the field of education. Professor Green has in this volume singled out Pestalozzi as an author of sufficient importance to be studied by himself. While there are suggestions regarding other influences in education, the treatment in a single volume of this one author will serve to emphasize once more the view which Quick so emphatically brought out in earlier days, that education advances just in the degree in which single individuals influence and modify social practices in the schools.

[1] *Life and Work of Pestalozzi.* By J. A. Green. New York: Warwick & York, 1915. Pp. 393.

The Teachers' edition of the *Elson-Runkel Primer*[1] aims to develop a method which the authors regard as relatively new and as a great improvement on earlier treatments of primary reading. The chief contention of this new method is that much preparatory oral work should be done before children take up the reading process in the first grade. This suggestion is psychologically sound. The reading process always follows the process of oral speech. The child's thinking is dominated by what he brings to the book in the way of oral language.

Whether the elaborate emphasis which is given in these suggested lessons on oral speech is necessary will have to be determined by the practical experience of teachers. The child has been acquiring during the period of home instruction a good deal of fluency in the use of words and sentences. It would seem as though this might be taken advantage of without so elaborate a scheme as is outlined in the book. There is certainly danger that the inexperienced teacher who takes this primer in hand and follows its methods will spend so much time on oral speech in the first grade that she will not get ahead with the main purpose of that grade in teaching the child a new form of acquisition of information and a new form of expression. Furthermore, it should be remembered that the outside activities of the school day furnish the child much opportunity for emphasis on oral language. While there can be no quarrel with the theoretical emphasis which is given to oral language, it still remains an open question whether this emphasis has not been overdone as a form of instruction.

The first part of the book which gives all of the reading exercises is another example of the attractive way in which modern reading-books are made. The illustrations and the text are above reproach on the mechanical side and make some use of those stories which have long been of interest to children. The first pages are of the conventional and somewhat formal type and will probably be open to the criticism that they do not furnish the interesting content that children get from some of the readers that begin immediately with the stories which they are used to repeating out of their common stock of folk-stories and rhymes.

[1] *Elson-Runkel Primer.* By William H. Elson and Lura E. Runkel. Chicago: Scott, Foresman & Co., 1914. Pp. 266.

This pamphlet[1] is the first of a series to be published by the Department of Education of Harvard University setting forth its relations with the Newton public schools, which are serving as a laboratory for a number of educational experiments. Many of these experiments relate to the high school, but an enumeration of them will suggest possibilities of similar work to be carried on in the elementary school. Thus an investigation is to be made of the possibilities of "differentiation in the treatment of pupils on the basis of the capacities they show for independent work in history, geography, and arithmetic." Another investigation is to deal with "the most advantageous disposition of the study period." There will be comparative studies of the best methods of teaching special topics such as long division, a study of the best methods of dealing with reviews, and so on.

There are so many higher educational institutions, such as colleges and normal schools, equipped with facilities for trying experiments of this sort that it seems surprising that the type of relationship suggested in this pamphlet is not more common. School systems should be persuaded to take advantage of the possibilities of affiliation with their immediate neighbors in carrying on the kind of research that will be immediately advantageous to the school systems themselves and also profitable for educational science.

Practical books on methods are very much in demand. Since the appearance of Bagley's *Educative Process* and McMurray's *Methods of the Recitation* a number of writers have tried their hand at this kind of application. The last effort[2] in this direction comes from an author whose experimental work in methods of study is of such a high character as to command attention for anything which she writes.

Miss Earhart has reviewed in the later chapters of her book some of the principles which she emphasized in her earlier experimental investigations. In addition she has brought together a

[1] *The School System as an Educational Laboratory.* "The Harvard-Newton Bulletins," Number 1. By William Setchel Learned. Cambridge: Harvard University Press, 1914. Pp. 50.

[2] *Types of Teaching.* By Lida B. Earhart. Boston: Houghton Mifflin Co., 1915. Pp. 277.

classification of different types of recitation and has presented the details of various plans for organizing and conducting recitations.

Miss Earhart is at the present time a principal of a public school in New York City and this book is the outgrowth of her effort to deal with her own teachers and others whom she is influencing in the direction of a more systematic treatment of the recitation.

The book presents its material in a very brief and sketchy form. The familiar distinction between inductive and deductive lessons is here to be found. The problem of assigning lessons and the various stages of the recitation are emphasized. Much is said about the social character of the recitation and the desirability of turning all of the school work in a direction which will cultivate a higher social appreciation and consciousness on the part of students. Indebtedness of the author to Professor Dewey and Professor Charters for much of the attitude expressed in the book is freely acknowledged and constantly exhibited.

The book will be found useful in the training of teachers who have had little or no experience in the actual conduct of recitations. It is very elementary in character and will undoubtedly make its appeal to a wide circle of readers.

The rural schools have been a subject of very vigorous discussion during the last five or ten years. The general changes in social conditions in the country and the necessity of a radical reorganization, both of the course of study and of the type of material equipment which will be tolerated for rural schools, have been commented on by every writer on general school conditions in America. The Bureau of Education has attempted to deal with this problem and numerous writers have taken up the theme. Dean Kennedy has attempted to call attention to the problems of rural life in a book[1] which is intended for the layman as well as for the technical student. Readers of his volume will miss some of the usual devices of the educational writer. The details of school organization which he would propose are suggested rather than carefully worked out. Yet there is an appeal in the book for a vigorous attack upon the problems of reorganization.

[1] *Rural Life and the Rural School.* By Joseph Kennedy. New York: American Book Co., 1915. Pp. 189.

In its style the book sometimes seems to appeal to analogies and to single incidents too strongly, but the reforms which it suggests are certainly needed.

The use of tests for normal and abnormal children has come to be so general that a summary[1] of the methods that have been suggested by students of educational science will be welcomed by those who are interested in getting a general view of this field. Stern is himself the author of a number of tests which are widely used. He has employed these tests in German schools more widely than any other single worker in Germany. He is fortunate in having a translator who is so completely familiar with work in this line.

Professor Whipple's statement in the translator's preface is that this "book affords the best, and in fact almost the only authoritative, critical and compact general survey of the literature of intelligence testing which is adapted for lay readers as well as for professional psychologists."

Three volumes of "Columbia University's Contributions to Education" may be commented upon briefly. The first[2] is a translation of Ebbinghaus' famous work on *Memory.* The influence of this book in suggesting methods of experimentation with the higher mental processes and the influence of Ebbinghaus' conclusions with regard to the rate of memorizing and forgetting are known to every student of educational psychology. Perhaps no single monograph of equal compass has exercised more influence on psychology than this. Its appearance in English dress will, therefore, be very welcome to many students who have not had access to the German original.

[1] *The Psychological Methods of Testing Intelligence.* By William Stern. Translated from the German by Guy Montrose Whipple. New York: Warwick & York, 1914. Pp. 160.

[2] *Memory.* By Hermann Ebbinghaus. Translated by Henry A. Ruger and Clara E. Bussenius. New York: Teachers College, Columbia University, 1913. Pp. 123.

Professor Davidson's summary[1] of the recapitulation theory puts into the hands of the critical student a general statement of all of the evidences which bear upon the problem of organizing the course of study for the elementary schools in terms of the history of the race.

Professor Davidson draws a sharp distinction between the biological processes which have to do with physical development and the social processes which have to do with inheritance of the intellectual type which brings to the individual the products of earlier civilization. This latter or intellectual inheritance is recognized as following different laws from those which are followed in biological evolution. It is also pointed out that even in biological evolution, the environment in which the individual grows up serves to modify very notably the structural changes which have been characteristic of the race in its longer development. The uncritical acceptance of the recapitulation theory will accordingly be checked from whichever point of view one proceeds.

The third volume[2] of this series is one on *Teachers' Marks, Their Variability and Standardization.* Here a summary is given of the evidence that grading systems are very uncertain in their significance and in the use which individual teachers make of them. School grades, examination marks, and the marks given with the aid of standard school scales are critically examined.

The following quotation will make clear the results.

> 1. A given grade or mark means many widely different things to different teachers when they are rating pupils for promotion. . . .
>
> 2. In rating examination papers very great differences of standards appear among supposedly equally competent judges. . . .
>
> 3. Probably no uniform test in arithmetic should be given to all ages of pupils.
>
> 4. Rating of papers by means of statistically derived scales, when the judges are unpracticed in the use of the scales, but experienced in marking by the common methods, produces different results for different subjects. In drawing, the variability is greatly reduced by the use of the scale. In composition, the variability is somewhat greater with the scale than without it.

[1] *The Recapitulation Theory and Human Infancy.* By Percy A. Davidson. New York: Teachers College, Columbia University, 1914. Pp. 105.

[2] *Teachers' Marks, Their Variability and Standardization.* By Frederick James Kelly. New York: Teachers College, Columbia University, 1914. Pp. 139.

CLASSROOM METHODS AND DEVICES

History for Prevocational Boys[1]

Many years ago Horace Mann said that, before its presentation to children, history should be rewritten. Quite recently, in his book entitled *The New History*, James Harvey Robinson, professor of history, Columbia University, pointed out that the writers of school textbooks were governed by tradition in the selection of material rather than by the "needs, capacity, interests, and future career of the boys and girls" to whom the history is to be taught. He shows, however, that some changes have been made in the right direction. He says:

> Our most recent manuals venture to leave out some of the traditional facts least appropriate for an elementary review of the past and endeavor to bring their narrative into relation, *here and there* [the italics are ours], with modern needs and demands. But I think that this process of eliminating the old and substituting the new might be carried much farther; that our best manuals are still crowded with facts that are not worth while bringing to the attention of our boys and girls and still omit in large measure those things that are best worth telling.

He intimates that it is possible to make such a selection of material "from the boundless wealth of the past" as will be peculiarly enlightening to a particular group of children, and he also suggests what this material should consist of if intended for children in the industrial schools.

In determining what topics should be included in a prevocational history course for children, the teachers of the experimental classes, noted in the initial article of this series, have been guided, first, by "the needs, capacity, interests, and future career of the boys," secondly, by the fact that an extremely limited amount of time was

[1] Acknowledgment should be made of the fact that this problem of history for prevocational classes has been made the subject of several studies by graduate students in the Department of Education, and that these studies have been of material help to the authors of this article. Especial mention is due Miss Miriam Besley, who worked out the initial course for our industrial class. The outlines submitted in this article, however, are those now in use in the prevocational classes of the Lane Technical High School.

available, and thirdly, by their opinions, clarified by careful and sympathetic experimentation, as to the most fruitful lessons which the past holds for the coming industrial workers of the country. While the topics may not agree closely with those suggested by Professor Robinson, it is believed that the plan, as a whole, well illustrates the principle of selection which he sets forth so clearly.

It has been noted previously that certain subjects, heretofore reserved for high school or even for college, have been given to prevocational classes. Of course they have been simplified and made concrete and have been brought within the comprehension of those children. One such subject is history and another is economics. The two in their interrelation form an eminently practical and a truly cultural study for prevocational pupils. In other words, these children should know something of history, but the particular phases of history which will be of genuine value to them are not the political or the military phases, nor even the industrial phases, narrowly considered, but those which tell of the relation of the worker to his work and to the rest of society. It is that history which tells of the methods by which the worker has maintained himself in life and has raised his class out of slavery to full citizenship. It is worthy of note that the American Federation of Labor has stated officially that industrial schools should teach the children, between fourteen and sixteen years of age, a sound system of "economics," including the theory of collective bargaining. The history, then, which is appropriate for these children is economic history and might well be entitled "A History of Work and Workers."

The Manhattan Trade School considers it necessary to include such instruction in its course of study, the subject being entitled simply "Industrial Conditions." The principal of the school, in commenting on the course, says:

> This course is designed to awaken in pupils an intelligent interest in industrial questions, and to acquaint them with the factory laws in such a way that they shall feel their responsibility in helping to enforce them.
>
> In order to give largeness of view, several talks are given on industrial history, starting with primitive forms of industry and leading up to the introduction of machinery which brought about the industrial revolution.
>
> A discussion of the industrial revolution and its effects shows how the need for factory laws arose, and these laws are then taken up for study. Copies

of the abstract posted in the factories are procured from the department of factory inspection and those portions which relate to conditions the pupils will meet in trade are read and discussed, and suggestions made as to ways in which workers can help in enforcing the laws.

Following this work comes a reading and study of some simple article explaining the principles of trade unions, with the twofold purpose of familiarizing the pupils with those principles and interesting them in literature along the lines of industrial problems.

As an additional step a brief sketch is given showing the nature of the work done by such organizations as the Consumers' League and the National Association for Labor Legislation in their efforts to improve industrial conditions.

The outline given below forms the basis for the work:

1. Primitive industries.
2. The industrial revolution.
3. Factory laws.
4. Trade unions.
5. The Consumers' League, etc.

In the preceding article it was shown that a study of industrial hygiene led inevitably to the conclusion that the lives of workmen are held more sacred year by year, and that greater efforts are constantly being made to conserve their interests. This fact, once established, may be taken as a starting-point for the study of "Economic History." In other words, the study of history in the prevocational class should be addressed to the problem of making clear to the children the social value of the workman as a human being. It must be shown that all other factors *may* be improved without advancing the interests of the workers at all. Such factors, for example, as cheaper raw materials of industry; better means of distribution; the fuller development of automatic machinery; the elimination of waste material or waste time—all these and other improvements *might* be brought about without essentially changing the lot of the masses of workmen. It cannot be denied that much of the instruction given in the schools under the name "Industrial History" entirely ignores the *workman* himself and merely relates to the wonderful development of modern industrial methods and the enormous increase in material commodities resulting therefrom. It should also be shown that unless the workers succeed in getting for themselves their share of the increasing benefits, at every state of industrial progress, these benefits will certainly go, in large measure, to the capitalistic class.

By making "the progress of the worker" the dominant factor in the course a vital element common to all times will be established, which element will serve to hold together and to relate *all* phases of history provided the study should be continued beyond the prevocational class. Professor Frank T. Carlton in his *History and Problems of Organized Labor* says:

> For indefinite centuries men have been seeking for the solution of various problems relating to the toilers. Students of ancient history have disclosed the struggles of the plebeian or slave class against the patrician or ruling class centuries before the Christian era. The labor problem is a problem of all nations, of all peoples, and of all centuries. The factors change but the problem remains. History is really a story of the struggle of the mass upward; true history is a chronicle of the relations of man to man in the struggle for existence and the subdual of natural forces.

The purpose of the following course, therefore, is to give the children an elementary appreciation of the various steps in the upward progress of the worker, and especially an understanding of the organizations of labor and of capital as they exist today, to the end that such study may ultimately produce workmen who will have a clear knowledge of their own conditions, their own rights, and their own duties. A brief outline follows:

I. INTRODUCTION

The course starts with an exposition of the more obvious features of *present-day* industrial conditions in order to develop a strong personal and practical interest in the study of the economic phases of history. These present-day features are as follows: the factory system of production and the saving effected by it; the modern methods of scientific management; the plan of organization of different business concerns, as, for example, the firm and the corporation; the relative advantages of working for each; the reasons for the corporation; the reasons for trade unions and for labor unions; and the relation of capital and labor.

II. THE STRUGGLE UP FROM SLAVERY

The next step is to outline the history of the masses as the workers have progressed through the following stages:

a) Slavery resulting from conquest of the weaker tribe by the stronger.

b) Slavery as a condition of birth. The slave class.

c) Essential features of feudalism and the condition of the land slaves.

d) The evolution of the craftsman and his emancipation through skill.

e) The craft gilds; apprentices, journeymen, masters; the employers and employed frequently in the same gild.

f) The rapid development of the factory method of production with its specialization, large-scale production, automatic machinery, child and woman labor. These methods of production had the effect of forcing down wages and of glutting the labor market, thereby reducing large numbers of workmen to a new kind of slavery.

III. ORGANIZED LABOR

The development of organized labor in America with its principles, problems, and history is then taken up as a means of studying the methods by which the worker is raising himself again, this time from an economic slavery to an economic freedom. This concludes with a brief mention of labor in politics with a discussion of the extent to which such movements have benefited the worker.

IV. THE WORKER AS A CITIZEN

The worker as a member of a labor organization sinks his identity. As a citizen he should stand as an individual. This conception introduces a brief study of civics in its more personal relations.

Some objection may be made to the foregoing outline on the ground that it seems to omit many fundamentals of United States history which all children should be taught. In working out the details of the course it will be found that, if there is enough time, ample opportunity is afforded for all necessary features of such history throughout the last half of the course. For example, early American history may be introduced as a part of Sec. II, beginning at *e*). This would include a study of the industries of the Colonial period, the condition of apprentices in New England, and the economic reasons for negro slavery in the South. Ample material for this will be found in chaps. ii and iii of Carlton's *History and Problems of Organized Labor*. Where there is a reasonable hope that the children are to remain in school for a sufficient time, and where a genuine interest has been secured, such excursions into the more general phases of United States history should undoubtedly be made, but the paramount importance of the development of industrial and social intelligence should always be kept clearly in mind. There are several history textbooks today which give some attention to the factors which this course makes central and paramount and these books can be used with great advantage. One such, for example, is *History of the United States*, by Bourne and Benton, which under such titles as "Immigration," "Indentured Servants,"

"Colonial Industries," etc., contains much interesting and pertinent material.

ILLUSTRATIVE ELABORATION OF OUTLINES

The limits of this article will not allow of the full elaboration of the outlines given above. Two illustrations of such elaboration are given for the purpose of showing what kind of facts have proved interesting to prevocational classes and of indicating roughly the methods which have been found effective in stimulating and holding the eager interest of the boys.

I. INTRODUCTION

What is history?

Why should we study history?

Besides the pleasure it gives us to know the story of how the civilized world has grown, and the help it gives us in understanding what is happening today, it also helps us to decide what we ought to do ourselves.

Some day we shall vote. A knowledge of history ought to help us to vote intelligently. One may be elected to a public office. In that case history should teach one how to be a more efficient officer.

But all of us have to work, and a knowledge of history really ought to make it possible for us to work more successfully, and to choose better what kind of work to do. Why?

Who did most of the work in the South before the Civil War?

Who did most of the work in ancient Greece?

Did these men decide what kind of work they would do or for whom they would work? Why?

Because they were slaves.

What is a slave?

What people do most of the work in Chicago today?

All of us.

Do most of us decide what we shall do and for whom we shall work?

In theory, yes. The wiser, stronger, better-trained men and women do choose to a large extent.

Why?

Because we are not slaves.

Can those who work in the large factories decide from day to day what they will do? Why not?

When and how did it happen that working-men became freemen instead of slaves? Would you like to know? History of the right kind will tell you. Shall we study it some day?

When you go to work would you like to decide what you will do and for whom you will work?

If you had the opportunity to choose would you know how?

Would you rather work for an individual, a firm, or a corporation?

What is a firm and what does partnership mean?

What is a corporation?

Can you bring to class next week the names of some (*a*) individuals who are in business and who employ others; (*b*) firms; (*c*) corporations? (*a*) is generally written thus: J. Jones, Hair Cutting; (*b*) thus: Jones & Smith, or Jones, Smith & Co.; (*c*) thus: The Jones-Smith Company, The Chicago Telephone Company.

Will you ask your fathers, brothers, and sisters who are at work whether they work for individuals, firms, or corporations?

How long have there been such things as industrial corporations?

Not many years, hardly more than two or three generations. The very large corporations are sometimes called trusts.

Why did men think of forming corporations?

The chief reason was that the production was getting to be on a larger and larger scale and few individuals could get money enough of their own to build and equip the plants, so they organized corporations, under charters from the state, and sold "shares" of stock. With the money thus secured they built factories and ran the business. The profits are divided among the "stockholders" in proportion to the number of shares they own. Thus large-scale production made the corporation necessary.

What is the advantage to the community of large-scale, factory production?

Lowers the cost.

Would it be interesting to know how, little by little, business and industry grew to its present state?

Will that help us to see how it will still further develop?

Is factory work and business under corporation form on the increase?

More than one-third of the wage-workers in the manufacturing industries of Illinois work for corporations which produce more than one million dollars worth of goods every year.

Before we go back to study the early days of industry, we ought to talk a little about the present times, and such facts as the foregoing help us to understand. Perhaps you can bring to class some interesting things about working conditions today.

Are there more men *directing* the corporations or more men *working* for corporations?

Which ones get the most money? Which have the most power?

What do you know about "capital" and "labor"? A very large question; but we must know some things about these terms and what they stand for. Capitalists control their own and *other* people's money.

Why do workmen "organize," that is, "form unions"?

It becomes necessary to do so because the corporation is a combination of capital, and labor must "combine" to hold its own.

Would you like to study a little about "labor unions" later?

Bring to class any information you can about them gained from relatives or friends, especially those in unions.

II. THE STRUGGLE UP FROM SLAVERY[1]

In telling about the life and progress of an individual we might describe what he did day by day or we might show what he had achieved at different stages in his development. For example, we could describe him when, as a boy of six years, he first went to school. We might next see him again when, at fourteen, he graduated from the elementary school and debated the question whether he would go to high school or go to work. Let us say that he took a two-year vocational course and that we find him at sixteen taking his first job. At twenty-one we see him, now a man, casting his first vote. At thirty he has perhaps just accomplished some worthy thing for which he has been working for years. Many years later we may see him, toward the close of life, looking back over it all and advising the younger men as to what things in life he had found satisfying.

In telling about the progress of the worker through the centuries we shall adopt this method and shall show his condition at six different periods of his development, remembering that many years or even centuries have passed between one stage and the next.

But first we may well ask the question, "Why are there those who have to work hard all the time and others who apparently do little or no laborious work?" Human nature seems to be such that few will do disagreeable work of any kind if they can make others do it for them. Furthermore, while there is almost always a better and an easier way of doing any kind of laborious work, the better way has almost always been "invented" or devised by the one actually engaged in doing the work. This requires ability and intelligence, and it seems that for many centuries men of ability apparently used their intelligence to get away from work by forcing the less able to do it for them. Thus a working class was firmly established. Throughout the history of the world, therefore, masses of men and women have been *compelled* to do the hard, dull, disagreeable, dangerous work—compelled in different ways, but always compelled. Do you know any of the different ways by which this compulsion has been exercised?

Another illustration that the weaker were obliged to do the drudgery may be found in the fact that the Indian "braves" did the hunting and compelled their women to do the "work." If the women had been the stronger, it might have been otherwise.

[1] The following is not intended to be read by the class or to the class, but is merely suggestive to the teacher.

The six stages in the progress of the worker will be pretty clearly understood by us if we talk over together the following facts and add to them from our own general knowledge and from what we can read in a few books. (Thurston's *Economics and Industrial History* will supply the necessary minimum for parts *c*) to *f*) of the following.)

a) *The Slave by Conquest*

Perhaps the first slavery, as we think of slavery today, was when one small tribe fought with and conquered another and weaker tribe, and then compelled the conquered tribe to do its menial work for it, and killed those who would not. The ancient Greeks and Romans had numerous slaves of this kind, men who were born free, but were "thrown into slavery."

b) *The Slave Class*

Little by little, however, there was developed a slave class. Children were "born into slavery" and educated to service. The most familiar example to us in the United States, of course, is the condition of negro slavery before the Civil War. Perhaps more interesting illustrations can be drawn from the history of Greece and Rome where many of the slaves were of very superior peoples, the equal intellectually of their masters.

c) *Feudalism*

Feudalism grew up under government too weak to preserve that order which the state should insure to all its citizens. As the government could not give this protection, the strongest men, in England called Earls, Barons, and Lords, with their soldiers and followers, were called upon by weak freemen and small landowners to accept their services and, in return, to give them protection. That is, the one asking for protection became, to a certain extent, a kind of slave. There were different classes among the people who acknowledged "fealty" to the Lords, but the conditions of those who tilled the soil were nearest to those of slavery as we know it. As illustrating the conditions of the serfs of the feudal system we may well take as example the villeins on the manors of England. (See Thurston, pp. 52–55.)

Of course this kind of "serfdom" or slavery varied in the different parts of Europe and in different centuries. (Note the date as given by Thurston for this English example. William Hard says that "in 1807 two-thirds of the inhabitants of Prussia were serfs, bound to the soil.")

d) *Freedom through Craftsmanship*

During the so-called "Home Period," individuals, while doing all the work required of the serf or villein, still had a little time to work for themselves. Again, these individuals sometimes developed special ability in some one craft. Thurston notes this in an interesting way by calling attention to several English names which clearly indicate this fact. While all had to be farmers, some became known as Carpenter, Baker, Butcher, Smith, etc., because they had become especially proficient in the craft in question. Suggest other names: Weaver, Webber, Mason, Fisher, Wheeler, Tailor, Tyler, etc.

In process of time the craftsman came to devote all his time to his trade. It also developed that these craftsmen gathered in towns where work could be found, since now the work was not done directly for the consumer. As the man became a craftsman instead of a farmer he was less restricted in his movements from place to place, though he was still subject to many regulations which workmen do not have today (Thurston, p. 176). He was much less a slave to a master, though he might be a slave of "circumstances."

The craft gilds imposed regulations, but the workman was a member of the gild and so had something to do with making these regulations. On the whole we may say that through the skilled craft the workman finally became a freeman.

e) The Worker and the Gild

How, for a time, the skilled worker maintained himself as a freeman, during the early days of the wage system, must be studied in the gilds. There is much that may be said about them but, for our particular study, i.e., the rise from slavery to freedom, it is most interesting and pertinent to note the discussion given in Thurston on p. 77. This shows that the skilled workman was, to a considerable extent, "his own master." It also shows that this condition cannot last long since it has in it the seeds of its own destruction. It also shows us why, and indicates that strength for labor can be permanent only by making it equal with capital. Although his position is not to last long our skilled workman is free. Has he, with the capitalist, forgotten the unskilled and the learners? Is this his weakness?

f) Conditions Leading to a New Slavery

The conditions which eventually broke down the advantage thus far gained by the skilled worker were specialization, large-scale production, and automatic machinery which utilized unskilled labor, including the labor of children and women.

These resulted in an over-supplying of labor, thus forcing down wages, making work irregular or uncertain, narrowing the "margin of safety," to say nothing of comfort, making the worker dependent on the capitalist for "the opportunity and the right to work," and actually producing, for many thousand people even in this rich country, what the socialists call "wage slavery."

This leads directly to the history and problems of organized labor, the purpose of which is to again enable the worker to struggle up, but this time, let us hope, with a larger percentage of all workers, not merely the highly skilled but all who can be helped by standing together for the good of all.

METHODS

This whole subject must be treated mainly by the "lecture method," since little reading can be expected of the boys, owing both to the nature of the material and to the extreme difficulty of finding any connected presentation of it simple and brief enough to come within their comprehension.

The value of the subject, however, will be all but lost unless the teacher can succeed in stimulating the imagination and thus making the subject vital and vivid. This can be done by interpreting the "lecture method" as a "story-telling method" and by enriching the material in every possible way. The teacher should be able to get from the few references, given at the end of this article, interest and information sufficient to carry the work to a successful issue, provided too much is not demanded of the pupils. Frankly, little of the traditional kind of reaction can be expected, but the thoughtful teacher will value far above this the eager and discriminating questions with which the young students of "economic history" ply their instructor. He will probably be unable to answer all these questions, but so much the better, because an entirely new relationship will have been established and both teacher and pupil have much to gain thereby.

But of course the boys must be given something to do. At the beginning, the principal source of information for the boys, aside from the "lectures," should be the people whom they can question outside the schools—their relatives and friends. It follows, therefore, that the school period must be almost wholly given to "story-telling" and "round-table" discussion. The teacher may be surprised at the amount and variety of information contributed by the boys.

A little later the pupils can be assigned short, well-chosen references to read. These should be carefully marked and definitely limited, and should be easily accessible. They can be chosen from a variety of sources, some of which will be noted at the close of this article.

From the beginning the pupils should keep notebooks. The "notes," however, should be largely dictated by the teacher at the close of the general discussion. If, in the beginning, these notes consist of but *one question a day*, together with the briefest possible answer, legibly written, the teacher should be satisfied. In this way a textbook, meager to be sure, is built up little by little. The joy of the pupils as they look back two or three weeks and realize that they know the answers to the various questions is, in itself, ample proof that the subject is vital and that the method is sound.

In place of the pupil's ability to give certain historical facts and dates, the teacher of this kind of history must be glad to accept an enthusiasm for the discussion of the question presented and a growing interest in and intelligence about our marvelous, complicated, twentieth-century industrial life. When carried out as above suggested and by an enthusiastic teacher, such results may be confidently predicted.

LIST OF GENERAL REFERENCES

James Harvey Robinson, *The New History*, chap. v. Macmillan.

Frank T. Carlton, *History and Principles of Organized Labor*. D. C. Heath & Co.

Washington Gladden, *The Labor Question*. The Pilgrim Press.

Arthur William Dunn, *The Community and the Citizen*. D. C. Heath & Co.

SPECIFIC REFERENCES

William H. Mace, *A School History of the United States*. Rand McNally & Co.

"Colonial Life" 95–117
Social Classes 98
How Social Differences Were Shown 99
Social Life 100–101
The Patroons 79
"Industrial and Social Development from Washington to Civil War" 279–94
"The New North West" 415–46
Corporations 439
Growth of Labor Organizations 439
Strikes 440–42
Railroad and Other Strikes (1877–1886) 440–41
Chicago Anarchists (1886) 441
Homestead Strike (1892) 441
Coal Strikes (1900–1902) 442

S. E. Foreman, *A History of the United States*. The Century Co.

"Early America a Place for Laborers and Work 100 Years Ago" 23–29
"Slaves and Indentured Servants" 82–83
"Occupations, 1700" 83
"Farm Implements, 1800" 179
"Inventions, Manufacture, and Transportation" 180–83
"Everyday Life" 183–84
"National Roads, 1818 207
"Steamboats" 207–8
"Life in the Middle West (in Early Days)" 210–12
"Development (Industrial), 1820–40" 239–48

Woodburn and Moran, *Elementary American History and Government.* Longmans, Green & Co.

Katharine Coman, *Industrial History of the United States.* Macmillan.
"Labor Organizations"

Frank M. Leavitt
Edith Brown

University of Chicago

THE WISCONSIN CONTINUATION SCHOOLS

H. E. MILES
President, Wisconsin State Board of Industrial Education, Racine, Wisconsin

In considering a new and great social movement we must first find and judge the concepts upon which it is predicated, and then measure the accomplishment by these concepts. For such a movement implies the acceptance of new standards, or a revaluation of old standards with a new emphasis upon their relative importance.

I have reason to think that it was in some such way that gentlemen who had under advisement the modification of the school system of the second city in the world, a system now costing $40,000,000.00 per year, visited the Milwaukee Continuation Schools in July, 1914, questioned the children, canvassed the situation with the teachers, with employers and representatives of labor, and expressed themselves as follows:

Said Professor Henry Suzzallo, chair of sociology, Columbia University:

> Two things struck me with reference to your situation: (1) Your fundamental laws had not hampered you in any way, neither had any preconceived notion of your own. (2) You are doing for every class of people that come to you what they most need, and doing it on a frankly experimental policy which admits the gross adjustment in many cases, but leaves the way open to the determination to refine that adjustment from day to day.
>
> As an educator approaching the whole problem from the standpoint of sociology, I distinctly approve of your whole series of policies.

Said Mr. Arthur Dean, New York state director of vocational education:

> The continuation school is a reality. I am tremendously impressed with the progress it has made. It is saving the children from the dead ends of industry. It is making education a continuous process in that there is and need be no set period for leaving school.
>
> It is an absurd idea to expect that just because a child is fourteen he is going to stop going to school and learning, and go on a job to earn and not

learn. I see into that future when everyone, old and young, will go to school, the little ones for the whole day, the older ones for a part of the day or night.

This continuation school is a regular educational, life-saving device for those who work and those who employ.

The demand that a minimum wage shall be paid means that thousands must earn what they are paid, but this efficiency can never be taught by preaching, it must be the result of instruction.

If there is anyone in this state who does not believe in the continuation work, let him talk with the little immatured girls who go to this school.

Said Mr. William G. Wilcox, of the Board of Education, New York City:

I am impressed with the simplicity and economy of the system, and the rational and effective basis it affords for mutual benefit and co-operation between employers and employees. Altogether, it seems to me more adapted to the immediate needs of New York than anything which I saw during our trip.

These expressions are typical. They are not mere opinions, but, like the diagnosis of the physician, they are based on broad and expert knowledge of fundamentals.

THE OLD CONCEPTION

Says Mr. Howell Cheney, in the December *Elementary School Journal:* "The industrial education problem had, previous to 1911 [the enactment of the Wisconsin statute] been largely a work of promoting an idea," through the establishment of all-day trade schools which "were realized to be tentative experiments" by many of their promoters. In the thirty years of effort, from 1880 to 1910, with 30,000,000 child workers entering the occupations meantime, and other millions of older workers, all educationally neglected, there were only about thirteen of these trade schools established, with a regular attendance all told of about 2,000 students, with a few thousand more in night schools which were mostly without vocational content worth while.

Meantime, more than half of all the children in America were leaving school, as they still are, by the end of the sixth grade, and stumbling into industry or into the streets, purblind, unaided, undirected by the educational authorities. The American public school, rightly said by President Eliot to be one of America's five great contributions to civilization, had brought substantially all of the children to the end of the fifth and sixth grades with some knowledge of the three R's. The country was just beginning to see that a further step is necessary for those who leave school at this point, and that it is as necessary to train each working child to an occupation as to train, at great expense, a favored few for the professions.

By way of illustration, it is said in the *Journal*, p. 202, that Connecticut "instead of accepting failure" in her elementary schools (as Wisconsin is assumed to have done), assured justice to her child workers educationally by refusing employment permits unless the child "had a grasp of the three R's, as expressed by an ability to read intelligently, write legibly, and to perform the simple operations in numbers, including decimal fractions." Was this Connecticut's conception of duty fulfilled to her child workers, her adult citizens of tomorrow, and did other states agree with her? Her streets contain substantially as many little semi-ignorant, hapless, industrial waifs as Wisconsin's did. Children who can only read and write do not read and write well. Wisconsin predicated failure upon that "definite standard" claimed above for other states. She begins with her working people, as such, where other states leave off. Better stated, Wisconsin did not "accept failure" at all; she merely progressed.

Information indicates that under the shadow of Yale University, 50 per cent of the children leave school ill prepared to use effectively the three R's, and without further help to advance by their use or otherwise in the vocations and in citizenship, and so do 65 per cent in the mill towns of Massachusetts, and majorities almost everywhere. The school people in New Haven, Boston, and elsewhere have come to see, with their Wisconsin fellows, the imperative need of the further extension of education for these youngsters, and their intelligent induction into industry by the co-operative effort of teachers, employers, and parents.

It seems inconceivable to many that, after the failure of the trade school to care for the workers generally, anyone should fail to rejoice in the happy development of continuation schools in Wisconsin, into which substantially every working child in cities of over 5,000 population is brought. Nor should her happiness be misjudged as pride, when she evidently has only adapted and used the experience of centuries in North Continental Europe.

The article which appeared in the *Journal* was written in January, 1914, when the concept of 1911 had not generally been replaced by the new demand that every child shall be made intelligent, efficient, and at home in a well-chosen occupation so far as may be. I had one bitter proof of this when I pleaded with a noted educator, who helped make the condemnatory "expert investigations" referred to in the *Journal* and is partly responsible for the statements there made. This official knew that there were some 50,000 child workers in his own state suffering for this education. His smile hurt as much as his words, as he said concerning them: "Oh! we must always have our hewers of wood and drawers of water"—a concept thousands of years old.

Mr. Cheney is a man of the rarest parts, an economist, a sociologist, and by profession a business man. It is with much regret that I endeavor to correct the exceedingly erroneous impression of the Wisconsin system and my statements concerning it that his article is likely to give. I consider it, however, a duty, as he has written me, to attempt to make fair correction, not for Wisconsin, certainly not for myself, but that the last child in industry may the more quickly come to his rights educationally, and that no one because of the article mentioned may conclude that one method is a mistake which is in fact easy, inexpensive, and universally applicable.

Mr. Cheney summarizes what he understands to be the claims made for the Wisconsin system in thirteen counts, based upon an article by myself in the *World's Work*, of October 1913. One would think that a criticism of those claims would be addressed to the thirteen counts, thus carefully set forth, but no, *mirabile dictu!* the counts are restated with material deflection in five other counts, followed by the words, "Stated as boldly as above, these claims would doubtless now seem as exaggerated to their authors as they here appear." This is evidence that the charges are in part inferential only. They are indeed so "boldly exaggerated" as to appear revolting, but if they were worth publishing, so is their correction.

They are:

Mr. Miles's Statement (p. 668)	Mr. Cheney's Statement of What Mr. Miles Said
The Wisconsin schools were operated in 1912–13 at a yearly cost per pupil of less than half that of the common schools, the expense varying in proportion to the size of the community and the number of pupils—from $7.00 to $15.00 a year for every pupil. The average for the entire state for the year was $10.00 per pupil.	1. That a good vocational education could be given for $10.00 a year.[1]

Herein is apparently the crux of what may be called the ill feeling and blind complaint against the *World's Work* article. The promoters of vocational education the country over were dominated by the thought of all-day trade schools and trade high schools, with a cost in the former of from $171.50 per pupil per year, as named by Mr. Cheney, up to $250.00; and $100.00 per pupil per year in the vocational high schools, including 5 per cent for interest and maintenance of plant. The Wisconsin figure is extremely significant. It was first announced by her director of vocational schools.[2] As said by the state superintendent of schools in Pennsylvania, the all-day method would bankrupt any state. It is a choice, as concerns at least 80 per cent of the million children who now leave school at the end of the sixth grade, whether they shall have no further consideration; or secondly, whether they shall be taken into continuation schools at a cost of $10.00 per year or thereabouts for the first few years, after which we may be able to spend more; or thirdly, whether they shall be taken into all-day schools at not less than $100.00 per pupil per year, plus a loss in the latter case of about $150.00 in wages and family income per child now working.

[1] Publishers write headlines. I fancy they know how. One preceded the *World's Work* article and read "Good Vocational *Teaching* for $10.00 a Year." As Mr. Cheney knew I had no knowledge of this headline, I assume he did not refer to that nor misquote it in his article.

[2] On October 26, 1914. He makes a similar statement for the next year: "In very general terms the per capita cost for the year 1913–14 was $11.00 and a considerable portion of this was for maintenance and miscellaneous expenditure."

That is \$10.00 versus \$250.00.[1] The first alternative means a wretched, unendurable loss in human values, in happiness, in moral and physical worth. The second means about \$10,000,000.00 in school expenditure. The third means \$100,000,000.00 in expenditure, plus \$150,000,000.00, more or less, in loss of wages. All these figures are to be doubled if we include the fourteenth and fifteenth years, and quadrupled if we add the sixteenth and seventeenth, as we must ultimately for many children. Furthermore, continuation schools must be thoroughly developed in any event for as many of the thirty-odd millions of older workers as will avail themselves of these schools.

New York City wants to know what it will cost to train her 97,000 fourteen- and fifteen-year-old industrial waifs. Answer: multiply \$10.00 by this number=\$970,000.00. This figure has been arrived at approximately by some of her own experts, by other methods. Even this small amount will strain her, and the proportional amount is deterring today many other municipalities. The other alternative, \$9,700,000.00, plus about \$14,000,000.00 wage loss (or any other estimated loss), is palpably impossible.

Wisconsin people never talk cost inside the state. They rest on the knowledge that the cost is minimum, joyously met, and bounteously repaid; however, those who hold to the old conceptions have to talk cost and have to neglect their youth until they get an acceptable cost. Philadelphia must figure for her 30,000, and Chicago for the 37,000, which Mr. Ayres calls a conservative estimate, based upon the federal census.

The assumption by the trade-school man that it is implied that this \$10.00 gives in value or in number of hours what the trade school does, or any other fixed quantity per child, is gratuitous and unfounded. It is a statement of financial fact only, a solution of the money question. Some children come for a very short time because they get their permits just before vacation, or just before they are sixteen. Others come for longer than the maximum statute requirement. No law can be drawn reasonably that will cause permits to be so issued that each child will be in school for

[1] I thought of making the jar less by saying "less than \$15.00" per year; but the contrast would have been about the same, so I stated the fact.

even a six months' period before he is sixteen. Mothers make birthdays not statutes.

Mr. Cheney estimates forty hours' average yearly attendance in 1913–14. I do not know. I do know that thousands of children could not be brought in that first year with legal promptness. The directors did not rent space in anticipation fast enough, etc. The average was one hundred hours for 1913–14, being the second year.

Moreover, the opening of a new school to care for fourteen- and fifteen-year-old children finds necessarily that the majority of these children have been neglected for a considerable time: fully one-fourth are already fifteen and one-half years old, and one-eighth are fifteen and three-quarters. Quality cannot be estimated by averages that year. In the second year, they were evidently caught immediately upon leaving school. This partly accounts for the increase in average attendance from forty hours to one hundred. Nor can quality be measured by a quantitative test.

The first year 12,000 persons were cared for, all told; the second year, 27,000; and an estimate of 35,000 for the third year was made at a legislative hearing recently—I know not with what accuracy. The average hours of attendance should be greatly increased this year, for many are coming four hours or more every day under the statutory requirement that children temporarily unemployed shall so attend. This makes unemployment a blessing instead of a curse.

2. "That the content of this training should not be the practice but the theory and art of a trade." I know of no man in Wisconsin who would subscribe to this statement, which is here ascribed to me. It is inferred from the fact that Wisconsin has emphasized the extent to which the practice of a trade may be and is acquired in the shop. She does not teach much of the practice in night school to men who have been practicing in shops all day. She does, however, insist that practice and theory must go together. Said Dean Schneider, "I have $15,000,000.00 of machinery in my school," meaning in the shops in which his students work. So has Wisconsin. In addition, her schoolrooms contain much machinery, and more is added right along. The permit children are thoroughly

familiar with the use of fundamental tools, if not expert. Milwaukee teaches twenty trades to men,[1] and as many of them as she well can to permit pupils. She has in one room six or eight power generators. She is publicly pledged to teach any trade to any twelve persons who will apply. Other towns seek to approach this accomplishment, some of them quite ambitiously. It is to be assumed that some schools may be far from admirable in this respect. I speak in terms of the purpose and the measurable accomplishment of the movement.

3. "That good teachers could be found in abundance of this content in the shops." It seems to be generally accepted in Boston, New Haven, Wisconsin, and elsewhere, that for the best technical instruction of the average worker it is best to take carefully picked foremen and workers, men and women, from the millions who are now working in the shops of the country, and either give them some ninety days of instruction in pedagogy before they enter the schools or teach them in connection with their school work. Recently there were fifteen picked mechanics so trained in night classes in Pratt Institute, waiting for employment as teachers. Wisconsin has classes for such mechanics occasionally in the School of Education, University of Wisconsin, in the Milwaukee branch of the University Extension, and is now preparing a summer course at Stout Institute for as many as will come. It is as possible to get hundreds of these teachers as to get a dozen. It only takes a longer and a wider search. There is no reason for waiting on this score. Delight at finding rarely good teachers offsets disappointments, and a free weeding-out brings satisfaction. Nor do we realize the hunger and the ignorance of vast numbers of the pupils, and the ease with which that hunger can be satisfied by an average ability, trained in the occupation taught. Some of these children have never owned a jack-knife or used hammer or saw. It doesn't take a genius to make the world look different to them and better, but

[1] Bakery, bookkeeping, carpentry, cabinet-making, concrete work, drafting, electrical work, mechanical trades, masonry, painting, pattern-making, printing, plumbing, power-plant work, sheet-metal work, steam-fitting, stenography, salesmanship, tinsmithing, the chauffer's trade, the drug business.

it does need someone who is very experienced with simple tools and can instruct simply.

Said Mr. R. L. Cooley, director of the Milwaukee schools, somewhat impatiently, "There ought to be a law passed that no one should speak of these schools until he has seen a thousand of these children gathered together; then there would be nothing to talk about."

It is surprising how many of these new teachers are found in the factories, who have risen high in college or technical school, or have even taught school.

4. "That the leaven of this new education would react upon and revolutionize our common-school systems." It is so reacting. The continuation school may be termed a laboratory for the common school. Courses and methods developed in the former are carried into the latter. A certain type of common-school pupil is allowed part time in the continuation school. Pupils who have rejected the common school are led back to it through the continuation school. It is fair to anticipate that in three or five years more the pedagogy and philosophy of the common school and the workaday vital experiences of the continuation school will bring about changes that philosophers cannot dream of, simple, fundamental, democratic. The 150 superintendents and teachers in charge of these schools had some thought of these reactions when they "unanimously and enthusiastically" declared that the Wisconsin or dual system is advantageous to both kinds of schools.

5. This is the broadside: "That, finally, Wisconsin had a vision which would abolish the blind-alley jobs, lead idle children away from the vices of the street, remove the sting of illiteracy, and give to every person in Wisconsin, from children to gray-haired men and women, 'the special training that he or she needs.'" Think of "abolishing jobs with a vision!" My statement was, "We are saving boys and girls from blind-alley jobs through compulsory attendance at our continuation schools," and that with these schools opened everywhere "there will be no idle children learning the vices of the streets." Says the president of the Racine Board, "There were 150 idle boys on our streets three years ago. There are none now." Says Judge Smeeding of Racine's

Juvenile Court, "We have almost no trouble with boys and girls in this court who are enrolled in your school. In the majority of instances, a delinquent boy or girl who can be induced to enrol in the industrial school ceases almost immediately his or her career of waywardness, and is greatly benefited."[1] This is the natural and general experience. In the present period of extreme unemployment, there are 130 boys and 39 girls in the all-day industrial school in Racine—as many as in the average all-day trade school of the country. Similar testimony comes from many cities. I have seen a ball game abandoned Saturday afternoon while all the youngsters were staring through the school windows at their luckier companions, street boys who were learning trades.

The educational expert of the Chicago Association of Commerce tells me that labor permits pass for twenty-five cents current at "craps" in the Chicago alleys. A permit once secured, the child is lost. A Wisconsin permit goes to the employer only and is returned by him to the authorities the moment the child quits. The child then attends the all-day school.

Wisconsin does not give to every person the training he needs. She offers it, and gives to those who will receive, from the simple fractions, that some folk think it "unvocational" to teach industrial workers, up to university courses through the Extension Division of the State University by correspondence and by traveling teachers, which Division, by the way, helps the continuation work by teaching more than fifty common trades.

The adaptability and flexibility of the continuation school is invaluable; witness classes for janitors of churches and schoolhouses; of Spanish for the workaday correspondents and stenographers who handle the business of Racine factories with South America; in leather work, including cobbling, in another city; in delivery work, including the care of horses; in dietaries at Wasau for poor wives unused to American markets, not unaccustomed to meals of potatoes and bread only, and to more varied but improperly prepared food; and, of course, the usual trades in wood and metal, electricity, home-making, etc., as the basis of the larger activities.

[1] Says the truancy officer in Milwaukee, Mr. Pestalozzi: "There are today 3,600 children in average attendance in our continuation schools. Without these schools my department would be in touch with less than 50 of these children. The rest would escape us."

It is insistently stated that Wisconsin seeks to raise the age limit to sixteen. Quite the contrary, except as she adds the five-hours-per-week continuation school from fourteen to sixteen. She is better satisfied than before in letting children leave the common schools at fourteen with the educational qualification required by Connecticut and other states upon the child's making a thoroughly good case before a carefully chosen permit officer, the place of employment being fully considered, and upon the new and further condition that the employer excuse the child until sixteen years of age for a half-day's vocational schooling per week, and that the child return without fail to the all-day school immediately upon leaving employment. Two years' experience finds this to be easy, practical, and effective. Simple, isn't it? How much and how intelligently does a state care for her children which fails to do as much as this?[1]

Raising the age limit and prevocationalizing in six trades settle nothing. Whenever children leave school they must be inducted into 47 trades and trained on and on so far as they wish through higher and higher continuation schools; and trained into new trades as old ones disappear, or are modified.

PER HOUR COST

No one can figure better or more considerably than the author of the *Journal's* article, but even he must understand the factors. The "$10.00 per child" includes rent, equipment, machinery, partitions, etc., purchased that year. This makes his figures entirely meaningless, and further justifies an expression of regret that the article was written without the author's ever seeing the schools, and published eleven months after it was written, evidence accumulating meantime that makes its appearance now an anachronism.

The costs are the lowest possible until the directors can divert their attention from larger considerations to a saving of relatively very petty amounts. Teachers are paid from $800.00 to $1,300.00,

[1] A bill is before the Connecticut legislature establishing continuation schools with compulsory attendance, doubtless with the approval of her educators. Many states are about to legislate to this effect.

thereby insuring quality so far as may be (some get less, some get $2,000.00). They work eight hours a day, five days in the week, from eight months a year to eleven in Milwaukee. With a class of twenty, and a $1,200.00 salary, the instruction would be under five cents an hour. Rent is minimum, in loft buildings, over stores, with factory conditions, every foot of space used for instruction except the director's office. Nothing for playgrounds, gymnasium, auditorium, great halls, or display. Equipment is simple, including machinery. There is none of the vocational high-school attempt to gratify an expanding imagination or rival a great industry, which is said by some school officers in a great city to have caused many of its children to "dislike their own homes, and hate work"—only the necessary machines simply installed.

Percentages deceive. In one city, the permit cost last November was twice the expected amount because half the children lost their jobs and went over into the all-day school, but the percentage translated into net figures was inconsiderable.

In Milwaukee, two splendid instructors, getting $2,000.00 each, both experienced in manufacturing, one formerly professor in a college of engineering, are, with two assistants, teaching 400 select, adult students, two nights a week, and providing them with two other nights of hard work at home. Such instruction keeps the average costs low, quality remaining high. So of the cost of instruction of thirty druggists' clerks in compounding and analysis by the proprietor of a drug-store who is a member of the State Pharmaceutical Board, and by a graduate chemist who is superintendent of a drug-manufacturing company.

The $2,000.00 men follow in a way the correspondence method, but with verbal lessons and personal contact instead of mail. Their value is somewhat indicated by the fact that 2,000 Milwaukee workers, mostly of high quality, have been buying such instruction by mail only, from one correspondence school for about $80,000.00 a year. These figures are low compared to some cities. In the correspondence courses, most pupils drop out soon. In the Milwaukee course the attendance is 85 per cent in the fifth month and many have petitioned that the course go on through the summer. Again we see how fatally ignorant we have all been of the opportunities and needs of these new schools. By way of cost contrast, another course could be named with costs of from $1.00 to $5.00 an hour, because it is being developed in a field that is new, with startling evidence of its necessity.

"ONLY FIVE HOURS A WEEK"

We shall honor ourselves when we realize that these five hours spent in instruction related and essential to the work of the other forty-three hours in employment makes in a way forty-eight hours of schooling. "These are not the children I sent you," said a department-store manager of 63 little cash and bundle girls; "you have made them over." "I can tell a boy in my factory who has been six months in continuation school, and I can distinguish from him a boy who has been twelve months," says Mr. Schultz, of the State Board. A few minutes' time has compassed many of life's great lessons. Let us concentrate our efforts upon the educational possibilities of school and employment tied together and not think of them as disassociated. The latter is as unfair as to over-mphasize the thoughtful estimate of Dr. Claxton, of the federal Bureau of Education, that the children in the elementary schools are affirmatively, actively occupied in recitation and study only about two hours a day or ten hours a week, and in the high schools fifteen hours a week, with, we may add, almost no correlation with the hours out of school.

"MAKING GOOD THE FAULTS OF THE COMMON-SCHOOL SYSTEM"

Might we not better say completing the work of the common schools by this new agency? Have not the common schools done their best up to the sixth grade, escaped fault at least, and do not the continuation schools merely continue in necessary and essential respects the equivalent of the seventh and higher grades? Very largely so, I believe.

APPRENTICESHIP

This is another and collateral movement which it has been impossible apparently even to attempt to develop seriously until now. Under supervision just established and hearty co-operation, the wisdom of the legislation is more than apparent. But the story is too long for this place.

THE CONDEMNATORY EXAMINATIONS

It would seem that a revision of those findings is evidenced in the later findings noted at the beginning of this article, and in the statement by one of the earlier critics to a Milwaukee official recently, after one or two later visits to the city, that Milwaukee is doing the biggest thing in the country, and another, "Your schools are simply great." A third spoke to like effect.

It would be pleasanter to quote the first gentleman in milder terms, but it is necessary to quote as we may as against an earlier and different judgment. So altogether splendid is the work of the Boardman Apprentice School in New Haven, Miss Marshall's School in New York, and many others, that it grieves one to make comparisons. It is only right to measure the Wisconsin movement in terms of its advantage to the great body of the working people, and in that respect it is necessary.

"THE SCHOOLMASTER'S CONTROL"—AND OPPORTUNITY

May we not find an element of satisfaction in the oft-repeated declaration that the schoolmasters are more in control than ever under the new dual or associate board? What better people could be in control? Witness Mr. Glynn and Miss Marshall, for instance. But the point is that the work is, and has to be, so satisfactory to the citizenship at large, to the industries that are brought into the work by compulsion of law, and to the representatives of labor, that each of these other elements may and do know that they are equally and as satisfactorily in control. All this simply indicates that the partnership is perfect. No element is subordinated. No essential element can feel that it is relegated to a mere tiptoeing, inferior, advisory capacity.

Says Mr. R. L. Cooley, director of the Milwaukee continuation schools, voicing the Wisconsin experience:

> The provision of the law, making the city superintendent of schools a member of the local Board of Industrial Education has added greatly to the strength and importance of his position in the community and has given the superintendent a new leverage with which to make his ability and personality felt in matters of education. He is usually the executive member of the Industrial Board in fact. His position is established by law and is one which gives him a clearly defined independence of action. He speaks both as a

member of the Board and as an expert on matters of education as questions arise, and in view of the composition of the Board is the element in the mortar which makes for compatibility as occasions require. The superintendent in this position is practically emancipated from many of the restrictions which kill his enthusiasm and bind his hands in his usual status.

Long may our schoolmasters, in the language of our state superintendent, "enthusiastically and unanimously" approve of this plan which makes them men of affairs, a new and big element in the day's work, outside the formal school as well as inside. It is equally fortunate and necessary that men of affairs and working people are joining in an educational development within their understanding and their ability to serve.

The statements in the *World's Work* are now simple and commonplace. Read with a recollection of the shock they gave to those who were grounded in the old conception and effort, they afford an interesting study in psychology.

THE QUALITY OF INSTRUCTION VERSUS THE SUBJECT-MATTER OF INSTRUCTION

FRANK P. BACHMAN, PH.D.
Committee on School Inquiry, New York City

EMPHASIS OF FACTS AND PREVALENCE OF DRILL

Within the last half-dozen years, some twenty school surveys have been made. These surveys, with scarcely an exception, have characterized the classroom teaching observed as on a low plane, or as appealing chiefly to memory, or as made up very largely of drill exercises.

In the survey of the schools of New York City, Dr. Frank McMurry says:

> According to the standards proposed for judging instruction, that now given in the New York City elementary schools is—in spite of many exceptions—on a low plane, poor in quality, and discouraging for the future. . . . . In instruction on the lower plane the comprehension and retention of facts and mechanical skill, rather than certain effects upon the more important habits of pupils, are the acknowledged goal. . . . .

In the survey of the schools of Springfield, Dr. Leonard P. Ayers says:

> In seven rooms out of each ten, the records show that in the judgment of the visitor the teacher was mainly engaged in hearing pupils recite what they had learned in the book. . . . . In eight out of each ten rooms the observers judged that the questions were predominately of such a nature that the pupil could answer them only by stating facts or giving definite information. . . . . In two out of each ten rooms the object of the questioning was mainly to get the pupils to describe or explain. . . . . The pupils in five rooms out of every ten answered mainly in single words, while in two cases they used phrases and in the remaining three the answers were mostly incomplete sentences. . . . . All of these records point in the same direction. They indicate that throughout the city the work of the teachers largely consists of hearing the pupils recite the lessons that they have studied in the textbooks.

"While some good teaching was observed," declared the surveyors of the schools of Butte, "there was altogether too much drill work and even this was often poor in quality."

In at least two out of the three cases cited, the criticism of the instruction in the particular system of schools is softened by the statement that after all the teaching in the particular system is probably no worse than in many other cities. This is only another way of saying—and most of us I think will agree—that, despite the emphasis during the last two decades on the professional training of teachers, actual classroom teaching, in the great majority of our schools, goes on emphasizing facts and mechanical detail, appealing strongly to memory, and pressing home what has been memorized through monotonous drill.

THE CAUSES ASSIGNED FOR POOR INSTRUCTION

When those who have been engaged in survey work seek to lay bare the reasons for the poor quality of the instruction observed, they assign as contributing causes the administration of the schools which fails to give freedom and permit of individuality among teachers, poor supervision, poorly prepared teachers, the course of study, lack of special classes, old textbooks, and the like. Each of these factors undoubtedly influences the work of the classroom, and improvement in any one of them would be reflected in the quality of instruction. But in our opinion, even if the administration of the schools permitted of the widest freedom among the teachers, even if the supervision were as good as any in the country, the teachers excellently prepared, the course of study equal to any in regular operation, the textbooks the best on the market, even if all these things were present in any one system of schools, even then, it is my opinion that the instruction would, in large measure, be subject to the same criticism as now. In other words, while each of the foregoing factors contributes to poor instruction, neither singly nor collectively are they the primary cause of the poor teaching observed in our schools, when this is judged in view of modern standards of good instruction.

INTIMATIONS OF A MORE BASIC CAUSE

If the above assigned causes were basic, one would expect to find in the practice departments of our normal schools only instruction of the highest type. Yet, it is a matter of common knowledge that there is little connection, at least in some of our normal schools, between the principles and methods of instruction taught in the department of theory and the actual teaching as carried on in the practice department. Moreover, it is a well-known fact that the materials of instruction used in the practice departments of those normal schools, colleges, and universities, where modern principles of education and methods of teaching are being applied, differ radically from the subject-matter taught in the ordinary public elementary school. How often we hear normal-school, college, and even university graduates say: "I enjoyed my work in the principles and methods of teaching, but I don't find that I can make very much use of it in my present position." Indeed, only last month I heard the president of one of the best normal schools of the East say: "Our present standards of judging instruction are all right in theory, but my girls, try as hard as they will, can't put them into practice." Here, then, is a paradox: Our normal schools, colleges, and universities are teaching principles and methods of instruction which, in some cases, have little influence on the classroom work of their own training schools, and which their graduates, when they take up ordinary school work, find hard to apply.

We have, at the present time, a number of excellent books by distinguished authors on the principles and methods of teaching. The best of these books include a number of illustrative lessons, showing how the principles and methods of instruction presented apply to the giving of actual lessons. Since these principles and methods of instruction are to guide teachers in their everyday work, it would be natural to expect that the materials for these illustrative lessons would be taken from textbooks in general use or that these materials would be such as the teacher is expected to teach in the ordinary school. If you examine these illustrative lessons you will find that, with few exceptions, the materials are not such as are taught in the average school, nor are they materials taken from textbooks in common use. An examination will show that these materials have as a rule been collected and organized with special reference to illustrating the application of given principles and methods of teaching. In other words, the principles and methods of teaching as laid down by our best authorities are not applicable, as a rule, to the presentation of the materials of instruction as prescribed by the ordinary course of study or as found in our standard textbooks. Hence, the paradox: Principles and methods of teaching which are not readily applicable to the presentation of the subject-matter which the teacher is ordinarily expected to teach.

It may be held that the teacher ought to be able, no matter what the course of study or the textbooks in use may be, to collect and organize the materials in the several studies of the schools so that she can teach according to the principles and methods of instruction as laid down by our best authorities. Here and there a strong teacher, under favorable conditions, will be able to do this and does do it. But in view of the number of different branches the grade teacher has to teach and the number of other claims on her time and energy, a large majority of teachers have neither the ability nor the energy to do more than present the materials of instruction as prescribed by the course of study and contained in the adopted textbooks. However much we may rebel against it, under the conditions under which modern school work is done, the quality of instruction is, and in my opinion will continue to be, determined very largely by the character and the organization of the subject-matter contained in the textbooks used. Eight out of every ten school men, I believe, will confirm the truth of this statement.

In view of the character and the organization of the materials of instruction in the very best of our present-day textbooks, what kind of instruction can be expected of the great majority of teachers in the elementary schools? This question can be answered most easily in view of materials taken from some of our best textbooks:

> Much gold is also mined on the coast just north of Sitka, the capital, and in other places as well. But the country is so far north that little food can be raised, and mining in many parts is not only difficult but dangerous.

This paragraph is typical of the other four paragraphs on Alaska and representative of a considerable portion of the remaining 250 pages of a home geography which is used extensively.

A paragraph from the advanced book of a very popular series is as follows:

> The cities in Great Britain that are most noted for iron and steel products are Birmingham and Sheffield in England, and Glasgow in Scotland. Birming-

ham manufactures jewelry, watches, firearms, bicycles, steam engines, etc. Sheffield has for centuries been distinguished for cutlery, the existence of grindstone quarries in the neighborhood being a partial reason for this particular industry. Why? It also manufactures steel rails and armor plate for warships. Glasgow, on the Clyde, is a center for shipbuilding and the manufacture of locomotives and machinery of various kinds.

This second book comprises more than five hundred pages of subject-matter not very different in character and organization from the foregoing quotation.

Do such materials carry in themselves any apparent reason why the child should master them? Do they afford opportunity for motivation? Are they rich in well-selected detail? Do they excite the imagination? Do they suggest problems which call for real thinking? Do they afford opportunity for the exercise of initiative and individuality? Yet such is the character of the subject-matter—hundreds upon hundreds of pages of it—which the elementary teacher is expected to teach, and her instruction is expected to be of good quality. If such materials have place anywhere it is in a geographical encyclopedia. After all, that is what even the best of our textbooks in geography are, and they bear about the same relation to geography which makes for intelligence and right conduct as the dictionary does to literature. Moreover, it is about as sensible to teach such materials and call them geography as it would be to teach the dictionary and call it literature.

With hundreds of pages of such materials to cover, what can the teacher do? She does as a rule the only thing that it is reasonable to expect her to do: she uses the "question-and-answer method" of instruction. "What is mined near Sitka?" "Gold." "Much or little?" "Much." Or, "What cities of Great Britain are noted for iron and steel products?" "Birmingham, Sheffield, and Glasgow." "What is manufactured at Birmingham?" "Jewelry, watches, etc." So on, recitation after recitation.

The following is taken from a popular primary history:

The English resolved to capture Fort Frontenac, now Kingston, Canada. Schuyler hastened with ship carpenters to Oswego and built a vessel to carry the cannon across the lake. Fort Frontenac fell, and the victory made easier Wolfe's great victory over Montcalm at Quebec the next year.

When the war was over Schuyler sailed for London on business. The captain of the ship died, and Schuyler was the only one on board who knew enough to take his place.

Mrs. Schuyler built a mansion on the banks of the Hudson, at Albany, while he was in England. The house still stands, and within its walls have been entertained some of the greatest men of America and Europe. During the next ten years, while looking after his business, Schuyler kept his eye on the rising quarrel between England and her colonies. He attended the dinner given by the New York Sons of Liberty to celebrate the repeal of the Stamp Act, in 1766.

The primary history from which the foregoing is taken covers the lives of some sixty great Americans. The average space given to each character is about six pages. This extract is typical, for the book as a whole, of the down-to-the-minute chronological treatment, of the variety of topics covered, of the poverty of detail, and of the abundance of meaningless generalization. Yet the book in question is undoubtedly to be ranked among the very best primary histories on the market.

The following is illustrative of the kind of materials found in our very best United States histories for the upper grades:

217. *Burr's conspiracy.*—While holding the office of vice-president, Aaron Burr—a brilliant and villainous man—killed Alexander Hamilton in a duel, because Hamilton had prevented him from being made president of the United States, and later from being elected governor of New York. Having failed to satisfy his political ambition in the East, Burr got together soldiers and adventurers from the western states, and sailed down the Ohio and the Mississippi to carry out some schemes not yet fully understood. It is thought that his plan was to establish a personal government in the Southwest, possibly including the Spanish possessions in Mexico. In due time he was taken and tried for treason, but was acquitted for lack of evidence. He died many years later, disgraced by his own acts and despised by the American people.

268. *Other aids to progress.*—Other aids to progress were furnished in the establishment of trans-Atlantic steamship lines and in the invention of the McCormick reaping-machine. The "Savannah," sailing from Savannah, Georgia, in 1819, was the first ocean steamship to cross the Atlantic. In 1838 two English steamships, the "Sirius" and the "Great Western," sailed from England to New York. Two years later the first regular trans-Atlantic steamship line, between New York and Liverpool, was established. This was the beginning of the well-known Cunard Line. Ocean steamship traffic greatly stimulated European immigration to this country.

The McCormick reaping-machine, which came into use in 1834, was destined to have a large influence upon the development of the West. By making farm-work easier and more profitable, it stimulated emigration to the fertile western lands.

The histories in most general use in the two upper grades contain about five hundred pages and treat on the average from 1,000 to 1,200 separate themes and sub-themes. This allows from 100 to 150 words to each topic. Such a treatment permits of the barest outlines containing a minimum of concrete details and a maximum of abstract interpretation. Yet the grade teacher is expected to take one of these historical dictionaries, give flesh and blood and life to the 1,000–1,200 skeleton outlines contained therein, and present them to the children in such form and in such a way that the children are taught right methods of work, taught how to evaluate historical materials, and how to think and judge. With the mass of teachers this is a physical and mental impossibility, and naturally enough history becomes as a rule a "memory grind."

When, in addition to the foregoing illustrations from geography and history, the mechanical character of much of the work in arithmetic, in spelling, in penmanship, and even in reading is taken into account, it will be granted, I believe, that the materials prescribed by our courses of study and supplied by even our very best textbooks are such that the only method applicable to any considerable extent to the presentation of such materials is the "question-and-answer method." The tendency of this method is to emphasize mechanical skill, to appeal to memory, and to give undue place to drill. Hence, the very character of the materials which the teacher is called upon to carry over to the child, with the exception of those contained in our reading-books, gives rise to a kind of instruction which is now condemned. In a word, the kind of instruction the surveyors of our public schools are finding is on the whole the only kind of instruction there is any good reason to expect to find.

Here, then, is a paradox of far-reaching significance: On the one hand, principles and methods of teaching and standards of judging instruction which emphasize richness of detail, careful organization of materials, motivation, thought-provoking problems, freedom of expression and judgment, initiative and individuality, and, on the other hand, materials of instruction of such a character and in such a form that teaching, except in the hands of the exceptional teacher, gravitates toward the level of appeal to memory and mechanical drill.

[*To be concluded*]

CURRENT EDUCATIONAL LITERATURE IN THE PERIODICALS[1]

IRENE WARREN
Librarian, School of Education, University of Chicago

Affleck, G. B. Selected bibliography of physical training and hygiene. Am. Phys. Educa. R. 20:90–100. (Fe. '15.)

Alt, Harold L. Mechanical equipment of school buildings. Am. School Bd. J. 50:13–15. (Mr. '15.)

Berns, Frederick H. The book-plate as a school problem. School Arts M. 14:527–29. (Ap. '15.)

Boyce, Arthur C. A method for guiding and controlling the judging of teachers. Am. School Bd. J. 50:9–10, 66–67. (Mr. '15.)

Bradford, Mary D. Motives for increasing professional interest and growth of teachers. Am. School Bd. J. 50:16–17. (Mr. '15.)

Brandenburg, George C. The language of a three-year-old child. Pedagog. Sem. 22:89–120. (Mr. '15.)

Brown, Elmer Ellsworth. Collegiate education as a national problem. School and Society 1:397–400. (20 Mr. '15.)

Brown, Robert M. The European war and geography. Educa. R. 49:248–57. (Mr. '15.)

Bryan, William Lowe. The share of the faculty in administration and government. School and Society 1:339–41. (6 Mr. '15.)

Burris, W. P. The opportunity of a municipal university in relation to the city schools. School and Society 1:295–300. (27 Fe. '15.)

Chancellor, William E. The selection of county school superintendents. School and Society 1:444–50. (27 Mr. '15.)

[1] *Abbreviations.*—Am. J. of Psychol., American Journal of Psychology; Am. Phys. Educa. R., American Physical Educational Review; Am. School Bd. J., American School Board Journal; Atlan., Atlantic Monthly; Educa., Education; Educa. R., Educational Review; El. School J., Elementary School Journal; English J., English Journal; J. of Educa. (London), Journal of Education (London); J. of Educa. Psychol., Journal of Educational Psychology; Kind. M., Kindergarten Magazine; Liv. Age, Living Age; Man. Train. and Voca. Educa., Manual Training and Vocational Education; Outl., Outlook; Pedagog. Sem., Pedagogical Seminary; Psychol. Clinic, Psychological Clinic; School Arts M., School Arts Magazine; Sci. Am., Scientific American; Sci. Am. Sup., Scientific American Supplement; Teach. Coll. Rec., Teachers College Record; Tech. World M., Technical World Magazine; Train. School Bull. (N.J.), Training School Bulletin (New Jersey).

Childe, Elizabeth. Parents and education. Outl. 109:539–41. (3 Mr. '15.)

Cohen, Julius Henry. The protocol and industrial education. Man. Train. and Voca. Educa. 16:465–71. (Ap. '15.)

Courtis, S. A. Objective standards as a means of controlling instruction and economizing time. School and Society 1:433–36. (27 Mr. '15.)

Crawford, Mary. The laboratory equipment of the teacher of English. English J. 4:145–51. (Mr. '15.)

Day, George Parmly. The function and organization of university presses. School and Society 1:370–77. (13 Mr. '15.)

Dean, Arthur D. A state program for industrial and social efficiency. School and Society 1:364–70. (13 Mr. '15.)

DeLong, Wahnita. The use of the conference hour. English J. 4:186–90. (Mr. '15.)

Dewey, John. A policy of industrial education. Man. Train. and Voca. Educa. 16:393–97. (Mr. '15.)

Dooley, L. W. The educational scrap heap and the blind alley job. Sci. Am. 112:247. (13 Mr. '15.)

Dooley, L. W. The educational scrap heap and the blind alley job. Sci. Am. Sup. 79:170–71. (13 Mr. '15.)

Downey, June E., and Anderson, John E. Automatic writing. Am. J. of Psychol. 26:161–95. (Ap. '15.)

Garver, Austin S. Aristotle's theory of art—a sketch. Pedagog. Sem. 22: 27–34. (Mr. '15.)

Goddard, Henry H. The adaptation board as a measure of intelligence. Train. School Bull. 11:182–88. (Fe. '15.)

Goudge, Mabel. A simplified method of conducting McDougall's spot-pattern test. J. of Educa. Psychol. 6:73–84. (Fe. '15.)

Gray, C. Truman. The training of judgment in the use of the Ayres scale for handwriting. J. of Educa. Psychol. 6:85–98. (Fe. '15.)

Haggerty, M. E. The analysis of an occupation. Man. Train. and Voca. Educa. 16:472–79. (Ap. '15.)

Henley, Faye. An experiment in the Francis W. Parker School of San Diego, California. Kind. M. 25:492–97. (Ap. '15.)

Hicks, Vinnie Crandall. The value of the Binet mental age tests for first grade entrants. J. of Educa. Psychol. 16:157–66. (Mr. '15.)

Hinckley, Alice C. A case of retarded speech development. Pedagog. Sem. 22:121–45. (Mr. '15.)

Hollingworth, H. L. Articulation and association. J. of Educa. Psychol. 6:99–105. (Fe. '15.)

How the English teach the war. Pedagog. Sem. 22:152–55. (Mr. '15.)

Johnston, Charles Hughes. High school terminology. Educa. R. 49:228–47. (Mr. '15.)

Keller, Eleanor. Need for correlation of Binet-Simon tests with other tests of doing. Psychol. Clinic 9:18–22. (Mr. '15.)

Keyser, Cassius J. Graduate mathematical instruction for graduate students not intending to become mathematicians. Science 41:443–55. (26 Mr. '15.)

Lane, Henry A. Standard tests as an aid to supervision. El. School J. 15: 378–86. (Mr. '15.)

Langenbeck, Mildred. A study of a five-year-old child. Pedagog. Sem. 22:65–88. (Mr. '15.)

Laughlin, E. V. The evolution of the American high school. Educa. 35: 446–49. (Mr. '15.)

Lodge, Gonzalez. Oral Latin and its relation to the direct method. Teach. Coll. Rec. 16:18–28. (Mr. '15.)

McCorkle, Charles E. Instruction in city schools concerning the war. Pedagog. Sem. 22:1–26. (Mr. '15.)

Mais, S. P. B. Public schools in war-time. Liv. Age 284:540–47. (27 Fe. '15.)

Merton, R. H. Why you are tall or short. Tech. World M. 23:154–56. (Ap. '15.)

Meusy, Mme. Notes on the education of backward children. Train. School Bull. (N.J.) 12:3–14. (Mr. '15.)

Meyer, H. Th. Matth. The German school work during the five months of the European war. Am. School Bd. J. 50:8, 67. (Mr. '15.)

Miller, G. A. Shamelessness as regards mathematical ignorance. School and Society 1:441–44. (27 Mr. '15.)

Montmorency, J. E. G. de. English education in the eleventh and twelfth centuries. J. of Educa. (London) Sup. 47:186–89. (1 Mr. '15.)

Moore, Earnest C. Shall Massachusetts equalize educational opportunity? School and Society 1:400–402. (20 Mr. '15.)

Nice, Margaret Morse. The development of a child's vocabulary in relation to environment. Pedagog. Sem. 22:35–64. (Mr. '15.)

Palmer, Herbert H. Thrift in the high school. What one Boston school is doing to encourage it. Educa. 35:422–26. (Mr. '15.)

Parsons, Elsie Clews. Nursery bugaboos. Pedagog. Sem. 22:147–51. (Mr. '15.)

Pillsbury, W. B. The function and test of definition and method in psychology. Science 41:371–80. (12 Mr. '15.)

Pine, John B. Notes on the building of a university. Educa. R. 49:217–27. (Mr. '15.)

Prichard, Mary Frothingham. The value of story-telling in the high-school course. English J. 4:191–93. (Mr. '15.)

Pritchett, Henry S. Standards and standardizers. School and Society 1: 336–39. (6 Mr. '15.)

Pyle, W. H. A psychological study of bright and dull pupils. J. of Educa. Psychol. 6:151–56. (Mr. '15.)

VOLUME XV NUMBER 10

THE ELEMENTARY SCHOOL JOURNAL

CONTINUING "THE ELEMENTARY SCHOOL TEACHER"

JUNE 1915

EDUCATIONAL NEWS AND EDITORIAL COMMENT

Vacation Schools

Many school systems are at this time planning the organization of vacation schools. A few of the items that indicate the scope of this work may be quoted as follows. Detroit has planned to open five buildings this summer instead of three, as was the case last year (*Detroit Journal*). Baltimore will also increase the number of its vacation schools (*Baltimore News*). St. Paul, Minnesota, has taken steps to insure opportunities for summer schooling (*St. Paul News*). Mason City, Iowa, will try the experiment of the "year-round" school, providing four terms of twelve weeks each in the year (*Burlington, Iowa, Hawkeye*). St. Louis has opened the largest open-air school in the United States. The session will be every week in the year and school will also be held on Saturday (*St. Louis Times*). Not more than three hours of the day will be devoted to academic work. The rest of the time will be devoted to industrial work and play. The school opens at 8 A.M. and closes at 3 P.M.

In the meantime, the city of Chicago is having a vigorous discussion as to the possibilities of continuing the vacation schools which for some years have been carried on by the Board of Education. Indeed, Chicago is suffering at the present time from a contest regarding school expenditures. Some members of the board and the superintendent seem to be in doubt as to the extent to which the schools are facing financial difficulty. All sorts of expedients of economy are being discussed. Either the teachers' salaries are to be reduced or some kinds of school activities are to be closed up. Among the activities listed for suspension are the vacation schools.

Junior High Schools

Indications continue to come from different parts of the country showing that the junior high-school movement is progressing. At a recent meeting of superintendents of leading Kansas cities it was decided to organize the seventh, eighth, and ninth grades as an intermediate school. As a part of the program it was decided that it is desirable to introduce prevocational subjects into the grades.

The *Salt Lake City Tribune* reports from that city that the superintendent of schools has recommended the extension of the junior high-school plan to twelve of the principal grade schools of Salt Lake City. The system has been in operation experimentally for several years in four of the larger schools and has proved successful.

The *Chronicle* of Spokane reports that at a recent meeting of the Inland Empire Teachers' Association a resolution was adopted recognizing the principal of differentiation at the seventh grade. This resolution favored the general plan commonly known as the six-six plan.

The request is frequently made that the course of study appropriate for a junior high school be given in detail. One of the earliest experiments in organizing such schools was at Concord, New Hampshire. In reply to an inquiry for the course of study, the accompanying schedule was sent to the *Journal* and may be of value to those who are organizing such courses.

Combination of Kindergarten and Primary Grades

The possibility of making a combination of the kindergarten and the primary grades has frequently been discussed. The advantages of this sort of arrangement are obvious to all who are not so wedded to the kindergarten that they regard that institution as entirely separate from the rest of the school. It is, however, difficult to bring about a real amalgamation between the kindergarten and the first grades. The following statement made

PROGRAM OF STUDIES, CONCORD HIGH SCHOOL

Junior High School

Grade	Course I: Classical	Course II: Academic	Course III: Commercial	Course IV: Mechanic Arts—Boys	Course V: Domestic Arts—Girls
Seventh Grade	English Literature 5 Arithmetic and Algebra 5 Latin ½ year, English Grammar and Composition ½ year 5 United States History 5 Manual Training Sewing Cooking	English Literature 5 Arithmetic and Algebra 5 English Grammar and Composition 5 United States History 5 Manual Training Sewing Cooking	English Literature 5 Arithmetic and Algebra 5 English Grammar and Composition 5 United States History 5 Penmanship (2) 1 Manual Training Sewing Cooking	English Literature 5 Arithmetic and Algebra 5 English Grammar and Composition 5 United States History 5 Mechanic Arts 6 *a*) Mechanical Drawing *b*) Elementary Cabinet Work	English Literature 5 Arithmetic and Algebra 5 English Grammar and Composition 5 United States History 5 Domestic Arts 4 *a*) Plain Cooking *b*) Sewing
Eighth Grade	English 5 Mathematics (Myers I) 5 Ancient History 5 Latin 5	English 5 Mathematics (Myers I) 5 French 5 Ancient History 5	English 5 Mathematics (Myers I) 5 Commercial Geography and History 5 Rhetoric 4 Penmanship (2) 1	English 5 Mathematics (Myers I) 5 Ancient History 5 Mechanic Arts 6 *a*) Mechanical Drawing *b*) Woodwork	English 5 French 5 Music and Art 5 Domestic Arts 5 *a*) Plain Cooking and Appliances *b*) Dressmaking and Design *c*) Millinery *d*) Embroidery

Senior High School

Grade	Course I: Classical	Course II: Academic	Course III: Commercial	Course IV: Mechanic Arts—Boys	Course V: Domestic Arts—Girls
Ninth Grade	English 5 Mathematics 5 Latin 5 Greek or German or French 5	English 5 French or German 5 Mathematics or Mediaeval and Modern History 5 Biology 5	English 5 Bookkeeping 5 Commercial Arithmetic ½ year, Stenography and Typewriting ½ year 5 French or Mathematics or Mediaeval and Modern History 5	English 5 Mathematics 5 French or Biology 5 Mechanic Arts 6 *a*) Mechanical Drawing *b*) Pattern-making *c*) Forging	English 5 French or German 5 Music and Art 5 Domestic Arts 5 *a*) Household Appliances *b*) Household Sanitation and Hygiene *c*) Dressmaking and Design
Tenth Grade	English 5 Latin 5 Greek or German or French 5 Physics or History 5	English 5 French or German 5 Physics 5 English History 5 or Review Mathematics 4	English 5 Bookkeeping 5 French or English History 5 Stenography and Typewriting 6 or Physics 5	English 5 Physics 5 French or English History 5 Mechanic Arts 6 *a*) Mechanical Drawing *b*) Machine Shop Practice	English 5 French or German 5 Music and Art 5 Domestic Arts 5 *a*) Physiology (scientific) *b*) Nursing
Eleventh Grade	English 4 United States History 4 Latin 5 Greek or German or French 5 Review Mathematics 4	English 4 United States History 4 French or German 5 Economics, Commercial Law, or Advanced Mathematics 4 Chemistry 5	English 4 United States History 4 French 5 or Bookkeeping 4 Economics ½ year, Commercial Law ½ year 4 Stenography and Typewriting 6 or Chemistry 5	English 4 United States History 4 Chemistry 5 Review Mathematics 4 Mechanic Arts 6 *a*) Mechanical Drawing *b*) Machine Shop Practice	English 5 French or German 5 Music and Art 5 Domestic Arts 5 *a*) Cooking (analytic) *b*) Household Economics *c*) Household Design and Decoration

in a kindergarten letter published by the Bureau of Education shows the progress of an experiment in Boston.

In the spring of 1913 Dr. Franklin B. Dyer, superintendent of schools in Boston, called for volunteers from among the kindergartners to try the experiment of doing advanced kindergarten work with the children of the primary grades for two afternoons a week. The response was immediate and cordial; in September there were 49 kindergartners at work at this problem in 30 school districts, with the children of 60 primary classes.

The organization varied somewhat, but the most common arrangement was for the kindergartner to take one division of the lowest primary grade for the first hour of the afternoon session and the other division for the second hour of the session, reversing the order of the divisions on the second day. Occasionally her work was with only the lower divisions of the two first grades, and again it extended into a second grade.

Great freedom was allowed in the choice of activities and arrangement of the program, though at Dr. Dyer's request all the teachers gave ample opportunity for the free conversations familiar in the kindergarten, but often lacking in the primary classes, with their larger numbers and more formal procedure. Advanced gift and hand-work were used in most classes, the former for free construction and for number work, the latter for hand-training and for free expression of experiences, drawing and paper-cutting proving especially valuable in this work. Games were played, stories were told, and many delightful excursions were taken to woods and parks and farms and beaches, both stories and excursions furnishing rich supplies of material for conversations and expression through hand-work.

The remainder of the letter is devoted to quotations from various reports made by teachers who have had experience with the experiment. All of them indicate that the results have been beneficial.

The School Lunch Movement

The movement to furnish inexpensive lunches to school children is gaining ground and at present practically all of our large cities and many of the smaller ones are serving lunches at cost to at least a portion of their pupils.

The *Journal of the American Medical Association* in a recent publication says of the movement:

School lunches have become established in a large number of our cities, and a defense for their institution is now unnecessary. The maintenance of such a service is no longer defended solely on the basis of the needs of the poorer classes, but is encouraged in ways to avert the criticism that the school lunch leads to pauperizing and to the neglect of maternal responsibility in the home. The unquestioned benefits of a well-chosen warm lunch, usually supplied at the cost of the materials and service, have impressed both teachers and parent, so that even the well-to-do commend and approve this latest innovation in the routine of the school day. As a rule, the school lunchroom provides better food than the street vender. In most places the foods are chosen by persons trained in the field of dietetics, and the variety of dietary articles offered at one cent a portion is frequently quite impressive. It includes soups, salads, sandwiches, fruits, puddings, and other dishes. The New York School Lunch Committee in co-operation with the Bureau of Welfare of School Children of the Association for Improving the Condition of the Poor, for example, has maintained a service available to over 24,000 children in seventeen public schools situated in districts in which the need of such service is pressing. The registration has run as high as 2,353. In addition to this noon warm lunch service, the committee has operated a special 3-cent warm lunch of milk and crackers at 10 A.M. for anaemic, ungraded, and crippled classes. It begins to appear that the school lunch movement has engendered certain features which promise to contribute to the general welfare in a direction almost as important as that of the proper nourishment of the body. Educational and social possibilities, at first unforeseen, are being brought to notice. The children of the well-to-do parents and the children of the poor have learned "to sit quietly as one family, to talk pleasantly with each other, to eat their food properly; and many acts of courtesy and generosity have been encouraged." The appeal which the school lunches have made has not infrequently been manifested by mothers who have had their interest in respect to special foods and dietary procedures aroused. Thus the school lunch scheme has fostered educational and social as well as economic purposes.

County Supervision and Administration

The movement to make the county the unit in the supervision and administration of rural schools is spreading. The United States Bureau of Education reports that Texas has recently passed a law providing that the general management and control of the public schools of each county shall be vested in five county school trustees elected by the people for four-year terms. These trustees are given power to fix subdistrict lines, to determine the location of high schools, to consolidate schools, and have the general control of the instructional work, conforming to regulations of the state department of education. The bill takes effect immediately. The Senate has passed a bill providing for the selection of the county superintendent of schools by the county school trustees, for a term of two years, at a salary fixed by the board of trustees, maximum $2,500. Counties of less than 2,000 school population might organize in groups (provided the combined school population should not exceed 3,000) and through the joint action of the boards of trustees select a county superintendent for the combined territory.

Utah has also recently passed a law extending the county unit of administration to all counties in the state. Eight counties had adopted the county unit in accordance with the provisions of the permissive law of 1905. Under the provisions of this new bill all counties must now adopt the county unit system of administration of rural schools.

Standards of Business Education

Increasing efforts are being made to analyze in a detailed way the needs of the community as a basis for a scientifically organized curriculum in the public schools. An example comes to hand from a letter recently issued by the United States Bureau of Education. A national committee, made up of representatives of leading organizations of business men and educators, has been incorporated, with the object of effecting a league of commercial schools (public and private) in co-operation with local organizations of business men for the purpose of placing commercial education on a more practical and scientific basis through the adoption of definite standards.

The employment managers of a number of large firms, among whose employees careful studies have been made, agree that the following requirements are indispensable for all beginners in the office (office boys and others of similar grade):

1. Ability to copy addresses accurately in legible handwriting.

2. Accuracy and some speed in adding, subtracting, multiplying, and dividing whole numbers, decimals, and the few easy fractions common in business.

3. Ability to spell a few hundred words common in business; to recognize and punctuate a sentence; and to correct a few of the grosser errors in grammar, use of words, and pronunciation.

For the suggested preliminary test in spelling, Dr. Ayres of the Russell Sage Foundation has formulated a list of 542 words that constituted seven-eighths of all the words in 2,000 business, professional, and social letters.

The foregoing attainments are suggested as prerequisites for admission alike to the business office as a beginner, and to any commercial course. After the completion of the commercial course in public or private school, there should be a series of advanced tests designed to demonstrate the following:

1. Knowledge of short cuts in arithmetic; habitual accuracy in handling figures, not below 95 per cent with a certain minimum speed, clerica accuracy as well as intelligence in filling out business forms, as the foundation upon which bookkeeping skill can be built up.

2. Accuracy on the typewriter approximating 99 per cent, with a speed of 20 to 35 words a minute (ability to use the typewriter is desirable for all office employees, and even salespersons); for stenographers, a speed of 100 words per minute in taking dictation, and ability to transcribe notes without making gross blunders, and not more than 2 or 3 minor errors per 100 words.

3. Ability to spell 75 to 90 per cent of words like those in an advanced list suggested by the committee and the habit of referring to the dictionary in all cases of doubt; to punctuate properly common business matter; to correct ordinary errors of grammar involving agreement of subject and predicate, reference of pronouns, relation of participial phrases and subordinate clauses, etc.

The National Committee has prepared a new set of tests of the type suggested above. Copies may be obtained upon application to the United States Bureau of Education.

School Surveys

Several surveys are under way which deserve special comment. In the city of Minneapolis the National Society for the Promotion of Industrial Education is carrying on a survey which will be made the subject of discussion at the next annual meeting of the society. This survey is being kept in the closest relation with the industrial side of the Cleveland survey. The two surveys are undertaking to elaborate in a much more complete fashion the analysis of the industries which was commenced in the Richmond survey. The Minneapolis survey is under the general direction of Mr. Prosser. The Cleveland survey is under the direction of Dr. Ayres of the Russell Sage

Foundation. Salt Lake City has undertaken a general survey of its school system under the leadership of Professor Cubberley. This work is to be done during the months of May and June.

Commission to Study Defectives

In accordance with a concurrent resolution of both houses of the Arkansas legislature, the governor has recently appointed an unpaid commission to investigate the conditions and needs of the feeble-minded in the state. The resolution for the commission was introduced after a special committee composed of representatives from both houses attended a lecture on the feeble-minded given by Alexander Johnson of the Vineland Training School.

Mr. Johnson has promised his hearty co-operation and will probably spend several months in Arkansas during the fall and winter.

It is probable that the federal Children's Bureau, which is doing some research work along these lines, will co-operate with the commission and extension department.

The plan as now outlined is to make a wide inquiry by questionnaire, followed by an intensive canvass of certain sections of the state, which will include the testing of many school children and others. This will be accompanied, or followed, by a publicity campaign to include public lectures, newspaper work, the formation of local committees and the like, the whole leading up to the presentation of a bill to the next session of the legislature to create an institution for all classes of mental defectives except the insane.

There are at present more than 100 feeble-minded persons in the state hospital for the insane, since the law allows counties whose full quota of insane patients in the hospital is not full to send feeble-minded persons there.

Not only does this afford too limited institutional provision for the probable number of feeble-minded individuals in the state, but also such an institution does not provide the proper care and training for these persons, where, no doubt, they are a conflicting and disturbing element.

Studies of Tenure in Louisiana

The question of the tenure of teachers is one that is deserving of the most careful attention of educators. Throughout the country, except in large cities, our teaching population is of a very migratory character. The teachers are continually wandering from place to place, if they remain in the profession itself long enough to do so.

A recent investigation in Louisiana, excluding New Orleans, sets forth quite clearly the situation in that state. The following facts regarding tenure are of interest.

Ten years, or more	2.14
Five years, only	2.76
Three years, only	9.49
One year, only	54.07

Thus it is seen that, as was pointed out in the investigation, "excluding the beginners who are teaching their first session, these figures show that more than 40 per cent of the teachers in the state outside of New Orleans, swap positions in every year."

These facts most certainly indicate a condition that should not exist, for it is undoubtedly true that the usefulness of a teacher grows as she comes to have a better understanding of the community that she serves. If school authorities would only realize this fact, they would make greater efforts to hold good teachers.

Legislative Hearings in Illinois

Before this item comes to its readers some action will probably have been taken by the legislature of Illinois on the bills on industrial education which are being considered by committees of both the House and the Senate. In both branches of the legislature the bill commonly known as the Commercial Club bill has been introduced, and also a bill from the Teachers' Association. The former aims to set up a dual school system, while the latter sets up a unified school system and supplies funds for the enlargement of industrial work. Both bills agree in that they provide for special boards to supervise the activities of industrial education. The bills differ radically in the fact that the Commercial Club bill, drafted by Mr. Cooley, provides for a separate state superintendent, separate funds, separate buildings, and a separate organization in general. The German analogy on which Mr. Cooley based his pleas in earlier days for the passage of this bill has not been pushed this year as emphatically as formerly. The Wisconsin plan has been frequently cited as an example of a successful system operating under the dual plan. Attention has frequently been called at the hearings to the fact that the Wisconsin plan does not provide for a separate organization in the sense in which the Commercial Club bill provides for separation. For example, in the state of Wisconsin the chief state officer is recommended by the state superintendent of education and acts as a deputy in the superintendent's office. It is proposed by the Cooley bill that there shall be an entirely separate officer, quite independent of the state superintendent.

The differences in the bills are doubtless familiar to most readers who will see this note. Indeed, it is the purpose of this note to comment not so much on the bills themselves as on the character of the hearings.

At the hearing of the Senate committee it was very interesting to listen to the contentions of one of the speakers who was brought by the Commercial Club interests to represent the bill. He was a lawyer, evidently unacquainted with the details of the Wisconsin plan and, furthermore, evidently quite unable to judge of the value of the measure to the community at large. He could hardly have had any personal interest in the passage of the bill and did not seem in any sense of the word qualified to inform the committee on the real merits of the case. It is interesting to ask the question why such a man should appear in defense of an educational bill. Teachers have from time to time been criticized for going into politics. They have sometimes been criticized for organizing committees on legislation. The hearing before the Senate committee is a perfectly clear demonstration of the desirability of organization on the part of teachers in order to insure satisfactory educational legislation. If hearings are to be attended by people who are evidently there to advocate cases without any special reference to the interests of the state at large, it evidently becomes the duty of the teachers of the state to come to the hearing with the facts on which intelligent discussions must be based.

EDUCATIONAL WRITINGS

The appearance of another book[1] on school discipline as a school problem shows a general movement on the part of students of education and practical school officers to give this important problem its due consideration. The *Journal* commented a few months ago on two other books[2] on this same subject. The present volume is by a district superintendent in New York City. It is interesting to note that he agrees entirely with the other authors that there should be a frank recognition on the part of school officers of the importance of discipline as a problem apart from instruction. He says, as did the other authors, that the young teacher must learn devices for keeping order in the room. Here, as in the other books, attention is called to the fact that a well-conducted recitation and a well-modulated voice are among the devices that can be employed incidentally in keeping proper order in the room. But it is also made clear that the problem is one which extends beyond the mere methods of instruction, and special attention is necessary to this problem if the work of the school is to go on without interruption.

Superintendent Perry's book is to be contrasted with the other books as very general and descriptive in its account of the problems. There is a chapter on the "Psychology of Conduct," one on "Intellect," one on "Feeling," and one on "Will." There is a chapter on "Heredity." There is a chapter on "Nature and Nurture," one on "Stages of Development in the Individual," and so on. In short, nearly half of the book is given over to general discussions which are collateral to the main problem of administering the school.

These general discussions are not very helpful to the student of this special problem because they seem very abstract in the presence of the urgent demand for a definite statement of what one should do in order to keep the school in order. An author can

[1] *Discipline as a School Problem.* By Arthur C. Perry, Jr. Boston: Houghton Mifflin Co., 1915. Pp. 273.

[2] *School Discipline.* By William Chandler Bagley. *The Discipline of the School.* By Frances M. Morehouse.

hardly write with technical accuracy on such a matter as heredity in the compass of the few pages that are devoted to the problem in this book. The same abstractness appears in the paragraphs in which Mr. Perry discusses some of the special problems of discipline. For example, one feels that there is nothing very final about such a discussion as the following.

> Rewards and punishments. All that has just been said applies alike to rewards and to punishments, so that the teacher has frequently to choose between the two as a means of discipline. In general, we may say that it is better to appeal to the pupil by way of reward than by way of punishment. The spirit of the pupil is better sustained by a minimum of punishment. Nevertheless, no pupil should be exempt from the operation of punishment, for punishment is an important and unavoidable fact in life. No pupil should be sent from the school into the business and social world with the idea that he is to be rewarded at every turn when he conducts himself properly or that there are no punishments meted out to offenders (p. 192).

Again, the following quotation is typical:

> Parents' associations. Parents' associations have their place in the scheme of co-operation. These are, of course, more effective if they develop on the initiative of the parents. If they do not evolve thus spontaneously, the principal may skilfully bring about their organization. He should be careful, however, not to take too active and prominent a part in their proceedings. In some schools associations comprising both the parents and the teachers are found effective.
>
> Even with a flourishing parents' organization, there will be many parents who are not brought into touch with the school. The only way in which they can be reached is through visitation either by the regular teacher or by a specially appointed visiting teacher (p. 226).

Such summary treatments of the problem of school discipline ought to be relieved by more careful studies of the different types of children and the different devices which can be employed in keeping them in order.

Superintendent Alderman has for some time been an enthusiast in favor of the movement which gives school credit for various forms of children's activity at home and during their leisure hours. In this book[1] he presents a very full statement of the different plans which are in operation throughout the states of Washington and

[1] *School Credit for Home Work*. By L. R. Alderman. Boston: Houghton Mifflin Co., 1915. Pp. 181.

Oregon for the giving of such credit. Sometimes the plan takes the form of a competitive exercise and the reward offered to the child under the supervision of the school is some kind of a prize. In many cases the reward offered is exemption from some kind of school work. For example, in one of the plans a student who does many of the things that are credited by the school is allowed to answer fewer questions in the examination than the child who does not carry on these outside activities.

What one misses in Superintendent Alderman's book is a clear statement of the effect of all of this on school work. To be sure, there is repeated assertion that in individual cases the work of the school, which up to the beginning of the outside credit was neglected, improved steadily under the stimulus of regular habits and better forms of thought about labor. There is much argument which goes to show that the work which the children undertake is very much benefited by the supervision of the school and the credit which is given by the school, but the essential matter, which is the infringement upon school time, needs to be very carefully studied. In one chapter, for example, in which Superintendent Alderman asks what is to become of algebra, he makes many assertions to the effect that algebra is distinctly improved by the outside credit. That is the result which would interest school people in general, but it seems obvious to many of us that if the school day is not increased at all in length and the requirements for graduation are absolved by giving credit for outside activities, these outside activities will reduce somewhat the amount of school work which will actually be regarded as essential by the school authorities for graduation. Children have always done a good deal of work outside of the school and there cannot be the slightest question that it is desirable to systematize and supervise this outside work. It would seem reasonable to suggest that if the school extends its activities so as to include for the advantage of the outside work these activities that formerly were not on the school program, the school should have some recognition for the extension of its work by being allowed to require more for graduation.

In short, if outside work could be interpreted as a device for extending the influence and scope of the school, there are many who would be in favor of it. If the supervision of the outside work is to distract the school from its primary function of giving instruction in certain lines that society has long regarded as valuable, then there is a genuine danger which must be safeguarded. On this point Superintendent Alderman's book does not seem to be at all conclusive.

One of the investigations which has of recent years been very productive in an experimental way is the investigation of children's habits of observation. The methods which have been employed are those which originated in Germany with the tests requiring children to describe the details of a picture which is exhibited to them. The selection which the children make of the objects in the pictures and the changes which are exhibited during the various periods of intellectual development can then be recorded in a form that is exact and illuminative. Mr. Winch,[1] who has made extensive studies in the English schools of the various characteristics of children's mental processes, has brought together in a monograph a series of experiments on children's observations of the picture which was used for many of the German tests. The picture itself is reproduced in the book, and the author thus opens a way for similar tests in schools in this country.

Without attempting to go into the details of the results, it may be pointed out that a rapid development is shown in the powers of observation in children up to the age of six or seven. At this point there seems to be a check in the development of perceptual processes. This check is undoubtedly related to the fact that the school training which begins at this point turns the attention of children away from their immediate observation of natural objects to the use of books and reading-matter.

The monograph will be found very suggestive to teachers who are interested in developing the perfectly natural tendency which children bring to the school of making observations, but who find that the ordinary school routine is likely to interfere with this natural tendency rather than cultivate it.

[1] *Children's Perceptions.* "Educational Psychology Monographs," No. 12. By W. H. Winch. Baltimore: Warwick & York, 1914. Pp. 245.

There is at the present time a large body of literature on religious education which is characterized by the desire on the part of religious educators to bring their special field into the closest possible relation to the general work of the school. These writers are prepared to give up many of the special types of instruction which were characteristic in earlier days of religious training. They are anxious to follow the best examples of the present-day public schools. A book[1] prepared by the secretary of the Religious Education Association can be described as typical of the whole series of such writings. Mr. Cope comments on practices of earlier days and practices which he wishes to recommend in a fashion which shows a disposition to be very liberal and yet at the same time a desire to perpetuate some of the older forms of instruction. Take, for example, the chapter on Sunday in the home. Sunday is to be made a day of enjoyment. In order to do this the modern attitude toward play is distinctly to be recognized. The children ought to play, but they ought to have a selected set of games differing from the games which they play on other days of the week. These Sunday games are to be characterized by religious content or by their deference to the needs of other people. The type of enjoyment which they give should be of a somewhat more elevated sort than that which attaches to the games during the rest of the week. The associations with parents ought to be somewhat more intimate than usual.

Take another example. The author wishes to advocate family worship. He says, "It is true that, in many homes, under modern conditions of business, it is almost impossible for the family to be united at the hour when worship used to be customary, following breakfast." Other devices, however, and other times can be adopted, and the chapter is full of suggestions as to the ways in which substitutes can be provided for this earlier family custom.

The book will be found full of suggestions of this type. Indeed, as a book of methods of meeting the exigencies of modern decline of family life, the book may be described as a textbook on the family organization rather than a textbook on religious education. There

[1] *Religious Education in the Family*. By Henry F. Cope. Chicago: The University of Chicago Press, 1915. Pp. 298.

are some chapters which give a general account of the sociological conditions which have arisen in the modern home. The book will be of interest to teachers who are constantly called upon to decide the questions of moral education in the school and in the family. These questions are so intimately related to the division of functions between the school and other agencies that it is frequently the duty of the teacher not only to settle questions of the division of labor here involved, but also to make suggestions to those who are at work on aspects of the problem which are outside of the school.

The effort to make Froebel appear to be an empirical psychologist of the modern type taxes the ingenuity of even an enthusiast for Froebel's system. A new book[1] on Froebel undertakes to prove that he is such a psychologist and at the same time to show that Froebel's system is not only useful in organizing primary and kindergarten work but also helpful to the teacher who is dealing with older children. We are reminded that the school at Keilhau was a school extending far beyond the kindergarten and that the influence of this school has been very great in liberalizing the course of study and the policy of discipline of all subsequent schools. The reader of the history of education would undoubtedly be willing to admit this contention, but to pass from that contention to the contention that it is the psychological foundation for the Froebelian system which explains the success of the school seems a long step which the book itself hardly justifies. In fact, after reading over laboriously some of the passages in which the author attempts to show by comparative quotations and brief explanatory discussions that Froebel is a modern psychologist, one comes more than ever to the conclusion that Froebel is capable of almost any interpretation which his reader wishes to put on him, especially in some of the vague general passages which are quoted in this book.

Modern empirical psychology has gone so far in developing a technique and body of results that it seems altogether unwise to try to prove the utterly unprovable thesis that men of three-quarters of a century ago knew what modern psychology has

[1] *Froebel as a Pioneer in Modern Psychology.* By E. R. Murray. Baltimore: Warwick & York, 1914. Pp. 230.

brought to light in regard to the functions and forms of mental life. It is not likely that even the kindergarten will benefit by any effort to revive and maintain the Froebel cult. The kindergarten ought to be free from any of the traditions that attach to the vague and metaphysical doctrines out of which it originally grew. What is needed today is a vigorous study of real children, not platitudinous statements or efforts to extract from psychologies of a bygone day some remote resemblances to modern statements. Every kindergarten teacher and every other student of Froebel ought to realize that Froebel would undoubtedly have encouraged all of his followers to progress as the school has progressed since his day. It will be very much better for teachers to spend their time reading William James or some good modern psychologist than to go back to this rehearsal of Froebel's doctrines.

The child-study movement in this country has been absorbed in the other forms of scientific study to such an extent that it is difficult to determine in advance just what an author means by the title "Child Study." The book[2] before us has used the title in a fashion which is hardly in keeping with the traditions of the name. The topics which are covered might very much better be indicated by some such phrase as "A Study of the Child's Home Relations." The book is intended to give suggestions to parents' associations and other organizations of this type which wish to make a study of the literature dealing with the child in his relation to the church, the members of the family, the playground, and other organizations and agencies which lie very largely outside of the school itself. There are outlines or studies on the father as the guardian of the home, the father and the alcohol problem, and the father as a handy man. There are outlines on the political status of motherhood, the pension system and motherhood, and so on. These topics, selected at random, indicate that the scope of this study is not that which would ordinarily be indicated by the title "Child Study."

The author is very enthusiastic about the organization of groups of parents who are to carry on these studies, and the book is intended

[1] *Outlines of Child Study*. By William A. McKeever. New York: Macmillan, 1915. Pp. 181.

as a handbook for leaders of organizations of this type. The selection of the references which are used for this purpose is, of course, a matter of a great deal of concern to the schools which will be influenced indirectly by the studies of such organizations. The criticism which suggests itself to the reader of the bibliography is that the material has not been very carefully selected. There are a number of excellent references in the list, but there are also a number of articles that are of very mediocre value. Furthermore, the list does not seem to have been selected with any special reference to the probability of the presence of most of the material in public libraries from which it will have to be drawn if it is used by such associations.

Professor Bagley is editing a series of books entitled "The Modern Teacher's Series." The first volume[1] of this series is entitled *The Lesson in Appreciation* and is from the pen of an English writer. In the course of this book the author makes numerous comments on the availability of music and painting as instruments of general education. He attempts to defend the thesis that these subjects should be introduced into the school with a view to cultivating the aesthetic appreciation of students. We are called upon to recognize the importance of this side of the child's nature and are urged to go about its cultivation with a great deal of directness. The book also purports to give us an account of the psychological character of this aesthetic appreciation. Some theory is distributed through the pages of the book. There are many references to the material which is available for instruction.

The book makes the impression on a reader who is not altogether sympathetic with its thesis that such books commonly do. There is an offhand reference to works of art that will be baffling to the person who does not immediately have access to all of these higher forms of culture. He will not know where to find them and he will not know what to do with them when he gets them. There is a certain vagueness in the definition of what is meant by appreciation and in the psychology of the processes themselves. There

[1] *The Lesson in Appreciation.* By Frank Herbert Hayward. New York: Macmillan, 1915. Pp. 234.

is no definite effort to tell just when these various items of experience should be introduced into the school course. In short, one is disposed to make a comment which has frequently been made with regard to art instruction in the school, that if it really is going to be successful it will have to be defined with somewhat greater precision than commonly appears in the writings of those who are most enthusiastic about its introduction.

Two English books which have just appeared would seem to indicate that the child-study movement is being emphasized in England rather more than in America at the present time. The first[1] of these is intended chiefly for Sunday-school teachers. It gives a very interesting summary of the differences between children of the primary years and children of the later years. There is some discussion of the development of infancy. All of the chapters are focused upon the problem of religious instruction.

The other volume[2] by Ellen Adamson is a general study of particular subjects of school instruction. Here one finds chapters on reading, writing, composition, history, etc. The book is a cross between a discussion of methods and a discussion of the results of child-study. Many practical suggestions are given in its pages. The impression one gets after reading the American literature on similar subjects is that the book is written on the basis of a large practical experience and a slight study of scientific work rather than the reverse. The practical suggestions are many of them very useful, but the general drift of the whole discussion is lost in the details which the author writes out of her practical experience.

[1] *Child Study with Special Application to the Teaching of Religion.* By Rev. C. H. Dix. New York: Longmans, Green & Co., 1915. Pp. 134.

[2] *The School, the Child and the Teacher.* By Ellen Winifred Adamson. New York: Longmans, Green & Co., 1915. Pp. 394.

CLASSROOM METHODS AND DEVICES

Problems in Geography—A Continent

In the March number of the *Journal* a number of problems based on the scale, direction, and legend of a map were suggested. The aim of the paper was twofold: to test the knowledge of the subject by the ability to make use of the knowledge and to show that it is possible to devise questions which will show processes of thinking rather than of memory. The present paper enlarges the scope of the former one and blazes a way for problems and test questions in the study of a continent—in this case, South America. Only such of the subject-matter is admitted here as will furnish an outline, and it is to be understood that where there appear to be flagrant omissions the material was not relevant to the problems undertaken, although it may be vastly important from another standpoint. There is good training in making generalizations from the outline and topography maps of South America in order to gain a good conception of the value of these controls, and from them some simple problems may be formulated, but for the purposes of this paper these maps together with the wind maps for July and January with isotherms inserted will be taken as the background of the first series of problems.

1. *Rainfall.*—The study of North America and of the wind belts in preparation for South America yields the following summary:

Rain is the resultant of an ascending current of air containing moisture—the mass of ascending air expands and cools mechanically, the moisture condenses and falls. Ascending currents are caused by:

A. Heated air, which, becoming lighter than the surrounding air, is pushed up, as in: (1) doldrum belt; (2) lows of prevailing westerlies.

B. A slope intercepting the winds, as on: (3) windward slopes.

Dryness, conversely, is the resultant of a lack of ascending currents and may occur under descending currents or surface winds.

A. Descending currents are caused by gravity: (1) doldrum belt; (2) highs of westerlies; (3) leeward slopes; (4) polar highs.

B. Surface winds are drying and cause dryness when they blow persistently over the land: (5) trade winds over land.

With a proper preparation, questions or tasks are possible which call for no great ability, but which demand thorough knowledge.

Locate a region of heavy rain; a region of light rain. What is the rainfall of southern Chile and why? On an outline map, make a rainfall map of South America—using solid blue for areas of heavy rainfall and leaving the regions of light rainfall uncolored. Areas not falling into the two classes may be considered as having a moderate rainfall and may be colored a light shade of blue.

The comparisons of the pupils' maps with an accurate rainfall map will show how far the reasoning process has been followed, and the errors in the maps will expose the weak points in the teacher's presentation or the pupil's comprehension.

2. *Temperature.*—The climatic controls are latitude, altitude, proximity to the sea, winds—especially direction, and whether or not they blow from land or water—and rainfall. In discussing the temperatures, there has been too much generalization; teachers have been satisfied with "hot," "cold," or "temperate" for answers. The word "temperate" has no virtue except to cover a vast amount of ignorance, and little knowledge of middle-belt climates can be gained unless the *ranges* of temperature between extreme seasons are considered.

Discuss the climate of Para from the standpoint of the five climatic controls. Compare the effect of each control on Para and the pupil's home town and establish the causes of the difference. Compare the temperatures of Para and Quito; of Para and Valparaiso. From the isotherms, state the annual range of temperature at Para and Rio de Janeiro. Account for the differences.

3. *Vegetation.*—As climate is the greatest factor in determining the distribution of plants and density of vegetation, the conditions affecting density and kinds furnish a preparation for another problem. Very roughly, regions of heavy rainfall yield forests;

regions of light rainfall or having periods of drought are treeless, but grasses thrive; regions of moderate but well-distributed rains are generally wooded (open forests) in their natural state, but offer excellent areas for agriculture; regions of little rain have desert plants.

What will be the vegetation at Para? at Iquique? at Quito? Locate grass areas in South America. What are the llanos? the pampas? the campos? Where will trees probably be found on this continent? Construct a map showing density of vegetation.

The emphasis in vegetation is less upon density than upon products of commercial value. Problems under this heading may be approached in two ways: first, given the conditions under which the staple products will grow, find the localities suitable for these in the country, or, secondly, knowing the conditions and locations, determine whether the conditions agree with the statements already made concerning the temperature, rainfall, altitude, and latitude of the areas.

Rice requires 60–80 degrees for ripening, an abundance of moisture, and is generally grown on low, alluvial lands in the tropics.

Sugar cane requires rich, moist soil; must be practically free from frost, even in winter; and thrives best in low places in the vicinity of the sea.

Coffee grows in well-watered mountainous regions, 1,000 to 4,000 feet high, in the tropics.

Wheat requires a mean summer temperature of 57 degrees and plenty of sunlight.

Which of these (and other) products will grow about Para? Rio de Janeiro? Quito? Buenos Aires? From a study of the maps already presented locate on an outline map the parts of South America which fulfil the requirements for rice. Find a rice map of the continent and note where rice is cultivated. Why are not all the areas capable of yielding rice used for rice culture? Do the same thing for the other products of South America.

Accurate vegetation maps showing density of vegetation cover and the distribution of important products should be presented. It is, of course, recognized that maps showing distribution of any staple of commerce are not in themselves sufficient and they should be supplemented by a graph or statement which shows the amounts of yield in the various localities.

4. *Animals.*—If the semi-arid localities, inasmuch as they are covered with sparse grasses, offer food for cattle, it will be possible to discuss the cattle industry of South America from the standpoint of the controls. Plot upon an outline map the areas which, because of a short seasonal or a slight yearly rainfall, are covered with grass and are thus suitable for grazing. Compare this with an animal map and account for the divergences.

Among the controls which should be presented before proceeding far in the study is the soil map, and this can be interpreted to mean not so much the character of the soil as the special soil products. In general terms, rainfall and topography furnish good criteria for the soil condition, but the distribution of important minerals in South America—the gold, silver, and sodium nitrate especially—is a large factor in the distribution of the people.

5. *Commerce and population.*—Areas of largest commerce are found where the staples of trade occur in greatest quantities and they are generally located near a convenient harbor or station; areas of moderate commerce follow the same law somewhat modified; inaccessible areas are undeveloped and barren areas are unproductive. Considering the presentations up to this point, it will be possible for the pupils to prepare a commerce map, showing the areas indicated above. Here, as in other cases when an accurate commercial map is presented, a number of points will probably have to be considered because of the departures of the pupils' maps from the true one. As commerce is to a great extent influenced by the density or sparsity of population, a map showing density of population could be made by the pupils.

6. *Exports and imports.*—The teaching of the exports and imports of a country from a tabulated list is a deadening process and rarely accomplishes anything. It is evident that a country will export products demanded in the world's commerce of which an excess over home needs is produced, and will import the necessities and conveniences of life which the land does not yield. The exceptions to this rule are relatively few, but prominent enough to call forth a special explanation. In South America, a review

of the chief products which the country possesses in quantities ought to make clear what the exports are; for instance, on the vegetation map wheat and grass lands for grazing were indicated for Argentina. There was a distinct absence of important products such as the United States finds of value, notably coal and iron, by which manufacturing is carried on. If this is true, then it must be evident that manufactured goods will be a need of Argentina; foremost among these are textiles, cotton and woolen cloths, and then come tools, implements, and manufactured foods. Argentina engaging largely in agriculture will undoubtedly need agricultural implements. What does Rio de Janeiro need? What are the exports and imports of Para? Iquique?

A general treatment of South America is frequently followed by a special treatment of specific important areas. On this continent this would include Rio de Janeiro and coffee, Buenos Aires and wheat and cattle, Iquique and sodium nitrate, and Para and rubber; or, as is at times the custom, the leading states, Brazil, Argentina, and Chile, are studied in more detail. In any case, the work is a review of generalizations, together with a few points of more definite knowledge. In the case of Chile the maps of position, topography, winds, rain, soil, commerce, and population of the continent tell the story and little more is needed except now and then a clearer picture of a few regions, which may fall into the category of type-studies. It is difficult at first for pupils to appreciate that the needs of the home locality are not the needs of all peoples under diverse conditions of life; that meat, an essential part of diet in parts of the United States, has no great place in the life of the people of Para, but considerable training should be given along this line. Questions and problems on the work may be from actual cases or may be hypothetical.

Draw the following areas: a map of a locality, 300 miles from coast to mountains, in the trade winds, which will be a desert; a map of a region with uniform temperature, indicating its climatic and topographic conditions and enough data to explain the climate; a map of a locality producing rice, wheat, and cattle, and possessing a harbor which has to be protected by artificial means from the winds; an area having a gold-export trade, but importing foods, textiles, and implements; a sketch map of Peru (exporting metals, sugar, and cotton and importing bread stuffs, hardware, and cotton cloth) showing the basis of her trade; a map showing the reason of the lack of rainfall about Lake Titicaca; a map of Chile which will explain her three types of climates, and at the same time will illustrate the industries of northern, central, and southern Chile.

ROBERT M. BROWN

RHODE ISLAND NORMAL SCHOOL
PROVIDENCE, RHODE ISLAND

PLANS FOR TEACHING A STORY TO SMALL CHILDREN

The place of literature in the elementary school is too well assured to admit of any argumentation; its function is too well established to require explanation. It is a fact, however, that even the most enthusiastic teacher occasionally wonders why she secures responses from so few of her pupils.

Aside from the fact that some children are more motor than others, it is just as true that some are more matured, or are naturally brighter than others, and the teacher in her exercises in story-telling makes her appeal directly to the favored few. The less fortunate children are required to do or say too much for their powers and consequently become hopelessly muddled in thinking and in expression. Should the teacher have a great aim in presenting the story, and then upon each repetition have a subordinate aim, she would be more successful in her results. By this means the children are led to picture the situations vividly, to think the process in orderly fashion, to express it clearly, and to live and love the story because of its being their very own.

The well-known story of "The Three Billy Goats Gruff" by Dasent is taken to illustrate the points made. The lessons do not have to be given upon successive days.

FIRST LESSON

Teacher's aim: So to tell the story that the children's attention will be gripped, their imagination quickened, and interest sustained to the end.

Method: How many of you have ever seen a billy goat? How many of you have one at home? What can yours do? [Free expression.] Do you think he is very bright? I know a story about three Billy Goats, and they were very interesting. Would you like to hear the story? Listen while I tell it. [Teacher tells the story with dramatic effect and without comment.] What do you think of these goats? [Free expression.] See if you can tell the story to your mothers when you go home.

SECOND LESSON

Teacher's aim: To clear up obscure points in the minds of the children and to assist them in getting a more definite idea of the story.

Method: You remember the story we had the other day about the Three Billy Goats. What were these Billy Goats named? Where did they go? Who tried to keep them from going? Some of you have seen billy goats, but some of you have not. I am sorry that I cannot show you a live one. I haven't any, but here are some pictures of billy goats. [Teacher shows several pictures.]

Would you like to hear the story again? I shall tell it if you help me. [Teacher tells, assisted by children; e.g.:]

(*Teacher*) Once upon a time there were—

(*Children*) three Billy Goats, etc.

(*Teacher*) Under the bridge there lived—

(*Children*) a great Troll.

(*Teacher*) What is a bridge? Where is one near here? This is the picture of a bridge—another picture. I am sure you never saw a Troll; they do not live now. We can only think how they looked. This Troll had eyes—

(*Children*) as large as saucers;

(*Teacher*) and a nose—

(*Children*) as long as your arm.

Shut your eyes and think of a Troll that looked like that. Think of him as under the bridge. I am sure we should be afraid to cross that bridge, but these little goats were not afraid. Help me to tell what Little Gruff did; Middle Gruff [etc., until the entire story has been told by teacher and children].

THIRD LESSON

Teacher's aim: To induce the children to think through the story, putting incidents in their chronological order.

Method: We know the story of the Three Billy Goats so well that today we shall try to tell it and not leave out anything. How does the story begin? [Once upon a time there were three Billy Goats.] Where were the Billy Goats? Where did they want to go? What was the trouble they would have in getting there? Which Billy Goat went first? Tell what the Troll said to him, and what he said to the Troll. Tell about the next Billy Goat. What comes next in the story? Tell about it. What are the Billy Goats doing when the story ends?

FOURTH LESSON

Teacher's aim: To lead the children to dramatize the story.

Method: We shall play one of our little stories today. Which one do you want? [This story will be selected at some time. The teacher can afford to let it wait until the children want to play it.] I am sure that we know the story of the Billy Goats Gruff well enough to play it today. What must we have? [Children will probably name the Three Billy Goats and the Troll.] We shall need something else besides animals. [Children will probably mention bridge, hill, and lowland.] Where shall we have the hill? What can we have for the bridge? Where shall be the plain where the Billy Goats were first eating? [Children arrange details. The actors may be selected (*a*) by teacher, (*b*) by a leader, or (*c*) may be volunteers. Several sets of children may play the parts before the period ends.]

Remember where the Goats are at first, where they are to go, and exactly what they are to say. Take places, etc.

FIFTH LESSON

Teacher's aim: To lead the children to tell the story with attention to order of events, in good language, and with vivid interest.

Method: I wonder if we can tell the story of the Billy Goats Gruff today. Tell of the three Goats, what they were doing, and what they thought they would like to do, John.

Tell of the trouble they would have in getting to the mountain and what Little Gruff did, Mary.

Tell what Middle Gruff did, Edward.

Tell what Big Gruff did, and how the story ends, Anna.

Tell the whole story, Edith.

SIXTH LESSON

Teacher's aim: To allow the class to give free expression to the story.

Method: What story do you want today? Shall we tell it or play it? [Volunteers to tell or play. Children arrange all details, etc.]

SUGGESTIONS

1. Tell some stories to the children without expecting any response from them other than the light upon their faces.
2. Often let the children volunteer to tell stories.
3. Often let them select the stories to tell or to be told.
4. Let the story-teller face the audience and try to interest them.
5. The audience should be free to clap or to show approval in any way if the story is pleasing to them.
6. The audience should be encouraged to ask questions at the close of a story.
7. The teacher in her favorable comment may take occasion to call attention to something which she is emphasizing with the class; e.g., "We enjoyed Ben's story. He spoke so clearly."
8. The teacher should draw the class as closely around her as possible.
9. A good story will stand many repetitions.
10. An uninteresting story should not be repeated.
11. Never forget that literature should give joy, joy, joy.

MATTIE LOUISE HATCHER

STATE NORMAL SCHOOL
BOWLING GREEN, KY.

THE QUALITY OF INSTRUCTION VERSUS THE SUBJECT-MATTER OF INSTRUCTION—*Concluded*

FRANK P. BACHMAN, PH.D.
Committee on School Inquiry, New York City

EDUCATION FOR CONDUCT VERSUS EDUCATION FOR KNOWLEDGE

The existence of this fundamental paradox is to be accounted for, I believe, by the fact that our standards for judging instruction and our ideas of the subject-matter of instruction belong to widely separated epochs in the history of education. The ends of education are now defined in terms of conduct, and good instruction is such as will influence behavior. Hence the insistence upon motivation, appeal to the emotions and to the imagination, large place for thought and judgment, opportunity for initiative and individuality, and emphasis upon doing, as the marks of good instruction. The aims we are endeavoring to achieve through the school thus belong to the twentieth century and are well founded in modern psychology and sociology. Our ideas of the materials of instruction, on the other hand, belong more nearly to the seventeenth century. They belong very largely to the age of "pansophia" or "encyclopedic education." They belong to an age when the question was not What can a man do and how does he behave? but What does he know? They belong to the age which gave rise to such adages as "Knowledge is power."

Educationally, most school men are much like the Indians, who in large numbers at different times in the early history of our country confessed the Christian faith and thereafter called themselves Christians, but who went on about as before, robbing, devastating, and reeking vengeance on their enemies. So with most school men, we confess to believe that the chief purpose of education is to influence conduct, but we go on making our courses of study encyclopedic in scope, insisting that our textbooks be encyclopedic in character, and measuring the results of our work in terms of knowledge. Acting on our twentieth-century belief in the aims of education, we condemn our schools and criticize our teachers, because instruction is poor. Acting on our seventeenth-century ideas of subject-matter, we set teachers the task of handling materials which by reason of their character and organization inevitably lead to poor instruction, when this is judged in terms of education for conduct.

IMPROVING THE QUALITY OF INSTRUCTION: GENERAL SUGGESTIONS

Until this basic paradox between the purposes that we are seeking to achieve and the subject-matter which we are using to attain our ends is removed, instruction will continue to be adjudged poor in quality.

A system of administration which permits of large freedom among teachers, better supervision, and better-prepared teachers, will help to improve classroom teaching, but even more important are:

First, there is need of bidding farewell, now and forever, to the encyclopedic conception of education and to the idea that there is a fixed and specific body of information, other than a command of the rudiments of the three R's, which everyone must possess to be intelligent. Intelligence implies knowledge, but no given body of knowledge. Aside from the technique involved in gaining the ability to read, write, and cipher, the elementary school should not give place to mere information or to materials which appeal merely to the intellect. Only such other materials should find place in the elementary course of study as, in addition to appealing to the intellect, will excite the imagination, grip the heart, and influence the taste, the aspirations, and the actions of children in ways socially acceptable. In a word, we should cease teaching knowledge for the sake of knowledge, and use knowledge merely as one of the means of influencing conduct.

Second, the subject-matter taught not only should fulfil the above requirements, but should be such in character and in organization as will permit of a ready application of modern principles and methods of instruction. We should do for the course of study of the ordinary school what the writers of our best textbooks on the principles and methods of instruction have done for particular lessons, or what the teachers of our best practice schools have done for given series of lessons, or are attempting to do for the curriculum as a whole. That is, we should select and organize the materials of instruction in view of the requirements of good teaching. This implies, of course, that the determining factors in the selection of subject-matter are the ends to be achieved and that what we teach is subordinated to these ends. Concretely, we should stop teaching United States history as history and select from the entire field and use only those portions which fit in with our purposes as defined in terms of conduct. In this way and in this way only will habits, ideals, and modes of behavior become the actual goal of our endeavors.

Third, there is need of getting away from the idea that anything has really been accomplished when changes are made in the course of study only. Too often such changes are acclaimed as educational achievements, when, as a matter of fact, no corresponding changes have been made in the subject-matter furnished the teachers, and in consequence classroom work goes on about as before. How often has this been the case, when such topics have been added to the curriculum as local history, local industries, local government, biographies of great men, stories of inventions, lessons in morals, and the like. Experience should long since have shown us that the chief way to influence the work of the schools is through the subject-matter taught. No change in the course of study is complete and effective, in the ordinary system of schools, until teachers are provided either in reference books or in textbooks with appropriate materials and these in such form and so organized that the principles and methods of good teaching can be easily applied in their presentation. Until such materials are supplied the work of the school will remain relatively unchanged and instruction will continue to be poor.

Fourth, there is need of superintendents, supervisors, and principals seeing that much of their work at the present time is without results, because they are working at their problems from the wrong side. There is little to be gained by talking to teachers, as is so often done, about how they ought to teach and about the characteristics of good instruction, when the very subject-matter which the teachers are called upon to present keeps them from doing what they are asked to do. Let superintendents, supervisors, and principals come to see that the most important part of their work is to provide teachers with materials of the right kind and these properly organized, and the questions of methods of teaching and of the characteristics of good instruction will largely take care of themselves, or at all events what they have to say about these things, when once appropriate materials are supplied, will yield results.

Fifth, there is need of a better appreciation on the part of all of the importance of the right kind of subject-matter. To determine the aims and purposes of education and to establish the principles and methods of instruction is only half of our problem. The other half, and, from the point of view of achieving the ends desired, quite as important as the first half, is the working-out of appropriate materials of instruction and putting these in such form that they are readily accessible both to pupil and to teacher. Persons especially fitted for this work should be given opportunity in the public school and especially in higher institutions interested in public education to work out and to organize such materials. The preparation of materials to be used in the classroom has been left, up to the present time, very largely to interested individuals. The preparation of such materials is vastly too important to be left to private enterprise and to chance, and should long since have been made an integral part of public education.

IMPROVING THE QUALITY OF INSTRUCTION: SPECIFIC SUGGESTIONS

To be more specific, if the quality of instruction in the ordinary school is to be improved, there is need of a better working appreciation of what is concrete to the child and of a better appreciation of the significance of the concrete in teaching. For instruction that is thought-provoking and inspiring and that fosters vigorous mental action must be concrete or at least deep-rooted in the concrete.

The concrete versus the abstract.—There is an inclination to think that subject-matter dealing with particular situations, objects, processes, actions, and persons is concrete; whereas the abstract is the principle, the rule, or the definition. Yet descriptions and narratives, though they deal with given situations, objects, and processes, may for particular children be abstract—abstract in the sense that they call to mind no vivid images nor carry for the child any meaning. Indeed, in this sense, the most specific statement of fact may be an abstraction. For example, the inventor of the telephone used the phonautograph and the manometric capsule. Unless one happens to be familiar with the phonautograph and the manometric capsule, this sentence is about as meaningless as the third law of motion would be to a first-grader. To be sure, only those materials are concrete which have to do with specific situations, objects, and processes, but materials of instruction, no matter how simple and vivid the treatment, are concrete to children, only when the children have, or can readily acquire, an abundance of experience in the light of which they can give meaning to the subject-matter in question.

To a boy in central Illinois who has plowed the land, prepared the soil, planted, cultivated, and harvested corn, geographical materials on "How Corn Is Raised" are concrete, but to the boy in the heart of New York City, who may never have had so much as a good-sized clod in his hand, who has never seen a cornfield, and who never in all his life cared for any kind of a plant, to such a boy, the very same materials are abstract. He may memorize what the teacher tells him or what the textbook says about "How Corn Is Raised," and he may talk parrot-like about corn-raising, but in reality the process means little or nothing to him, and the mastery of such materials has little if any educational significance. Similarly, to the girl who has planted, tended, picked, put up, and sold an acre of tomatoes, to such a girl, problems in arithmetic having to do with tomato-raising are concrete, but to the girl who has never had anything to do with raising and marketing garden products, these same problems are abstract. The attaching of names to numbers does not make problems concrete. For whether or not a given body of subject-matter is concrete or abstract depends entirely upon the experiences of the particular group of children to whom it is presented.

From this point of view, a considerable part of the contents of our textbooks for the primary grades, to say nothing of the contents of those for the upper grades, cannot be other than abstract to at least a part of the children to whom such subject-matter is taught. The following paragraph is from a chapter in a home geography, on "What the Cow Furnishes Us":

> Do you know how cheese is made? The milk is first curdled by putting into it some liquid rennet. Rennet is the name given to a preparation made from the inner coating of the calf's stomach. The curd is separated from the watery part of the milk, which is called whey, and then pressed into solid cakes. The curd is then called cheese.

To the few children who have seen cheese made in this way or who have actually made it in this way, the foregoing paragraph is concrete, but to those who have not had this experience and to whom this experience is not supplied this paragraph is about as meaningful as the rule for extracting cube root found in our older arithmetics. To take children under these conditions over page after page of such materials is a waste of good time and a travesty on education which is expected to educate.

If, then, instruction is to be more than memory work and drill, it is incumbent on us to make sure that our materials of instruction are really concrete, and concrete to the particular group of children to whom they are presented.

Concreteness, a factor in the selection of topics.—How can much of the material which we are expected to present ever be made concrete to children? asks the teacher. It should be confessed that as long as we hold to an encyclopedic conception of education, a large part of what we teach the children can never be made real to them. If, however, we take the position that, apart from the mastery of the basic elements of the three R's, there is no other knowledge which all children must of necessity have to be intelligent, to be good citizens, and to be started on a self-supporting career, then the problem is not so difficult. We can make concreteness, or the possibility of making given materials of instruction real to particular groups of children, an important factor in the selection of the topics of instruction, and that is what we should do, in so far as we can.

It is almost a hopeless task for a teacher in New York City to attempt to make real to her children copper-mining, but how different in Butte, Montana, where copper-mining is the very life of the city, indeed, the very life of the children themselves. Copper-mining might well be ignored in New York City, whereas in Butte it should be given special attention. There is little opportunity in Fall River, Massachusetts, to make real to children iron- and steel-making, but Fall River offers a splendid opportunity for teaching spinning and weaving. Irrigation can be made concrete to children in Colorado; wheat-growing to children in North Dakota; lumbering to children in northern Minnesota; cotton-growing to children in Alabama; corn-growing to children in central Illinois, and so on, but there is little hope that instruction in these topics will ever be other than on the lower plane so long as we require teachers to present such topics where it is impossible to make them concrete.

There is large opportunity in all the important common-school branches to select subject-matter in view of making it real to particular groups of children. To be sure, the fundamentals of arithmetic are the same for all, but when we come to socialize arithmetic, to give to children worth-while problems, to make arithmetic a means of acquiring knowledge of social and industrial life, the field of application must be concrete to the children in question. Fall River, Massachusetts, might well teach the arithmetic of spinning and weaving, but such arithmetic would be an empty and formal exercise to the children of Whitehall, Montana. At Whitehall, the arithmetic of irrigation could be made real, but to teach the arithmetic of irrigation at Fall River would be worse than useless. Reading likewise affords abundant opportunity for such selection of materials. What better materials in reading could be presented to children who are familiar with ships and whose fathers and brothers work on ships or are engaged in ship-building than materials such as are suggested on "Ships and Ship-building" by Edith P. Parker in the October number (1914) of the *Elementary School Journal*. Similar groupings of materials can be made for children who live on the prairies, in the heart of a mountain region, by the great lakes, or on the banks of a river, or for children whose fathers and brothers are farmers, or miners, or mill-workers, or common laborers. Indeed, it is possible to select materials for reading which can be made real to children of every type and kind.

To select materials of instruction in view of the possibility of making them concrete to particular groups of children is therefore within limits altogether possible, and just to the extent that this is done have we reason to hope for better teaching in the ordinary school.

Richness of details versus meagerness of details.—By reason of the encyclopedic character of our textbooks, it would be possible to select from them a series of topics which could be made real to a particular group of children. But if a superintendent or principal or teacher made such a selection, it would be found that at least in certain subjects, such as arithmetic, physiology, geography, and history, the topics selected would be treated in barest outline. Relatively, a very few problems are given in our arithmetics under the arithmetic of the farm. A few paragraphs or possibly a few pages are devoted in our geographies to lumbering, or to mining, or to any one of the other of our basic industries, and in our histories a treatment equally short seemingly is regarded as adequate to tell the life-story of one of our national characters or to give the historical background of any one of our present-day social or industrial problems. Indeed, one is scarcely aware of the meagerness of the details in our standard textbooks, unless the question has been given special attention.

This meagerness of details is brought clearly to view if the materials on cotton-raising in our best geographies are contrasted with the materials contained in *Cotton-raising* by Bronson, or if the details in our geographies on lumbering are compared with the details on this subject in *The Blazed Trail*, by Stewart Edward White, or if the barren outline of the life of one of our great men, for example, Cyrus Hall McCormick, as sketched in our primary histories, is placed alongside the rich and suggestive treatment of McCormick's life by Herbert N. Casson. Equally striking is the contrast between the dry-as-dust outline statements about the closing scenes of the Civil War, found in our advanced histories, and the heart-gripping descriptions of the same events in the first chapters of *The Leopard's Spots* by Thomas Dixon.

These outlines with their meagerness of details may have answered when the ideal in education was to impart knowledge and a little of it about many things. But in an age when knowledge is looked upon as a tool and to be acquired in most part when there is special interest or when needed for practical reasons, and in an age when the purposes of education are to develop in children the ability to collect and organize materials and to think rightly, to fix habits of action, attitudes of mind, and ideals of conduct, in such an age these outlines by no means meet the requirements of the school.

If the teacher is to make real and significant topics of instruction to particular groups of children, there must be at hand, it will be admitted by all, an abundance of well-selected details. For only as children are led to acquire of themselves or there is presented to them upon the topic in hand materials rich in detail do they become really interested, do they have opportunity to weigh the value of materials, do they find of themselves problems and work out their solutions, are their imaginations fired, their emotions aroused, and their ideals of conduct influenced. Children may, to be sure, be swamped by too many details, however well selected these may be. This, however, seldom occurs. The materials presented, if instruction is to be of good quality, should at least be sufficiently rich in details to enable the children to form vivid mental pictures, mental pictures as real and vivid as the different scenes of a moving-picture and at least adequate to enable them to do real thought-work.

Before any great improvement in classroom work can reasonably be expected, teachers will need to be supplied with an abundance of materials rich in details and these materials in such form that they can be readily used. To provide such materials is a difficult task and at best it will be a slow process. In the meantime, teachers should be encouraged to do all they can of themselves, and generosity should be exercised in judging of the quality of instruction.

Fertile topics versus barren topics.—Topics of instruction might be selected which could be made concrete to given groups of children and an abundance of well-selected details might be provided, yet the topics chosen might be of such a kind that they lack thought-provoking characteristics, or lack those qualities which appeal to the imagination and stir the emotions, or fail to carry in themselves lessons which will influence the conduct of children in desired ways. Teachers recognize these differences, for how often the teacher apologizes for a poor lesson on the ground that the particular subject-matter gave no opportunity for good teaching, and all too often the teacher is right.

There is the very widest difference in the teaching possibilities between a series of lessons on cube root and a series of lessons on the arithmetic of the farm. The fourth-grade teacher who is called upon to teach the names of the states, the capital of each, and one other important city may perform this formal task with great skill, but it is almost foreordained that her instruction will be on the lower plane, whereas the instruction of a teacher of very much less native ability may well be of good quality when she is presenting a series of lessons on "How Corn Is Raised." There is only about one thing that even the very best teacher can do who is called upon to teach the skeleton and the bones of the human body, but what magnificent teaching opportunities are afforded in a series of lessons on bacteria. The "Panic of 1837" as a topic in history is barren of thought-provoking situations, of the qualities that appeal to the imagination and that carry vivid life-lessons when compared with a topic such as the "Invention of the Reaper."

So long as we hold that there is a specific body of knowledge apart from the basic elements of the three R's, which all children must have, naturally enough we proceed to impart this information irrespective of the teaching opportunities the particular materials may offer. This, of course, makes the giving of specific information the primary work of the school. By the same token, if our working aim is to develop, in children, methods of work, ability to think rightly, proper attitudes of mind and standards of conduct, then, to be logical, to be consistent, the topics of instruction selected should be such as will contribute to the achievement of these ends.

When one glances over the prescribed topics in the courses of study of even our most progressive cities and when one turns over the pages of the textbooks which are used to carry into effect the requirements of these courses of study, one is struck by the number of topics which are primarily informational and which afford a minimum of opportunity to do good teaching when this is judged in terms of education for conduct.

The topics which teachers are called upon to teach, if the aim of the modern school is to be realized, should be rich in the opportunity they afford children to exercise initiative and individuality, rich in opportunity to try out different methods of work, rich in thought-provoking situations, rich in those qualities that fire the imagination, and rich in vivid life-lessons. In a word, topics of instruction should be selected, not so much from the point of view of information, as from the point of view of the teaching possibilities they afford.

Few topics versus many topics.—If there is any one mark particularly distinctive of our courses of study in the elementary school, it is the number of the prescribed topics of instruction. Not infrequently these prescribed topics follow closely the chapter headings of the adopted textbooks and it is not uncommon for teachers in attempting to carry out the prescriptions of the curriculum to follow their textbooks almost chapter by chapter and paragraph by paragraph. The number of topics covered in our standard textbooks is therefore at least suggestive of the number of topics actually taught. A popular home geography covers, for example, forty-eight different subjects, giving an average of five pages including illustrations to each theme. A popular primary history, in a little less than four hundred pages, sketches, as we have seen, the life-story of some sixty great Americans. What is true of the multiplicity of topics in the textbooks for the lower grades is even more true of those for the higher grades. It should also be taken into account that these different topics are as a rule treated in quite complete outline, with the result that effort is made to squeeze into a short paragraph the essence of what is presented in more comprehensive works in a chapter of length—in a word, our textbooks, reading excepted, are epitomes.

There can be but one effect, as pointed out above, upon the quality of instruction of this effort to cover in miniature a multiplicity of topics. Under such conditions, there is no time to guide children in collecting or acquiring of themselves an abundance of rich details about the questions in hand; there is no time to give children an opportunity to organize and weigh the worth of materials; there is no time to permit children to abide with a subject until they are sufficiently familiar with it to discover problems and to work out their solution, or to see the relations of the given subject to other subjects and to understand its significance for individual and social life; there is no time to permit children to become so saturated with a theme that it has its way with their imaginations and emotions; there is no time to permit a subject to carry over and to impress its lessons. With a large number of topics to cover, all of necessity is hurry. Indeed, the work of the schoolroom reminds one of a public reception; the topics of instruction are the honorable persons to be met, and the children are the guests. The children are introduced, as it were, to a great subject, they abide with it from eighty to a hundred minutes and then pass on to a new theme, to forget all too often that they have ever studied the given subject.

Present-day standards of instruction demand a procedure diametrically opposite to this. They demand concentration on a few large topics in order that children may have the time to acquire the needed richness of details, may have opportunity to exercise initiative and individuality, may learn to think rightly with different materials and under different conditions, and may have opportunity to put to use what they have learned and to act upon the impulses that have been aroused.

So long, then, as teachers are required to take children over a multiplicity of topics, so long will instruction appeal to memory and emphasize drill, and only when teachers are permitted to concentrate on a few rich topics can we expect them to do teaching which will meet present-day standards.

Kind of subject-matter and textbooks needed.—We need then, by way of summary, if the quality of instruction is to be improved, to concentrate upon a few fundamental topics, upon topics that are to the human mind what the mountain ranges and great rivers are to a continent; these basic topics should not only be selected in view of the information to be acquired through their mastery, but they should be selected particularly in view of the opportunity they give children to participate in the right kind of educative activities, hence, in view of the teaching opportunities they afford; these topics should be clothed in a richness of well-selected details; and the particular topics to be taught to a given group of children should be chosen in view of the possibility of making the given topics concrete and real to the children in question.

Our textbooks, with the exceptions of reading, contain, as we have seen, very little of such subject-matter. They have been prepared rather in view of giving something, however little it may be, about every topic that might possibly be taught in any considerable number of places. Their growth has been, on the whole, by mechanical addition, for most new authors have felt constrained, for practical reasons, to include in their books the themes which successful writers have covered in similar books, and few old authors have ever been brave enough to eliminate any considerable number of old topics. Our textbooks are thus dominated by practical rather than educational considerations. They are made to sell and not necessarily to meet real and particular educational needs. Private interest is thus left in a way to dominate an important aspect of public education.

It goes without saying that our textbooks should be prepared solely in view of educational considerations. Even were this done, there might well be certain books, such as readers, arithmetics containing the fundamental operations and the like, and geographies made up largely of maps, which would serve for the country as a whole. There might be other books, such as spellers, physiologies, and histories, that would meet the needs of a considerable number of places. There would, however, remain a considerable part of the subject-matter of instruction for the elementary school which should be prepared in view of the educational requirements of particular groups of children and particular localities. For example, if arithmetic is to afford to children opportunity to pursue right methods of work and to do genuine thinking, if arithmetic is to be made a "content" as well as a "tool" subject, and thus become a medium of giving children valuable insights into industrial processes and business operations, we should have arithmetic in the form of booklets which treat separately the arithmetic of each of our basic industries and the particular commercial transactions arising therefrom. If geography is to be a worth-while subject, we need, in addition to good atlases, a goodly number of special geographies, the geography of irrigation, of cotton-growing, of corn-raising, of copper-mining, of lumbering, of New Orleans, of New York City, and the like. If history is to carry over its vital lessons, the ordinary outline on McCormick and the reaper is not sufficient for the children of the Middle West or the Northwest, nor will the common treatment of the inventions of Hargreaves, Ackwright, and Crompton answer in New England towns having as their principal industry spinning and weaving. Similarly, the civics applicable to a large city is by no means suited to given small towns or to given rural districts. Likewise, a physiology adapted to teach the requisite lessons on hygiene and sanitation in a dry, cool climate like that of North Dakota will not serve the needs of the school in a wet, hot climate such as is to be found in Florida. Moreover, all of our textbooks should be prepared not so much from the point of view of treating a few great topics in rich detail, as from the point of view of bringing children face to face with vital life-problems and of providing them with the materials which will enable them to think these problems through for themselves.

School men as a whole, it will be granted, are, at the present time, far from accepting the position taken in this paper—that, aside from a mastery of the elements of the three R's, there is no specific body of information which all elementary-school pupils should have to be intelligent, to be good citizens, and to be started on a self-supporting career. Our subject-matter of instruction as embodied in even our very best textbooks is surely far from the kind we are maintaining should be used. Nevertheless, there is a rapidly growing number of school men who believe that the school must follow along the general lines here suggested, if classroom instruction is to contribute its full share toward achieving the purpose of education.

KINDERGARTEN VERSUS NON-KINDERGARTEN CHILDREN WITH RESPECT TO CERTAIN TRAITS OF CHARACTER

L. ALDEN MARSH
Edgewood, Pittsburgh, Pennsylvania

This is a study of 380 grade children, in twelve grades, all of the Edgewood Public School. The method is one of comparison based on teachers' estimates of certain traits of character enumerated in Table I. There is no attempt to take into account native ability.

Conditions for the study are favorable for the following reasons: (1) Edgewood is a residence town having an unusually even class of children—all come from good homes, all have intelligent parents; (2) the kindergarten children are not from more favored homes than the non-kindergarten; (3) the kindergarten has been established for sixteen years; (4) the kindergarten instruction has been good. For seven years it has been directed by the present recently elected assistant supervisor of the Pittsburgh kindergartens.

To save space in the tables and to avoid repetition, K in this paper signifies kindergarten children, NK, non-kindergarten.

In obtaining the materials for the study, a form similar to Table I was given to each teacher. They were asked to write in the first column the names of their pupils and to grade them in each of the seventeen qualities as conscientiously as possible. No teacher knew that the study had anything to do with kindergartens. The forms were collected and afterward the kindergarten children were marked with a star. No prejudice on the part of a teacher with regard to kindergarten could affect the result as they had no idea of the purpose of the classification.

The report from each school was summarized as at the bottom of Table I. Under column 1, self-confidence, the average of the K is 1.9; of the NK is 2. The smaller number of course denotes the higher standing. As only 1, 2, and 3 are used, the decimals are significant. In the last column the summaries of all the qualities are compared. In Table I the NK are surpassed by 0.17 of a point.

Table II tabulates the averages of all the schools after each was footed up as in Table I.

In Table III the differences in favor of either K or NK, as shown in Table II, are placed in columns. The sums of the variations of all the schools are given below each quality, and the difference of these sums is marked K if the difference is in favor of the kindergarten children, and NK if in favor of the non-kindergarten. The amount of variation may not be so significant, but the remarkable uniformity of results in every school could hardly be accidental. Since the sum of the differences is taken, in Table III the larger sum represents the greater degree of difference.

K children show greater self-confidence in every room but two. In moral attitude the NK surpass in seven rooms out of twelve and show a total difference of 0.33. In love of nature K surpass in every school but two. In ability to mix K surpass in every school but one. In friendliness K are ahead. Their advantage in interest is small but the NK are far ahead in attention. The K surpass in ability to think, in originality, in observation, in response to ideas, in response to directions, in cleanliness, in oral expression, and in ability to play. The NK surpass in but four points: namely, moral attitude, attention, manual ability, and orderliness.

The most remarkable differences in favor of K are in ability to mix, in originality, and in response to ideas. The difference is high in favor of K in self-confidence, love of nature, friendliness, observation, oral expression, and in ability to play.

The big advantage shown by these tables in favor of K, and the fact that the advantage is true in nearly all the schools, could hardly occur by chance. If, in a study of 380 children in twelve groups rated by different teachers independently, the results are so emphatically in favor of K, there is no reason to suppose that the same result would not be obtained in any group of children if they were of an even class. Native ability would not affect these tables, as they are based on averages and there is no more reason

TABLE I

GRADES: VERY HIGH, 1; MODERATE, 2; LOW, 3

1. Self-Confidence
2. Moral Attitude
3. Love of Nature
4. Ability to Mix
5. Friendliness
6. Interest
7. Attention
8. Ability to Think
9. Originality
10. Observation
11. Response to Ideas
12. Response to Directions
13. Manual Ability
14. Cleanliness
15. Orderliness
16. Oral Expression
17. Ability to Play

Name	1	2	3	4	5	6	7	8	9	10	11	12	13	14	15	16	17	Total
A. B.	2	2	1	1	1	2	2	2	2	2	2	2	3	3	3	2	1	
B. E.	1	1	2	2	1	1	1	1	2	1	1	3	2	1	1	2	2	
B. W.	1	1	1	1	2	2	2	1	1	1	1	2	1	1	3	2	2	
etc.																		
etc.																		
21 K.	1.9	1.57	1.43	1.71	1.33	2	1.9	2.05	1.95	1.57	1.9	1.57	1.81	1.52	1.95	2.09	1.57	1.75
9 NK.	2	1.22	1.33	1.55	1.11	1.44	1.33	1.44	2.22	1.77	1.55	1.22	1.77	1.55	1.55	2.11	1.66	1.58

TABLE II

Grade		1	2	3	4	5	6	7	8	9	10	11	12	13	14	15	16	17	Average
I	K	1.75	1.47	1.75	1.66	1.16	1.66	1.78	1.87	2.06	1.75	2.03	1.66	1.69	1.41	1.44	1.66	1.37	1.71
	NK	1.80	1.40	1.80	2.00	1.40	1.40	1.60	1.60	2.20	1.80	2.20	1.40	1.40	1.00	1.00	1.00	1.60	1.56
I A	K	1.16	1.33	1.00	1.33	1.42	1.33	1.75	1.17	1.75	1.75	1.50	1.75	1.83	1.17	1.25	1.42	1.17	1.42
	NK	1.43	1.43	1.00	1.71	1.86	1.29	1.43	1.29	2.71	1.17	1.57	1.43	1.71	1.29	1.29	2.00	1.71	1.55
II B	K	1.50	1.20	1.00	1.40	1.20	1.50	2.00	1.80	2.40	1.80	1.70	2.00	1.70	1.40	1.50	2.10	1.20	1.62
	NK	1.27	1.55	1.00	1.75	1.82	1.64	2.00	1.73	2.18	1.73	2.00	2.00	1.64	1.64	1.91	2.18	1.55	1.74
II	K	1.75	1.79	1.39	1.86	1.64	1.61	1.75	1.70	1.82	1.82	1.39	1.39	1.79	1.25	1.79	1.82	1.29	1.64
	NK	1.82	2.00	1.54	2.09	1.63	1.54	1.82	1.82	2.09	1.82	2.00	1.72	1.64	1.55	1.63	2.18	1.73	1.80
III	K	1.68	1.23	1.50	1.36	1.36	1.32	1.82	1.45	1.59	1.32	1.36	1.50	1.77	1.00	1.82	1.77	1.41	1.49
	NK	2.00	1.17	1.50	1.58	1.50	1.58	1.83	2.00	1.75	1.50	1.67	1.84	1.67	1.00	1.50	1.92	1.50	1.62
III A	K	1.78	1.56	1.44	1.50	1.06	1.72	2.17	2.22	2.00	1.33	1.39	2.06	1.89	1.39	2.11	2.00	1.67	1.69
	NK	1.75	1.63	1.63	1.63	1.25	2.00	2.25	2.00	2.13	1.75	1.88	2.13	2.38	1.63	2.00	1.75	1.50	1.80
IV	K	1.90	1.57	1.43	1.71	1.33	2.00	1.90	2.05	1.95	1.57	1.90	1.57	1.81	1.52	1.95	2.08	1.57	1.75
	NK	2.00	1.22	1.33	1.55	1.11	1.44	1.33	1.44	2.22	1.77	1.55	1.22	1.77	1.55	1.55	2.11	1.66	1.58
V	K	2.04	1.75	1.54	1.79	1.79	1.79	1.83	1.96	2.00	1.75	1.79	1.38	1.63	1.29	1.42	1.79	1.17	1.69
	NK	2.33	1.55	2.11	1.88	1.88	1.55	1.55	2.11	2.55	2.11	2.11	1.88	1.77	1.33	1.67	1.88	1.33	1.86
VI B	K	1.56	1.16	1.08	1.56	1.32	1.52	1.56	1.72	1.96	1.52	1.64	1.48	1.16	1.16	1.64	1.80	1.48	1.49
	NK	2.00	1.13	1.13	1.75	1.13	1.75	1.75	2.00	2.13	1.75	2.00	2.00	1.38	1.00	1.38	2.38	1.63	1.66
VI	K	1.83	1.00	1.17	1.75	1.75	1.25	1.17	1.50	1.75	1.58	1.50	1.17	1.33	1.00	1.50	1.75	1.75	1.37
	NK	1.88	1.00	1.24	1.82	1.71	1.35	1.41	1.65	1.77	1.59	1.47	1.24	1.12	1.59	1.59	1.77	1.12	1.49
VII	K	2.00	1.50	1.38	1.75	1.44	1.63	1.69	1.69	1.81	1.69	1.75	1.56	2.00	1.13	1.31	1.56	1.56	1.62
	NK	2.24	1.29	1.71	2.05	1.71	1.76	1.57	1.81	2.05	1.86	1.81	1.43	1.62	1.13	1.29	2.05	1.71	1.71
VIII	K	1.68	2.00	1.84	1.42	1.37	1.79	1.95	1.84	1.74	1.63	1.84	1.89	2.00	1.26	1.79	1.58	1.32	1.69
	NK	1.86	1.86	1.82	1.59	1.55	1.86	1.86	1.91	2.05	1.91	1.82	1.77	1.73	1.27	1.50	1.73	1.36	1.74

TABLE III

	Self-confidence		Moral Attitude		Love of Nature		Ability to Mix		Friendliness		Interest		Attention		Ability to Think		Originality	
	K	NK	K	NK	K	NK	K	NK	K	NK	K	NK	N	NK	K	NK	K	NK
I	0.05	...	...	0.07	0.02	...	0.34	...	0.24	...	...	0.26	...	0.18	...	0.27	0.14	...
I A	.27	...	0.10	...	0	0	.38	...	.44	...	...	.04	...	.32	.12	...	.96	...
II B	...	0.23	.35	...	0	0	.33	...	.62	...	0.14	...	...	.10	...	.07	...	0.22
II	.07	...	.21	...	.15	...	.23	...	...	0.01	...	.07	0.07	...	.12	...	.27	...
III	.32	...	...	.06	0	0	.22	...	.14	...	.26	...	.01	...	.55	...	.16	...
III A	...	.03	.07	...	.19	...	.13	...	.19	...	.28	...	.08	...	...	.22	.13	...
IV	.10	...	...	.35	...	0.10	...	0.16	...	.22	...	.56	...	.57	...	.61	.27	...
V	.29	...	...	.20	.57	...	.09	...	.09	...	...	.24	...	.28	.15	...	.55	...
VI B	.44	...	...	.03	.05	...	.19	...	...	.19	.23	...	.19	...	.28	...	.17	...
VI	.05	...	0	0	.07	...	.07	...	...	.14	.10	...	.24	...	.15	...	.02	...
VII	.24	...	...	.21	.33	...	.30	...	.27	...	.13	...	...	.12	.12	...	.24	...
VIII	.18	...	...	.14	...	.02	.17	...	.18	...	.07	...	...	.09	.07	...	.31	...
Summary	2.01	0.26	0.73	1.06	1.38	0.12	2.45	0.16	2.17	0.46	1.21	1.17	0.59	1.66	1.56	1.17	3.22	0.22
Difference	1.75K	...	...	0.33NK	1.26K	...	2.29K	...	1.71K	...	0.04K	...	...	1.07NK	0.39K	...	3.00K	...

TABLE III—*Continued*

	Observation		Response to Ideas		Response to Directions		Manual Ability		Cleanliness		Orderliness		Oral Expression		Ability to Play		Summary	
	K	NK	K	NK	K	NK	N	NK	K	NK	N	NK	N	NK	K	NK	K	NK
I	0.05	...	0.17	...	...	0.26	0.29	...	...	0.41	...	0.44	...	0.66	0.23	...	...	0.15
I A	...	0.58	.07	...	...	.32	...	0.12	0.12	...	0.04	...	0.58	...	.54	...	0.13	...
II B	...	.07	.30	...	0	0	...	.06	.24	...	.41	...	.08	...	.35	...	.12	...
II	0	0	.61	...	0.33	...	...	.15	.30	...	...	.16	.36	...	.44	...	.16	...
III	.18	...	.31	...	.34	...	...	.10	0	0	...	.32	.15	...	.09	...	.13	...
III A	.42	...	.49	...	.07	...	.49	...	.24	...	...	.11	...	.25	...	0.17	.15	...
IV	.20	...	...	0.35	...	.35	...	.04	.03	...	...	.40	.02	...	.09	...	...	.17
V	.36	...	.32	...	.50	...	.14	...	.04	...	.25	...	.09	...	.16	...	.17	...
VI B	.23	...	.36	...	.52	...	.22	...	...	.16	...	.26	.58	...	.15	...	.17	...
VI	.01	...	...	.03	.07	...	...	.21	.59	...	.09	...	.02	...	...	.63	.12	...
VII	.17	...	.06	...	...	.13	...	.38	0	0	...	.02	.49	...	.15	...	.09	...
VIII	.28	...	...	.02	...	.12	...	.37	.01	...	...	.29	.15	...	.04	...	.05	...
Summary	1.90	0.65	2.69	0.40	1.83	1.18	1.14	1.43	1.57	0.57	0.79	2.00	2.52	0.91	2.24	0.80	1.29	0.32
Difference	1.25K	...	2.29K	...	0.65K	...	...	0.29NK	1.00K	...	...	1.21NK	1.61K	...	1.44K	...	0.97K	...

to assume more native ability among the 235 K than among the 145 NK. Neither would the fact that there are more K affect the averages.

In Table IV we have the averages of the same children in their school subjects given by the same teachers. The grades in one subject, arithmetic, are also given. This table shows a difference of 0.9 in average and 0.6 in arithmetic in favor of K.

TABLE IV

Grade	Average K Pupils	Average NK Pupils	Math. K Pupils	Math. NK Pupils	Number K Pupils	Number NK Pupils
	Per Cent	Per Cent	Per Cent	Per Cent		
I.	82	81	82	83	32	5
I A.	83	83	84	84	22	18
II.	84	84	83	84	28	11
III.	87	85	87	85	22	12
III A.	79	78	68	70	18	8
IV.	84	85	78	80	21	9
V.	81	80	77	77	19	14
VI B.	81	78	76	68	26	8
VI.	86	85	86	85	12	17
VII.	88	86	87	83	16	21
VIII	85	85	78	81	19	22
Totals . .	83.6	82.7	80.6	80	235	145
Difference in favor of K	0.9	. . . .	0.6	. . . .	. . . .	. . . .

The school grades show no such variation in favor of K as the record of the characteristics. It will be seen that the following qualities would have great bearing on the lives of the individuals but would not be observable in their influence on school subjects: ability to mix, friendliness, cleanliness, ability to play. The following would affect school grades only indirectly and do not have the appreciation they should in school work: self-confidence, moral attitude, love of nature, originality, observation. The qualities in which the K excel that would be expected to affect school grades are interest, ability to think, response to ideas, response to directions, and oral expression.

The study shows a decided advantage for K in qualities which make for richer, larger living. If such qualities as love of nature,

TABLE V

		1	2	3	4	5	6	7	8	9	10	11	12	13	14	15	16	17	Av.
Grade III, 1914	22K	1.68	1.23	1.50	1.36	1.36	1.32	1.82	1.45	1.59	1.32	1.36	1.50	1.77	1.00	1.82	1.77	1.41	1.49
	12NK	2.00	1.17	1.50	1.58	1.50	1.58	1.83	2.00	1.79	1.50	1.67	1.84	1.67	1.00	1.50	1.92	1.50	1.62
Grade III, 1915	18K	1.61	1.11	1.28	1.11	1.17	1.22	1.55	1.44	1.50	1.44	1.33	1.44	1.50	1.00	1.72	1.67	1.17	1.37
	11NK	1.55	1.00	1.18	1.18	1.18	1.27	1.73	1.55	1.45	1.36	1.36	1.36	1.45	1.00	1.27	1.73	1.27	1.35
Grade VII, 1914	16K	2.00	1.50	1.38	1.75	1.44	1.63	1.69	1.69	1.81	1.69	1.75	1.56	2.00	1.13	1.31	1.56	1.56	1.62
	21NK	2.24	1.29	1.71	2.05	1.71	1.76	1.57	1.81	2.05	1.86	1.81	1.43	1.62	1.13	1.29	2.05	1.71	1.71
Grade VII, 1915.......	17K	1.76	1.35	1.59	1.88	1.41	1.59	1.76	1.76	1.82	1.59	1.65	1.59	1.53	1.12	1.35	1.47	1.76	1.59
	15NK	1.93	1.40	2.13	1.80	1.60	1.80	1.87	1.80	1.73	1.73	1.80	1.33	1.53	1.06	1.40	2.00	1.73	1.68

sociability, originality, observation, response to ideas, oral expression, ability to think, and ability to play have no significance in our grade schools, our curricula and bases of measurement should be readjusted. The grade schools are evidently not close enough to vital experiences of life.

The NK show an advantage in manual ability, in orderliness, in moral attitude, and in attention, all of which have been claimed as especial aims of the kindergarten. If in these respects improvement is needed, I am sure the kindergarteners would be the first to seek means to arrive at it.

EXPLANATION OF TABLE V

To check up the results of this work it seemed desirable to repeat the judgments at a later date. It so happened that a year later two of the teachers were teaching the same groups as in 1914, when the study was first tabulated. These were asked to repeat the process, leaving out new children not considered before. The teachers reported that their judgments would differ considerably because of their better knowledge of the children. There is some variation, too, because the groups are not identical, some having moved away.

In Grade III the judgment is reversed in four qualities: self-confidence, originality, observation, and response to directions. Even the average is reversed, although NK surpass K by only 0.02 of a point. It will be observed that all of the reversals were changed by only a small decimal of a point. In thirteen qualities the conclusion is the same as that reached in 1914.

In Grade VII there are reversals of five qualities: moral attitude, ability to mix, originality, orderliness, and manual ability, but the averages vary in the same order and by exactly the same difference, 0.09.

BOOKS RECEIVED

AMERICAN BOOK CO., NEW YORK

Rural Life and the Rural School. By JOSEPH KENNEDY. Illustrated. Cloth. Pp. 189.

COMSTOCK PUBLISHING CO., ITHACA

The Natural History of the Farm. By JAMES G. NEEDHAM. Illustrated. Cloth. Pp. 348. $1.50.

GINN & CO., BOSTON

Beacon Third Reader. By JAMES H. FASSETT. Illustrated. Cloth. Pp. 288. $0.50.

Young and Field Literary Readers. By ELLA FLAGG YOUNG and WALTER TAYLOR FIELD. Illustrated. Cloth.

Book Three, pp. 288, $0.48.

Book Four, pp. 320, $0.52.

Intermediate Song Reader. By JAMES M. MCLAUGHLIN. Cloth. Pp. 128. $0.32.

Graded Writing Textbooks. Book Two. By ALBERT W. CLARK. Paper. Pp. 32. $1.25 per dozen.

HENRY ALTEMUS CO., PHILADELPHIA

Bed-Time Bible Stories for Little Children. By GERTRUDE SMITH. Illustrated. Cloth. Pp. 192. $0.50.

HENRY HOLT & CO., NEW YORK

New Practice Book in English Composition. By ALFRED M. HITCHCOCK. Illustrated. Cloth. Pp. 226. $0.80.

Sir Roger de Coverley Papers. From the Spectator. Edited by NATHANIEL EDWARD GRIFFIN. Cloth. Pp. 204.

HOUGHTON MIFFLIN CO., BOSTON

The Eskimo Twins. By LUCY FITCH PERKINS. Illustrated. Cloth. Pp. 192. $0.50.

Types of Teaching. By LIDA B. EARHART. Cloth. Pp. 277. $1.25 net.

Vocational Arithmetic. By H. D. VINCENT. Cloth. Pp. 126. $0.55 net.

LITTLE, BROWN & CO., BOSTON

In Toyland. By LOUISE ROBINSON. Illustrated. Cloth. Pp. 127. $0.40.

Pretty Polly Flinders. By MARY FRANCES BLAISDELL. Illustrated. Cloth. Pp. 188. $0.40.

A. J. NYSTROM & CO., CHICAGO

A Teacher's Manual. Accompanying the Sanford American History Maps. By ALBERT H. SANFORD, M.A. Paper. Pp. 95.

J. B. LIPPINCOTT CO., PHILADELPHIA

Wonderland Stories. Simplified by ELIZABETH LEWIS. Illustrated. Cloth. Pp. 153. \$0.50.

Lippincott's New Picture Composition Book. By J. BERG ESENWEIN. Illustrated. Cloth. Pp. 111. \$0.50.

PUTNAM, NEW YORK

Handbook of English. By D. B. NICOLSON. Cloth. Pp. 107. \$0.50 net.

SEMINAR PUBLISHING CO., SPRINGFIELD, MASSACHUSETTS

Tales of Telal. By HANFORD M. BURR. Illustrated. Cloth. Pp. 116. \$0.75.

PSYCHOLOGICAL REVIEW CO., PRINCETON, NEW JERSEY

Mental and Physical Measurements of Working Children. By HELEN THOMPSON WOOLLEY and CHARLOTTE RUST FISCHER. Paper. Pp. 247.

RUSSELL SAGE FOUNDATION, NEW YORK

'West Side Studies": *The Middle West Side.* By OTHO G. CARTWRIGHT. *Mothers Who Must Earn.* By KATHARINE ANTHONY. Illustrated. Cloth. \$2.00, postpaid.

"West Side Studies": *Boyhood and Lawlessness.* By RUTH S. TRUE. *The Neglected Girl.* By RUTH S. TRUE. Illustrated. Cloth. \$2.00, postpaid.

A Scale for Measuring the Quality of Handwriting of Adults. By LEONARD P. AYRES. Paper. Pp. 11. \$0.05.

THE UNIVERSITY OF CHICAGO PRESS, CHICAGO

School Review Monograph VI. Work in Education in Colleges and Universities. Rating, Placing, and Promotion of Teachers. Lists of Investigations and Other Information of Interest to Members. Papers by CARTER ALEXANDER, C. H. JOHNSTON, WILLIAM C. RUEDIGER, HARLAN UPDEGRAFF, F. E. THOMPSON, F. L. CLAPP, and A. C. BOYCE. Paper. Pp. 94. \$0.50 net.

MISCELLANEOUS

Annual Report of the Board of Regents of the Smithsonian Institution for the Year Ending June 30, 1913. Illustrated. Cloth. Pp. 804.

The General Education Board: An Account of Its Activities, 1902–1914. Illustrated. Cloth. Pp. 240.

Rural School Libraries at Small Cost. By HARRIET B. OSBORN. Paper. Pp. 7.

Swift and Company Spelling Book. Paper. Pp. 52.

School and Home Gardening: For Use in Primary Grades. Bulletin No. 31 (Revised), 1913, Bureau of Education. Paper. Pp. 115.

Report of the President of the Board of Education of New York City, September 1, 1914. Paper. Pp. 66.

Report of the Industrial Conference in the City of New York, June 29, 1914. Paper. Pp. 61.

Stories of the Schoolroom. By C. W. BARDEEN. Cloth. Pp. 235+xxxii.

Anales de Instrucción Primaria, República Oriental del Uruguay, 1913–1914. Paper. Pp. 979.

Experiments. By PHILIP E. EDELMAN. Illustrated. Cloth. Pp. 256. $1.50.

Biennial Report of the Coroner of Cook County, Illinois. Illustrated. Paper. Pp. 176.

Efficient Causes of Crime. By RUFUS BERNHARD VON KLEINSMID. Paper. Pp. 12.

Report of the North Bennet Street Industrial School for 1913. Illustrated. Paper. Pp. 58.

Report of the State Superintendent of Public Schools of the State of Maine, for the Year Ending June 30, 1913. Illustrated. Cloth. Pp. 279.

CURRENT EDUCATIONAL LITERATURE IN THE PERIODICALS[1]

IRENE WARREN
Librarian, School of Education, University of Chicago

Ayres, Leonard P. School surveys. School and Society 1:577–81. (24 Ap. '15.)

Bardwell, Darwin L. Phases of the work of a modern high school. Educa. R. 49:367–78. (Ap. '15.)

Bliss, D. C. Open window classes. Psychol. Clinic 9:29–38. (Ap. '15.)

Bonser, F. G. Berea, an example of American educational ideals. School and Society 1:597–601. (24 Ap. '15.)

Bowden, Witt. Education for power and responsibility. Educa. R. 49:352–66. (Ap. '15.)

Butler, Nicholas Murray. Concerning some matters academic. Educa. R. 49:391–99. (Ap. '15.)

Carrington, W. T. The study of education in a normal school. School and Society 1:477–81. (3 Ap. '15.)

Chancellor, William E. Written examinations: the scientific view. J. of Educa. (Bost.) 81:451–56. (29 Ap. '15.)

Collins, Joseph V. The chief aim in education. Educa. 35:522–28. (Ap. '15.)

Cooley, Edwin G. Welfare of working youth in Germany. Educa. R. 49:337–51. (Ap. '15.)

Coons, Charles S. The teaching of science to children in the Gary public schools. School and Society 1:546–52. (17 Ap. '15.)

Dennett, Mary Ware. The right of a child to two parents. Cent. 90:104–8. (My. '15.)

(The) Department of Superintendence. Am. School 1:102. (Ap. '15.)

Evans, Frederick H. The essence of success in evening vocational work. School and Society 1:593–97. (24 Ap. '15.)

Flower, Elliott. Sounding the retreat. Harp. W. 60:417–18. (1 My. '15.)

[1] Abbreviations.—Am. School, American School; Atlan., Atlantic Monthly; Cent., Century; Educa., Education; Educa. R., Educational Review; El. School J., Elementary School Journal; English J., English Journal; Harp. W., Harper's Weekly; J. of Educa. (Bost.), Journal of Education (Boston); Man. Train. and Voca. Educa., Manual Training and Vocational Education; Pop. Sci. Mo., Popular Science Monthly; Psychol. Clinic, Psychological Clinic; R. of Rs., Review of Reviews; School R., School Review; Sci. Am., Scientific American; Sci. Am. Sup., Scientific American Supplement.

Freeman, Frank N. An analytical scale for judging handwriting. El. School J. 15:432–41. (Ap. '15.)

Gardner, Lucy M. Training children to read good literature. English J. 4:248–53. (Ap. '15.)

Graham, Edward Kidder. Inaugural address at the University of North Carolina. School and Society 1:613–21. (1 My. '15.)

Gruenberg, Benjamin C. Why vocational guidance? Sci. Am. Sup. 79:275. (1 My. '15.)

Haight, Harry W. The case system of teaching hygiene and preventive medicine in the upper grades. Educa. R. 49:503–9. (My. '15.)

Haniphy, Joseph A. Juvenile courts. Educa. R. 49:489–502. (My. '15.)

Heck, W. H. The mission of universities and colleges in stimulating the development of an esprit de corps among high school students. School and Society 1:541–46. (17 Ap. '15.)

Hicks, Frederick C. Library problems in American universities. Educa. R. 49:325–36. (Ap. '15.)

Horton, D. W. A plan of vocational guidance. School R. 23:236–43. (Ap. '15.)

Hosic, James Fleming. The essentials of composition and grammar. School and Society 1:581–87. (24 Ap. '15.)

Jones, Adam Leroy. Memoranda from the records of a few college freshmen. School and Society 1:626–30. (1 My. '15.)

Jungmann, A. M. Teaching defective children. Sci. Am. 112:361. (17 Ap. '15.)

Lull, Herbert G. Vocational instruction in the high school. Man. Train. and Voca. Educa. 16:529–36. (My. '15.)

Manny, Frank A. Initiative in education. Educa. 35:489–90. (Ap. '15.)

Marrinan, J. J. The education of youth for democracy. Educa. R. 49:379–90. (Ap. '15.)

Miller, H. L. Report on the sixty-minute class period in the Wisconsin high school. School R. 23:244–48. (Ap. '15.)

Mitchell, H. Edwin. Time-articulation between high school and college. School R. 23:217–24. (Ap. '15.)

Moore, Ernest C. The administration of the public schools of New York City. Educa. R. 49:469–88. (My. '15.)

Newton, Peter. The toy theater: a children's playhouse where fairy tales come true. Craftsman 28:36–41. (Ap. '15.)

Otis, Margaret. Moral imbecility from a respectable family. Psychol. Clinic 9:51–55. (Ap. '15.)

Owen, William Bishop. Vocational education in Illinois; the contest. Am. School 1:99–102. (Ap. '15.)

Pearse, C. G. Gary; the city which has seen a great light. Am. School 1:104–7. (Ap. '15.)

Pintner, Rudolph, and Paterson, Donald G. The factor of experience in intelligence testing. Psychol. Clinic 9:44–50. (Ap. '15.)

Reed, Katharine Speer. New open-air vocation for women in horticulture. R. of Rs. 51:579–80. (My. '15.)

Richards, Robert H., and Bailey, Henry Turner. Value of manual training. Man. Train. and Voca. Educa. 16:537–43. (My. '15.)

Snedden, David. High schools—new and old. School and Society 1:621–26. (1 My. '15.)

Spaulding, F. E. Problems of vocational guidance. School and Society 1:481–84. (3 Ap. '15.)

Strong, Edward K., Jr. Teacher training. School and Society 1:587–93. (24 Ap. '15.)

Talbert, E. L. The play attitude and the school fraternity. Pop. Sci. Mo. 86:472–77. (My. '15.)

Taylor, Joseph S. Report on Gary (Ind.) schools. Educa. R. 49:510–26. (My. '15.)

Wald, Lillian D. The house on Henry street. III. Education and the child. Atlan. 115:649–62. (My. '15.)

Weir, Irene. A new kind of art school. Art and Progress 6:217–19. (My. '15.)

Williams, Gertha. A group of children as clinical problems. Psychol. Clinic 9:39–43. (Ap. '15.)

Woolley, Helen T. Child labor and the school. Am. School 1:103. (Ap. '15.)

Yocum, A. Duncan. The compelling of efficiency through teacher training. School and Society 1:469–77. (3 Ap. '15.)

Volume XV JUNE 1915 Number 10

The Elementary School Journal

Continuing "The Elementary School Teacher"

THE UNIVERSITY OF CHICAGO PRESS
CHICAGO, ILLINOIS, U.S.A.

AGENTS
THE CAMBRIDGE UNIVERSITY PRESS, LONDON AND EDINBURGH
KARL W. HIERSEMANN, LEIPZIG
THE MARUZEN-KABUSHIKI-KAISHA, TOKYO, OSAKA, KYOTO

The Elementary School Journal

CONTINUING "THE ELEMENTARY SCHOOL TEACHER"

EDITED BY

THE FACULTY OF THE SCHOOL OF EDUCATION

WITH THE CO-OPERATION OF

THE FACULTY OF THE FRANCIS W. PARKER SCHOOL

Vol. XV **CONTENTS FOR JUNE 1915** **No. 10**

The Elementary School Journal is published monthly from September to June by the University of Chicago at the University Press. ¶ The subscription price is $1.50 per year; the price of single copies is 20 cents. Orders for service of less than a half-year will be charged at the single-copy rate. ¶ Postage is prepaid by the publishers on all orders from the United States, Mexico, Cuba, Porto Rico, Panama Canal Zone, Republic of Panama, Hawaiian Islands, Philippine Islands, Guam, Samoan Islands, Shanghai. ¶ Postage is charged extra as follows: For Canada, 30 cents on annual subscriptions (total $1.80); on single copies, 3 cents (total 23 cents). For all other countries in the Postal Union, 46 cents on annual subscriptions (total $1.96); on single copies, 6 cents (total 26 cents). ¶ Remittances should be made payable to The University of Chicago Press, and should be in Chicago or New York exchange, postal or express money order. If local check is used, 10 cents must be added for collection.

The following agents have been appointed and are authorized to quote the prices indicated:

For the British Empire: The Cambridge University Press, Fetter Lane, London, E.C., England. Yearly subscriptions, including postage, 8*s.* each; single copies, including postage, 1*s.* each.

For the Continent of Europe: Karl W. Hiersemann, Königstrasse 29, Leipzig, Germany. Yearly subscriptions, including postage, M. 8.25 each; single copies, including postage, M. 1.10 each.

For Japan and Korea: The Maruzen-Kabushiki-Kaisha, 11 to 16 Nihonbashi Tori Sanchome, Tokyo, Japan. Yearly subscriptions, including postage, Yen 4.00 each; single copies, including postage, Yen 0.50 each.

Claims for missing numbers should be made within the month following the regular month of publication. The publishers expect to supply missing numbers free only when they have been lost in transit.

Business correspondence should be addressed to the University of Chicago Press, Chicago, Ill.

Communications for the editors and manuscripts should be addressed to the Editors of THE ELEMENTARY SCHOOL JOURNAL, The University of Chicago, Chicago, Ill.

Entered as second-class matter, October 12, 1903, at the Post-office at Chicago, Illinois, under the Act of Congress of March 3, 1879

www.ingramcontent.com/pod-product-compliance
Lightning Source LLC
LaVergne TN
LVHW010521100826
845148LV00001B/64